SUSE Linux® 10 Bible

SUSE Linux® 10 Bible

Justin Davies
Roger Whittaker
William von Hagen

WILEY

Wiley Publishing, Inc.

SUSE Linux® 10 Bible

Published by
Wiley Publishing, Inc.
10475 Crosspoint Boulevard
Indianapolis, IN 46256
www.wiley.com

Published simultaneously in Canada

ISBN-13: 978-0-471-75488-6
ISBN-10: 0-471-75488-9

Manufactured in the United States of America

10 9 8 7 6 5 4 3 2

1O/RZ/QR/QW/IN

For general information on our other products and services or to obtain technical support, please contact our Customer Care Department within the U.S. at (800) 762-2974, outside the U.S. at (317) 572-3993 or fax (317) 572-4002.

Library of Congress Cataloging-in-Publication Data

Davies, Justin, 1979–
  Suse Linux 10 bible / Justin Davies, Roger Whittaker, and William von Hagen.
    p. cm.
  Includes index.
  ISBN-13: 978-0-471-75488-6 (paper/dvd)
  ISBN-10: 0-471-75488-9 (paper/dvd)
  1. Linux. 2. Operating systems (Computers) I. Whittaker, Roger, 1955– II. Von Hagen, William. III. Title.
  QA76.76.O63D34992 2006
  005.4'32—dc22
                            2005027885

About the Authors

Justin Davies has been a user of Linux since the age of 15, after getting frustrated at the (lack of) features of DOS. After University, he joined SUSE Linux as a Technical Consultant where he became very interested with Linux on non-Intel architecture. After a stint as a Unix Administrator post-SUSE, he joined the world of the value-added reseller and now works for SCC as an Enterprise Solutions Architect, helping organizations realize that Linux is a viable business solution.

After working as a teacher of Mathematics and Deputy Head of an independent school in London, **Roger Whittaker** discovered Linux in 1996 and became increasingly interested (some would say obsessed with) in the software. When SUSE Linux opened the company's UK office in 1999, he changed careers and worked as a technical and training consultant until early in 2004. He now works in London as a Linux consultant. He is a Council member of UKUUG, the UK's Unix and Open Systems user group.

William von Hagen has been a Unix system administrator for 20 years and a Linux fanatic since 1993. He has also worked as a systems programmer, product manager, writer, application developer, drummer, and content manager. Bill has written books on such topics as Linux filesystems, Red Hat Linux, GCC, SGML, Mac OS X, Linux system administration, and hacking the TiVo. He has written numerous articles on Linux, Unix, and open source topics for publications including *Linux Magazine*, *Linux Journal*, *Linux Format*, and *Mac Format*. An avid computer collector specializing in workstations, he owns more than 200 computer systems.

Credits

Contributor
Paul Weinstein

Executive Editor
Carol Long

Acquisitions Editor
Debra Williams Cauley

Development Editor
Kevin Kent

Technical Editors
Lenz Grimmer
Rob Foster
Peter Macmillan

Copy Editor
Michael Koch

Editorial Manager
Mary Beth Wakefield

Production Manager
Tim Tate

**Vice President and Executive
Group Publisher**
Richard Swadley

**Vice President and
Executive Publisher**
Joseph B. Wikert

Project Coordinator
Michael Kruzil

Graphics and Production Specialists
Carrie A. Foster
Lauren Goddard
Denny Hager
Joyce Haughey
Stephanie D. Jumper
Barbara Moore
Heather Ryan
Alicia South

Quality Control Technicians
David Faust
Leeann Harney
Joe Niesen
Brian H. Walls

**Media Development
Associate Producer**
Rich Graves

Media Development Specialist
Kate Jenkins

Media Development Coordinator
Laura Atkinson

Proofreader
Sossity R. Smith

Indexing
TECHBOOKS Production Services

Foreword

My Brothers and Sisters,

Should we accept that this book is indeed a *Bible*? Let us use a dictionary to see what the definition of a *Bible* is.

The first definition is marked obsolete, and just means "a book." I think that anyone would agree that this tome is a *Bible* by that definition.

The second definition was the one that most know, "The Book by way of eminence . . . accepted as of divine authority and origin." Well, Linux has long been known for its gurus who hand out small snippets of sage advice. Sometimes that sage advice is in many books, and beginners are often told RTFM (Read The Freaking Manual). Easy enough for the guru to say, but when there are so many manuals, HOWTOs, and other pieces of information scattered about, how do you put it all together?

Therefore, a Bible is necessary. Hopefully it carries information pertinent to your own religion, or in this case distribution. If the Bible tries to cover the information in every distribution, the reader may become lost. That is why this is *SUSE Linux 10 Bible*, and not some other brand of Linux.

Some people say that Linux and Free and Open Source (FOSS) are a religion, and that the people that support it are religious zealots. I don't think that is true, for the people I know in FOSS are multifaceted. But when it comes to programming, we believe that Linux and FOSS offer education, government, and business the most flexible, powerful, and lowest-cost solution. All you have to do is reach out and accept that fact.

Like any good religion you have to practice it, study it, and really understand what is being said to you. You also have to apply it to your life. Look for ways in your life that this software can help you, whether to organize your life or your business better.

Many people think that Total Cost of Ownership (TCO) is simply made up of the cost of the hardware, software, and services of the solution you pick. How naive. TCO is also made up of the cost of *not* picking a better solution, one that is flexible enough for you to solve 99 percent of your problems instead of 80 percent of your problems. How much does it cost you not to be able to solve that 19 to 20 percent?

The Freedom that you get when you use FOSS is the key to this savings, or (in reverse) the additional earning power. To be able to fully tailor the software to meet your needs is the greatest value of FOSS. But you can't do this without knowledge.

This is where this *Bible* comes in, to give you the knowledge to go out and explore further.

So, my brothers and sisters, throw off the shackles of proprietary software and learn how to make software do what *you* want it to do. Open the pages of this *Bible* and see your life change. Welcome to the bright side of "The Force."

Carpe Diem!

Jon "maddog" Hall
President, Linux International

Preface

Welcome to *SUSE Linux® 10 Bible*! This book is for anyone who is interested in running a SUSE Linux system—at home or at work, for fun or for profit. It covers all the currently available versions from SUSE: The *10* in the title refers to Enterprise Server 10, SUSE Linux 10.*x* and OpenSUSE 10.*x*. Most of the content applies equally to previous versions as well, however. We shall also describe other SUSE and Novell business products: the Novell Linux Desktop and the Open Enterprise and OpenExchange Servers.

The book aims to supplement the documentation provided by SUSE and to show the reader how best to carry out a particular task on a SUSE system, making full use of the SUSE configuration utilities. Many Linux books and how-to documents provide generic instructions for carrying out particular tasks; however, it often turns out that these are either incorrect in the details or unnecessarily complicated when applied to a particular distribution. In this book we aim to describe the best ways of working with SUSE in a wide variety of situations, making full use of the SUSE configuration tools.

Too often, computer books tend to be written only from the standpoint of how to perform a task and fail to provide a real understanding of the underlying principles. Our aim in this book is to combine a description of the steps necessary to perform a particular task with a real understanding of what is being done.

While we discuss the use of SUSE Linux in enterprise applications, with examples based on our own consulting experience, the book is also for home users getting to grips with Linux for the first time. In short, we aim for *SUSE Linux 10 Bible* to be what you need to run your SUSE Linux system, whatever your situation might be.

How This Book Is Structured

We've organized this book into five parts:

+ **Part I: SUSE Linux Basics**—This part introduces SUSE Linux by describing the installation of a SUSE system and discussing the fundamental concepts of Linux.

+ **Part II: The SUSE System**—This part describes the use of YaST for system configuration, explains Linux networking, system logs, the X Window system, and helps you to find further documentation.

♦ **Part III: Using the Command Line in SUSE Linux**—This part covers the power of the Linux command line, with chapters covering text editing and tools for manipulating text files, as well as package maintenance and advanced networking.

♦ **Part IV: Implementing Network Services in SUSE Linux**—This part describes the setup of the major network services on a SUSE system, including setting up web servers, mail servers, and file and print servers.

♦ **Part V: SUSE Linux in the Enterprise**—This part describes the place of SUSE Linux in the modern enterprise and covers the use of storage area networks (SANs). The configuration of the kernel is also covered. The SUSE OpenExchange server is described in detail, and an overview is offered of the Novell Open Enterprise Server. The Novell Linux desktop is also discussed.

Conventions Used in This Book

Throughout the book, special typeface indicates code or commands. Commands and code are shown in monospace type:

```
This is how code looks.
```

Additionally, the following icons are used to call your attention to points that are particularly important.

A Caution warns you to be careful when executing a procedure or you could damage your computer hardware or software.

A Cross-Reference refers you to further information on a subject that you can find outside the current chapter.

A Note provides extra information to which you need to pay special attention.

A Tip shows a special way of performing a particular task or introduces a shortcut to ease your way.

We hope you enjoy working with your SUSE Linux system as much as we enjoy working with ours, and we know that *SUSE Linux 10 Bible* will be an invaluable tool to help you get the most out of it.

DVD and Web Site

This book comes with a DVD containing a full copy of SUSE 10.0 for computers with x86, AMD64, or EM64T processors. Additionally, check out this book's web site at `www.wiley.com/go/suselinux10bible` periodically for additional and updated content. For more great books on Linux from Wiley, you can point your browser to `www.wiley.com` or `www.wrox.com`.

Contents at a Glance

Contents

• •

Part II: The SUSE System   107

Chapter 4: Booting the System. 109

Chapter 5: Documentation 135

Part III: Using the Command Line in SUSE Linux   267

Chapter 10: Text Manipulation. 269

Chapter 30: SUSE Linux OpenExchange Server 739

Introduction

What is Linux? There was a time (not so long ago) when the first page of every book and the first slide of every presentation on Linux had this obligatory question. We have come a long way since that time, and we certainly no longer feel that we have to start our own presentations with that slide. However, in a book like this, a brief introduction to Linux in general can provide an appropriate entry into our discussion of SUSE Linux in particular.

Linux is a multiuser, multitasking, multiplatform computer operating system (strictly speaking, an operating system kernel) that has been developed by an open source, collaborative process involving large numbers of people all over the world. Linux is a Unix-like operating system. This means that it conforms closely to a set of conventions and standards associated with Unix; however, Linux does not contain any of the original Unix code.

Linux has been developed using the open source development model. What that means is that all the work that is done by Linux developers is open and shared. It is open to peer review, which encourages honesty and means that each developer is able to build upon work that has already been done by others. Although this method is often still seen as revolutionary in the field of software development, it is effectively the same method that has been used by science in the Western world since about the time of Newton. The development of Western science has been spectacularly successful precisely because it is based on the same values of openness and shared results and because of the quality assurance provided by the scrutiny of peer review.

This model works so well both in science and software because openness leads to scrutiny, and scrutiny leads to improvement and the correction of errors. Openness also means the ability to build on the results of others. Newton himself said that if he saw further than others, it was "by standing upon the shoulders of giants." This sums up very well the power of collaborative development in any field. It contrasts strongly with the traditional closed source development model: a group of programmers working in secrecy with deadlines for work to be handed to a manager. In such a situation, a team member who knows that his work has a bug in it has no incentive to tell anyone; when the program is finally released, no one outside the small development group can look at the code to understand why it does not work as advertised. In contrast, Eric Raymond coined a phrase to describe the power of having a large open source developer community to debug code: "Given enough eyeballs, all bugs are shallow."

The dramatic success of Linux and of other associated open source projects such as the Apache web server and Samba are proof of the power of the open source development method.

Linux has come a long way since its beginnings in the early 1990s. In 1991, it was one man's hobby: Ten years later, in 2001, IBM announced that it was investing one billion dollars in its Linux strategy.

Linux History

The beginning of Linux is usually dated to August 25, 1991, the date on which Linus Torvalds sent a posting to the comp.os.minix newsgroup describing the work he had done so far. He subsequently invited others to join the project, made the code available by FTP, and offered it under a license allowing free redistribution (originally a license that he wrote himself, but soon afterward moved to the GNU GPL).

A worldwide community quickly arose, working on the Linux kernel and submitting code and patches back to Torvalds to be incorporated into the kernel. As time went on, the number of people working on Linux grew rapidly, and systems were put in place to filter and channel the incoming code; however, Linus Torvalds has stayed in charge of the whole project, which has remained independent of any particular vendor.

The remarkable rate at which Linux grew and matured is well known: Linux is living proof of the power of the open source development model.

Both the history of Linux and descriptions of the workings of open source development are described in many other publications. Glyn Moody's *Rebel Code: Linux and the Open Source Revolution* has a very good history of Linux and the open source movement generally. The classic exposition of why and how the open source development model works so well is in Eric S. Raymond's *The Cathedral and the Bazaar*.

Both of these books are recommended to any readers who want to know more about the history of Linux and open source software, and particularly to anyone who has residual doubts about whether free and open source software can really be secure or reliable.

In the first few years of Linux, a number of distributions of Linux emerged. It is important to understand that, properly speaking, the term *Linux* refers only to the kernel. To create a system that you can install and run, much more is required, including in particular the whole range of GNU utilities and a method of installing the system. A *distribution* of Linux is a complete set of packages built to work together around a Linux kernel, combined with a method of easily installing the system to the hard disk.

Many of the early Linux distributions have been forgotten. But a few companies formed in the early years began to produce important commercial versions of Linux: the most important then were Red Hat, Caldera, and SUSE. The most influential early noncommercial (or possibly semicommercial) distribution was Slackware, which played an important part in the early life of SUSE (and which still exists). The Debian project began at around the same time and also continues to this day as the purest Linux distribution from the point of view of the ideology of software freedom.

Red Hat's IPO (stock market flotation) in mid-1999 was perhaps the event that put Linux on the map for the wider world. The subsequent dramatic rise and equally dramatic fall of the stock price were perhaps at the same time somewhat unfortunate because it gave the perception that Linux was part of the Internet bubble—just another bright idea lacking a coherent business model.

However, the continual increase in the uptake of Linux by business and its endorsement by some of the giants of the computer industry made its importance clear even to the doubters. Oracle announced support for Linux in mid-1998; Oracle installations on Linux are a significant factor in the acceptance of Linux in the enterprise market. IBM began to take Linux very seriously from 1998 onward and started offering ports of its software to Linux the following year (including the DB2 database and Domino server); now it forms a major part of the company's strategy.

The past few years have brought us to a point where Linux is regarded as mainstream. All major industry players in both the hardware and software sectors (apart from Microsoft and its close collaborators) have adopted Linux or have a Linux strategy.

The takeover of SUSE by Novell at the end of 2003, and Novell's enthusiastic conversion to Linux, is a logical part of that process and is certain to accelerate Linux adoption globally.

SUSE History

SUSE is the oldest existing commercial distribution of Linux. The company was founded in 1992 near Nuremberg in Germany. The first release of a Linux distribution by SUSE was early in 1994.

A very frequently asked question is "What does *SUSE* stand for?" *SUSE* is a German acronym for *Software und System Entwicklung* or Software and System Development (not a terribly original or gripping name for a software company). However, the full name is never used; the company has been known as SUSE since the earliest days. More accurately, the company has been known as S.u.S.E., then as SuSE, and now SUSE as the marketing people gradually got to work on the corporate image of the company. In what follows, for simplicity we use the current form, SUSE, at the risk of anachronism.

The company was founded on September 2, 1992. The founders were Roland Dyroff, Thomas Fehr, Burchard Steinbild, and Hubert Mantel, all in their mid-twenties at the time. Three of the founders were still at University studying mathematics: Thomas Fehr had already graduated and was working as a software engineer. The original intention was that the company would do consulting work and software development for clients; according to Hubert Mantel's account, this did not work out very well as work was in short supply, and after a while the group had the idea of distributing Linux. Initially the company distributed a version of Linux called SLS (Soft Landing Systems). Later they switched to Slackware, producing a German-language version in cooperation with Slackware's founder, Patrick Volkerding.

According to the recollections of Bodo Bauer (one of the very earliest SUSE employees), the SUSE people decided that rather than constantly fixing bugs in Slackware before shipping their translated and enhanced version, it would be better to produce their own distribution. They also felt the lack of a good installation and configuration tool in Slackware. The result was that SUSE took Florian LaRoche's Jurix distribution as a starting point and began to develop YaST. (Florian also joined the SUSE team.)

The first true SUSE distribution was released in May 1996 and was numbered 4.2 (an intentional reference to the use of the number 42 in *The Hitchhiker's Guide to the Galaxy* by Douglas Adams).

At the time that early versions of Red Hat (and Red Hat clones) were ubiquitous in the United States, SUSE Linux gained popularity in Europe. SUSE became a worldwide company with the establishment of offices in the United States (1997) and in the United Kingdom (1999).

SUSE never attempted an IPO, although there were rumors that this would happen at one stage. Instead, the company went through a number of rounds of funding from venture capitalist and industry sources. Over-optimism and too rapid an expansion led to a point in 2001 when the company was forced to downsize significantly to survive. After that time, stricter financial discipline, the release of the enterprise versions, and the growing uptake of Linux by business put the company on a sound footing. With the takeover by Novell in 2003, the investors recouped their investment, while the market's approval became very clear in the dramatic and sustained rise in Novell's stock following the announcement.

Originally SUSE provided one product (simply known as S.u.S.E. Linux), which was released about three times a year and was available for the $x86$ platform only. The current SUSE Professional is the direct descendant of this, and the current version number of 10.0 is one of a series that goes back to the original 4.2.

In 2000, the SUSE offering was split into Professional and Personal versions, and versions for other hardware platforms (Alpha, Sparc, and PPC) were released.

The following year, SUSE released the Enterprise Server 7 version, and in due course, versions of Enterprise Server for IA64 (Itanium), PPC (intended for the IBM iSeries and pSeries), S/390, and zSeries were released. SUSE developed powerful tools to aid in the process of porting Linux to other platforms, and there was close collaboration with IBM in the production of versions for the PPC-based iSeries and pSeries and for the S/390 and zSeries mainframes. SUSE also worked with AMD on the development of a version for the Hammer chip (now known as the Opteron and Athlon 64). The story goes that an entire distribution for this architecture was completed and tested using emulation before AMD had any hardware to offer; when the first machine arrived at SUSE from AMD, the installation CD booted and installed flawlessly. SUSE uses a system known as AutoBuild that takes the same source code for all packages and builds the distribution for all platforms from it. This ensures a high degree of compatibility between versions on different platforms and is one of the key advantages of the SUSE Enterprise Server.

SUSE also released a series of mail server products leading up to the SUSE Linux OpenExchange Server 4, a mail and groupware server allowing integration with popular desktop clients, including Outlook and, hence, becoming a competitor to Microsoft Exchange Server. OpenExchange was developed jointly by SUSE and Netline, who wrote the groupware element. This has now been released as a separate product under the GPL, and can be run on other Linux versions as well as SUSE.

Enterprise Server 7 was succeeded by Enterprise Server 8 (available on *x*86, IA64, AMD64, iSeries, pSeries, and zSeries) in November 2002.

Prior to the release of Enterprise Server 8 (in November 2002), the UnitedLinux consortium was established, with SUSE, Connectiva, Turbolinux, and SCO as members. UnitedLinux was an agreed core, developed by SUSE for enterprise distributions to be issued by the other vendors in the consortium. Following the defection of SCO from the Linux community and its extraordinary decision to take legal actions against IBM and Linux distributors and users, the UnitedLinux consortium lost its importance and is now only of historical interest.

Enterprise Server 8 was followed by Enterprise Server 9 in August 2004, continuing a pattern of Enterprise releases separated by less than two years. These releases overlap each other in time: the full life cycle of each enterprise release is five years from initial release until the final end of support and maintenance, which means that at any one time there are two fully supported versions of the Enterprise Server, one of which is approaching its end of life. The next version in the Enterprise Server line is expected to be released in the first quarter of 2006.

March 2005 saw the release of the Novell Open Enterprise Server (based on SLES 9), marking the fulfillment of Novell's intention of integrating its NetWare product with Linux: the Open Enterprise Server makes NetWare's core functionality a service running on Linux rather than an operating system in itself and provides versions of Novell's directory services and management software on top of this platform.

In the early days, SUSE appeared to be simply one of a large number of Linux distributions. However, unlike many of the other distributions, SUSE had a developer team of real quality and strength in numbers. This fact was not lost on IBM when they increasingly cooperated with SUSE in development work for their high-end platforms, and it gradually became apparent that there were really only two Linux companies that really mattered—namely, SUSE and Red Hat.

Historically, however, there were some differences between the two companies' philosophies. Both Red Hat and SUSE provided boxed versions of their consumer version for sale. Red Hat offered ISO images identical to the CDs in the boxed product for download; SUSE did not, but allowed an FTP installation. SUSE somewhat controversially placed a licensing restriction on the redistribution of the YaST installation and administration tool; while the source remained open, it was not permissible to redistribute YaST on media offered for sale. This prevented a proliferation of SUSE clones in the way that there were numerous Linux distributions "based on Red Hat." Since the takeover of SUSE by Novell, however, the YaST license has been changed to the GPL, and more recently ISO images have been made available by FTP. Both these changes can be seen as signs of Novell's confidence in SUSE's leading place in the Linux market.

SUSE made a clearer distinction between the company's enterprise and consumer versions than Red Hat did. Red Hat was already offering a commercial software maintenance and support system on its boxed product (Red Hat 7.*x*, 8.*x*, and so on) when it introduced its enterprise versions (Advanced Server and Enterprise Server). Its subsequent withdrawal of all support for the boxed versions was something of a PR disaster for Red Hat and left many commercial users feeling very dissatisfied and looking for other options. A considerable proportion of these users migrated at that time to SUSE.

The SUSE Family of Products

Now that we have introduced some of the history behind what this book is about, it's time to take a look at the SUSE software that Novell currently offers. Novell divides its SUSE Linux products into Enterprise and Personal. This is essentially the distinction between the versions that are sold with a paid-for software maintenance system and those that are not.

Personal

The Personal category now consists of just one product, SUSE Linux Professional. (In the past there was a cut-down version of SUSE Linux Professional known as SUSE Linux Personal; with the release of 9.3 this product was dropped. Do not confuse Novell's customer category Personal with SUSE's former product SUSE Linux Personal.)

SUSE Linux Professional

SUSE Linux Professional now contains versions for both the *x*86 (Intel-compatible PC 32-bit) and *x*86-64 (Athlon 64, Opteron, and Intel EM64T) platforms. It consists of five CDs and two double-layer DVDs. The five CDs form is an installation set for *x*86 machines. One of the DVDs is an installation DVD for both *x*86 and *x*86-64; the other DVD provides the source packages. The Professional version contains a wide range of software, including desktop and server software and development tools. It actually contains considerably more packages than the Enterprise Server versions but should be regarded as essentially an unsupported version, but limited installation support is included in the price of the boxed set. A new version of SUSE Linux Professional appears twice a year.

A Live DVD version (it's been a DVD since version 9.2; previously this was a Live CD) is released with each version. This is available by FTP and can be burned to disk. This version cannot be installed, but booting a PC from this DVD provides a live Linux system that can be used to evaluate SUSE Linux without installing it or, if you want, as a way of carrying a Linux system around with you (perhaps with a USB stick to hold your files).

Traditionally SUSE did not provide ISO images of the distribution for download. This changed in the summer of 2005 when the full ISO images for version 9.3 were provided in this way. The Professional version has always been made available in an FTP version that allows for network installation, either directly from the FTP site or using a local mirror.

Recently, SUSE has also begun to offer a DVD ISO image (by FTP) of a cut-down installable version of the Professional distribution. This should be thought of as an evaluation edition, or as a replacement for the old Personal edition. This version is made available rather later in the product cycle than the FTP version and is known as the FTP DVD version.

openSUSE

Although the software concerned was almost all open source and freely distributable, the development of SUSE Linux was traditionally a closed process. Beta testing was done internally by the company with the help of volunteers from partner companies and the members of the public who carried out the testing under non-disclosure agreements.

When the first beta version of 10.0 was ready in August 2005, the beta testing process and the development of SUSE was opened up with the start of the openSUSE project. This is intended to create a community around the development of SUSE Linux and make the cutting-edge version of SUSE an entirely free one. In some ways the concept is similar to the Fedora project, which plays a similar role in the development of Red Hat; however, openSUSE aims to draw in a wider genuine participation by outside users and developers and has an interest in desktop usability and the needs of end users.

Future versions of SUSE Linux (at least in the short term) will be available both from openSUSE and as boxed versions that will include the traditional manuals and additional non-free software (such as Sun Java, Adobe Acrobat Reader, proprietary drivers of certain kinds, and so on).

Enterprise

The most important difference between SUSE Linux Professional and the enterprise versions is the way that you pay for them. SUSE's Enterprise Server and the other business products are offered only together with a subscription to a paid-for software maintenance system.

SUSE Linux Enterprise Server

The flagship product of SUSE is the SUSE Linux Enterprise Server (SLES). SUSE Linux Enterprise Server is, as its name implies, a version of Linux intended for use in an enterprise environment.

The latest version of SLES is due in early 2006.

While the Professional version focuses on being cutting-edge (containing the latest versions of software) and experimental, the Enterprise Server concentrates on being stable, supportable, and certified. So the software packages that make up the Enterprise Server have been carefully chosen, and the entire distribution is subject to very careful quality control and testing. This includes the all-important certifications by hardware and software vendors. Hardware from the major vendors, and particularly complete server systems from IBM, HP, Dell, Fujitsu Siemens, and others is certified against SLES. Certified software includes a wide range of IBM products and software from SAP and Oracle. Perhaps the most important of these from a business point of view is the certification by Oracle. Details of all certifications can be searched at `http://developer.novell.com/yessearch/`.

SLES is available for the following hardware platforms:

+ *x*86

+ *x*86-64 (AMD64 processors: Opteron and Athlon 64, and Intel EM64T)

+ Itanium

+ IBM iSeries and pSeries

+ IBM mainframe (S/390 and zSeries)

On each of the supported hardware platforms, the kernel and package version numbers are the same; the entire environment is the same apart from those details that are hardware specific. This consistency is guaranteed by the SUSE Autobuild system, which is a method used internally to create the software distribution from source code. As a result, you can develop on one hardware platform and deploy on another, or you can move production servers from one architecture to another and have the assurance that everything will continue to work as expected.

SUSE Linux OpenExchange Server and Netline OPEN-XCHANGE

Over the years SUSE has offered a series of mail server offerings based around the Cyrus IMAP server. The SUSE eMail Server 3 was the first of these to offer groupware capabilities. The SUSE Linux OpenExchange Server 4 was the first to provide a groupware offering that could integrate with the Microsoft Outlook client, providing mail and shared calendars in a way that was almost indistinguishable from the user's point of view to a connection to a Microsoft Exchange Server.

SUSE Linux OpenExchange Server 4 (SLOX) is based on the SUSE Linux Enterprise Server 8. The groupware functionality is provided by Netline's groupware server (previously known as Comfire).

With the release of SLES 9, Novell and Netline agreed to a different model: Netline has released their OPEN-XCHANGE server under the GPL, while Novell will market and support a commercial, maintained version of this software on behalf of Netline. This is an updated version of the application server that provides the groupware capabilities in SLOX.

The original SLOX is a standalone product. It is based on the same Linux version as SLES 8 and uses Postfix as its mail transport agent; Cyrus as the IMAP and POP server; and OpenLDAP for user information, address books, and authentication. Groupware data is stored in a PostgreSQL database.

On the other hand, OPEN-XCHANGE is an application that can be installed on a variety of different Linux distributions and other Unix and Unix-like operating systems, but provides the same functionality. As time goes on, existing supported SLOX installations will be offered an upgrade path to OPEN-XCHANGE. This enables the customer to move at the same time to a newer underlying operating system (typically this will be SLES 9, but as noted previously, with OPEN-XCHANGE you are not tied to a SUSE Linux version).

Virtually any mail client on any platform will operate as a client to SLOX or OPEN-XCHANGE. To access the groupware information, you have the choice of using the web interface or using Microsoft Outlook in essentially the same way as it is used in conjunction with a Microsoft Exchange Server. The ability to offer this functionality is a major selling point, particularly at a time when support for older versions of Microsoft Exchange is being discontinued.

Cross-Reference

SUSE Linux OpenExchange Server and Netline OPEN-XCHANGE are covered in detail in Chapter 30.

Novell Linux Desktop

Whether (or when) Linux becomes a serious contender on the business desktop
has been controversial for some time. In terms of usability, the latest versions of
the KDE and GNOME desktops are comparable to Windows for most tasks. In terms
of manageability, running Linux on desktops in place of Windows could save companies money in license fees and take away a wide range of administrative headaches,
particularly in terms of security and software licensing and auditing. OpenOffice
and StarOffice are now capable of almost everything that Microsoft Office can do.
However, the devil is in the detail. A very powerful factor preventing change is the
use of particular specialized applications that may be available only on Windows.
(In practice, as we will discuss in Chapter 32, the need for particular Windows
applications can often be handled fairly easily, particularly in a larger organization.)
Other factors inhibiting the switch to Linux desktops are a common strong psycho-
logical resistance and the cost of change.

The move towards Linux desktops has been led by certain European government and
local government organizations: it was the decision in principle by the city of Munich
in Germany to make this change that got a lot of press in mid-2003. That project is
still in progress, although surprisingly now that the implementation phase has been
reached, the decision has been made to use a Debian-derived distribution rather than
SUSE. Although there are a large number of organizations in which Linux is being
used on the desktop, there is still a feeling that the move to Linux on the desktop
is proceeding slower than had been hoped. It is notable however that both Novell
(quickly) and IBM (rather more slowly) have been moving towards internal use of
desktop Linux. In the case of Novell, that change is virtually complete.

Some months before buying SUSE, Novell acquired Ximian. Ximian's central involvement in the GNOME desktop project and particular applications for it (notably the
Evolution mail client) was undoubtedly one factor in that decision and signals that
the enterprise desktop is certainly part of Novell's thinking.

Time will tell, and while even the authors of this book differ among themselves
about the question of how soon Linux desktop adoption will take off in business,
we have no doubt that Novell is committed to Linux on the desktop.

SUSE first provided a commercial desktop version in the guise of the SUSE Linux
Desktop (SLD), which was based on SUSE 8.1 Professional and was binary compatible
with SLES 8. This was a business desktop version offered with a software maintenance agreement and with licensed copies of Sun's StarOffice and CodeWeavers'
CrossOver Office (for running Windows applications) and a Citrix client.

Since then, the Novell Linux Desktop 9 has been released. This stands in roughly
the same relationship to SUSE Professional 9.1 as did SLD to 8.1 and is the first fruit
of Novell's combined ownership of both Ximian and SUSE, in the sense that it inte-
grates Ximian's GNOME desktop and the Evolution mail client. The Novell edition
of OpenOffice.org 1.1 is included, as is support for Novell's iFolder, iPrint, and the
option to use Novell's ZENworks for managing multiple desktop machines.

It is expected that a Novell Linux Desktop version 10 will be released alongside the next Enterprise Server release in early 2006.

The Novell Linux Desktop is discussed in more detail in Chapter 32.

Novell Open Enterprise Server

As noted previously, Novell has recently re-invented NetWare. NetWare, historically Novell's core product, is a network operating system for Windows clients that held a position of dominance in the market in the early and mid-1990s but gradually lost market share to Windows NT and its derivatives. NetWare is still widely used, however, and Novell's Linux strategy is two-fold: to offer Linux as such in the form of SLES while at the same time replacing NetWare as an operating system by NetWare's services as services on Linux. In this way, it will no longer be necessary for NetWare to include low-level hardware support; the NetWare developers can concentrate on the network and file-serving functionality.

The Novell Open Enterprise Server was released in March 2005 and is available in two versions: running on a NetWare kernel and running on SLES 9 as its underlying operating system. In this book we cover the basic installation and configuration of Open Enterprise Server on SLES and look at some of the software and services that it provides. This is necessarily a brief introduction to a large subject; however, we will refer you to Novell's documentation and other relevant books on the subject, as well.

Novell also offers the Novell Linux Small Business Suite; based on SLES 9, this includes Novell's Groupwise mail and collaboration suite as well as directory services and is bundled with copies of the Novell Linux Desktop for the users.

The Novell Open Enterprise Server is discussed in Chapter 31.

Standards Compliance

As multiple Linux distributions became available, users began to express concern that multiple distributions would lead to a fragmentation of Linux. The concern was based on the history of fragmentation within proprietary Unix, where the different vendors each developed their own versions in incompatible ways. To prevent this, standards (initially for the layout of files and directories on the system, but since covering much more than that) were proposed.

LSB

All current SUSE versions comply fully with and are certified against the Linux Standards Base. The Linux Standards Base is a set of standards agreed to by representatives of the Linux community and documented at www.linuxbase.org.

The LSB provides detailed specifications for the behavior of system libraries, package formats, system commands, and the filesystem hierarchy. The existence of the LSB is a powerful preventative against the fragmentation of Linux, and it is encouraging that both Red Hat and SUSE have supported the LSB, helping to prevent the kind of fragmentation that occurred in the world of commercial Unix. The LSB standard includes POSIX (Portable Operating System Interface) compatibility tests. These essentially indicate compliance with (but not certification against) the POSIX standards, which are a standard adhered to by the commercial forms of Unix. The POSIX standard facilitates the porting of code between compliant systems.

SUSE has been a strong supporter of the LSB and has been active within it as part of the process of proposing and agreeing standards. Not surprisingly SUSE has always aimed at full compliance, believing that common standards for Linux encourage wider adoption and benefit all Linux vendors.

EAL Security Certifications

The EAL certifications are provided by a body (the Common Criteria Evaluation and Validation Scheme) that was set up under international agreements. SLES 8 was certified EAL3+ at the beginning of 2004. Novell, with the help of IBM, has been working towards higher levels of security certification, and SLES 9 on IBM hardware achieved the CAPP/EAL4+ certification in the spring of 2005. (CAPP stands for Controlled Access Protection Profile under the Common Criteria for Information Security Evaluation.)

The acquisition of the EAL certifications is part of a process that is leading to wider industry acceptance for SUSE Linux. Accelerated adoption by governments and the military will also promote more general acceptance elsewhere.

Grade Linux

Recent Enterprise versions all conform largely to the latest standards set for carrier-grade Linux by the Open Source Development Labs (for the needs of the telecom industry).

Licenses, Maintenance, and Support

The licensing of Linux and open source software is a complicated subject and one that can cause serious confusion as well as controversy. Even the term *open source* is controversial. We have referred here to *open source software* and the *open source community*; not all users of Linux and free and open source software would like that terminology. Some prefer to refer simply to *free software* or to *FOSS* (free and open source software) or *FLOSS* (free, libre, and open source software).

The most important free software licenses are the the GNU General Public License (GPL) and the BSD license, but several other licenses are regarded as free software licenses. There are differing views in the open source community as to which licenses should be accepted, but licenses that are accepted by the Free Software Foundation (FSF) Free Software Definition (`www.gnu.org/philosophy/free-sw.html`) or according to the Debian Free Software Guidelines (`www.debian.org/social_contract .html`) will be accepted as free or open source software by most people.

What all these licenses have in common is that they allow the right to free redistribution and modification of the software. Where they differ is in the responsibilities that are tied to that right. The GPL in particular requires that any modifications that you make to a program be distributed under the same license. This prevents GPL-licensed software from being incorporated into commercially licensed products, while the BSD license does not have this requirement.

The Linux kernel itself is licensed under the GPL. However, all Linux systems include a large number of packages, and not all of these are licensed under the same license. The packages included in SUSE Linux Professional and SUSE Linux Enterprise Server are almost all licensed under one of the licenses mentioned previously. However, SUSE Linux Professional includes a small number of packages that are commercial demo versions, or that SUSE has been given permission to distribute in binary form, although they are not free software. Examples from SUSE Professional 9.3 include the TextMaker word processor and the PlanMaker spreadsheet from SoftMaker.

Until recently YaST (the SUSE installation and administration tool) was licensed under a special license, which meant that although the source was open, it was not free software under the definitions mentioned previously. As noted earlier, this prevented unauthorized copies of SUSE installation disks from being legally sold and stopped other distributions from being based on SUSE in the same way that the original Mandrake distribution was based on Red Hat, for example. Since the release of SUSE Professional 9.1, YaST has been licensed under the GPL.

As noted previously, the groupware application server included in OpenExchange Server 4 (SLOX) was licensed by Netline under a traditional commercial software license. However, the newer OPEN-XCHANGE version is licensed under the GPL (although Netline licenses the Outlook plug-in client under a commercial license).

Maintenance

The Enterprise versions and the other SUSE business products are offered only in conjunction with a maintenance agreement. There is an important distinction to grasp here (although to some people's minds it might appear a rather fine and legalistic one). When you buy a copy of an Enterprise version of Linux from Novell, you are not paying for a license to use the software. What you are paying for is an agreement to use the software maintenance system. The price of that agreement depends on the hardware platform and in some sense is set by an arbitrary decision on the part of SUSE/Novell. But it means (as you might expect) that running an enterprise version of Linux on an IBM mainframe will cost you more in the payments you make to Novell than running the equivalent software on an Intel server.

The software maintenance agreement allows you access to a customer area on the SUSE/Novell web site where you can find support articles and other information regarding the particular version you have registered, as well as details of bugs and security issues and patches to fix them. More important, it provides you with the ability to get patches for your version directly through the YaST online update service. SUSE's record on fixing security issues is remarkably good; patches for the maintained products are regularly provided as a matter of urgency often within hours of the vulnerability first becoming known.

It is for precisely this reason that business customers choose to run SLES rather than SUSE Linux Professional, Debian, or some other non-maintained distribution. They like the assurance that a guaranteed maintenance system offers. In addition, the fact that SUSE can provide commercial support is of the greatest importance to those who are running business-critical applications.

The maintenance agreement is a renewable one; you have to renew every year.

The question of whether you need to run a maintained version or whether you can get by using the SUSE Linux unmaintained version (or some other "free of charge" Linux such as Debian or Gentoo) as opposed to the enterprise version depends on your application. If you are running just a web server serving static pages and you are aware enough to look out for security issues with Apache and SSH, then you may be happy to run on any distribution and pay nothing in maintenance. On the other hand, if you are running Oracle, you won't get any support from Oracle unless you are running on an Oracle-certified platform. Clearly, all kinds of scenarios exist between these two extremes, where the more you know and the more capable you are, the less you need a software maintenance program. In any case, the SUSE/Novell maintenance program can give you peace of mind.

Support
Novell offers commercial support on the Linux business products at two levels: Premium Support and Standard Support. Details are available at `http://support.novell.com/linux/index.html`.

This is an additional service on top of maintenance; the maintenance fee that you pay for an enterprise copy of Linux does not qualify you for support beyond installation support. These services are available only on the business versions; you cannot obtain this type of commercial support from Novell for the SUSE Linux unmaintained version.

YaST

YaST is the SUSE installation and administration program. YaST stands for *yet another setup tool*, and it is fair to say that YaST is really what distinguishes SUSE Linux from other flavors. YaST is what makes SUSE SUSE.

YaST is a modular program—there is a YaST core and a large number of modules that it can call. Third parties can also write YaST modules. This has been made easier by the new GPL license for YaST; SUSE's major hardware and software partners can now easily write modules to control their products.

YaST has been written with a useful degree of abstraction. You can use it either in graphical or text mode, with exactly the same functionality. This is important and enables you to administer a machine over a text-only remote SSH connection. YaST can also operate in Virtual Network Computing (VNC) mode, even during installation so that you can connect to a YaST session graphically from a VNC client running on any platform. This means you can start the installation and then control it remotely across the network.

Internally, YaST makes use of a special scripting language called YCP, which was invented by the YaST developers for the purpose of simplifying the development of the YaST modules.

As an installer, YaST is extremely easy to use; it has powerful hardware detection capabilities and generally does the right thing. As an administration tool, YaST is sometimes criticized for being too monolithic—it attempts to control every aspect of the system and with each release adds modules to configure yet more services. These criticisms have some substance, but there are two points to be made here: First, each advance in YaST has made SUSE Linux easier to administer in practice, and second, YaST modules have been very carefully written so that you are almost always made aware if you have made a manual configuration change that might be overwritten by YaST. Note that you are not forced to use YaST for configuration; you can choose to make all the changes to configuration files manually. But when you use YaST, it will respect the manual changes you have made by creating alternative copies of the changed configuration files.

In many cases YaST writes directly to configuration files, but for certain high-level options, YaST uses the /etc/sysconfig directory to hold configuration information. When YaST exits, it first runs a utility called SuSEconfig that propagates the changes that have been made in this directory through the system.

YaST includes tools that make it easy both to create an installation server and to run completely automated installations from that server (using AutoYaST).

 Cross-Reference Further details of the use of YaST are included throughout the book, and particularly in Chapter 9.

Now that we've introduced you to the subject of the book, it's time to delve into Chapter 1, where you will start to realize what a powerful and versatile operating system you have in SUSE Linux. Enjoy!

SUSE Linux Basics

]

◆　◆　◆　◆

◆　◆　◆　◆

Part I introduces SUSE Linux by describing the installation of a SUSE system, by discussing the fundamental concepts of Linux, and by delving into how to work with partitions, filesystems, and files.

Installing SUSE 10

The most important part of getting Linux up and running is installing the system. Unfortunately, this is also where most users encounter problems because of differences between the types of information that you need to know when installing Linux versus Windows. This chapter demystifies the process by helping you through the installation, pointing out any stumbling blocks that you may hit upon, and offering suggestions for resolving them.

The program used to install SUSE Linux is known as YaST, which stands for Yet another System Tool. (The "Yet another . . ." naming convention is a standard Unix/Linux naming convention, intended to reflect humorously on the number of similar tools that different people and companies have developed to do specific tasks in their favorite, customized fashion. YaST provides a framework that supports independent modules that perform a variety of administrative tasks, including modules for installation, all system administration and configuration tasks, and subsequent system updates. The YaST interface that you use for installation is therefore very similar to the interfaces that you will use for system configuration and administrative tasks when you have completed your SUSE Linux installation. Powerful and well designed, YaST will quickly become your friend.

Selecting Your Installation Method

You can install SUSE in numerous ways. Different installation methods are useful in different circumstances. The most common and recommended installation method is to use the installation media provided with the boxed SUSE Linux product. This book focuses on installing SUSE Linux 10 through the CDs provided with the SUSE Linux product. Installing SUSE Linux using the DVD that is also provided in the boxed SUSE product follows essentially the same process, but with the added bonus of not having to switch CDs.

Different Installation Sources

This chapter focuses on installing SUSE Linux from the DVD that was packaged with this book or from the installation discs you have purchased. However, your installation discs and the installation DVD that is packaged with this book (like all SUSE installation media) also support a number of other installation sources. If you want to make sure that you get the latest SUSE installation on your system, you may want to select Manual Installation from the initial menu of the boot DVD, select the Start Installation option, and then select the Network source medium. This enables you to select from a variety of different installation sources, including FTP installation, which enables you to install SUSE from a network source, such as one of SUSE's up-to-date repositories. (Other network installation mechanisms include HTTP, NFS, SMB, and TFTP, although FTP is the most common.) To install SUSE from a network source, you must have used the installer's Network Modules screen first to install the drivers for the network card in your computer, and the computer on which you are installing SUSE must also be connected to the Internet. Although this requires some knowledge about your computer system's hardware, it is a great way to get the latest and greatest version of SUSE Linux. As noted earlier, the DVD packaged with this book provides the most recent version of SUSE Linux Professional Edition available at the time that this book was written. To get the latest and greatest version of SUSE Linux and all of its patches, you can always install this version and then update it using the YaST Online Update module that is discussed in Chapter 9.

Note   The DVD included with this book provides the SUSE Linux 10 distribution.

You can install SUSE Linux in the following ways:

✦ **Compact disc** — The easiest and most common form of installation, because almost every modern computer system includes a CD drive. This is the standard way to perform a fresh installation of SUSE Linux on a computer system.

✦ **DVD** — A popular form of installation that saves you from having to swap out multiple CDs, but the computer system on which you are installing SUSE must contain a DVD drive. Because of the amount of storage available on a DVD, the SUSE Linux DVD also includes some packages that are not available on the CD installation set.

✦ **Manual installation** — Manual installation requires that you boot from a SUSE CD but provides more control over the source of the packages used when installing SUSE Linux. For example, this installation method enables you to install SUSE from a centralized network repository where the SUSE Linux packages are located, using network protocols such as FTP (File Transfer Protocol), HTTP (Hypertext Transfer Protocol), NFS (Network File System), SMB (Server Message Block, the Windows file sharing protocol), and even TFTP (Trivial File Transfer Protocol). This is a common installation method when you want to install SUSE on a large number of networked computer systems. Manual installation also enables you to install SUSE from an existing hard drive partition where the SUSE packages are installed. You can use Manual installation to install SUSE from a portable, external hard drive.

✦ **AutoYaST** — AutoYaST is an advanced installation method that enables a system administrator to create a profile file that can be used to automate installing SUSE Linux on any number of identically configured systems.

As you can see, each installation method has its own advantages and disadvantages, and some are specifically targeted toward technically sophisticated users or system administrators who are installing SUSE into existing networked environments. The remainder of this chapter focuses on installing from CD or DVD, but also provides an overview of using SUSE's network-based installation.

Starting Your Installation

Inside your SUSE box you should find the SUSE manuals (which are considered among the best Linux manuals available) and the media case.

The media case contains five CDs and two double-sided DVDs. One of the installation DVDs is installable, while the other contains the SUSE Linux source code. The installable DVD has two sides, one used to install SUSE on standard Pentium-class PCs, and the other containing an installable version of SUSE Linux for 64-bit systems. Each side of the DVDs is labeled in extremely fine print around the center ring of the DVD. Depending on the hardware in your computer system, installing from DVD is the least time-consuming installation method.

Insert the first CD or the bootable DVD in your system's optical drive. If you are booting from DVD, make sure that the side that you want to boot from is facing up in your DVD drive.

Next, enable booting from the optical media drive on your computer to start the installation routine. During the bootup routine, you need to enter the BIOS and set the order in which your system will probe attached devices looking for bootable media. You can enter your system's BIOS setup routines by pressing a special key when booting the machine. Typically, this is the F2, Delete, or F1 key — check your system's boot screen for BIOS Setup instructions, which are usually displayed at the bottom of the screen. When you've entered the BIOS setup screens, different BIOS have different ways of configuring your system's boot sequence. You may find the options you are looking for under Startup Items, Boot Options, or under your Advanced settings. Make sure that your CD or DVD drive is probed before your floppy disk, hard drives, or network. Once set, save the new settings, and your machine will reboot.

At this point, your system should boot from the first SUSE CD or the DVD, and you will see the welcome screen (see Figure 1-1).

Figure 1-1: The SUSE Welcome screen

Tip   If your system does not display a screen like the one in Figure 1-1, reboot and hold down the Shift key while your computer system boots. This will reboot your system into a text-mode installer that follows the same general sequence as the graphical boot process described in this chapter, but has fewer dependencies on the capabilities of the graphics card in your machine.

Selecting Boot Options

When the boot splash screen has finished, you will be asked to select how you want to install SUSE, as well as some other helpful options for booting your system (see Figure 1-2).

The boot menu offers more than just installation options, although the most common selection is the standard Installation item. We discuss the other six options in detail because at some point in the life of a SUSE user you will likely need to use the others.

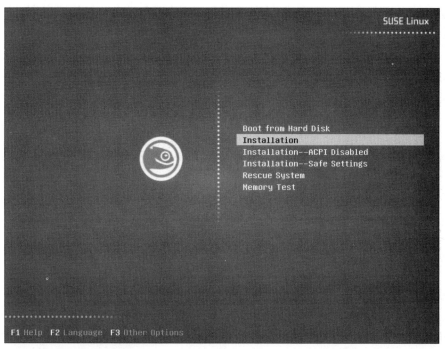

Figure 1-2: Boot options

✦ **Boot from Hard Disk** — This is the default setting if you do not interact with the boot sequence. It's the default because your system automatically reboots as part of the installation process to load the kernel that is installed on your hard drive during the initial phases of the installation process. If you forget to remove the installation media, the system will still boot off the hard disk and the install routine can continue.

✦ **Installation** — This is the standard option that most users should select. It will boot from the CD and start the install routine (YaST). We discuss the rest of the process in the remainder of this chapter.

✦ **Installation — ACPI Disabled** — Advanced Configuration and Power Interface (ACPI) is a feature of most new processors that controls power management and the way interrupts are handled by the system hardware. You should select this option if you encounter problems during the installation process, such as if your computer system goes to sleep (blanks the screen and powers down the drives) and if pressing the appropriate keystroke does not wake it up again.

✦ **Installation — Safe Settings** — As with the ACPI Disabled installation method, this turns off some of the features of the kernel that can cause problems with buggy or old system hardware. You should select this option if you encounter problems during installation, and they do not seem related to power management.

✦ **Rescue System** — The Rescue System enables you to correct system problems, such as disk corruption or lost passwords, by booting from the installation media and subsequently correcting system problems. The Rescue System is quite a feature-rich system that you can use to load and edit filesystems, as well as change the settings of an installed system.

✦ **Memory Test** — SUSE has been very kind and integrated a memory test suite in the system boot menu. The memory test will run long and exhaustive tests on your system's memory and warn you of any anomalies that it encounters on the way. We have used this a few times with systems that don't quite seem to be running as we expect, and it has been able to tell us that a DIMM (Dual In-Line Memory Module) has indeed failed.

In this chapter, we select the standard Installation option in the boot menu.

Note

SUSE has changed the original boot splash screen to be something more akin to the Windows bootup (see Figure 1-3). While this is fine for first-time users, it is something that will infuriate hard-core Linux users. SUSE is aware this may be a problem for some users, and pressing ESC while the system boots up will allow you to see the kernel and init messages.

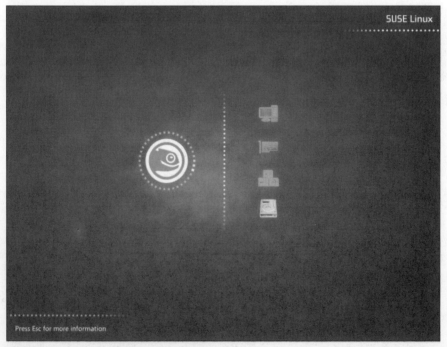

Figure 1-3: Booting SUSE installation

So far, the system has booted a minimal Linux kernel that is sufficient to run the installation process and execute the SUSE installer and the various utilities that it uses to probe and configure your system. SUSE's YaST installer now begins to collect information that it will use to configure your system to match your personal and hardware requirements.

Tip   The installer uses a very different boot process from that used by a standard SUSE Linux system. The standard Linux boot up sequence will be discussed in more detail in Chapter 4.

Configuring Language Settings

When the system has booted, you will be asked to configure your language settings (see Figure 1-4). SUSE has put a lot of effort into supporting as many languages as possible to accommodate a large audience. All language options are shown in their respective dialects and associated fonts. When your language has been selected, the installer will instantly change the system language and allow you to continue the installation process in that language.

When you've selected your language, click the Next button or use the keyboard shortcut Ctrl+N.

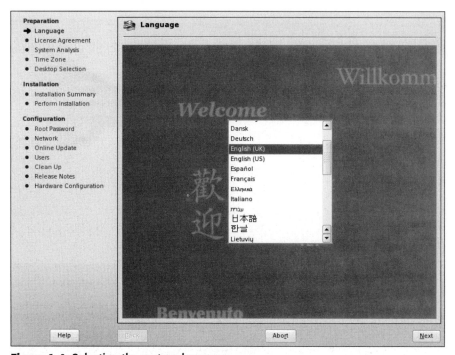

Figure 1-4: Selecting the system language

During the installation routine, you can control the screen with your keyboard using *accelerators*. Any option on the screen can be selected by pressing the Control key (Ctrl) and the accelerator code, signified by an underlined character in a button or a GUI element. For example, in Figure 1-4, pressing Ctrl+R will abort the installation while Ctrl+N will accept the setting you selected and proceed to the next screen.

Media Check

Before starting the installation process, you will be asked whether you want to check the media you are using during installation. With any mass produced optical media, there is always a possibility that something might be wrong with your disks (if there is, SUSE will replace them for you). The media check (see Figure 1-5) is a precautionary measure for you to check that everything is ok before formatting your hard drive and potentially being left with an unusable system until you get your new SUSE disks.

You can either skip the check by clicking Next or check your media by clicking Start Check. We will skip the check as we know our media is good.

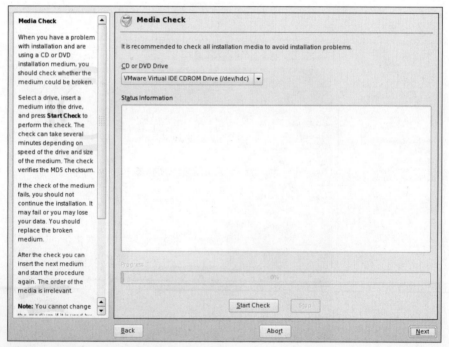

Figure 1-5: SUSE media check

Next, as with most software products, you have to agree to the SUSE license before using the system.

Customizing the Installation

For SUSE to operate correctly, the system time must be correct (you may get quite confused when the system says something happened at 3 a.m. when in fact it happened at noon!). Before partitioning your disks and setting up your system, you will need to select your time zone, check your date and time, and also your location (see Figure 1-6).

Selecting Your Desktop Environment

A new change to the SUSE installation is the option to select your desktop environment during installation (see Figure 1-7). If you are a GNOME or KDE fan, you can select one of those here. If you prefer another desktop environment (for example, Window Maker), then click Other and then Select. . . .

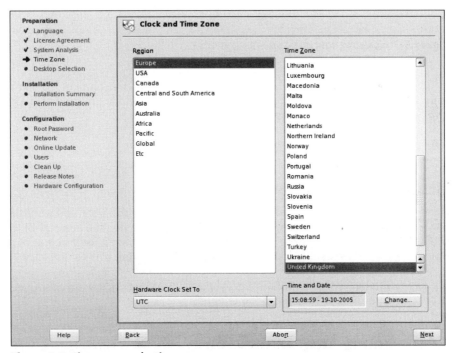

Figure 1-6: Time zone selection

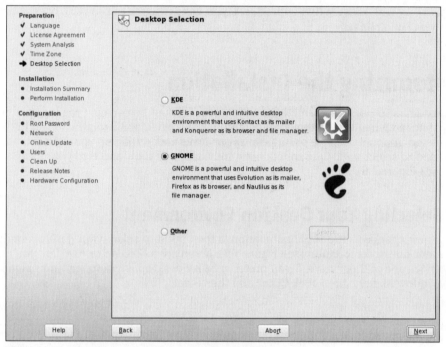

Figure 1-7: Selecting your desktop environment

You will be given the option of either a minimal desktop environment, or text mode only. If you are installing SUSE as a server, then these options are the best to go with as it minimizes unnecessary packages being installed.

For this installation we will choose GNOME.

Installation Overview

After you have made the decision about the desktop environment you want to use, YaST will then give you an overview of what it is going to do (see Figure 1-8). If you are installing on a new system with no other operating system, or you do not need any other packages installed, you can check the installation profile and click Next.

If you want to tweak the installation system, change the partition layout, or install other packages, follow the rest of the chapter.

Customizing Your Installation

To be able to get a broader overview of what you can change in the installation, click the Expert tab. This displays all available options rather than the few shown in the Overview tab.

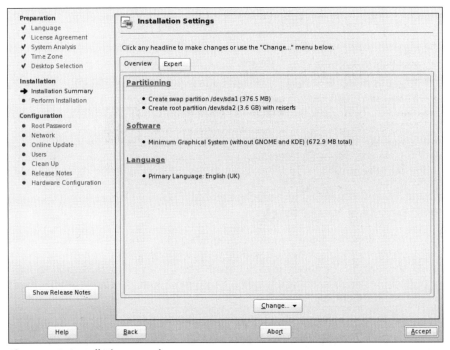

Figure 1-8: Installation overview

Clicking any heading in the Installation Overview section enables you to modify that aspect of your installation. Similarly, selecting the Change button displays a pop-up menu from which you can select any of the headings on this screen to change or examine the relevant aspects of the installation to guarantee that they meet your requirements.

✦ **System** — Displays a dialog box showing the hardware that the installer detected in your system. You cannot change these values.

✦ **Keyboard layout** — Select the keyboard set used for the system and the installation process.

✦ **Partitioning** — One of the most important aspects of installing a Linux system. Partitioning configures the target hard drive for the installation of an operating system.

✦ **Software** — Selection of predefined software profiles, as well as individual software packages.

✦ **Booting** — Configuration of the Linux boot loader. The boot loader bootstraps a loader at bootup that enables the user to boot not only Linux, but also any other operating systems in the system.

✦ **Time zone** — Set the time zone of the system based on either your location or specifically setting the GMT offset.

✦ **Language** — Set the language of the system and also the installation process. This was already set earlier in the installation process.

✦ **Default Runlevel** — Set the initial boot runlevel for the system. Runlevels are discussed in Chapter 4. For now, the default value (runlevel 5) is acceptable.

✦ **Reset to defaults** — Remove all changes you have made and start from scratch. This is useful for testing installation mixtures and seeing how these affect your system. This is accessible from the Change button at the bottom of the screen.

Throughout the remainder of the installation, we talk in more detail about what these settings do to your system and we also discuss the ways in which you can change these settings.

Partitioning Your Disks

YaST initially chooses a partitioning scheme based on your disk layout. It is very likely that the installation default will be fine (see Figure 1-9) for a first-time user. For other users, YaST enables you to control the layout of partitions on the disk, the type of filesystems that are used on those partitions, and any options that will be used when mounting them.

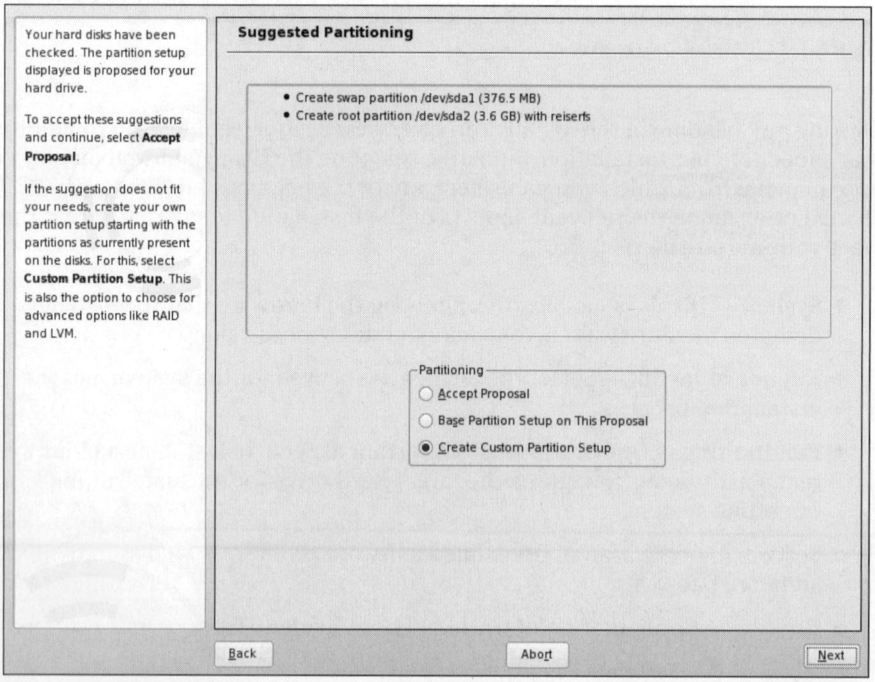

Suggested Partitioning

Your hard disks have been checked. The partition setup displayed is proposed for your hard drive.

To accept these suggestions and continue, select **Accept Proposal**.

If the suggestion does not fit your needs, create your own partition setup starting with the partitions as currently present on the disks. For this, select **Custom Partition Setup**. This is also the option to choose for advanced options like RAID and LVM.

- Create swap partition /dev/sda1 (376.5 MB)
- Create root partition /dev/sda2 (3.6 GB) with reiserfs

Partitioning
- ○ Accept Proposal
- ○ Base Partition Setup on This Proposal
- ◉ Create Custom Partition Setup

Back   Abort   Next

Figure 1-9: Partitioning

One key thing to know when defining and experimenting with disk partitioning is that none of the changes that you are defining are actually performed until you explicitly tell YaST to proceed with the installation. You can make as many changes or experiment with different partitioning schemes as much as you want without actually committing those changes. Aborting the SUSE Linux installation at any time before this point will leave your system's disk exactly as it was when you started the installation process.

What you do next depends on your requirements:

✦ If you want to accept the default partition layout selected by YaST, select Accept proposal as-is, click Next, and skip ahead to the section of this chapter entitled "Selecting Software for Installation."

✦ If you are an experienced Linux user, or you just want to specify your own customized partitioning scheme, select Create custom partition setup and click Next. Then, select the Custom partitioning - for experts option, and click Next (see Figure 1-10). This presents you with the option to create and delete partitions, as well as other advanced options such as software RAID and cryptographic filesystems.

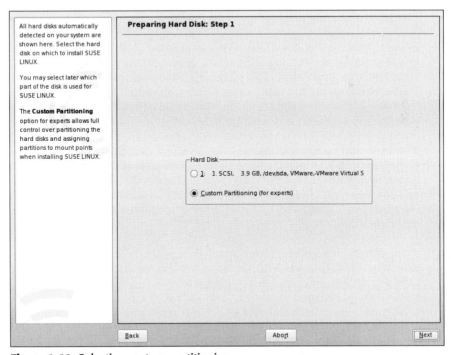

Figure 1-10: Selecting custom partitioning

If you are creating your own partitioning scheme and do not already have an operating system on your computer that you want to preserve, skip to the section "Primary and Extended Partitions."

Resizing Existing Operating System Partitions

Nowadays, it is quite common to have systems that can boot multiple operating systems. Such computer systems enable users to take advantage of the power and applications available in each operating system by selecting between available operating systems when you boot the system. These are typically referred to as *dual-boot* systems because most people install at most two operating systems on a single machine. However, because more than two operating systems can be installed on a single disk, the proper name is *multiboot*, which is the term used in this section. The number of operating systems that you can boot and run on a single computer is really limited only by the amount of disk space available on your computer system.

With SUSE Linux, the most common type of multiboot system is a system that can boot either SUSE Linux or some version of Microsoft Windows. Windows will be used as an example throughout the rest of this section, although the same general concepts are true when setting up multiboot systems that will run SUSE Linux and any other operating system.

Explaining how to install Windows on an existing SUSE Linux system is not relevant to a discussion of installing SUSE Linux. However, the reverse is not true. Installing SUSE Linux on a system that already runs Windows, and on which you want to be able to continue to run Windows, is a common wish. This is quite easy to do and involves only resizing your existing Windows partition(s) so that sufficient contiguous space is available for installing SUSE.

If you are running a new installation on a system that already contains an operating system such as Windows that you want to preserve, and if the disk or Windows partition in that system has sufficient free space to install SUSE Linux, YaST will propose a solution based on resizing your existing Windows partition and automatically creating appropriate swap and root partitions. If at all possible, you should accept this default selection.

If you do not have sufficient free space to install SUSE Linux and YaST cannot automatically resize your existing operating system partitions, your only alternative (besides adding another disk to your system) is to abort the SUSE install process, remove the installation media, and reboot into your other operating system. You must then free up sufficient disk space and clean up the organization of your operating system's partition(s) using a utility such as Windows' Disk Defragmenter. If there is sufficient unused space on your Windows partition, you should be able to restart the SUSE installation process and let YaST select appropriate partitioning and resizing values for you.

Cross-Reference For more on setting up dual-boot (multiboot) systems, see Chapter 4.

Primary and Extended Partitions

In this section, we start with a clean disk to create the partitions needed to install SUSE. If you want to remove the partitions on an existing installation of an operating system, select the partition and press the Delete button. You will be asked to confirm this, and the partition will be removed.

If you select Create, you are prompted for the type of partition you want to create (see Figure 1-11). In the PC world, the BIOS can access only four primary partitions. These can be thought of as four physical boundaries on the disk, with separate data and filesystems on each. With Linux, you need at least two partitions, and if you have Windows on another partition, and a data or home disk on the other, you may quickly run out of ways to expand the way your disk is laid out. To combat this, logical and extended partitions were designed. An *extended partition* is a placeholder for further logical partitions, and it is a good idea to create one extended partition (which takes up one of your primary partitions) and create logical partitions to accommodate further partitioning schemes in the future.

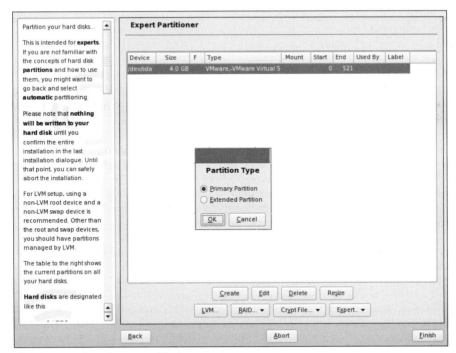

Figure 1-11: Creating a partition

The most common way to partition disks for home Linux use is to have one primary partition for the Linux root partition, a second primary partition for the swap partition, and then an extended partition for any other (logical) partitions that may be needed. Using extended and logical partitions grows the amount of total partitions you can have in a system to 16, which is usually more than enough.

Select the Primary partition option and click OK to proceed.

Defining Filesystems

After a primary partition has been created, you need to define the format in which a filesystem should be created on that partition, its size, and the mount point for that filesystem. Linux and Unix use the definition of mount points in the same way that Windows uses drive letters. The advantage with Linux is that the whole system is hierarchical in nature, and therefore access to data on disks, network drives, and partitions can be kept under one manageable tree structure.

Swap Partitions

The first partition you need to create is the *swap partition*. Most modern operating systems use swap partitions, also referred to as *swap space*, to support virtual memory. Virtual memory is a technique for enabling a system to use more memory than is physically available to the operating system. Processes on the system that are inactive or are waiting for input are copied from physical memory into swap space, known as *swapping out a process*. At this point, the physical memory associated with those processes can be reused by the operating system. When the process can run again, such as when input is available, it is copied from the swap space back into memory and continues execution. This is known as *swapping in a process*. The way in which processes are swapped in and out of memory is simple in theory, but is triggered by a number of internal metrics that are maintained and constantly updated by the kernel.

You should always create a swap partition on a Linux or Unix machine as the workload on any system can never be fully quantified beforehand and running out of physical memory without swap space causes processes to crash or be unable to execute in the first place.

The window to create a filesystem/partition can be quite daunting for new users (see Figure 1-12). SUSE and the other distributions try to make the process as simple and usable as possible. Selecting the format of the filesystem is primarily a concern when creating data partitions or for advanced users, as discussed in the next section. When creating a swap partition, you must select Swap as its format. You will notice that the mount point will also change to be swap because the swap partition is not mounted like a data partition but is used internally by the Linux system.

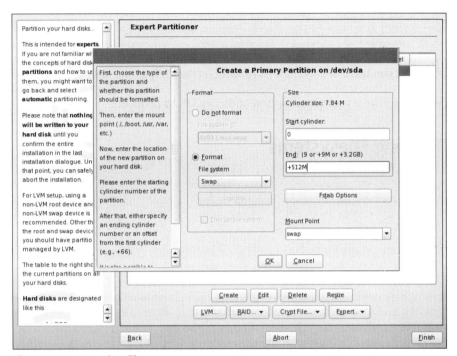

Figure 1-12: Creating filesystems

Cross-Reference

Filesystems are discussed in more detail in Chapter 3.

Start and end cylinders are often new concepts to new Linux users who are used to data sizes being defined in mega- and gigabytes. YaST enables you to enter the size of a partition in human readable form, such as MB and GB. The start cylinder, as this is the first partition on the disk, is 0 (the start of the usable space on the disk), and the end cylinder is what we need to change. It is usually customary to select a swap size that is 1.5 times the amount of physical RAM in the system, but this is subject to much conjecture. A reasonable swap size should be considered based on the work-load of the machine you will be using, and as most modern PC systems have at least 512MB, it is safe to use the standard 1.5 times physical memory. To specify that you want the swap partition to be 750MB, enter **+750M** in the End cylinder entry box. The + signifies that you want to add space, the number is the unit of space needed, and the *M* specifies that the amount of data is expressed in megabytes. You can also specify *G* for gigabytes, which you will be using in the following example of creating a root partition.

After entering the size of your new swap partition, click OK to proceed.

Tip

At a bare minimum, the filesystems that need to be created are the swap space and a root (/) filesystem. However, for ease of use and manageability, the creation of a /home partition can help keep your personal data separate from the system partition and also enable you to keep your data in the unlikely event that you want to do a total reinstall of Linux. See the section on "Data Partitions" later in this chapter for more information.

In this example you are creating the bare minimum, the swap and root partitions.

The Root Partition

After the swap space has been created, you need to configure the root (/) partition (see Figure 1-13). The root (/) partition is the most important data partition on any Linux or Unix system, and is the only non-swap filesystem partition that is required in order to boot a Unix or Linux system. The *root partition* takes its name from the fact that it is the partition mounted at the root of the Unix/Linux filesystem, which is the directory known as /. A filesystem must be mounted on this directory to successfully boot a Linux system. The root filesystem contains core directories required to boot Linux, such as the directory through which devices are accessed (/dev); the directory containing system administration, configuration, and initialization files (/etc); the directory in which critical system libraries, kernel modules, security, and internationalization information are located (/lib); and directories containing critical system binaries (/sbin, /bin, and so on).

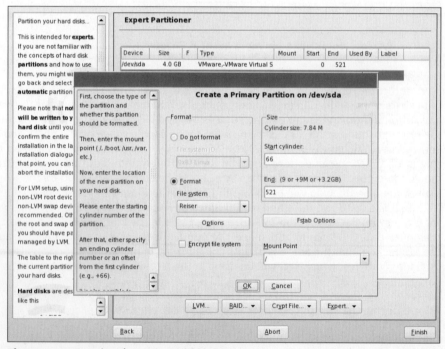

Figure 1-13: Creating the root partition

By default, creating this partition will automatically use the remaining unallocated space on the hard drive, which is fine for our example. However, if you need to create another partition — /home, for example — you specify the size of the partition explicitly as you did with the swap space. See the next section, "Data Partitions," for an overview of why you may want to create additional partitions.

The default type of filesystem used in SUSE is the Reiser filesystem, often referred to as the ReiserFS. It was one of the first available journaling filesystems for Linux, and a lot of the work was funded by both SUSE and mp3.com. A *journaling filesystem* dedicates a specific part of the filesystem for use as a cache of pending writes to the filesystem; this ensures that filesystem updates occur in a clean, atomic fashion; and allows a fast recovery if the system is not cleanly shut down. Ordinarily, when a Linux system is shut down, it ensures that all pending writes to each filesystem have completed, and then detaches the filesystems (known as *unmounting* them) to guarantee that all system data is consistent before the system is turned off. Using a journaling filesystem does not mean it is safer to just power off the machine, as data loss can still occur when data is not completely written to the disk.

After the root partition has been created, you can review your changes (see Figure 1-14) and proceed with the software installation by clicking Finish. If you want to create additional filesystems during the installation process, read the next section before clicking Finish.

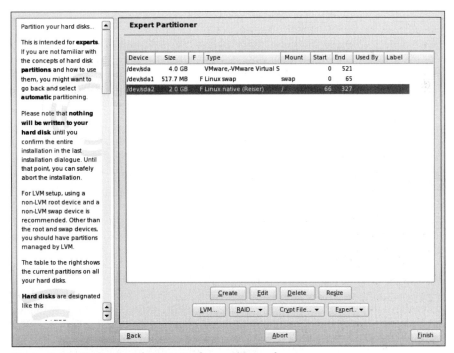

Figure 1-14: Reviewing changes to the partition scheme

Data Partitions

Data partitions is a generic term for partitions that are formatted as a filesystem and in which both the system and its users can store data. The partition designated as the root filesystem is a special case of a data partition because it is required in order to boot a Linux system.

The preceding sections explained how to create the swap and root partitions that must be present to successfully boot a Linux system. However, you can also create other data partitions, format them as filesystems, and specify their mount points during the installation process. On Linux systems, a *mount point* is simply a Linux directory through which a filesystem is made available to the system, known as *mounting* that filesystem. Using regular directories as mount points is a clever part of the design of Unix and Linux. If you run out of disk space on a given partition, you can add another disk to your system, create data partitions there, copy the data from existing directories to those partitions, and then mount the new partitions on the directory where the data was originally located, effectively increasing the amount of storage available to an existing system.

Today's larger disks make it attractive to create other data partitions. You have several reasons to consider creating multiple data partitions on today's disks:

✦ When you boot a Linux system, the system checks the consistency of each of its filesystems (as defined in the file /etc/fstab — more about this in Chapter 3). Checking the consistency of a single, huge, nonjournaled filesystem can take quite a bit of time.

✦ Filesystem corruption can occur as a result of a number of problems, such as a system crash, sudden power loss, or hardware problems. Whenever a filesystem is corrupted, repairing it (which is mandatory) can cause you to lose data. Creating multiple partitions reduces the extent to which filesystem corruption can affect a single data partition.

✦ Keeping data on multiple partitions limits the chance that you can lose data during a subsequent system upgrade. Some upgrades reformat the root partition or recreate its directory structure. If your user data is stored on other data partitions, they will not be affected by changes to the root filesystem.

✦ Some Linux backup software backs up data on a per-partition basis. Backing up a single huge partition can take quite a bit of time. Also, if your backups fail (such as when a tape is corrupted), you may not be able to use the backups to restore your system. Creating multiple partitions limits problems related to a backup failure to a single partition.

Chapter 3 provides more detail about creating multiple partitions and the types of filesystems supported by Linux and provides additional reasons why you may want to create multiple partitions on your Linux system. Most types of Linux filesystems can be resized once they have been created, enabling you to customize your system's partitioning, even after the system has been installed and is running.

If you want to create multiple partitions during the installation process, you can do this by making sure that the root partition does not completely fill your disk and then creating additional partitions in the remaining space on your disk. Common parts of a Linux system that you may want to put on separate data partitions are /boot, /home, /opt, /tmp, /var, /usr, and /usr/local. For more information on these partitions and the types of information stored there, see Chapter 3.

Selecting Software for Installation

The software that is automatically selected as part of a default SUSE installation provides you with nearly every type of software required for day-to-day work. This section offers additional details about the other types of installations provided by the SUSE installer to provide a full and thorough SUSE learning experience.

To customize the software that is included as part of your SUSE installation, you must click the Software heading in YaST's Installation Settings panel, or click Change and select Software from the pop-up menu. Doing either of these displays the pane shown in Figure 1-15.

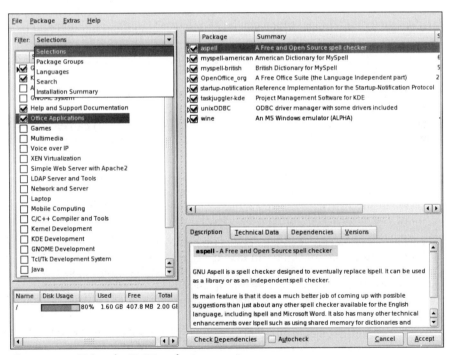

Figure 1-15: Using the YaST package manager

The left panel of the package selection screen gives a broad overview of packages and disk space used, and also indicates how much space will be required when installing all selected packages.

The Filter drop-down list box provides a powerful way to limit what packages you can select. As we stated in the Introduction, we ourselves differ on our views of a few Linux idiosyncrasies, including text, desktop environments, and also Linux on the desktop in general. SUSE is aware of differing views throughout the whole Linux community, and therefore using package selections enables users to specify things such as which desktop environment and editor they want to install — why waste disk space if you're not going to use something? The same is true for games, multi-media, and specific server software. The amount of disk space required to install your system can be reduced or enhanced by selecting specific packages.

We will keep the default package selection as chosen by SUSE and add a new package that is not installed by default.

Selecting Search from the drop-down list box enables you to enter search criteria for a package and returns all results based on the Search in criteria selected. Figure 1-16 shows a search for the Blackbox window manager. As you can see, YaST returned not only the package Blackbox but also other packages that contain the word *blackbox* in their summary definitions, which can be seen in the Description window.

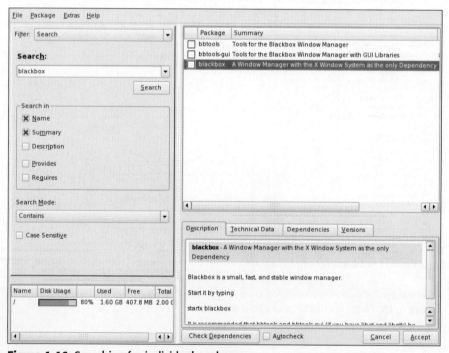

Figure 1-16: Searching for individual packages

When a package is selected, your disk usage will be increased to reflect the size of the install domain.

Select Accept to add those packages you select to the install list and take you back to the package installation summary screen.

Selecting a Boot Loader

The next item you can change is the configuration of the boot loader. A boot loader is central to the deployment of Linux as it controls the booting of operating systems on the PC. To customize the boot loader that is used by your SUSE installation, you must click the Booting heading in YaST's Expert Installation Settings panel, or click the Change button (under the Expert Tab) and select Booting from the pop-up menu. Doing either of these displays the pane shown in Figure 1-17, YaST's Boot Loader Settings screen.

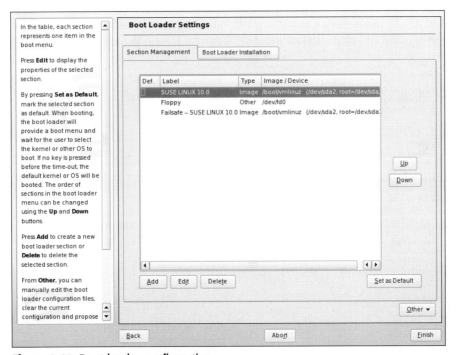

Figure 1-17: Boot loader configuration

Linux systems typically use one of two boot loaders, LILO (Linux Loader) or GRUB (Grand Unified Boot Loader). Both are very powerful and flexible, and are controlled by easily edited configuration files (/etc/lilo.conf and /etc/grub.conf, respectively). The key difference between the two boot loaders is how they interact with these configuration files. If you use LILO and update its configuration file, you must rerun the lilo command to update the system boot information that is stored on your disk. GRUB automatically rereads its configuration file whenever you boot your system and therefore does not require that you update any other system boot information.

A few years ago, the general consensus was to move away from the LILO boot loader to the GRUB boot loader. GRUB provides a more robust boot loader, and the default configuration is fine for most users. If YaST detects a Windows installation, it adds this as a boot option, providing a means to dual-boot Windows and Linux on the same system.

YaST will already have configured your boot loader, depending on your system configuration. This also includes any Windows installations that have been found. To edit a boot loader entry, select the relevant entry and click Edit. You will be presented with the boot item configuration screen shown in Figure 1-18.

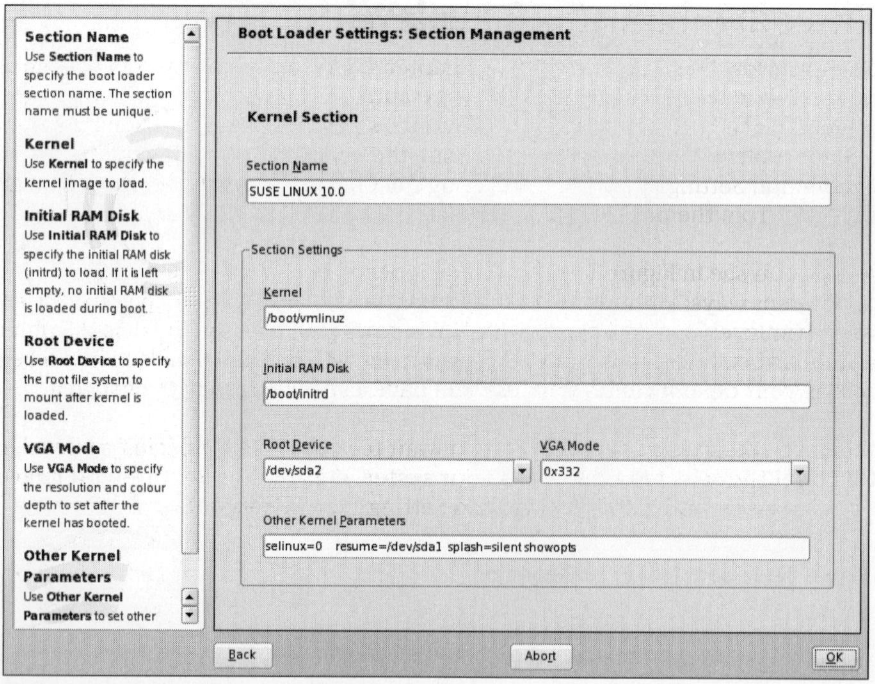

Figure 1-18: Editing a boot loader entry

One of the most important reasons for editing the default boot loader configuration is to add a Linux kernel option at startup. If your hardware manufacturer has notified you that a certain value must be passed to the Linux kernel at boot time, you would append it to the "Other kernel parameters" section of the configuration dialog box. When you are happy with the boot loader item configuration, click OK to return to the boot loader overview screen.

Note

A few very common kernel parameters that we have come across in recent years are noht and noacpi. Both of these parameters are relevant to modern machines. The first, noht, will turn off Linux's support of the Intel processor's hyperthreading feature. In certain processor-bound workloads, it is better to turn off hyperthreading to improve performance. The second, noacpi, turns off Linux's ACPI infrastructure. ACPI is the Advanced Configuration and Power Interface and is a standardized way for an operating system to control machine power, BIOS settings, and so on. In some situations ACPI actually stops Linux from booting on certain machines. Using the boot loader configuration to set these parameters enables you to control this before a system is installed.

When you make any changes that you want on the Boot Loader setup screen, click the Finish button to return to the standard YaST installer screen.

Changing the Default Runlevel

Runlevels are discussed in detail in Chapter 4. As a quick summary, a system's *runlevel* determines the services that are automatically started when your system boots. The YaST Expert Installation Settings screen can be used to change the default runlevel of the system by clicking the Default Runlevel heading in YaST's Installation Settings panel or by clicking the Change button and selecting Default Runlevel from the pop-up menu.

As you can see in Figure 1-19, you can choose to boot your SUSE system in a variety of different ways: without networking functionality (runlevel 2), multiuser with network (runlevel 3), or multiuser with X Windows (runlevel 5). The default runlevel in a standard installation is runlevel 5, multiuser with X Windows. You should keep this as your default runlevel unless you have a specific reason to change it.

When you make any changes that you want to your system's default runlevel, click OK to set the selected runlevel as your system default. The Set Default Runlevel pop-up closes, and YaST's Installation Setting panel displays.

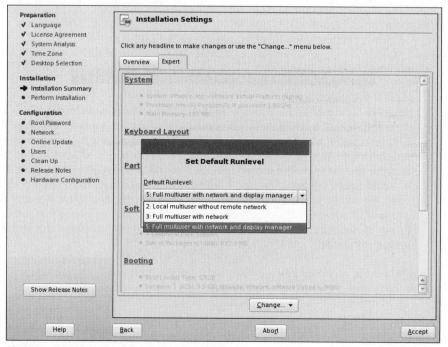

Figure 1-19: Changing the default runlevel

Running the Installation

When you've made any changes to the installation, select the Accept button in the Installation Settings window, and the installation process begins. You will be asked if you definitely want to create the partitions you defined and the filesystems that sit above them (see Figure 1-20). Partitioning the disk is a destructive process and *will* remove any data that those partitions replace.

Caution   This is your last chance to abort your installation without making any changes to your disk. You should continue only if you are sure that the selected settings are correct. If you are installing SUSE for the first time on a new computer system, you have nothing to worry about. If you are installing SUSE on an existing computer system on which you need to preserve existing data, double-check your settings before proceeding. You can double-check that your partitioning scheme is, in fact, correct for your environment and make changes as necessary by selecting Partitioning from the Installation Settings screen Then triple-check your selections before proceeding.

Selecting Install will destructively create the partitions and filesystems and installs the packages you selected.

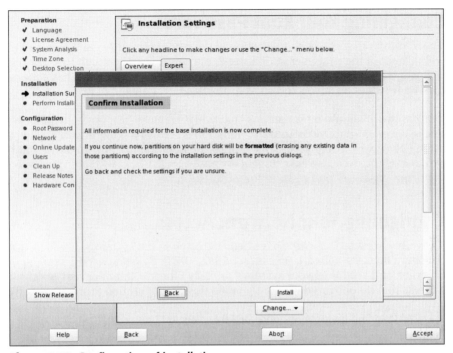

Figure 1-20: Confirmation of installation

During package installation, you can view the progress, the CDs needed, and also an overview of the package use by selecting the Details button. To switch back to the slideshow, select the Slideshow button.

This may be a good time to get a coffee, as nothing interesting happens while packages are installed. If you are installing from CDs, after the packages from CD 1 are installed, the system will automatically reboot itself to use the specific kernel for your architecture, as well as to commit packages installed on the system.

If you think back to the discussion of the install boot options at the beginning of the chapter, you will remember that the default is to boot off the hard drive first. This helps a lot if you leave the install media in the drive and are drinking your coffee in another room.

When the system has rebooted, YaST asks you for the remaining media to install the rest of the packages. In the case of a minimal installation, or all packages being installed, YaST proceeds automatically to the system configuration.

Configuring Your Root Password

The first item that needs configuration is the root password (see Figure 1-21). We will talk about the root user in Chapter 2, but for now it is enough to know this is the user who has the privileges to change anything on the system, has access to all files on the system, and is known as a *superuser*.

The password should be something that you can remember, but also difficult to guess. A combination of letters and numbers is always a good way of making a strong password. Using your name, family member names, and so on should be avoided as these can be easy targets for passwords. Click Next after you've entered your root password and re-enter for verification.

Configuring Your Network Access

If any network interface cards have been detected in the system, you will be asked to configure them for network access (see Figure 1-22). By default, YaST sets the first Ethernet card it finds as your system's primary Ethernet interface and assigns it an address that is configured via the Dynamic Host Configuration Protocol (DHCP).

 Cross-Reference   You can find discussions about DHCP servers in Chapter 20.

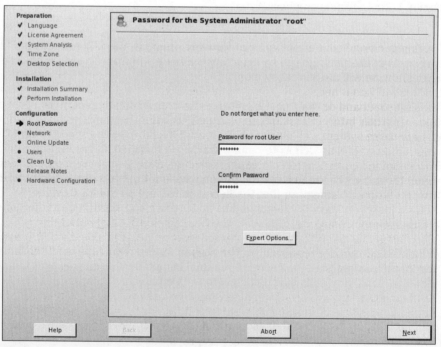

Figure 1-21: Setting the root password

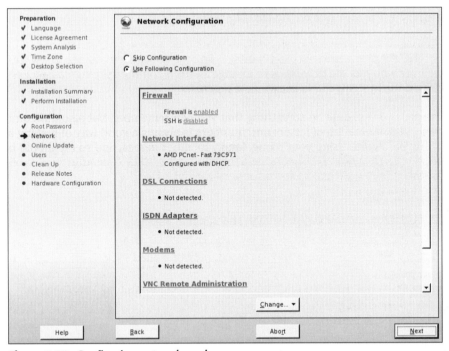

Figure 1-22: Configuring network cards

For most people using SUSE in a business environment, a DHCP server may already be running, and an address, domain name system (DNS) server list, and router configuration will already be available. Home users and users setting up a server system will find it necessary to configure these details manually. Home users with simple broadband or dial-up connections often automatically receive this information from their Internet service providers (ISPs) and therefore may not need to change these settings.

To change the configuration of the network card, click "Network Interfaces" and select the network card in question (if you have multiple network cards), and click the Edit button. A screen similar to the one shown in Figure 1-23 appears.

In this example configuration, we set the IP address of the network card to 192.168.0.1/255.255.255.0, with a router/gateway of 192.168.0.8 and a DNS server of 192.168.0.254. If you are unfamiliar with these terms at this stage, see Chapter 6 for additional information.

To change the configuration of the network card from automatic to manual, select Static address setup. This enables you to edit the IP and subnet mask fields. As you can see in Figure 1-23, we have set the IP address/netmask to that of the configuration we talked about in the preceding paragraph.

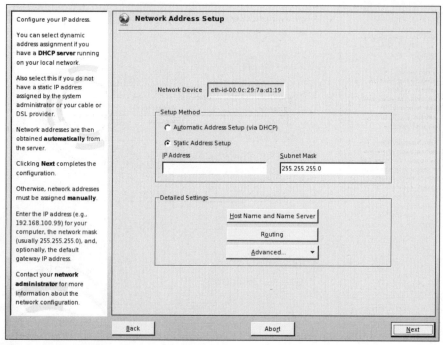

Figure 1-23: Configuration of network cards

Setting Up Your Host Name and DNS Addresses

To set up the host name of the Linux machine and the addresses of your Domain Name System servers, select the Host name and name server button. A screen like that shown in Figure 1-24 appears.

The host name of your Linux machine can be anything you like, such as a person's name, a descriptive name, or something random. The only thing that you have to bear in mind is that the host name and domain name can contain only letters and numbers as well a hyphen or an underscore. The host name can be only one string of characters and cannot contain a space or a period. As the name suggests, the domain name dictates the network domain that this machine falls into. This domain may well be something in line with your company's policy or could be something you have set up yourself.

Tip   When integrating a new system into an existing networked environment, you should always follow the same naming conventions that are already being used, especially for the domain name. If you do not, other systems on the network may not be able to locate your system correctly, and certain services on your system may not be able to interoperate with existing network services.

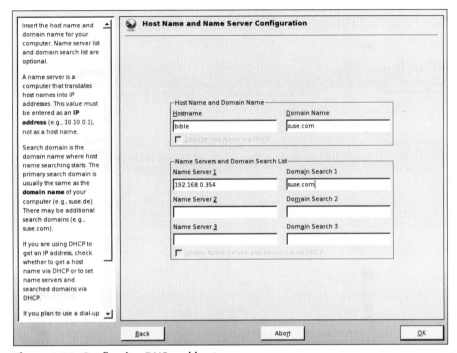

Figure 1-24: Configuring DNS and host name

Enter the name server address into the Name Server 1 field. You can also enter up to two other separate DNS server entries. Your administrator or ISP should be able to give you this information.

The Domain Search entry is used to control how your machine looks up the address of other machines connected through TCP/IP. For example, if you use a Domain Search entry such as suse.com, you can communicate with any machine in the SUSE domain by just its host name. For example, with suse.com as the Domain Search entry, you can communicate with the machine you are setting up in this example by just using the host name of bible. If you do have suse.com as a Domain Search field, however, you have to specify the fully qualified domain name of the machine you want to communicate with (in the case of this example, that is bible.suse.com).

When you have set the DNS configuration for your system, press OK to save your changes.

Configuring the Default Gateway

Next, you will probably need to configure the router/gateway for your system. To do this, click the Routing button. You will see a screen similar to the one shown in Figure 1-25.

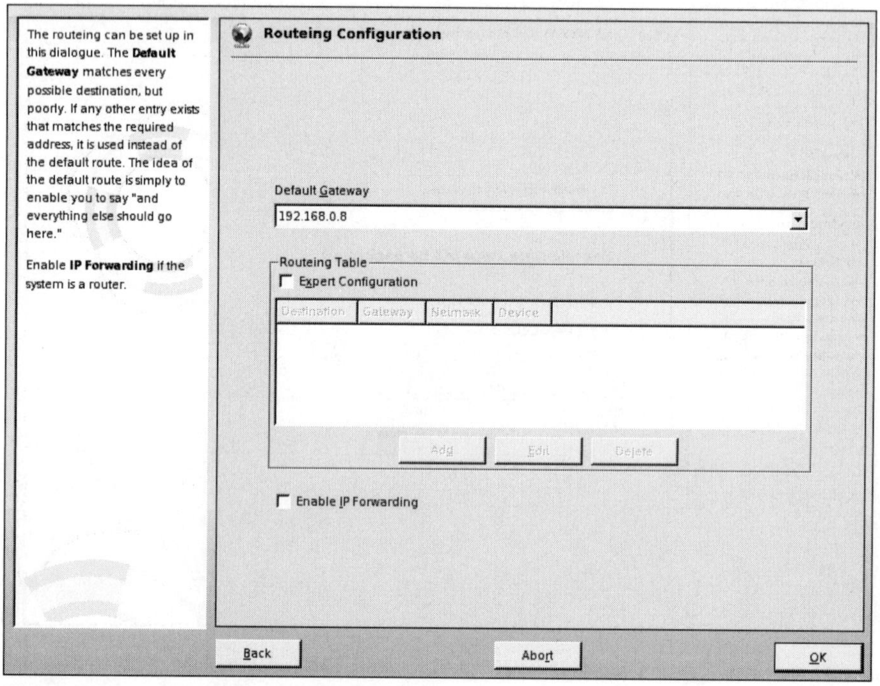

Figure 1-25: Configuring a default gateway

Your default gateway address is the IP address of the host to which TCP/IP packets that are not destined for your local network are sent for further processing. For example, your gateway address will be that of your asymmetric digital subscriber line (ADSL) router if that is how you connect to the Internet. In other cases, your network or system administrator will be able to provide you with this information.

When you have set the gateway address, click OK to proceed. You will then be returned to the Network Address Setup screen. If you are happy with the network card configuration, click Next.

When you have finished configuring all of the network cards that you need to configure, click Next in the Network Configuration screen. This tells YaST to save the changes to your network configuration and restart the system networking.

Testing Your Connection and Online Updates

Taking a page from the "other" operating systems, SUSE now enables you to run the update service as soon as the system has been installed (see Figure 1-26). Online updates are discussed in more detail in Chapter 9 and are not discussed here as part of our sample installation. If you are feeling adventurous, then testing your Internet connection and running the online update is a good idea, but it is not necessary as part of the installation process. Click Next after you have made your choice.

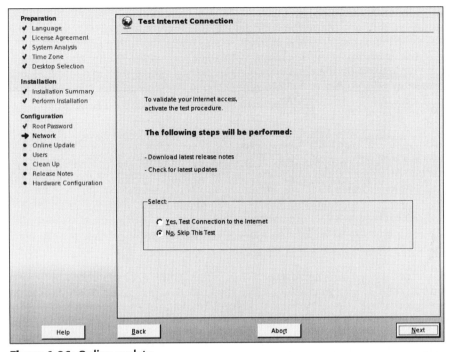

Figure 1-26: Online update

Configuring Your Modem

Modems are notorious for being something of a problem area for Linux because many of the internal PCI modems that are on sale are not true modems, but are what is known as *winmodems* or *soft modems*. The idea behind winmodems is that some of the functionality of the modem can be offloaded from hardware into software — the software in question being the Windows operating system. As these devices are designed to work only with Windows and in theory require a Microsoft operating system to work, it is not surprising that there are difficulties getting them to work on Linux. So there are three possibilities:

- ✦ **You have an old-fashioned external serial modem.** These will always work under Linux.

- ✦ **You have a winmodem.** This may or may not work with Linux.

- ✦ **You have an internal true hardware modem.** In almost all cases this will work with Linux.

Winmodem support has improved considerably, and some previously unsupported modems now work with Linux. SUSE supports at least the SmartLink and Lucent ltmodem types. During the installation, if YaST detects that you have a supported winmodem, it will install the necessary package to provide driver support.

Assuming that your modem is supported, YaST asks you for the necessary information to set up the modem and your dial-up connection. In the first screen of the setup you are asked for a dial prefix if necessary (a prefix you might need to get an outside line, for example) and to choose between tone dialing and pulse dialing (tone dialing will be the correct choice unless your telephone exchange is very antiquated). The other two choices here (Speaker on and Detect Dial tone) you will almost certainly want to leave as they are (selected by default).

The next screen asks you for your country and offers a small selection of preconfig- ured providers (ISPs). This means that the access number is already known to the system for these providers. One or two have gone further and enable you to use a preconfigured username and password to sign up with them, or even to get full anonymous access with payment being collected through your phone charges.

If you already have an account with an ISP that is not listed, you need to press the New button and add the details of the provider's name, the access phone number, and your username and password.

When this is done, press Finish and the modem configuration should be complete. You will then be able to connect using the kinternet program, which you can access through the KDE menu (Internet ⇨ Dialup). You can set kinternet to run whenever you log in to KDE; if you do this, you can log in by clicking its tiny icon, which will be resident in the system tray area of the KDE panel (by default in the bottom-right corner of the screen).

Note   More information about using winmodems under Linux can be obtained from w w w .linmodems.org. You may be able to obtain a driver for your modem from this site, even if it is not supported by SUSE. You can also download a tool called scanModem, which detects the exact type of modem that you have. When you know this, you can search the site for information about whether it is possible to get it working.

ISDN and ADSL Connections

SUSE has very good support for internal Integrated Services Digital Network (ISDN) cards, and these can also be set up at this point in the installation. In most cases, the card will be automatically set up, and you just have to provide the specific information given to you by your ISP.

Asymmetric digital subscriber line (ADSL) providers sometimes offer a particular hardware device to connect with. These are sometimes USB devices. Unfortunately, there are a large number of different types and not all of them work with Linux. There are also different standards in different countries, and as a result, getting these devices to work on Linux has always been something of a problem. If YaST detects such a device during the installation, it attempts to set it up, but there are still many cases in which USB ADSL devices fail to work with SUSE Linux.

If at all possible, rather than using a USB device for ADSL, you should choose one of the ADSL routers with Ethernet output. This type of ADSL connection will always work, and if your provider offers the choice, you should definitely go for this type of connection. If your provider offers a wires-only service, you can buy such a router and use it to connect; again, there should be no problems at all. All you need to do is follow the instructions provided by the manufacturer or ISP for setting up your network connection to talk to the router and make the necessary settings in YaST's networking module.

Adding a New User

Just as Windows provides the infrastructure to authenticate users through a central database, the Unix world can use the Network Information System (NIS) or Lightweight Directory Access Protocol (LDAP) to store user account details. Most home users need to configure only a standalone machine and should select that option (see Figure 1-27).

See Chapter 25 for more information on the configuration of LDAP.

Click Next to create a new local user, and the Add a New Local User screen appears (see Figure 1-28). Most of the information needed for creating a new user is self-explanatory.

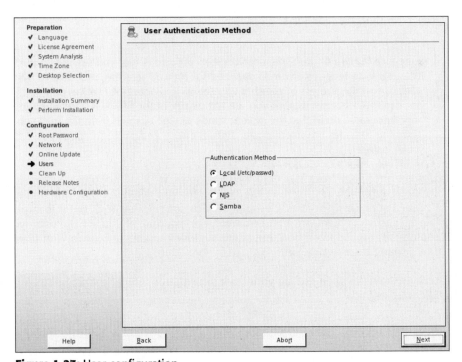

Figure 1-27: User configuration

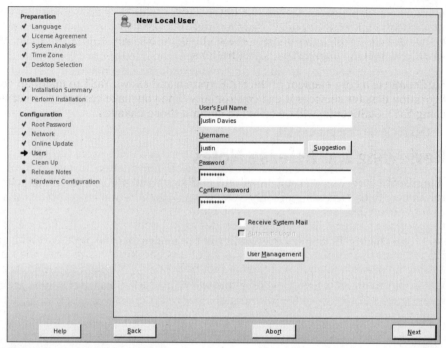

Figure 1-28: Creating a local user

Tip   One nice feature of the SUSE user creation process is that you can set yourself as the user who receives any mail destined for root by selecting the Receive System Mail option. Regardless of whether you set up this option, it is always a good idea to read the root user mail (if you are the owner of the root user account!) to see any automated mails that the system sends as well as mails from the mail subsystem. This includes bounced emails, system errors, and package updates that have been installed.

Taking another page from Mac OS X and Windows XP, SUSE enables you to set up an account to automatically log in to the system for you when the machine boots up. For home users, this provides a simpler way to use their system, but it is impractical and insecure in business environments. For example, if you are the user who is automatically logged in on boot up, someone else can gain access to your files simply by turning the machine on.

When you have finished adding your user information, click Next to continue, and SuSEconfig will run.

SuSEconfig

The SUSE system configuration is controlled by SUSE-specific control files that the system application SuSEconfig uses to write application-specific configuration files.

This enables the user to configure services and server processes without having to understand application-specific configuration files. When all packages have been installed, SuSEconfig picks up the default configuration files installed by SUSE and writes out specific application configurations.

SuSEconfig is a core element of the SUSE system and allows YaST to maintain configuration files for services it can control. Any time you make changes to a service using YaST, SuSEconfig will be called to commit those changes.

Reviewing the Release Notes

When SuSEconfig has finished its initial installation, you will be shown the SUSE release notes (see Figure 1-29). These notes contain general information about changes from previous versions of SUSE Linux, as well as a technical overview of the previous version. This file also provides errata from the SUSE manual and is worth a read to get a general idea as to what has happened since the last release. Ninety percent of users at this point have not touched the included manuals with SUSE, except perhaps to move them out of the way when locating the installation media, so this at least gives you an introduction to the features and functionality of the product.

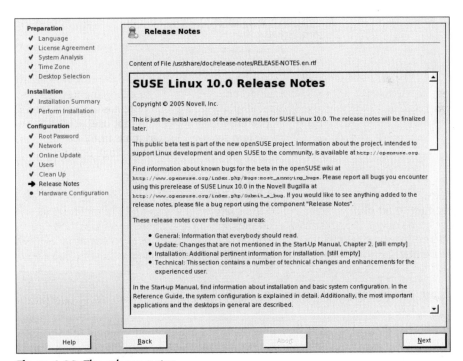

Figure 1-29: The release notes

Configuring Your Hardware

When you have read the release notes, click Next and you will be asked to configure your hardware (see Figure 1-30). The YaST installer and the YaST system configuration manager runs the same modules to configure hardware. For now you will configure the video card so that you can use X/KDE/GNOME.

YaST in SUSE 10 has changed the way it detects your graphics capabilities. YaST will automatically sense what your current configuration is and will then allow you to change those individual settings.

Configuring Your Monitor

To change your monitor configuration from what YaST detected, click on the monitor listed under "Graphics Cards." You will be presented with a list of available monitors from which you can choose (see Figure 1-31).

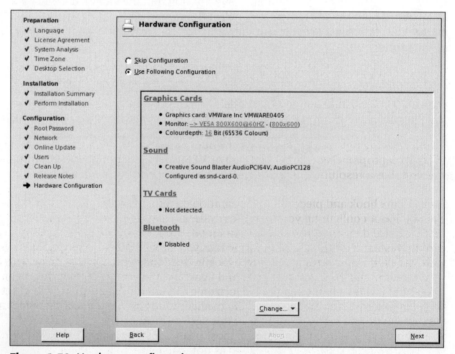

Figure 1-30: Hardware configuration

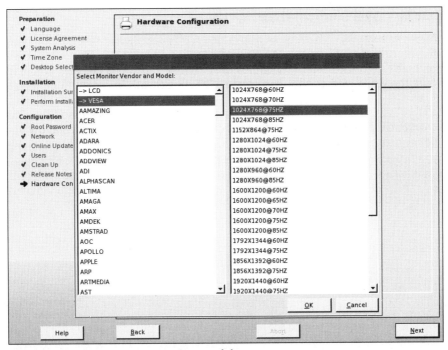

Figure 1-31: Choosing your monitor model

If your specific monitor is listed in the vendor list, select it. If not, choose either LCD (for laptop or flatscreen monitors) or VESA (for CRT monitors). It is usually a safe bet that a resolution of 1024 × 768 will be supported by your monitor.

Every Linux book and piece of documentation on X Windows configuration has a disclaimer about configuring your graphics system. This book is no different because there are real dangers if you set up your monitor incorrectly. Because the graphics card drives the monitor, it is imperative that you either configure the graphics system with standard lower settings, or take a look in the documentation that came with *both* your monitor and your graphics card and figure out the correct settings for them. Sax2 comes with well-defined Video Electronics Standards Association (VESA) settings for general setup and also specific configurations from the major manufacturers of graphics systems. The remainder of this section discusses a low-specification graphics setup that should be safe for most people. However, you really should know how hard you can push your system so as not to damage your monitor by overdriving what your graphics card gives to it. Most of today's monitors have built-in settings to protect against hardware damage, but you should be especially careful when configuring the X Window system on an older monitor.

Graphics Card Configuration

As you have changed the resolution of your monitor, you will also need to change the resolution of your graphics card to reflect the monitor settings. To do this, click on the resolution (in Figure 1-30, this is 800 × 600). You will be presented with a small drop-down box asking you for the resolution you wish to run X with (see Figure 1-32).

Configuring Your Sound Card

YaST will detect the sound card and will set it up automatically. During a standard installation, you are not required to intervene in this process; it just happens. In almost all cases, that is all you need to know. The rest of this section concerns what you can do after installation if it turns out that sound was not configured correctly during the installation.

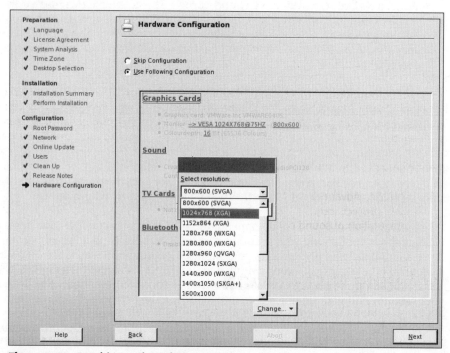

Figure 1-32: Graphics card resolution

After the installation is complete, confirm that sound is working by attempting to play a music CD or music file (for example, an MP3 file using the xmms player program). If you don't hear sound at this stage, first check the physical connection to the speakers. Then (if you are using KDE) check that the KDE volume control is at a sensible setting and not disabled or turned down to zero. In the unlikely event that sound still fails to work, you can rerun the YaST sound module in expert mode. The sound module is found in YaST's Hardware section. You will find three possible setup modes:

✦ **Quick automatic setup** — This is the default and is the one that is used during installation.

✦ **Normal setup** — This enables you to test the sound card. There is a volume control and a test button. When you have set the volume, a test sound is played when you press test.

✦ **More detailed installation of sound cards** — If you choose this option, you will be taken to a screen where any configurable options for the particular sound card that has been detected can be set. Depending on the particular card, these may include settings to enable a joystick and MPU (midi processing unit) port settings.

If even experimentation with the detailed installation options fails, you can try the low-level alsaconf program. As root, type **alsaconf** to start the program. It is a text-based program that, in fact, provides the back end for YaST's sound configuration module, but running it standalone gives you the opportunity to use its command-line options, including alsaconf -l, which writes a log file to /tmp/alsaconf.log that may give a clue as to the problem.

Tip   The ALSA (Advanced Linux Sound Architecture) home page can be found at w w w .alsa-project.org. This is the best place to start if you have any difficulties with configuration of sound on Linux.

Completing Installation

Once you have finished with your hardware configuration, click Next.

It has been a long road, but you have successfully installed SUSE at this point (see Figure 1-33). Pat yourself on the back if you are a brand-new user to the world of Linux. You have done a lot of new things by installing SUSE — not the least of which is that you have begun a journey on which you'll learn lots of new ideas and philosophies, as well as giving you a stable operating system to use.

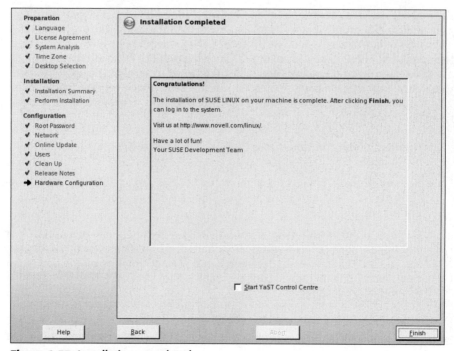

Figure 1-33: Installation completed

If you are an experienced Linux user, you should be quite happy about how much SUSE has come along from other distributions and how easy it has been to install it. Don't worry, however; as with everything Linux-related, you can make it as easy or as hard as you like, and you will see how in later chapters.

Just to whet your appetite, Figure 1-34 shows an image of what you will see once your system has booted up to the system proper.

As this is a new installation with default settings, typing in your username and password and pressing the login button automatically loads the K Desktop Environment. The version of KDE that SUSE ships with has been optimized to integrate with the SUSE system, and you will see how well a job the developers have done in Chapter 8. Enjoy, play around with the system, and as the developers in Germany say: Have a lot of fun!

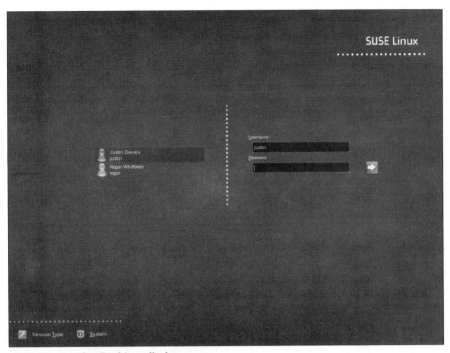

Figure 1-34: The final installed system

✦   ✦   ✦

Linux Fundamentals

CHAPTER

2

◆   ◆   ◆   ◆

In This Chapter

Command line 101:
The shell

Getting help for Linux
commands

Working with files
and directories

Common
administrative tasks

Working with
software packages

Connecting over the
network

◆   ◆   ◆   ◆

T*he Linux Gazette* (`http://linuxgazette.net`) used to have a regular feature called "Clueless at the Prompt." That title will almost certainly ring a bell with anyone who remembers his or her first interactions with Linux or any other form of Unix.

Someone who wants to use Linux only as a desktop system may not need to know too much about using the command line. You can log in to the graphical login screen (typically `kdm`) and you see a user interface (typically KDE — K Desktop Environment) that is remarkably similar to the Windows interface. There is a Start button with cascading menus. Some icons are on the desktop, and you can start programs either from the Start menu or by clicking the icons. There is a file manager (typically Konqueror) that allows drag-and-drop support for moving files. For many end users (and future users of Linux desktop systems), this may be all they need to know. In our experience, a desktop user new to Linux can start working — doing normal office work and saving and managing files — without any real need for training.

We assume that you will want and need to do much more than this. A number of books are available that serve as guides to using the KDE interface. These rarely do much more than describe how to interact with the KDE user interface, which, although it has some subtleties, is fairly intuitive and user friendly these days. From the command-line point of view, some other books are basically "command references" for Linux. These can be very helpful, particularly for learning useful commands that you might not have known about or whose syntax you can never remember. Again, this is not such a book. This book does not provide exhaustive lists of Linux commands but focuses on discussing the important ones in context and in detail.

Command Line 101: The Shell

Commands issued at the command line on any computer system are read and executed by a program known as a *command interpreter*. A command interpreter does the following:

✦ Reads the commands and any options and arguments that you provide

✦ Translates or expands any special characters such as the * and ? used as wildcard characters on Linux and Unix systems (more about these in the next section)

✦ Locates the command that you want to execute on your system

✦ Executes that command with the appropriate options and arguments and displays any output of that command

On Linux and Unix systems, a command interpreter is known as a *shell*. Linux and Unix systems offer many different shells, each of which has its own special features and devotees.

There are several shells included in the SUSE system, including ash, csh, ksh, tcsh, and zsh. They all have their advantages and disadvantages, and some users have strong preferences for one shell over another. However, bash has become the effective standard on Linux systems, and from now on all the examples in the book will assume that you are using the bash shell.

Tip   On Linux systems, the list of "legal" shells is maintained in the file /etc/shells. The contents of this text file list the possible shells that can be started when you log in on the system.

In addition to being able to execute standard Linux commands for you, each of these shells supports its own command language. Command files written in the command language provided by a shell are known as *shell scripts*. The first line of a shell script typically identifies the shell that should be used to run the command script. If no shell is identified in the first line, a shell script is executed by the sh shell, which is usually the same thing as the bash shell on Linux systems.

Commonly Used Shell Features

By default, when you use the command line on a SUSE system, you are using the bash shell. If you have not used bash or a similar shell much in the past, and particularly if you have bad memories of the DOS command line, you may not realize just how powerful working at the command line can be. Experience shows that people who come to Linux from a Windows background tend to start by trying to use graphical tools (for example, copying files by dragging them from one Konqueror window to another) but gradually realize that the command line is both a quicker and easier way to perform many tasks.

The bash shell provides a powerful command-line interface that offers many features that the DOS command line lacks. The most important of these are command history and command completion:

✦ **Command history** — You can see a history of the commands you typed by pressing the up arrow key repeatedly. You can then edit the command and reuse it.

✦ **Command completion** — If you type part of a command and then press the Tab key, bash will complete the command as far as it is able to do so uniquely.

These two features taken together make working with the shell extremely quick and easy with a little practice. The command history is also searchable in more than one way: If you type the command history, you will see a listing of the last commands you have typed. Each of these is numbered: If you type ! followed by the number of the command, you can run it again. If you press Ctrl+R (hold down the Control key and press *r*), you can search the command history by typing part of the command you are looking for. If the first command that appears is not the one you had in mind, repeat the Ctrl+R until it appears. You can also repeat a previous command by typing ! followed by the first letter or letters of the previous command.

Advanced Shell Features

If useful shell features such as command history and completion intrigue you, just wait! This section highlights some of the other powerful capabilities that are built into the bash shell. Most of these features are present in the other shells discussed earlier in this chapter, but this section focuses on bash because it is the standard shell used on Linux systems.

Note   You may want to skip over this section if you are new to Linux and are just trying to learn how to perform some standard tasks. When you have become more experienced with Linux, you can always come back and read this section to find out how to get even more power out of the Linux command line.

Environment Variables

As you can guess from the discussion of command history in the previous section, the bash shell maintains a significant amount of information about the commands that it has executed, the settings for various configuration parameters, the environment in which it is operating, and so on. Much of this information is stored in variables in the shell environment, which are therefore known as *environment variables*. You can display all of the environment variables set within your current shell and their definitions by typing the printenv command, as in the following example:

```
$ printenv

HOSTNAME=home.vonhagen.org
TERM=xterm
SHELL=/bin/bash
HISTSIZE=1000
WINDOWID=31457294
ENSCRIPT=-r2G
PRINTCMD=enscript -r2G
PATH=/home/wvh/bin:/opt/timesys/timestorm/2.4.1:/usr/local/firefox:/usr/local/bin:/usr/local/
Acrobat5/bin:/home/wvh/cxoffice/bin:/opt/OpenOffice.org1.1.0:/usr/local/textmaker:/usr/java/b
in:/usr/sbin:/sbin:/usr/kerberos/bin:/bin:/usr/bin:/usr/X11R6/bin
INPUTRC=/etc/inputrc
PWD=/home/wvh/personal/writing/SUSE/OLD
JAVA_HOME=/usr/java
LANG=en_US.UTF-8
PS1=[\u@\h:\W]\$
HOME=/home/wvh
DISPLAY=:0.0
XAUTHORITY=/home/wvh/.Xauthority
_=/usr/bin/printenv
```

As you can see from this example, the names of environment variables typically comprise uppercase and underscore characters and are used in a variety of ways. For example, the value of the HOME environment variable is a single string that contains the name of a user's home directory. The PATH environment variable is a colon-separated list of directories that the shell searches in order when looking for a command that you have executed. The PS1 environment variable defines the structure and content of the prompt that is displayed by the shell. The '_' environment variable (the last line of the code example) holds the full path of the last command executed within the shell — in this case, that of the printenv command you just ran.

Environment variables can be set in a number of places:

✦ System-wide configuration files such as those located in /etc/profile, /etc/profile.local, and the directory /etc/profile.d on a Linux system. These are system-wide files that are executed to help initialize your working environment each time you log in.

✦ System-wide configuration files such as /etc/bashrc. These are typically executed by a user's personalized bash configuration file each time that you start a new shell and set system-wide shell configuration variables.

✦ User-specific configuration files such as .bashrc that are read each time you start a new shell.

✦ Within shell scripts for use within those scripts or to be exported back to the command-line environment.

✦ From the command line for your convenience or within shell functions executed by the shell.

Environment variables that you want to make available to all subsequent shells are made available to the parent shell using the `export` command. For example, suppose that you want to set an environment variable named `SAVEME` to the name of the current directory so that you can remember it. If the current directory is `/home/wvh`, you can set the `SAVEME` environment variable to this directory with the following command:

```
export SAVEME=/home/wvh
```

One common task involving environment variables is to add a new directory to the column-separated value of the `PATH` environment variable so that your shell looks in that directory for executables. For example, suppose that you've just installed the popular Linux Firefox browser on your system. Firefox is typically installed in the directory `/usr/local/firefox`, and the binary program that you actually execute to run the browser is `/usr/local/firefox/firefox`. You can always execute Firefox by typing the full path of the `firefox` command, but that's a bit tedious. A better solution is to add the directory `/usr/local/firefox` to the value of your `PATH` environment variable (generally referred to as "adding it to your path"). You can do this within the current shell by executing the following command:

```
export PATH=$PATH:/usr/local/firefox
```

After typing this command, you can execute the `firefox` command from that shell by simply typing `firefox` and pressing Return.

Tip   The sample `export` command tells the shell to export a new value for the `PATH` environment variable, where that value consists of the directory `/usr/local/firefox` prefixed to the previous value of the `PATH` environment variable. The first reference to the `PATH` variable identifies the name of the variable that you want to set. Any environment variable preceded by a `$` means that you are referring to the value of that variable, not its name.

When you've customized the value of your `PATH` environment variable, you will probably want to do that same customization each time you log in and in every shell that you start (in each Konsole window, each `xterm`, and so on). You can do this by adding the previous command to any existing `PATH` setting in your bash startup file, which is the file .bashrc in your home directory, or by putting this as the last command in your .bashrc file. See the section "Configuring User Preferences" later in this chapter for more information about the .bashrc configuration file.

Tip

When you've set an environment variable, you can unset it at any time using the unset command. The unset command removes the environment variable and its associated value from the shell in which you execute it. You would not want to unset an environment variable such as the PATH environment variable because the shell would not know where to find commands. However, you may find it useful to unset environment variables that are used only by certain programs. For example, the ENSCRIPT environment variable, shown in the previous sample output of the printenv command, is used to specify personalized arguments for the enscript command, which produces nicely formatted output from text files. To execute the enscript command without those arguments (in other words, using its internal default values), you could execute the command unset ENSCRIPT before printing.

Wildcards and Pattern Matching

All Unix and Linux shells support several ways of locating file and directory names that match a specified pattern. As you might expect, when working from the command line, one of the most common things that you will want to do is to specify the names of one or more files as arguments to other commands. To make it easier to identify specific files without requiring that you type every filename in its entirety, Linux shells provide a number of different ways to specify patterns that can be used to match specific filenames.

The most basic pattern matching provided by Linux shells such as bash are two special characters known as *wildcards*, which means that these characters can match any other character. Linux shells support two basic wildcards:

✦ **Asterisk (*)** — Also referred to as the star, can represent any number of characters (including none at all) in a row

✦ **Question mark (?)** — Represents any single character

In addition to these wildcards, Linux shells support two other ways to match specific patterns within filenames:

✦ By specifying ranges of values separated by a dash within square brackets. For example, the expression [1-3] will match any instance of the numbers from 1 to 3, inclusive.

✦ By specifying lists of comma-separated values enclosed within braces (also known as *curly brackets*). For example, the expression {1,3} will match either the number 1 or the number 3.

A few examples will help clarify how you can use these to identify certain files in your directories. Suppose that a directory contains the following files:

✦ file1

✦ file1.doc

✦ file2

✦ file2.doc

✦ file3

✦ file3.txt

✦ file8

✦ other_file.doc

Given this list of files, Table 2-1 shows how you can use wildcards, ranges of values, and lists to match specific files. As you'll see later in this chapter, pattern matching is especially useful when listing filenames and directory names that match specific patterns.

Table 2-1
Pattern Matching in Linux Shells

Pattern	Matching Filenames
*	file1, file1.doc, file2, file2.doc, file3, file3.txt, file8, other_file.doc
file?	file1, file2, file3, file8
*.doc	file1.doc, file2.doc, other_file.doc
file?.doc	file1.doc, file2.doc
file?.*	file1.doc, file2.doc, file3.txt
file[1-3]	file1, file2, file3
file{1,3}	file1, file3
file{1,3}.{doc,txt}	file1.doc, file3.txt

Note As explained later in this chapter, in the section "Listing Files," Unix and Linux systems do not list files that begin with a period by default. Therefore, the wildcard * will match only all visible files in a directory (files whose names do not begin with a period), even though the * matches the period in the middle of a filename.

Connecting Commands and Redirecting Input and Output

Unix and Linux commands are designed with a KISS *(Keep It Simple, Stupid)* philosophy. Some operating systems feature thousands of specialized commands that perform many specific, but similar, tasks. Unix and Linux take the opposite approach, providing many small, simple commands that you can combine to perform complex tasks.

For example, some operating systems might provide a specialized command to print a listing of the current directory. On a Linux system, you would perform this task by combining the existing list (ls) and print (lpr) commands into a single sequence of commands in which the output of the ls command was provided as input to the lpr command by connecting the two commands using a special symbol known as a *pipe* (|), as in the following example:

```
ls | lpr
```

Linux shells provide this capability by connecting the output from one command to the input expected by another. In Linux terms, this is *connecting the standard output from one command to the standard input of another.* The pipe symbol automatically ties the two commands together and sends the output of the first to the second as input.

Linux actually provides two different ways of specifying that the output of one command is the input to another—by using a pipe to connect the two commands, or by what is known as *redirecting IO,* which stands for *redirecting input/output.*

The output of a file can also be redirected to a file, using the greater than sign (>), which simply creates a file containing the output of the command, as in the following example:

```
ls > listing.out
```

This command takes the output of the ls command and sends it to the file listing.out.

Linux supports combining commands and redirecting input and output by recognizing three different aspects of program input and output:

 ✦ **stdin**—The *standard input* stream that is read from by a program

 ✦ **stdout**—The *standard output* stream to which program output is sent

 ✦ **stderr**—A specialized output stream known as *standard error* to which program error messages are written

You will encounter these terms as you become more familiar with executing shell commands because these are the cornerstones of creating complex commands by stringing together simple ones. Like the regular expressions discussed in the previous section, redirecting input and output is an extremely powerful feature of most

Linux shells. Entire books have been written about shells such as bash and tcsh —
search your favorite online bookseller for these if you want to become a true shell
expert and amaze your friends with various complex shell tricks.

Getting Help for Linux Commands

The man and info commands are basic ways to view program documentation on
Linux. To view the man or info help for a specific command, you use the man or info
command followed by the name of the command that you want help on.

The man command provides access to the traditional Unix and Linux online manual,
displaying formatted help that you can page through. The info command is a newer
online help mechanism that displays text help for commands inside a customized
version of emacs with hypertext capabilities that enable you to jump from one topic
to another. Many commands now maintain their online help only in info format rather
than supporting both. In general, info help for a command is always at least as up-to-
date and complete as the equivalent man help for that same command.

The info interface is a little confusing for beginners; it is actually a form of hypertext. SUSE also offers pinfo, which is slightly easier to use, and also the ability to
view man and info pages using the Konqueror browser. See Chapter 5 for more
details.

  ✦ man ls — Views the man page for the ls command

  ✦ man -k disk — Looks for man pages referring to the word *disk*

  ✦ info coreutils — Looks at the info page for the coreutils package

Tip   A number of excellent books and online references are available that provide
detailed information about standard Linux commands, Linux shells, and so on.
One of the best sources of online information about Linux is the Linux
Documentation Project, available at www.tldp.org. In the true spirit of Linux, the
Linux Documentation Project provides hundreds of free documents, HOWTO files,
and compilations of frequently asked questions (FAQs) documents that explain
different aspects of using standard Linux systems.

Working with Files and Directories

A very large proportion of all the work most users do from the command line, even
advanced users, consists of few key activities and a fairly small number of common
commands. Most of these have to do with locating, listing, creating, editing, and deleting files and directories. This section provides an overview of the most common file-
and directory-related tasks and the commands that you use to perform them.

Note You will notice that most of these very common commands have short two-, three-, or four-letter names. Note also that you can use the shell's command completion feature to type a few letters, press the Tab key, and bash will complete the command (for example, type **ema**<Tab>, and bash displays the command emacs).

If you're unfamiliar with the basic commands used in the rest of this chapter, your best plan is to experiment. Just as the best way to learn a language is to speak it, the best way to learn Linux commands is to use them. Experiment as freely as possible and play.

Listing Files

The ls (list) command lists files in the current directory. The command ls has a very large number of options, but what you really need to know is that ls -l gives a "long" listing showing the file sizes and permissions, and that the -a option shows even "hidden" files — those with a dot at the start of their names. The shell expands the * character to mean "any string of characters not starting with '.'." (See the discussion of wildcards in the "Advanced Shell Features" section earlier in this chapter for more information about how and why this works.) Therefore, *.doc is interpreted as any filename ending with .doc that does not start with a dot and a * means "any filename starting with the letter *a*." For example:

✦ ls -la — Gives a long listing of all files in the current directory including "hidden" files with names staring with a dot

✦ ls a* — Lists all files in the current directory whose names start with *a*

✦ ls -l *.doc — Gives a long listing of all files in the current directory whose names end with .doc

Copying Files

The cp (copy) command copies a file, files, or directory to another location. The option -R allows you to copy directories recursively (in general, -R or -r in commands often has the meaning of "recursive"). If the last argument to the cp command is a directory, the files mentioned will be copied into that directory. Note that by default, cp will "clobber" existing files, so in the second example that follows, if there is already a file called afile in the directory /home/bible, it will be overwritten without asking for any confirmation. Consider the following examples:

✦ cp afile afile.bak — Copies the file afile to a new file afile.bak.

✦ cp afile /home/bible/ — Copies the file afile from the current directory to the directory /home/bible/.

✦ cp * /tmp — Copies all nonhidden files in the current directory to /tmp/.

✦ cp -a docs docs.bak — Recursively copies the directory docs beneath the current directory to a new directory docs.bak, while preserving file attributes and copying all files including hidden files whose names start with a dot. The -a option implies the -R option, as a convenience.

✦ cp -i — By default, if you copy a file to a location where a file of the same name already exists, the old file will be silently overwritten. The -i option makes the command interactive; in other words it asks before overwriting.

✦ cp -v — With the -v (verbose) option, the cp command will tell you what it is doing. A great many Linux commands have a -v option with the same meaning.

Moving and Renaming Files

The m v (move) command has the meaning both of "move" and of "rename." In the first example that follows, the file afile will be renamed to the name bfile. In the second example, the file afile in the current directory will be moved to the directory /tmp/.

✦ m v afile bfile — Renames the existing file afile with the new name bfile

✦ m v afile /tmp — Moves the file afile in the current directory to the directory /tmp

Deleting Files and Directories

The r m (remove) command enables you to delete files and directories. Be warned: r m is a dangerous command. It doesn't really offer you a second chance. When files are deleted, they're gone. You can use r m -i as in the last example that follows. That at least gives you a second chance to think about it, but as soon as you agree, once again, the file is gone.

Note Some people like to create an alias (see Chapter 14) that makes the r m command act like r m -i. We would advise at least to be careful about this: It will lull you into a false sense of security, and when you're working on a system where this change has not been made, you may regret it.

Doug Gwyn, a well-known Internet personality, once said, "Unix was never designed to keep people from doing stupid things because that policy would also keep them from doing clever things." You can, of course, use r m to delete every file on your system as simply as this: r m -rf /. (You have to be logged in as a user, such as the root user, who has the privileges to do this, but you get the idea.) Some better examples of using the r m command in daily use are:

✦ r m afile — Removes the file afile.

✦ r m * — Removes all (nonhidden) files in the current directory. The r m command will not remove directories unless you also specify the -r (recursive) option.

✦ r m -rf doomed — Removes the directory doomed and everything in it.

✦ r m -i a * — Removes all files with names beginning with *a* in the current directory, asking for confirmation each time.

Changing Directories

You use the cd (change directory) command to change directories:

✦ cd ~ — Changes to your home directory

✦ cd /tmp — Changes to the directory /tmp

Tip

On most Linux systems, your prompt will tell you what directory you're in (depending on the setting you've used for the PS1 environment variable). However; if you ever explicitly need to know what directory you're in, you can use the pwd command to identify the working directory for the current process (process working directory, hence pwd).

Making Directories

You can use the mkdir (make directory) command to make directories. For example:

✦ mkdir photos — Makes a directory called photos within the current directory.

✦ mkdir -p this/that/theother — Makes the nested subdirectories named within the current directory.

Removing Directories

The command rmdir will remove a directory that is empty.

Making Links to Files or Directories

In Linux, you can use the ln (link) command to make links to a file or directory. A file can have any number of so-called "hard" links to it. Effectively, these are alternative names for the file. So if you create a file called afile, and make a link to it called bfile, there are now two names for the same file. If you edit afile, the changes you've made will be in bfile. But if you delete afile, bfile will still exist; it will disappear only when there are no links left to it. Hard links can be made only on the same filesystem — you can't create a hard link to a file on another partition because the link operates at the filesystem level, referring to the actual filesystem data structure that holds information about the file. You can create a hard link only to a file, not to a directory.

You can also create a *symbolic* link to a file. A symbolic link is a special kind of file that redirects any usage of the link to the original file. This is somewhat similar to the use of "shortcuts" in Windows. You can also create symbolic links to directories, which can be very useful if you frequently use a subdirectory that is hidden several levels deep below your home directory. In the last example that follows, you will end up with a symbolic link called useful in the current directory. Thus, the command cd useful will have the same effect as cd docs/linux/suse/useful.

✦ ln afile bfile — Makes a "hard" link to afile called bfile

✦ ln -s afile linkfile — Makes a symbolic link to afile called linkfile

✦ ln -s docs/linux/suse/useful — Makes a symbolic link to the named directory in the current directory

Concatenating Files

The command cat (concatenate) displays files to standard output. If you want to view the contents of a short text file, the easiest thing to do is to cat it, which sends its contents to the shell's standard output, which is the shell in which you typed the cat command. If you cat two files, you will see the contents of each flying past on the screen. But if you want to combine those two files into one, all you need to do is cat them and redirect the output to the cat command to a file using >.

Tip Linux has a sense of humor. The cat command displays files to standard output, starting with the first line and ending with the last. The tac command (cat spelled backward) displays files in reverse order, beginning with the last line and ending with the first. The command tac is amusing: Try it!

✦ cat /etc/passwd — Prints /etc/passwd to the screen

✦ cat afile bfile — Prints the contents of afile to the screen followed by the contents of bfile

✦ cat afile bfile > cfile — Combines the contents of afile and bfile and writes them to a new file, cfile

Viewing Files with more and less

The more and less commands are known as *pagers* because they allow you to view the contents of a text file one screen at a time and to page forward and backward through the file (without editing it). The name of the more command is derived from the fact that it allows you to see a file one screen at a time, thereby seeing "more" of it. The name of the less command comes from the fact that it originally began as an open source version of the more command (before more itself became an open source command) and because it originally did less than the more command (the author had a sense of humor). Nowadays, the less command has many added features, including the fact that you can use keyboard shortcuts such as pressing the letter *b* when viewing a file to move backward through the file. The man page of less lists all the other hot keys that can be used for navigating through a file while reading it using less. Both more and less use the hot key *q* to exit.

✦ more /etc/passwd — Views the contents of /etc/passwd

✦ less /etc/passwd — Views the contents of /etc/passwd

Viewing the Start or End of Files

The head and tail commands allow you to see a specified number of lines from the top or bottom of a file. The tail command has the very useful feature that you can use tail -f to keep an eye on a file as it grows. This is particularly useful for watching what is being written to a log file while you make changes in the system. Consider the following examples:

✦ head -n5 /etc/passwd — Prints the first five lines of the file /etc/passwd to the screen

✦ tail -n5 /etc/passwd — Prints the last five lines of /etc/passwd to the screen

✦ tail -f /var/log/messages — Views the last few lines of /var/log/ messages and continues to display changes to the end of the file in real time

Searching Files with grep

The grep (global regular expression print) command is a very useful tool for finding stuff in files. It can do much more than even the examples that follow this paragraph indicate. Beyond simply searching for text, it can search for regular expressions. It's a regular expression parser, and regular expressions are a subject for a book in themselves.

When using or administering a system, you often need to look for lines in a file that contain a certain string. In the first example that follows, you simply find the lines in the file that contain the string *bible*. The examples with tail are examples of *piping* the output from one command to another: a very powerful concept that was also introduced in the section "Advanced Shell Features," earlier in this chapter. In the first case, you get the output from the tail command, and you just select the lines that contain *404*. In the second, you select the lines that do *not* include the string *googlebot*; the -v option indicates "not." In the last example, the ^ symbol represents the start of a line, so you see only the lines that do not start with the symbol `#`. (The `#` character identifies lines that are comments in shell scripts and most Linux configuration files. This example therefore displays the lines of the configuration file that are actually active.)

✦ `grep bible /etc/exports` — Looks for all lines in the file `/etc/exports` that include the string *bible*

✦ `tail -100 /var/log/apache/access.log|grep 404` — Looks for the string *404*, the web server's "file not found" code, in the last hundred lines of the web server log

✦ `tail -100 /var/log/apache/access.log|grep -v googlebot` — Looks in the last 100 lines of the web server log for lines that don't indicate accesses by the Google search robot

✦ `grep -v ^# /etc/apache2/httpd.conf` — Looks for all lines that are *not* commented out in the main Apache configuration file

Finding Files with find and locate

The `find` command searches the filesystem for files that match a specified pattern. The `locate` command provides a faster way of finding files but depends on a database that it creates and refreshes at regular intervals. The `locate` command is fast and convenient, but the information it displays may not always be up-to-date — this depends on whether its database is up-to-date. To use the `locate` command, you need to have the package `findutils-locate` installed.

`find` is a powerful command with many options, including the ability to search for files with date stamps in a particular range (useful for backups) and to search for files with particular permissions, owners, and other attributes. The documentation for `find` can be found in its info pages: `info find`.

✦ `find . -name *.rpm` — Finds RPM packages in the current directory

✦ `find . |grep page` — Finds files in the current directory and its subdirectories with the string *page* in their names

✦ `locate traceroute` — Finds files with names including the string *traceroute* anywhere on the system

Editing Text with vi and emacs

The `vi` (visual) and `emacs` (editor macros) text editors are the two most important text editors in Linux. You probably need to learn basic text editing using `vi` whatever you do because it is almost always available on Unix and Linux systems. The `emacs` editor has immense power but may not be installed on every system you use.

✦ `vi /etc/exports` — Edits the file `/etc/exports` with `vi`

✦ `emacs /etc/exports`— Edits the file `/etc/exports` with `emacs`

The key differences between these two editors lie in their command sets and their approach to editing files. The `vi` editor is a modal editor, in which you are either in edit mode, typing characters into a file, or in command mode, moving around in the file or executing commands on portions of the file. The `emacs` editor is a modeless editor in which you are always in edit mode—you use special key sequences known as *control* and *escape* sequences to move around in or execute commands on portions of the file. The arguments between devotees of the two editors and approaches to editing text are legendary, and we shall not get into those discussions here.

Cross-Reference See Chapter 11 for more details on these text editors and the similarities and differences between them.

Common Administrative Tasks

The tasks in this section are common ones that you may need to do when setting up your system and beginning your new life as the system administrator of your own Linux system.

Basic User and Group Concepts

Linux is a truly multiuser operating system. The concept of users and groups in Linux is inherited from the Unix tradition, and among other things provides a very clear and precise distinction between what normal users can do and what a privileged user can do (such as the root user, the superuser and ultimate administrator on a Linux system, who can do anything). The fact that the system of users and groups and the associated system of permissions is built into the system at the deepest level is one of the reasons why Linux (and Unix in general) is fundamentally secure in a way that Microsoft Windows is not. Although modern versions of Windows have a similar concept of users and groups, the associated concept of the permissions with which a process can be run leaves a lot to be desired. This is why there are so many Windows vulnerabilities that are based on exploiting the scripting capabilities of programs that are run with user privileges but that turn out to be capable of subverting the system.

Tip If you're interested in the differences between the major operating systems, Eric Raymond, noted open source guru and philosopher, offers some interesting comparisons and discussion at `www.catb.org/~esr/writings/taoup/html/ch03s02.html`.

Every Linux system has a number of users accounts: Some of these are human users, and some of them are system users, which are user identities that the system uses to perform certain tasks.

The users on a system (provided it does authentication locally) are listed in the file /etc/passwd. Look at your own entry in /etc/passwd; it will look something like this:

```
roger:x:1000:100:Roger Whittaker:/home/roger:/bin/bash
```

This shows, among other things, that the user with username roger has the real name Roger Whittaker, that his home directory is /home/roger, and that his default shell is /bin/bash (the bash shell).

There will almost certainly also be an entry for the system user postfix, looking something like this:

```
postfix:x:51:51:Postfix Daemon:/var/spool/postfix:/bin/false
```

This is the postfix daemon, which looks after mail. This user can't log in because its shell is /bin/false, but its home directory is /var/spool/postfix, and it owns the spool directories in which mail being sent and delivered is held. The fact that these directories are owned by the user postfix rather than by root is a security feature—it means that any possible vulnerability in postfix is less likely to lead to a subversion of the whole system. Similar system users exist for the web server (the user wwwrun) and various other services. You won't often need to consider these, but it is important to understand that they exist and that the correct owner-ships of certain files and directories by these users is part of the overall security model of the system as a whole.

Each user belongs to one or more *groups*. The groups on the system are listed in the file /etc/groups. To find out what groups you belong to, you can simply type the command **groups** (alternatively look at the file /etc/group and look for your user-name). By default, on a SUSE system, you will find that you belong to the group users and also to a few system groups, including the groups dialout and audio. This is to give normal human users the right to use the modem and sound devices (which is arranged through file permissions as you shall see later in this chapter).

Creating Users and Groups

You can most simply create a new user using YaST's user module. Start YaST and choose the users and groups option. You might want to create a user with the user-name guest and the real name Guest User. YaST will create the user according to your instructions and also create a home directory /home/guest for the new user with a skeleton of configuration files in it.

This skeleton is copied from the directory /etc/skel but has the ownership of the new user (user guest, group users) applied to it once the new user's home direc-tory has been created.

You can also create a new user from the command line with the command useradd. The equivalent command would be:

```
useradd -m guest -c "Guest User"
```

The useradd command has options that allow you to specify the groups to which the new user will belong.

In a similar way, you can create or modify groups through YaST, and there are equivalent command-line commands called groupadd (to add groups) and groupmod (to modify existing groups).

As always, you can get complete and detailed information about the useradd, groupadd, and groupmod commands by looking at their man pages (for example with the command man useradd).

Working with File Ownership and Permissions

The users and groups discussed in the previous section are useful only because each file on the system is owned by a certain user and group and because the system of file permissions can be used to restrict or control access to the files based on the user who is trying to access them.

 Cross-Reference   The section that follows is a crash course in file permissions; we go into greater detail in Chapter 13.

If you look at a variety of files and directories from across the system and list them with the ls -l command, you can see different patterns of ownership and permissions. In each case the output from the ls command is giving you several pieces of information: the permissions on the file expressed as a ten-place string, the number of links to the file, the ownership of the file (user and group), the size of the file in bytes, the modification time, and the filename. Of the ten places in the permissions string, the first differs from the others: The last nine can be broken up into three groups of three, representing what the user can do with the file, what members of the group can do with the file, and what others can do with the file, respectively. In most cases, these permissions are represented by the presence or absence of the letters r (read), w (write), and x (execute) in the three positions. So:

✦ r w x means permission to read, write, and execute

✦ r-- means permission to read but not to write or execute

✦ r-x means permission to read and execute but not to write

and so on.

Note   Permission to write to a file includes the right to overwrite or delete it.

So for example:

```
ls -l screenshot1.png
-rw-r--r--  1 roger users 432686 2004-05-17 20:33 screenshot1.png
```

This file can be read and written by its owner (roger), can be read by members of the group users, and can be read by others.

```
ls -l /home/roger/afile
-r--------  1 roger users 0 2004-05-17 21:07 afile
```

This file is not executable or writable, and can be read only by its owner (roger). Even roger would have to change the permissions on this file to be able to write it.

```
ls -l /etc/passwd
-rw-r--r--  1 root root 1598 2004-05-17 19:36 /etc/passwd
```

This is the password file—it is owned by root (and the group root to which only root belongs), is readable by anyone, but is group writable only by root.

```
ls -l /etc/shadow
-rw-r-----  1 root shadow 796 2004-05-17 19:36 /etc/shadow
```

This is the shadow file, which holds the encrypted passwords for users. It can be read only by root and the system group shadow and can be written only by root.

```
ls -l /usr/sbin/traceroute
-rwxr-xr-x 1 root root 14228 2004-04-06 02:27 /usr/sbin/traceroute
```

This is an executable file that can be read and executed by anyone, but written only by root.

```
ls -ld /home
drwxr-xr-x  6 root root 4096 2004-05-17 19:36 /home
```

This is a directory (note the use of the -d flag to the ls command and the d in the first position in the permissions). It can be read and written by the root user, and read and executed by everyone. When used in directory permissions, the x (executable) permission translates into the ability to search or examine the directory—you cannot execute a directory.

```
ls -ld /root
drwx------  18 root root 584 2004-05-14 08:29 /root
```

In the preceding code, /root is the root user's home directory. No user apart from root can access it in any way.

```
ls -l /bin/mount
-rwsr-xr-x 1 root root 87296 2004-04-06 14:17 /bin/mount
```

This is a more interesting example: notice the letter s where until now we saw an x. This indicates that the file runs with the permissions of its owner (root) even when it is executed by another user: Such a file is known as being *suid root* (set user ID upon execution). There are a small number of executables on the system that need to have these permissions. This number is kept as small as possible because there is a potential for security problems if ever a way could be found to make such a file perform a task other than what it was written for.

```
ls -l alink
lrwxrwxrwx  1 roger users 8 2004-05-17 22:19 alink -> file.bz2
```

Note the l in the first position: This is a symbolic link to file.bz2 in the same directory.

Numerical Permissions

On many occasions when permissions are discussed, you will see them being described in a three-digit numerical form (sometimes more digits for exceptional cases), such as 644. If a file has permissions 644, it has read and write permissions for the owner and read permissions for the group and for others. This works because Linux actually stores file permissions as sequences of octal numbers. This is easiest to see by example:

```
 421421421
-rw-r--r-- 644
-rwxr-xr-x 755
-r--r--r-- 444
-r-------- 400
```

So for each owner, group, and others, a read permission is represented by 4 (the high bit of a 3-bit octal value), a write permission is represented by 2 (the middle bit of a 3-bit octal value), and an execute permission is represented by 1 (the low bit of a 3-bit octal value).

Changing Ownership and Permissions

You can change the ownership of a file with the command chown. If you are logged in as root, you can issue a command like this:

```
chown harpo:users file.txt
```

This changes the ownership of the file file.txt to the user harpo and the group users.

To change the ownership of a directory and everything in it, you can use the command with the -R (recursive) option, like this:

```
chown -R harpo:users /home/harpo/some_directory/
```

The chmod command is used to change file permissions. You can use chmod with both the numerical and the r w x notation we discussed earlier in the chapter. Again, this is easiest to follow by looking at a few examples:

- ✦ chmod u+x afile — Adds execute permissions for the owner of the file
- ✦ chmod g+r afile — Adds read permissions for the group owning the file
- ✦ chmod o-r afile — Removes read permission for others
- ✦ chmod a + w afile — Adds write permissions for all
- ✦ chmod 6 4 4 afile — Changes the permissions to 644 (owner can read and write; group members and others can only read)
- ✦ chmod 7 5 5 afile — Changes the permissions to 755 (owner can read, write and execute; group members and others can only read and execute)

If you use chmod with the r w x notation, u means the owner, g means the group, o means others, and a means all. In addition, + means add permissions, and - means remove permissions, while r, w , and x still represent read, write, and execute, respectively. When setting permissions, you can see the translation between the two notations by executing the chmod command with the -v (verbose) option. For example:

```
chmod -v 755 afile
mode of `afile' changed to 0755 (rwxr-xr-x)

chmod -v 200 afile
mode of `afile' changed to 0200 (-w-------)
```

Using umask

When a user creates a file, it is created with certain permissions. You can create an empty file with the touch command:

```
touch newfile
```

If you then list the file, you will see something like this:

```
ls -l newfile
```

```
-rw-r--r--  1 roger users 0 2004-05-18 10:00 newfile
```

So the file has been created with the permissions 644. What controls the permissions with which a new file gets created is something called the umask.

By default on a SUSE system, a normal user's umask is 022, which means that the permissions for a new file added to 022 will make 666, while the permissions for a new directory added to 022 will make 777.

SUSE's defaults are relatively generous and open—the fact that the users you create are by default all members of the same group (users) and that the default umask is 022 means that files created by one user can be read by another. If you want to change a user's umask, you can change it in the .bashrc file; see the section on user preferences that follows.

Configuring User Preferences

Linux stores most user preferences in so-called "dot files" in the user's home directory. If a filename starts with a dot, it will not be displayed by the ls command unless you use the -a option and is therefore regarded as a "hidden" file. Both dot files and dot directories are used to hold preferences for most of the programs you use. Many programs will write a new dot file in your home directory when you run them for the first time.

Many of these dot files have names that include the letters rc—this comes from the initial letters of *run command* and is an old Unix legacy. The same letters rc will be seen in the SUSE commands used for starting and stopping services.

In particular, the KDE desktop uses a directory .kde in a user's home directory to store preferences for all KDE programs as well as your desktop settings. This directory contains multiple subdirectories and preference files for many KDE applications.

The behavior of the bash shell is determined by the user's file .bashrc. Exactly how bash preferences are set is complicated; as mentioned earlier, the system-wide files /etc/profile and /etc/profile.local are also read, and the user's file .profile is read at login.

You can modify various aspects of how bash behaves by editing .bashrc. In particular, you could change your umask simply by adding a line at the end of .bashrc like this:

```
umask 077
```

If you were then to log in and create a file, you would find that it had permissions -rw------- or 600, so it would be not be readable or writable by any other user (apart from root). Similarly, if you created a directory, it would have the permissions drwx------, so that it could not be explored by any other user.

The file .bashrc can also be used to control the appearance of the prompt and set paths and environment variables.

The user's file .xinitrc (if it exists) controls the behavior of the X Window system when it is started by the user. In particular, the window manager to be used could be specified with lines in .xinitrc near the end of the file similar to this:

```
WINDOWMANAGER=/usr/X11R6/bin/twm
exec $WINDOWMANAGER
```

You probably don't want to make exactly that change, but it serves to illustrate what is possible. You might also want to include a command to start an xterm, which is a command-line terminal application that runs within the X Window system, immediately before starting the window manager:

```
WINDOWMANAGER=/usr/X11R6/bin/twm
xterm &
exec $WINDOWMANAGER
```

It can sometimes be useful to remember that if you are having difficulties with the behavior of programs as a user, removing (or better, hiding) the relevant dot file may help you diagnose the problem. So for example, you could do this:

```
mv .emacs .emacs.trouble
```

The next time you start emacs, it will start without a preferences file so you can look through your previous one to try to solve the problem.

Mounting and Unmounting Filesystems

Mounting a filesystem is what you need to do to make the files it contains available, and the mount command is what you use to do that. In Linux, everything that can be seen is part of one big tree of files and directories. Those that are on physically different partitions, disks, or remote machines are "grafted" onto the system at a particular place—a mount point, which is usually an empty directory.

To find out what is currently mounted, simply type the command **mount** on its own.

We discuss the mount command further in Chapters 14 and 22.

 Note SUSE Linux now uses subfs to mount removable devices such as CD-ROMs and floppy disks. This means that you no longer have to mount them explicitly; for example, if you simply change to the directory /media/cdrom, the contents of the CD will be visible.

✦ mount 192.168.1.1:/home/bible/ /mnt — Mounts the remote network filesystem /home/bible/ from the machine 192.168.1.1 on the mount point /mnt

✦ mount /dev/hda3 /usr/local — Mounts the disk partition /dev/hda3 on the mount point /usr/local

✦ umount /mnt — Unmounts whatever is mounted on the mount point /mnt

Working with Software Packages

All the packages that SUSE supplies are offered in RPM format.

Note   RPM (officially, but not very helpfully) now stands for the RPM Package Manager. Its original name was the Red Hat Package Manager, and it was developed originally by Red Hat, but it has been widely adopted by other distributions. SUSE adopted RPM at an early stage. Not all Linux distributions use RPM; the best-known alternative is the one used by the Debian distribution and its derivatives.

An RPM package is a packed archive containing the files that need to be installed on the system as well as necessary information about the package, particularly about *dependencies* (which other packages the package depends on).

If you are installing SUSE packages, then the best way to do this is to use YaST. YaST will sort out the dependencies for you during the package installation and generally "do the right thing." You can start YaST and use the package installation screen to see what packages are available and choose the ones you want to install. Alternatively, if you know the name of the package that you want to install, and the installation source is available to the system, you can simply type the following:

```
yast -i <packagename>
```

Checking What's Installed

The command:

```
rpm -qa
```

will list all the RPM packages that are installed on the system. To check whether a particular package is installed (for example, apache), combine this with grep:

```
rpm -qa | grep apache
```

Examining RPM Packages

When you hear of an interesting piece of software that you would like to test out, your first reaction should be, "Is there a SUSE package?" Checking this first can save you a good deal of trouble.

Third-party packages that are distributed in RPM format may not work on SUSE for a variety of reasons. Whether they will or not depends on their complexity and what other packages they depend on.

The command:

```
rpm -qpl foreignpackage.rpm
```

will list the files that `foreignpackage.rpm` will install. For example, SUSE does not offer an `mpage` package. If you examine the `mpage` package from the Fedora distribution in this way, the result is as follows:

```
rpm -qpl mpage-2.5.3-7.i386.rpm
warning: mpage-2.5.3-7.i386.rpm: V3 DSA signature: NOKEY, key ID 4f2a6fd2
/usr/bin/mpage
/usr/share/doc/mpage-2.5.3
/usr/share/doc/mpage-2.5.3/CHANGES
/usr/share/doc/mpage-2.5.3/Copyright
/usr/share/doc/mpage-2.5.3/NEWS
/usr/share/doc/mpage-2.5.3/README
/usr/share/doc/mpage-2.5.3/TODO
/usr/share/man/man1/mpage.1.gz
/usr/share/mpage
/usr/share/mpage/CP850.PC
/usr/share/mpage/ISO+STD+OTH
/usr/share/mpage/ISO-8859.1
/usr/share/mpage/ISO-8859.15
/usr/share/mpage/ISO-Latin.1
/usr/share/mpage/ISO-Latin.2
```

Through this output you can see that this installation is not going to interfere with any existing files on the system, so you can simply install the package with the command:

```
rpm -Uvh mpage-2.5.3-7.i386.rpm
```

Extracting Files from Packages

The easy way to extract files from packages is with m c (midnight commander), a text-based file manager that has the nice feature that explores inside various types of archives and packages, including RPM packages. So if you start m c in a directory in which there is an RPM package, as shown in Figure 2-1, you can examine the package using m c as shown in Figure 2-2 and copy or read a text file from within m c.

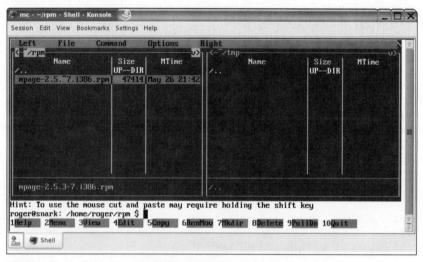

Figure 2-1: A directory containing an RPM in mc

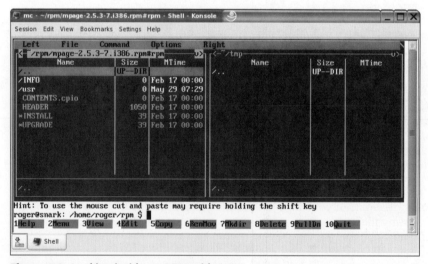

Figure 2-2: Looking inside an RPM with mc

Working with Source RPMs

There will be occasions when a SUSE RPM of a particular package exists but not for the particular SUSE version you are using. If you are running SLES 9 on x86, you should be able to install a binary RPM taken from SUSE 9.1 Professional without any problems, because these two versions are binary compatible. But in many other cases although you may not be able to install the binary RPM, you may be able to take a source package and rebuild it according to your needs. In the simplest case, you would do this (as root):

```
rpmbuild --clean --rebuild packagename.src.rpm
```

You will then find that in the directory /usr/src/packages/RPMS, in the subdirectory corresponding to your architecture (i586 if you are on x86), there is a brand-new binary RPM package that you can install. Again, you need to have the development tools installed for this to work.

 Cross-Reference   Working with packages is covered in detail in Chapter 12.

Compiling Source Packages

You will very often find materials distributed as gzipped tar archives. These are files that will usually have names such as filename.tgz or filename.tar.gz. To extract all the files from this archive, copy it to an empty directory somewhere and use the tar command to unpack it, something like the following example:

```
mkdir unpack
cp filename.tgz unpack/
cd unpack
tar zxvf filename.tgz
```

Usually, you will then find that a new directory has been created with all the contents of the package inside — if you are lucky, there will be a document there giving you details about how to build the package. Very often (but not always) the way to proceed will be to do the following commands:

```
./configure
make
make install
```

You will need to have the development tools installed for this to work.

Connecting over the Network

Traditionally the way to connect to a remote machine and work on it was Telnet. Telnet is inherently insecure because it sends passwords in plain text across the network; SUSE systems do not have a Telnet server enabled by default. If you want to log in remotely, you should use ssh (secure shell).

If you are logged in to the machine bible as user `fred` and you want to log in to the machine faraway as user `guest`, this is what you would do:

```
fred@bible:~> ssh guest@faraway
```

You will be prompted for the password, and you will be logged in.

If you use `ssh` with the option `-X` you will be able to run graphical programs on far-away and see the display on bible.

If you need to connect to your Linux machine from Windows, you can still use `ssh` provided you have installed an `ssh` client for Windows: the best known of these is `putty`. You will find a version of `putty` in the `dosutils` directory on the SUSE DVD that is included with this book. The latest version of putty is always available online from `www.chiark.greenend.org.uk/~sgtatham/putty/`.

Similarly, the traditional way to move files from one system to another was FTP. Again, SUSE systems do not have FTP enabled by default because of security concerns; you should use either `scp` or `sftp`:

✦ `scp` is most convenient when you are copying files from the local machine to the remote one:

```
scp myfile root@faraway:/tmp/
```

✦ `sftp` enables you to list files and navigate directories on the remote machine just like FTP. You can then use the `get` and `put` commands within `sftp` to transfer the files.

The Konqueror browser has a very nice feature called fish, which allows you to browse files on a remote machine using `ssh`, effectively combining the functionality of the `ssh` tools into a graphical remote access client. In the Konqueror location bar, type **fish://faraway**. Konqueror will then try to log you in under your current user-name to the machine faraway and display your home directory there. You can then drag files across to another Konqueror window or to the desktop. If you need to use a different username on the remote machine, you can type, for example, **fish://root@faraway** into the location bar.

If you are regularly logging into one or more machines by `ssh`, you may want to consider creating an `ssh` key and copying it to the remote machine to allow a secure passwordless login:

```
ssh-keygen -t rsa
```

When prompted for a password, you can simply press Return. This will create files `id_rsa` and `id_rsa.pub` in the directory `.ssh` under your home directory. If you copy (or append) the file `id_rsa.pub` (the public key) to the file `.ssh/authorized_keys2` under your home directory on the remote machine, you will be able to log in simply by typing `ssh faraway`.

Backing Up, Restoring, and Archiving Files

After you've done any real work on your SUSE system, you want to make sure that you've backed it up somewhere in case of hardware failure or accidental deletion of your data. Linux provides a variety of ways to create archive files that contain files and directories. You can then copy these archive files to another machine over your network or write them to removable media such as a CD-ROM to protect yourself against calamities. This section introduces some of the most popular commands used to create archive files on a Linux system, either as a standard Linux archive file or as an ISO file that you can subsequently burn to a CD for archival purposes.

Creating and Reading Simple Archives

We mentioned gzipped tar archives earlier — if you want to back up the current state of a directory with all file permissions, date stamps, and symbolic links preserved, creating such an archive may be the best way to do it. To create a gzipped tar archive of the directory `work`, execute a command such as the following:

```
tar zcvf work.tgz work/
```

The options `zcvf` mean "compressed, create, verbose, file," respectively. If you copy the archive somewhere else and you want to unpack it:

```
tar zxvf work.tgz
```

where `zxvf` means "compressed, extract, verbose, file."

If your aim was simply to back up the directory on a remote machine, you can create the file on your local machine and copy it elsewhere as explained in the previous section. You could also use `ssh` and `tar` together to copy the directory tree across, like this:

```
tar cvf - work/|ssh faraway "cd /home/bible/incoming; tar xvf -"
```

What this does is to create a tar archive of the directory work on standard output, which is pushed through the pipe (|) to `ssh`, which changes directory and unpacks the archive that it is receiving on standard input.

SUSE includes a very nice tool called `pax` that can both create archives and very easily move a directory tree from one place to another, preserving all file attributes. To create a `pax` archive of the directory `work`, you can do this:

```
pax -wf work.pax work/
```

To unpack this again, do the following:

```
pax -rvf work.pax
```

One of the nice features of pax is that it can deal with archives in both the traditional Unix formats tar and cpio. It is also a very convenient tool for copying a directory tree unchanged from one place to another, like this:

```
pax -rwv work /tmp/
```

Another useful tool for synchronizing directory trees, whether locally or remotely, is rsync. For example:

```
rsync -r localdir faraway:/home/bible/incoming/
```

will create a copy of the directory localdir on the remote machine faraway under the directory /home/bible/incoming/. One of the advantages of rsync is that it is economic with bandwidth because it sends only changes to files across the network. If you make changes in one file in localdir and run the preceding command, only the changed file (actually only parts even of that) will be transmitted across the network. rsync has other features including a server mode where it runs as a daemon and allows other machines to synchronize against a directory tree.

Creating an ISO Image to Burn to CD

An ISO file is a file that essentially contains the image of an ISO 9660–compliant CD. If you create archive files in this format, you can then burn those files to a CD for offsite archival purposes.

To create an ISO image of the directory work that you can subsequently burn to CD, do this:

```
mkisofs -J -r -o work.iso work/
```

To mount the image and check that it is correct, use the following:

```
mount work.iso /mnt -o loop
```

You can then umount the image (umount /mnt) and then burn the image to CD using cdrecord from the command line or KDE's k3b tool.

Ultimately, this chapter has attempted to introduce the most common commands and concepts that you will need when working with a SUSE Linux system. Much of the material that has been covered here will become clearer as it is used again in other chapters of the book.

It is often said that the only way to learn a language is to use it. In the same way, if the commands and ideas in this chapter were new to you, the best advice is to use them, experiment with them, and gain knowledge by experience, with the examples in this chapter as a guide.

Partitions, Filesystems, and Files

Partitions are physical or logical portions of a disk; a *filesystem* is the logical arrangement of data on a physical or logical partition so that your computer system can access and store data there. Partitions and filesystems are nothing new to the computer world, but you will find that these parts of the operating system are much more visible and important as you use Linux. One of the great things about Unix in general is that it is hands on. This may be daunting at first, but it enables you to have as much or as little control over how your system works as you want, optimize your system to meet your needs, and fix any problems that may crop up.

Windows users have pretty much had it easy with regards to installing their operating systems, which is a testament to Microsoft's ability to provide a high-level installer that still performs low-level tasks without low-level user involvement. Of course, this can be a burden, too, as any high-level interface provides less access to the low-level commands that may be necessary when optimizing your system for your specific requirements.

The next few sections cover partitions, how to use them, why you use them, and where you use them. Later in this chapter, you will use this basic knowledge about partitions to create a filesystem in which you can actually create and store files and directories.

Partitions

We touched upon partitions during the installation of SUSE in Chapter 1, and the configuration and creation of these is relatively easy with the new graphical installers to help users along. Before graphical interfaces such as YaST were readily available, more low-level tools such as `fdisk` were available to simplify working with and partitioning disks. This book is designed to teach you the ways of SUSE. However, because you already know how to create partitions graphically with YaST as discussed in Chapter 1, we will use the `fdisk` command from now on to get additional insights into the low-level aspects of working with disks and partitions.

Tip   You can still access SUSE's graphical partitioning utility after system installation by running the Control Center, selecting the YaST2 Modules entry, selecting System, and clicking the Expert Partitioner. This enables you to create new partitions in unallocated space. To resize existing partitions, you can use the `/usr/sbin/parted` (partition editor) utility.

Most operating systems enable users to split a disk into sections that are known as partitions. Disks are partitioned for several different reasons. In many operating systems, such as older DOS/Windows systems, the operating system software lagged behind the manufacturing capabilities of disk drive manufacturers, so partitions were necessary to divide large disks into sections that the system could address correctly. In general, partitions provide both manageability and logical separation of data for any computer system. Dividing a disk into partitions makes it easier to back up data because backups are generally done on a per-partition basis. Partitioning also limits the potential problems related to partial disk failures. Even if a portion of your drive becomes unwritable, data on other portions (partitions) of the disk is still accessible. Finally, separating a disk into partitions makes it easier to administer and reallocate disk space. Data can be moved between partitions as needed, and partitions can be managed and added into the overall filesystem more flexibly thanks to the way in which Unix and Linux systems make partitions available by mounting them on directories. For example, if a system supports a large number of projects and one project uses substantially more disk space than others and often fills up an existing partition, its data can be moved to its own partition, which can then be mounted on its home directory.

Types of Partitions

There are three types of partition definitions, and each provides different functionality for different situations:

✦ **Primary partitions**—These are the standard physical partitions you would use if you did not need to segment your disk too much. Linux supports a total of four primary partitions on a disk, which is usually a limitation for people with large disks who would like to have some segmentation in the way they organize their data or critical files.

✦ **Extended partition** — An extended partition is a portion of a disk in which logical partitions can be created (see the next bullet item). It is a special type of partition because it cannot directly hold any data itself but contains other partitions that can themselves hold data.

✦ **Logical partitions** — This is a special type of partition that is not a single physical portion of your disk, as a primary partition is, but instead resides inside an extended partition. After creating an extended partition, creating subsequent partitions will offer you the choice of creating either a primary partition (remember, only four per disk) or a logical partition that resides in an extended partition.

If you have never encountered partitions before, they can be very daunting. With this in mind, Figure 3-1 shows a logical view of sample partitions on a hard disk. This is not necessarily how partitions are physically laid out on disks but provides a good conceptual view of how they work together.

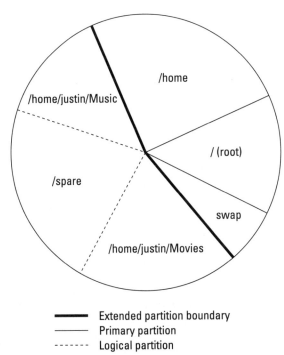

Figure 3-1: Conceptual view of partitions

After a partition has been created, it is represented in Linux by a device name. Devices are represented by files in /dev, and the devices we are interested in at the moment are the block devices that represent disk systems. We will concentrate on the common IDE (/dev/hdx) and SCSI (/dev/sdx) disks.

Character and Block Devices

Two types of devices can represent physical and virtual devices in Linux:

✦ *Character devices* are those whose communication is based on a serial communication character by character. Common character devices are your serial ports (/dev/ttyS0, /dev/ttyS1, and so on) and the /dev/random device, which is a virtual device that if read will just feed out a string of random bytes. The latter is useful for creating an empty file that contains actual data.

✦ *Block devices* are those whose communication is based on multiple bytes that are read and written as a unit known as a block. All disk devices are block devices.

You will come across more block and character devices throughout the book.

Creating Partitions

This section uses the fdisk command to view, edit, and create partitions on a sample SUSE system. If you do not have available, unallocated disk space to experiment with on your existing system, this section provides examples of the most common reasons you would use fdisk to carry out partitioning work so that you can see how and when you might use fdisk in the future.

Caution   Partitioning and creating filesystems is a destructive procedure, and if not done correctly, it will destroy data. It is quite likely that you have used up all of the space on your disk(s) when you installed SUSE, which may mean that you will not have any space left on the disk to experiment with the processes in this chapter. If you are new to Linux, it is possible that playing with the system over time and prodding and poking system elements such as partitions and filesystems could accidentally destroy your SUSE system (it happens to all of us who like to learn by playing). If a reinstallation is needed, you could create your SUSE system with space left over to test out these practices. If you are worried about your data and SUSE installation, we cannot stress enough that playing around with partition tables and filesystems can lead to data corruption, or at worst, the destruction of all data on a disk. If you have a spare computer, you may want to consider using it as a test system rather than experimenting on a system that you are using for real work and which stores your personal data.

Your disk controllers and existing disk drives were detected and configured when you installed SUSE Linux on your system. When using fdisk or any other partitioning software, the most important thing to find out is that you are working with the correct disk on your system. SUSE provides a few ways to do this, but the easiest is to use a feature of fdisk that prints out all of the disks detected by the system along with their partition maps. As shown in Listing 3-1, the fdisk -l command tries to query all disks attached to the system and their respective partition maps. The sample system used in this chapter has only one disk.

Listing 3-1: **Output of the fdisk -l Command**

```
# fdisk -l
Disk /dev/hda: 82.3 GB, 82348277760 bytes
255 heads, 63 sectors/track, 10011 cylinders
Units = cylinders of 16065 * 512 = 8225280 bytes

   Device Boot    Start      End    Blocks   Id  System
/dev/hda1    *        1       13    104391   83  Linux
/dev/hda2            14      268  2048287+   83  Linux
/dev/hda3           269      395  1020127+   82  Linux swap
/dev/hda4           396    10011  77240520    f  Win95 Ext'd (LBA)
/dev/hda5           396     2945 20482843+   83  Linux
/dev/hda6          2946     4857 15358108+   83  Linux
/dev/hda7          4858     6132 10241406    83  Linux
/dev/hda8          6133    10011 31158036    83  Linux
```

The output of fdisk -l shows you the size of the disk, how many cylinders it has, and the disk's block and cylinder size. As the development of fdisk has progressed, the usability of the tool has increased, showing users human-readable information regarding the disk subsystem. We will use human-readable sizes when creating partitions, as this is the easiest and safest way to create new partitions.

Note

As you can see from the output of fdisk -l, the partitions within a disk are numbered incrementally. As a partition is added to a disk, the partition number is increased. As you can see from the fdisk -l output, we have eight partitions, 1–8. Partition 4 is not an actual partition but is the definition for the extended partition that actually houses logical partitions 5, 6, 7, and 8. You can determine this by looking at the partition name or by comparing the starting and ending block numbers for these partitions.

Disks themselves are referenced using different drive letters within each type of I/O interface (IDE, SCSI, and so on). The first IDE disk on the system is named hd**a**. The first SCSI disk on the system is named sd**a**. As more disks are added to the system, subsequent letters are used within each of your system's storage interfaces. For example, hd**b** would be the second IDE disk on the system's first IDE interface, hd**c** would be the first drive on the systems second IDE interface, sd**b** would be the second disk on the system's SCSI interface, and so on.

To set up partitions using fdisk, you need to specify the disk itself on the command line. After fdisk has loaded, you will be dropped to its command line to continue working on the disk. At any time while in the fdisk command prompt, entering m followed by Return will display a help screen that lists all available fdisk commands.

What Does fdisk Really Do?

The fdisk command displays and modifies the *partition table*, often referred to as the *partition map*, for one or all disk drives. The partition table is stored on disk and is just a list of the cylinders, sectors, and blocks associated with each existing partition on the disk. When you start fdisk in interactive mode, it reads your disk's partition table into memory and enables you to make changes to that in-memory copy. Changes to the partition table are not actually written back to the disk until you explicitly use the w (write) command to do so. Do not issue the w command unless you are absolutely sure that you want to update a disk's partition map.

So let's go ahead and load fdisk with /dev/hda as the disk we will be working with (see Listing 3-2). (We're using a different disk in the following examples from the one we used in Listing 3-1, so don't worry about the discrepancy between this listing and the previous fdisk -l example.)

Listing 3-2: **Using fdisk to Edit /dev/hda**

```
bible:~ # fdisk /dev/hda

The number of cylinders for this disk is set to 31207.
There is nothing wrong with that, but this is larger than 1024,
and could in certain setups cause problems with:
1) software that runs at boot time (e.g., old versions of LILO)
2) booting and partitioning software from other OSs
   (e.g., DOS FDISK, OS/2 FDISK)

Command (m for help): p

Disk /dev/hda: 16.1 GB, 16105807872 bytes
16 heads, 63 sectors/track, 31207 cylinders
Units = cylinders of 1008 * 512 = 516096 bytes

   Device Boot      Start         End      Blocks   Id  System
/dev/hda1              1        1041      524632+   82  Linux swap
/dev/hda2    *      1042        7283     3145968    83  Linux
/dev/hda3          7284       11445     2097648    83  Linux

Command (m for help):
```

As you can see in the preceding listing, fdisk presents you with a warning about the size of the disk. The warning relates to older systems and disks and is not especially relevant these days. Older operating systems used to talk to the disks in a system by directly querying its BIOS for a specific coordinate on the disk expressed in terms of a cylinder, head, and sector address. With space being at a premium in the old days, the amount of space allocated to actually store those coordinates was very low (10 bits). For those of you who haven't done some binary math in your head, that equates to a total of 1,024 possible addresses on the disk, and this is the problem fdisk is telling us about. DOS is an OS that is therefore unable to handle these larger disks, and even the Linux LILO boot loader had this limitation until a few years ago. It is unlikely that this limitation will affect you as most modern computer BIOSes have resolved these issues.

After starting the fdisk command and seeing any introductory messages, you are presented with its internal prompt, Command (m for help):. We issued the p command to print out the partition map. This produces the same output as the fdisk -l command, but only for the disk specified on the command line (/dev/hda).

The following example shows how to create an extended partition and logical partitions within it. Listing 3-3 shows a transcript of this fdisk session, with our sample responses highlighted in bold.

Listing 3-3: **Creating an Extended Partition**

```
Command (m for help): n
Command action
   e   extended
   p   primary partition (1-4)
e
Selected partition 4
First cylinder (11446-31207, default 11446): <CR>
Using default value 11446
Last cylinder or +size or +sizeM or +sizeK (11446-31207, default 31207): +2G

Command (m for help): p

Disk /dev/hda: 16.1 GB, 16105807872 bytes
16 heads, 63 sectors/track, 31207 cylinders
Units = cylinders of 1008 * 512 = 516096 bytes

   Device Boot       Start         End      Blocks   Id  System
/dev/hda1                1        1041      524632+  82  Linux swap
/dev/hda2     *       1042        7283     3145968   83  Linux
/dev/hda3             7284       11445     2097648   83  Linux
/dev/hda4            11446       15321     1953504    5  Extended

Command (m for help):
```

To create a partition, press n (new partition). After entering n, fdisk prompts you for the type of partition that you want to create: p (for primary) or e (for extended). As you already have three partitions, creating an extended partition will use all of your available primary partitions. However, as you are creating an extended partition, you can add more logical partitions when needed.

After entering e to create an extended partition, fdisk prompts you with a suggested value for the starting cylinder for the new partition. This is always the first available cylinder on the disk — the first cylinder that is not already allocated to an existing partition. Unless you have a specific reason not to do so, you should always accept the suggested first cylinder by simply pressing Return to accept the default value (shown in Listing 3-3 as <CR>, for carriage return).

Next, fdisk prompts you for the size or ending cylinder of the partition that you are creating. You enter +2G to show that you want to create a 2GB partition, at which point the fdisk prompt redisplays. After entering p to print the new partition map, you can see that you have created a 2GB-sized extended partition. This enables you to create logical partitions within it totaling no more than 2GB collectively.

Caution

As mentioned previously, it is safe to experiment with fdisk on your primary system as long as you *never* write out the updated partition table. When you start fdisk, it creates an in-memory copy of the partition map for the specified disk and makes all of its changes there. It never updates your disk until you actually issue the w (write) command. *Never* issue the write command in fdisk unless you want to save your changes and update your disk's idea of its partitions. This can usually be undone, but if you have accidentally updated the partition table for your system's boot drive, and have changed any existing partition definitions, your system may well crash the next time that it tries to read from disk. If you accidentally save an updated partition table, you may be able to recover by booting from a rescue disk and manually recreating the old partition table within fdisk before you attempt to check the consistency of the drive (by using fsck). Unfortunately, this is impossible to guarantee, so be very careful when experimenting with fdisk.

Now, let's go ahead and create a logical partition to hold a filesystem, as shown in Listing 3-4.

Listing 3-4: **Creating a Logical Partition**

```
Command (m for help): n
First cylinder (11446-15321, default 11446): <CR>
Using default value 11446
Last cylinder or +size or +sizeM or +sizeK (11446-15321, default 15321): +200M

Command (m for help): p

Disk /dev/hda: 16.1 GB, 16105807872 bytes
16 heads, 63 sectors/track, 31207 cylinders
```

```
Units = cylinders of 1008 * 512 = 516096 bytes

   Device Boot      Start        End     Blocks   Id  System
/dev/hda1               1       1041    524632+   82  Linux swap
/dev/hda2      *      1042       7283   3145968   83  Linux
/dev/hda3            7284      11445   2097648   83  Linux
/dev/hda4           11446      15321   1953504    5  Extended
/dev/hda5           11446      11834    196024+  83  Linux

Command (m for help):
```

Enter n to create a new partition. Because you have used up all the primary partitions you can on the disk and now have one extended partition, fdisk is clever enough to realize that you cannot create a primary partition, and therefore automatically determines that you can create only a logical partition within the empty extended partition. Although you have the ability to create many more partitions, this example simply creates a small logical partition of 200MB for a test filesystem.

Printing out the partition table now shows you five partitions. The Extended partition cannot store data or be accessed by Linux as anything but a container for logical partitions.

Updating a Disk's Partition Table

After you have created a partition, you need to save the updated partition table for your disk. As mentioned before, do not do this on a live system unless you are allocating previously unused space. If the disk you are working on is currently in use (as may well be the case on a small home machine), then the partition table will be saved but cannot be reread by Linux. To solve this problem, you need to reboot your machine. If you were partitioning a disk that was not in use (no filesystems mounted), then saving and rereading the table will work without a problem. Listing 3-5 shows the q (quit) command in fdisk, followed by messages from fdisk indicating that the system must be forced to update its idea of the disk's partition table.

Listing 3-5: **Saving the Partition Configuration**

```
Command (m for help): q
The partition table has been altered!

Calling ioctl() to re-read partition table.

WARNING: Re-reading the partition table failed with error 16: Device or
resource busy.
The kernel still uses the old table.
The new table will be used at the next reboot.
Syncing disks.
bible:~ #
```

Changing Partition Types

As you can see from the output of fdisk -l and the p command in fdisk in the preceding sections, there are a variety of different types of partitions. Linux, Linux swap, and Extended all refer to a specific type of partition. Many operating systems, including Windows and Linux, have different types of partitions. The most common ones that every Linux system uses are the Linux (type 83 in fdisk) and Linux swap (type 82 in fdisk) types. Linux handles partitions of different types in different ways.

Any Linux filesystem you create on a partition must be created on a partition whose type is Linux (type 83). The swap partition must be of type Linux swap. When creating partitions, type 83 is the default partition type for all physical or logical partitions. If you want to create a partition of a different type, you must create it (using fdisk or YaST) and then modify its type.

Why would you want to do this? You may want to create a partition of a different type if, for example, you are adding a new disk to a system that can boot both Linux and another operating system and you want to use a portion of your new disk as a standard partition for that other operating system. For example, Linux knows about Windows partition types, but Windows does not know about Linux partition types, so you would want to partition the disk using Linux but then format the Windows partition under Windows. Linux recognizes (and can access) an incredible number of different types of partitions, which enables you to use fdisk to create disks that you can share with a wide range of other types of computer systems.

To change the type of a partition in fdisk, use the t command and enter the number of the partition that you want to modify. You will then be prompted for the type of partition that you want to change the partition to. This prompt takes a hexadecimal number as a type; you can view the list of available partition types by entering L when prompted for the hex code for the new partition type.

Filesystems

Filesystems provide a base for your files to be stored on the physical disk. A good analogy is that a disk is like the building that houses your local library, while the filesystem is its infrastructure—the shelves that hold the books and the card catalog that enable you to find a particular title. Linux supports many different types of filesystems, each of which has its own internal structure and access methods. To access a specific type of filesystem, Linux uses kernel software known as a *driver* that understands the internal structure of a specific filesystem. If you are trying to read a disk from another type of system, Linux might also need to load additional drivers to be able to interpret the disk partition tables used by some types of disks and associated filesystems.

To provide access to a wide range of different types of filesystems, Linux provides a general method that is easily extended. Linux provides a virtual filesystem (VFS) layer that a filesystem driver hooks into to provide file-based access to information. Whether it is listing the files in a directory, reading the data from a file, or providing other functionality such as direct file access (not using the filesystem buffers), VFS and the filesystem driver provide a uniform application program interface (API) to deal with files in different types of filesystems. This is nothing new, and Unix and all other operating systems that support multiple filesystems provide this virtual filesystem interface in one way or another.

When you have created partitions, you must usually create a filesystem in that partition to make use of the newly allocated space. Many different types of filesystems are available for this purpose, but this section focuses on types of filesystems that are available out of the box with SUSE Linux.

The most common and preferred filesystem used with SUSE is the Reiser filesystem (ReiserFS). ReiserFS was the first stable incarnation of a journaling filesystem on Linux. The development of ReiserFS was partly funded by SUSE as they realized that enterprise class storage (at least large storage pools) needed a journaling filesystem.

What Is a Journaling Filesystem?

A *journal*, with respect to filesystems, is an area of the disk that is used to store information about pending changes to that filesystem. Filesystems contain two general types of information: the actual files and directories where your data is stored, and filesystem *metadata*, which is internal information about the filesystem itself (where the data for each file is physically stored, which directories contain which files, and so on). When you write to a file in a journaling filesystem, the changes that you want to make are written to the journal rather than directly to the file. The filesystem then asynchronously applies those changes to the specified file and updates the filesystem metadata only when the modified file data has been successfully written to the file in question. Journaling helps guarantee that a filesystem is always in a consistent state. When you reboot a Linux system, Linux checks the consistency of each filesystem (using a program called fsck, for *file system consistency check*) before mounting it. If a filesystem requires repair because its consistency cannot be verified, the fsck process can take a long time, especially on larger disks. Enterprise systems tend to require journaling filesystems to minimize the time it takes to restart the system because downtime is generally frowned upon.

Historically, the most popular Linux filesystem is EXT2, which is a fast, simple filesystem that does not have a journaling feature. When a system that uses EXT2 filesystems crashes, the EXT2 metadata must be scanned thoroughly and compared to the data that is actually on the disk to correct any chance of data corruption. On a large system, this consistency check can take at best minutes and at worst an hour or two. Journaling filesystems introduce a small overhead for all write operations, but the greater assurances of data consistency and the fact that modern drives are very fast make them an attractive choice for use on most modern Linux systems.

There are certain situations where the use of a journaling filesystem can be a bad idea — most notably with databases that store their data in a standard Linux filesystem but that keep their own log of changes to those data files and are able to recover data using their own internal methods. Oracle is a good example of a database that provides its own methods to guarantee the consistency of its data files.

EXT2

EXT2 has been the de facto Linux filesystem for many years and is still used for initial ramdisks and most non-journaling filesystems. Because of its age, EXT2 is considered extremely stable and is quite lightweight in terms of overhead. The downside to this is that it does not use any journaling system to maintain integrity of data and metadata.

EXT3

EXT3 is a journaling version of the EXT2 filesystem discussed in the previous section. It adds a journal to the EXT2 filesystem, which can be done to an existing EXT2 filesystem, enabling easy upgrades. This is not possible with other journaling filesystems because they are internally very different from other existing filesystems.

EXT3 provides three journaling modes, each of which has different advantages and disadvantages:

✦ **journal** — Logs all filesystem data and metadata changes. The slowest of the three EXT3 journaling modes, this journaling mode minimizes the chance of losing the changes you have made to any file in an EXT3 filesystem.

✦ **ordered** — Logs only changes to filesystem metadata, but flushes file data updates to disk before making changes to associated filesystem metadata. This is the default EXT3 journaling mode.

✦ **writeback** — Logs only changes to filesystem metadata but relies on the standard filesystem write process to write file data changes to disk. This is the fastest EXT3 journaling mode.

Beyond its flexibility and the ease with which EXT2 filesystems can be converted to EXT3 filesystems, another advantage of the EXT3 filesystem is that it is also backward compatible, meaning that you can mount an EXT3 filesystem as an EXT2 system because the layout on disk is exactly the same. This enables you to take advantage of all the existing filesystem repair, tuning, and optimization software that you have always used with EXT2 filesystems should you ever need to repair an EXT3 filesystem.

ReiserFS

The ReiserFS filesystem was mentioned earlier; this section provides more in-depth information about its advantages and capabilities. ReiserFS is one of the most stable Linux journaling filesystems available. Although occasional problems have surfaced in the past, the ReiserFS filesystem is widely used, and problems are therefore quickly corrected.

ReiserFS does not allocate and access files in the traditional block-by-block manner as do other filesystems such as EXT2, but instead uses a very fast, balanced b-tree (binary tree) algorithm to find both free space and existing files on the disk. This b-tree adds a simple but elegant mechanism for dealing with small files (files that are smaller than the filesystem block size, generally 4 kilobytes) in ReiserFS. If a file is smaller than a filesystem block, it is actually stored in the binary tree itself instead of being pointed to. Retrieving the data for these files therefore takes no more time than is required to locate them in the b-tree, which makes ReiserFS an excellent choice for filesystems in which large numbers of small files are constantly being created and deleted, such as mail directories or mail servers.

ReiserFS also provides other optimization that can lead to dramatic space savings compared to traditional filesystems.

When a file is stored on a filesystem, filesystem blocks are allocated to actually store the data that the files contain. If you had a block size of 4K, but wanted to store a file of 6K on the disk, you would be wasting 2K of disk space because a block belongs to one file only and in this case you would have to occupy two, wasting 2K and therefore not optimally using the space. ReiserFS can also store these fragments in its b-tree by packing them together, which provides another way of minimizing disk space consumption in a ReiserFS filesystem. Later in the chapter, we look at some published benchmarks comparing filesystems in different situations.

JFS

JFS is a port of IBM's Journaling Filesystem to Linux. JFS was originally developed for IBM's OS/2 operating system and later adapted for use as the enterprise filesystem used on its pSeries/AIX-based systems. IBM released the source code for JFS to the open source community in 2000 and has actively participated in the continuing development and support of this filesystem for Linux since that time.

JFS is similar to ReiserFS in that it uses binary trees to store information about files. JFS is heavily based on transactions, in much the same way that databases are, using these as the basis for the records that it maintains in its journal. JFS provides a very fast method of data allocation based on extents. An *extent* is a contiguous series of data blocks that can be allocated, read, written, and managed at one time.

JFS also makes clever use of filesystem data structures such as the *inode* (information node) data structure that is associated with each single file or directory in the filesystem. At least one inode exists for every file in the filesystem, but JFS creates them only when files and directories are created. In traditional filesystems, the number of inodes (and thus the number of files) on a filesystem was dictated at filesystem creation time. This could lead to a situation in which no more files could be created because there was nowhere to store information about the file. Creating inodes as files and directories means that a JFS filesystem can contain an essentially unlimited number of files and allows a JFS filesystem to be scalable in the traditional sense. As JFS is a 64-bit filesystem, it is also able to allocate space for extremely large files, unlike existing 32-bit filesystems that can create files only up to 4GB in size because of addressing issues.

XFS

XFS is SGI's high-performance 64-bit filesystem, originally developed for use with its IRIX operating system. SGI machines have traditionally had to work with large data sets on machines with many processors, which is reflected in the way that XFS works. One of the best features of XFS is that it offers independent domains of data across the filesystem. This allows a multiprocessor system to access and change data in different allocation groups independently of each other. This also means that instead of a single write happening to the filesystem at one time, multiple reads and writes can take place at the same time. This provides a significant performance boost for enterprise level data storage. This may not sound like something that would work in the traditional sense of a single disk on a home PC, but if you have a storage area network in which multiple data streams are provided by many disks, the idea works very well.

Like ReiserFS, XFS uses its journal to store information about file metadata and employs binary trees to handle allocation of data. An added feature of XFS is that it also uses a binary tree to store information about free space. This helps speed up block allocation for new information. As you would expect from a filesystem originally developed for machines that process huge amounts of multimedia data, XFS is especially good at allocating and managing huge files.

XFS is truly an enterprise filesystem and may not prove overwhelmingly attractive for a home user, but for large amounts of data and high-end machines, it really is an excellent choice.

VFAT/NTFS

Virtual File Allocation Table (VFAT) and New Technology File System (NTFS) are the Microsoft filesystems that are found in Windows 98/95, NT, and 200x operating systems. NTFS filesystems are readable by Linux systems, although writing NTFS filesystems is a recent addition to the Linux kernel that is still being developed and debugged. Support for the VFAT filesystem is quite stable in Linux and enables a user to mount and reliably read and write to VFAT filesystems, which is especially convenient if you are using a machine that can boot both Linux and Windows. SUSE Linux is usually quite good at finding a Windows installation and, depending on its support for the version of NTFS used on your disk(s), will create a mount point for your Windows filesystems so that you can access your files while running Linux.

Creating Filesystems

As you can see from the previous sections, the choice of filesystems provided by Linux is quite large, and they all perform relatively well. A journaling filesystem is always recommended when quick restart times and maximized data integrity are significant factors, and the ReiserFS, EXT3, JFS, and XFS are all excellent filesystems to consider. In enterprise environments, optimizing data access and creation times are especially significant features, with both XFS and JFS providing potential performance advantages, especially when creating large files. For home users, getting the most out of your storage devices is often a primary concern, in which case ReiserFS is a good choice. If you want to migrate existing EXT2 filesystems to Linux or are simply concerned about having the richest possible set of diagnostic and debugging tools, the EXT3 filesystem is probably your best choice.

Those of you familiar with other forms of Unix will be expecting to find `mkfs` scripts to create new filesystems. As Linux is a form of Unix, it does indeed use the notion of `mkfs` to create new filesystems. On Linux systems, the `mkfs` program is actually a wrapper for filesystem-specific versions of `mkfs`, which have names such as `mkfs.ext2`, `mkfs.reiserfs`, and so on. When you execute the `mkfs` command, you must specify the type of filesystem that you want to create using the -t (type) option, which the `mkfs` command then uses to locate the version of the `mkfs` command that will create the specified type of filesystem. The following list shows the filesystem-specific versions of `mkfs` that are found on a standard SUSE system:

```
# ls -1 /sbin/mkfs*
/sbin/mkfs
/sbin/mkfs.bfs
/sbin/mkfs.ext2
/sbin/mkfs.ext3
/sbin/mkfs.jfs
/sbin/mkfs.minix
/sbin/mkfs.msdos
/sbin/mkfs.reiserfs
/sbin/mkfs.vfat
```

Having already created partitions to house our filesystems earlier in this chapter, we can now use these to experiment with different types of filesystems. The next few sections show how to create different types of journaling filesystems and provide some guidance on mounting and using these types of filesystems.

Tip

The utilities used to create EXT2 and EXT3 filesystems (`mkfs.ext2` and `mkfs.ext3`) are actually hard links to the `mke2fs` utility (as is the `mkfs.ext3` utility discussed in the next section). The `mke2fs` utility was written long ago, before the `mkfs.filesystem-type` naming convention was developed. The `mke2fs` utility therefore takes different options and behaves differently depending upon how it is invoked from the command line.

Creating an EXT2 Filesystem

The version of `mkfs` for each type of Linux filesystem provides some options that are specific to that type of filesystem. One of the most interesting options for the `mkfs.ext2` command is the `-T` option, which enables you to invoke predetermined filesystem configuration definitions that are designed to optimize the filesystem for a specific usage pattern. The `mkfs.ext2` man page lists the following `-T` options:

✦ **news**— One inode per filesystem block. In this case, each inode would have a 4K block space allocated for data. If you have a large amount of small files on your system (less than 4K), this will provide one inode per filesystem block.

✦ **largefile** — One inode per 1MB of data allocation. This would be used where most of your files are about 1MB in size. This makes the dispersal of data across the filesystem less granular but optimizes the amount of inodes needed.

✦ **largefile4** — One inode per 4MB of data allocation. If your filesystem will primarily store huge files, this will optimize the amount of inodes needed on your system for larger files.

If you are using this filesystem for general purposes, such as to hold the operating system itself, it is a bad idea to use these options because they are not designed for general purpose environments. Linux system partitions such as the root filesystem contain a diverse mixture of small and large files. Under- or over-allocating inodes can prove either disastrous or overzealous for general-purpose use.

Listing 3-6 shows the output of the `mkfs.ext2` command when creating an EXT2 filesystem with default settings.

Listing 3-6: **Creating an EXT2 Filesystem**

```
bible:~ # mkfs.ext2 /dev/hda5
mke2fs 1.34 (25-Jul-2003)
Filesystem label=
OS type: Linux
Block size=1024 (log=0)
Fragment size=1024 (log=0)
49152 inodes, 196024 blocks
```

```
9801 blocks (5.00%) reserved for the super user
First data block=1
24 block groups
8192 blocks per group, 8192 fragments per group
2048 inodes per group
Superblock backups stored on blocks:
    8193, 24577, 40961, 57345, 73729

Writing inode tables: done
Writing superblocks and filesystem accounting information: done

This filesystem will be automatically checked every 36 mounts or
180 days, whichever comes first.  Use tune2fs -c or -i to override.
bible:~ #
```

By default, the block size of the EXT2 filesystem is 1 kilobyte, with a total of 49,152 inodes. The number of inodes available for the filesystem is dictated by the amount of space on the partition and the block size of the device. If you are making an EXT2 filesystem with default settings, as we did, bear in mind that the number of inodes available on the filesystem dictates the number of files that can be created. Once you have created an EXT2 filesystem, you have no way to extend the number of inodes available on that filesystem.

Tip For a complete list of the options that are available when creating an EXT2 filesystem, see the online manual page for the `mkfs.ext2` or `mke2fs` utilities, available by typing `man mkfs.ext2` from a Linux command line.

Creating an EXT3 Filesystem

As mentioned at the end of the "Creating Filesystems" section, the same utility is used under the covers to create both EXT2 and EXT3 filesystems; it is simply invoked differently by the `mkfs` wrapper command. Therefore, the same options are available when creating an EXT3 filesystem.

The easiest way to create an EXT3 filesystem is to use the `mkfs` wrapper command, specifying `ext3` as the type of filesystem that you want to create. Listing 3-7 shows the output of the `mkfs` command when creating an EXT3 filesystem with default settings. Note that the output of this command is exactly the same as that shown when creating an EXT2 filesystem in the previous section, with the exception of the following line:

```
Creating journal (8192 blocks): done
```

This line indicates that a journal was created for the new partition, and that it is therefore an EXT3 partition.

Listing 3-7: **Creating an EXT3 Filesystem**

```
bible:~ # mkfs -t ext3 /dev/hda5
mke2fs 1.34 (25-Jul-2003)
Filesystem label=
OS type: Linux
Block size=1024 (log=0)
Fragment size=1024 (log=0)
49152 inodes, 196024 blocks
9801 blocks (5.00%) reserved for the super user
First data block=1
24 block groups
8192 blocks per group, 8192 fragments per group
2048 inodes per group
Superblock backups stored on blocks:
    8193, 24577, 40961, 57345, 73729

Writing inode tables: done
Creating journal (8192 blocks): done
Writing superblocks and filesystem accounting information: done

This filesystem will be automatically checked every 36 mounts or
180 days, whichever comes first.  Use tune2fs -c or -i to override.
bible:~ #
```

Tip When creating an EXT2 or EXT3 filesystem manually, you should write down the location of the superblock backups that were created as part of the filesystem. A good place to write these is on a label that you then attach to the top of the disk. You may need to know this information if the primary superblock on your filesystem ever becomes corrupted. For information about how and when to use these superblock backups, see the section "Common EXT2 and EXT3 Mount Options" later in this chapter.

Upgrading an EXT2 Filesystem to an EXT3 Filesystem

Because EXT2 and EXT3 filesystems share the same internal structure (with the exception of whether or not a journal exists), you can easily convert an existing EXT2 filesystem to an EXT3 filesystem to take advantage of the journaling capabilities of the latter. You may want to do this if you decided to play things safe and created all of your filesystems as EXT2 filesystems when you installed SUSE on your system, or if you are upgrading an older, existing Linux system that uses EXT2 filesystems to the latest revision of SUSE Linux. Either way, converting an existing EXT2 filesystem to EXT3 is a painless operation involving two steps: using the `tune2fs` command to add an EXT3 journal to each existing EXT2 filesystem that you want to upgrade and then updating your system's filesystem table (`/etc/fstab`) to identify the upgraded partition(s) as EXT3 filesystems rather than EXT2 filesystems. The structure of the `/etc/fstab` file is explained in detail later in this chapter in the section "Mounting Filesystems Automatically." Upgrading an EXT2 filesystem to an EXT3 filesystem is a completely safe operation to perform on any existing EXT2 filesystem. The EXT3 filesystem was designed with this sort of upgrade in mind and is a truly impressive piece of work.

Caution   As mentioned earlier, you should not upgrade EXT2 filesystems to EXT3 filesystems in certain circumstances, specifically if your EXT2 filesystem holds data files such as Oracle database files that have their own built-in journaling mechanism. Running two journaling mechanisms on the same file may cause data corruption or may cause your database system to crash.

Listing 3-8 shows the output from using the `tune2fs` command to upgrade an existing EXT2 filesystem to an EXT3 filesystem. When this command completes, simply bring up the file `/etc/fstab` in your favorite text editor, search for the line related to each partition that you upgraded, and change the value `ext2` to `ext3`. After saving the file, you can reboot your system to take advantage of the journaling capabilities of your new EXT3 filesystems.

Listing 3-8: **Updating an EXT2 Filesystem to EXT3**

```
bible:~ # tune2fs -j /dev/hda5
tune2fs 1.34 (25-Jul-2003)
Creating journal inode: done
This filesystem will be automatically checked every 26 mounts or
180 days, whichever comes first. Use tune2fs -c or -I to override.
```

Tip   As its output suggests, the `tune2fs` command enables you to adjust many other parameters for EXT2 and EXT3 filesystems. As you become more familiar with Linux, the `tune2fs` command can help you further fine-tune your EXT2 and EXT3 filesystems. See the online manual page for the `tune2fs` command for more information about other available options and why you might want to use them.

Creating a ReiserFS Filesystem

In most cases, you will create ReiserFS partitions when you first install your system. However, if you subsequently add a new disk drive to your system, you will need to partition it and create filesystems on those partitions. The ReiserFS filesystem is an excellent choice for most Linux filesystems, especially user filesystems and mail or web server partitions where you will be creating and deleting large numbers of small files. As discussed earlier, the design of the ReiserFS makes it a fast filesystem in which to locate files and also helps you get the most out of your available storage by handling small files (less than 4K) specially.

Tip   Unfortunately, there is no automatic way to convert an existing filesystem of some other type to a ReiserFS filesystem. To convert an existing filesystem to ReiserFS, you would have to back up all existing data from one of your existing partitions, create a new ReiserFS partition on that partition, and then restore your data there.

Listing 3-9 shows commands (and related output) used to create a ReiserFS filesystem from scratch on `/dev/hda5` using the default parameters. Although this example uses the `mkfs.reiserfs` command directly, you could do exactly the same thing by executing the command `mkfs -t reiserfs /dev/hda5`.

Listing 3-9: **Creating a Reiser Filesystem**

```
bible:~ # mkfs.reiserfs /dev/hda5
mkfs.reiserfs 3.6.13 (2003 www.namesys.com)

A pair of credits:
BigStorage(www.bigstorage.com) contributes to our general fund every month,
and has done so for quite a long time.

Alexander Lyamin keeps our hardware running, and was very generous to our
project in many little ways.

Guessing about desired format.. Kernel 2.6.4-52-default is running.
Format 3.6 with standard journal
Count of blocks on the device: 48992
Number of blocks consumed by mkreiserfs formatting process: 8213
Blocksize: 4096
Hash function used to sort names: "r5"
Journal Size 8193 blocks (first block 18)
Journal Max transaction length 1024
inode generation number: 0
UUID: 4af72c6a-3f9c-4097-bbce-3124bc0c214a
ATTENTION: YOU SHOULD REBOOT AFTER FDISK!
    ALL DATA WILL BE LOST ON '/dev/hda5'!
Continue (y/n):y
Initializing journal - 0%....20%....40%....60%....80%....100%
Syncing..ok
ReiserFS is successfully created on /dev/hda5.
```

As you may have noticed, the creation of the ReiserFS filesystem makes doubly sure that you are aware that you will erase data on your partition once the filesystem has been created. As ReiserFS is a large project for a small amount of people to look after, it is funded by various organizations. The developers have been lucky that major organizations rely heavily on the success of ReiserFS and have bought support contracts that directly help maintain the development of ReiserFS.

Filesystem Benchmarks

Choosing the type of filesystem that you want to use on your system can be tricky. Throughout the earlier sections of this chapter, we have explored the capabilities of various Linux filesystems and suggested the types of tasks that each is best suited to. However, nothing shows the performance of a filesystem better than benchmarks that you can run against each, and then simply compare the results. Various books and articles on Linux filesystems provide just this sort of comparison. Justin Piszcz, the author of one such article for the online *Linux Gazette,* kindly gave us permission to reproduce the benchmark results from his article. Figure 3-2 shows some of the more general benchmarks he ran that highlight some of the most important results. To see the full benchmark, you can view the full article at `http://linuxgazette.net/102/piszcz.html`.

FILESYSTEM	EXT2	EXT3	JFS	Reiser	XFS
1 UNTAR KERNEL 2.4.26 TARBALL	24.49	31.73	34.64	12.36	23.79
2 TAR KERNEL 2.4.26 SOURCE TREE	17.86	23.4	27.06	22.81	24.85
3 REMOVE KERNEL 2.4.26 SOURCE TREE	4.24	7.26	10.86	3.18	4.48
4 COPY 2.4.26 TARBALL 10 TIMES	18.28	46.68	38.17	49.16	26.22
5 CREATE A 1GB FILE	18.93	22.35	28.87	25.8	20.49
6 COPY A 1GB FILE	45.04	62.48	54.46	71.06	55.89
7 CAT 1GB FILE TO DEV NULL	21.7	23.52	20.4	23.28	21.13

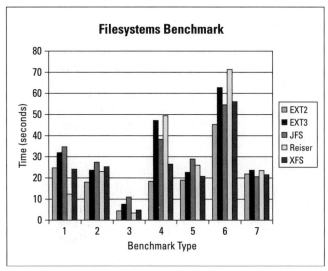

Figure 3-2: Benchmark results

The benchmarks represented in the graph are as follows:

1. Untar the kernel 2.4.26 kernel. This represents a large amount of small files being created on the filesystem.

2. Tar the same source tree. This shows a large amount of small files being queried and read.

3. Remove the kernel source tree. This represents a large amount of files being removed from the filesystem.

4. Copy the kernel tarball ten times. This represents the reading of a large file many times over and shows both filesystem performance and the performance of the read-ahead buffer.

5. Create a 1GB file. This shows how well the filesystem handles the creation of a large file. This is especially good at showing how well the filesystem deals with allocating a large amount of space over a large span of the disk.

6. Copy a 1GB file. This represents how well the filesystem deals with both reading and writing a large file. This is valuable for fileservers that have to deal with large files.

7. Stream data from a 1GB file to the null device. The null device is a black hole that is able to read in any data and drop it immediately. This represents how well the filesystem can read a file.

As you can see in the benchmarks, ReiserFS is very good at dealing with small file operations, whereas EXT2 is good at reading larger files. XFS copies large files sequentially very well (not as well as EXT2), whereas JFS proved the best at reading the 1GB file.

These tests are by no means conclusive, but they are here to give you an idea of how well the filesystems perform comparatively. Choosing among them is a matter of judging how data is manipulated on your system and how you see that changing in the future. For general information about the capabilities and design of each of the types of filesystems shown in Figure 3-2, see the section that introduces that filesystem earlier in this chapter.

Mounting Filesystems

After a filesystem has been created, you will probably want to use it. The process is different from that of other operating systems, such as Windows, where all available filesystems are automatically loaded. In Unix, a filesystem has to be *mounted* by the operating system. Mounting is the process where the root of the filesystem is attached to your system's file hierarchy by associating it with a directory. This may seem like an archaic way of accessing your data, but it does provide you with a transparent way of accessing all the data (local and remote) under a single administrative domain.

The filesystems that you can access from a Linux system can be grouped into two general types — local and remote. Local filesystems are filesystems that are located on storage devices that are directly connected to a particular Linux system. Remote filesystems are those that are attached to other Linux systems but that you can access from your system by using a networked filesystem protocol such as the Network File System (NFS), which is the most common network filesystem on Linux and Unix systems.

Cross-Reference   For more information about NFS, see Chapter 22.

Filesystems can be mounted either manually or automatically when your system boots. Mounting filesystems automatically is discussed later in this chapter, in the section "Mounting Filesystems Automatically." Filesystems are mounted manually by using the mount command. The mount command attaches a filesystem to the filesystem hierarchy and allows you to pass parameters to the filesystem driver that specify how it should use the filesystem. Issuing the mount command with no arguments lists all of the filesystems that are currently mounted on your system, as shown in Listing 3-10.

Listing 3-10: **Mounting an EXT2 Filesystem**

```
bible:~ # mount -t ext2 /dev/hda5 /mnt
bible:~ # mount
/dev/hda3 on / type reiserfs (rw,acl,user_xattr)
proc on /proc type proc (rw)
tmpfs on /dev/shm type tmpfs (rw)
devpts on /dev/pts type devpts (rw,mode=0620,gid=5)
/dev/hda2 on /home type reiserfs (rw,acl,user_xattr)
/dev/hdc on /media/dvd type subfs
(ro,nosuid,nodev,fs=cdfss,procuid,iocharset=utf8)
/dev/fd0 on /media/floppy type subfs
(rw,nosuid,nodev,sync,fs=floppyfss,procuid)
usbfs on /proc/bus/usb type usbfs (rw)
/dev/hda5 on /mnt type ext2 (rw)
```

As most commonly used, the mount command takes two arguments, the block device that the filesystem resides on and the directory you want to mount it under. The /mnt directory is a general-purpose directory that is present on most Linux systems and is used for mounting filesystems that you want to use for a single session only. For filesystems that you want to use regularly, it is customary to either create a directory under /mnt if you want to mount a filesystem or follow the procedure to mount a filesystem on a regular basis discussed later in this chapter in the section entitled "Mounting Filesystems Automatically." If you want to mount filesystems permanently for specific purposes, it is a good idea to create or identify a directory that is permanently associated with that specific filesystem. For example, if you want to store the /var hierarchy on a different disk, you would mount it permanently outside of /mnt.

The mount command's -t option enables you to specify the type of filesystem that you are mounting but is unnecessary in many cases because the kernel tries to automatically sense the filesystem type. If the kernel cannot determine the filesystem type automatically and you are unsure of the type of filesystem that is located on a device, you can use the guessfstype utility, which examines the superblock on a specific partition to try to determine the type of filesystem that it contains. You can then explicitly identify the type of filesystem that a partition contains by using the -t type option when you issue the mount command.

Mount Options

Depending on the type of filesystem you are using, you can pass mount options that impact the way the filesystem is used. These are functional parameters that change the way that the filesystem works or that provide optimizations for specific scenarios.

This section provides an overview of the most significant mount options that are available for the EXT2/EXT3 and ReiserFS filesystems, as well as a discussion of some general mount options that can be useful regardless of the type of filesystem that you are using. The online manual page for the mount command provides complete information about all of the general and filesystem-specific options that are supported by the mount command.

Common EXT2 and EXT3 Mount Options

As discussed earlier in the chapter, the EXT2 and EXT3 filesystems share the same basic data structures and differ largely only in terms of whether a journal is present (and the journaling option is enabled in the filesystem superblock). For this reason, they also share a large list of mount options that can be used with either. Of these shared mount options, the most significant is the sb option, which enables you to specify an alternate superblock to use when checking the consistency of the filesystem using the fsck utility.

As shown earlier in Listings 3-6 and 3-7, a number of backup superblocks are created when an EXT2 or EXT3 filesystem is created. A *superblock* is the cornerstone of a Linux filesystem and provides key information about a filesystem such as the number of free inodes, a pointer to the list of free blocks, and various attributes that specify the configuration of that particular filesystem. The size of a filesystem determines the number of backup superblocks created by the mkfs.ext2 or mkfs.ext3 utilities when you created the filesystem.

Backup superblocks are useful when the primary superblock for a filesystem (generally the first 512 bytes of the filesystem) has become corrupted or otherwise damaged. If a filesystem's primary superblock has become corrupted, you must specify an alternate superblock to use when checking the filesystem's consistency using `fsck`, and then again when you mount the filesystem. The mount option `sb=n` tells the `mount` command to use block n as superblock instead of block 1. The block number must be supplied in terms of 1K units. Therefore, to use logical block 32768 as a replacement superblock on a filesystem that uses 4K blocks, you would specify the mount option `sb=131072`.

Tip   If you don't know the location of the backup superblocks in your EXT2 or EXT3 filesystem, don't panic. Block 8193 is almost always a superblock backup.

As an example, the following `mount` command mounts the partition `/dev/hda5` on the directory `/mnt` as an EXT2 filesystem using the alternate superblock at block address 8193:

```
mount -t ext2 -o sb=8193 /dev/hda5 /mnt
```

EXT3-Specific Mount Options

Although the EXT2 and EXT3 filesystems share the same general organization, the EXT3 filesystem supports various attributes that are specific to its support for journaling. These attributes are stored in the superblock of an EXT3 filesystem.

The most interesting of these attributes are those that control the journaling mode used by a mounted EXT3 filesystem. The three journaling modes supported by the EXT3 filesystem were discussed earlier in this chapter in the section "EXT3." Each EXT3 filesystem is assigned a default journaling mode when that filesystem is created; by default, all EXT3 filesystem are created with a default journaling mode of `ordered`, which means that only filesystem metadata changes are logged to the journal, but all pending changes to filesystem data itself are written to disk before filesystem metadata changes are committed.

You can use the `mount` command's `data=mode` option to override the default journaling mode assigned to an EXT3 filesystem when it is mounted. Possible values for *mode* are the three journaling modes `journal`, `ordered`, and `writeback`. As an example, the following `mount` command mounts the partition `/dev/hda5` on the directory `/mnt` as an EXT3 filesystem with the `writeback` journaling mode:

```
mount -t ext3 -o data=writeback /dev/hda5 /mnt
```

ReiserFS Mount Options

When introducing ReiserFS earlier in this chapter, we discussed the way that ReiserFS can optimize the storage requirements of files smaller than the filesystem block size and the ends of files that are not aligned to the block size by actually storing those files in the b-tree. The latter saves space overall but can add some overhead because of the need to allocate space for the b-tree and balance the tree.

If you wanted to stop this from happening at a slight sacrifice of disk space (about 5 percent or 6 percent of the filesystem), you can pass the notail parameter when you mount the filesystem using -o notail:

```
mount /dev/hda5 /mnt -o notail
```

Another option that you can specify when mounting a ReiserFS filesystem is to disable journaling. To turn off journaling, add the nolog parameter to the options that you supply to the mount command. At the time of this writing, the Reiser filesystem actually still executes its journaling algorithm internally when this option is specified but simply does not write this data to disk, so this option provides only a slight increase in performance at the potential detriment of reliability should your system crash while a process is writing to the filesystem.

General Mount Options

The mount options discussed in the previous sections were specific to certain types of filesystems. This section discusses mount options that can be used with any type of filesystem and are therefore generally useful options to consider when fine-tuning your system.

When a file in a filesystem is accessed by the system or an application, its access time is updated in the entry associated with that file. This information is stored in the file's inode for Unix and Linux filesystems, or in the filesystem-specific data structure for other types of filesystems. If you and your applications do not need to know when the file was last accessed (either by writing to the file or by simply reading it), you can tell the filesystem that it should not update this. If you are accessing thousands of files, this can add up to a tremendous savings in processing time and can dramatically improve performance when an application deals with a large number of files.

To stop the access time from being updated each time you simply examine a file in a mounted filesystem, you can mount the filesystem with the noatime option, as in the following example:

```
mount /dev/hda5 /mnt -o noatime
```

If you share external disks with other Linux systems, you might want to consider disabling the use of the s bit on executables in the filesystems on the external disk. The s bit (set user ID on execution) was explained in Chapter 2. You can disable all uses of the s bit within a single filesystem by mounting it with the nosuid option, as in the following example:

```
mount /dev/sda1 /mnt -o nosuid
```

This command mounts the partition /dev/sda1 on the directory /mnt and ensures that no programs in that filesystem whose s bit is set will be able to take advantage of that fact to execute as a privileged (or specific other) user.

Three final `mount` options that are generally useful are `ro`, `rw`, and `remount`. When mounting external or remote partitions, you may occasionally want to mount them read-only so that you cannot accidentally change their contents. You would do this by specifying the `ro` (read-only) option when mounting the filesystem, as in the following example:

```
mount /dev/sda1 /mnt -o ro
```

After examining the filesystem, you may find that you want to modify some of the files that it contains or simply add other files to that filesystem. You can always do this by unmounting the partition and remounting it without the `ro` option. However, the `mount` command provides some shortcuts in this process, enabling you to automatically remount a mounted filesystem in a different mode (such as `rw`, read-write) by using the `rw` and `remount` options together, as in the following example:

```
mount /dev/sda1 /mnt -o rw,remount
```

This command simply updates the mode in which the filesystem is mounted without explicitly unmounting it.

Mounting a CD or DVD

DVD and CD devices are slightly different from hard drives because they can consist of only a single partition and cannot be written to when mounted. Mounting a CD or DVD in SUSE is now automated, as the system senses when a new disk has been inserted. When you actually try to access the CD or DVD, the kernel mounts the device automatically for you. This is something that Windows and Macintosh users will be used to, because they have had this luxury for quite a while.

To mount a CD or DVD manually, you can also use the `mount` command. SUSE will create a directory under `/media` that represents your optical device. Different directories will be created under `/media` depending on the optical disk that you are mounting. For example, if a CD with the volume name of SUSE_BIBLE was inserted, the directory `/media/SUSE_BIBLE` would be created, and the CD would be mounted under this directory. A device-specific directory may also be created. For example, on an IBM Thinkpad X21 with an external CD drive, the `/media` directory also contains a directory named `usb-storage-0000000001194703:0:0:0`, whose name was created from the USB type and device information for that external CD drive.

Because optical devices do not have partitions, you access the whole disk. IDE-based CD or DVD devices are associated with a `/dev/hdx` device in the same way as any other IDE device. If your CD/DVD drive is connected to the first port on the secondary IDE bus (as is usual on most PC systems) you would access it through `/dev/hdc`. You could therefore mount the disk manually by issuing the command `mount /dev/hdc /media/cdrom`.

Note SUSE now uses HAL and `subfs` to automatically sense media inserted into the computer. In the case of an optical device, its volume name is used. In the case of other storage mediums (USB keys, removable drives, and so on) the device string is used (comprising the hardware address of the device). If you want to create a directory under `/media` for manual mounts (for example, mounting a CD-ROM under `/media/cdrom`), you would have to first create that directory and then manually mount the media.

During the installation, YaST actually creates a link to your optical media device in `/dev` so that you do not have to deal with the details of where your optical drive is. If you have a standard CD drive, this is linked to `/dev/cdrom`. For a CD recorder this is `/dev/cdrecorder`, and for a DVD drive it is `/dev/dvd`.

Mounting Filesystems Automatically

The `/etc/fstab` file is used to store information about filesystems that have been permanently defined for the system. This includes the swap partition and the root partition, as well as any other partitions created during installation. The `fstab` file proves very useful if you create new partitions that you will be using on a perma-nent basis and that need to be integrated into the system whenever the system is booted. During bootup, the initialization of the system attempts to mount all of the filesystems in the `fstab` file unless the `noauto` option has been added to the options for a specific filesystem.

In this example, we add a new Reiser filesystem we created, and we mount it under `/spare` automatically at each system boot.

Cross-Reference To edit the `/etc/fstab` file or files like it, you need to work with a text editor. For more information on text editors, take a look at Chapter 11.

To add a filesystem to be mounted automatically at bootup, you need to add a line to the `fstab` file that specifies the partition, mount point, filesystem type, your options, and some system information about backups and mount order:

```
/dev/hda5   /spare   reiserfs    default    0 0
```

The line you add to `fstab` is made up of the following fields:

✦ **Column 1** — The partition you want to mount.

✦ **Column 2** — The directory you want to mount the filesystem under.

✦ **Column 3** — The filesystem type (the same that is passed to `mount -t`).

✦ **Column 4** — A comma-delimited list of filesystem options (`noatime`, `notail`, and so on).

✦ **Column 5**—Specified dump priority. The value "0" in this field means "do not back up this filesystem."

✦ **Column 6**—The order in which the filesystem should be checked. If this is a journaling filesystem, this is not needed as a filesystem check is run when the filesystem is mounted by the filesystem driver. The value "0" in this field means "do not perform this check."

Unmounting Filesystems

The discussions of mounting filesystems in the previous sections wouldn't be complete without a parallel discussion of unmounting those filesystems. Unmounting a filesystem removes the association between that filesystem and the directory in which it was mounted. In the case of removable media such as a CD, you will not be able to remove a manually mounted CD from your drive unless it is first unmounted.

Unmounting a filesystem is done using the umount command (note the missing *n*). You must be the root user or be executing using root privileges to unmount a filesystem. To unmount a filesystem, simply specify the name of the partition, filesystem, or its mount point on the umount command line. For a USB CD drive (/dev/cdrom) that is actually the physical device /dev/sr0 and is mounted at /media/cdrom, the following three commands are equivalent:

```
# umount /dev/cdrom
# umount /dev/sr0
# umount /media/cdrom
```

The one catch when unmounting a filesystem is that you cannot unmount a filesystem when any process is using any file on that directory. This includes processes that you might easily overlook, such as a bash shell in which you have simply used the cd command to change disks to somewhere in the filesystem that you want to unmount. Before unmounting a filesystem, you must use the cd command to exit that filesystem or terminate any processes that are using that filesystem in any way.

Identifying the processes that are using or accessing a mounted filesystem can be tedious, especially if you have multiple applications, konsole windows, or xterm windows open on your system. To save time, SUSE provides two convenient commands as part of its Linux distribution, the lsof (list open files) and fuser (find user) commands.

✦ To use the lsof command to identify the files open on a specific filesystem, simply provide the name of that filesystem or its mount point as an argument to the lsof command, as in the following example:

```
# lsof /dev/cdrom
```

```
COMMAND  PID USER    FD    TYPE DEVICE SIZE    NODE NAME
bash    4317 root    cwd    DIR   11,0 2048 710656 /media/cdrom
vi      4365 root    cwd    DIR   11,0 2048 710656 /media/cdrom
```

The output of this command shows that the root user has two active processes that are using the filesystem on your CD device: a bash shell (process ID 4317) and the vi text editor (process ID 4365). You can either terminate the processes manually by using the kill command and specifying the IDs of the processes that you want to terminate, or you can use the fuser command to do this for you.

✦ The fuser command shows any processes associated with a specific file on a mounted filesystem. For example, to see any processes that have the file /media/cdrom/Future_ReadME.txt open, execute the fuser command with the name of this file as an argument, as in the following example:

```
# fuser -m /media/cdrom/Future_ReadME.txt
/media/cdrom/Future_ReadME.txt:   4317c   4365c
```

The -m option is required to specify the name of the file that you want information about. To terminate this process, you can add the fuser command's -k option, as in the following example:

```
# fuser -mk /media/cdrom/Future_ReadME.txt
/media/cdrom/Future_ReadME.txt:   4317c   4365c
```

Tip   Be very careful when using the fuser command's -k option. This option terminates any processes that are accessing any component of the full path of the filesystem that you specify, which is generally fine for a path such as /media/ cdrom, but which can kill many more processes than you expect if you specify a path such as /home. The processes you can kill are restricted to those you are authorized to terminate — which is all processes if you are logged in as root.

Filesystems are an integral part of Linux and operating systems in general, and understanding them and how they work is very important to the use, performance, and optimization of a system. Filesystems are the lifeblood of a system because the primary purpose of computers is to create, manipulate, and display data, which must be stored in a filesystem of some sort. The filesystems created during the SUSE installation process are set up with default settings. As you become more of a Linux expert or simply want to experiment, you may find it interesting to see how the different mount options and types of filesystems discussed in this chapter can help improve the performance or reliability of your system. Faster is always better, so understanding the types of filesystems to use and how to use them is something that a system administrator has to deal with at every juncture of his or her career, and if you are working with SUSE on you home computer system, you are officially a system administrator.

✦   ✦   ✦

The SUSE System

The chapters in this part describe booting your Linux system and help you understand your Linux network. Documentation sources, logging, and the X Window system are also covered. Finally, the use of YaST for system configuration is considered.

Booting the System

Booting a machine is something most of us do every day. The routine of sitting in front of the machine with the morning coffee, turning it on, and waiting for the operating system (OS) to load so that you can read your email is something most of us take for granted.

It may seem that the whole thing is easy, smooth, and predictable day in, day out, but the reality is that booting the operating system is no small feat, and the OS has to make sure that the system is in a consistent state for you to do your daily work.

This chapter explains how SUSE and most other Linux distributions boot and start a set of predefined processes and services, grouped together by what is known as a runlevel. We discuss the boot loader (the software that actually helps your machine load the operating system), what Linux actually does during the boot process, how to configure your system to boot two different operating systems, and how to diagnose and correct problems in the boot process.

Booting Concepts

The term *booting* comes from the saying "Pull yourself up by your bootstraps," which is fundamentally what a machine must do. When power is applied to the processor, it carries out a self-check to make sure it is healthy and jumps to a predefined address in memory called the BIOS (basic input-output system) to load and initialize the system hardware. The BIOS is the piece of code that checks your system memory, initializes hardware, and checks to see if you have a bootable operating system.

This section discusses booting in terms of x86 systems. SUSE also supports other hardware architectures, such as the PowerPC (PPC) architecture used by Macintosh and IBM RS6000 systems, where the boot process is slightly different due to hardware and firmware differences. Regardless of the underlying architecture, the Linux boot process is identical with the exception of the boot loaders, which are architecture specific.

You can usually access the BIOS to make modifications to the devices it enables and to the order to check for bootable disks (hard drive, floppy disk, CD-ROM, or maybe the network) during BIOS initialization. On some machines, you access the BIOS by pressing F2, the Delete key, or some other key combination when your machine is first switched on.

Your system documentation has details on how you access your machine BIOS. Nearly every BIOS on a machine will also tell you what key to press during system initialization by showing a message like, "Press F2 to access BIOS."

For example, during the installation of SUSE, you would have to make sure that your system attempts to boot from the CD-ROM (or DVD) device before attempting to boot from your hard disk. This is necessary so that your system starts the installation process from the CD or DVD rather than booting any existing operating system that might be installed on your hard disk.

After your system initializes its hardware, the BIOS attempts to find a bootable device and load a small piece of executable code called a *boot manager*, or *boot loader*, from that device. The boot manager typically reads some configuration information from the boot media to locate and load an operating system, such as the Linux kernel. On a CD/DVD installation of SUSE, this piece of code is called ISOLINUX. ISOLINUX is a boot loader for removable media that allows a user to create a bootable Linux system. ISOLINUX is a simple yet powerful tool that automatically loads the Linux kernel and an initial ramdisk so that you can continue installing SUSE.

Initial Ramdisk

You have come across the term *initial ramdisk* quite a few times in this book. An initial ramdisk is an integral part of both the installation of SUSE and also the day-to-day booting of the operating system. An *initial ramdisk* is a file containing a compressed image of a small filesystem, and it is uncompressed into memory at boot time so that it can be used as an initial filesystem during the Linux boot process. It takes its name from the fact that the filesystem is uncompressed into an area of memory that the system can use as a disk (with an associated filesystem) during the first stages of the boot process. This Linux filesystem contains startup commands that bootstrap the main SUSE installation by preparing disk devices (by loading device drivers) and making sure your system has enough memory to continue with a SUSE install. Throughout the book we talk about initial ramdisks and their possible uses when booting and using a SUSE system.

Tip   The SUSE boot CD/DVD media is preconfigured to use ISOLINUX. Although you don't need to know the details of how ISOLINUX works in order to use it, you can get more information about ISOLINUX from the ISOLINUX home page at http://syslinux.zytor.com/iso.php. We have found ISOLINUX to be of most use when building bootable CD Linux distributions for things like firewalls, automated Linux builds, and so on.

Once the boot loader has loaded and executed in memory, you are usually presented with options about what operating system you want to load. This panel typically also enables you to pass additional, optional arguments to the operating system before it loads and initializes.

Figure 4-1 shows the boot screen of the SUSE installer that you saw in Chapter 1. As you can see, you are presented with quite a few options that we discussed before. This is the ISOLINUX boot loader on the SUSE install media.

Figure 4-2 shows the SUSE boot loader that is installed by default after successfully installing SUSE. This screen provides fewer, and different, options than those shown in Figure 4-1 because they refer only to the installed operating system and a fail-safe Linux system (which you can use in case your main SUSE boot configuration is corrupted).

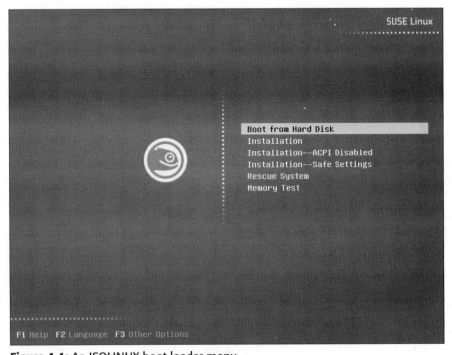

Figure 4-1: An ISOLINUX boot loader menu

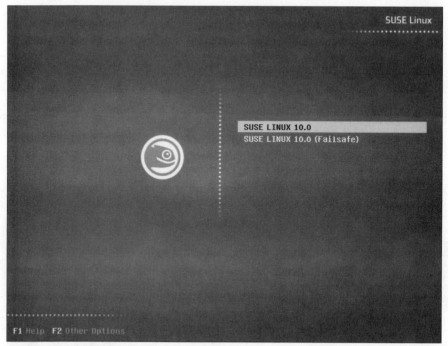

SUSE Linux

SUSE LINUX 10.0
SUSE LINUX 10.0 (Failsafe)

F1 Help F2 Other Options

Figure 4-2: The SUSE system boot loader

Selecting the default boot option, Linux, after SUSE has been installed will load the kernel and the initial ramdisk in memory. If you do not specify anything at this menu, the system automatically boots the default choice after ten seconds. The processor will then jump to the start of the kernel in memory and execute it. The execution of the kernel is usually very quick, within five seconds. After the kernel has loaded, you will see the initial ramdisk being mounted, and the small Linux distribution takes over and loads any drivers that are needed to load your Linux installation from the disk. SUSE hides much of the boot process behind a graphical screen that simply displays a progress bar. You can press F2 at any time during kernel loading and initialization to see detailed status messages that explain exactly what the system is doing.

Note

The initial ramdisk usually contains essential drivers that are needed to mount your / (root) filesystem. The kernel binary includes the basic drivers for IDE disk devices, so these are not loaded by the initial ramdisk, but the drivers for IDE CD-ROM devices are often loaded from the initial ramdisk. Similarly, the drivers for SCSI devices can either be compiled into the kernel or loaded through the initial ramdisk. The driver for the type of filesystem used on the initial RAM disk must also be compiled into the kernel, but you can load additional filesystem drivers from the initial ramdisk if you want to keep your kernel as small as possible. Either the kernel or the initial ramdisk must contain the driver for the type of filesystem used in your on-disk root filesystem.

The reason drivers have to be loaded from the initial ramdisk is that the kernel is unable to access the / (root) filesystem if it does not contain the filesystem drivers to do this. Compiling drivers into the kernel is always safe but creates a larger kernel (which therefore uses more memory). The Linux kernel image contains enough drivers to be able to load and mount at least an initial ramdisk for further disk controller access.

If you lose your initial ramdisk, you may not be able to load the root filesystem in order to complete the boot process. In this case, you will need to use the SUSE Rescue System. We discuss this later in the chapter.

Once the initial ramdisk has loaded any drivers needed to access the root filesystem, it is unmounted and the kernel reclaims the memory associated with the initial ramdisk. When this has been completed, the root filesystem is loaded and the boot process proceeds as normal by reading the default runlevel from the file `/etc/inittab` and then starting up the processes associated with the default runlevel.

Runlevels

The term *runlevel* in Unix is used to describe a set of predefined processes and services that are associated with a specific mode of Unix system operation. The processes associated with a certain runlevel are started by the `/sbin/init` process, as explained in the next section.

Most Linux systems, including SUSE Linux, provide eight runlevels that you can use, numbered 0 through 6 and including runlevel s or S, which is shorthand for single-user mode and is equivalent to runlevel 1. Table 4-1 shows the general description of each runlevel.

Runlevels are an extremely important part of the Linux system, and any administrator must know how they work when managing a system. The administrator of a multiuser system must know how to take a system down to runlevel 1 in order to perform many administrative tasks without the possibility that other users can change data on the system. Runlevel 2 can be useful when trying to diagnose system problems that manifest themselves only in multiuser mode, but again without the possibility that other users could log in over the network and change data on the system. If you are your own system administrator for a home Linux system, you may want to set your system up to use runlevel 3 by default if you are experimenting with optimizing or upgrading your X Window system installation.

Table 4-1
Runlevels and Their Descriptions

Runlevel	Description
0	This runlevel is used to halt a system. The machine is shut down, and all services are terminated.
1, s, S	Single-user mode. Only the root user is allowed to log in. No services are running.
2	Multiuser, no network. Users can log in only locally. No network services have been exported.
3	Multiuser, with network. The network has been initialized and any user can log in locally or over the network.
4	Unused.
5	Multiuser with X Windows and network. Same as runlevel 3, but the X Window system is loaded, allowing users to use a window manager, GNOME, KDE, and so on.
6	Reboot. This runlevel shuts down all services, the network, and so on, and reboots the machine.

Switching Runlevels Manually

If you want to switch runlevels, you can use the init or telinit commands, which are located in the /sbin directory on SUSE systems. The telinit command is a symbolic link to the init command. The init command therefore behaves slightly different when invoked as telinit, taking the -t flag followed by an integer number of seconds. The init command will wait the specified number of seconds before switching to the specified runlevel.

The init process is fondly referred to as the *grandfather process* on Unix and Linux systems, as it is the first process started by the kernel after the kernel has finished initializing and is the process that controls the startup of all processes on the system. The init process always has process ID number 1and always exists on a Linux system.

When init is executed by the kernel, it reads the system's default runlevel from the file /etc/inittab. The entry for the system's default runlevel in this file looks like the following:

```
id:3:initdefault:
```

The number in the second field identifies the system's default runlevel, which is the runlevel that the system will boot to whenever it is powered on and allowed to start up normally.

When the init process identifies the runlevel that it will enter by default, it checks the remainder of the /etc/inittab file to determine what to execute for each runlevel. The entries in /etc/inittab for each runlevel look like the following:

```
l0:0:wait:/etc/rc.d/rc 0
l1:1:wait:/etc/rc.d/rc 1
l2:2:wait:/etc/rc.d/rc 2
l3:3:wait:/etc/rc.d/rc 3
l4:4:wait:/etc/rc.d/rc 4
l5:5:wait:/etc/rc.d/rc 5
l6:6:wait:/etc/rc.d/rc 6
```

These entries tell the init process to go to a directory in /etc whose name is based on the runlevel it needs to load, and execute any startup commands that it finds there. Table 4-2 shows the correlation between the number of a runlevel and the directory it searches for command files to execute, highlighting the fact that the runlevel directly determines the name of the directory used to specify what to start on your system.

Table 4-2
Runlevels and Their Respective Directories

Runlevel	Directory
0	/etc/init.d/rc0.d
1	/etc/init.d/rc1.d
2	/etc/init.d/rc2.d
3	/etc/init.d/rc3.d
4	/etc/init.d/rc4.d
5	/etc/init.d/rc5.d
6	/etc/init.d/rc6.d

The directories associated with different runlevels contain both scripts that the init process will execute when entering a runlevel (known as "Start" scripts) and scripts that it will execute when it leaves a runlevel (known as "Kill" scripts). Start scripts are scripts whose name begins with an uppercase S. Kill scripts are those whose name begins with an uppercase K.

Note When we say *enters* and *leaves* with respect to runlevels, we are talking about changing from one runlevel to another using the init or telinit process, or booting or shutting down the system.

You never just stop a runlevel in Unix—you always move from one runlevel to another. For example, if the system loads into runlevel 5 by default, it will continue to run at that runlevel until you tell it to move to another one. So if you wanted to shut down the machine, you would move into runlevel 0. This would trigger init to run all of the Kill scripts in /etc/init.d/rc5.d and then run all of the Start scripts in /etc/init.d/rc0.d (of which there are none).

The Start and Kill scripts in a runlevel directory are actually symbolic links to files in the /etc/init.d directory, which are all of the service scripts for daemons and processes that can be controlled by init. Using symbolic links rather than runlevel-specific scripts enables the system to share basic scripts across different runlevels. The directory associated with each runlevel that wants to start a specific service can simply contain a symbolic link to the same master script, saving disk space and simplifying maintenance of the master service scripts. Updating the master service script in /etc/init.d automatically makes those changes available to any other runlevel that refers to the same Start script.

The files in /etc/init.d contain a few features that are unique to the init system. The scripts are nearly always bash shell scripts that take at least two arguments, start and stop. If you directly ran one of these scripts with the start option, it would try to load up the application that the script controls. Similarly, if you pass the stop parameter to the script, it attempts to shut down the application cleanly. In the SUSE world, we use rcservicename scripts to control this behavior instead of accessing the /etc/init.d directly. For example, if you wanted to stop the Apache web server process, you could type the command rcapache2 stop. To start the process, you would execute the command rcapache2 start.

If you move back to the specific runlevel directory and take runlevel 3 as an example, you will see many symbolic links in /etc/rc.d/rc3.d that begin with an S or a K, but you will note that some of these point to the same script in the directory /etc/init.d.

When the init process runs a Start script, it calls the script that the link points to with the argument start. When the init process runs a Kill script, it calls the script that the link points to with the argument stop.

Start and Kill scripts usually have numbers after the S or K. This number signifies the relative order that the scripts are executed in. A lower number means that the scripts are executed earlier than one with a higher number when entering or leaving a runlevel. Sequencing Start and Kill scripts is a very significant part of the boot process. If a service needs the network to be initialized before it can run (for example, the Apache web server), then its start order will have to be higher than that of the network. Similarly, to cleanly shut down Apache, you would have to have it shut down before the network when leaving the runlevel.

When all the Start scripts associated with a specific runlevel have finished executing, the system is said to be in runlevel *x*. This means it has successfully completed initializing all associated services and is now in the specified runlevel.

When the system is in a specific runlevel, you can control a switch to another runlevel with the init or telinit processes. If you were in runlevel 5 and wanted to cleanly shut down X Windows and move to runlevel 3, you would issue the command init 3. If you wanted to be able to wait ten seconds before beginning to move to runlevel 3, you would issue the command telinit -t 10 3. Thinking back, you should now be able to trace what the init program does with regards to these "init scripts" (a common name for runlevel scripts). The init process executes all of the scripts in sequence in the directory /etc/rc.d/rc5.d that start with a K in the order of the numbering in the filename. When it has finished killing processes, it then runs all of the scripts in /etc/rc.d/rc3.d that begin with an S in the sequence specified by the filename numbering. When it has completed these Start scripts, the system will successfully be in runlevel 3.

> **Note** If you ever find that you need to change the default runlevel before your system boots, you can pass the desired boot runlevel to the boot loader (for example, append a 1 to the boot parameters in GRUB).

If there are services that should be running in runlevel 3 that were running in runlevel 5, the system is clever enough to not kill off those services and allows them to continue because it knows those services are common to both runlevels.

Using chkconfig to Control Runlevels

Those of you familiar with Red Hat may recognize the chkconfig system script. This is a program that allows you to add and remove services from the runlevel directory of a specific runlevel. If this program did not exist, you could create your own links to move from one runlevel to another—for example, in the directory /etc/init.d/rc3.d or /etc/rc.d/rc3.d (these are the same directory) to /etc/init.d to make sure a process starts and stops in an order you dictate. The services that you can control with the chkconfig command are all of the scripts in the /etc/init.d directory.

> **Note** The chkconfig command is actually a wrapper to the SUSE insserv command. The innserv command provides more granular control over the SUSE init scripts. For more information on innserv, take a look at the man page.

The `chkconfig` command takes a few arguments that you will probably use quite a lot. To list all of the applications in runlevels that are controlled by `init` with details of whether they are on (started in a runlevel) or off (not started in a runlevel), you can just run `chkconfig --list`.

Tip
When you are viewing all the output of `chkconfig -list`, you will see a list of all processes controlled by init with their status scroll by on the screen. You can use the pipe (|) process to push the output through less by issuing `chkconfig -list |less`. This will enable you to move up and down with the cursor keys and see all of the output regardless of whether the output is longer than the screen you are viewing it on. This is something that can be used with any textual output that scrolls past you because there is too much data. You can read more about `less` and other common command-line activities you might want to perform on a regular basis in Chapter 2.

The `chkconfig -list` produces a useful summary of what is running in your runlevels. You may find that you want only certain programs running in your default runlevel. If this is the case, you can stop services from loading in your runlevel by using `chkconfig -d service` (delete) to turn off the named service. Similarly, you can use `chkconfig -a service` (add) to add a service to all multiuser runlevels. As a shortcut, you can use the command `chkconfig service on|off` to activate (`on`) or deactivate (`off`) the named service at all multiuser runlevels. To specify that a named service be started at one or more specific runlevels, you can append those runlevels to the `chkconfig` command. For example, both of the following `chkconfig` commands configure your system to start the apache web server at runlevels 3 and 5:

```
chkconfig apache2 on
chkconfig apache2 35
```

When explicitly specifying the runlevels at which Apache should start, the `on` command is implied.

Customizing Runlevels for Different Types of Systems

As a general rule, if you are running a server using SUSE (or any other operating system for that matter), you should turn off any services that are not needed for the running of that specific server. For example, if you were running a web server for your organization, you would not run X Windows because it is not needed to run Apache. In this situation, you would probably run in a default runlevel of 3 (multiuser, with network, no X Windows) and turn off (or better, remove) any non-essential services using the `chkconfig` program. Listing 4-1 shows the output of `chk-confg -list` after we have turned off any services that are not needed to run Apache.

Listing 4-1: **Output of chkconfig -list with a Customized Runlevel**

apache2	0:off	1:off	2:off	3:on	4:off	5:on	6:off
cron	0:off	1:off	2:on	3:on	4:off	5:on	6:off
fbset	0:off	1:on	2:on	3:on	4:off	5:on	6:off
kbd	0:off	1:on	2:on	3:on	4:off	5:on	6:off
network	0:off	1:off	2:on	3:on	4:off	5:on	6:off
nscd	0:off	1:off	2:off	3:on	4:off	5:on	6:off
postfix	0:off	1:off	2:off	3:on	4:off	5:on	6:off
random	0:off	1:off	2:on	3:on	4:off	5:on	6:off
resmgr	0:off	1:off	2:on	3:on	4:off	5:on	6:off
splash	0:off	1:on	2:on	3:on	4:off	5:on	6:off
splash_early	0:off	1:off	2:on	3:on	4:off	5:on	6:off
splash_late	0:off	1:off	2:on	3:on	4:off	5:on	6:off
sshd	0:off	1:off	2:off	3:on	4:off	5:on	6:off
syslog	0:off	1:off	2:on	3:on	4:off	5:on	6:off

If you are customizing a runlevel for a specific purpose (again, for Apache in this example), you should choose the runlevel that is closest in principle to what you need to run just for Apache and then customize it to your situation. Because we do not need X Windows, but we do need a multiuser system with networking, we choose runlevel 3 as a default and then customize it down.

Boot Managers

We will now go back to the beginning of the boot process and talk about boot managers. As you saw earlier in the chapter, the boot manager helps the system load other operating systems. You should see it as a stepping stone from the BIOS to the operating system itself.

Two boot loaders are used in Linux—the traditional LILO boot loader and the newer GRUB boot loader.

LILO

The Linux Loader (LILO) was one of the first boot loaders available for Linux. It is a relatively simple loader that was designed from the start for simplicity and stability. One downside to using LILO is that its configuration information is stored in the MBR (Master Boot Record) for your primary hard drive. Any changes you make to the configuration means that your MBR has to be updated every time. Changing your MBR is something that should not be taken lightly because if you corrupt it, the system will not boot. The MBR is what the BIOS looks for on a hard disk to see if it can boot from it. If this is corrupt or does not exist, the BIOS *will not* boot from the media.

The configuration file for LILO is stored in /etc/lilo.conf. The layout of the lilo.conf file is relatively easy to read, and we will set up a simple LILO configuration for a Linux system and a Windows system for dual-booting purposes (see Listing 4-2).

The lilo.conf file has a general configuration section that sets default values for LILO, followed by specific entries for different boot configurations that can be used to boot operating systems. Each boot configuration in the lilo.conf file is referred to as a *boot profile* because it specifies all of the custom options associated with booting a specific Linux kernel or other operating system.

Listing 4-2: **Sample lilo.conf Configuration**

```
message = /boot/message
timeout = 80
prompt
default = Linux
boot = /dev/hda

image = /boot/vmlinuz
   label = Linux
   initrd = /boot/initrd
   root = /dev/hda3


image = /boot/vmlinuz
   label = Failsafe
   initrd = /boot/initrd
   root = /dev/hda3
   append = "noresume nosmp noapic"

other=/dev/hda2
   label=Windows
```

Table 4-3 explains the entries in the /etc/lilo.conf file and describes what each of these entries means so that you are able to create a custom boot configuration if needed.

Table 4-3
Sample lilo.conf Configuration Description

lilo Parameter	Description
boot = /dev/hda	Defines the default boot device for the system.
default=Linux	If there has been no user intervention, this is the profile that is loaded when the timeout value has been exceeded.
image = /boot/vmlinuz	The kernel image for the profile.
initrd = /boot/initrd	The initial ramdisk for this configuration.
label = Linux	The name of the profile. This is used to select this profile at the lilo prompt.
other=/dev/hda2	To boot "other" operating systems, you can specify the other clause. LILO will simply load and execute the boot sector of the specified partition at boot time. As with the standard Linux profile, a label can be added to allow you to load the profile for a specific operating system, in this case, Windows.
message	Defines the file containing a text message that is displayed by LILO.
prompt	Causes LILO to display its prompt, enabling you to specify a nondefault boot profile.
root = /dev/hda3	The root filesystem used for this profile. This is the / (root) partition that we discussed earlier in the chapter.
timeout = 80	The timeout value until the default profile is used when there has been no user intervention.

When the edit of the lilo.conf file configuration has been completed, you then need to commit those changes to the MBR on the hard disk by typing **lilo** at the command prompt as the root user. Adding -v to the lilo command line will print out verbose messages describing what lilo is doing. As this is an intricate part of the system, we recommend you always run lilo with the -v option to make sure it has executed successfully and diagnose any problems you may find.

Tip

In general, many Linux commands support a -v (verbose) option. When you are first learning Linux, using the -v option with commands such as m v, chown, and others can help you see exactly what a command is doing, especially if you are using a single command to work with multiple files, such as the contents of a directory.

GRUB

Since its emergence, the Grand Unified Boot Loader (GRUB) has become the de facto boot loader for Linux on the PC for several reasons:

✦ It allows the user to have much more granular control over the configuration of the boot loader as well as the boot process as a whole.

✦ GRUB requires that the MBR be updated only once, when installing the bootstrap for GRUB. All GRUB boot configuration data is read directly from the GRUB configuration file, /etc/grub.conf. This eliminates the need to execute a command to refresh the boot loader after making any changes to its configuration file.

✦ GRUB provides advanced features for logically swapping and hiding partitions, which can be very useful in multiboot environments or for security purposes.

✦ All of the options for the boot process can be edited from the GRUB boot loader during the boot process. This enables you to make one-time modifications to the boot process when diagnosing or correcting problems. With LILO, if you made a configuration error in your boot configuration file, your system would not boot. With GRUB, you can temporarily make configuration changes to fix those problems and continue booting the system.

All of these features have managed to make GRUB the boot loader of choice in most modern Linux distributions.

The primary GRUB configuration file is the file /etc/grub.conf. The grub.conf file is very similar to LILO's lilo.conf configuration file in that it provides both general boot loader configuration settings and specific booting options for operating systems. In SUSE, the configuration of GRUB is actually controlled via the file /boot/grub/menu.lst — if you examine the /etc/grub.conf file, you will see that it performs some initial setup and then passes control to the /boot/grub/menu.lst file. The /etc/grub.conf file and SUSE's /boot/grub/menu.lst file, therefore, support exactly the same commands and syntax because the /boot/grub/menu.lst file is simply a SUSE extension to the more standard /etc/grub.conf file. Listing 4-3 shows an example of a SUSE /boot/grub/menu.lst file.

Listing 4-3: **Sample menu.lst Configuration File**

```
color white/blue black/light-gray
default 0
timeout 8
gfxmenu (hd0,2)/boot/message

title Linux
   kernel (hd0,2)/boot/vmlinuz
```

```
    root=/dev/hda3
    initrd (hd0,2)/boot/initrd

title Windows
    root (hd0,1)
    makeactive
    chainloader +1
```

Table 4-4 takes the default "Linux" entry in `menu.lst` and breaks it down so that you can create your own GRUB entry if needed.

Table 4-4
Sample menu.lst Configuration Description

Parameter	Description
`chainloader +1`	Because Windows has its loader in the MBR of the partition it was installed into, its boot loader needs to be loaded. The `+1` signifies that GRUB should start loading the boot loader from the first sector in the partition.
`Default`	Identifies the default profile that is used if no user interaction takes place. As with other things in GRUB, the entries start from 0, so the default used in the previous example is the "Linux" profile.
`gfxmenu (hd0,2)/boot/message`	Specifies the location of the graphical file used as a background against which to display the GRUB menus.
`initrd (hd0,2)/boot/initrd`	The initial ramdisk that is used for this kernel.
`kernel (hd0,2)/boot/vmlinuz`	The location of the kernel. The `hd(0,2)` signifies hard drive 0 (the first hard drive), partition 3 (partition numbers in GRUB start at 0). If you look in the `/boot` directory, you will see the `vmlinuz` kernel file.
`Makeactive`	When you are booting Windows, it installs a boot loader into the MBR of the partition that it is installed into. To actually load this MBR, GRUB has to temporarily make the partition "active" for booting. This clause makes sure this happens when the Windows profile is selected.
`root=/dev/hda3` *or* `root (hd0,1)`	For a Linux boot profile, specifies the partition that the kernel will attempt to mount as its root filesystem. This is the partition that is to be mounted at / (root) that we have talked about previously in this chapter. For non-Linux boot profiles, specifies the hard drive and partition that holds the alternate bootable operating system.

Continued

Table 4-4 *(continued)*

Parameter	Description
Timeout	The number of seconds that GRUB waits before automatically booting the default profile.
title Linux	This is how the entry looks in the GRUB menu that is shown to the user at boot up.

If you are modifying or updating the /etc/grub.conf or /boot/grub/menu.1st files manually, you can embed comments in the file by beginning each comment line with a hash mark (#), as in the following example:

    # This line is a comment.

As we talked about before, once a change is made to any GRUB configuration file, you do not need to run any specific command to commit those configuration changes because GRUB loads its configuration at boot time from the configuration file(s).

Dual Booting

As mentioned during the installation process described in Chapter 1, it is quite common to have systems that can boot multiple operating systems. Such computer systems enable users to take advantage of the power and applications available in each operating system by selecting between available operating systems when you boot the system. These are typically referred to as *dual-boot* systems because most people install at most two operating systems on a single machine. However, because more than two operating systems can be installed on a single disk, the proper name is *multiboot*, which is the term used in this section. The number of operating systems that you can boot and run on a single computer is really limited only by the amount of disk space available on your computer system.

The most common type of multiboot system is a system that can boot both SUSE Linux and some version of Microsoft Windows. The following sections discuss how to install Windows and SUSE on the same computer system, and how to add SUSE to a system on which some version of Windows is already installed.

Installing Windows and Linux on a New System

Windows is designed to be the primary operating system on your computer and isn't all that smart about alternate scenarios. If you have a new machine and want to install both Windows and SUSE, you should always install Windows first.

Different versions of Microsoft Windows interact with the disks in a system differently:

✦ Windows Me systems do not provide the opportunity to partition the disk during installation, but simply format it all as a single large partition in Windows FAT32 (a 32-bit version of the Windows file allocation table — FAT — filesystem) format.

✦ Windows NT, 2000, and XP systems enable you to partition the disk during installation. When installing Windows, you can simply leave unallocated space on the disk after allocating sufficient space for your Windows installation.

After installing any of these versions of Windows, you can follow the instructions in the next section, "Installing Linux on an Existing Windows System," to install SUSE. If your entire disk is currently dedicated to a Windows partition, the SUSE installer will automatically offer to shrink the size of your existing Windows partition and will use the space that it has reclaimed to install SUSE Linux. If you were able to leave space unallocated when installing Windows NT or 2000, the SUSE installer will offer to partition the unallocated space and install SUSE Linux there.

Tip   The BIOS used by some older systems cannot directly address more than 1,024 cylinders (528MB) of disk space. If you have one of these systems, the partition containing the Linux kernel — either / or a separate partition mounted as /boot — must be located within the first 528MB of the disk. When the kernel is loaded, the Linux disk drivers can address disks of essentially any size, but your BIOS must be able to find and load the kernel in order for that to occur.

Installing Linux on an Existing Windows System

If you are installing SUSE for the first time on a system that already contains an operating system, such as Windows, that you want to preserve, and if the disk or Windows partition in that system has sufficient free space to install SUSE Linux, the SUSE installer will propose an instant solution based on resizing your existing Windows partition and automatically creating appropriate swap and root partitions. If this is the case, installation proceeds normally after the partition has been resized, and the SUSE installer also sets up the correct GRUB or LILO settings to enable you to choose between operating systems at boot time.

Tip   Before installing Linux on a system where any version of Windows is already installed, always boot the system into Windows and run the Windows Disk Defragmenter software to pack your Windows data into the Windows partition(s) as efficiently as possible. This makes it easier for tools such as the SUSE installer (discussed in this section) or `parted` (discussed in the next section) to resize an existing disk as efficiently as possible.

If you do not have sufficient free space to install SUSE Linux and YaST cannot automatically resize your existing operating system partition(s), you have the following alternatives:

✦ Add another disk to your system and install SUSE there.

✦ Reuse an existing Windows partition after manually moving the data from that partition into another Windows partition. To move data from one Windows partition to another, you must boot Windows and then drag and drop files and folders from one partition to another. For example, you can consolidate the data from any Windows partition other than your C: drive to the C: drive. You cannot use this method to move the contents of your Windows boot drive to another partition and subsequently expect your system to be bootable because you must also move hidden files that cannot be selected for drag and drop. Also, any applications that were directly installed on the Windows partition that you are clearing out may no longer function correctly because of internal references to its drive letter.

✦ Abort the SUSE install process, remove the installation media, and reboot into your other operating system. You must then free up sufficient disk space and clean up the organization of your operating system's partition(s) using a utility such as Windows' Disk Defragmenter. If there is sufficient unused space on your Windows partition after this cleanup, you should then be able to restart the SUSE installation process and let YaST select appropriate partitioning and resizing values for you.

These are really your only options for installing Linux on an existing Windows system where sufficient space to install Linux is not available or cannot be reclaimed from your Windows partitions by the SUSE install process.

Manually Partitioning an Existing Windows System

If the SUSE installer cannot repartition an existing Windows partition automatically, you can always use the Linux `parted` (Partition Editor) utility to manually resize an existing partition, usually when your entire disk is occupied by a Windows partition. The `parted` utility is available from the SUSE install disk when you select the Rescue System option from the main menu of the SUSE install CD or DVD. For more information about booting the rescue system, see the section "The SUSE Rescue System" later in this chapter — this section focuses on repartitioning after you have booted in this fashion.

Caution

Before using software such as `parted` that directly manipulates partitions, you should make sure that you have a full backup of any critical data on the partition that you are resizing, and that the backup is readable. The `parted` utility is quite stable, but problems do occur, and we can't think of anything more depressing than finding that you cannot use a backup that you were depending on in order to restore critical data that may have taken you years to amass.

Before using parted to repartition an existing Windows partition, boot the system into Windows and run the Windows Disk Defragmenter software to pack your Windows data into the Windows partition(s) as efficiently as possible. This will make it easier for parted to resize an existing disk as efficiently as possible. After defragmenting, right-click the icon for the Windows partition that you are resizing (probably C:), and write down the amount of space used on that partition, as well as the amount of free space remaining. You can then shut down your Windows system and reboot into the SUSE Rescue System.

After you boot and log in to the system in rescue mode, you can use the fdisk -l command to identify the name of the disk containing the partition that you want to resize, usually /dev/hda (IDE drive) or /dev/sda (SCSI drive) in a single-disk Windows system.

You would then start the parted utility, using the name of the drive that you want to repartition as an argument, as in the following example:

```
# parted /dev/hda
GNU Parted 1.6.6
Copyright (C) 1998, 1999, 2000, 2001, 2002, 2003 Free Software Foundation, Inc.
This program is free software, covered by the GNU General Public License.

This program is distributed in the hope that it will be useful, but WITHOUT
ANY WARRANTY; without even the implied warranty of MERCHANTABILITY or
FITNESS FOR A PARTICULAR PURPOSE.  See the GNU General Public License for
more details.

Using /dev/hda
Information: The ... geometry on /dev/hda is 10011/255/63.
Therefore, cylinder 1024 ends at 8032.499M.
(parted)
```

When running parted, its internal prompt is (parted), as shown in the preceding example. You can then use the parted command's print command to display a listing of the current partitions on your disk, as in the following example:

```
(parted) print help
Disk geometry for /dev/hda: 0.000-78533.437 megabytes
Disk label type: msdos
Minor   Start      End    Type     Filesystem Flags
1        0.031  78528.669  primary  fat32        boot
```

Tip   Write down the output of the print command in case you need to undo your partitioning changes later. I've never had to do this, but forewarned is forearmed.

After you have identified the Windows partition that you want to resize, you can use the `parted` command's `resize` command to resize the partition. The `resize` command takes three arguments:

✦ The minor number of the partition that you want to resize

✦ The starting position of the filesystem in megabytes

✦ The end of the resized filesystem in megabytes

The end of the resized filesystem must be some number greater than the amount of used space in your Windows partition that you wrote down earlier in this section. This guarantees that the resized filesystem is large enough to hold all of the files that are currently used by Windows in the original partition. Remember to make this number slightly larger than the amount of used space in your Windows partition so that you will be able to create new files under Windows.

For example, to resize the partition shown in the previous example to 3GB, you would enter a command such as the following:

```
(parted) 1 0.031 3000
```

When this command completes, use the `print` command to verify that your partition has been correctly resized, and then use the `exit` command to leave the `parted` program. You should then reboot your system into Windows, and make sure that Windows still boots correctly.

If this is the case, you can then shut down your Windows system, boot from the SUSE install CD or DVD, and proceed with installing SUSE Linux into the space that you freed up on your disk.

Sharing Data on Windows and Linux Partitions

The previous sections explained how to install both Windows and Linux on a single system in various different scenarios. This section summarizes the different types of partitions that are used by each operating system and the extent to which you can access the partitions used by one operating system from the other. If you have a dual-boot system, it's inevitable that at some point you will need to use data under one operating system that is actually stored in the filesystem(s) used by the other. Because both operating systems can't be running at the same time on a dual-boot system, you will need to be able to mount or simply explore one operating system's filesystem while running the other operating system.

Note   For background information about the different types of filesystems used on Linux and Windows systems, see the discussion of EXT2, EXT3, and VFAT/NTFS in Chapter 3. Chapter 3 also discusses other types of Linux filesystems, but at the time of this writing, only the EXT2 and EXT3 filesystems can be accessed successfully from Windows systems.

Accessing Windows Partitions from Linux

Linux has provided support for FAT and FAT32 (another name for the VFAT filesystem) filesystems for quite some time. Support for NTFS filesystems existed for the 2.4.*x* series of Linux kernels but has been directly integrated into the 2.6 series of Linux kernels (such as those used on SUSE 9.1 and greater).

Reading NTFS filesystems under the 2.6 kernel works fine, but writing to them is still experimental and should be done with caution.

To mount a Windows partition under Linux, you use the `mount` command discussed in Chapter 3. The following is a sample command to mount a VFAT Windows partition on the Linux directory `/mnt/c` (which must be created before attempting to mount the drive):

```
mount -t vfat /dev/hda1 /mnt/c
```

If you are mounting an NTFS partition and do not need to write to it, you can use a command such as the following to mount it in read-only mode:

```
mount -t ntfs -o ro /dev/hda1 /mnt/c
```

Accessing Linux Partitions from Windows

Accessing Linux partitions from Windows is slightly trickier than the reverse because Windows does not provide any built-in support for any of the types of partitions used by Linux. However, a number of utilities and drivers are available for Windows systems that enable you to mount and access EXT2 or EXT3 filesystems under Windows. These range from commercial products to public domain and open source utilities:

- ✦ **Explore2fs** (http://uranus.it.swin.edu.au/~jn/linux/explore2fs .htm) — EXT2 filesystem access from Windows 9x, NT, 2000, XP, and ME.

- ✦ **EXT2 IFS** (http://uranus.it.swin.edu.au/~jn/linux/ext2ifs.htm) — Installable filesystem driver for EXT2 and EXT3 under Windows NT, 2000, and XP.

- ✦ **Ext2fsnt** (http://ashedel.chat.ru/ext2fsnt/) — EXT2 access from Windows NT. This driver code has been incorporated in Paragon Software's Mount Everything utility.

- ✦ **FSDEXT2** (www.yipton.demon.co.uk/content.html#FSDEXT2) — Mounts EXT2 partitions on Windows 95, although read-only. (No longer under active development, but then neither is Windows 95.)

✦ **Paragon Mount Everything** (www.mount-everything.com/) — Mounts EXT2 and EXT3 filesystems under Windows 9x, NT, 2000, and XP. Paragon Software Group's home page is at www.paragon-gmbh.com.

We highly recommend Explore2fs as an open source solution and Paragon Software Group's Mount Everything as a commercial solution. Many people have reported success with the other packages listed in the previous list, but the we have no direct experience with them.

Troubleshooting Booting

Unfortunately, an important part of system administration is fixing problems, and the authors have all spent many hours fixing configuration problems for customers. This section explores what to do if you have trouble booting your system.

Fixing Boot Problems Using Runlevels

We discussed runlevels earlier in this chapter, and if you have a corrupt system, or a runaway process that is loaded in the init process, one way to fix this is to force the system into a specific runlevel to stop that process from running. This is achieved by passing the runlevel number to the boot loader at boot time. Both LILO and GRUB are capable of passing parameters to the kernel before it is loaded, which is a feature that every Linux user should know how to use.

The kernel is able to take parameters in the same way that a normal application or program can once Linux is loaded. To do this, the kernel must know this information before it is loaded and executed so that it can make changes based on what you need to do. The kernel itself does not deal with what runlevel the system boots up in. This is up to the init process, as defined in the /etc/inittab file by default, but it can be overridden from the boot manager. The feature of the kernel that allows this is that any parameter you pass to it that it does not understand will be passed on to the first program that the kernel calls after it has finished initializing. In the case of Linux, this is the init process. If you remember, the way to change a runlevel is to use the init process with the runlevel as a parameter. If you add the runlevel number to the kernel command line before booting, this number is sent to the init process, which therefore boots the system into the specified runlevel.

To pass an init parameter to LILO, you can specify linux 1 on the LILO prompt to load up the boot profile called Linux.

In GRUB you do this by selecting the profile you would like to edit and entering the number of the runlevel into which you want to enter at boot-up (see Figure 4-3).

In both cases, the 1 tells init to load up the system in runlevel 1. This, as you may remember, is the runlevel that signifies single-user mode with no network. This is the lowest usable runlevel that is needed only if there is a problem with the system.

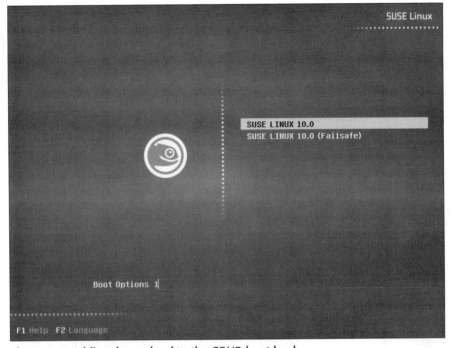

Figure 4-3: Adding the runlevel to the GRUB boot loader

If, on the other hand, you know your runlevel configuration is sound, but you want to manually stop a certain service starting up, you can add PROMPT_FOR_CON-FIRM=
"yes" in /etc/systconfig/boot.

As shown in Figure 4-4, you will be asked for the root password to log in to the system (this is why you should *never* forget you root password). Once logged in you can then turn off processes as we talked about with the chkconfig script or fix any other problems that the system has. Once fixed, you can then reboot the system normally. Because specifying a runlevel to GRUB and LILO is a temporary change, you are able to let the system start up normally without having to interrupt the normal operation of LILO or GRUB.

The SUSE Rescue System

We have talked about fixing system problems by changing the boot runlevel of the system temporarily, but what if you encounter a dire problem such as forgetting the root password! This requires another approach because you will need the root password at some point.

```
/dev/fd0 on /media/floppy type subfs (rw,nosuid,nodev,sync,fs=floppyfss,procuid)    done
Loading required kernel modules                                                     done
Restore device permissions                                                          done
Activating remaining swap-devices in /etc/fstab...                                  done
Setting up the CMOS clock                                                           done
Setting up timezone data                                                            done
Setting scheduling timeslices                                                     unused
Setting up hostname 'bible'                                                         done
Setting up loopback interface        lo
     lo        IP address: 127.0.0.1/8
                                                                                    done
Cleaning up using /sbin/modify_resolvconf:
restored /etc/resolv.conf from /etc/resolv.conf.saved.by.dhcpcd                     done
Enabling syn flood protection                                                       done
Disabling IP forwarding                                                             done
Creating /var/log/boot.msg                                                          done
System Boot Control: The system has been                                          set up
Skipped features:                                                             boot.sched
System Boot Control: Running /etc/init.d/boot.local                                 done
INIT: Entering runlevel: 1
Boot logging started on /dev/tty1(/dev/console) at Mon May 24 18:28:17 2004
Master Resource Control: previous runlevel: N, switching to runlevel:                  1
Hotplug is already active  (disable with  NOHOTPLUG=1 at the boot prompt)           done
coldplug scanning input:                                                            done
             scanning pci: *W..**                                                   done
             scanning usb:                                                          done
      .   .   .   .   .   .   .   .   .   .   .   .   .   .   .   .                   done
ehci-hcd ohci-hcd uhci-hcd usb-ohci usb-uhci
Loading keymap querty/uk.map.gz                                                     done
Start Unicode mode                                                                  done
Loading console font lat9w-16.psfu  -m trivial (K                                   done
Sending all processes the TERM signal...                                           done
Sending all processes the KILL signal...                                           done
INIT: Going single user
INIT: Sending processes the TERM signal
Terminated
Give root password for login: _
```

Figure 4-4: Logging in to init 1

SUSE realizes the need to be able to repair a Linux system, which generally requires Linux tools and access to the ailing Linux system using those tools, and so has included a Rescue System on the first CD or DVD in your SUSE installation set. To load the Rescue System, use the optical media, and select Rescue System from the initial boot menu. The kernel from the CD will load, and an initial ramdisk containing a fuller Linux system will be loaded. This Rescue System has built-in support for the types of Linux filesystems discussed in this book, as well as to IDE hard drives. If you are using a SCSI disk, this ramdisk also includes the main modules for loading a SCSI disk.

As an example of using the SUSE Rescue System, we will take the case of a forgotten root password and reset this with the Rescue System.

Caution   Some of you might see a large security problem with what we are about to do. If malicious users have physical access to a server, they are quite able to reset the root password of the machine using this method. This is why the physical security of a machine is as important as the security of the machine from an operational standpoint.

To reset the root password from the SUSE Rescue System, follow these steps:

1. When the Rescue System has loaded, you will be prompted to select the keyboard map that you are using (which defines the type of keyboard that you are using). After the kernel executes, loads the initial ramdisk, and starts various system processes, you will then be asked to log in. Just enter **root** as the username, and you will be dropped into the Linux system from the initial ramdisk.

2. At this point, you need to identify the partition that contains /etc. This will usually be your / (root) partition. Mount the partition under /mnt. The following example uses /dev/hda3 as the root partition:

   ```
   mount /dev/hda3 /mnt
   ```

3. When mounted, you need to edit the file /mnt/etc/shadow to reset the root password. You can edit this file using any text editor, although vi is the only screen-oriented text editor that is provided in the SUSE Rescue System. Remember that you mounted your system's root partition under /mnt; which is why the location of the /etc/shadow file has changed.

Note   The shadow file is a system file that contains encrypted passwords of the users on the system. The file can be read and written to only by the root superuser.

4. When loaded, you need to find the entry for the root user. Find the encrypted password, which is the second field (fields in the file are separated by a colon). When found, delete the password so that there are just two colons next to each other (::), and save the file.

5. After the file has been edited, change the directory to / (root) and unmount the filesystem by issuing the following:

   ```
   umount /mnt
   ```

6. When unmounted, you can reboot the system by typing **reboot** and pressing the Enter key, or just pressing the reboot key on the machine. Remember to remove your optical media as the system reboots, or you may accidentally boot from it.

You will find that you can now log in to the system as root without a password. As soon as you are logged on, set the password immediately—and try to remember it.

The Rescue System is something every administrator and user should have in his or her arsenal as it can help you fix pretty much any lethal problem you have on a Linux system, regardless of whether it is SUSE-based or not.

This chapter has provided a great deal of information about the Linux boot process and the way in which you can start various services by associating them with Linux runlevels. You learned how to customize the boot process for both Linux-only and dual-boot Windows/Linux systems. The last section explained various ways to correct boot process configuration problems. All in all, this chapter should have you well on your way to becoming a Linux system administrator (or the administrator of your own home Linux system). The only thing remaining is experience, which you will accumulate as you perform more and more of your daily activities on your SUSE Linux system.

✦   ✦   ✦

Documentation

O ne of the misconceptions that are still fairly widespread about Linux is that it is not well documented. This goes with the preconceptions that people have about the nature of open source software: they think that while proprietary systems come with copious glossy manuals, with Linux you have to be a programmer who can read the source code to understand the system.

The truth is much more refreshing and interesting. In our experience it is usually much easier to find relevant and specific information about Linux and open source software than about proprietary products. The spirit of open source means that there are a variety of sources of "good" information about the software—from official documentation provided by commercial vendors to mailing lists, newsgroup postings, and other ephemeral information.

Finding Help on Your SUSE System

Although this chapter surveys a whole spectrum of information sources about SUSE Linux and associated utilities, we will start with documentation that you can find on your system or in your purchased package of SUSE Linux, including the official SUSE documentation.

The SUSE Manuals

Your copy of SUSE Linux or SUSE Linux Enterprise Server comes with official printed documentation. Versions of SUSE up to 9.3 contained two printed books: *SUSE Linux Administration Guide* and *SUSE Linux User Guide*. These were also included on the installation disks in electronic form in both HTML and PDF formats with the package names `suse-linux-adminguide_en`, `suse-linux-adminguide_en-pdf`, `suse-linux-userguide_en`, and `suse-linux-userguide_en-pdf`. When installed, these documents can be found under the directory `/usr/share/doc/manual/`.

In This Chapter

Using the SUSE manuals

Using man and info pages

Using the SUSE Help Center

Package documentation

Reviewing Linux Documentation Project resources

Finding help online

With the release of SUSE 10.0, the printed documentation has been slimmed down, so that the boxed copy includes only the book entitled *SUSE Linux 10.0 Start-up*. The other documentation has been combined into a single package called suselinux-manual_en. This package installs all the SUSE-specific documentation (the book *SUSE Linux Reference* and *SUSE Linux 10.0 Start-up*) in HTML format to the directory /usr/share/doc/manual/. The main book consists of 49 chapters. The PDF versions of both books are in the directory docu/ in the root directory of the installation media.

The SUSE manuals have their strengths and weaknesses. They are very well produced and clearly printed; and the look and feel of both the printed and the HTML versions is elegant and easy to read. The main manual *SUSE Linux Reference* should be regarded (as its name implies) as a reference book. Its coverage of the system as a whole is remarkably good, and certain chapters provide good information that is hard to find elsewhere. The installation chapter covers most common problems and includes short sections on setting up Logical Volume Management (LVM) and software RAID (Redundant Array of Inexpensive Disks). The network section includes subsections on Samba, Lightweight Directory Access Protocol (LDAP), and Network Information System (NIS), and a good introduction to setting up the Domain Name System (DNS). All of this information is somewhat pared down, as a whole book could be written on any one of the topics, but the advantage is that there is a good description of setting up these services specifically on SUSE Linux, using the YaST modules.

The *Start-up* book is a 275-page introduction to installing and using SUSE Linux, aimed mainly at the new desktop user. There are a good general description of YaST and introductions to the main features of both the KDE and Gnome desktops. The chapter entitled "Getting to Know Linux Software" gives a useful comparison between the desktop applications available on Linux and the commonly used Windows equivalents.

The SUSE Linux Enterprise Server 9 printed manual is similar to the *Administration Guide* that was issued with the SUSE 9.*x* versions.

Man Pages

Man pages (man is short for *manual*) are the original form of online Unix documentation. Traditionally, command-line programs have associated man pages that are installed as part of the package that the program belongs to. To access a man page (for example the man page of the cp command), type **man cp**:

```
user@bible:~> man cp
```

The man command displays a somewhat terse but usually complete and accurate summary of the options and usage of the command. A large number of commands have man pages, which provide a quick and easy way of checking on command syntax and usage. Many man pages include command examples, which can be quite useful. The man pages are normally stored in directories under /usr/share/man and are normally stored as gzipped files to save space on your system. Man pages are written in a simple markup language known as nroff that is interpreted by the man command to produce nicely formatted output for the screen. You can print a text version of a man page by using a command such as the following:

```
user@bible:~> man cp | lpr
```

You can also create a more nicely formatted printed output by using the man command's -t option, which processes the man page using a formatter (groff — GNU roff) and generates output in the PostScript printer format, as follows:

```
user@bible:~> man -t cp | lpr
```

If you want to save the nicely formatted output as a PostScript file so that you can print or display it later, you can redirect the output of the man -t command into a file, as in the following example:

```
user@bible:~> man -t cp > manpage.ps
```

To find out more about the use of the man command, you can, of course, look at its man page:

```
user@bible:~> man man
```

To search for a man page, you can use the man command with the -k (keyword) option:

```
user@bible:~> man -k copy
```

This will list one-sentence summaries of man pages that are relevant to the word *copy*. It does this by searching a database of man page summaries known as the whatis database. You can use this summary to determine which man page you may want to view in full.

Another command that does essentially the same thing is the apropos command, which searches the same database of available man pages used by the man -k command, looking for a specified phrase. An equivalent example of using apropos is the following:

```
user@bible:~> apropos copy
```

Working with Man Page Sections

On Linux systems, man pages are divided into ten general sections according to the type of information that they provide. The ones that you are most likely to use frequently are sections 1 (User Commands), 5 (File Formats), and 8 (System

Administration). Man pages are stored under a single directory hierarchy, the directory /usr/share/man on Linux systems. (Older Linux and other Unix-like systems often store these under the directory /usr/man.) Each section has its own subdirectory—for example, man1, man2, man3, and so on.

Table 5-1 lists the man pages sections and their corresponding types of information.

Table 5-1 Man Pages Sections	
Section Number	**Type of Man Pages**
1	User commands
2	System calls
3	Subroutines and library functions
4	Devices, special files, device drivers, and associated file formats
5	File formats
6	Games
7	Miscellaneous
8	System administration commands
9	Kernel
N	New

In certain cases, man pages may have the same name but different content in different sections. Thus, for example, you will see the man page for the crontab program with the following:

```
user@bible:~> man 1 crontab
```

However, you will see the man page describing the structure of a crontab file with the following:

```
user@bible:~> man 5 crontab
```

When searching for man pages on a particular command-line program, you may therefore want to consider the type of information that you are looking for and provide a specific man page section to zero in on the information. As mentioned in the previous section, you can use the `man -k` command to list all relevant man pages for a given topic, as in the following example of the output from the `man -k crontab` command:

```
crontab     (1)  - maintain crontab files for individual users (V3)
crontab     (5)  - tables for driving cron
```

Working with Man Pages Graphically

If you are working graphically, you may prefer to use Konqueror as your viewer for man pages. If you type the location `man:/` into Konqueror's location bar, Konqueror displays a top-level index of manual pages on the system, showing clearly the hierarchy (see Figure 5-1).

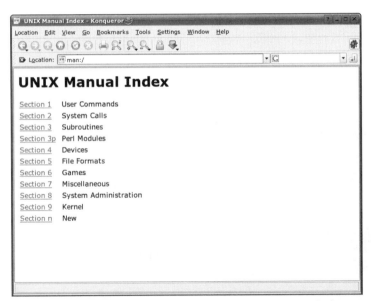

Figure 5-1: Konqueror displaying the top-level man pages index

If you use Konqueror as your man page viewer, you can browse all the pages in a particular section simply by clicking the link, or you can find a page or pages by typing, for example, `man:/crontab` in the location bar (see Figure 5-2).

Of course, you can also print man pages like the one shown in Figure 5-3 from Konqueror if you want (although they won't actually look as good as if you printed them from the command line, as described earlier in this chapter).

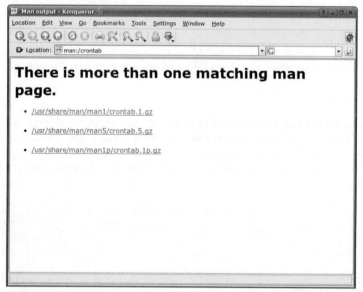

Figure 5-2: Konqueror displaying the choice of man pages for crontab

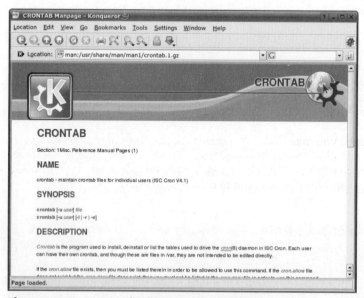

Figure 5-3: Konqueror displaying man 1 crontab

Info Pages

Info pages are another form of online documentation that work in a similar way to man pages, but that include a type of hyperlinking even in text mode on the console. These are particularly associated with the GNU utilities. For example, the command

```
user@bible:~> info ls
```

displays the info page for the ls command in an emacs-like viewer. If you move the cursor so that it is positioned over an asterisk, and then press Enter, you will follow that link to a linked page. The info command also provides a number of keyboard shortcuts to move around in the hierarchy of pages. Some of the most commonly used shortcuts are the following:

✦ **Tab**—Skip to the next hyperlink in the current info page

✦ **n**—Move to the next node in an info page

✦ **p**—Move to the previous node in an info page

✦ **q**—Quit info and return to the command prompt

✦ **u**—Move up a level

✦ **?**—Split the current window and display help containing a list of available info commands in the bottom half. To exit from this help window, press Ctrl+X+0.

The command

```
user@bible:~> info
```

gives you a menu that lets you reach all the info pages on the system.

As with man pages, you may find it convenient to use Konqueror as a viewer if you are working graphically. If you just type **info:/** into the location bar in Konqueror, you will get a menu of all available info pages. For example, if you type **info:/du** you will see the info pages for the du command (see Figure 5-4).

The SUSE Help Center

In the default SUSE KDE desktop, there is a menu item and a panel icon (which looks like a life preserver) labeled "SUSE Help Center." This calls the program khelpcenter. The Help Center displays the release notes for the current version and the official SUSE manuals in HTML format. It also replicates the tree of applications included in the cascading menus on the KDE start button and displays help information about a wide range of KDE applications. It also offers the man and info page display discussed previously in the chapter and a variety of other documentation. Essentially this is a useful way to bring together many of the various sources of information installed on the system and to view the documentation in one place. The Help Center is searchable; the first time you attempt a search it will build an index under `/var/cache/susehelp/`. Figure 5-5 shows what the Help Center looks like.

/usr/share/doc/packages/

Many packages on the system install at least some related documentation in the directory `/usr/share/doc/packages/`. Occasionally, badly behaved third-party packages will use `/usr/share/doc/`. The quality of the documentation found here varies. In many cases you will simply find a copyright notice and installation instructions that are irrelevant because they apply to building and installing from source. However, some packages install serious documentation here in the form of printable manuals in PostScript or PDF format. For example, if you install the `unison` package (a file synchronization program), you will find a file `/usr/share/doc/packages/unison/unison-manual.ps` that is a 56-page PostScript manual for the program, which you can print or view with `gv` or `kghostview`.

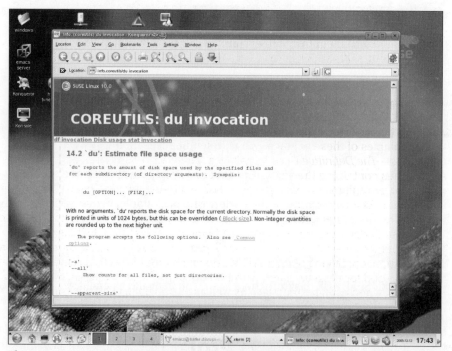

Figure 5-4: Konqueror displaying the info page for du

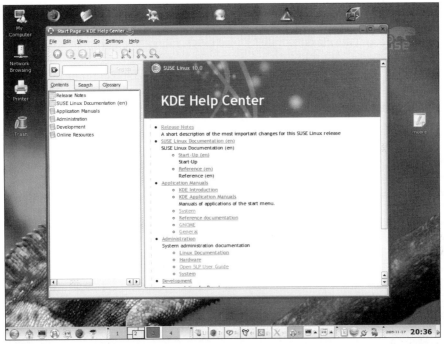

Figure 5-5: The SUSE Help Center

Other Documentation Packages

Some of the packages included in the SUSE distribution contain only documentation. Good examples of these are the `perlref` (reference book for Perl) and `docbook-tdg` (*Docbook—The Definitive Guide*) packages. There are a number of other packages with names containing the string `-doc` that provide documentation relevant to a particular program—for example, `apache2-doc`, `gawk-doc`, `openssl2-doc`, and `samba-doc`. As an indication of the variety of types of documentation that can be installed on the system, the first of these installs a directory containing multiple HTML files under `/usr/share/apache2/manual/`, the second installs some PostScript files under `/usr/share/doc/packages/gawk-doc/`, the third installs a directory tree containing text and HTML document files as well as sample code and files in the pod format associated with Perl documentation, while the last installs sample code and configuration files as well as a large book in HTML format.

Linux Documentation Project Resources

To quote from the Frequently Asked Questions (FAQ) file, the Linux Documentation Project (LDP) is ". . . a loosely knit team of volunteers who provide documentation for many aspects of Linux." That's a classic example of an understatement. The

Linux Documentation Project web site (www.tldp.org) provides an incredible amount of extremely useful information about using Linux, using specific programs, performing specific classes of tasks, and much more. The LDP provides this information in several different forms:

✦ FAQs, which are sets of frequently asked questions on various topics

✦ Guides, which are books or medium-length documents on a variety of topics

✦ HOWTOs, which literally explain how to use a specific application or perform specific types of tasks

✦ Sets of man pages

All of these are often available in multiple languages and are also provided in a variety of formats such as plain text, HTML, PDF (Adobe's Portable Document Format), PostScript, and SGML/XML source code (where relevant). The LDP site also provides back issues of the *Linux Gazette* (www.linuxgazette.com/) and *LinuxFocus* (www.tldp.org/linuxfocus/index.shtml) online magazines.

The LDP is the writer's side of the open source movement — open source documentation that rivals and sometimes exceeds commercial documentation on using Linux. As with any open source project, your mileage may vary — the LDP documentation is contributed by a variety of people with varying levels of expertise. To make the documentation that it provides as useful as possible, documents such as the guides provided by the LDP are divided into two general classes — Current/Maintained and Older/Unmaintained guides. This helps you determine how recent and up-to-date the information contained in these guides may be. The LDP is also a distribution-neutral project, which means that most of the documentation provided there is not specific to any Linux distribution. You may find that some of the documentation provided there recommends configuration changes that may be out of date or unnecessary because your Linux distribution (such as SUSE) may have already implemented them. Regardless, the Linux Documentation Project is a world-class effort to provide detailed documentation about using Linux, provide a central source for locating that documentation, and deliver it in as many different languages as possible.

The next few sections provide details on the types of documents provided by the LDP, locations for finding the most up-to-date lists, and, where relevant, information about how these documents are delivered with SUSE Linux.

FAQs

The Linux Documentation Project site also hosts a number of FAQs, which are sets of frequently asked questions on various topics — along with the answers to those questions, of course. FAQs are available on topics ranging from general Linux information (www.tldp.org/FAQ/Linux-FAQ/index.html) to detailed information about using specific applications, window managers, system administrative topics such as RAID, and so on. The index of available FAQs in HTML form on the LDP site is available at `www.tldp.org/FAQ/`.

HOWTOs

The Linux Documentation Project publishes a large number of documents known as HOWTOs. These are included in SUSE in the packages `howto` (plain text versions) and `howtoenh` (HTML versions). The latest definitive versions are always available in a variety of formats (including nicely formatted PostScript and PDF versions for printing) at the Linux Documentation Project site. The index for available HOWTOs at this site is located at `www.tldp.org/HOWTO/HOWTO-INDEX/howtos.html`.

Tip It is worth checking the dates of the HOWTOs carefully. In some cases information may be out of date or may recommend configuration changes that won't be necessary because they are already incorporated into your SUSE system. Regardless, there is a lot of useful information in the HOWTOs.

Linux Documentation Project Guides

The Linux Documentation Project provides a large number of freely distributed books on Linux. Some of these are included in the SUSE package named books (see the next section in this chapter). The index of available guides at the LDP site is located at `www.tldp.org/guides.html`. The listing for each available guide includes the date that it was last updated and a list of the formats and languages in which each guide is available.

The following are some or our favorite current guides:

✦ *Advanced Bash-Scripting Guide* by **Mendel Cooper** — An excellent document that provides both reference material and tutorials on how to accomplish various tasks in Bash shell scripts.

✦ *Bash Guide for Beginners* by **Machtelt Garrels** — An excellent introductory document to using `bash` on a daily basis.

✦ *Introduction to Linux: A Hands on Guide* by **Machtelt Garrels** — A document oriented to new Linux users that provides a good deal of fundamental information that helps new users explore and become comfortable with Linux.

✦ *Linux Network Administrator's Guide, Second Edition* by **Olaf Kirch and Terry Dawson** — Although an older document (last updated in 2000), this document provides a good introduction to fundamental administrative tasks related to using a networked Linux system.

✦ *Linux System Administration Made Easy* by **Steve Frampton** — An even older document (1999), this guide provides a good introduction to fundamental administrative tasks.

✦ **Linux System Administrators' Guide by Lars Wirzenius, Joanna Oja, Stephen Stafford, and Alex Weeks** — A detailed document that provides a good deal of information about performing standard system administrative tasks on a Linux system, without focusing on the administrative tools provided by any single distribution.

✦ **Windows+BSD+Linux Installation Guide by Subhasish Ghosh** — If you're interested in multibooting, this document goes into detail about how to set up a system that can boot into Windows, Free/OpenBSD, and Linux. Can't make up your mind which operating system to use, or want to do different tasks using different operating systems? This document is for you!

The documents in the preceding list are general documents about using and administering Linux, primarily as a desktop operating system. In addition, the LDP site hosts some documents targeted toward specific segments of the Linux community other than desktop users. Some good examples of these are the following:

✦ **Custom Linux: A Porting Guide — Porting LinuxPPC to a Custom SBC by Shie Erlich** — If you're interested in using Linux in an embedded environment, this document provides a good deal of general information about porting Linux to new hardware.

✦ **EVMS User Guide by Christine Lorenz, Joy Goodreau, and Kylie Smith** — A great document on the Enterprise Volume Management System, the latest generation of Logical Volume Management (LVM) for Linux. This document is extremely useful for system administrators who are responsible for enterprise Linux systems.

✦ **Guide to Managing Media and Public Relations in the Linux Community by Sheldon Rose, The Linux Professional Institute** — This is an interesting meta-document about Linux that discusses how to create and maintain positive public relations and news media coverage for Linux.

✦ **Linux From Scratch by Gerard Beekmans** — Provides good insights and suggestions on customizing and personalizing an existing Linux distribution and using an existing Linux distribution as the foundation for creating your own distribution.

✦ **LDP Author Guide by Mark F Komarinski, Jorge Godoy, David C. Merrill, and Emma Jane Hogbin** — A great document on how to write, submit, and maintain LDP documentation.

✦ **Linux Kernel Module Programming Guide by Peter Jay Salzman and Ori Pomerantz** — A great document that provides a variety of information about developing loadable kernel modules for the 2.4 and 2.6 Linux kernels. Targeted toward driver writers and aspiring kernel hackers.

✦ **Pocket Linux Guide by David Horton** — A hands-on guide that provides a good deal of fundamental information about the organization of a Linux system and how to build a Linux distribution from scratch. This document uses a project known as Pocket Linux as the foundation for its examples; when you finish the document, you've actually built a small distribution!

The SUSE Books Package

This package includes works such as the following, which are mostly current or "classic" (in some cases quite old, but still valuable) books from the Linux Documentation Project:

✦ *Linux Installation and Getting Started* by Matt Welsh

✦ *Linux Kernel 2.4 Internals* by Tigran Aivazian

✦ *Linux Kernel Module Programming Guide* by Ori Pomerantz

✦ *Linux Network Administrator's Guide, Second Edition* by Olaf Kirch and Terry Dawson

✦ *Linux Programmers' Guide* by Sven Goldt and Sven van der Meer

✦ *Linux System Administrators' Guide* by Lars Wirzenius, Joanna Oja, Stephen Stafford, and Alex Weeks

✦ *Linux Users' Guide* by Larry Greenfield

The books package (whose full name is `books-2004.4.16-3.noarch.rpm` at the time this book was written) is available on the DVD if you purchased a boxed copy of the SUSE distribution but can also be downloaded from any SUSE FTP site, such as those that you can access through the SUSE portal discussed later in this chapter. After retrieving this package, you can install it using a command similar to the following:

```
rpm -Uvvh books-2004.4.16-3.noarch.rpm
```

The `rpm` switches used in this example simply update any previously installed version of this package (`U`) and provide very verbose (`vv`) feedback that includes a histogram composed of hash marks (`h`) as each file in the package is installed.

Once installed, these documents (and more) are available as PostScript or PDF files under `/usr/share/doc/Books/`.

Finding Help Online

The Internet gives you access to a host of additional sources for information about anything, including Linux and SUSE Linux. This section surveys some of the best sources of information about SUSE Linux that you can find online and highlights some of the ways that you can find detailed answers to questions that may not be covered in the official SUSE documentation.

The SUSE Portal

Like most companies today, SUSE provides a central site for people searching for customer support, answers to questions about SUSE Linux, software updates and patches, and so on. Located at http://portal.suse.com, the SUSE Portal site (see Figure 5-6) requires that you first create an account in order to access the site, but then provides centralized access to many SUSE-related sources of information.

From the SUSE Portal site, you can do any or all of the following:

✦ Search the SUSE knowledge base of common questions, hot tips, and information gleaned from previous customer support questions

✦ Submit your own customer support questions, provided that you have registered a SUSE product and are still within the free support window provided by that product, or if you have paid for customer support

✦ Browse a list of supported hardware, which is software that is known to work with SUSE Linux

✦ Access the SUSE FTP servers and their mirrors to retrieve product updates and upgrades

✦ Find shortcuts to SUSE web servers and general-purpose SUSE sites

Figure 5-6: Konqueror displaying the SUSE Portal login page

The SUSE Portal is a great resource and an excellent place to start when trying to resolve a problem you've encountered when using SUSE, or when you need answers to general questions and can't wait for some kind soul to respond to your post on a mail list, newsgroup, or blog.

SUSE Public Mailing Lists

SUSE runs a number of public mailing lists. You can subscribe to them at `www.suse .com/en/private/support/online_help/mailinglists/`. The lists are archived at `http://lists.suse.com/`.

The general-purpose SUSE list in English is the `suse-linux-e` list. This mailing list is a general technical discussion list with a high volume of messages. The quality of responses is high, and it is well worth joining provided you are prepared for the large number of mails you will receive. Other interesting and lively SUSE lists include `suse-oracle` and `suse-slox-e` (the English language mailing list for the SUSE Linux OpenExchange Server). Also of particular interest are the `suse-autoinstall` list, which is a valuable source of information about the use of AutoYaST, and the `suse-security` and `suse-security-announce` lists. If you are running SUSE Linux on a 64-bit AMD (or Intel EM64T) processor, you will be interested in the `suse-amd64` list.

The Unofficial SUSE FAQ

An unofficial SUSE FAQ is maintained by Togan Müftüoglu. It is available at `http://susefaq.sourceforge.net/`.

The FAQ is based on traffic from the `suse-linux-e` list and is constantly being expanded and enhanced.

Other Unofficial SUSE Help Sites

The SUSE Linux forums (in English) at `http://forums.suselinuxsupport.de/` are a useful resource. Damian Smith who also runs the site `www.suseroot.com/` has recently set up an unofficial SUSE Wiki at `www.susewiki.org/`.

Other SUSE Documents

While various SUSE sites provide a number of useful documents, some of them are hard to find. This section can help you track down a few of these useful but elusive gems. (Many thanks to Lenz Grimmer for his help with finding these links.)

✦ The full documentation for AutoYaST by Anas Nashif is hidden away at:

`www.suse.com/~nashif/autoinstall/`

and also at:

`http://forgeftp.novell.com/yast/doc/SLES9/autoinstall/index.html`

✦ "Update-Media-HOWTO" by Henne Vogelsang and others is at:

`ftp://ftp.suse.com/pub/people/hvogel/Update-Media-HOWTO/index.html.`

✦ "Working with the SUSE 2.6.x Kernel Sources" by Andreas Gruenbacher is at:

`www.suse.de/~agruen/kernel-doc/`

✦ "The YaST2 Screen Shot HowTo" by Stefan Hundhammer is at:

`www.suse.de/~sh/yast2/screen-shots/index.html`

✦ "Large File Support in Linux" by Andres Jaeger is at:

`www.suse.de/~aj/linux_lfs.html`

Finally, Novell has centralized their online SUSE Linux documentation at:

`www.novell.com/documentation/suse.html`

SUSE Linux OpenExchange Server and OPEN-XCHANGE Web Sites

In addition to the `suse-slox-e` mailing list mentioned previously, if you are dealing with the OpenExchange Server (SLOX) or Netline's open source OPEN-XCHANGE, you have two useful web sites you can check out:

✦ `www.oxhelp.org/` is an unofficial user-supported site where users can post questions and answers. To post questions you need to create a login.

✦ `http://mirror.open-xchange.org/ox/EN/community/` is an official site provided by the Netline developers. There is a rapidly growing quantity of documentation there, particularly installation instructions for different platforms.

Topic-Specific Sites

Certain topics, both in the area of hardware support and particular software projects, have a major web site with definitive information.

Scanners

For information on scanner support under Linux, go to `www.sane-project.org`.

Printing

For printing on Linux, the definitive sites are www.linuxprinting.org and www.cups.org.

Winmodems

A *winmodem* is a modem that performs much of its digital signal processing in software, rather than in hardware as traditional modems do. Offloading signal processing to software is cost-effective for the manufacturer because the physical modem requires less hardware and is therefore cheaper and easier to manufacture. However, winmodems are a constant cause of irritation to those who want to use dial-up modems with Linux because most of the software components for these modems are available for Windows only (hence the name). The definitive site to turn to for help is www.linmodems.org.

Wireless Support

There is high-quality information on wireless support at www.hpl.hp.com/personal/Jean_Tourrilhes/Linux/.

Graphics

For definitive information about support for graphics hardware under X, see www.xfree.org.

Major Software Projects

Many of the major pieces of software you might use on your SUSE system provide a wealth of information at the home pages for these software projects, in the form of documentation, mailing lists, and so on. Any time that you are going to be using a particular piece of software extensively, it pays to check on the project's web site for the latest information on that software. Some key software projects to check out include:

✦ **Apache** — www.apache.org

✦ **Samba** — www.samba.org

✦ **Squid** — www.squid-cache.org

✦ **Postfix** — www.postfix.org

✦ **OpenLDAP** — www.openldap.org

✦ **MySQL** — www.mysql.com

Cross-Reference For detailed information about these topics without searching the web, see the chapters dedicated to these software projects in Part IV of this book.

Some of the key Desktop Linux software projects also have their own web sites. The information provided at those sites is well worth checking out because project sites are typically the most up-to-date source of information about those projects.

✦ **KDE**—www.kde.org

✦ **GNOME**—www.gnome.org and www.ximian.com

✦ **OpenOffice.org**—www.openoffice.org

Finding Software

Some key web sites that should be among your first places to look if you are looking for open source software are:

✦ http://freshmeat.net—The FreshMeat web site and associated mailing list provide information about recently updated software packages and projects.

✦ http://packman.links2linux.org—A great German site that is nicely organized into logical groups of packages (development, finance, games, and so on).

✦ www.rpmfind.net—A great site for locating and downloading packages in RPM format for almost any Linux package.

✦ http://sourceforge.net—SourceForge is the home for thousands of Linux software projects, providing a collaborative environment and disk space to the open source community.

 Tip   The first place to look is actually on your SUSE disk set. The software you are looking for may well have been there all along!

IBM

IBM provides some extremely useful Linux materials, including tutorials and in-depth technical articles, so-called IBM Redbooks, training materials for the Linux Professional Institute exams, and much more.

Good starting points in looking for this information are:

✦ www-1.ibm.com/linux/

✦ www-1.ibm.com/linux/whitepapers/

✦ www-136.ibm.com/developerworks/linux/

✦ http://publib-b.boulder.ibm.com/redbooks.nsf/portals/LinuxRedbooks

Other Distributions

Much of the documentation provided by other Linux distributions can be useful and relevant, although it may take experience to be able to judge in detail which parts apply to SUSE and which do not. In particular, Debian (`www.debian.org`), Gentoo (`www.gentoo.org`), Ubuntu (`www.ubuntulinux.org`), and Red Hat (`www.redhat.com`) have good materials available on their web sites.

News Sites

The leading sites for Linux news are `http://slashdot.org` and `http://lwn.net`. Some others of interest are `http://linuxtoday.com`, `www.osnews.com`, and many others. Some readers may also be interested in the lives of SUSE people as described on `www.planetsuse.org`.

IRC

If you use IRC, there is a SUSE channel `#SuSE` on `irc.freenode.org`.

Finding Further Information

In a word: *Google*.

The amount of information "out there" about Linux is enormous. A web search for a command, an error message, or information about a specific Linux command will always unearth a huge number of hits: the more specific the search the more likely that the result will be useful to you. If you are having a specific problem with Linux, an Internet search should be your first instinctive response.

The fact that there is so much information "out there" is another tribute to the power of open source. Open source encourages a cooperative attitude and state of mind among users as well as developers. The fact that nothing is hidden also means that the vendors have nothing to hide. Taken together, this means that Linux provides and fosters a culture in which users, developers, and vendors are all on the same side, unlike in the world of proprietary software, whereas getting information out of a vendor is often like getting blood out of a stone.

Whatever your SUSE Linux question, you should have no trouble finding documentation, support, or a friendly SUSE user to help you answer it.

✦   ✦   ✦

Understanding Your Linux Network

The network is a big place. It encompasses the Internet, wide area networks, metropolitan area networks, local area networks, and any other network type you can think of. In its simplest terms, the network is a source of connectivity between two systems. It could be a proprietary link between two legacy machines, or open protocols all the way with the latest generation of networked enterprise systems, Linux.

Regardless of what you think a network is, the likelihood is that you have a fair idea of what it encompasses. Ten years ago, there weren't that many people familiar with the term "network" in a digital communications sense. With the emergence of the Internet, that has all changed. Try finding a 12-year-old who does not know what the Internet is.

We all know what a network is, but how systems interact and become a network is something most people take for granted. Linux is a big player in the Internet. It provides a huge amount of the web servers you see out there. Apache itself serves more of the Internet than any other web server, and it is all open source. The TCP/IP protocol is an open protocol, so are the many services based on TCP/IP.

One thing about the Internet that we sometimes forget is that it was and in some sense still is a frontier for the technical elite to be able to define and sculpt technology in an open forum, in view of peers. This leads to technological advances that would not be possible in a closed environment.

We will keep the history lesson about the Internet to a minimum, but in this chapter we want to give you a brief overview of where it came from and why it is as it is. After that, this chapter is all about working protocols. We will not talk about the specifics of networking Linux, which we cover in Chapter 15. To be able to understand what you are doing when you network Linux, you need to understand how it works under the hood.

We have seen a lot of network configuration and, even worse, firewall configuration in which the user has had no regard for how a network actually works and has either set up the network wrong or left gaping holes in the security of their systems. This chapter provides the information to help you avoid that pitfall.

Internet 101

The Internet as it stands today is a marvel to look at. You are able, at the click of a mouse, to load a web page from Australia and display it in front of you in the United Kingdom with seamless ease. Moving large files around the world is a snap. Video conferencing over the Internet actually works now. All of these functions rely on the resilience of the Internet and the technology that has driven it to help the Internet become an important part of our society.

In the early 1960s, the U.S. government was aware that the Cold War could actually affect homeland security such that one part of the United States would not be able to communicate with another. Lack of communication in that type of environment would prove disastrous to say the least. What was needed was a communications network that was resilient to those types of disasters, and the U.S. government decided to commission the Defense Advanced Research Projects Agency (DARPA) to design this resilient, scalable technology. DARPA's goal was to use technology in defense and give the United States a competitive advantage in times of war.

This was no small feat in those days, and some of the best minds in the world worked on this problem for many years. These minds managed to design not only the physical layout of this resilient system, but also the protocol used to move data from one machine to the next. The protocol eventually became know as the Transmission Control Protocol/Internet Protocol (TCP/IP).

The original Internet was known as the ARPANET (Advanced Research Projects Agency Network) and consisted of fewer than ten main routing points across the United States in universities and government sites. These routing points were the backbone of the communications network that grew steadily over time to connect many educational establishments to each other. This pushed the growth of the technology that drove the Internet, both physically and logically. Applications were designed to work with the new TCP/IP protocol, from simple file transfer (FTP — File Transfer Protocol) to mail (SMTP — Simple Mail Transport Protocol).

The sharing of information drove the expansion of the Internet to exponential proportions with *Request for Comment* documents (RFCs). RFCs solicited feedback on proposed standards and then, once comments were integrated, formed the basis of standards for Internet technologies. These are still used to this day to put feelers out to peers over new enhancements to protocols and new technology that helps make the Internet what it is today.

Note   If you are interested in reading the RFCs that formed the basis of the Internet as we know it today (and many newer ones), search www.rfc-editor.org and www.rfc.net.

The Internet is a place for pioneers to shape society in one form or another; it has provided users with something that has truly revolutionized the way we communicate and work.

TCP/IP

In the previous section, we discussed how TCP/IP was designed as a resilient network protocol and about how moving data from one part of the world to another is seamless. This is no easy task, and TCP/IP is able to do this for two fundamental reasons — it is simple in its design, and it is open.

A protocol is classified as *open* when every single person in the world is able to see how it works, right down to the wire.

TCP/IP is based on a layered architecture, as are many network protocols. These layers form the basis of network abstraction. By abstracting layers from each other, you can make sure the technology can grow to meet the demands placed upon it.

Imagine that the TCP/IP protocol was designed and implemented over 20 years ago. With most things in computing, a lot changes in 10, let alone 20 years, but TCP/IP has managed to keep up with trends in computing and networking. This is because as network speeds got faster, the protocol's abstractive nature has managed not to be tied to a technology that is 20 years old.

The ISO OSI Model

Every abstracted network protocol adheres to, either loosely or strictly, the International Organization for Standardization's (ISO) standard seven-layer *Open Systems Interconnect (OSI) model* (see Figure 6-1). It provides a general layered architecture that defines a way to design a network protocol.

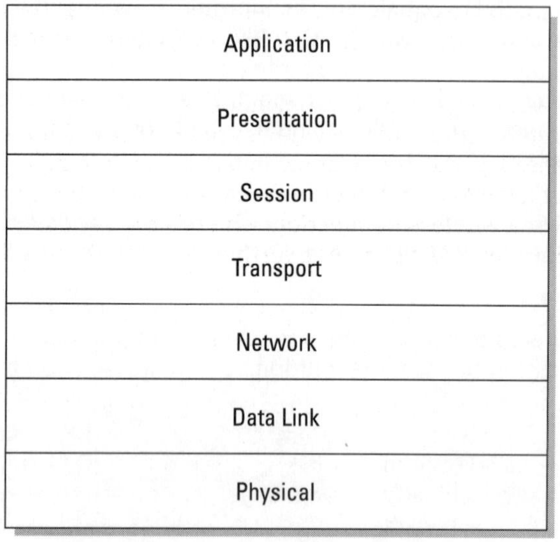

Figure 6-1: The ISO OSI seven-layer model

From the bottom up, you find the following layers:

✦ **Physical layer**—Deals with how information is transmitted over a medium, whether it is copper or fiber Ethernet, wireless networking, or satellite transmission. This layer has no concept of the upper layers and does not need to have, as it is concerned only about getting information safely from one place to another over a medium.

✦ **Data link layer**—Concerned with the encapsulation of data from the upper layers in preparation for moving to the wire. Protocols in this layer could be Ethernet or token ring.

✦ **Network layer**—The network layer is used to define addressing schemes for nodes and networks. It is not concerned with the accuracy of the data it is encapsulating or what format the data is in. Its only concern is that the data is able to get from A to B.

✦ **Transport layer**—Concerned about how data is moved from A to B. Protocols in this layer could be TCP or User Datagram Protocol (UDP); it also deals with the integrity and retransmission of data in the event of a failure.

✦ **Session layer**—Concerned with making, you guessed it, a session between two machines, to be ready for sending data that is passed to it by upper layers using the lower layers to transport this data to its destination.

✦ **Presentation layer**—Concerned with how data is represented. For example, HTML, JPEG, or MP3 formats would all reside here.

✦ **Application layer**—Concerned with applications that use the network protocol. Applications could be SMTP, Hypertext Transport Protocol (HTTP), and FTP.

It may still be unclear to you how this model helps abstraction and furthers the protocol. We hope that the following example will help you understand.

Suppose I am sitting in my garden on a sunny day in London (amazing, but we do get sun here!) writing this chapter. I am running a wireless network in my house, so I can check my email, surf the web, and listen to some music on my laptop. None of this would be possible without a layered architecture because I am using so many different protocols running over a wireless connection, which is then connected to an asymmetric digital subscriber line (ADSL) router, further connected to a firewall.

I am in my garden, and I need to send a chapter to my editor at Wiley. To do this, I need to open an FTP connection to the Wiley server. Here is what happens.

I initiate an FTP connection, with the IP address of the server I want to connect to. My machine sees that the machine I want to communicate with is not on its local network and sends the FTP request over to my router, which needs to get it to Wiley. My router knows that it does not specifically understand where the FTP server I need to talk to is, so it then sends the packet to its default router, and so on. This will carry on, with each hop through a router getting me closer and closer to the destination. When the packet hits Wiley's FTP server, TCP/IP creates a network session so that the FTP server knows that this specific connection is coming from my IP address.

When this connection is established, I have a virtual circuit to the FTP server — that is, according to my laptop I have a connection to Wiley, regardless that it is not a physical connection, but is rather traversing many routers, the Atlantic, and many firewalls. This is all transparent not only to the user, but also to the client machine. My FTP client does not care how a connection is made to Wiley; it is only concerned that a connection *can* be made.

Connection Versus Connectionless Protocols

The transport layer has two protocols used to transport data from A to B — TCP and UDP, which are connection- and connectionless-based protocols, respectively. Most TCP/IP application layer services use the reliable TCP protocols to transport data. TCP maintains a connection to the server as long as is needed to fulfill a request. During this time, if a checksum error is found in a packet, the TCP protocol requests a retransmission. To the upper layers, this is transparent and guarantees data consistency. Where short data bursts are needed, or where the upper layers take care of data loss or error, UDP can be used to reduce overhead, at the sacrifice of data consistency. UDP is commonly used for Domain Name System (DNS) lookups (small packet size, where the upper layer is capable of requesting data again in the event of failure) and also for streaming Moving Picture Experts Group (MPEG) streams. (The MPEG protocol is able to deal with quite a high amount of data loss and errors itself.)

When the FTP connection is established, I then need to upload a text document that is in a certain format (Word). I use FTP commands to create a new directory and to upload my document to the FTP server. Again, using FTP commands, I close the connection to the FTP server, which closes my TCP/IP connection, and the transfer is over.

We used pretty much all of the OSI layers in this one transaction. Table 6-1 comparatively shows the correlation between an action in the example and the OSI layer used.

Table 6-1 OSI Layers and Their Uses	
Layer	*Action*
Application	The FTP protocol is an application layer protocol.
Presentation	The transfer of my Word document in a format that is understandable by both servers. In addition, the way a Word document is constructed internally is a presentation layer protocol.
Session	When my laptop initially communicates with the FTP server, it has to create a TCP/IP session. This has no bearing on the upper FTP protocol because FTP works "on top" of a TCP/IP session.
Transport	The TCP/IP connection that is established in the session layer will be a connection-based protocol that lasts for the time of the FTP connection. Transporting packets is handled by the transport layer, which encapsulates the data from upper layers into manageable chunks. It also deals with the integrity of the data and retransmission of lost packets.
Network	When I specify an IP address to connect to, the network layer deals with establishing a route through my firewall, across the Atlantic, and to the FTP server at Wiley. This involves addressing schemes and routing.
Data link layer	After packets have been encapsulated by the upper layers, they are prepared by the data link layer to be transported over a wireless connection from my laptop to the base station. This involves packaging data from the upper layers into 802.11 protocol packets and also deals with any encryption scheme that I have between my laptop and the base station.
Physical layer	This would deal with frequencies, signal strength, and so on of my wireless connection, as well as timing for sending packets over a wireless network.

We talk a lot about encapsulation in Table 6-1, and this is an important part of a layered network model. *Encapsulation* is a means to wrap data packets inside layer-specific headers and footers. For example, an application layer packet is encapsulated into a transport packet, which is encapsulated into a network packet, which is finally encapsulated into a data link packet, and then sent via the physical layer.

You may have noticed that we don't have encapsulation of presentation and application layers. This is because these layers do not deal with packets of data; they are holders for standards of data—for example, XML, FTP, HTTP, and DOC.

The way a network connection is made makes no difference to the FTP program you use, whether it is over gigabit or wireless networks. This fact allows the TCP/IP protocol to expand to growing demands. For example, FTP has no idea about gigabit Ethernet because the technology is quite new. FTP, on the other hand, was around way before gigabit. A layered network model allows this abstraction to not impact the upper layers, as only the lower layers need to understand gigabit technology. This is why we can *bolt on* new technologies without having to worry about upper layers.

The DoD Model

In reality, the TCP/IP standard does not adhere 100 percent to the OSI model. As we said, the model is only a reference guide, and protocols do not have to follow it exactly. The TCP/IP model fits more closely to the DoD (Department of Defense) model of a network protocol shown in Figure 6-2. TCP/IP is not as abstracted as the OSI model, and many of the components fit into the DoD model. For example, the TCP/IP application usually takes care of the format of the data that is sent and also the creation of a TCP/IP session.

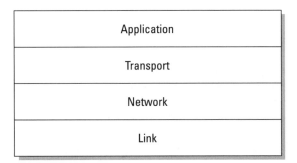

Figure 6-2: The DoD model

Note We spent so much time on the OSI model because everyone refers to it as the standard representation of how a network protocol can be implemented. You will see people refer to the OSI model more often than the DoD model.

The DoD model is so named because it was a TCP/IP four-layer protocol originally developed by the United States Department of Defense when defining TCP/IP. The seven layers of the OSI network model have a many-to-one mapping to the four layers used in the DoD model.

Tip   For additional information about the OSI and DoD networking models and the relationships between the various layers that they define, see Internet sites such as www.comptechdoc.org/independent/networking/guide/netstandards .html **and** www.novell.com/info/primer/prim05.html.

So there you have it, a TCP/IP conceptual overview. The information will become clearer as we progress through the chapter.

Note   A wealth of good books about TCP/IP are available, as well as a plethora of Internet resources. This chapter provides an overview of networking theory to make it easier to understand how Linux uses networks and what aspects of networking you may need to configure. This is not a networking book, so we've provided only as much detail as necessary for basic understanding.

IP Addresses

Every machine that takes part in a TCP/IP network such as the Internet has an *IP address*. If you dial up and check your email, you are given an IP address to distinguish you from other machines so that machines you communicate with know how to find you.

An IP address is something called a *dotted decimal number*. We will take a private IP address (which we talk about later in the chapter) of 192.168.0.1 as an example.

192.168.0.1 is a dotted decimal number. The dots split up the number into separate entities, so the address is 192 168 0 1, all separate from each other. It is not 19216801!

This distinction between the numbers in an address is very important and should never be overlooked as it plays an integral role in the way that IP works. IP is the network layer protocol in the TCP/IP suite and provides addressing facilities.

IP has classes of addresses. This splits the address space up into manageable chunks and provides a way for users to allocate those addresses coherently. Table 6-2 shows classes and their uses.

Each section of an IP address expressed as a dotted decimal number is referred to as an *octet* because each section of an IP address is actually internally stored as an 8-bit binary number. As there are 8 bits, you have a total number of 256 (2^8) possible combinations in each octet. As with most digital numbering systems, you have a range of 0–255, giving you the smallest IP address of 0.0.0.0 and the largest of 255.255.255.255. Both of these addresses are reserved for internal IP use, and we will talk about those later in the chapter.

Table 6-2
IP Address Classes

Class	IP Range	Description
A	1.0.0.0 to 126.0.0.0	Large organizations, many host addresses
B	128.1.0.0 to 191.254.0.0	Midsized organizations, many host addresses
C	192.0.1.0 to 223.255.254.0	Small organizations, small amount of host addresses
D	224.0.0.0 to 239.255.255.255	Multicast addresses
E	240.0.0.0 to 254.255.255.255	Reserved for experimental use

Classes D and E are out of bounds for normal IP addressing use, and we will not discuss those further; we list them for reference purposes only.

An IP address is split into a network and a host component:

✦ **Network component** — Specifies a network of hosts

✦ **Host component** — Refers to a specific host on that network

To distinguish between both, you use a *network mask*. A network mask is core to the way routing of packets is calculated. We discuss that in the "Routing" section later in the chapter.

In a class-based IP model, there are defined network masks, as shown in Table 6-3.

Table 6-3
Address Classes and Network Masks

Class	Network Mask
A	255.0.0.0
B	255.255.0.0
C	255.255.255.0

So if you take the IP address of 192.168.0.1, you can refer to Table 6-2 and see that this is a Class C address. And in looking up the network mask, you see it is 255.255.255.0 for a Class C address.

To find a distinction between network and host components, the routing algorithm in the Linux kernel needs to do binary math. It does a logical AND operation on the network mask and the IP address. We discuss the math needed later in this chapter, but for now we will deal with class-based host/network distinction as this can be done with standard decimal math.

Wherever there is a 255 in the network mask, you effectively highlight the network component of the address. What you are left with is the network component of the IP address minus the host portion. So for a Class C address, like the example address used here, with a netmask of 255.255.255.0, you can see that 192.168.0 is the network component. You can, as a matter of deduction, see that the host component of the address is .1. You write the network component as a zero-padded address, so the network address of 192.168.0.1 is, in fact, 192.168.0.0.

So, you can now say that the address 192.168.0.1 is in the network 192.168.0.0 and is host number 1 in this network.

Every IP address must have a network mask to be able to function. One cannot live without the other.

Special IP Addresses

Earlier in the chapter, we talked about the IP addresses 0.0.0.0 and 255.255.255.255. These are reserved addresses and are used to signify *all* IP and broadcast addresses, respectively.

✦ The 0.0.0.0 address is a way of saying "all networks" and is commonly seen when we define a default route in Linux.

✦ The 255.255.255.255 address is a catchall address that is called a broadcast address. All IP addresses on a network will listen to this address, as well as their own IP address for broadcast traffic.

✦ The 192.168.0.0 address (in the example we are discussing) is called the network address and again is reserved for internal use in TCP/IP. This is the same as the 0.0.0.0 address, but refers to the specific network as opposed to all networks.

Note

The term *broadcast* is used to describe a way of communicating with many machines simultaneously on a network. In the case of 192.168.0.1, the broadcast address of 192.168.0.255 is used to broadcast to all machines in the 192.168.0.0 network. The term *unicast* refers to a one-to-one communication to a specific host. Therefore, if you communicated directly to 192.168.0.1, you would be performing a unicast operation. The term *multicast* refers to a broadcast to a selected group of hosts, such as all hosts on the 192.168.0.0 network.

To sum up, you can say that the IP address of 192.168.0.1 has a network address of 192.168.0.0 and a broadcast address of 192.168.0.255.

Network Address Translation

NAT is a technology that allows you to "hide" your private IP network from the Internet. All traffic, whether it is to a web server or a mail server or so forth is seen by the Internet to come from your NAT box. The NAT box then does the reverse translation when the server you are communicating with needs to send you data back and will change the destination IP address to that of your private machine. The web/mail server you are communicating with has no idea that the request is coming from a private address and sends all requests back to the routable address of your NAT box. We talk about constructing a NAT box in Chapter 24.

In Table 6-2 we listed the number of hosts per network. In Table 6-4, we take this a step further now and specify based on the network mask how many hosts are available in each network.

Table 6-4
Network Class and Host Allocation

Class	Hosts Available
A	Using 2.0.0.0 as the network component, you have 16,581,375 ($2^8 * 2^8 * 2^8$) hosts.
B	Using 130.1.0.0 as the network component, you have 65,025 ($2^8 * 2^8$) hosts.
C	Using 192.5.1.0 as the network component, you have 256 (2^8) hosts.

Remember that .255 and .0 are reserved, so the actual number of hosts available is two less than those stated.

If an organization has been given a Class A network for its use, it has an awful lot of hosts it can use. It takes a lot to be allocated a Class A address and is normally reserved for Internet service providers (ISPs). Even then, it would have to be an extremely large organization to justify the allocation of over 16 million public IP addresses. Most organizations have Class B or Class C networks.

Non-routable IP Addresses

Every machine that is directly connected to the Internet must have a *public* IP address, commonly known as a *routable address*. A routable address is one that a connection can be made to from anywhere on the TCP/IP network, in this case, the Internet. For example, any web site you visit that is on the Internet has a routable address. If it were non-routable, packets would not be able to be routed to it. Each IP address class has its own *non-routable address* (they cannot be routed on the Internet), which can be used in a private IP network (one that is not on the Internet). Non-routable addresses are commonly used in an organization or a home network that is not directly connected to the Internet. It is customary (and cost effective, as routable IP addresses cost money!) to have a Network Address Translation (NAT) box that acts as a gateway to the Internet for your non-routable addresses.

There is one very special address that you will find on every TCP/IP host, and that is 127.0.0.1. The address is commonly referred to as the *loopback address* and is a virtual network that exists only on your local machine. The loopback address is used for testing a TCP/IP network and is useful if you want to test whether or not your network services are working. It also helps any process that needs to communicate over TCP/IP to a service locally on the machine because that process can use the loopback address. The loopback address is not linked to a physical network device, but to a logical lo (loopback) device on your system. If you type `ifconfig` on the command line of your SUSE host, you will see the loopback device listed with an address of 127.0.0.1. Uses of the loopback device will become apparent when we talk about implementing network services later in Part III of this book.

As each class of IP network has its own non-routable address space (see Table 6-5), you can base how you would use those private addresses in your organization (or at home) on how network assignments work in the routable space of that class.

Table 6-5
Non-Routable Classed Networks

Class	Non-Routable Addresses
A	10.0.0.0–10.255.255.255
B	172.16.0.0–172.31.255.255
C	192.168.0.0–192.168.255.255

If your organization needed a flat IP address space, you could assign a non-routable Class A address range to all of your internal machines. However, this is usually wasteful and a network manager's nightmare because there is no logical distinction between departments or machine use. One way to combat this is via subnetting, which is the subject of the next section.

It is common that if you have a small to medium organization, you could set up your network as in Figure 6-3. This would use the networks 192.168.0.0, 192.168.1.0, 192.168.2.0, and 192.168.3.0. As these are using a subnet mask of 255.255.255.0 (the default for a Class C network), these networks are seen from a networking standpoint as being separate entities.

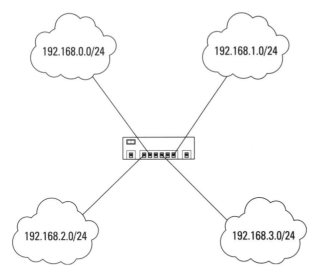

Figure 6-3: Network layout with Class C non-routable addresses

Tip

You can use any network layout you feel comfortable with, but you should always use a pen and paper to design the logical layout before even touching a network cable. Any mistakes in the early stages of designing a network will come back to haunt you as your network grows.

Subnetting

If you need more granular control over your network layout, *subnetting* allows you to break the mold of the class-based IP address schemes. Subnetting is a classless addressing methodology that allows you to choose your own network mask (subnet mask). In the traditional class-based network, you would have a strict amount of hosts in a network. With subnetting, you can specify multiple networks, sacrificing the amount of available hosts.

We will use the network 192.168.0.0/255.255.255.0 (IP address/network mask) and subnet this down further.

Note

The notation of IP/netmask is a common one in networking circles, but a more shorthand version is 192.168.0.0/16. The 16 is the number of bits used in the network mask.

Whereas with a class-based network, you would have a single network, 192.168.0.0, and 253 available hosts, you can specify multiple networks by using a subnetwork mask.

Figure 6-4 shows how the number 248 is represented in binary. The binary number system is capable of representing any number using a combination of 0s and 1s, and this should be apparent in the figure. Anywhere that a 1 is present signifies that this number should be added to the overall decimal number represented by binary.

128	64	32	16	8	4	2	1
1	1	1	1	1	0	0	0

Figure 6-4: Binary representation

128+64+32+16+8=248

As each octet is represented in its barest form as a binary number, you can make a comparison of a network mask to a subnet mask.

You can see in Figure 6-5 that a subnet mask is, in fact, a further extension of the network mask at the sacrifice of the host portion of the IP address. We are using four bits of the host address, which takes the amount of hosts in a Class C address (253) down to 14 per network (of which there can be 14 networks).

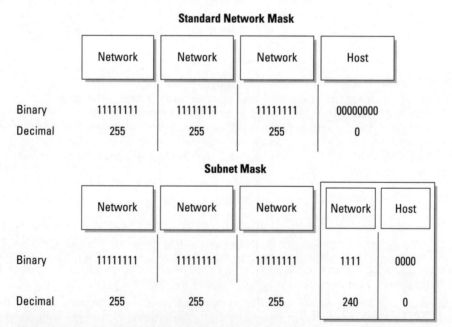

Figure 6-5: Comparison of a network and subnet mask

If you correlate the bits in the new subnet mask to a decimal number, you can see that the network mask of the subnetted network is 192.168.0.240.

Subnetting is something that we have not come across that often in the real world, as the class-based network design is usually enough to represent a logical network layout. Most small/medium organizations are capable of splitting their departments into a rough estimation of the IP class system. In larger organizations, you will find that classless IP addressing is quite common, although such organizations usually limit the network based on an IP network alignment — that is, a traditional non-routable Class A network is subnetted down with a Class C subnet mask.

One thing that you should take away from this discussion of subnetting is that it is controlled on a local level. The Internet routers rarely know about how an administrator has subnetted a network because there is no way to propagate this information about the network to the whole Internet.

> **Note** CIDR is an exception to this rule. CIDR is Classless Interdomain Routing, and this is an interim solution to the lack of IPv4 addresses that are available. CIDR is a group of subnetted addresses that are controlled by larger organizations and have been registered by ISPs as being a domain of control. This is further subnetted by the ISP to provide a larger number of IP networks, but a lower number of hosts. Usually if you ask your ISP for a few routable IP addresses, they will give you a subnet mask as opposed to a network mask. It is up to the ISP to distinguish between the standard class-based system and the classless addressing scheme. It is unlikely that an organization would need 253 routable addresses, so ISPs can split their allocation of public addresses down to the 4 or 8 addresses that you really need.

Routing

We have talked about the addressing of hosts on a network, but what about communicating with hosts on a different network. This is an important part of TCP/IP and is how the protocol is so scalable. Even though you can have non-routable addresses, you still have to make sure these machines are able to communicate with machines on other logical networks (whether subnetted local networks or public Internet machines) and the Internet.

The Linux routing table contains network routes for a few specific networks. Whenever you add an IP address for a specific network interface, a route is created based on the IP address and network mask you assign. If TCP/IP communication is needed to a machine that is in the same network or subnetwork as your machine, the traffic will be sent out through that network interface for local delivery.

If the routing algorithm is not able to find the destination address of the machine in your routing table based on the network mask, it attempts to send the TCP/IP packet to your default route.

To see the kernel routing table, use `route -n` (see Listing 6-1). This displays your routes without looking up host names (this saves a lot of time).

Listing 6-1: **Output of route -n**

```
bible:/usr/sbin # route -n
Kernel IP routing table
Destination    Gateway       Genmask        Flags Metric Ref    Use Iface
192.168.131.0  0.0.0.0       255.255.255.0  U     0      0        0 eth0
169.254.0.0    0.0.0.0       255.255.0.0    U     0      0        0 eth0
127.0.0.0      0.0.0.0       255.0.0.0      U     0      0      0 lo
0.0.0.0        192.168.131.254 0.0.0.0      UG    0      0        0 eth0
```

In this example, the IP address of the machine called bible is 192.168.131.70/
255.255.255.0. As you can see from the routing table, there is a route to the
192.168.131.0 network through the eth0 device.

The 0.0.0.0 IP address we talked about before can be seen in the code output, and
this refers to the default router we are using if our routing table does not understand how to communicate with a machine we specify.

In this case, the default route is 192.168.131.254. This is the IP address of a router
that connects to the Internet.

When a packet is received by your router, it will do roughly the same thing with
your TCP/IP packet, distinguishing if it knows how to send the packet directly to
a network it is connected to or whether it should send the packet to a preferred
route.

Depending on what capabilities the router has and where the router is on the
Internet, it may know the best route for the network you are trying to communicate
with directly. This usually happens only on larger core routers, but this is how a
packet eventually ends up at its destination. Larger routers know roughly where to
send a packet to because they are more intelligent and have more connections to
core parts of the Internet. This kind of router is usually your ISP's router, which has
a link into the backbone Internet connection of a country or region.

And Breathe . . .

TCP/IP is not an easy technology to comprehend, but you should now have enough
information to understand the basics of TCP/IP and how it relates to Linux throughout the rest of the book.

✦   ✦   ✦

Logging

✦   ✦   ✦   ✦

In This Chapter

Explaining log files

Using various loggers

Managing log files

✦   ✦   ✦   ✦

Few Linux books provide separate chapters on logging, discussing log files only in the context of the applications that create them. In reality, because Linux stores all of the log files for system applications in a single directory, examining logging as a general concept provides some good insights should you ever need to try to diagnose a system problem on your SUSE system.

Logging is the way that Linux tells you what is happening, from general status information to error logging. This proves very useful for day-to-day diagnostics and should be the first port of call for any anomalies that you find on your system.

We will talk about the de facto logging facility in Linux, syslog; the newer and more versatile syslog-ng (next generation); logrotate (for managing the log files once written); as well as about future directions in Linux logging such as evlog, the enterprise logging facility brought over from AIX by IBM.

Why Log?

Logging is the only way you can find out what your system and processes are doing. Linux, like any other Unix operating system, takes logging very seriously, and regardless of whether you are an administrator or a home user, you will have to deal with system logs at one point or another.

Most logs are written to the /var/log directory. This is the standard place you will find logs on your system. *Log files* themselves are plain text files that contain information in a semi-standardized fashion, so it is usually the case that if you know how to read one type of log file, you can read them all. Disseminating the information that is logged is something that is specific to the facility that logged the message. In this chapter, we talk briefly about the most popular core system logging processes such as kernel, mail, and authentication errors, because most people need to understand what they are to be able to act upon those messages.

The Files in /var/log

Our initial installation was based on the default, so the contents of /var/log should be very similar to what we will talk about in this section. If you have installed other applications, such as Samba or BIND, you will find more log files on your system.

Core services such as Apache, Samba, and BIND log to a subdirectory under /var/log as their files can grow quite large, and the subdirectory structure provides a more structured view of your system. Having a single directory that all of your applications log to can prove confusing, especially when applications write more than one log file for different purposes. Listing 7-1 shows a long listing of the /var/log file on our default system using the ls -l command.

Listing 7-1: **Listing of /var/log**

```
bible:/var/log # ls -l
total 828
drwxr-x---  2 root  root      48 2004-04-05 19:33 apache2
-rw-r-----  1 root  root       0 2004-07-30 07:42 boot.log
-rw-r--r--  1 root  root   17886 2004-08-30 06:05 boot.msg
-rw-r--r--  1 root  root   20540 2004-08-20 06:06 boot.omsg
-rw-r--r--  1 root  root     586 2004-07-30 07:42 convert_for_getconfig.log
drwxr-xr-x  2 lp    lp        80 2004-07-30 19:08 cups
-rw-------  1 root  root   24024 2004-08-30 06:05 faillog
drwxr-xr-x  2 root  root      48 2004-04-05 18:27 ircd
-rw-r--r--  1 root  root    8915 2004-08-16 22:16 kdm.log
-rw-r--r--  1 root  tty   292292 2004-08-30 06:05 lastlog
-rw-r--r--  1 root  root    1128 2004-08-10 21:54 localmessages
-rw-r-----  1 root  root   12563 2004-08-30 06:05 mail
-rw-r-----  1 root  root     276 2004-07-30 19:06 mail.err
-rw-r-----  1 root  root   12563 2004-08-30 06:05 mail.info
-rw-r-----  1 root  root    2143 2004-07-30 19:06 mail.warn
-rw-r-----  1 root  root  164497 2004-08-30 06:05 messages
drwxr-xr-x  4 news  news     272 2004-07-30 07:41 news
-rw-r--r--  1 root  root       0 2004-07-30 09:03 ntp
drwxr-xr-x  2 root  root      48 2004-07-21 03:01 samba
-rw-r--r--  1 root  root   70421 2004-08-10 05:48 SaX.log
-rw-r--r--  1 root  root    1876 2004-08-08 17:45 scpm
drwxr-x---  2 squid root      48 2004-04-06 10:54 squid
-rw-r--r--  1 root  root   15426 2004-07-30 18:57 update-messages
drwxr-xr-x  2 root  root      48 2004-04-05 10:18 vbox
-rw-r--r--  1 root  root   12376 2004-08-30 06:05 warn
-rw-rw-r--  1 root  tty   267648 2004-08-30 06:05 wtmp
-rw-r--r--  1 root  users  24358 2004-08-20 06:05 XFree86.0.log
-rw-r--r--  1 root  root      15 2004-08-10 05:30 xvt
drwx------  2 root  root     352 2004-07-30 18:55 YaST2.
```

The names of most of the entries in this directory indicate the contents of each log file or the program or type of program that created them. For example, mail refers to the Mail Transfer Agent (MTA) such as Postfix or sendmail that is running on your system. In much the same way, if you had Apache on your system, you would find an `apache2` subdirectory in `/var/log` that contains Apache-specific log files.

Most log files do not contain secure system or private user data so they can be read by anybody on the system. Certain files do contain information that should be readable only by the superuser on the system and refer to kernel messages, authentication messages, and mail messages. To find out what files normal users are able to access on the system, do a long listing on the `/var/log` directory (as we have done in Listing 7-1).

Cross-Reference   For more information on listing files, see Chapter 13.

Logging with syslog

The standard Linux logging facility is *syslog*. The syslog daemon intercepts messages logged to the system logging facility and then processes those messages based on the configuration specified in `/etc/syslog.conf`. The other side of syslog is the klogd process, the kernel logging process that processes kernel-specific messages such as kernel crashes or a failure in a component of the kernel (for example, a kernel module).

Note   Not all processes use the syslog method of logging. You will see in this chapter that syslog has some limitations. To get around these, many applications provide their own logging facilities and use their own logging mechanisms. The way that such applications handle logging is therefore application-specific, and does not use the syslog process.

The configuration file for syslog is relatively simple to read, and you will see why it is limited in its use in modern systems based on this.

When a process asks the kernel to log information, it passes a logging facility to the kernel system call. This logging facility tells the kernel and the user what type of log entry it is. In the case of mail, the logging facility is MAIL. For FTP logging, it would be FTP. A total of 20 logging facilities are available to the system, 12 of which are used for specific purposes (see Table 7-1) and 8 for local use only. (When we talk about local use, we mean that you can tell your application to use one of the local logging facilities to customize how those log entries are saved and interpreted.)

Table 7-1
Logging Facilities and Their Uses

Logging Facility	Description
AUTH	Deprecated. Replaced by AUTHPRIV.
AUTHPRIV	Authentication logging.
CRON	Logging for the CRON and AT daemons.
DAEMON	General logging for daemons that do not have their own facility (BIND, OpenLDAP, and so on).
FTP	Logging for FTP daemons.
KERN	Kernel logging.
LOCAL0 – 7	Custom logging facilities for local use.
LPR	Printing system logging facility.
MAIL	Mail Transfer Agent (MTA) logging.
NEWS	Network News Transfer Protocol (NNTP) logging facilities.
SYSLOG	Internal syslog logging facility. Used for syslog to log messages it generates itself.
USER	Generic user messages.
UUCP	Logging for Unix-to-Unix Copy Protocol (UUCP) services.

Information for this table was taken from the syslog(3) man page.

Predefined logging facilities can cover the main services a Linux server is used for, but if you are hosting a large number of services on a server, you will find that you will run out of logging facilities to use. For general use, syslog serves the purpose well. But for larger systems, or a central logging server, it may prove very difficult to separate logs in a coherent fashion.

Each logging facility also has a log level that can be associated with the severity of the message (see Table 7-2). A world of difference exists between the MAIL facility's logging that mail has been received and that there is a critical configuration problem that has stopped the mail system from running. To distinguish between these scenarios, you can specify in the `syslog.conf` file how to handle those different situations. Of course, it is up to the mail system to specify the severity of the messages, not syslog.

As an example, we will work with an entry for the mail subsystem (see Listing 7-2) and examine how the logging via syslog is configured.

Table 7-2
Log Levels

Log Level	Description
EMERG	Dire emergency. The system in question may not be capable of continuing.
ALERT	Action must be taken immediately.
CRIT	A critical error has occurred.
ERR	Standard error.
NOTICE	General notification level. This is something that someone should see and perhaps act upon if the need arises.
INFO	General information.
DEBUG	Debugging information. Usually very high traffic.

Information for this table was taken from the syslog(3) man page.

Listing 7-2: Mail Facility Logging via syslog

```
#
# all email-messages in one file
#
mail.*                        -/var/log/mail
mail.info                     -/var/log/mail.info
mail.warning                   -/var/log/mail.warn
mail.err                      /var/log/mail.err
```

The format of the `syslog.conf` file is relatively simple. The first field (on the left in Listing 7-2) specifies the name of the logging facility, followed by the logging level. The second field (on the right in the preceding listing) is the file or host to log this message to.

Note You will find that a lot of naming conventions in Linux, and Unix in general, are standardized in an unofficial way. The *suffix.prefix* notation is found in a few configuration files. In the syslog configuration file, the `mail.info` notation means the MAIL logging facility, with a log level of INFO.

In reference to the file that the `mail.info` log facility writes log data to, the dash (-) means that all input/output (IO) on this file will be synchronous. *Synchronous IO* means that all data is forced to the disk for committal immediately. This could, in fact, degrade the performance of the process that is logging the messages (and thus the system in general), but it does guarantee that the messages are logged. It is up to the user's discretion whether logging of the messages is as important as the performance of a process. For example, you would likely want to log all failed authentication attempts on the system, regardless of the performance impact to the application that logged the errors. For mail, it may not be as important to you.

For each entry that refers to the logging facility (`mail`, `ftp`, `lpr`, and so on), you can specify a catchall (`*`) or a specific log level to log data to. In the example of the mail facility shown in Listing 7-2, SUSE by default logs all of the messages about MAIL to `/var/log/mail` and splits out the log levels of info, warning, and error to separate files at the same time. You will find that messages in `/var/log/mail` are also in the separate log level files. This offers a centralized location for all of your MAIL messages, but allows you to see any serious errors with your mail system if needed.

Listing 7-3 provides an idea of where the LOCAL facilities are used on SUSE systems. As SUSE has commented, many `init` scripts use the LOCAL log facilities for their logging purposes. Such facilities are also a catchall for foreign programs that are not controlled via the normal logging facilities and that need to use the LOCAL specification.

Listing 7-3: **Local Specification**

```
#
# Some foreign boot scripts require local7
#
local0,local1.*                    -/var/log/localmessages
local2,local3.*                    -/var/log/localmessages
local4,local5.*                    -/var/log/localmessages
local6,local7.*                    -/var/log/localmessages
```

Tip   Most users and administrators view `/var/log/messages` to see if any errors have been caught before looking in the other log files, as `/var/log/messages` contains information about most system errors and anomalies.

Logging with syslog-ng

In the previous section, we talked about the shortcomings of the syslog method of logging. The syslog-ng method goes further with the logging process by allowing you to specify regular expressions based on what the message contains for logging and by logging to specific files based on what the message contains. For example, the Linux firewall command `iptables` enables you to specify a logging prefix. If you were to use syslog-ng, you could specify that if the message that was intercepted by syslog-ng contained your logging prefix, you could write that message to a specific file.

Another really useful feature of syslog-ng, especially if you are setting up a centralized logging host, is that you can save the messages to a specific file in a specific directory based on where the messages originated. All of these things add up to a more granular experience for organizing your log files with syslog-ng.

To configure syslog-ng, we will take a slight deviation because the /etc/syslog-ng .conf file that is read by syslog-ng on startup is, in fact, maintained by SuSEconfig by default. To edit the file but also maintain control of the syslog-ng file by SuSEconfig, you need to edit the template file for syslog-ng. This is not a bad thing because only a few macro entries are used by SuSEconfig to control the workings of syslog-ng (relating to the source of the messages controlled by syslog-ng).

To edit the configuration of syslog-ng, you need to edit the file /etc/syslog-ng/ syslog-ng.conf.in.

Note

YaST is a very capable configuration manager when it comes to services; it is able to control them in a user-friendly fashion. If you feel uncomfortable letting YaST control the configuration of your services, you can turn this off. By default, YaST automatically starts a process named SuSEconfig to dynamically update your system based on the contents of the files in /etc/sysconfig to ensure that the system can maintain your configuration changes. If you do not want YaST to maintain a particular service, find the file that controls the general use of the service you are interested in, in /etc/sysconfig. For example, for syslog-ng, open the file /etc/sysconfig/syslog, find the line SYSLOG_NG_CREATE_CONFIG="yes", and change "yes" to "no". This ensures that YaST will not change your syslog configuration files.

The syslog-ng file contains three important definitions that make up a log profile:

✦ **The log source** — The program or system capability that generates the log data

✦ **The filter** — Any filters that should be applied to the messages that are being logged

✦ **The log destination** — The local file or network designation to which log messages should be sent

In the default syslog-ng configuration that is installed, all of the default log profiles used in syslog are also in the syslog-ng configuration. As an example, we will examine the components that make up the iptables logging rules — the log source, the filter, and the log destination — as they describe the three main components of syslog-ng and also show the regular expression features of syslog-ng.

The Log Source

Listing 7-4 shows an example of a log source.

Listing 7-4: syslog-ng Configuration for iptables — Source

```
source src {
    #
    # include internal syslog-ng messages
    # note: the internal() source is required!
    #
    internal();

    #
    # the following line will be replaced by the
    # socket list generated by SuSEconfig using
    # variables from /etc/sysconfig/syslog:
    #
    unix-dgram("/dev/log");
    unix-dgram("/var/lib/ntp/dev/log");

    #
    # uncomment to process log messages from network:
    #
    #udp(ip("0.0.0.0") port(514));
};
```

Listing 7-4 shows the source definition for the entire syslog-ng process. This example shows two logging sources, /dev/log (for the standard kernel logging device) and /var/lib/ntp/dev/log. A separate entry is necessary because the NTP service runs in a chroot jail and its log source has to reside under this jail so that the ntp executable can access it.

This example also shows a UDP entry that SUSE has commented out. This is a logging source entry for a network port. This is how you can set up a central logging server for your organization. By setting a source to be UDP on port 514, you are enabling your machine to accept messages for logging from remote hosts. TCP/IP port 514 on UDP is the standard port entry for syslog messages. If you uncomment this entry, you are able to receive messages from remote hosts.

Cross-Reference   For more information on TCP/IP and specifying addresses and ports in Linux, see Chapters 6 and 15.

The Filter

Listing 7-5 gives an example of a syslog-ng filter.

Listing 7-5: **The Filter**

```
filter f_iptables   { facility(kern) and match("IN=") and match("OUT="); };
```

A filter in syslog-ng is the same as the first field in the syslog.conf file but has the capability to be much more granular. In the example shown in Listing 7-5, you are defining a filter named f_iptables. This filter filters out messages that have the logging facility of KERN (kernel) and uses a regular expression comparison to match a message if it contains the words IN or OUT. The regular expression capabilities of syslog-ng enable you to eliminate or redirect logging messages based on examining their contents.

Cross-Reference

We talk about firewalls and iptables in detail in Chapter 24. For now, you can tell iptables to log messages about a TCP/IP packet with a message prefix. For example, you can say that if a message has been denied INto your machine/network, then the message is prefixed with the word IN. The same is true for any messages that have been denied OUT of your network. In this case, you could tell syslog-ng to log these facts into a separate file for your perusal at a convenient time.

The Log Destination

Listing 7-6 shows an example of a log destination.

Listing 7-6: **The Destination**

```
destination firewall { file("/var/log/firewall"); };
```

By default, SUSE comments this line out in order to send these messages to its default location. With most services in SUSE, all the output is sent to the /var/log/ messages file because there is not a logging facility for each specific service. So, we assume we have uncommented the destination definition for use on our system so that firewall messages go to a specific destination. The destination specifies that the custom definition firewall will write log messages to the file /var/log/firewall. This enables you to examine firewall-related messages (produced by the iptables facility, which filters network packets) by simply examining a specific log file.

The Log Definition — Tying It All Together

These three definitions may all sound well and good in principle, but are you getting the feeling that there should be something to bring these three definitions together? This is the final piece in the puzzle of syslog-ng. You need to configure a log parameter that will use these definitions and bring them into a coherent specification for a logging trigger, which is a log definition that ties a log source, specific filter, and specific destination together.

Listing 7-7 brings together our disparate example definitions of log source, filter, and log destination into a final log definition.

Listing 7-7: **Log Definition**

```
log { source(src); filter(f_iptables); destination(firewall); };
```

For any log entry you want to make, you need to specify the logging source (in this case /dev/log and /var/lib/ntp/dev/log), the filter (anything from the kernel that contains either IN= or OUT=), and the destination (in this case the file /var/log/firewall).

You should now have enough information to help you set up simple syslog-ng rules and to distinguish why and where you would use syslog-ng and its more granular control compared to what syslog offers. As you can likely see, you can ultimately do powerful things with syslog-ng by combining network sources with complicated filters.

Future Directions for Linux Logging

Although this chapter discussed two different system logging applications for Linux, there are actually many more, each designed to solve or simplify different types of logging concerns.

One of the more interesting developments in system logging is the evlog (Event Log) application originally developed by IBM for use in its enterprise AIX environments and later released to the open source community. Although still maturing, the evlog project is an ambitious effort that is POSIX-compliant and platform-independent, and can significantly simplify logging in a complex multi-machine environment.

Note   `evlog` has been part of the SUSE system since version 9.3.

For information about the current state of the `evlog` project, see its home page at `http://evlog.sourceforge.net`. For an overview of the `evlog` project, its goals, and its approach to unifying enterprise logging, see the overview documentation at `http://evlog.sourceforge.net/linuxEvlog.html`.

Managing Your Logs with logrotate

Having these logging technologies is great for accessing the information at your fingertips, but a time will come when you do not need the logs in their original form and would like to archive them off. This can be handled manually, but if you have a large number of logs, automation is the way to go.

Logs, left to their own devices, especially those on a large active system, can run riot with your disk space. The logrotate application can automate the management of log files by copying and archiving them based on rules.

SUSE includes logrotate scripts for most active logging processes, and these can be found in `/etc/logrotate.d`. The directory contains a logrotate configuration file for each process logrotate manages. The main configuration file for logrotate is `/etc/logrotate.conf` and contains archiving defaults as well as an entry to link all of the configuration files for logrotate-aware applications.

Any files located in `/etc/logrotate.d` will be opened and interpreted as logrotate directives when logrotate is executed.

Executing Processes Automatically on Linux Systems

The Linux `cron` process automatically executes tasks at various times based on the contents of configuration files stored in user-specific subdirectories of the directory `/var/spool/cron` or in the system-wide configuration file `/etc/crontab`. This file runs processes in the directories `/etc/cron.hourly`, `/etc/cron.daily`, `/etc/cron.weekly`, and `/etc/cron.montly` on an hourly, daily, weekly, and monthly basis, respectively. These automatically scheduled and executed processes perform many essential cleanup and maintenance tasks on most Linux systems. For more information about `cron` and the format of its configuration files, check the online reference information by executing the commands `man cron` and `man 5 crontab` on your SUSE system.

logrotate is executed daily at 4:14 a.m. by cron, which is a Linux process that automatically executes specified processes at a specified time. logrotate loads the configuration files in /etc/logrotate.d and then decides if it needs to rotate any of the log files it manages.

In this section we take Apache as an example of a logrotate entry. Looking at what logrotate can do with an Apache logrotate entry will give you an idea of how powerful and helpful the utility can be. Listing 7-8 displays the Apache logrotate entry for access_log. (The Apache access_log contains information about who has accessed any files available via the HTTP server process.)

Listing 7-8: **Apache logrotate Entry for access_log**

```
/var/log/apache2/access_log {
    compress
    dateext
    maxage 365
    rotate 99
    size=+4096k
    notifempty
    missingok
    create 644 root root
    postrotate
     /etc/init.d/apache2 reload
    endscript
}
```

As you can see in the listing, a given logrotate entry is made up of multiple directives. Each of these directives gives logrotate some instruction as to how to behave toward the log files covered by that particular logrotate entry. Table 7-3 details each of the directives in this file and the actions they inspire.

Note   Each file that you would like to be rotated must have a specific logrotate entry. You cannot specify a directory to rotate all files, but you can identify groups of log files by using the syntax /full/path/to/log/file/*, which is essentially the same thing.

If you have an active web site, you can see that your access_log will get rotated quite regularly with the settings in the example. In essence, your logs will be rotated and compressed once the file reaches 4MB. With these directives, logrotate gives you great control over when and how you archive, what you archive, and even how long you keep that archive.

Table 7-3
logrotate Directives

Directive	Description
Compress	Compress the file when it is rotated.
dateex (SUSE only)	Add a date extension to the rotated log file. For example, access_log.20040527.gz.
maxage 365	If previously rotated log files reach this age, then remove them. Age is expressed as an integer number of days.
rotate num	If a file is rotated *num* times, then remove the oldest rotated file.
Size	If a file to be rotated grows above the size specified, then rotate it. Size can be specified in various units, such as kilobytes (k) and gigabytes (g).
notifempty	Do not rotate the file if it is empty.
missingok	If a file to be rotated does not exist, then issue an error and continue.
create 644 root root	The file permissions to create the new file with.
Postrotate /etc/ init.d/apache2 reload endscript	When a rotation has taken place, execute the following. In this case we are telling Apache to reload its configuration. This forces Apache to reopen its log file, completing the rotation process.

Analyzing Your Logs with logcheck

When your applications are logging to specific files, and the logs are being rotated, you can then manage and view your system statistics daily. If you would like to automate analysis of your log files for major occurrences, logcheck is here for you.

logcheck scans through your log files and searches for telltale security and error messages and emails you its findings at predefined times through cron. The logcheck process uses a bookmark feature to send you only its findings since the last logcheck run so that you do not receive the same errors for the same log file time and again.

Cross-Reference

logcheck is not included in the SUSE distribution, so the authors have created an RPM at www.palmcoder.net/files/suse-rpms/wiley. See Chapter 12 for more information on installing RPM packages. You can also find the logcheck RPM on the book's companion web site at www.wiley.com/go/suselinux10bible.

When installed, the logcheck RPM creates an entry in /etc/cron.hourly. Any executable scripts in /etc/cron.hourly will be run every hour. This is appropriate for most busy systems as one logcheck run per day would produce a very large email sent to the root user.

When logcheck runs, it will email the root user to tell him or her of any problems it has come across. It is up to the administrator to act upon the email and either fix or investigate the logcheck reports.

The /etc/logcheck directory contains four files. Two of these files are used to search through log files in the logcheck.sh file and identify specific types of log messages to report, while the other two are used as lists of messages to ignore in the log files specified in the logcheck.sh file. If a line in an ignore file is found, its appearance will not be reported. If on the other hand a line contains an entry in the logcheck.hacking or logcheck.violations, its appearance is reported to the administrator.

logcheck does not actually use a configuration file, but is controlled by the logcheck.sh script, located in /usr/sbin/logcheck.sh. By default, the script will scan /var/log/messages, /var/log/warn, and /var/log/mail. To add or remove entries in the logcheck.sh file, open the script and find the $LOGTAIL entries in the middle of the file. Listing 7-9 shows an example.

Listing 7-9: Entry for logcheck Log File to Monitor

```
$LOGTAIL /var/log/messages > $TMPDIR/check.$$
$LOGTAIL /var/log/warn >> $TMPDIR/check.$$
$LOGTAIL /var/log/mail >> $TMPDIR/check.$$
```

These entries direct logcheck to append messages from various system log files to a temporary file for later analysis. It is important to realize that the first $LOGTAIL entry copies the log file since the last read and the last two concatenate /var/log/warn and /var/log/mail into the temporary file. The $LOGTAIL environment variable is used to call the logtail application, which will read in a text file and output only new data since it was last passed through logtail. This stops you from receiving old warnings about log activity.

When the temporary file has been created, the whole file is compared against the hacking and violation files we talked about before.

It is a relatively involved process to get logcheck customized, and we have done the hard work for you to get it working with the SUSE RPM we build in Chapter 12. We recommend you use this RPM as opposed to using the source distribution available unless you know what you are doing.

Listing 7-10 displays an example of mail sent to the root user by the logcheck script. Take note that under the heading Security Violations are two entries referring to failed login attempts via SSH.

Listing 7-10: logcheck Example Mail

```
From root@bible.suse.com  Thu May 27 23:23:41 2004
X-Original-To: root
Delivered-To: root@bible.suse.com
Date: Thu, 27 May 2004 23:23:39 +0100
To: root@bible.suse.com
Subject: bible 05/27/04:23.23 system check
User-Agent: nail 10.6 11/15/03
MIME-Version: 1.0
Content-Type: text/plain; charset=us-ascii
Content-Transfer-Encoding: 7bit
From: root@bible.suse.com (root)


Security Violations
=-=-=-=-=-=-=-=-=
May 27 23:23:35 bible sshd[5019]: error: PAM: Authentication failure
May 27 23:23:35 bible sshd[5019]: error: PAM: Authentication failure

Unusual System Events
=-=-=-=-=-=-=-=-=-=
May 27 23:23:35 bible sshd[5019]: error: PAM: Authentication failure
May 27 23:23:35 bible sshd[5019]: error: PAM: Authentication failure
May 27 23:23:10 bible postfix/pickup[3881]: E47F918D21: uid=0 from=<root>
May 27 23:23:10 bible postfix/cleanup[4941]: E47F918D21: message-
id=<40B66A4E.mail3V41ZYZPX@bible.suse.com>
May 27 23:23:11 bible postfix/qmgr[3882]: E47F918D21: from=<root@bible.suse.com>,
size=1161, nrcpt=1 (queue active)
May 27 23:23:11 bible postfix/local[4944]: E47F918D21: to=<root@bible.suse.com>,
orig_to=<root>, relay=local, delay=1, status=sent (delivered to mailbox)
May 27 23:23:11 bible postfix/qmgr[3882]: E47F918D21: removed
```

How often you set logcheck to run depends on how much data you receive in the email. If you have an active system, we recommend that you increase the frequency of the logcheck runs. If you have a relatively small system, running logcheck once a day will produce a manageable email that can be handled when things are quiet.

Using Webalizer

Another popular log analyzer is webalizer. Webalizer was specifically written to produce an HTML page with graphing statistics for access to a web site. Figure 7-1 shows a webalizer page for a busy site.

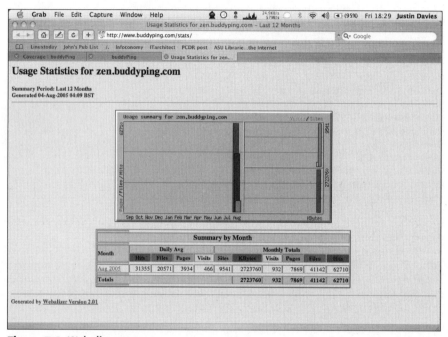

Figure 7-1: Webalizer output

The webalizer page is quite long and contains information on the amount of traffic served; how many hits per month, per day, per hour; ranking of the most popular pages; and so on. To access specific information about a certain month, you can click its entry and you will be presented with a screen similar to Figure 7-2.

Webalizer outputs all of its data by default into /var/lib/webalizer, which is linked to /srv/www/htdocs/webalizer for serving via Apache.

Cross-Reference   Apache configuration is covered in Chapter 16.

This enables you to automate the running of webalizer on a foreign system and, at the same time, enables you to access the results via the web server you are analyzing.

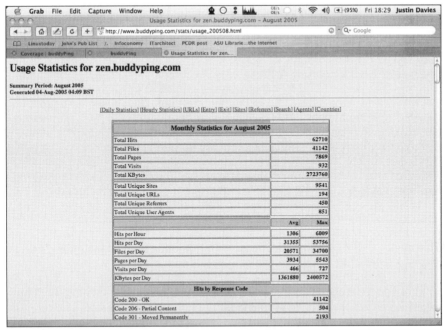

Figure 7-2: Month output in webalizer

We will not talk about the configuration of webalizer here, because the configuration file /etc/webalizer.conf is extremely well documented, and the default setting suits 99 percent of people who need to analyze their web traffic.

Reading Log Files

This chapter has covered what logging on a SUSE Linux system means and what you can do with the messages that are generated both by the kernel and processes that you run.

However, reading log files is a skill in itself. There is no good way to teach people how to read log files; rather, it is something that comes with experience. We will give you our short rundown of common entries you will find in /var/log/messages and explain how to interpret them to help you on your way. The following line is an example of a log entry indicating an SSH login failure:

```
May 27 23:23:35 bible sshd[5019]: error: PAM: Authentication failure
```

From this example, you can see certain things about log entries that are generic to all of them. The first entry is the date and time this entry was created, with the host name of the machine that the message originated from (in this case, bible). The next entry is usually the process that actually created the log entry (in this case the ssh daemon). The number you see next to the process name is the process number, followed by the message itself.

The message you see in this example is self-explanatory, saying that there was an authentication error. The PAM: entry is something you will see with most authentication errors in Linux as PAM (Pluggable Authentication Modules) is used to take a username and password for a process and decide if this user with the password they have entered is actually allowed to log in to the system.

This next example is an informational message from the kernel after a kernel driver has been loaded:

```
May 27 22:19:22 bible kernel: IPv6 over IPv4 tunneling driver
```

This means that the driver that deals with tunneling IPv6 traffic over IPv4 has been loaded successfully.

So here you have seen two extremes of what you might find in a log file. The latter example is a general informational message telling you all is fine. The other is a bit more serious, telling you that someone attempted to log in to the system but failed because they provided the wrong authentication information (wrong username or password).

Log files are there to help you in your running of your Linux system. You have to be vigilant in your efforts to keep the system running nicely, and log files help you with this.

Have you checked your logs recently?

✦   ✦   ✦

The X Window System

The graphical interface that comes with Linux is provided by an implementation of the X Window system. The *X Window system* is a set of protocols and standards for a cross-platform, network-transparent graphics display system. On Linux, the implementation chosen has traditionally been that from the XFree86 project. Recent arguments about licensing have resulted in the major Linux distributors' switching from XFree86 to the X.org project from `www.x.org`. In the case of SUSE, this change was made with the release of the 9.2 version. However, this makes no difference to the principles discussed here.

Note   Historically, the original developers of the X Window system have been very insistent about the fact that it is a window system named X, and thus should not simply be referred to as X. In this book, we refer to the X Window system as X because it is more convenient and common to do so. Computer history fans should note that the designation X originally came from the fact that the project that inspired the X Window system was the W Window system from Stanford University — X is simply the next letter of the alphabet.

The big difference between X and (for example) the graphics display systems found in Microsoft Windows or Mac OS X is that X is inherently network-transparent and is designed from the ground up as a client-server system. That means that, using X, you can run a graphical program in one place and display its output somewhere else. This is a capability for which you need to pay for special add-ons in the Windows world, but that is built into Linux. The "somewhere else" where you will be displaying the graphical output can be any platform for which an X server implementation is available, which includes virtually any operating system capable of TCP/IP networking and running a graphical display. In a typical Linux desktop situation, you will of course be running the display on the same machine that the applications are running on; however, the network transparency of X provides huge benefits that we shall examine further in this chapter.

The common complaints that are often heard about X are the problems of configuration (largely but not entirely a thing of the past), problems with fonts (antialiased display of fonts in all situations took a long time to become available on Linux), lack of direct support for hardware acceleration, and other performance issues. Some of these difficulties are directly related to the fact that implementations of X have to be backward-compatible and standards-compliant.

Largely through the efforts of open source operating systems such as Linux, FreeBSD, OpenBSD, and NetBSD, X Window system configuration today is quite easy, rivaling the ease of installing and configuring graphics on any modern operating system. The XFree86 project's generic `xf86config` utility is quite easy to use but requires some knowledge of your system's graphical capabilities. The X.org project's `xorgcfg` utility is very similar and has similar information requirements. The vendors that sell and support Linux and BSD distributions have stepped in to make things even easier. Applications such as the `sax2` utility developed by SUSE and provided with all SUSE Linux distributions provide a simpler, almost automatic mechanism for configuring and fine-tuning X on a modern Linux system.

X Window System Concepts

When using X, a user is running a graphical application, say an xterm. The xterm is the client; it communicates with an X server, which does the job of displaying it. There is no requirement that the client and the server must run on the same machine; the client and the server simply need to be able to communicate with each other. In addition, the X server needs to be willing (from a security point of view) to display the output of the client, and the client needs to be started in an environment that includes suitable information about how it will display its output (typically the `DISPLAY` environment variable).

In most simple cases (including cases in which you are explicitly logging in remotely by `ssh`), you don't need to think about any of this — everything just works.

Window Managers

The X server itself knows how to display the output of a program, but it does not know how to manage the different programs that it is displaying — that is the job of the window manager. The *window manager* looks after the behavior of the application windows, their "decorations," the look and feel of their borders and control widgets (such as close and maximize buttons), the way they interact with the mouse and keyboard, and so on.

There are a variety of window managers that range from the very minimal, such as TWM and MWM, to the integrated desktop environments, such as KDE and GNOME.

Traditionally, a window manager on the X Window system on Unix was not particularly pretty, to say the least; if you log in to your SUSE Linux system and choose TWM as the window manager rather than the default, you will see what we mean.

If you choose the installation option Minimal with X11, you get a system with the `fvwm` window manager and the `xdm` login manager. You may want to do this if you are installing SUSE on a server for which you do not need the use of a full-blown desktop but may occasionally need to run a graphical program (such as certain monitoring tools or the Oracle installer, for example).

KDE and GNOME

Back in 1996, there was a general feeling that the available window managers running on X were sparse and lacking in features compared to the graphical environments available on Windows and the Mac. A primary concern was that X Window system window managers were fine at creating and managing windows and the graphical applications that created them, but did not support the greater ease of use that users of systems such as Microsoft Windows and Mac OS have come to expect. This led to the start of the KDE project. The idea of KDE was to go beyond a window manager that simply handled mouse and keyboard interactions and to create a unified desktop environment for users. In this unified environment, clicking a file in the file manager would launch the correct application, drag and drop would work between compliant applications, all applications would share a common look and feel, and so on.

KDE made rapid progress but became involved in controversy because it is based on the Qt toolkit (produced by Trolltech), which was issued under a license that was regarded by many as unacceptable. (Although the source code was open, it did not qualify as a free software license because it did not permit the redistribution of modifications.) Some people also feared that Trolltech could unilaterally change the terms on which it offered the toolkit, thereby derailing the project. The rival GNOME project with similar aims was started shortly afterward, partly in reaction to the controversy over the Qt license. GNOME used the GTK+ toolkit, which was part of the GNU project and licensed under the GNU Library General Public License (LGPL).

In due course the controversy surrounding KDE was solved by a change in the license. At first, Trolltech sought to solve the problem by offering a free edition of Qt under a special open source license (the QPL), but controversy continued until Trolltech agreed to release Qt under a dual license (GPL and QPL), a solution that was satisfactory to all parties.

Window Managers and Desktops

In the context of the X Window system, *window managers* manage the creation and manipulation of the windows created by various applications. *Desktop environments* such as GNOME and KDE go one step further — each includes a window manager but adds a variety of software that extends its support for graphical interaction between applications. As mentioned previously, desktop environments provide capabilities such as file managers, which support graphical browsing of files and directories and also support capabilities such as drag and drop, where dragging a file's icon onto an application's icon launches the application and automatically opens a specified file, or where clicking a file in a file manager launches the correct application and opens the specified file, and so on. Many hardcore Linux users prefer simply using a window manager because window managers typically consume fewer system resources than desktop environments. One of the core benefits of Linux is that you can use whatever you want to do your work, and switching between using a window manager and desktop is easy, as explained later in this chapter.

Both KDE and GNOME are now mature desktop environments. Traditionally, SUSE distributions have offered both, but with a definite bias toward KDE, whereas Red Hat has shown a bias toward GNOME. This may be related to the percentage of the developers of these respective desktop environments that work at these companies.

In mid-2003, Novell acquired Ximian (the commercial company employing many GNOME developers). Novell's stated position is that both KDE and GNOME will continue to be supported in the future; however, it seems at least likely that when the next desktop version aimed at business users appears, it will be based on Ximian's version of GNOME.

Configuring X

Traditionally, X configuration was a common, major problem; grown men have been known to weep over it. Such problems are largely a thing of the past, and in almost all cases you will find that the configuration that occurs automatically during the installation gives you a good working setup.

The most likely reason why X configuration might fail these days is that you are using a very new graphics adapter that is not natively supported by XFree86 or X.org. Fortunately, even in this case there is usually a workaround, which is to use framebuffer graphics (see the section on this topic later in the chapter).

Getting Hardware Information

In most cases, the hardware will be automatically detected. If necessary, you may have to refer to your monitor's manual to check its capabilities. To get the relevant information from the system, the command

```
hwinfo --monitor
```

may be useful for getting information about the monitor, while any of the following commands may be useful for getting information about the graphics card:

```
lspci -v
sax2 -p
hwinfo --gfxcard
```

Using sax2

To configure or reconfigure X on SUSE, you can use SUSE's sax2 tool. It is best (but not essential) to switch first to runlevel 3, so type as root:

```
init 3
```

Then, again as root, issue the command

```
sax2
```

The sax2 tool then starts its own graphical environment that offers you choices for configuring the graphics, and from here on, everything should be simple. Certain problems can occur, however. In particular, it is possible that limitations of the graphics card or monitor may prevent sax2 itself from displaying. If this happens, you should look into the various options that sax2 offers. Type the following:

```
sax2 --?
```

This shows you a list of options for the sax2 command. The most useful options if sax2 is not displaying properly are -l and -V. The command sax2 -l (or sax2 --lowres) runs sax2 in low resolution mode (640 × 480). This is useful if your monitor is not being correctly detected, which leads to a wrong resolution or frequency being sent to it as sax2 tries to start. Use this option if you see only a blank screen when sax2 starts. The -V option allows you to choose the resolution and frequency at which sax2 runs. So for example

```
sax2 -V0:1024x768@85
```

runs sax2 at a resolution of 1,024 × 768 and a frequency of 85 Hz. So if sax2 is not displaying when you run it without options, you can run it at a resolution and frequency that you know your hardware can handle.

Note that what we are talking about here is the resolution at which the `sax2` tool itself displays, not the eventual resolutions that we are going to configure.

Occasionally it may be necessary to run `sax2` with the option `- m`, which allows it to choose an appropriate module to run with using a command like this:

```
sax2 -m 0=s3virge
```

The available modules can be found by listing the directory `/usr/X11R6/lib/modules/drivers/`.

When `sax2` starts, you will see something like Figure 8-1.

In general, `sax2` is able to detect your monitor and check its capabilities against its database; if not, you can use the monitor section to set the monitor type (in the worst case you may need to set the monitor's capabilities manually based on the frequency and resolution that its documentation tells you that it is capable of). Figure 8-2 shows the screen that `sax2` displays to let you specify the graphics resolution that your monitor is capable of.

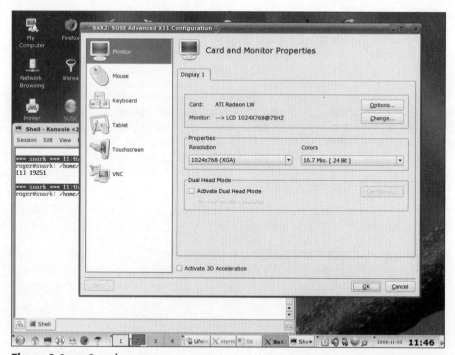

Figure 8-1: sax2 main screen

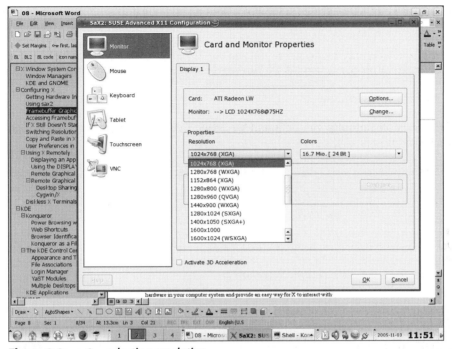

Figure 8-2: sax2 — selecting resolution

Similarly, the graphics card is also typically detected automatically. However, you have the option to set it manually, either specifically by name (this should be unnecessary because typically `sax2` is capable of detecting it automatically) or generically (which may be necessary if the card is really unsupported).

Framebuffer Graphics

Any VESA2-compliant graphics adapter is capable of providing framebuffer graphics. Framebuffer graphics provide an abstraction layer for the graphics hardware in your computer system and provide an easy way for X to interact with and control your graphics hardware. If nothing else works, this is your best chance of getting graphics configured, but may not take advantage of any specialized features of your hardware.

If you need to use framebuffer graphics, you can specify a graphical resolution at boot time through a boot parameter, such as `vga=791`, which sets the resolution to 1,024 × 768 at 16-bit color depth (a common and reasonably safe option). Having booted with this boot parameter, you can then run `sax2` and force the graphics mode to be framebuffer by using the command line:

```
sax2 -m 0=fbdev
```

You should then find that you have no choice of resolution and you can test and save the configuration. You should then be able to start the X server with the command `startx` to check that everything is working.

The easiest way to set the `vga` parameter at boot time is to press the spacebar as soon as the SUSE boot screen displays. This suspends the boot process, enabling you to specify additional boot parameters at the bottom of the boot screen.

Table 8-1 lists common resolutions with the relevant `vga` parameter codes.

Table 8-1 Framebuffer vga= Parameters				
Color Depth	Resolution			
	640 × 480	800 × 600	1,024 × 768	1,280 × 1,024
256 (8-bit)	769	771	773	775
32,768 (15-bit)	784	787	790	793
65,536 (16-bit)	785	788	791	794
16.7 million (24-bit)	786	789	792	795

When you are sure that the configuration works, you can set the `vga=` parameter in the file `/boot/grub/menu.1st` so that it will take effect at the next boot. You should make this change in the default configuration, so you need to edit the first instance of `vga=` in that file. Note that if you have configured framebuffer graphics, they simply will not work unless the system is booted with the correct `vga=` parameter.

Accessing Framebuffer Graphics after Installation

Because SUSE's installer automatically starts the X Window system in graphical mode, you may believe that you've correctly specified your graphics hardware during installation. Unfortunately, you may then find that X (and `sax2`) will not start or execute correctly on your system. This is especially common when installing SUSE on laptops, which frequently use custom, low-power versions of well-known graphics chips.

To start `sax2` using framebuffer graphics, use the following command:

```
sax2 -m 0=fbdev
```

If this doesn't work, you can use the following command to tell `sax2` to experiment with various graphics modes until it finds one that works correctly:

```
sax2 -r -m 0=fbdev
```

One of these commands should cause `sax2` to start correctly. You can then save your configuration file and start the X Window system using a command such as `startx`.

When you've managed to get the X Window system to work on your system, you may find that the system doesn't take advantage of all of the available screen space. Once again, this is especially common on laptops. Most laptops provide built-in functions that control the behavior of your hardware. For example, on many IBM ThinkPad laptops, you can press the Function and F8 keys at the same time to toggle between different display modes until you find the one that works best for your hardware.

If X Still Doesn't Start

By default, a SUSE installation is set to boot into runlevel 5, which means that networking and graphics are both running when the system starts, and that a graphical display (login) manager is launched (usually `kdm`). It occasionally happens that immediately after the first time the system boots following installation, X either fails to start, or (worse) starts but fails to display on the monitor because it has been incorrectly configured during the installation. This can be distressing, not to say depressing, because it appears that you have gone through the whole installation and now nothing works. Don't despair; if this happens, log in as root on one of the text consoles (hold down Ctrl+Alt+one of the keys F1–F6). Then type:

```
init 3
sax2
```

and start again with X configuration.

Switching Resolutions

If you have more than one resolution configured, X typically starts in the highest of these. You can switch resolutions by pressing Ctrl and Alt together with the plus (+) or minus (–) keys from the numeric keypad. You can also (rather brutally) kill the X session with Ctrl+Alt+Backspace. This kills all running graphical programs without saving anything.

Copy and Paste in X

Windows users are used to using Ctrl+C and Ctrl+V for copying and pasting between applications. Almost all X applications follow the principle that selecting with the left mouse button copies and clicking with the middle button pastes. This is one reason why you should really make sure that you have a genuine three-button mouse when you run Linux. However, many applications, including KDE applications, also use the Ctrl+C/Ctrl+V system. KDE has a clipboard application (`klipper`) that maintains a history of recent copies and allows you to select them for the next paste operation.

Tip

One aspect of copying and pasting text between the X Window system and various desktop environments that is often confusing to users is that the cut and paste buffer used when selecting text in many X applications using the mouse is a different clipboard buffer from that used by GNOME/KDE applications. If you have problems cutting and pasting between X and GNOME/KDE applications, you can use an intermediate application such as `xclipboard` as a bridge between the two. For example, you can start `xclipboard`, select text in an `xterm` using the mouse, paste it into `xclipboard`, and then easily paste it into any GNOME/KDE application.

User Preferences in X

The file .xinitrc in your home directory holds the information about what will happen when you start X. You may find that the file itself does not exist but that there is a file .xinitrc.template. You can copy this to .xinitrc and make changes to it. One useful and very simple thing you may want to do is to add a command near the end of the file to start an xterm before the window manager is executed. This is simply a question of adding the following line just before the line that reads exec $WINDOWMANAGER:

```
xterm &
```

Making this change means that if a problem with the window manager arises, you will at least have somewhere to type commands to rectify the situation, rather than seeing the frustrating gray screen with an X pointer on it and nothing else.

The .xinitrc file is automatically invoked when starting X. In general, you can use this file to specify any other commands that you want to start when the X Window system starts. Many people use this file to automatically start web browsers or other popular applications when starting X. Because this file is a standard Linux shell script (command file), you can simply list any other applications that you want to start before the line that says exit 0 — make sure to follow each of these with an ampersand (&) to indicate that the X Window system starts them as background processes, rather than interrupting the execution of the .xinitrc file.

Using X Remotely

As we hinted earlier, the fact that X is a network-transparent protocol means that you can run a program in one place and display it somewhere else.

Understanding the DISPLAY Environment Variable

As you'll see in the next few sections, the `DISPLAY` environment variable tells X Window system applications which device they should contact in order to display their output. In most cases, you won't have to set this variable because the default is always your local machine. However, in general, the `DISPLAY` environment variable is declared using a command such as the following:

```
DISPLAY=displayname; export DISPLAY
```

The *displayname* specification uses the following form:

```
hostname:display_number:screen_number
```

When specifying a `DISPLAY`, *hostname* specifies the machine on which the display is running and must be either a machine name or the machine's network address, as listed in `/etc/hosts`. The *display_number* variable specifies one of the displays on *hostname*. Each display on a system is assigned a *display_number*, beginning with 0. The variable `screen_number` specifies the screen on which the display is running. In most cases, you can specify a *displayname* as `hostname:0`. For example, you would execute the following command to display output on the host foo:

```
export DISPLAY=foo:0.0
```

Displaying an Application Remotely

Suppose, for example, that you are logged in at the machine bible, and you log in via ssh to the machine wiley:

```
user@bible:~> ssh wiley
Password:
user@wiley:~>
```

You now try to start an xterm:

```
user@wiley:~> xterm
xterm Xt error: Can't open display: snark:0.0
```

If, instead, you start out by using the -X option to ssh, everything works as expected and hoped—the DISPLAY variable is correctly set and ssh does X forwarding:

```
user@bible:~> ssh -X wiley
Password:
user@wiley:~> xterm &
```

You will now see an xterm running on wiley and displaying in front of you (on the monitor attached to bible).

If you simply want to run single graphical applications remotely, this is all you need to do.

Note Many systems that support SSH deactivate X11 forwarding in their SSH daemon's configuration files or in their X server's configuration files. If you have problems getting X11 forwarding to work, check your system and X server configuration settings.

Using the DISPLAY Environment Variable

Suppose that you are logged in at the machine bible and you check the value of the DISPLAY environment variable:

```
user@bible:~> echo $DISPLAY
:0.0
```

You can set that variable to point to a display on another machine and try to run a program:

```
user@bible:~> export DISPLAY=wiley:0
user@bible:~> xterm &
```

Typically you will see something like the following:

```
xterm Xt error: Can't open display: wiley:0
```

However, if on wiley you allow clients from bible to connect to the X server with the following:

```
user@wiley:~> xhost +bible
```

and now if you run

```
user@bible:~> xterm &
```

you will see an xterm starting on wiley.

Note, however, that the capability to do this is now switched off by default in SUSE; you will need to make the following configuration change to make it work. In the file /etc/sysconfig/displaymanager, change the line:

```
DISPLAYMANAGER_XSERVER_TCP_PORT_6000_OPEN="no"
```

to read:

```
DISPLAYMANAGER_XSERVER_TCP_PORT_6000_OPEN="yes"
```

and run SuSEconfig. Note that this functionality is switched off by default because it is a potential security risk; for most purposes, using ssh -X allows you to do all the remote displaying that you need to do.

Remote Graphical Login

It is also possible to log in graphically and remotely to wiley from bible and see exactly what you would see if you were in front of wiley's monitor.

To make this possible, you need to do some configuration on wiley; its kdm (or if you are not using KDE, its gdm or xdm) configuration file needs to be fixed so that it allows remote graphical logins.

1. For kdm, on wiley, edit the file /etc/opt/kde3/share/config/kdm/kdmrc and in the section headed [Xdmcp] change the line

   Enable=false

   to

   Enable=true

2. Now, assuming that no graphics are running on bible (you have issued the command init 3 and you are logged in at a text console), do this:

   user@bible:~> X -query wiley

You should now see wiley's graphical login screen; you can log in to wiley as any user on wiley and work in your desktop there.

If graphics are running on bible but you want to be able to log in graphically to wiley (and switch between the two sessions), that is possible also. Simply specify a display on bible that is not in use:

   user@bible:~> X -query wiley :1

This starts a new X session with wiley's login screen on bible's second display (the first display is number 0, the second is number 1). You can even run the preceding command from within the existing graphical session. The existing display on bible will still be there, and you can switch to it with Ctrl+Alt+F7. You can switch to the new display with Ctrl+Alt+F8.

Tip
To do the same sort of thing automatically, you can modify SuSEconfig environment settings or use the yast2 Remote Administration panel. Setting the appropriate SuSEconfig variable is done by changing the value of the DISPLAYMANAGER_ REMOTE_ACCESS variable to "yes" in the file /etc/sysconfig/displaymanager or by using the yast2 Network Services ➪ Remote Administration panel.

Remote Graphical Connection from Windows

There are ssh clients for Windows, the best known of which is PuTTY. If you want to view your Linux desktop from a remote Windows machine, one easy way is to use PuTTY together with Virtual Network Computing (VNC). You will need to have the tightvnc package installed on Linux, and you will need to have PuTTY and a VNC

viewer available on Windows. These applications are provided in the `dosutils` directory on your SUSE distribution media, but you can always get the latest and greatest versions directly from their home sites. PuTTY is available from `w w w .`
`chiark.greenend.org.uk/~sgtatham/putty/`. A VNC viewer for Windows is available
from `www.realvnc.com`. It appears that version 3.3.5 of the Windows viewer works
best with the `tightvnc` package included in current versions of SUSE.

Use PuTTY to log in to your Linux machine from Windows. When you are logged in,
do this:

```
user@bible:~>vncserver
You will require a password to access your desktops.
Password:
```

When you have set the password, you will see something like this:

```
New 'X' desktop is bible:1
Creating default startup script /home/user/.vnc/xstartup
Starting applications specified in /home/user/.vnc/xstartup
Log file is /home/user/.vnc/bible:1.log
```

You can now start the VNC viewer on the Windows machine and connect to `bible:1`
(or the appropriate IP number followed by `:1`). The `:1` is the display number; the
VNC server takes the next available display number, and you have to supply the
same number to connect to it. You will see a Linux desktop (in fact, running `t w m` as
a window manager). If you normally use KDE and you would like to see your usual
KDE desktop, you need to edit the file `~/.vnc/xstartup` and replace `t w m &` with
`startkde &`.

Note that you can also connect to the VNC server through a (Java-enabled) browser
by using the address `http://bible:5801`—the port number is 5800 plus the display
number.

Tip   You can do the same thing by activating Remote Administration capabilities in YaST.

Desktop Sharing

The `krfb` desktop sharing program is also included as part of KDE in SUSE; this
allows you to share your *current* session with another user through the VNC protocol. The `krfb` program creates a session password and offers the invitation for a
limited period of time. Someone can connect to the session from any VNC client
elsewhere on the network, but in this case they will be literally sharing the same
desktop session—both users can use the keyboard and mouse and the effects will
be seen on both displays.

Of course, you can also run a VNC server on Windows and access the Windows desktop using the Linux vncciewer or krdc programs, or you can use these to access your Linux desktop from another Linux machine.

Alternatively, you can run a full X server in Windows. Free alternatives include the Java-based weirdx, which is included in the dosutils directory on the SUSE distribution, and cygwin/X, which is part of Cygwin, which provides a complete Unix-like environment on Windows.

Cygwin/X

Cygwin/X is available from http://x.cygwin.com/ and is easy to install and run on Windows. When you run the installer, you will find that because of dependencies, you install a considerable proportion of the entire Cygwin environment in order to run X. You can then click the Cygwin icon to get a shell, type (for example) X -query wiley, and you can log in graphically to the remote Linux machine.

There are also a number of proprietary X server implementations for Windows. The best and most affordable of these is Labtam's XConnectPro software, available from www.labtam-inc.com. Other companies, such as Hummingbird Communications Exceed (www.hummingbird.com/products/nc/exceed/), provide similar capabilities for Windows users who require interoperability.

Diskless X Terminals

To act just as a display for programs that are running elsewhere does not require a great deal of physical resources; the idea of using legacy hardware just to do this is an interesting one. We won't discuss this in any detail, but interest is growing in a thin-client approach to desktop computing using Linux.

In a true thin-client situation, the client machine uses network booting to get its kernel, mounts its directory tree entirely across the network from a server by NFS (the Network File System), and runs programs on the server, with only the display taking place locally. In certain variations, some applications are executed locally.

The best-known method for doing this is the Linux Terminal Server Project (LTSP) at www.ltsp.org. At present, LTSP is not included in the SUSE distributions. However, recent rumors (which have been confirmed) suggest that Novell's Linux desktop team is interested in improving LTSP and offering it as part of an Enterprise desktop solution.

LTSP consists of a directory structure on the server that is exported by NFS to the clients and an adapted kernel. The clients boot by using either PXE booting (Intel's Preboot Execution Environment) or etherboot (which allows a network card to boot across the network either from a special boot floppy or from a bootrom added to the card).

Installation and setup of LTSP is relatively easy, and LTSP has huge advantages. The hardware used for the clients can be machines that otherwise you would throw away, but the user experience will be similar to a new machine provided the server is powerful enough to support all the clients. No configuration is needed on the clients — if hardware fails, you can simply replace a client machine and everything will still work. All user files are, of course, on the server.

Note   Another similar (and very ingenious) method of running diskless Linux X terminals is provided by Michael Brown's `nymph` **package** (`www.fensystems.co.uk`).

KDE

The K Desktop Environment (KDE) is traditionally the default graphical environment on SUSE. Currently at version 3.2, it provides a very complete desktop environment with many nice features. It offers among other things:

✦ A consistent look and feel between applications

✦ A start button with cascading graphical menus

✦ Icons

✦ A panel bar

✦ Multiple desktops

✦ Themes

✦ A clipboard

✦ Drag-and-drop support

✦ Copy-and-paste support between applications

Additionally, SUSE has integrated YaST into the KDE menus and contributed toward the partial integration of OpenOffice. Figure 8-3 shows a default KDE desktop.

Caution   The functionality of an integrated desktop environment comes at a price in terms of resources; a considerable amount of infrastructure has to be started before you actually do anything in KDE. For machines with a limited amount of memory, a more minimal X Window system environment such as a window manager (discussed later in this chapter) may therefore be a better choice.

It is not our intention to document all the features of KDE here. That would be superfluous (because most of the functionality of KDE is indeed as intuitive as it is intended to be) and would also take up far too much space. However, we discuss some particularly useful features that may not be apparent at first glance.

Figure 8-3: A new user's default KDE desktop

Konqueror

Konqueror is a universal browser. It is both a web browser and a file manager, and much more. Konqueror is probably the most important achievement of the KDE team, and as a web browser it is very pleasant to use. Konqueror's HTML rendering engine has been incorporated by Apple into the Safari browser on Mac OS X.

As a browser, Konqueror includes nice features such as tabbed browsing (where you can open various web sites within a single browser, each of which is created as a separately selectable entity known as a tab) and split windows. You can drop a URL onto the main window with a middle-click to go straight to a URL that you have copied. Another nice feature is the Clear location bar button just to the left of the location bar. This button clears whatever URL is already entered, allowing you to easily enter a new one, something that other browsers might do well to copy.

Power Browsing with Split Windows

A very nice feature of Konqueror is that you can split the window into two panes and view every result of clicking a link in the left pane in the right one. To achieve this, do the following:

1. Click Window and then choose Split View Left/Right.

2. Link the two panes by clicking the small box you see at the bottom right of each. A chain icon should appear in both panes.

3. Right-click that chain icon in the left pane and choose Lock to current location.

Now, whatever link you click in the left pane will be opened and displayed in the right pane.

Web Shortcuts

Konqueror includes several built-in shortcuts for accessing particular search engines and other sites. You can define these in the Konqueror Settings dialog box under Configure Konqueror ⇨ Web Shortcuts. For example, you can directly get a Google query for the word *SUSE* by typing gg:SUSE in the location bar. You can search CPAN for Perl modules containing the word *text* with cpan:text and so on. (Using gg for Google can certainly become a habit that leads to irritation when for some reason you happen to be using another browser that doesn't support these web shortcuts.)

Browser Identification

Just occasionally, you may need to set Konqueror to identify itself as another browser to particular sites that absurdly test the browser identification and lock you out if they don't like what they see. You can set this on a per-site basis in Settings ⇨ Configure Konqueror ⇨ Browser Identification.

Konqueror as a File Manager

Again, if you want to use Konqueror to move files around, it can be useful to split the window; entering something such as /home/ in the location bar takes you into the local file system. You can click the other pane and enter another path there and drag and drop files to copy or move them.

If you type an FTP location into Konqueror, it behaves as expected, and you can drag files from the FTP server and onto your desktop or into another Konqueror window.

A very useful feature of Konqueror is that it can integrate ssh functionality. If you type a location in the form fish:someone@somewhere, Konqueror attempts to use ssh to authenticate as user someone on the remote machine somewhere. If the authentication is successful, you will see the files in the home directory of someone on the machine somewhere. Then, subject to permissions, you can drag and drop files to and from this window. While in general we don't really favor dragging and dropping files, this is particularly useful. It is the equivalent of scp combined with sftp, but better because filename and path completion on the remote system don't work with the scp command, and sftp doesn't do command completion and history properly. This way you see everything on the remote side directly.

Tip   If you have the package `kdenetwork3-lan` installed, you can type `lan:/` in the location bar, and all machines on the network that are running an `ssh` daemon or offering NFS or Samba/Windows shares should be visible. You should then be able to click the appropriate machine and type of share.

The KDE Control Center

KDE's Control Center gives the user a great deal of scope for altering the look and feel and behavior of the KDE environment. Most of the customizations that can be made are fairly self-explanatory, but we would like to highlight a few interesting features.

Appearance and Themes

This dialog box enables you to customize the look and feel of KDE to your heart's content. To select this configuration option, select the Control Center from SUSE's Start menu and then select the Appearances and Themes option in the left pane.

File Associations

In general, you don't want to make many changes here, but it is certainly useful to know that you can, and to know where to find this feature. You can do two useful things:

✦ You can change the default application that opens a given type of file when you click it in Konqueror.

✦ You can alter whether the file will be viewed by an external application or by a viewer embedded into Konqueror if such a viewer exists.

Login Manager

This set of dialog boxes (in the System Administration menu) is certainly easier to use than editing the configuration file by hand. To select this configuration option, select the Control Center from SUSE's Start menu and then select the System Administrator option in the left pane, followed by the Login Manager option. You will need to run this in administrator mode (by clicking the Administrator Mode button and entering the root password) to do anything very useful. A particularly nice feature is that it allows you to drop a photo of a user into the dialog box; this photo then appears on the `kdm` login screen.

YaST Modules

SUSE has integrated YaST so that you can access it through the KDE Control Center menus if you want. To access YaST modules, select the Control Center from the SUSE Start menu and then select the System Administrator option in the left pane, followed by the Login Manager option. You will need to run this in administrator mode (by clicking the Administrator Mode button and entering the root password) to do anything very useful.

Multiple Desktops

By default, you get only two desktops (between which you can move by clicking the desktop switcher applet in the panel). This dialog box (under the Desktop menu) enables you to increase this number to as many as 16.

KDE Applications

KDE comes with a large number of KDE-compliant applications, far too many to list here. They vary in quality, and quite a number are simply KDE front ends to well-known tools. The best are excellent, others are very promising, and some are not particularly useful:

✦ The kwrite application is an excellent graphical text editor with syntax coloring and highlighting for a variety of languages. It can export to an HTML file showing the syntax highlighting, and it shows outlines and document structure by default (so that you can collapse or expand loops in programming languages or tagged sections in HTML documents). Even so, it is probably unlikely to tempt many people away from emacs, for example.

✦ In something of the same spirit, the KOffice programs — kword, kspread, and so on — have progressed enormously and are very usable, but are unlikely to tempt many people away from using OpenOffice.org, simply because the ability to import Microsoft Office documents lags somewhat behind.

✦ Every KDE user has used the konsole terminal emulator, an exceptionally good and configurable terminal emulator. A nice feature is that simply by clicking an item in the File menu you can bring up m c (the Midnight Commander text-based file manager) in the current directory. Similarly, you can start an ssh session from the same menu, which remembers previous user and hostname settings. It even supports "print screen" — a useful feature.

✦ SUSE's help system (susehelp) is well integrated into the rest of the desktop. We discuss this further in Chapter 5.

✦ A recent addition to the SUSE distribution is the rekall database system. This answers a long-felt need for a desktop database front end roughly comparable to Microsoft Access.

✦ KDE's kmail, kaddressbook, and korganizer programs do exactly what you would expect, and do it well, but we often hear negative comparisons in relation to GNOME's Evolution. Work is currently going on to combine these applications into a unified client to the Kolab project's mail and groupware server.

Note   The Kolab project (http://kolab.org/) promises to establish a standard and show how the functionality of shared calendaring and email can be established in the open source world, thus offering the intended functionality of the Microsoft Exchange/Outlook combination without the notoriously appalling performance and security problems.

✦ The k3b application is a front end to the various programs needed for creating and burning ISO images to CD or DVD.

✦ The kooka application is well featured for controlling a scanner.

GNOME

The other desktop environment for Linux is GNOME. There is something of a tradition of dichotomies in this world: the disagreement between the devotees of vi and emacs. In the area of scripting languages there is a similar split between the followers of Perl and those who use Python. On the desktop, it is KDE versus GNOME.

As noted earlier, GNOME began as a reaction against KDE and the license of the Qt toolkit. The ideological battle is long over — the Qt license as used in KDE is now acceptable to all. It is worth noting nonetheless that there is still a significant license difference in that GNOME applications can be (and are) compiled and offered on the Windows platform; the Qt license does not allow the same to be done with KDE applications, although it is possible in principle.

Traditionally, because KDE was the default on SUSE, SUSE's GNOME packages tended to be less well looked after, and less well integrated into the rest of the system. There was also a tendency for them to be somewhat less up-to-date than the comparable KDE versions. Indeed, on at least one occasion the timing of a SUSE release was calculated to be exactly in time to carry a major KDE release.

As with KDE, GNOME attempts to provide an entire desktop environment in which compliant applications can cooperate in drag-and-drop, copy-and-paste, and other tasks. Again, as with KDE, this means significant costs in overhead before any programs are actually run. Discussions abound about which approach is technically better and about which environment has a better look and feel and better programs.

 Tip

The free desktop project at www.freedesktop.org focuses on interoperability between different desktop environments for the X Window system. The project's goal is to provide a common infrastructure that KDE, GNOME, and others can agree upon and build upon. The motivation for the founding of the project was partly the widely shared feeling that the differences between GNOME and KDE were likely to hinder the adoption of Linux as a desktop system by businesses.

SUSE provides an up-to-date version of GNOME in order to support the latest and greatest GNOME applications. Some of the key GNOME applications are the Nautilus file manager, the Evolution mail client, the GIMP graphics package, the AbiWord word processor and Gnumeric spreadsheet, the Inkscape vector graphics package, and (slightly tangentially as they are not strictly part of the project) the Mozilla browser and popular derivatives such as Firefox.

Parallel to the official SUSE GNOME packages is the Ximian GNOME (Ximian Desktop 2) distribution, a version of which is available for SUSE. The only problem at present with using this version is that it means you will have to be very careful about what online updates you permit.

Another set of GNOME packages for SUSE systems is available from `www.usr-local-bin.org/`. These packages are produced by a former SUSE employee in the UK and are very popular.

In many ways, from the user's point of view, there is little difference when choosing between KDE and GNOME (see Figure 8-4).

However, some differences do exist and a couple of notable ones are as follows:

✦ One difference that you will immediately notice is that by default KDE is a one-click interface: Clicking an icon once launches the application or action. In most cases, this is intuitive and corresponds well with the one-click nature of web links, but it is still difficult for the user coming from Windows. It can cause problems occasionally when it seems that you need to first select an item and then do something with it. In most cases a right-click enables you to do what you want. GNOME's double-click default is perhaps easier for Windows refugees (though KDE can be reconfigured to use double-clicks, as well).

Figure 8-4: A new user's default GNOME desktop

✦ Another key difference between GNOME and KDE is that technically GNOME does not include its own window manager; it requires a GNOME-compliant window manager. These days that means the metacity window manager, although in the past GNOME was normally used with the sawfish window manager. KDE can also use other window managers, although it uses its own, `kwn`, by default.

Nautilus

Nautilus should be thought of as a file manager. It is capable of rendering web pages, but it does this by calling an embedded external viewer, and by default out of the box, it views the HTML source rather than the rendered page.

As a file manager, Nautilus is attractive. By default, it shows files in an intuitive and friendly way; as with Konqueror, image files and various other types are shown as thumbnails or miniature copies of themselves. Selecting and copying files using the copy-and-paste or drag-and-drop features works as expected, but there is no means of splitting the main window. If you want to drag files from one directory to another, you need to have each directory open in a separate window.

Epiphany

By default, the GNOME desktop web browser in SUSE is Epiphany, one of the cut-down browsers based on Mozilla (another is Galeon). It should probably be considered a disadvantage that, unlike in KDE, in GNOME it is not natural to "do everything in one place." You can, of course, browse the file system with Epiphany, but you cannot use it to move files around.

Evolution

Evolution is the GNOME mail client; people who use it tend to be very fond of it. It is deliberately similar in look and feel to Microsoft Outlook and has integrated calendaring capabilities. Ximian's Evolution Connector (a piece of software allowing Evolution to connect to a Microsoft Exchange server and exchange calendar information) has recently been released as open source by Novell.

Gnucash

Gnucash is a personal finance application with similar features to some of the commercial proprietary applications in this field.

AbiWord

AbiWord is a word processor with many advanced features. However, as in the case of `kword`, mentioned previously, poor importing of Microsoft Word files means that it does not compare well with OpenOffice.org.

Gnumeric

Gnumeric is an impressive spreadsheet program. Similar considerations regarding importing other file types that we mentioned when discussing AbiWord apply, however. OpenOffice.org certainly seems to have the edge in that regard, although as a standalone spreadsheet, Gnumeric compares very well in terms of features with the OpenOffice.org spreadsheet and with Microsoft Excel. It also offers some scientific calculation functions, such as its Solver for linear equations and its Simulation and Statistical Analysis capabilities, that are not currently available in other spreadsheet applications.

Note   Of course, there is nothing to stop you from running applications designed for one of the major desktops within the other. The design of the menus tends to push you toward one set of programs rather than the other. In addition, if you are going to run Konqueror, for example, within a GNOME environment, it will start a fairly large proportion of the KDE infrastructure in the background simply to support it. Integration between the two environments has improved, and each finds and displays programs from the other in its menu structure.

Other Window Managers

If you decide not to use either KDE or GNOME, a variety of X Window system window managers are available. Essentially, your choice is about balancing beauty against simplicity.

✦ If resources are limited, one of the fairly minimal window managers may suit you. Also, if you are in the habit of starting everything from the command line, then complex menus and icons may not be so useful to you. At the very minimal end of the spectrum, TWM, and Fluxbox (discussed later in this chapter) provide an environment where you can start an xterm and do everything else from there. Apart from the ability to move and minimize and maximize windows, there is not a great deal of other functionality.

✦ On the other hand, a window manager such as Xfce offers complex menus, a great deal of configurability, and a lot of eye candy, but uses a good deal of resource and lacks the nice built-in file management capabilities of GNOME and KDE.

Window managers such as IceWM and Blackbox fall somewhere in between the two extremes. In general, if you use one of these window managers you are going to find yourself spending a fair amount of time doing configuration to get the look and feel the way you want and the menus the way you want: At least some of this work will be spent editing text files by hand.

MWM and FVWM2

MWM (the Motif Window Manager) is minimalism in action (see Figure 8-5). If you are installing a server and you just need to have X available so that, for example, you can run the graphical Oracle installer later, you may choose the Minimal + X11 installation option, which uses the FVWM2 window manager by default but also installs MWM. Figure 8-5 shows the MWM window manager.

A good site for additional information about the Motif Window Manager is `w w w .plig.org/xwinman/mwm.html`.

Blackbox

Blackbox is elegant minimalism of the "less is more" school of thought (see Figure 8-6). Based on the window manager provided on NeXT computer systems (NeXTStep), Blackbox is a powerful and elegant window manager.

Figure 8-5: MWM

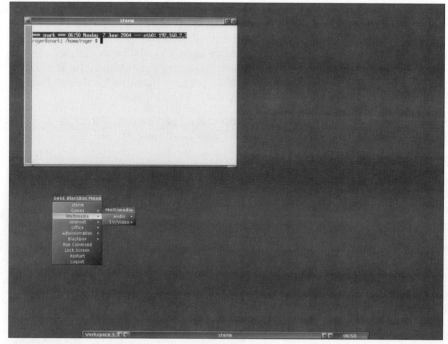

Figure 8-6: Blackbox

A good site for additional information about the Blackbox window manager is `http://blackboxwm.sourceforge.net`. The Openbox window manager is based on Blackbox and also included with SUSE Professional (see also `http://icculus.org/openbox/`).

IceWM

IceWM is very configurable in terms of the look and feel of window decorations and menus, and offers a start button and cascading menus. It also offers multiple desktops and the capability to switch between them by clicking a panel applet.

A good site for additional information about the IceWM window manager is `http://icewm.sourceforge.net/`. IceWM is a great window manager with low resource requirements.

XFCE

XFCE is in a similar tradition but has a launcher panel rather than menus. It comes with its own file manager called `xftree`. XFCE is actually more of a low-resource desktop environment than a simple window manager because it provides lightweight functionality for drag-and-drop support and other desktop capabilities.

The primary web site for XFCE is `www.xfce.org`.

Window Maker

Window Maker has some strong advocates; it offers themes, menus, and icons, and is based on the look and feel of the NeXTStep environment.

The primary web site for Window Maker is `www.windowmaker.org`.

FVWM

FVWM, shown in Figure 8-7, is another old favorite. In the early days of Linux it tended to be the default. It has a launcher rather than cascading menus, and multiple desktops with a nice desktop pager.

For more information, go to `www.fvwm.org`.

Figure 8-7: FVWM

Building Your Own X Applications

While SUSE includes a huge selection of the most popular X Window system desktops, window managers, and applications, you may eventually encounter an X application or window manager that you'd like to experiment with but which is not available as part of the SUSE distribution or as an update. Compiling your own X applications from their source code is actually quite easy — SUSE includes all of the tools and development infrastructure necessary to do so.

The following sections discuss the packages that you must install on your system to build X applications, provide a general discussion of building and installing X applications, and then show you how to build and install a popular window manager that is not provided as part of your SUSE distribution.

Development Requirements for X Applications

Being able to compile X applications under SUSE requires that you install a fairly small set of packages. All of these are available on the SUSE DVD or CDs. The basic requirements for X application development are the following:

✦ binutils — The assembler, linker, and other applications that provide the infrastructure required by the GNU C compiler

✦ gcc — The C compiler from GCC, the GNU Compiler Collection

✦ make — Applications that can perform sequential compilation steps and follow dependencies as expressed in a compilation command file known as a Makefile

✦ xorg-x11-devel — X11 header (include) files that provide basic definitions used in X source code

Compiling and running X applications has other requirements, such as the presence of the GNU C library (glibc), but these are satisfied by the basic SUSE installation on your system.

Building Fluxbox

Fluxbox is a small, lightweight, and powerful window manager based on the source code for the Blackbox windows manager, discussed earlier in this chapter. The home page for Fluxbox is www.fluxbox.org.

Unlike Blackbox, Fluxbox is actively under development, and new versions of Fluxbox are frequently available from the Fluxbox web site. In addition to providing a fast window manager with relatively low memory and systems requirements, Fluxbox is also *theme-able*, which means that you can download and easily apply alternate graphical and menu configurations. Figure 8-8 shows a sample Fluxbox screen using one of the default themes, BlueNight.

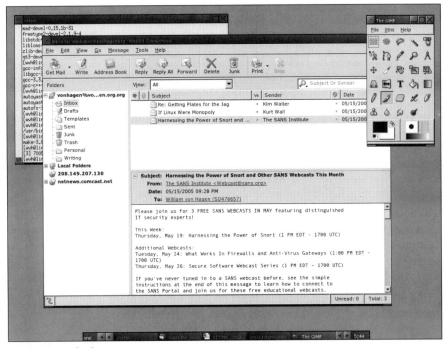

Figure 8-8: Fluxbox

The first step in building and installing any X application is to obtain its source code. The source code for the latest version of Fluxbox is always available from the Fluxbox site's download page, which is located at www.fluxbox.org/download.php. The version of Fluxbox used in the rest of this section is 0.9.13, which was available from http://prdownloads.sourceforge.net/fluxbox/fluxbox-0.9.13.tar.gz at the time this book was updated.

After downloading the source code, you must unpack the archive using the standard Linux tar command, as in the following example:

```
$ tar zxf fluxbox-0.9.13.tar.gz
```

This will create a directory named Fluxbox-0.9.13 in the current directory. Use the cd command to change to this directory, and run the configuration script provided with Fluxbox by executing the command ./configure. (The ./ prefix ensures that the shell runs the configure script that is found in the current directory.) This command will produce very verbose output as it explores your system to ensure that all of the correct components for compilation are present on your system and constructs a Makefile that you can use to build Fluxbox. The following is some sample output from the configure script:

```
# ./configure
checking for a BSD-compatible install... /usr/bin/install -c
checking whether build environment is sane... yes
checking for gawk... gawk
checking whether make sets $(MAKE)... yes
checking for gcc... gcc
checking for C compiler default output file name... a.out
```

Next, all you have to do is run the `make` command. The `make` command uses the `Makefile` created by the configure script to build all of the components of the Fluxbox window manager in the right order. The following is some sample output from the `make` command:

```
# make
cd . \
 && CONFIG_FILES= CONFIG_HEADERS=config.h \
    /bin/sh ./config.status
config.status: creating config.h
config.status: config.h is unchanged
config.status: executing default-1 commands
make  all-recursive
```

After compilation has finished, you can install Fluxbox by executing the command `make install` using `sudo` or as the root user. By default, Fluxbox and all of its themes and other requirements will be installed to the appropriate subdirectories of `/usr/local` on your system. The Fluxbox executable is installed as `/usr/local/bin/Fluxbox`.

Using Fluxbox

After you have installed Fluxbox, you'll want to experiment with it. The easiest way to experiment with different window managers on your SUSE system is to create a file called .xinitrc (located in your home directory) that starts the X applications and window manager of your choice. If you are using a graphical display manager such as `kdm` (the default on SUSE systems), the specified applications and window manager will start automatically the next time you log in on your system. If you are using your system at run level 3 (non-graphical mode), you can start the X applications and window manager by executing the `xinit` command from the command line.

First, create a sample .xinitrc file in your home directory using your favorite text editor. A simple .xinitrc file that starts a single X terminal (`xterm`) application and then starts the Fluxbox window manager is the following:

```
/usr/X11R6/bin.xterm&
exec /usr/local/bin/fluxbox
```

After you have created this file, exit the text editor and log out. This should redisplay the standard SUSE graphical login screen. Log back in, and the system will execute the .xinitrc file in your home directory to start an xterm and the Fluxbox window manager.

When you are running Fluxbox, click the right mouse button to display its application and configuration menu.

The contents of this menu are determined by the file ~/.Fluxbox/menu, which is a text file that is located in your home directory. To add other commands to this menu, simply edit the file and add those commands to the menu. To switch between different Fluxbox themes, select Fluxbox menu ⇨ System styles from the main Fluxbox menu and select any of the other styles that are listed on that menu.

If, after experimenting with Fluxbox, you decide that you prefer the desktop environment or window manager that you were previously using, simply remove the .xinitrc file from your home directory and your system will return to using its previous graphical defaults.

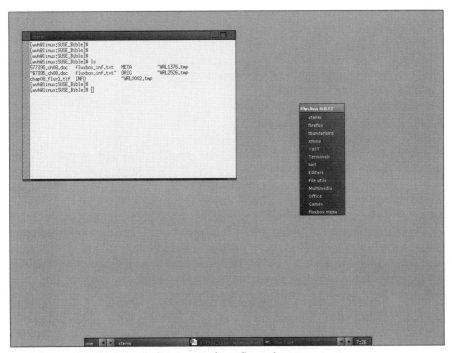

Figure 8-9: The Fluxbox application and configuration menu

Wrapping Up

The X Window system is the de facto graphics standard for modern Unix-like systems. SUSE Linux provides complete, integrated support for the most popular open source X Window system desktop environment, KDE and GNOME, and also provides a complete spectrum of window managers for users who prefer a graphical user interface with lower hardware and memory requirements. If you've installed GCC, you can even easily build and use other open source window managers and desktop environments. This combination of built-in, supported packages and flexibility is a primary factor in the rich user experience that SUSE Linux has always been famous for.

✦   ✦   ✦

Configuring the System with YaST

C H A P T E R

◆ ◆ ◆ ◆

In This Chapter

YaST and YaST modules

Keeping time with NTP

Configuring a printer

Online updating with YaST

Installing additional software with YaST

Installing other systems from yours

SUSE has always had a great configuration tool, YaST. Over the years it has moved from being a small configuration tool to being able to control the configuration of most aspects of the system. With each new release, the capabilities of YaST have grown.

YaST can be executed in a terminal-oriented, a non-graphical mode, or an X Window system mode, the difference being that one consists of purely text-based menus for remote configuration and the other is a GUI running under X.

Note The name YaST stands for Yet another Setup Tool, another example of the humorous program names that are common in the open source world.

Since the release of SUSE 9.1, YaST has been published under the General Public License (GPL). As we discussed in the Introduction, the YaST license had previously been a bone of contention because people felt it restricted the distribution of the SUSE operating system.

With the release of YaST under GPL, it means that the powerful configuration modules can now be ported to other versions of Linux. Other distributions do not have the wealth and breadth of configuration modules for system configuration as YaST does, so we hope this will help speed up the use of Linux by both home users and enterprise deployments.

Note We talk about YaST in GUI mode in this chapter, but the differences between YaST on the command line and YaST under X are only cosmetic. YaST has been designed so that regardless of the way you view it, the functionality is the same.

Figures 9-1 and 9-2 show the same YaST view from both the text and GUI system.

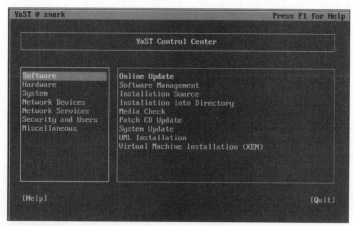

Figure 9-1: YaST running under text mode

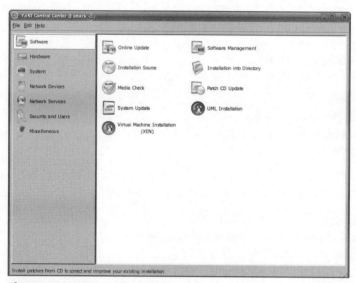

Figure 9-2: YaST running in GUI mode

There are numerous ways you can start YaST, either from a terminal directly or via the GNOME/KDE menus. Chapter 8 details how to load YaST from the desktop environment menus.

To load the GUI YaST interface, type **yast2** (as user root) at the command prompt. If YaST detects that X is running, it loads the GUI. If not, it runs the text-based interface. If you want to force the text-based interface, use the su command to become the root user and type **yast** at the command prompt.

When loaded, you will see the main YaST menu, as in Figures 9-1 and 9-2, depending on what version of the interface you have chosen.

From now on we will deal with the GUI-based YaST system.

YaST Modules

The YaST system is split into seven menu topics, each one opening up another list of menus for direct configuration of the chosen module.

Tip   If you want to load a YaST module without loading the main menu, you can enter yast2 modulename. For a list of modules available in your installed YaST environment, type **yast2 -l**.

The available topics for YaST configuration are as follows (with the YaST module name in brackets to load directly with yast2 modulename):

✦ **Software**

- Control the installation and removal of software packages (sw_single).
- Update your SUSE system to the latest patch level from the SUSE servers (online_update).
- Add a SUSE installation source (FTP, HTTP, SAMBA, directory, and so on) (inst_source).
- Use a patch CD to update your system (online_update '.cd_default').
- Install SUSE into a directory (dirinstall).
- Install SUSE into a directory for Xen (xen-dirinstall).
- Media check (test SUSE CDs or DVDs) (checkmedia).
- Change the characteristics of your system (package defaults, system language, and so on) (update).
- UML installation (install a User Mode Linux instance) (uml).

✦ **Hardware**

- Configure Bluetooth (bluetooth).
- Configure CD/DVD mount points, and so forth (cdrom).
- Configure your SCSI disk controller (controller).
- Configure your graphics card and monitor (x11).

- Get a general overview of your current hardware configuration (`hwinfo`).
- Enable/disable the direct memory access mode of your IDE disk (`idedma`).
- Configure infrared ports (`irda`).
- Configure your joystick device (`joystick`).
- Configure keyboard settings (`keyboard`).
- Configure your printer (`printer`).
- Configure your scanner (`scanner`).
- Configure your mouse (`mouse`).
- Configure a sound card (`sound`).
- Configure a TV Tuner card (`tv`).

✦ **System**

- Configure YaST-based services configuration in `/etc/sysconfig` (`sysconfig`).
- Configure a boot loader (`bootloader`).
- Change system language (`language`).
- Create a boot/rescue floppy disk (`bootfloppy`).
- Change the date and time (`timezone`).
- Configure the Logical Volume Manager (`lvm_config`).
- Partition disks (`disk`).
- Configure kernel tweakable settings (`powertweak`).
- Set up and control system profiles (`profile-manager`).
- Configure system backup (`backup`).
- Restore a system backup (`restore`).
- Enable and configure power management (`power-management`).
- Change runlevel configuration (`runlevel`).

✦ **Network devices**

- Configure a DSL (Digital Subscriber Line) connection to the Internet (`dsl`).
- Configure a modem for fax capabilities (`fax`).
- Configure your ISDN connection (`isdn`).
- Configure a modem (`modem`).

- Configure voice capabilities in your modem (`answering_machine`).
- Set up your network cards (`lan`).

✦ **Network services**

- Set up a DHCP server (`dhcp-server`).
- Set up a DNS server (`dns-server`).
- Configure DNS name resolution (`dns`).
- Configure an HTTP server (`http-server`).
- Configure host names (local name resolution) (`host`).
- Set up a Kerberos client (`kerberos-client`).
- Set up an LDAP client for a user database (`ldap`).
- Configure your mail server (`mail`).
- Set up an NFS mount point (`nfs`).
- Set up an NFS server (`nfs_server`).
- Set up an NIS client (`nis`).
- Set up an NIS server (`nis_server`).
- Control automatic time updates with NTP (`ntp-client`).
- Configure network services controlled via `inetd` (`inetd`).
- Set up a system-wide web proxy configuration (`proxy`).
- Set up remote administration (`remote`).
- Configure your network routes (`route`).
- Search for SLP-aware devices on your network (Service Location Protocol — SLP — is the same technology that drives Apple's Rendezvous automatic network configuration protocol) (`slp`).
- Set up a Samba client (Windows Shares) (`samba-client`).
- Set up a Samba server (`samba-server`).
- Set up a Trivial FTP server (`tftp-server`).

✦ **Security and users**

- Create and remove users (`users`).
- Create and remove groups (`groups`).
- Configure the SUSE firewall (`firewall`).
- Configure system security (file permissions, and so on) (`security`).

✦ **Misc (Miscellaneous)**

- Configure automatic installation services with AutoYaST (`autoyast`).

- Create an installation server (`instserver`).

- Load a vendor driver from the vendor's CD (`vendor`).

- Post a support request with SUSE (`support`).

- View the kernel startup log (`view_anymsg`).

- View the system log (`view_anymsg '/var/log/messages'`).

Phew! As you can see, you can configure a huge amount of the Linux system via YaST without having to touch a configuration file. This is a testament to the SUSE developers who have designed the SUSE system to be easily configured.

Going through every YaST module would take up a whole book, and as we are going to be guiding you through the configuration of some services later in the book, we deal with specific configurations for services in their respective chapters. In this chapter, we discuss some of the main modules that you use on a day-to-day basis.

The Software section of YaST controls the installation, removal, and control of the software installed on the SUSE system. One of the most important parts of the section is the Install/Remove package that we discussed during the installation of SUSE in Chapter 1. Taking this further, we add a new installation source and also show how to use the SUSE online update to make sure your system is up to the latest patch level.

Configuring Installation Sources

You are able to install SUSE from a network, CD, or DVD. Installing SUSE using an FTP server and other network-related sources is discussed briefly in Chapter 1. When the system is installed, you can also configure other installation sources for the SUSE packages. This is a common scenario when you have a few SUSE servers that all run from the same installation media.

To specify alternate installation sources, select the Software icon after starting YaST, and click the Change Source of Installation icon in the right pane.

To set up a central Network File System (NFS) server for installing SUSE, copy the DVD or each CD-ROM into a directory on your NFS server and export it.

Cross-Reference For more information on setting up an NFS server, see Chapter 22.

To set up an installation source from the NFS server:

1. Select Software ⇨ Change source of installation in YaST. You will be presented with a list of the current installation sources. It is likely you will see the source you used to install SUSE set as the default.

2. To add a source, select the Add drop-down box and NFS (see Figure 9-3).

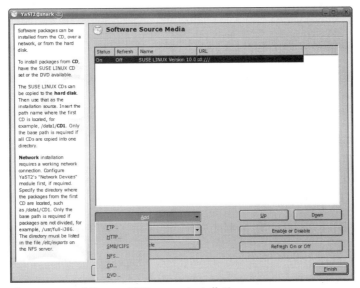

Figure 9-3: Adding an NFS server installation source

3. When the source is selected, you will be asked for the host name of the NFS server holding the SUSE packages and the directory on the server that contains the SUSE distribution (see Figure 9-4).

Figure 9-4: Configuring the NFS server parameters

Tip

If you are setting up an NFS source for installation (and have the installation CDs), you should create a directory to hold the current version of your SUSE installation media, and then copy each CD from the SUSE installation set into a separate directory in that directory, with names such as CD1, CD2, CD3, and so on.

4. When you have entered the information, you then need to select OK. YaST then attempts to mount the NFS server directory and checks the validity of the install source. If all goes well and YaST likes what it sees, you see the NFS installation source appear in the Software Source Media window, as it is in Figure 9-5.

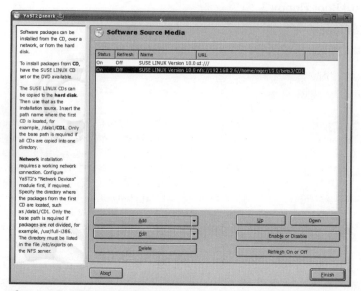

Figure 9-5: NFS installation source added to the source list

Creating and Using Boot and Rescue Floppies

The installation media contain a set of floppy disk images for starting an installation if for some reason you cannot boot from the CD-ROM. There is also a rescue floppy image. These are in the directory /boot on the DVD or CD1. YaST contains a module for creating floppy disks from these images. It can also write out an arbitrary floppy image to disk. Clearly, this is not useful for a new installation if you do not already have another SUSE system set up, but it may be useful to have a full set of boot, module, and rescue floppies available.

Note   If you need to create the floppies from the installation media and you don't have a SUSE system available, you can use the dd command on any Unix or Linux system (see Chapter 14). If you need to do this on a DOS or Windows system, you can use the rawrite or rawwritewin programs, which are in the /dosutils directory on the installation media.

This module is in the System section of the YaST menu, or it can be started from the command line with the command `yast2 bootfloppy`. You are then simply asked which floppy you want to create. The choices are as follows:

✦ Standard Boot Floppy 1

✦ Standard Boot Floppy 2

✦ Standard Boot Floppy 3

✦ Rescue Floppy

✦ Modules Floppies

✦ Custom Floppy

✦ Download Floppy Image

These do exactly what they say they do: They create the floppy disks from images on the installation media. YaST will use whatever installation source has already been set up to write out the floppy disks. Whichever of the options you choose, you are prompted for the floppy device (typically `/dev/fd0`), and the disk image is then written out to the floppy. There is an option to format the disk first. If you choose Modules Floppies, you are prompted for which one you want to create. Usefully, the menu tells you which floppy supports which hardware. There is more information in the files `/boot/modules1.txt`, `/boot/modules2.txt`, and so forth on the installation media.

If you want to use the floppies that you have created to start an installation or the rescue system, just boot from the first boot floppy. Depending on your hardware, you may be prompted for one or more of the modules floppies. If you choose the rescue system at the initial boot screen, you will later be prompted for the rescue floppy.

 Note If you want to run the rescue system from the set of floppies, after all three boot floppies and possibly the modules floppies have been inserted, you will see a message similar to "Make sure that CD1 is in your drive." Instead of OK, choose Back, select your language settings, and then select rescue system. You will then be prompted for either the CD or the rescue floppy.

Setting Up Proxy Settings

If your company uses a proxy, or you use a proxy at home, you can set a global system proxy that a large proportion of network utilities will try to honor.

You can set up either an anonymous proxy or one with user credentials. The proxy configuration itself is not intelligent because all it does is inform your applications that the proxy should be a certain host with a username and password (if specified). It does not impact how the application communicates with the server.

To set up your proxy configuration, select the Network Services icon after starting YaST, and select Proxy from the right pane. Next, enter your server addresses for your HTTP and FTP proxying services. If you need to configure a specific port number on your proxy, you can add this by appending a colon to the host name with the port number (see Figure 9-6).

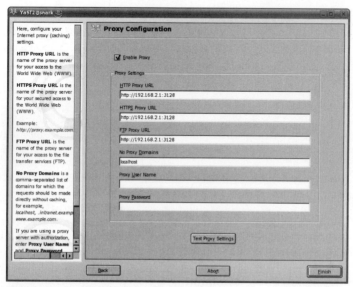

Figure 9-6: Configuring local proxy settings

Using NTP Time Services

Network Time Protocol (NTP) synchronizes your machine time with a centralized time server of your choosing. Time servers available on the Internet are usually a secondary source to a machine that acts as a central time server. Central (or primary) time servers are usually linked into an extremely accurate clock mechanism. To specify an NTP time source, select the Network Service icon in the left pane after starting YaST, and then select the NTP Client option from the right pane.

Selecting the NTP Client option causes you to be prompted for the host name of an NTP source (see Figure 9-7). An excellent list of NTP primary and secondary sources is available at www.eecis.udel.edu/~mills/ntp/clock2b.html. To ensure that your system automatically synchronizes itself with an NTP server, you should select the When Booting System option button—the default selection is Never, which effectively disables the use of NTP by your system.

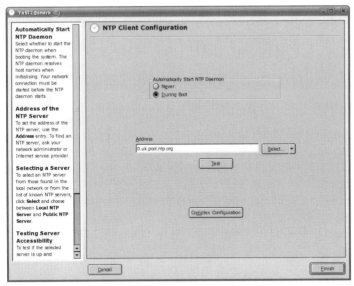

Figure 9-7: Configuring an NTP source

It is customary to source your NTP synchronization to a secondary time server, and for primary servers to synchronize to secondary servers only for general use.

When configured, your machine will attempt to synchronize to the NTP server specified in the configuration window. If you want to synchronize to more than one server, select the Complex Configuration button. Unless you are running a server that is extremely sensitive to time fluctuations, the default usually suffices.

Tip   If you are running an SLP-aware NTP server in your network, clicking the Lookup button causes the system to attempt to discover an NTP service for you.

Printer Configuration

One of the biggest things that annoyed Linux users in the past was the configuration of printers. In the Windows world, the addition of a printer is painless, but in Linux it seemed the process was always marred by problems with drivers and configuration options.

The Common Unix Printing System (CUPS) print drivers have helped to provide a unified printer architecture for Unix in general, and with distributions such as SUSE providing configuration front ends, the problems have become less apparent.

A more detailed and theoretical description of CUPS is given in Chapter 19.

To configure your printer:

1. Select Hardware from the initial YaST menu, and then Printer from the right pane. YaST displays the Printer Configuration screen (see Figure 9-8). It then attempts to discover local printers connected to your machine and guide you through the installation of the printer as a default on your system.

We will concentrate on the configuration of a network printer, but the principles are still the same if you are configuring a local printer.

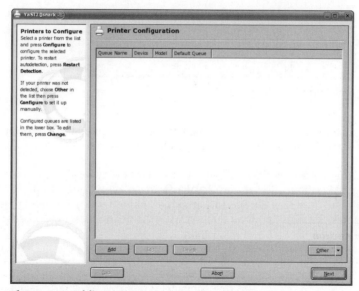

Figure 9-8: Adding a new printer to the system

2. If your printer is not local to the system, you will have to manually configure it. This is not as difficult as it used to be and is now as easy to do as it is in other operating systems. Click the Configure button, and you are taken to the Printer Type screen, shown in Figure 9-9, to select the type of printer you are configuring.

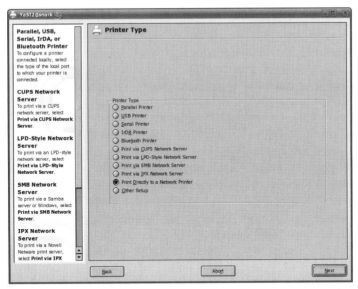

Figure 9-9: Selecting printer type

As you can see from Figure 9-9, you have a large range of print options available to you. Table 9-1 briefly describes those options.

Table 9-1
Printer Connections

Printer Connection	Description
Parallel printer	Until recently, parallel printers were the standard for PC printing. If you have a parallel/centronics printer connected to your computer, you should select this option.
USB printer	Fast becoming the *de facto* standard. If you have a USB printer connected to your machine, select this option.
Serial printer	Serial printers are quite rare nowadays and have been superseded by USB printers. If you have a printer that connects to the serial port on your machine, select this option.
IrDA printer	Especially prominent on laptop machines. If you are using the infrared port to connect to a printer, select this option.
CUPS Network	If you have a CUPS server on your network that is acting as a central print server, select this option.

Continued

Table 9-1 *(continued)*

Printer Connection	Description
LPD Network	Similarly, if you are using the traditional Unix print server as a central printing resource, select this option.
SMB Network	If you are trying to connect to a printer connected to a Windows machine, select this option.
IPX Network	If you are on an IPX/NetWare environment and the printer is IPX-based, select this option.
Network printer	Most high-end printers can connect directly to the network. If you have a network/JetDirect printer, select this option.
Other	If none of the preceding options fits your bill, you can select this option. With this you can set a CUPS class or a pipe-based print queue, or you can enter a unique URL for a printer to see if it will work.

3. Select Print Directly to a Network Printer. Click Next and you are prompted for the protocol used for printing to this network printer (see Figure 9-10).

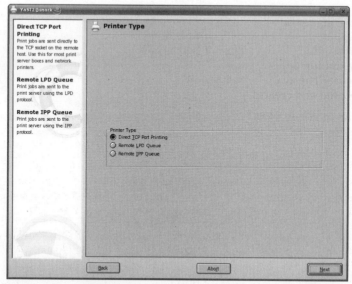

Figure 9-10: Printing protocol

- **Direct Printing**—Sends the printing job in raw form. This is usually safe for most modern network printers.

- **LPD Protocol**—If your network printer understands the Unix LPD protocol, then you can use this option.

- **IPP Printing**—Sends print jobs to the printer with the Internet Printing Protocol.

4. Select the direct printing protocol and click the Next button.

5. You are prompted for the IP address of the network printer to which you want to connect, or you can attempt to scan for available network printers on your network with the Lookup button.

6. If your printer has been detected successfully on the network, you can click the Test Socket Access button to see if the printer accepts print jobs before continuing.

7. Click the Next button to move on to configuring the printer name, description, and location (see Figure 9-11). These are free-form strings that will help you identify the printer from your applications. Two options of note are Do Local Filtering and Automatically Propose Multiple Queues.

- **Do Local Filtering**—Relevant when the remote printer you are connecting to is not intelligent enough to prepare a print job before putting ink to paper. In this case, to take the burden away from your printer, you can do the preparation of page layout and so forth on your local machine and then send the finished, prepared job to the printer.

- **Automatically Propose Multiple Queues**—Used when the system that hosts your printer uses different queues to reflect different printer configuration options, such as black and white printing, color printing, and so on. The available printer queues are usually contingent on those supported and created by the printer driver.

As we are doing local filtering in this example, we are unable to print a test page at this point because we need to set up our specific printer model. If your printer is intelligent enough to handle raw print jobs, you can attempt to print a test page. Otherwise, you may find your printer printing out garbage.

8. Click Next to view the Printer model page (see Figure 9-12). On the left you will be presented with a list of printer manufacturers. When you select a manufacturer, you will see a list of specific printer models on the right.

In the unlikely event that your printer is not listed, you may be able to use the PPD printer file that your printer uses in Windows to define your printer configuration.

If you have a PPD file, select Add PPD File to Database. You can either select the PPD file locally (on your filesystem), or you can download a PPD file from an FTP server.

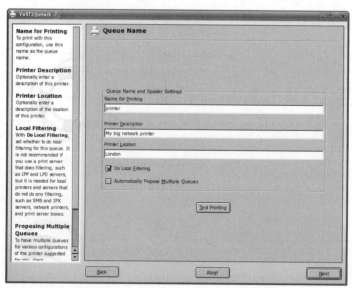

Figure 9-11: Selecting printer queue and descriptions

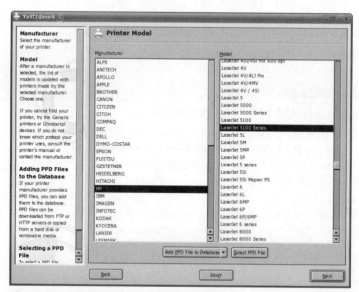

Figure 9-12: Selecting your printer model

PPD Files

PostScript Printer Description files (PPD files) control how information is sent to your printer in its native format. These files are relevant only to printers that require output in Adobe's PostScript printer language. Printers that do not use PostScript, such as Hewlett-Packard's PCL (Printer Control Language) printers, do not require a PPD file.

To find your printer definition file, take a look at the driver disks that were provided with your printer. PPD files may also be found by searching the Internet. Google is your friend!

Adobe has a great resource of third-party PPD files on its web site at www.adobe.com/products/printerdrivers/winppd.html.

9. When you have selected your printer model, click the Next button to view an overview of your printer settings so far.

10. If all of the information is correct, you can now test the printer configuration by sending a test page to the printer. Click the Test button to see if your configuration will work with your printer (see Figure 9-13).

   If you are not happy with your printer configuration, either select the item that is incorrect and press the Edit button, or press the Back button to go back and change settings.

   When you click Test, you are presented with an option of what you want to print as a test page. This could be a photo, graphics with no photo, or just text. Make your selection and your job is sent to the printer for your perusal.

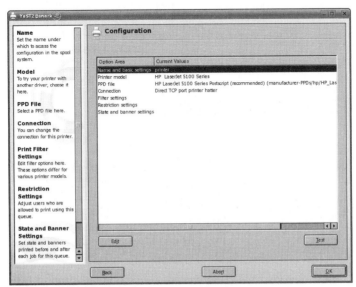

Figure 9-13: Testing printer configuration

Note   If your printer is printing garbage, you are given the option to stop the print job by YaST once the job has been received by the printer.

If anything is not correct with your test page, go back and try to change any settings that may affect the quality or the use of your printer.

11. If you are happy with your printer configuration, press OK to return to the printer overview screen that you were presented with when you started the printer configuration.

12. Press the Finish button to complete the configuration and save your changes to the system.

Setting Up a Scanner

YaST's scanner module automatically detects and sets up a scanner if it can; USB and SCSI scanners are supported, as well as Hewlett-Packard's all-in-one (scanner-printer-fax devices) USB devices and network scan stations. The ancient parallel port scanners are not supported and cannot be configured with this module. In most cases, if a USB or SCSI scanner is detected, YaST sets it up automatically. One or two USB scanners require a firmware file to be installed; if this is required, YaST warns you of the fact, but you may have to obtain this file from the installation media that came with the scanner or from the manufacturer's site. When the scanner is set up correctly, you can use it most easily by running the program kooka (KDE's scanning tool) or, if you prefer, xsane.

Note   The definitive source of information about using a scanner with Linux is www.sane-project.org. You may also find information about problems with specific scanners by searching for the word *scanner* on the SUSE portal's support database: http://portal.suse.com/PM/page/search.pm.

Boot Loader Configuration

We talked in Chapter 4 about configuring the boot loader of the system using the boot loader configuration files directly. Here we will quickly use YaST to install a new boot option into the GRUB boot loader for the installation of a new Linux kernel.

Note   We hope that as you move through this chapter you will see there is more than one way to do things in Linux — the easy, the interesting, and the downright hard way. We have concentrated on the easy and the interesting ways throughout the book and will continue to do so.

1. To bring up the Boot Loader Settings screen (see Figure 9-14), select System ⇨ Boot Loader Configuration.

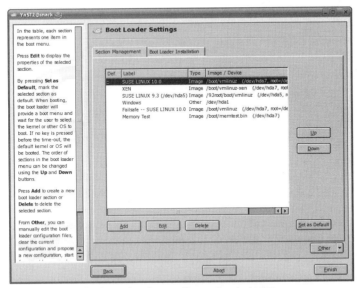

Figure 9-14: The boot loader configuration in YaST

2. To add a new boot option, select Add. This brings you to a configuration screen that enables you to create a new configuration, either by cloning an existing boot loader entry or by creating a standard Linux, Xen, or Chainloader configuration. A Chainloader configuration is what you need if you want to boot a Windows system (see Figure 9-15).

3. Now click the Next button to produce a new configuration.

4. As this is another Linux kernel being installed, change the kernel and initial ramdisk entries to reflect the newly installed kernel and initial ramdisk by selecting the `kernel` and `initrd` lines and changing the location of the kernel image and ramdisk (see Figures 9-16 and 9-17).

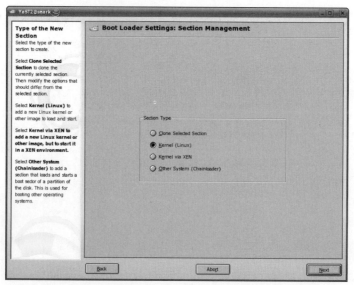

Figure 9-15: Boot loader settings: creating a new section

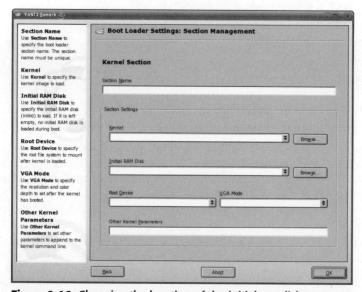

Figure 9-16: Changing the location of the initial ramdisk

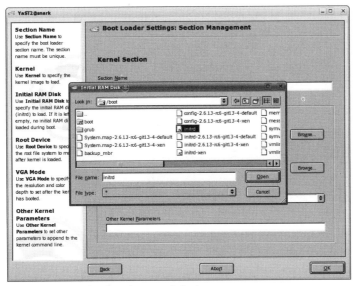

Figure 9-17: Selecting the new initrd

5. When you have finished configuring the location of the kernel and initial ramdisk, click OK to return to the boot loader profile list window.

6. If you are happy with the overall look of the profiles, press OK to return to the boot loader configuration window. You can see the entry we just created in the Available Sections part of the configuration list.

7. To save the configuration, press the Finish key. Your GRUB configuration will be saved and your entry will be available at next boot.

Setting Up SCPM

SUSE Configuration and Profile Manager (SCPM) is a profile manager for the SUSE system. Profiles control what runs on the system and the configuration of your system. For example, if you used a laptop and needed to use a DHCP client with a certain proxy configuration in your office, but a static IP address and no proxy at home, you could configure this with SCPM and switch profiles when needed.

We will configure this same environment as a quick introduction to what can be achieved with SCPM. It is an extremely powerful component of the SUSE system that can profile any system configuration you can think of for future switching.

1. To start SCPM, select System ⇨ Profile Manager.

   When you start SCPM for the first time, it is likely that the system process is not running (as is the default). You will need to start SCPM before you can continue with the addition and configuration of profiles (see Figure 9-18).

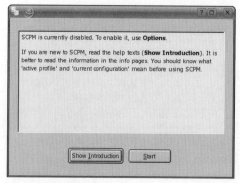

Figure 9-18: Starting SCPM

2. When SCPM starts, it creates a default profile (see Figure 9-19) based on your current system configuration. At the moment, the system has an IP address configured to use DHCP and a proxy setting (discussed earlier in the chapter). You will change the name of the profile to Work.

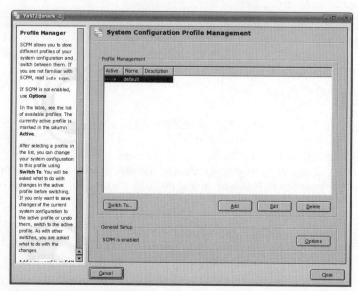

Figure 9-19: SCPM profiles

3. When your default profile has been created, you can edit its settings by selecting the default entry and clicking Edit. The screen in Figure 9-20 shows the default profile with its name changed to Work.

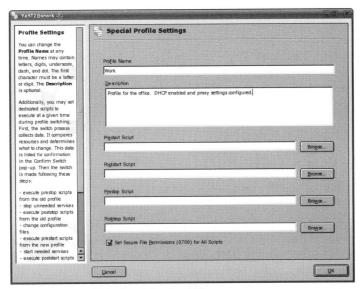

Figure 9-20: Editing the default profile

In this screen, you can set the new title and a description for the profile using the boxes provided. You can also add scripts that are executed upon entry and exit of the profile. It is beyond the scope of the book to go into it in detail, but you can make powerful scripts to customize aspects of the system — for example, copying a specific configuration file for a service you need to control (that is not controlled by SUSE) or running an application that checks for security settings.

4. When your Work profile has been created, you need to create one for Home. To do this, you can use YaST's modules to change to a static IP address and remove your proxy settings.

   We won't show you how to do this with YaST here, because we have discussed network configuration during the installation and discussed proxy configuration earlier in the chapter.

5. When you have changed your system to how you need it for another profile, you need to click the Add button to define a new profile. You will be prompted for how you want to add this profile (see Figure 9-21). Select The Current System Configuration. If you want to make this the active profile, then select Make the Added Profile Active, but for this example, because we spend more time at work than at home, we will leave this unselected.

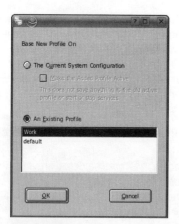

Figure 9-21: Adding a new system profile

6. When you have clicked OK, you are presented with the profile title and description screen you saw before to configure the display information, this time for your Home profile.

7. When you are happy with the title and description, click OK to save it. YaST then analyzes your current profile (as configured via YaST for network and proxy settings) and saves the profile.

8. YaST then returns you to the profile list screen where you can now switch between the profiles when needed.

9. Click the Close button to commit your changes to SCPM and return to YaST.

Tip

It is not always pertinent to load YaST to change your profile. To change your profile from the command line to the Home profile, enter scpm switch Home. SCPM analyzes your system for changes that need to take place and then makes the necessary changes for the new profile.

Runlevel Editor

Throughout the book, we have talked about enabling services at boot time. This is a very important concept when dealing with Unix systems. A mail server would be useless if the server process itself did not start up at boot time. You would have to manually start the mail server every time the system booted, which is inefficient and time-consuming. The Runlevel Editor can be used to turn on and off system services at system boot in different runlevels. To load the Runlevel Editor, start YaST and select System ➪ System Services (Runlevel).

The Runlevel Editor loads the current system configuration for the services and then displays what services are currently enabled. You have two options to edit the runlevel configuration, Simple and Expert mode:

✦ **Simple mode** — You can select the service and either enable or disable it. You do not have control over the specific runlevel it starts in because YaST enables the service in its default runlevels.

✦ **Expert mode** — Use Expert mode if you want to enable or disable a service in a specific runlevel.

In Figure 9-22, for example, in Expert mode, we have selected the Postfix service. At the bottom of the screen you can see a description of the service (although the Postfix service's description is rather nondescript). Below the service description, you can set the levels that this process is enabled in. We have selected runlevels 3 and 5 (networking and networking with X, respectively).

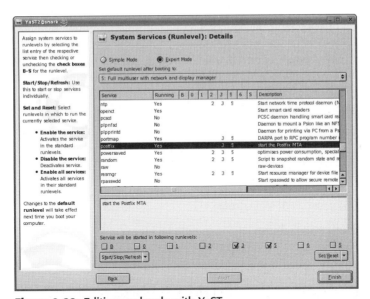

Figure 9-22: Editing runlevels with YaST

When you are happy with the runlevel editing, press the Finish button to continue.

Your runlevel configuration is now saved and will take effect when your system next boots up. You can always manually start up Postfix or any other system service with the rc script. For Postfix, you use rcpostfix.

Cross-Reference   Runlevels are discussed in more detail in Chapter 4.

Configuring DHCP

To load the configuration for both the DHCP server and the client, you need to edit different system settings. For the DHCP server, choose Network Services ➪ DHCP Server. For the DHCP client, you need to edit your network card configuration by selecting Network Devices ➪ Network Card.

We discuss DHCP client and server services in Chapters 1 and 20, so we will not go into detail here. Suffice it to say, you can edit these settings using YaST.

Users and Groups

As well as editing users and groups directly, as described in Chapter 2, you can use YaST to edit these files in a more user-friendly fashion.

Adding or Editing Users

To edit users, select Security and Users ➪ Edit and create users. You will be presented with a list of users currently in the system (see Figure 9-23).

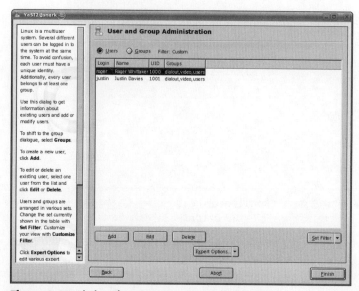

Figure 9-23: Listing the current users on the system

When the user list has loaded, you can either edit (select the user and press Edit) or create a new user. We will go ahead and create a new user, Roger Whittaker.

To create a new user:

   1. Click Add. You will be presented with a dialog box very similar to what you see when you install SUSE, with YaST asking you about the user (see Figure 9-24).

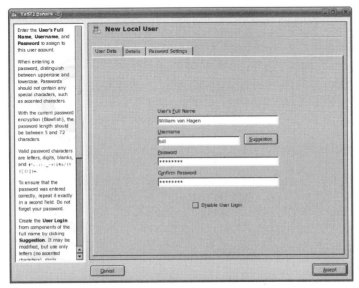

Figure 9-24: Creating a new user

   2. To create the user, click Create. If you want to set specific settings for the user, you can select either Password Settings or Details.

   a. You can change quite a few things about how the user's password is used in the system. Click Password Settings.

   In Figure 9-25, you can see that you can set the amount of days before the user is warned of a password expiry (where they need to change their password), the amount of times the user can log in to their account after their password expires (use -1 to allow them to always log in to their account once the password has expired), and the amount of days the same password can be valid, along with the minimum. You can also set the amount of time the account itself is active.

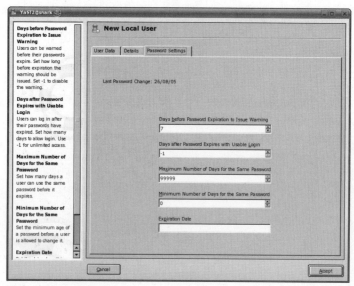

Figure 9-25: Editing password settings

For example, if you had a contractor on site for the next two weeks, you could set the expiry date to be two weeks in the future (in the format of YYYY-MM-DD).

To save the password settings, click Next.

b. To set specific account information for the user roger, click the Details button. You will be presented with a screen, shown in Figure 9-26, enabling you to change the User ID, home directory, the gecos field (a free-form field allowing you to enter any information about the user, such as their description and so forth), the default login shell, and also the user's default group, along with any other groups the user should be part of.

One of the most important parts of this section is the Additional Group Membership. If you have created other groups or are going to separate your users into specific groups, you can add the user to the group here. By default, normal users are associated with audio (to access the sound card), dialout (to access the modem), uucp (to access the terminal), and video (to access advanced features of the video card).

3. When you are happy with the settings for the user account, click Next. You are returned to the user information screen, where you can click Create to save the user to the system.

4. To return to YaST, click Finish.

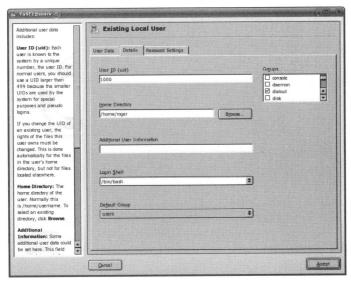

Figure 9-26: Changing account settings

Adding or Editing Groups

To create or edit groups in your system, select Security and Users ➪ Edit and create groups. Similar to the User section, you are presented with a list of groups currently on the system (see Figure 9-27). You can select a group from the list and click Edit to change settings for that group, or click Add to create a new group.

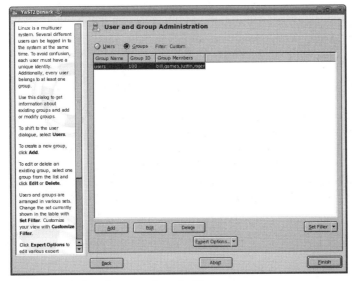

Figure 9-27: List of groups installed in your system

If you click Add to create a new group, you are presented with the screen in Figure 9-28. Here you can enter the group name, the group ID (it is safe to use the default), and also the option to use a password for the group.

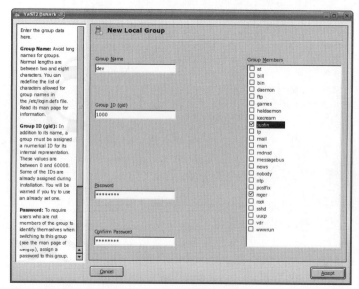

Figure 9-28: Adding a new group to the system

Note   Users are able to change their default group for a session by using the `newgrp` command. For example, if user `justin` wants to change his default group from `users` (the default) to `dev`, he can use the command `newgrp dev`. If a password is set for this group, he must enter it before he can change to this new group.

If you want to add any users to this group, you can select them from the right-hand pane. When you are happy with the new group, click Next. You are returned to the group list, where you will see your new group in the list. Click Finish to return to YaST.

Installing Additional Software with YaST

Unless you installed every available package when you installed your SUSE system, you'll eventually hear (or read about) some additional software package from the SUSE distribution CDs or DVD that you wish you'd installed. Chapter 12 explains how to install additional software packages from the command line, but if this software is on the SUSE distribution CDs or DVD, you'll have to figure out where to find it first. Luckily, SUSE's YaST tool makes it easy to both locate and install additional software from your SUSE distribution media.

YaST's Install and Remove Software module can be started from within YaST by selecting the Software icon in YaST's left pane and then selecting Software Management from the left pane or the Install and Remove Software icon in YaST's right pane. You can also start this module by typing:

```
# yast2 sw_single
```

If you start the module from within the KDE Control Center, YaST prompts you for the root password before allowing you to continue.

When the module starts (see Figure 9-29), it displays a dialog that makes it easy to search for packages by name, within the summary text that describes the package, within their short description, and so on.

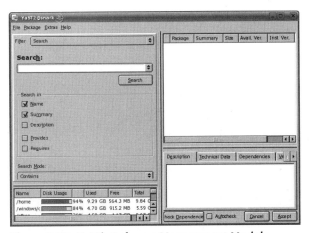

Figure 9-29: YaST's Software Management Module

As an example, suppose that you've read about emacs in this book and want to see what emacs-related packages are available on your SUSE distribution. To do this, enter **emacs** in the Search text box and click Search. The Install and Remove Software window redisplays, showing all packages with the string *emacs* in their Name or Summary. A check mark displays to the left of the names of all packages that are already installed, as shown in Figure 9-30.

To install a package that is not yet installed, click the check box next to its name in the package listing pane and then click Accept to proceed with the installation process. For example, to install the qemacs (Quick Emacs) package, a small, lightweight version of emacs, click the check box next to its name and then click Accept. YaST analyzes any dependencies required by the selected package, adds those to the list of packages to install, and proceeds to install the selected packages. If the media from which you installed SUSE is not in your CD or DVD drive, YaST prompts you for the appropriate disk, as shown in Figure 9-31.

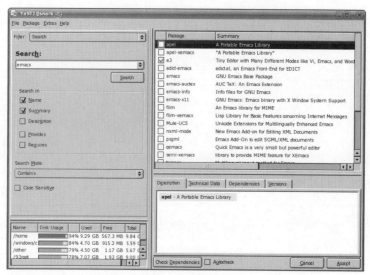

Figure 9-30: Installed packages matching emacs

Figure 9-31: Prompt for necessary media

After the selected package(s) have been installed, YaST runs SuSEconfig to ensure that any libraries installed along with the package are available to the system and prompts you as to whether you want to install additional packages. Click Install More to search for and install additional packages, or click Finish to close the Install and Remove Software dialog box.

YOU – The YaST Online Update

Software is one of those things that is never finished. In the open source world, we tend to be more honest about this fact than elsewhere; Linux and all the software running on it is in a constant state of change and improvement. At the same time, there are security issues. Again, the open source mentality makes for openness about the fact that these security issues exist and provides very rapid fixes.

For several years, SUSE has provided an online method of updating the system; this operates by collecting patch RPMs from a server and installing them through the YaST online update module. The beauty of patch RPMs is that they need to contain only the changed files from an RPM that has been updated, very significantly reducing the bandwidth involved in the update procedure.

YOU on SUSE Professional and on SLES

The online update on SUSE Linux Enterprise Server (SLES) and the other SUSE business products is the means by which the paid-for software maintenance system is applied to your server. As such, it requires authentication; your 14-digit maintenance key and password need to be put into the YaST Online Update (YOU) module for it to authenticate against the server in Germany. SLES 9 offers a YaST module to assist with setting up a local YOU server.

In the case of Professional, although the online updater comes with no guarantees, it is a free part of the system, there is a choice of installation servers offering the patch RPMs, and no registration is required to use it.

susewatcher

SUSE Linux Professional includes a system tray applet called susewatcher. This displays an icon that indicates whether an update is required. It does this by checking the state of the system against a remote server. If Automatically check for updates is selected in the susewatcher main screen (see Figure 9-32), then susewatcher will regularly check whether any updates to the currently installed set of software are available. If updates are available, it changes the appearance of its icon in the system tray:

✦ A red icon with an exclamation mark indicates that security updates are required.

✦ A smiling geeko icon indicates that all available updates have been made.

✦ If there is a green icon with a white page symbol overlaid on it, all available updates have been applied, but you have not yet read the update messages by clicking the susewatcher Show Messages button.

Figure 9-32: The susewatcher main screen

The YaST Online Update Module

YaST's online update module can be started from within YaST by selecting the Software icon in YaST's left pane and then selecting the Online update icon in YaST's right pane. YOU (Yast Online Update) can also be started either from the susewatcher Start online update button (which of course requires you to type a root password) or by typing:

```
# yast2 online_update
```

When the module starts (see Figure 9-33), it first gets a list of possible online update servers. You may want to change the server from the default that is offered if, for example, you find that you get slow updates from that server. YaST then examines the system against the patches available, and in the main screen it informs you of the patches that you may want to install. An indication of priority is given: Security patches are given prominence (see Figure 9-34).

When you have agreed to install the patches, the installation proceeds almost exactly like a YaST software installation. At the end, YaST runs SuSEconfig and the update is complete.

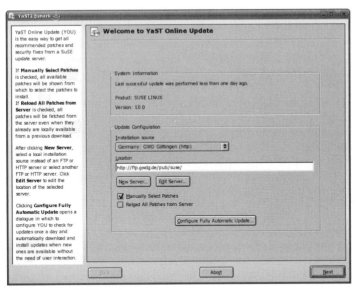

Figure 9-33: YOU main screen

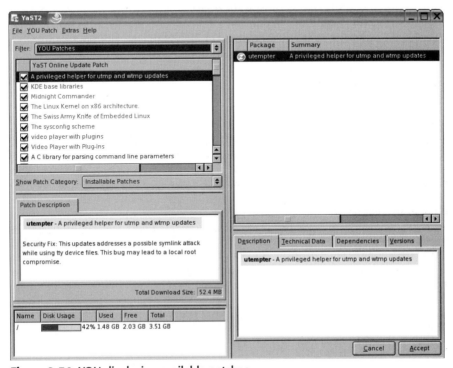

Figure 9-34: YOU displaying available patches

YOU Dangers

It is important to realize that if for some reason you have installed third-party versions of packages having the same name as SUSE packages, a careless YOU update could overwrite them.

When running a mission-critical system, although you should always be aware of security issues and be ready to apply relevant security patches to any publicly available machine as a matter of priority, you should also be extremely careful not to apply all patches without serious thought. Some kernel patches in particular can totally break the functionality of third-party commercial software, which may at best mean that you need to reconfigure the software and at worst could lead to a situation where you have real difficulty in getting back to a working system.

The online_update command

The command online_update can be used for a noninteractive update. However, the previous comments about the dangers of careless updating apply even more to this procedure because it does not allow you to select and deselect patches. Running the command with the -h option (online_update -h) will give a list of options.

fou4s

Fast Online Updater for SUSE (fou4s) from http://fou4s.gaugusch.at/ is another command-line alternative to YOU. It has similar functionality, but claims additional speed and can be run either interactively or automatically from a script or cron job.

The YaST Installation Server Module

An *installation server* is a machine that offers the installation set across the network. If you are likely to want to install a large number of machines, this gives you a way of reducing the amount of work involved in installing systems; after the new system has been booted, it can access the installation set across the network, and the bulk of the installation can be done unattended. If you set up autoinstallation (see the next section) and network booting, then the installations can in fact be totally automatic.

There are two features that were introduced by SUSE at the time of the release of SLES 9 that make these processes easier than they were before. In the past, it was necessary to create and populate the directories on the installation server manually with materials from the installation CDs. It was also necessary to manually set up NFS, FTP, or HTTP serving for those directories. When performing an installation across the network, it was also necessary to select the installation source manually. The two features that make the whole process easier are:

✦ The YaST installation server module

✦ The use of SLP (Service Location Protocol)

Service Location Protocol allows services to advertise themselves across the network and be discovered by clients. In the case of the installation server, this means that the client machine that is being installed can discover any installation server on the network without the need to type in an IP number or directory designation. All that is required is that when you start the installation on the client, you choose SLP as the source (rather than the other alternatives such as CD, NFS, local disk, and so on). The client will then discover the installation server and access the installation source through whatever protocol it is being offered, without further manual intervention.

Setting Up an Installation Server

The package name of YaST module that simplifies the process of setting up an installation server is `yast2-instserver`. This is not installed by default, so the first thing you will need to do if you want to use it is to install it in the usual way.

Once installed, the module can be started from the Misc section of YaST, or using the command

```
yast2 instserver
```

You will see the screen in Figure 9-35.

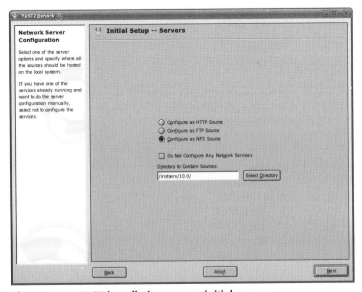

Figure 9-35: YaST installation server: initial screen

You are offered three choices for how you want to offer the installation source across the network: you can make it available by HTTP, FTP, or NFS. In the module itself these are mutually exclusive choices, but there is no reason why you could not offer the sources by more than one of these protocols. However, there would be some extra manual setup required to do so.

The choice of which protocol to use depends on your circumstances. If the installation server is not on the same network as the clients that are to be installed, then HTTP or FTP (which can be accessed through a proxy) are the likely choice. If the installation server is on the same network and directly accessible by the clients, then NFS is probably the right answer.

In Figure 9-35, we have chosen NFS, and we have selected a location where the installation set is going to be created (/instserv/10.0/).

You are then asked for a name for the installation source (a server may be advertising more than one source, so it is necessary for each to have an individual name — this will also be the name given to the directory in which the sources are placed).

You can either use the installation CDs or DVD to create the installation source, or, if you have ISO images available, YaST can create it from those. Service Packs can also be integrated into the installation source if they exist.

The same screen offers the option Announce as Installation Server with SLP. When you select this option, the installation server will use SLP to announce itself on the network, making the installation process simpler on the clients as described previously.

You will then be prompted for the installation media (CDs or DVDs, or if you opted to use ISO images, you will be prompted for the path to find those images on the hard disk). You will be prompted to change the media until the installation source has been completed. The necessary NFS, FTP, or HTTP server will be set up or modified automatically for you, and will be started automatically.

When the process is complete, if you go to a Konqueror window on the local machine or elsewhere on the network and type the location slp:/, you will see a window similar to the one in Figure 9-36.

This window provides a description of the SLP source being offered. It is, of course, possible that you might have more than one SUSE installation source advertising itself by SLP on the network.

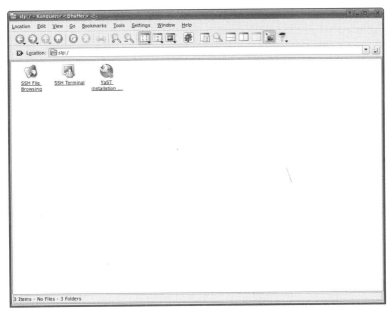

Figure 9-36: Konqueror displaying SLP information

If you click on the YaST Installation source icon, you will see a window similar to the one in Figure 9-37.

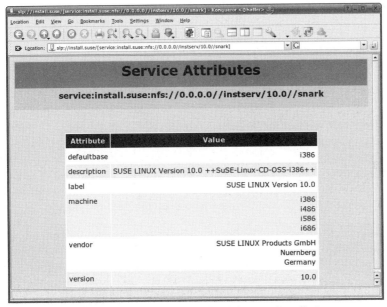

Figure 9-37: Konqueror showing details of the SLP installation source

Installing from the Installation Server

Assuming that you have set up an installation server as described previously and it is available on the network, you can install a new client from it very easily. Ideally there should be a DHCP server on the network (see Chapter 20). Then when the client boots, it will get an address and will be able to see the installation source directly without further intervention.

If the new machine is booted from the standard SUSE installation media, the first screen you see will offer a set of choices (by pressing F3) for the source to use. These include NFS, FTP, HTTP, local directory, and so on. If you set up the installation source with SLP, and if a DHCP server exists on the network, then everything is easy. In the first screen, select SLP, choose Installation, and as soon as the machine gets an IP address, it will also find any SUSE installation servers that are available on the network by SLP. You will then be asked the select the one you want and the rest of the installation will be done from the installation server.

Autoinstallation — AutoYaST

A common scenario is the need to install the operating system on a number of machines in an identical way or perhaps in a predefined way. Where the hardware is exactly identical, it can sometimes be simplest to use the "ghosting" approach: copying an image of one hard disk to all the others. However, it may well be that there are significant differences between the machines, but you want to install a known set of packages on each, possibly with some other predefined configuration. In such a case, automatic installation may well be the best approach.

Another way of looking at this is the well-known dictum that if you find yourself repeating a task more than a few times, the best thing to do is to find a way of automating the task. That is exactly what SUSE has done by providing the ability to do automated installations with YaST: the AutoYaST method.

Principles

Provided you have a means of booting a machine that you are trying to install, and if at the same time you can tell it where to find the installation set, the rest of the installation can be done across the network. If at the same time you can tell the installer the answer to each and every question in the interactive installation, the installation would be truly unattended and automated.

AutoYaST does exactly this: It is a highly configurable method of implementing automated, unattended network installations. The details of the installation required for each machine are held in an XML file on the installation server. The

XML file allows for a very high degree of detailed control over the installation of the particular machine: Different machines can have different specific XML control files. Essentially, the XML file contains an answer to every question that the installer asks the user in an interactive installation.

Mode of Operation

The machine that is being installed has to be booted somehow. The possibilities are to boot it from a floppy disk, from a bootable CD-ROM, or by PXE network booting.

✦ SUSE provides a GRUB boot floppy for starting an installation that is capable of network booting in conjunction with a Trivial FTP (TFTP) or Dynamic Host Configuration Protocol (DHCP) server.

✦ Alternatively, the system can be booted from an installation CD, but can be given a boot parameter such as `install=nfs://192.168.1.1/suse-install/`. If a DHCP server is available, the machine obtains an IP address and then finds the installation files from the information given at boot time. This information can also be placed in an info file held on a floppy disk to be read at the start of the installation.

✦ The most elegant method, if it is available, is PXE booting (supported by most modern hardware). In this case, a little more is needed on the installation server side: You need to run a DHCP server and a TFTP server together with the special files (from the package `pxe`) required to start the boot process. The DHCP server offers an IP address based on the client's hardware address; the TFTP server then gives a file based on the IP address, which references the XML installation control file on the server.

In any of these cases, when the installer has booted and obtained the relevant XML file, the XML file controls the rest of the installation just as if a human were interacting with the installer.

The installation server can offer the installation files by HTTP, NFS, or FTP. In the case of SUSE Professional, it is sufficient that the contents of the installation CDs or DVD (or a mirror of the installation set on the FTP site) be available by one of these methods.

The YaST Autoinstallation Module

The purpose of this module is to help you create the AutoYaST XML control file. You can start the module with:

```
# yast2 autoyast
```

or by selecting the icon in the YaST Misc screen (the one with the wonderful pineapple icon). When you start the module you will see a screen like Figure 9-38.

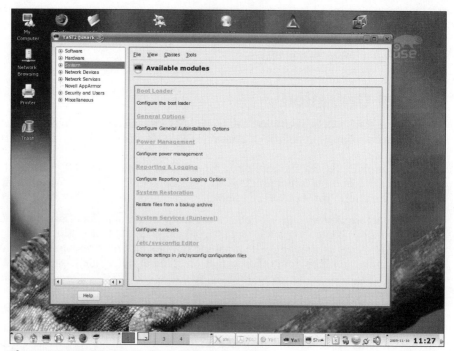

Figure 9-38: YaST's AutoYaST module main screen

The module enables you to create a configuration by going through any or all of the possible steps that would be taken during a real installation, using an interface almost identical to YaST during installation.

Alternatively, you can create a configuration based on the current machine, which you can use as a starting point or template for your XML files (see Figure 9-39). Here you can choose which aspects of the current machine's configuration you want to copy to the reference profile. You can then base your final configuration on this by making suitable changes. You can at any stage view the XML file itself or go through the elements of an interactive installation and modify the file (see Figure 9-40).

When you have a basic XML file, you may want to refine it by editing it by hand (see Figure 9-41); this can be done with the emacs editor with the psgmls package installed. This makes emacs a true XML editor, which can find and parse the XML DTD and help you in many ways to avoid creating an invalid file.

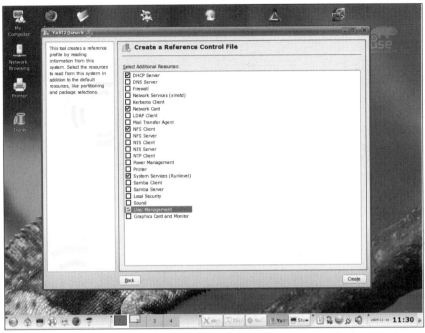

Figure 9-39: Creating a reference file based on the current machine

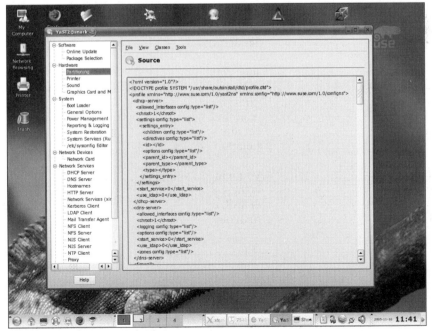

Figure 9-40: Viewing the XML source

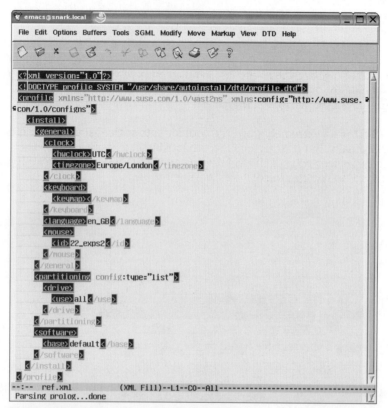

Figure 9-41: Editing the control file with emacs

Using Pre-Install, chroot, and Post-Install scripts

AutoYaST enables you to include scripts in the XML file (as CDATA sections). The three phases of the installation at which the scripts can be run are: before the installation proper begins (pre-scripts); while the installation system is in memory, but before the first reboot (chroot scripts); and after the first reboot of the system (post-scripts). Using such scripts, which are usually shell scripts, means that essentially anything is possible. For example, during the main part of the installation, the hard disk partition to which the packages are being written is mounted in the installation system on /mnt, so during this phase you can use a script to copy additional packages or files across the network from the installation server and into /mnt/tmp. After the first boot, this directory will be /tmp. A post-script can be used to install, copy, or manipulate the files in any way that might be required.

By such methods, any kind of configuration that is not allowed for in YaST can be done automatically as part of the autoinstallation server, and the only limit on this process is your own ingenuity.

Further Information

The author of AutoYaST is Anas Nashif of SUSE; the main documentation for it is located at www.suse.com/~nashif/autoinstall/. There is an active mailing list at suse-autoinstall. To subscribe to the list, send an empty mail to suse-autoinstall-subscribe@suse.com, or use the form at www.suse.com/en/private/support/online_help/mailinglists/.

SUSE's AutoYaST is an extremely powerful tool for automatic installation and is difficult conceptually. But it is certainly worth looking at and can be very useful in various Enterprise scenarios, including the easy deployment of desktop systems and the installation of nodes in clusters, to name but two.

✦   ✦   ✦

Using the Command Line in SUSE Linux

Part III covers the power of the Linux command line in more detail, with chapters covering text editing and tools for manipulating text files, as well as package maintenance and advanced networking.

Text Manipulation

In This Chapter

Reading and extracting lines from files

Working with text file fields

Searching for text within files

Formatting text files for printing

This chapter introduces some of the text manipulation tools available on Linux. They provide a remarkably powerful way of getting information out of text files, or altering those files in useful ways.

Typically, you might have a file containing information in the form of text items that are laid out with a certain structure, but you want to view only certain parts of that structure, or you want to transform the information into some other format.

For example, you might want to take a log file from some application and extract certain interesting parts of it while ignoring the rest. Or you might want to extract or summarize the important information from the file and format it in some other way. A great many tasks are of this general kind, and while the more difficult tasks may require complex scripting, a very useful set of tools is available for text processing tasks, which can save you the trouble of writing a script.

These tools can often be combined together to make a single command line perform a relatively complicated text manipulation. Indeed, they have been designed with that in mind; each tool does a particular job well, in a clearly understood way, and the output from one tool can form the input to another so that a well-designed combination can perform a clever task.

In this chapter we describe some of these tools and offer examples of how they work in simple cases. Space does not allow us to list all of the options that are available for each command, and you can find these from the man and info pages. Here we want to give you a taste of the power of this set of tools so that you will want to play with it and find out more.

Reading Lines from Files

Most of the commands introduced in this section are part of the coreutils package and are the GNU versions of commands that have long been part of the standard Unix toolkit.

cat

The cat command is so called because (in the words of its man page) it "con*cate*-nates files and prints them to standard output." So the command:

```
cat /etc/passwd
```

simply prints the content of the file /etc/passwd to the screen.

If you cat a number of files, you will see them printed to the screen in the order they are named:

```
cat file1 file2 file3
```

So far, this is not very useful, but you can now redirect the output to a new file:

```
cat file1 file2 file3 > bigfile
```

You now have a combined file bigfile containing the contents of the three original files.

Numbering Lines in a File

The cat command has the sometimes-useful capability of being able to number the lines in a file. This is done with the -n option. So if you have a file fruits:

```
user@bible:~> cat fruits
apple
banana
cherry

user@bible:~> cat -n fruits
     1  apple
     2  banana
     3  cherry
```

The -b option numbers only non-blank lines. It quite often happens that for some reason you have a file that contains hundreds of blank lines as well as some infor-mation you actually want: You could simply use cat -b and direct the output to a new file.

Replacing Blank Lines and Tabs

Another useful option is -s, which replaces any number of blank lines with a single blank line (removing unwanted white space from the file, while keeping the structure).

So, for example:

```
user@bible:~> cat gapfruits
apple



orange
peach


pear

user@bible:~> cat -s gapfruits
apple

orange
peach

pear
```

The -T replaces tabs with visible characters (↑):

```
user@bible:~> cat morefruits
kiwi    mango
pear    quince

user@bible:~> cat -T morefruits
kiwi^Imango
pear    quince
```

There was a tab on the first line and spaces on the second. Sometimes the distinction between tabs and spaces really matters: in the case of makefiles and tab-separated files, for instance. The -T option enables you to tell the difference easily.

Making Sense of Binary Files

If you use cat on a binary file that contains nonprintable characters (for example, an executable file or a file created by an application such as Microsoft Word), you will typically see a lot of "garbage" on the screen, and in some cases your terminal will be messed up so that the characters before the prompt display incorrectly. The -v option to cat avoids the garbage by displaying nonprinting characters more intelligibly. So cat -v wordfile.doc is a better way of peeping inside such a file than plain cat. See also the sections in this chapter on the commands strings and anti-word.

Tip   If your terminal settings get messed up so that your prompt is made up of weird characters, you can usually remedy the situation by typing the command `reset`. As you type it, you may see the wrong characters appearing on the screen, but as soon as you press Return, the terminal should be back to normal. This applies whether you are using a text console, an `xterm`, or a KDE `konsole` window.

tac

The `tac` command does almost the same as `cat` but presents the lines of the file in reverse order:

```
user@bible:~> cat fruits
apple
banana
cherry

user@bible:~> tac fruits
cherry
banana
apple
```

Note that `tac` does not offer all the same options as `cat`.

zcat

The `zcat` command uncompresses a gzipped file and then does the same as `cat`. For example, the `INDEX.gz` file on the SUSE installation disk(s) is a gzipped text file containing an index of packages on the disks. `zcat INDEX.gz` will view its contents.

head

The `head` command outputs part of a file starting at the top. By default it outputs the first ten lines, but with the option `-n` followed by a number it can output any number of lines. So, for example, `head -n5 file1` outputs the first five lines of `file1`.

tail

The `tail` command outputs part of a file including its end. Again, by default it outputs the last ten lines, but if used with a numerical option it can output any number of lines in the same way as described previously for the `head` command.

A very useful option is `-f` (for *follow*), which outputs the appended data as the file grows. This allows you to watch a log file, for example, while you make a change somewhere else:

```
# tail -f /var/log/messages
```

Combining head and tail clearly gives you an easy way of getting certain particular lines from within a file:

```
user@bible:~> cat file1
line  1
line  2
line  3
line  4
line  5
line  6

user@bible:~> head -n5 file1| tail -n2
line  4
line  5
```

So you've extracted the last two of the first five lines of the file.

expand

The expand command converts tabs in the file to spaces. Let's use the same example we used in the section "Replacing Blank Lines and Tabs":

```
user@bible:~> cat morefruits
kiwi      mango
pear      quince

user@bible:~> cat -T morefruits
kiwi^Imango
pear      quince

cat morefruits | expand | cat -T
kiwi      mango
pear      quince
```

By piping the contents of the file through the expand command, you have converted the tabs to spaces. The output of cat -T shows that the tabs have gone away. This is a convenient way of tidying up a file that contains white space that is a random mixture of tabs and spaces.

nl

The nl command outputs the file with line numbers added, as in cat -n. But nl has various options regarding the format of the line numbers and how they are applied. For example:

```
user@bible:/media/cdrom/ > zcat INDEX.gz |nl -n rz | head -n1000| tail -n3
000998   ./CD1/suse/i586/ethtool-1.8-123.i586.rpm
000999   ./CD1/suse/i586/evlog-1.6.0-31.i586.rpm
001000   ./CD1/suse/i586/evlog-devel-1.6.0-31.i586.rpm
```

In this example, you get the last 3 of the first 1,000 lines of the uncompressed INDEX.gz file (the index file from the SUSE installation media), numbered with the leading zeros option to nl. The -n option enables you to specify a numbering format. Here we have chosen rz for the numbering format, which indicates *right justified with leading zeros*.

uniq

The uniq command outputs a file with adjacent identical lines removed. It does not remove non-adjacent duplicate lines. For example:

```
user@bible:~> cat fish
angelfish
bream
bream
cod
dogfish
cod

user@bible:~> uniq fish
angelfish
bream
cod
dogfish
cod
```

The uniq command can skip a certain number of fields or characters before starting its check for uniqueness. For example:

```
user@bible:~> cat numberedfish
1       angelfish
2       bream
3       bream
4       cod
5       dogfish
6       cod

user@bible:~> uniq -f1 numberedfish
1       angelfish
2       bream
4       cod
5       dogfish
6       cod
```

The -f1 option here tells the uniq command to skip the first field in the file when deciding whether the lines match. Because lines 2 and 3 were identical, line 3 has been dropped.

sort

The sort command does what it says — it sorts the lines of a file. An alphabetical sort is the default, as you can see in the second code block that follows. In the third code block, you can see that the -r option has made the alphabetical sort into a reverse sort, sorting the files from *z* to *a*:

```
user@bible:~> cat animals
cobra
aardvark
zebra
duck
elephant

user@bible:~> sort animals
aardvark
cobra
duck
elephant
zebra

user@bible:~> sort -r animals
zebra
elephant
duck
cobra
aardvark
```

There are many options: the most important are -n (sort numerically) and -u (for *unique*: skip duplicate lines).

Extracting Lines from Files

In this section, we look at the slightly more difficult challenges of extracting exactly the lines or parts of lines that you want from a text file, based on certain criteria.

grep

The grep command is the *global regular expression printer*. What that means is that it cannot just search for a particular string in a file and output the lines where that string occurs, but can search for text that follows a particular pattern and output the matching lines. For example, the pattern could be a single capital letter followed by two or more digits, a British postcode, a valid U.S. Social Security number, a line beginning with a number of spaces followed by a lowercase letter, or virtually anything that you can describe in similar terms.

In the simplest case, you can use `grep` to output the lines of a file that contain a certain particular string:

```
user@bible:~> cat file2
albatross
bat
bit
Batman
bathroom
debit
ding
doubt
   dingbat

user@bible:~> grep bat file2
albatross
bat
bathroom
   dingbat
```

The lines containing the exact string `bat` have been selected. Note that you don't see `Batman` in the output because by default `grep` is case-sensitive. To search without case sensitivity, you use `grep -i`:

```
user@bible:~> grep -i bat file2
albatross
bat
Batman
bathroom
   dingbat
```

grep Options

In regular expression notation, a dot represents a single character, so an expression such as b.t represents a letter *b* followed by any other character, followed by a letter *t*. The command that follows searches for any lines containing such a sequence:

```
user@bible:~> grep b.t file2
albatross
bat
bit
bathroom
debit
   dingbat
```

To search for lines beginning with the letter d:

```
user@bible:~> grep ^d file2
debit
ding
doubt
```

Here, the symbol ^ represents the start of a line. Similarly, the symbol $ represents the end of the line, so bat$ searches for the string bat at the end of a line:

```
user@bible:~> grep bat$ file2
bat
    dingbat
```

To search for lines containing a letter d followed by any number of characters followed by a letter t, use the following:

```
user@bible:~> grep d.*t file2
debit
doubt
    dingbat
```

The * symbol represents zero or more repetitions of the previous character.

And these examples just scratch the surface of what can be done.

grep -v means output lines not containing the expression. For example, here you find the lines that do not contain the string bat and do not start with the letter d:

```
user@bible:~> grep -v bat file2| grep -v ^d
bit
Batman
```

The following is a more practical example:

```
# grep 09\/Jun /var/log/2/access.log| grep -v -i ooglebot
```

This (probably) lists all entries in the Apache log file dated 9 June that do not refer to accesses from the Google search engine robot. Of course, this is slightly naive; you are not specifying in which field of the log file the string ooglebot is appearing.

Extended Regular Expressions and grep

Looking for relevant lines in a log file is the kind of use that you find yourself employing grep for the most. It's also in this situation that you are likely to build up long command lines of the form grep |grep |grep -v | . . . .

Take, for example, a grep involving United Kingdom (UK) postcodes. UK postcodes look something like these: OX5 2AZ, N1 5JJ, and AL13 4RG. To search (again naively) for strings of this type in a file, you might use the following:

```
# grep -E '[a-zA-Z]{1,2}[0-9] *[0-9]{1,2}[a-zA-Z]{1,2}' file
```

grep -E means that you are using extended regular expressions. Here you are looking for one or two letters followed by a digit, any number of spaces, one or two digits, and one or two letters.

U.S. Social Security numbers look something like this: 012-34-5678. So (again naively because there are rules about which numbers in this format are valid ones) a command like this could be used to match them:

```
# grep -E '[0-9]{3}-[0-9]{2}-[0-9]{4}' file
```

It is beyond the scope of this book to explore regular expression syntax in any detail. Indeed, entire books have been written on the subject. But it should be clear that grep (particularly in combination with the other tools mentioned in this chapter) can be a very powerful tool.

Note   There is good but somewhat terse documentation for using regular expressions with grep in the regular expressions section of the grep info page; type **info grep**. There are a number of tutorials on the web including one on IBM's Developer Works sites at www-106.ibm.com/developerworks/linux/edu/l-dw-linuxregexp-i.html.

zgrep

The zgrep command is to grep as zcat is to cat: in other words, it does the job of grep on gzipped files. Here is a genuinely useful example:

```
user@bible:/media/cdrom/ > zgrep kernel-source INDEX.gz
./CD1/suse/i586/kernel-source-2.6.4-52.i586.rpm
./CD2/suse/src/kernel-source-2.6.4-52.src.rpm
```

The full listing of every SUSE version is contained in a gzipped text file INDEX.gz on the distribution media. Here we have used zgrep to find a particular package.

grepmail

The grepmail command is a grep-like tool that looks for a string or regular expression in a Unix-style mailbox and outputs the entire mail or mails that contain the pattern. If you redirect the output to a new file, that file will be a mailbox consisting of exactly the mails you were looking for, which you can open in your mail client.

Here is a simple example:

```
user@bible:/home/user/Mail > grepmail Linuxbier inbox
From person@somedomain.com Tue Aug 10 09:14:34 2004
Return-path: <person@somedomain.com>
Envelope-to: person@somedomain.com
Delivery-date: Tue, 10 Aug 2004 09:14:34 +0100
Received: from person by somedomain.com with local (Exim 3.35 #1 (Debian))
    id 1BuRmE-0007tX-00
```

```
    for <person@somedomain.com>; Tue, 10 Aug 2004 09:14:34 +0100
Date: Tue, 10 Aug 2004 09:14:34 +0100
To: person@somedomain.com
Subject: Mail with special word included
Message-ID: <20040810081434.GA30335@somedomain.com>
Mime-Version: 1.0
Content-Type: text/plain; charset=us-ascii
Content-Disposition: inline
User-Agent: Mutt/1.3.28i
From: Roger Whittaker <person@somedomain.com>
Status: RO
Content-Length: 106
Lines: 5

This mail includes the word "Linuxbierwanderung".
It also contains some other words.


--
Roger Whittaker
```

You see the entire mail (or mails) with full headers from the inbox file that matches the expression given. The grepmail command has options that also enable you to add date and size specifications to the search.

sgrep

The sgrep command is *structured grep* and enables you to extract sections from structured files (rather as grepmail does, but allowing for much more general types of files). It enables you to extract particular sections from, for example, XML or HTML files (based on the content and the markup surrounding them) or from program source files, mailboxes, or any file with a known and defined structure. The reason for mentioning it here is to alert you to its existence; it may be by far the quickest way to extract information from files with a known structure and save you from having to write complex scripts.

Here is a very simple example:

```
user@bible:~ > cat index.html
<html>
<head>
<title>Web Page Title</title>
</head>
<body>
...

user@bible:~ > sgrep '"<title>"__"</title>"' index.html
Web Page Title
```

Here you are searching for text enclosed by the opening and closing HTML title tags, and the command outputs the relevant string.

split

The split command does what it says: It splits a file into parts. By default it splits the file into pieces, each of which has 1,000 lines with names xaa, xab, xac, and so on. The split command can also be used to split up a binary file into equal sized pieces; this can be useful in those cases where the only way to get a file off a machine is to copy it to a floppy disk, and the file is too big. To reassemble the file, use cat. Consider the following examples:

```
user@bible:~ > split -l 100000 ARCHIVES
```

This first example splits the file ARCHIVES into pieces with 100,000 lines each, with names xaa, xab, xac, and so on.

```
user@bible:~ > split -b 1024k kernel-source-2.6.4-52.i586.rpm
```

This second example splits the file kernel-source-2.6.4-52.i586.rpm into pieces 1MB in size with names xaa, xab, xac, and so on. Assuming that these files have all been copied into a directory elsewhere, to reassemble the original file, you simply use the following command:

```
cat x* > kernel-source-2.6.4-52.i586.rpm
```

Because the shell interprets the x * as a list of all matching files in alphabetical order, the files will be concatenated in the right order and the result will be identical to the original.

csplit

The csplit command enables you to split the file wherever a pattern is found in a line:

```
user@bible:~ > cat birds
albatross
blackbird
chaffinch
duck
eagle
fieldfare

user@bible:~ > csplit birds /finch/
20
31

user@bible:~ > ls -l
```

```
-rw-r--r--  1 user users 51 2004-06-10 10:47 birds
-rw-r--r--  1 user users 20 2004-06-10 12:20 xx00
-rw-r--r--  1 user users 31 2004-06-10 12:20 xx01

user@bible:~ > cat xx00
albatross
blackbird

user@bible:~ > cat xx01
chaffinch
duck
eagle
fieldfare
```

In this example, you have split the file according to the pattern finch. This was found in the line containing chaffinch, so that line became the first line of the second file when the file was split.

The pattern on which we split the file could be a regular expression. One obvious use for this is to break up a structured file that has a standard separator for sections. In this example, you will also use {*} to indicate a split on the same pattern as many times as possible:

```
user@bible:~ > cat file
line 1
line 2
==
line 3
line 4
line 5
==
line 6

user@bible:~ > csplit file /==/ {*}
14
24
10

user@bible:~ > ls
file  xx00  xx01  xx02

user@bible:~ > cat xx00
line 1
line 2

user@bible:~ > cat xx01
==
line 3
line 4
line 5

user@bible:~ > cat xx02
```

```
= =
line 6
```

Note that every time the string = = was encountered, a new file was started.

Working with Fields from Text Files

The commands discussed in this section enable you to work with text files in which each line is regarded as being made up of a number of fields separated by white space or by a particular *delimiter* character.

cut

If you have a file that consists of lines of text that are split into fields by white space or a delimiter character, cut can get a particular field or fields from every line of the file. For example, in /etc/passwd the file is delimited by the colon character (:). The cut option -f tells it which field or fields you are selecting, and the -d option tells it what the delimiter character is. The file /etc/passwd is made up of lines like this:

```
user:x:1001:100:Guest User:/home/user:/bin/bash
```

To get just the real name (the fifth) and the shell (the seventh) fields from the file, you could do this:

```
user@bible:~ > cut -d: -f5,7 /etc/passwd
```

This would produce many lines of output like this:

```
Guest User:/bin/bash
```

You can also select particular characters from each line, using the -c option:

```
user@bible:~ > cat file
first
second
third
fourth

user@bible:~ > cut -c2-4 file
irs
eco
hir
our
```

paste

The `paste` command takes corresponding lines from a set of files and puts them together into lines in its output. These examples should be enough to give you a general idea:

```
user@bible:~ > cat file1
1
2
3

user@bible:~ > cat file2
A
B
C

user@bible:~ > cat file3
X
Y
Z

paste file1 file2 file3
1    A    X
2    B    Y
3    C    Z
```

In this first example, you have put together corresponding lines from the three files in the order given, with white space between them.

```
paste -d: file1 file2 file3
1:A:X
2:B:Y
3:C:Z
```

In this next example, by specifying -d: you have forced the delimiter in the output to be the colon, rather than the default spaces.

join

The `join` command takes two files with lines split into fields, and where a particular field is identical, it takes the other fields from both files and combines them. What follows is a simple example. (There are, of course, options to control which field is regarded as the key.)

```
user@bible:~ > cat file1
001 beef
002 beer
003 pies
```

```
user@bible:~ > cat file2
001 water
002 wine
003 apples

user@bible:~ > join file1 file2
001 beef water
002 beer wine
003 pies apples
```

awk

awk is something rather bigger than the tools we have been discussing up to now; it is an entire language. awk is an interpreted scripting language; in other words, programs written in awk do not need to be compiled before they are run. We shall present a few simple uses of awk just as a command line here. You will see it used (also usually as a simple single line command) quite often in system shell scripts, and it is certainly useful to know about its existence. But if you want to do the kinds of things that awk does well (selecting and replacing text in text files according to rules that you program), you should consider whether the task could be done more simply and easily by another and more powerful scripting language (such as Python or Perl). On the other hand, awk is a much smaller program and is always available:

```
user@bible:~ > cat foods
boiled carrots
fried potatoes
grilled onions
grated carrot

user@bible:~ > awk /carrot/ foods
boiled carrots
grated carrot
```

Here awk has simply selected the lines that match carrot:

```
user@bible:~ > awk `{print $1}' foods
boiled
fried
grilled
grated
```

In this example, awk has printed the first field of each line, as defined by `{print $1}'. Using $2 here gives us the second field, while $0 represents the whole line.

You can also define the separator to be something else. In the example that follows, the option -F\: specifies that the field separator is a colon, allowing you to select a particular field (the fifth, which is the user's real name) from /etc/passwd, which is a colon-separated file.

```
user@bible:~ > awk -F\: '{print $5}' /etc/passwd
root
bin
[...]
Guest User
```

awk has various useful built-in functions. For example:

```
user@bible:~ > cat morefoods
boiled carrots and fried bacon
fried potatoes and grilled sausages and mushrooms
grilled onions
grated carrot

user@bible:~ > awk 'NF > 2' morefoods
boiled carrots and fried bacon
fried potatoes and grilled sausages and mushrooms
```

NF represents the number of fields; in this example, by using 'NF > 2' you have selected the lines with more than two fields. This could be useful, for example, if you are trying to solve a problem of importing structured data into an application where the import fails because of some lines having the wrong number of fields:

```
user@bible:~ > awk 'NF > 2 {print $4}' morefoods
fried
grilled
```

So in the preceding example, you have printed the fourth field of each line, which has more than two fields.

```
user@bible:~ > awk '{ print NF ":" $0 }' morefoods
5:boiled carrots and fried bacon
7:fried potatoes and grilled sausages and mushrooms
2:grilled onions
2:grated carrot
```

Now in this example, you have printed the number of fields followed by a colon and the whole line (which is represented by $ 0).

An awk script can be run from the command line with a command such as awk -f scriptname file. For example, save the following as script.awk:

```
{print $1 ":" $2 ":" NF
}
END{print NR}
```

Then do this:

```
user@bible:~ > awk -f script.awk morefoods
boiled:carrots:5
fried:potatoes:7
grilled:onions:2
grated:carrot:2
4
```

The first two fields of each line of the file have been printed, with a colon between them, followed by another colon and the number of fields (NF) in the line. Then the END section has printed the value of NR (the number of records) after finishing looping through the file.

GNU awk has documentation on the system in the form of an info file; type **info awk** to view it. The latest version of the GNU awk manual is always available at www.gnu.org/software/gawk/manual/. You can find a number of books available on awk, including *sed & awk* by Dale Dougherty and Arnold Robbins (O'Reilly, 1997).

Getting Statistics about Text Files with wc

The wc command counts the lines (strictly the number of newline characters, which may be one less if the last line does not end in a newline character), words, and bytes in a file:

```
user@bible:~ > cat file
the quick brown fox
jumped
over the lazy dog

user@bible:~ > wc file
2  9 44 file
```

The file has 2 newline characters, 9 words, and 44 characters in all (made up of 36 letters, 6 spaces, and the 2 newline characters; there is no newline character at the end of the file).

Replacing Text

This section deals with ways of replacing text in a file according to given rules, either at the level of strings or of individual characters.

sed

sed is the stream editor; that means that you can use it to edit a stream of text (from a file or from the output of a different program) according to rules that you define. In fact, these rules can be very complex and you can do very clever things with sed, but we suggest that for the more complex tasks these days, a modern scripting language (Python or Perl according to taste) may sometimes be a better option. For simple tasks (such as replacing all instances of a string in a file with a replacement string), however, sed is easy to use and quick.

To simply replace all instances of a string in a file, the command is:

```
sed 's/oldstring/newstring/g' file
```

For example:

```
user@bible:~ > cat file
red elephant, red wine
blue mango
red albatross

user@bible:~ > sed 's/red/pale green/g' file
pale green elephant, pale green wine
blue mango
pale green albatross
```

The s is for substitute; the g tells sed to do so globally (that is, every time the string to be replaced occurs in a line). Without the g, the first instance in a line will be replaced:

```
user@bible:~ > sed 's/red/pale green/' file
pale green elephant, red wine
blue mango
pale green albatross
```

You can also choose which instance of the string you want to change:

```
user@bible:~ > sed 's/red/pale green/1' file
pale green elephant, red wine
blue mango
pale green albatross

user@bible:~ > sed 's/red/pale green/2' file
red elephant, pale green wine
blue mango
```

```
red albatross
```

Also, you can combine more than one command to sed:

```
user@bible:~ > sed 's/red/yellow/2; s/elephant/rhinoceros/' file
red rhinoceros, yellow wine
blue mango
red albatross
```

You can choose to make the replacement only if a line matches certain criteria. For example:

```
user@bible:~ > sed '/albat/s/red/yellow/g' file
red elephant, red wine
blue mango
yellow albatross
```

Here you selected only the lines containing the string albat to make the replacement.

If you have more sed commands, they can be combined into a file (say sedscript), and then you can run a command like the following:

```
sed -f sedscript file
```

The documentation for GNU sed on the system is in the form of an info file; type **info sed** to view it. There is a great deal of useful material on sed at http://sed .sourceforge.net/, including a list of sed tutorials at http://sed.sourceforge .net/grabbag/tutorials/. The book *sed & awk* mentioned earlier in the chapter is also useful.

tr

The tr command replaces (or deletes) individual characters from its input and passes the result to its output. For example, if you wanted to replace lowercase *e* with uppercase *E*, or all lowercase letters with uppercase letters, you could use the following command lines:

```
user@bible:~ > cat file
red elephant, red wine
blue mango
red albatross

user@bible:~ > cat file|tr e E
rEd ElEphant, rEd winE
bluE mango
rEd albatross
```

```
user@bible:~ > cat file|tr a-z A-Z
RED ELEPHANT, RED WINE
BLUE MANGO
RED ALBATROSS
```

However, for this example, it is probably better to do the following:

```
user@bible:~ > cat file | tr [:lower:] [:upper:]
```

This has the same effect as the previous example, but does the right thing if we include accented characters in our file. For example:

```
user@bible:~ > echo 'éléphant' |tr a-z A-Z
éLéPHANT
```

```
user@bible:~ > echo 'éléphant' |tr [:lower:] [:upper:]
ÉLÉPHANT
```

Note Exactly how the range of characters in the preceding examples is interpreted may depend on the locale, in other words the language settings in the current environment.

```
user@bible:~ > cat file |tr a-z mnopqrstuvwxyzabcdefghijkl
dqp qxqbtmzf, dqp iuzq
nxgq ymzsa
dqp mxnmfdaee
```

Here, the `tr` command performs the simple *rot13 cipher* on the lowercase letters — each letter is moved forward 13 places in the alphabet. Repeating the command restores the original text.

With the option -d, `tr` simply removes the characters that are listed:

```
user@bible:~ > cat file | tr -d abcde
r lphnt, r win
lu mngo
r ltross
```

With the option -s, `tr` removes repeats of the characters that are listed:

```
user@bible:~ > cat repeats
aaabcd
abbbcd
abcccd
abcddd

user@bible:~ > cat repeats|tr -s ab
```

```
abcd
abcd
abcccd
abcddd
```

Repeated *a*'s and *b*'s have been lost.

dos2unix and unix2dos

DOS and Windows have a different convention for newline characters from Unix and Linux. In DOS, the newline character is a carriage return and a line feed, whereas in Unix it is just a linefeed. What this means is that there can be problems when dealing with files from one system on the other. The programs dos2unix and unix2dos will convert (by default in place) a file from one system of newlines to the other.

For example:

```
user@bible:~ > unix2dos INDEX
```

This will silently overwrite the original file with its Unix-style line endings with the DOS version (which you can give to your friend so he can read it in Notepad without embarrassment).

If you want to keep the original file, both dos2unix and unix2dos have a -n option that enables you to specify an output file:

```
user@bible:~ > unix2dos  -n INDEX INDEX.txt
unix2dos: converting file INDEX to file INDEX.txt in DOS format ...~
```

You can, in fact, achieve the same result as dos2unix with tr like this:

```
cat file.txt |tr -d '\15' >outfile
```

This removes the carriage return character that has the decimal value 13 represented by octal \15.

Formatting Text Files for Viewing and Printing

The commands illustrated in this section offer ways to take plain text files and tidy them up or present them differently for display or printing.

pr

The pr command takes a text file and splits it into pages of text separated by a number of newlines with a header on each page. Optionally, it can add a form feed character between the pages for sending the output directly to a printer. For example, using the command with no options:

```
user@bible:~ > pr README.txt
```

will output pages with a header on each looking like this:

```
2 0 0 4 -0 8 -10 12:26              INDEX                   Page 1
```

fold

The fold command reformats a text file by breaking long lines. By default, the lines will be set to a maximum width of 80 characters. You can set the width of the lines you want in the output with the option - w, but if this is too small, the output may look bad.

A case where the fold command is useful is when you have saved a word processor document as plain text. In the text file, each paragraph will be a single line. A command such as fold - w 7 6 file.txt will break these lines sensibly.

fmt

The fmt command takes some text (say an article that you have written in a text editor) and does some sensible reformatting to it. Provided that you have separated paragraphs by empty lines, fmt will combine broken lines and make all lines a sensible length. It can also ensure that words are separated by one space and sentences by two. In the example that follows, the -u option forces uniform spacing—in other words, one space between words and two spaces between sentences.

```
user@bible:~ > cat badfile
This is a
file with some extra space and its line endings are in         a
mess.  We
need to
reformat it somehow.

user@bible:~ > fmt -u badfile
This is a file with some extra space and its line endings in a mess. We
need to reformat it somehow.
```

groff -Tascii

The document formatting system groff is used by the man page system to create formatted man pages (which are written in plain text with markup) from their source. It can also produce nicely formatted printed output.

This is not the place to talk about groff in general. However, you may have seen those nicely justified text files with a straight right-hand margin and wondered how they are produced. The same effect is seen in man pages, and this is no accident because you can use groff (which is used to format man pages) with the -Tascii option to produce text formatted in that way. It adds spaces to reduce the need for splitting words and hyphenation, and hyphenates reasonably sensibly. The output certainly looks nice, and if you are writing a file that will be read in text format (for example, a long README file to distribute with some software), it gives a nice impression to format it in this way.

```
user@bible:~ > groff -Tascii filename
```

a2ps

The a2ps command converts a text file to PostScript and either creates a file or sends it to the printer. If you simply type **a2ps file**, the file will be printed with a nice header and footer showing the filename and datestamp, the name of the user who printed it, and the date of printing. You can control the way a2ps works with a huge variety of options; for example, this command:

```
a2ps -j -B -R --columns=1 file -o outfile.ps
```

creates a PostScript file outfile.ps showing the text of the original file, and with a nice border around the page (the -j option), but no other header or footer. (The

psnup and mpage

Although technically off topic for this section, this is a good place to mention psnup and the other PostScript utilities in the psutils package. psnup can take a PostScript file and create a new file with multiple pages per physical page. If you want to save trees and toner, this is something you may often want to do. For example:

```
psnup -4 file.ps>file4up.ps
```

puts four pages of file.ps per physical page in the output file.

For reasons known only to SUSE, SUSE distributions do not ship with mpage, which does what psnup does, but often does it better. The mpage RPM shipped with the current version of Fedora Linux should install and run correctly on SUSE.

headers are suppressed by -B, while -R forces portrait format. The -o option speci-fies the output file.)

enscript

The enscript command does the same thing as a2ps. The default output from a2ps looks nicer. However, enscript has some other clever capabilities, including adding syntax highlighting to code in certain languages, and also producing output in HTML and RTF formats. For a list of all the options, see the man page.

Comparing Files

Very often you will have different versions of the same file, and you need a way to find the exact difference between them. This section focuses on that activity. In par-ticular, the diff and patch commands are very important to programmers who often distribute changes to an existing program in the form of a *diff* (in other words, a file containing the differences between an existing version and a newer version). The existing version can then be brought up to the level of the newer version using the patch command. This applies the changes that it finds in the diff file to the existing version, bringing it up to date. These ideas also underlie all version control sys-tems.

cmp

The cmp command compares two files and tells you how they differ, but not in a particularly useful way. If you type the command **cmp file1 file2** and you get no out-put, then the files don't differ. Otherwise, cmp can list the bytes that differ. For almost all purposes, diff is a better tool.

diff and patch

The diff tool compares two files and produces output that describes precisely the difference between the files, containing all the information needed to restore one from the other. In the simplest case, if the two files are identical, the command diff file1 file2 produces no output.

The diff command can report the differences between the files in more than one format; here you use diff without options:

```
user@bible:~ > cat file1
red elephant, red wine
blue mango
red albatross
```

```
user@bible:~ > cat file2
red elephant, pink wine
green plums
blue mango
red albatross

user@bible:~ > diff file1 file2
1c1,2
< red elephant, red wine
---
> red elephant, pink wine
> green plums
```

If you direct this output to a file, it can be used later as input to the patch command.

```
user@bible:~ > diff file1 file2 > diff12
```

We have simply written that record of the differences between the two files (the output of the diff command) to a file. This file, together with file1, can act as input to the patch command, which applies the differences to file1. The file file1 will then have the necessary changes applied to it to make it identical to file2.

```
user@bible:~ > patch file1 diff12
patching file file1

user@bible:~ > cat file1
red elephant, pink wine
green plums
blue mango
red albatross
```

So, you have patched file1, and it is now identical to file2.

If you try the patch the other way round, patch detects this and offers to try a reverse patch:

```
user@bible:~ > patch file2 diff12
patching file file2
Reversed (or previously applied) patch detected!  Assume -R? [n]
```

If you type **y**, you will find that file2 is now identical to the original file1.

If you use diff with the option -c or -u, you can apply the patch more simply as all the information about how the diff file was created is within it. So you just run patch with diff12 as input. patch can see from the contents of this file that it was created as a diff between the two files concerned, so it can easily decide how to do the correct thing.

```
user@bible:~ > diff -c file1 file2 > diff12
user@bible:~ > patch < diff12
```

```
patching file file1
```

Now `file1` is identical to the original `file2`.

The `diff` and `patch` commands can also be used (and generally are) at the level of directories. If you have a directory containing a large number of source code files, and an updated version of the same directory, the `diff` command can combine all differences between files in the two directories into a single file, which can be applied as a single patch.

The `diff` and `patch` commands are the basis for all revision control and versioning systems and are of massive importance to programmers. Changes to kernel source files are generally distributed as `diff` files and applied using `patch`.

There is a manual describing the use of `diff` and `patch` at `www.gnu.org/software/diffutils/manual/`.

Getting Text out of Other File Formats

A common problem is that you receive a file in a format that you cannot easily read because you don't have an appropriate application. This is particularly irritating in the case of binary files that are intended to be read only by a particular application but that you know actually contain text and formatting instructions. The most common case of this problem is that you want to retrieve the text from a Microsoft Word file. But equally, you may want to extract the text from a file that has been sent to you in PostScript or PDF format; you can display the file beautifully on the screen, but it's not always obvious how to retrieve the text. The tools discussed in this section can help with this common problem.

antiword

The typical Windows user has no idea what a Microsoft Word file contains. It is a binary file with bits of text mixed in with very strange stuff; try viewing a .doc file with something like `emacs` or (better) a hex editor such as `ghex2`. Among other things, it may often contain a lot of stuff the author does not suspect is there, things she thought she had deleted, for example. Quite a few people have been surprised by this feature, having unsuspectingly distributed .doc files, and then been confronted with contents that they didn't know were there.

From the point of view of Linux users, what is more important is that when people send you .doc files, you don't necessarily want to go through opening them with OpenOffice.org or a similar program. You may just want to extract the text. Fortunately `antiword` does this very well. All you need to do is type:

```
antiword filename.doc
```

You will see the file in text format.

Note The `antiword` package is no longer included in the SUSE Professional version. It can be obtained from `www.winfield.demon.nl`. Provided you have the necessary tools installed, it is very quick and easy to install: unpack the archive and run `make` and `make install`. You can install it as a user without root privileges; the binary will be copied to your `~/bin` directory.

ps2ascii

The `ps2ascii` command tries to extract the full text from a PostScript (or PDF) file. In general this works quite well, but there may be problems in the output with missing spaces where newlines were, and (depending on how the PostScript file was created) there may be some unrecognized characters. For example:

```
user@bible:~ > ps2ascii filename.ps
```

will write to standard output, while

```
user@bible:~ > ps2ascii filename.ps outfile.txt
```

will write the output to a file.

ps2pdf

If you want to convert PostScript files to the PDF format so that people who use Windows can easily view them, then `ps2pdf file.ps` is all you need. This command creates the PDF version with the name `file.pdf`.

dvi2tty

DVI (device independent) files are files produced by the TeX and LaTeX typesetting system (explained in the next section) that can then be printed using a suitable driver to an output device. Most typically on Linux they are converted to PostScript using the command `dvips` and then printed directly. DVI files can be viewed directly using a program such as `kdvi`.

You can extract the text from a DVI file with the command `dvi2tty`. Similar caveats to those mentioned for `ps2ascii` apply: The text you get out might not be exactly the text that was put in. A command such as

```
user@bible:~ > dvi2tty filename.dvi
```

extracts the text to standard output. You can, of course, redirect it to a file.

detex

TeX is a text formatting system developed by Donald Knuth. LaTeX is an extension of TeX. These systems are widely used for typesetting mathematical and scientific books and also in creating printable versions of open source documentation. A TeX or LaTeX source file is a plain text file with added markup.

The detex command tries to remove all markup from a TeX or LaTeX source file. It can also be called as delatex. For example:

```
user@bible:~ > detex filename.tex
```

outputs the stripped text to standard output.

acroread and xpdf

acroread and xpdf are PDF viewers:

✦ acroread—Has a text selection tool on its toolbar that enables you to select text with the cursor and copy it and paste it into another application.

✦ xpdf—Has similar functionality; you can select rectangles of text with the mouse cursor and paste them elsewhere. This can be a very convenient way of getting text out of a PDF file, particularly if it is a complex one with a number of columns or separate boxes of text.

html2text

If you have an HTML file and you just want the text without markup, you can of course display the file in Konqueror and copy the text and paste it into a new file. However, if you want to do a similar thing for a large number of files, a command-line tool is more useful.

The html2text command reads an HTML file and outputs plain text, having stripped out the HTML tags. You can even run it against a URL:

```
user@bible:~ > html2text http://news.bbc.co.uk
```

Text Editors

Plain text is our favorite file format. It is readable everywhere and depends only on the universally understood ASCII (and these days, possibly Unicode) format. You are not limited to a specific program to read or create plain text, or to view it.

In the world of Windows, the naive user thinks (and this is what the application vendor wants him to think) that just to write a shopping list, he should use a proprietary word processing application. When he sends that shopping list to his friend by email, he attaches the binary file (which requires a copy of the original application or a filter built into another one) to read it.

The Windows registry consists of binary files (which again require special tools for manipulation). Most Windows applications store their files in binary formats.

In Linux, almost all configuration files, log files, and other system information are held in plain text. The only exceptions are one or two databases (for example, the file /var/log/wtmp, which holds the history of logins that can be accessed by the command last). In the case of applications, most native Linux applications that have their own file formats use a form of modified text, rather than a binary format. For example, the Gnumeric spreadsheet uses an Extensible Markup Language (XML) format (gzipped to reduce the file size). So does the GNOME diagram editor, Dia. OpenOffice.org documents are zipped archives containing XML files. XML is a sensible format for this kind of thing because it is a natural way of creating structure in a file that is pure text. And the beauty of it is that we can read all the information from the file (and process it and manipulate it in various ways) without having the original application. In some ways, open file formats (and other related open standards) are as important for computing freedom as open source.

Because of the importance of plain text as a format, and because of the need to edit all kinds of text files on Linux, the question of which text editors are available and which ones to use becomes important.

The Politics

A large number of text editors are available for Linux. SUSE Linux includes at least the following: e3, ed, emacs, fte, gedit, jedit, joe, kate, kvim, kwrite, mined, nvi, pico, qemacs, the, uemacs, xcoral, yudit, and zile.

Each of the major graphical user environments, GNOME and KDE, comes with its own graphical text editor(s): GNOME has gedit and KDE has kate and kwrite. Others, such as mined, joe, and pico, are editors that run in a console. Some of these are more user friendly than others.

In practice, however, for people who do a lot of general text editing, only two editors really matter, and the vast majority of users tend to prefer one or the other or one of their variants. These two are vi and emacs. As with certain other preferences in the Linux world, there are strong views on each side, sometimes so strong as to be described as constituting "religious wars."

Without taking sides in those wars, we shall describe the main features of the two editors and leave readers to make their own choices.

Note   In some ways, the situation is not quite symmetric. You may or may not *like* vi, but in practice you cannot get away from it. You will have to at least be able to use it, even if it is not your editor of choice. The reason for that is that in a minimal installation of Linux (or any Unix system), you can rely on vi being installed and available, whereas emacs may not be there until or unless you install it.

vi/vim

The vi text editor started off as a project for Bill Joy (who went on to great things with BSD and Sun Microsystems) when he was hacking the ed editor and incorporating features of e m (editor for mortals) while still a student.

One advantage of the vi/vim text editor is that it is installed both in the rescue and main SUSE installed system by default. The vim editor is relatively lightweight on system resources, but extremely powerful at the same time. Incorporating syntax highlighting and regular expression handling, vim is an all-around nice guy of the text-editing world.

By default, the `vim` editor is installed (`vi` improved). It adds extra functionality to the traditional `vi` text editor.

One of the first things that may stump you when you first start using `vi` is the fact that you cannot enter any text when you just type **vi** at the command line. This is one of the reasons that a lot of people do not like `vi` and move to `emacs`. However, before you move on, let us explain what's happening: `vi`/`vim` uses a command mode and a text mode. In command mode, you can manipulate the text with commands, save and quit files, and open files without "entering" text into your document. To actually edit text with the traditional methods (insert, delete, and so on), you need to move out of command mode.

This may seem quite alien at first, but we hope that with some examples you will see that it is a quite powerful way to do things, and for people who work more quickly on the command line, it can dramatically speed up your text-editing needs.

Figure 11-1 is what you will see when you type **vi** or **vim** at the command prompt. As soon as `vim` has loaded, it is automatically in command mode. To move into insert mode, press the *i* key. If you want to insert a new line at the current position, use the *o* key. This inserts a new line and puts you in insert mode.

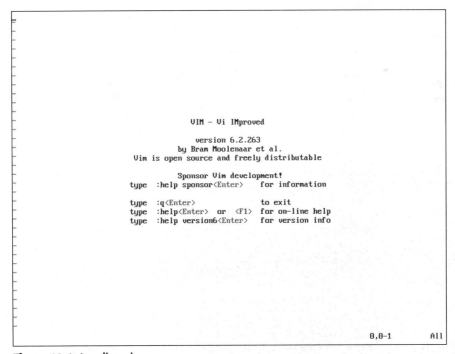

Figure 11-1: Loading vim

In the bottom-left corner of the screen, you will see the word INSERT. This signifies you are in insert mode. You can now type text until your heart is content.

One of the great things about vi is that it can be used pretty much anywhere. If you are on an old terminal, and you have access to alphanumeric characters only, you can control the cursor with the *k*, *h*, *l*, and *j* keys (up, left, right, and down, respectively) to navigate the screen (as opposed to the cursor key we have come to rely on so much).

In most cases, the Backspace key will enable you to delete characters. If your terminal (an xterm, telnet session, or ssh session) is not capable of using the common keys you are accustomed to, you will have to use other methods to edit your text.

It may seem backward to not use the backspace and cursor keys to edit your text, but vim is very good at adapting (or should we say, being adapted) to any situation you throw at it. This is an extremely powerful feature that will help you if you are in a tight spot with connectivity issues.

Using Command Mode

We briefly touched on the INSERT mode of vim, which is where most things happen because it's where the addition of text occurs. After all, that is why you use a text editor.

However, apart from the traditional editing features, we want to talk about the command mode editing features of vim as well. To enter the command line, press the Escape key. The INSERT keyword in the bottom-left corner of the screen disappears. You are now in the realm of the vi command mode. You can use the cursors (or the *k*, *h*, *l*, and *j* keys) to move around the text, but you cannot insert anything.

The next sections discuss some basic keys that you can use in command mode that prove very useful.

Moving Around the Text

We have talked about using the cursor to move around the text while in command mode. To speed up your text editing, you can use shortcuts to move quickly to blocks of text, the start and end of a file, and to the start and end of a line of text.

Moving to the Start and End of a File

To move to the end of a file (and this applies to quite a few text-based applications in Linux such as man and less), press Shift+g. To move to the start of the file, press g+g. You can also go to a specific line in the file by entering the number of the line that you want, followed by g+g. For example, 15g+g would take you to line 15 of the file that you are editing.

Moving Around a Line of Text

To move around a line of text, you can use w to move to the next word, $ to move to the end of the line, and Shift+a to move the cursor to the end of the line and enter append mode.

It is very useful to combine the end-of-line operation with the append operation to add text to the end of the line.

Figures 11-2 and 11-3 demonstrate this. Keep an eye on the location coordinates at the bottom-right corner of the screen to see how the Shift+g and Shift+a operations affect the cursor.

To move to the start of the current line, use the zero (0) key or the Home key.

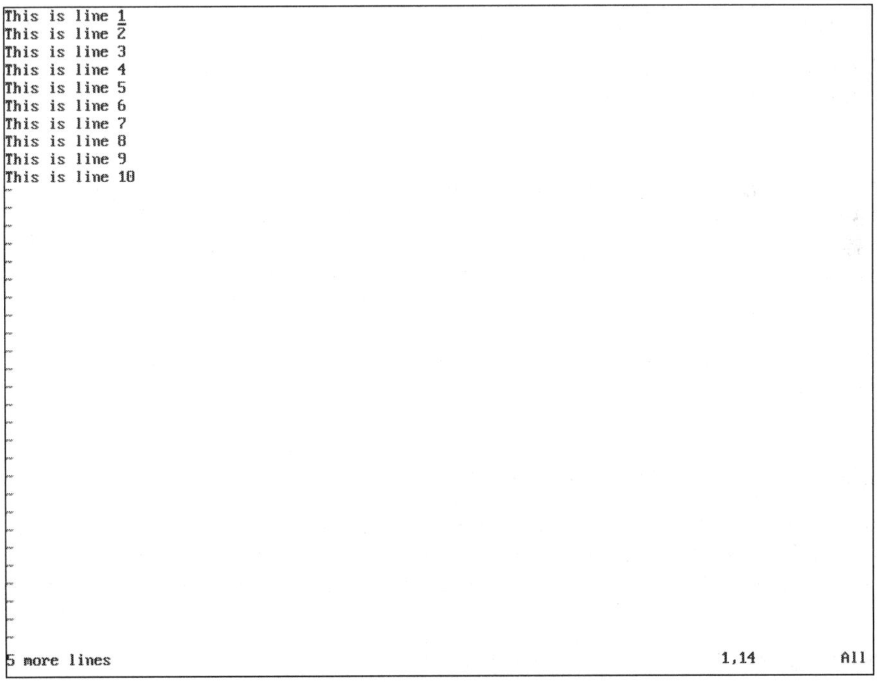

```
This is line 1
This is line 2
This is line 3
This is line 4
This is line 5
This is line 6
This is line 7
This is line 8
This is line 9
This is line 10
~
~
~
~
~
~
~
~
~
~
~
~
~
~
~
~
~
5 more lines                                          1,14          All
```

Figure 11-2: Starting at the end of line one

```
This is line 1
This is line 2
This is line 3
This is line 4
This is line 5
This is line 6
This is line 7
This is line 8
This is line 9
This is line 10_
~
~
~
~
~
~
~
~
~
~
~
~
~
~
~
~
~
~
~
~
~
~
~
~
~
-- INSERT --                                           10,16        All
```

Figure 11-3: Using Shift+g and Shift+a to move to the end of the file

Tip   All of the keys on the Insert/Delete/Home/End/PageUp/PageDown keypad perform
           the actions you'd expect in `vim`.

Deleting Text

To remove a character from a string of text, press the *x* key. A comparison of
Figures 11-4 and 11-5 shows you the results.

You can see in the figures that the *s* in *insert* was removed. The *x* key in command
mode can be thought of as a replacement for the Backspace key. You will find after
repeated use of `vi` that you will not use the Backspace key at all. We have even used
the x command in Word as we are in the mindset that we are editing text and we
should use the *x* key to remove text. We hope that the editors of this book will spot
any erroneous *x*'s in the text!

Deleting More Than One Character at a Time

Often you want to remove whole lines of text, and `vi` enables you to do this very
quickly with the d command.

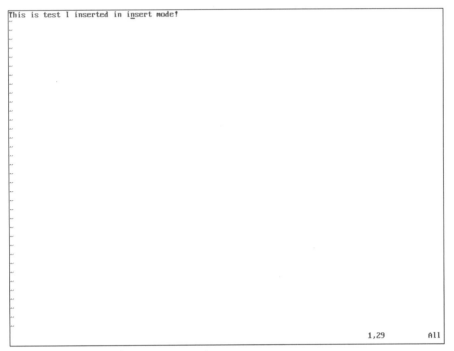

Figure 11-4: Before character removal

The d command can be used to remove a whole line, a word, part of a word, multiple lines, and multiple words.

To remove a word of text (text surrounded by a space), move the cursor to the start of the word and press d+w sequentially. If you wanted to remove the part of a word, position the cursor at the character you want to remove to the end of the word and use the d+w command.

> **Tip** It may be slightly confusing to put these commands into practice in your head, so we advise that you find a text file (or create your own) full of text and play around with the commands we talk about here.

To remove a full line of text, press d+d sequentially. The double d removes the whole line of text, until it finds the end of the line. It may be that you cannot see the entire text on the line if it is longer than your terminal display, so be careful when you remove a line.

To remove all text from the cursor position to the end of the current line, press d and then $ sequentially.

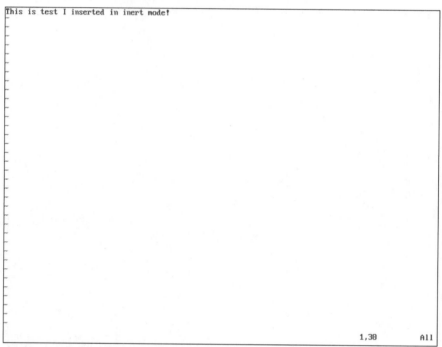

This is test I inserted in inert mode!

1,38   All

Figure 11-5: After character removal

Undoing and Redoing

The vim editor also features an undo command that proves very helpful. If you have made a mistake (for example, removing a line you didn't mean to), pressing u while in command mode will undo the last operation you made. Pressing u again will undo the previous operation before this and so on. To redo an operation you have undone, press the Ctrl+r key (redo).

Removing Multiple Times

To remove multiple times, you can specify a number to work with the previous commands. For example, to remove five lines of text, press 5+d+d sequentially. In Figure 11-6, you can see a series of lines before the five lines of text are removed. In Figure 11-7, the operation 5+d+d has been used to remove Line 3 through Line 7.

You can use this operation to remove characters (*number*+x), lines (*number*+d+d), and also to remove characters to the end of a line (it will remove all text from the subsequent lines).

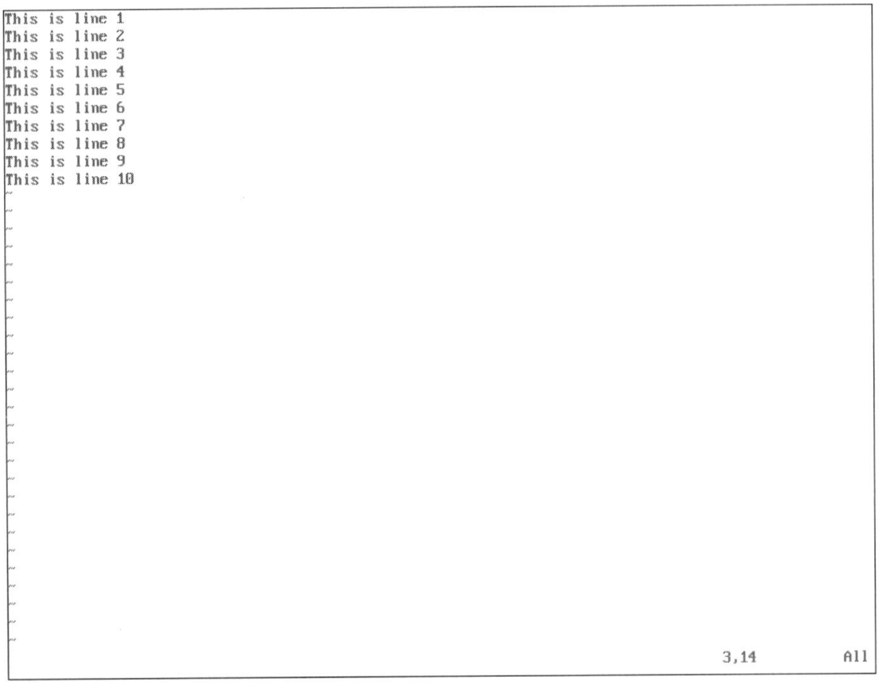

```
This is line 1
This is line 2
This is line 3
This is line 4
This is line 5
This is line 6
This is line 7
This is line 8
This is line 9
This is line 10
~
~
~
~
~
~
~
~
~
~
~
~
~
~
~
~
~
~
                                                3,14          All
```

Figure 11-6: Removing multiple lines of text (before)

Copying and Pasting

Entering copious amounts of text into a file is never a fun thing, and the copy-and-paste idea has helped to speed up repetitive text entry. In most graphical user interface (GUI) applications, a simple right-click for the text menu enables you to copy and paste text. When you are working on the command line, this is not possible, and you have to do it a little bit differently.

In vim, you call a copy a *yank* (as in, you are yanking the text). With this in mind, you may be able to guess what you use to yank the text, a y+y combination. To copy a line of text, place your cursor on the line you want to copy and press y+y. This copies the text into the buffer. To paste the line to another place in the file, press the p key (for paste).

If you wanted to paste multiple copies of the line, you can use the multiplier. For example, to paste a line five times, use 5+p.

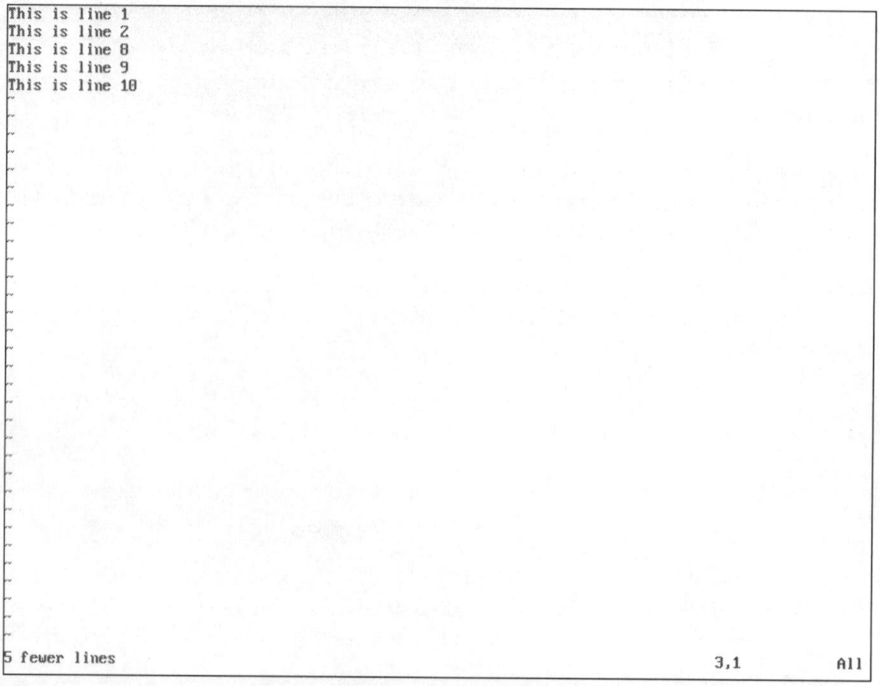

```
This is line 1
This is line 2
This is line 8
This is line 9
This is line 10
```

`5 fewer lines`   `3,1`   `All`

Figure 11-7: Removing multiple lines of text (after)

Inserting and Saving Files

If you are editing a file and you realize that you want to pull in text from another file, you can use the :r command in vi command mode.

For example, if you want to read the contents of the file /tmp/myfile into the current document at the current cursor position, you enter command mode with the Escape key and type **:r /tmp/myfile**.

To save a file, you use the : w command. To save a file you just edited to /home/justin/mynewfile, you enter **:w /home/justin/mynewfile**.

Tip

Entering commands with the colon (:) specified first with the command will show you what you are typing. If the colon is not used, as we have been doing, then you do not see the command you are using. The colon commands are usually used to manipulate text in a way that enables you to edit the command before you run it (by pressing Enter).

Searching and Replacing

To search for a string in your text, you can use the forward slash (/) and question mark keys (?).

To search from your current position forward in the file, use the / key. For example to search for the word *apples* from the current cursor position to the end of the file, enter **/apples** and press Enter in command mode.

To search backward, to the start of the file, use the ? key. To search for *apples* from the current cursor position to the start of the file, enter **?apples** and press Enter in command mode.

If you are looking for more than one occurrence of the word *apples* in the text, press the n key to move to the next occurrence.

> **Tip** As we talked about before, Shift+g and g+g can be used in less and man to move to the end and start of a file. The /, ?, and n commands can also be used in these applications to search forward and backward in a file.

Replacing text globally in a file is quite easy to do and is very powerful, if you know what you are doing. To replace text in the whole document, you need to use the substitution command, :s.

For example, to replace the word "apples" with "pears" in the current document, enter **:%s/apples/pears/g**.

The :%s command is quite powerful in its ability to search and replace. In the example command, we used % to tell vim to check every line of the document for the occurrence of "apples". Adding the g tells it to replace all occurrences of "apples" on a line with "pears".

If you are worried that you could be replacing text you do not want to replace, you can add the c command onto the g to get vim to ask for confirmation of a replace.

This may seem quite a big step from some of the single commands we have talked about in this chapter so far, but we want to highlight how powerful vim can be with more abstract commands.

> **Note** A good introduction to vim is included in the package; to run it, type **vimtutor** at the command line. If you want to access the online help, go into command mode and enter :h and press Enter. To exit the online help, enter :q in command mode and press Enter.

Using the vim Initialization File

If you want to customize how vim works, you can add startup commands to the file .vimrc in your home directory. This file is used to set the profile for how vim works for you and is a very useful file.

One popular feature of vim is its syntax highlighting. If you are editing C, or maybe Perl, vim can colorize your text so it is easier to read. Open the .vimrc file (it may not exist, which means you'll have to create it) and add the following to the file:

```
syntax on
```

It is usually nice to be able to use the Backspace key to delete characters for us folks who like to be able to edit interactively.

```
set backspace=2
```

This tells vim that when it is in insert mode, the Backspace key can be used to delete text as you can in Windows Notepad, for example.

And finally for programmers out there, it is useful to indent your code when typing so that you can structure your code; vim can be told that it should remember the current place you are indented to by setting the autoindent parameter in your startup file:

```
set autoindent
```

Now, when you press Enter for a new line, vim returns to the column you are indented to (using the Tab key).

You can set many options in your .vimrc file, and it would take up a whole book to describe them all. An excellent vim tutorial at http://newbiedoc.sourceforge .net/tutorials/vim/index-vim.html.en can be of help.

Exiting vim

To exit vim, you need to use the :q command. This will quit the current session as long as you have saved your work (that is, all text buffers are written to disk).

If you want to quit and save the current file to disk, use :wq. This works only if you have assigned a filename to the file you are working with. If you have not, you will see an error message. To remedy this, you can pass the name of the file you want to save with :wq filename. In the case of the example file we used previously in this section, entering **:wq /home/justin/mynewfile** will successfully save the file and exit vi cleanly.

To exit `vim` without saving the file, you can use `:q!`. This will not ask for confirmation and will exit `vim` immediately. Use with caution.

emacs

There is a strong contrast between `vi` and `emacs`, both in terms of philosophy and the user's experience. While `vi` is essentially small and efficient, `emacs` is large and powerful. One of the things that many people find most irritating about `vi` is the need to switch between command mode and text-entry mode. The `emacs` editor operates differently; you access commands through key combinations involving the Ctrl and Meta keys (on Linux for Meta, read Alt).

`emacs` is much more than a text editor; it aims to be an entire working environment. You can use `emacs` as your mail client. You can use it as a complete integrated development environment (IDE). You can even use it as a web browser (we don't recommend this — but try it if you must: You will need to have the `emacs-w3` package installed).

`emacs` dates back to 1976, when it was first developed by Richard Stallman and others at MIT's Artificial Intelligence Lab. The name was derived from the phrase *editor macros*. GNU emacs is part of the GNU project. The history of the project and of the split between `emacs` and XEmacs is well documented on various web sites, including the emacs Wiki site and `www.xemacs.org`.

What to Install

A bewildering variety of packages have "emacs" in their names. It is important to realize that there are two distinct versions of emacs included in SUSE: `emacs` and `xemacs`. This sounds as if one is for use in the text console environment and one in X, but it isn't as simple as that.

GNU emacs (the package called `emacs`) runs in the graphical environment as well. At some point in history, there was a fork in the development of emacs, and a version of emacs with (at that time) better support for the graphical environment split off. This was at one time called Lucid emacs and is the ancestor of `xemacs`. In the case of GNU emacs, you can install the package `emacs` and `emacs-x11` or you can install `emacs` and `emacs-nox`. By default, you will get `emacs-x11`, and if `emacs` detects that X is running, it will start in graphical mode by default. If X is not running, you will get emacs in text mode. If you want the text mode version all the time, you should install `emacs-nox` and not `emacs-x11`.

You can independently also install `xemacs` if you want to have both `emacs` and `xemacs` on your system. In general, `emacs` and `xemacs` can use the same package files and (by a clever trick) can share their user configuration files.

Almost everything we say here about `emacs` applies to `xemacs` also. It used to be that `xemacs` had a much nicer look and feel than GNU emacs when running graphically. That is no longer the case. As far as editing commands and modes are concerned, in almost all cases what we say applies to both.

Starting emacs

If you start `emacs` from the command line (by typing **emacs**), then if `emacs-x11` is installed and X is running, you will see something like Figure 11-8.

If you want to start `emacs` in an `xterm` or `konsole` window, type:

```
emacs -nw
```

The `-nw` option (think *no window*) prevents it from starting in its own window and forces it to run in text mode inside the `xterm` or `konsole` window. You will see something like Figure 11-9.

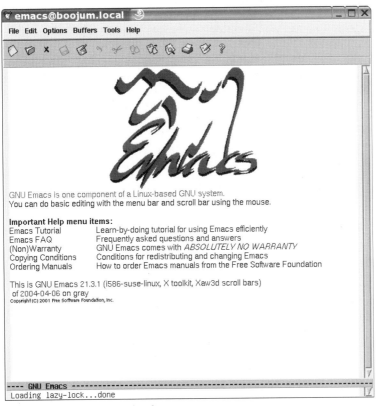

Figure 11-8: emacs starting in X

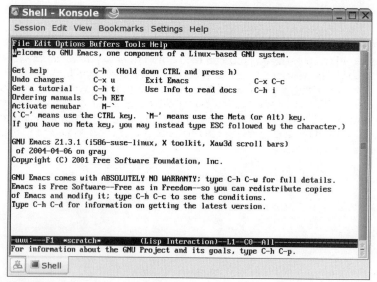

Figure 11-9: emacs -nw starting

It is more likely that you will want to start `emacs` by opening a particular file. To do that, type the following:

    emacs file

or

    emacs -nw file

If the file that you name does not exist, it will be created when you first save the file.

You can then start editing the file. Typing will instantly type to the editing buffer, which you see. Just doing "what comes naturally" will work fine now: The arrow keys or the mouse will reposition the cursor as expected and the Backspace key will delete backward while the Delete key will delete forward.

Controlling emacs

To issue commands to `emacs`, you use key combinations. In describing these, it is the convention to use C for the Ctrl key and M for the Meta key, which can be either Alt or Esc. For example, to save a file, you do Ctrl+x Ctrl+s; this is normally written as C-x C-s. If you are running the graphical form of `emacs`, you can do some of the most common actions (such as saving a file) by clicking menu items (File ➪ Save).

Note
Note that the commands here are the default ones. The emacs editor is totally configurable, which means that you can bind a particular keystroke to any command you want. For example, C-x C-f is bound to the command find-file, which you can also run with M-x find-file. You can break that binding and bind the command to a different keystroke. You can also bind a keystroke to a command that you find yourself using regularly that has no binding (or one that you find inconvenient). To make such a change permanent, you need to add a line to your .gnu-emacs-custom file.

The most important basic emacs commands are as follows:

✦ C-x C-f — Find a file (that is, open it).

✦ C-x C-s — Save the current buffer.

✦ C-x C-w — Write the current buffer to a file ("Save as").

✦ C-x C-c — Quit.

✦ C-k — Kill the rest of the current line.

✦ C-y — Yank (that is, copy) the last killed text.

✦ M-w — Copy the selected text.

Moving Around

If you are using emacs in a graphical session, the mouse works both for selecting text and for moving around the file. But you can also navigate with the keyboard using the following keystrokes:

✦ C-f — Move to next character.

✦ C-b — Move to previous character.

✦ M-f — Move to next word.

✦ M-b — Move to previous word.

✦ C-a — Move to beginning of line.

✦ C-e — Move to end of line.

✦ M-a — Move to beginning of sentence.

✦ M-e — Move to end of sentence.

✦ C-Home — Move to top of buffer.

✦ C-End — Move to bottom of buffer.

✦ M-x goto-line — Move to a line number that you specify.

It is assumed that sentences are separated by a dot and two spaces.

Undo

`C-_` or `C-x u` will undo your last command or typing; `emacs` remembers everything you do, so you can do a sequence of undo commands.

Replacing Text

`M-x replace-string` will globally replace one string with another in the whole buffer or in the selection. You can also do a conditional replacement of text with `M-%` or `M-x query-replace`. This prompts you as to whether you want to make each change.

Searching

`C-s` starts an incremental search. What this means is that if you type **C-s Li**, for example, you see the next instance of *Li* highlighted in the text. If you type another letter (for example *n*), you will now be searching for *Lin*. If you press `C-s` again, you will move to the next instance of this new search string.

You can also do a non-incremental search by typing `C-s` followed by pressing Return. Whatever you now enter will be the search string and `emacs` will jump to the next occurrence of it. Regular expression searches are also possible. The command `M-C-s` starts a regular expression search. If you then type a regular expression, `emacs` searches for the next matching text in the buffer. (See also Chapter 10 for more on regular expressions.)

Making Corrections

`M-c` capitalizes the next word, and `M-u` makes the next word all caps. `M-l` does lowercase. `M-t` switches the order of two words. `M-x ispell-buffer` checks the spelling of the entire buffer. You can check the spelling of a single word with `M-x ispell-word`.

Using Word Completion

One of the very useful features of `emacs` is the way that it knows what you are going to type. (Well, not quite literally, but good enough.) If you are working on a file and you start a word and then type **M-/**, `emacs` tries to complete the word for you, based on previous words in the file. If it chooses the wrong one, simply type `M-/` again until you get the one you want and then continue typing. This is an extremely powerful feature, not just because it can save you a lot of typing, but more importantly, if you are writing code, you can use it to ensure that you don't make mistakes when typing variable names that you have already created.

Using Command Completion and History

If you start to type an emacs command with **M-x** and a couple of characters, emacs will show you all the available completions. So, for example, if you type **M-x fin** and then press the Tab key, you will see all the emacs commands that start with fin. There are a lot of them!

If you type **M-x** and then an up arrow, emacs offers you the last command you gave it. Another up arrow will take you to the one before, and so on.

emacs Modes

This is where emacs really comes into its own. emacs provides different sets of key bindings and functions that are automatically associated with different types of files. The set of key bindings and functions for a particular type of file is known as a *mode*. For example, if you are editing HTML, emacs has a mode for HTML. If you are editing Perl code, emacs has a mode for Perl. In the same way, there are modes for all major programming languages, for shell scripts, for Makefiles, for almost anything you can think of. And these modes are highly intelligent. For instance, in the example shown in Figure 11-10, we are editing Python code. The emacs editor understands the Python syntax and colorizes the code based on its knowledge of the key words in Python. It also automatically indents the code as you type (in Python, the structure of the program is shown by the indentation; emacs helps you get the indentation right). It also helps you get the syntax right by refusing to indent a line correctly following a syntax error.

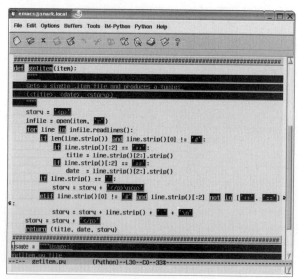

Figure 11-10: emacs editing python code

In most modes, `emacs` has special commands to do things that make sense in that context. For example, in XML mode, `C-c /` closes the currently open tag (so it will look back in the file for the last open tag, and type for you the correct closing tag).

In almost all cases, `emacs` loads the correct mode for the file that you are editing when it opens it. If it doesn't do so, you can select a mode with a command like `M-x xml-mode`.

Similarly, in HTML mode (see Figure 11-11), `emacs` colorizes the code in a way that helps you distinguish tags from text. There are numerous special key commands for this mode that allow you, for example, to insert common opening and closing tags with a single key combination and to call an external program to view the file.

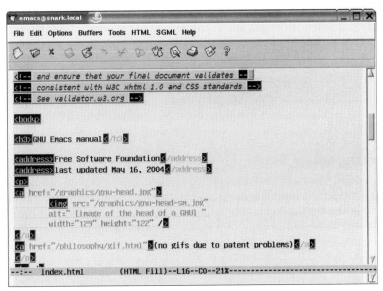

Figure 11-11: emacs editing HTML

The modes are implemented by files of lisp code that are installed in directories under /usr/share/emacs. You can, of course, install additional modes. If you use a language for which there is no mode included in the SUSE emacs packages (fairly unlikely, but possible), you can always add it. We always have to add magicpoint mode (for editing source files for magicpoint, a nice slide display tool that uses a markup format).

The magicpoint mode that we use was written by Christoph Dalitz and comes in a file called mgp_mode_cd.el. To make this work and be automatically loaded when you open a magicpoint file (with a name such as file.mgp), you need to copy mgp_mode-cd.el to the directory /usr/share/emacs/site-lisp/ and add the following lines to the emacs startup file .gnu-emacs-custom in your home directory:

```
(autoload 'mgp-mode "mgp-mode-cd" "MGP mode." t)
(add-to-list 'auto-mode-alist '("\\.mgp$" . mgp-mode))
```

As one would hope, the instructions for making this work are included as comments in the mode file itself.

Note   You can (of course) write your own emacs modes. But to do so you need to become familiar with some Lisp programming.

These comments just scratch the surface of what emacs modes can do, but they do give you a clear idea of what an intelligent editor emacs can be. For additional information about the emacs customization file and customizing emacs, see "Customizing emacs" later in this chapter.

Using the Calendar

The command M-x calendar displays a calendar in emacs. When the calendar is displayed, with a date highlighted, if you type **p p** you will get that date translated into the Persian calendar. If you type **p i**, you will get the Islamic date, and **p e** will give you the Ethiopic date.

In a way, this sums up exactly what people both love and hate about emacs. It does everything, but as a consequence it is very complex, and some would say bloated.

Customizing emacs

If you've ever gone to the desk of any emacs aficionado and used emacs there, you've probably noticed that it doesn't seem to work the same way for them as it does on your system. The reason for this is that emacs is the most configurable editor in existence. Not only does emacs provide a rich configuration language for changing the commands that different keys are associated with (known as key bindings), but it also includes a complete implementation of the Lisp programming language that makes it easy for serious emacs users to write their own commands or modify the behavior of existing ones.

Most Linux systems store all per-user emacs customization information in the file .emacs in the user's home directory. SUSE provides a slightly richer model for emacs customization and configuration. When a user account is created, YaST copies the files .emacs and .gnu-emacs from the system's /usr/skel directory into the user's new home directory. The ~/.emacs file is primarily just a loader that determines whether you are running standard X11 emacs or the more graphical version of emacs known as XEmacs, and automatically loads the contents of appropriate startup files for each of these emacs implementations. If you are running the standard X11 emacs (which is what this section focuses on), the .emacs file loads the ~/.gnu-emacs file whenever you start emacs. If you are running XEmacs, the .emacs file loads a configuration and customization file called ~/.xemacs/init.el (if the file exists). You can modify the contents of the appropriate file to fine-tune the characteristics of how emacs works for you.

In addition, if you are running the standard X11 emacs and you want to further customize how emacs works on your system, you can create a file called ~/.gnu-emacs-custom to hold your specific key bindings, functions, and other customizations. Because this section focuses on the standard X11-aware version of emacs, the customizations discussed in the rest of this section should be put in this file.

The next few sections highlight the basic types of customizations that you can make in an emacs configuration file, providing examples of each. A number of excellent sites on the web provide much more detailed information about customizing emacs, such as http://jeremy.zawodny.com/emacs/emacs-4.html and http://linuxplanet.com/linuxplanet/tutorials/3166/4/.

Changing Key Bindings

Whenever you execute an `emacs` command, you are actually executing a Lisp function. As explained earlier, `emacs` is configured to execute specific commands in response to combinations of the Control or Escape keys and the standard keys on your keyboard. These are known as *key bindings* because they associate (bind) a specific function with a specific key sequence. However, if you're already familiar with another editor that also used commands consisting of combinations of the Control or Escape keys and the standard keys on your keyboard, your fingers are probably used to typing certain keys to execute certain commands. The most common customization made to `emacs` is therefore to change the keys to which commonly used commands are associated.

Though `emacs` enables you to change key bindings globally or within a specific mode, it is more common to customize a specific key binding so that it works regardless of the mode in which you are using `emacs`. The `emacs` configuration command to globally set a key binding is `global-set-binding`. For example, to globally set the
key sequence Ctrl+z to a function that scrolls the current buffer up one line rather than attempting to suspend `emacs`, you would put the following command in your `~/.gnu-emacs-custom` file:

    (global-set-key "\C-Z" 'scroll-one-line-up)

In Lisp fashion, you must preface the name of the function that you are referring to with a single-quotation mark (not the back-quote). If you're interested, the scroll-one-line-up function is provided as an example in the section "Defining Your Own Functions" a bit later in this chapter.

Note   When specifying key bindings, the Control key is represented by `\C-` and the Escape key is represented by `\M-`.

Setting Variables

`emacs` uses a number of internal variables to control its behavior. These variables can be modified using the `setq` command. For example, to cause `emacs` to scroll more smoothly in one-line increments, you could add the following line to your `~/.gnu-emacs-custom` file:

    (setq scroll-step 1)

As another example, the default settings in `emacs` cause it to automatically save your files each time you have typed or modified 300 characters. To decrease this value to every 100 changes, you could add the following line to your `~/.gnu-emacs-custom` file:

    (setq auto-save-interval 100)

Specifying Modes

As discussed earlier, emacs provides different key bindings and functions based on the type of file that you are using; these are known as modes. The default mode used by emacs when you start emacs without specifying the file that you want to edit is known as Fundamental mode. You may want to customize emacs to always use a different mode by default, regardless of the name of the file. For example, to make text mode the default mode each time you start emacs, you could add the following line to your ~/.gnu-emacs-custom file:

```
(setq default-major-mode 'text-mode)
```

As you can see from this example, the name of the default mode in emacs is defined through an emacs variable, default-major-mode, which in this case requires the name of an emacs function rather than a numeric value as shown in the examples in the previous section.

Each emacs mode also enables you to specify other actions whenever you use that mode. For example, to turn on auto-fill (wrapping words to the next line when you reach a certain column on your screen), you could add the following line to your ~/.gnu-emacs-custom file:

```
(add-hook 'text-mode-hook 'turn-on-auto-fill)
```

Changing File Associations

As discussed earlier, emacs automatically enters specific modes when you open files with a specific extension, just like many GUIs do when you click a specific type of file. You may occasionally want to have emacs automatically enter a specific mode when you open files that the specified mode is not traditionally associated with. For example, emacs automatically enters text mode when you edit files with the .txt or .text extensions. But what if you typically name text files with the .inf extension and want emacs to automatically enter text mode when entering files of that type?

The file extensions associated with different emacs modes are stored in a list of extension/mode-name pairs. Therefore, to add the .inf extension to the list of extensions associated with text mode, you would simply append that extension to the list of extensions associated with text mode, as in the following example:

```
(setq auto-mode-alist
  (cons '(".inf" . text-mode) auto-mode-alist))
```

This example uses the Lisp cons function to append the pair .inf and text-mode to the list of automatic file associations, and then uses the setq function discussed in the previous sections to set the auto-mode-alist variable to the new, expanded list.

Working with Packages

Originally, there was no such thing as a package in Linux. It was a dark time for people who have a penchant for an organized, manageable, and above all clean system.

A *package* is a file containing all the files of an application, library, or anything else with data in it that can be installed, removed, queried, and managed as one entity. The RPM (Red Hat Package Manager) format has undoubtedly become the *de facto* package standard on Linux (and is available on other operating systems, too).

In the dark days, when you needed to install new applications, you downloaded the source code, untarred it, configured the build environment, and compiled it. When it came to installing the application, you had no way of telling what file belonged to what application. This led to orphaned files existing on a system when you wanted to remove the application or upgrade it.

Enter RPM to solve this issue. *RPM* uses a central database that contains information about all software installed on the system. You can query this database to find out what packages are installed, their versions, and also what files they own. If you want to upgrade the package, you can download the RPM and simply tell RPM that you want to upgrade the software to a later revision. This helps to control and curb orphaned files and provides a quick and easy way to see what software is installed on the system.

This chapter covers package maintenance and manipulation using RPM. RPM is a very powerful system, not only to install and manage packages, but also to automate the build process of software to produce a binary RPM.

Binary RPMs

An RPM contains the binary, configuration, and documentation for an application. It also contains information about what it depends on and what it provides to the system (so that other packages can depend on the RPM you are dealing with if needed). Whereas with source code you have to resolve and figure out any dependencies that are needed, the RPM contains all of this information for you in the package itself.

When you install SUSE, a large number of RPM files are installed with the software you have selected. These RPMs may rely on other RPMs for functionality and so on. The process of controlling dependencies is handled by YaST automatically. For example, if you want to install Mozilla, YaST knows from the RPM file that Mozilla depends on the X libraries, among others. YaST creates a dependency tree for RPMs that need to be installed and resolves any dependency needs as well as any conflicts.

This feature of YaST is something that proves extremely useful because it means that the user does not need to resolve package dependencies manually when installing software.

Note RPM manages packages directly, installing, querying, and building RPMs. YaST, on the other hand, takes the features of RPM and builds an installer system around it. YaST will resolve dependencies, give you information about the packages, and enable you to search all SUSE packages on the media to find what you need to install.

Dependencies are an important part of the RPM process. The fact that the RPM system manages dependencies takes away the cumbersome and sometimes difficult process of manually resolving dependencies of the source code.

Installing an RPM

To install an RPM, you can use the YaST package selection tool we talked about in Chapter 1 or install manually. Installing an RPM manually involves using the command-line features of rpm as opposed to using the YaST package manager. We will talk about installing, querying, and removing RPM packages manually so that you are proficient in managing and checking installed software.

The rpm command is used to control all package operations on the system. To install a package, you need to use the -i (install) parameter. Doing a straight install is fine in most situations, but if the package is installed already (albeit a lower version), you will either need to remove the package and then install the higher version or use the -U (upgrade) parameter.

Tip   Doing an upgrade on a package that does not have a lower version install will do a straight install, so we usually just use the upgrade parameter.

To illustrate the dependency problem we talked about in the previous section, Listing 12-1 shows an install of the bb-tools package. The bb-tools package is a group of applications that act as helpers to the Blackbox window manager. If you want to use Blackbox, we recommend that you also install the bb-tools package.

Listing 12-1: **Installing the bb-tools RPM Package**

```
bible:/media/dvd/suse/i586 # rpm -Uvh bbtools-2005.1.24-3.i586.rpm
error: Failed dependencies:
     blackbox is needed by bbtools-2005.1.24-3
```

We used the -U (upgrade), -v (verbose output), and -h (show hashes) parameters. The -v and -h parameters are usually very helpful in giving you active feedback of the installation of a package.

The bb-tools package depends on quite a few other software packages; thankfully, most have already been installed during the installation of SUSE. However, you can see that we do not have the Blackbox window manager installed, as RPM's dependency tree can tell this from the RPM itself.

To be successful, you need to install both Blackbox and bb-tools. The RPM system is able to install multiple RPM files and will take into account whether the packages to be installed depend on one another. This proves very useful in these situations. Listing 12-2 shows an installation of both bb-tools and the Blackbox RPM.

Listing 12-2: **Installing Both bb-tools and Blackbox**

```
bible:/media/dvd/suse/i586 # rpm -Uvh bbtools-2005.1.24-3.i586.rpm blackbox-
0.65.0-313.i586.rpm
Preparing...              ######################################### [100%]
  1:blackbox              ######################################### [ 50%]
  2:bbtools               ######################################### [100%]
```

Take note that even though we specified bb-tools before Blackbox, RPM was able to see that Blackbox had to be installed first during the preparation phase of package installation.

Querying RPM Packages

To find out information about an RPM package, you must *query* the RPM database or the RPM package directly. You do this with the -q command-line option. If you are querying an installed RPM, you just need to use the -q parameter with the query type you want to use. If you need to query an RPM package file directly, you have to add the -p (package) directive.

Querying RPMs is a very important part of administrating an RPM-based system because you may need to see what version of the software is installed, determine whether a file you have come across on your system is owned by an RPM package, or list the files that belong to an RPM.

Listing Files in an RPM

It is quite useful to see what files are in an RPM package, both before and after the package has been installed. To do this, you need to query (-q) the package for its files (-l), as in Listing 12-3.

Listing 12-3: **Querying a Package for Its File List**

```
bible:/media/dvd/suse/i586 # rpm -ql blackbox
/usr/X11R6/bin/blackbox
/usr/X11R6/bin/bsetbg
/usr/X11R6/bin/bsetroot
/usr/share/blackbox
/usr/share/blackbox/menu
/usr/share/blackbox/nls
/usr/share/blackbox/nls/C
/usr/share/blackbox/nls/C/blackbox.cat
/usr/share/blackbox/nls/POSIX
```

Blackbox contains a lot of files, and we have cut the list short to conserve space.

Even though the RPM file itself is called blackbox-0.65.0-313.i586.rpm, you need to query only the package name itself. The rest of the filename refers to the version (0.65.0-313) and the architecture it was compiled for (i586).

If you want to see what files belong to an RPM before it is installed, you need to query the package directly, and not the RPM database. To do this you use the -p (package) option (see Listing 12-4).

Listing 12-4: **Querying a Package Directly for Its File List**

```
bible:/media/dvd/suse/i586 # rpm -qlp blackbox-0.65.0-313.i586.rpm
/usr/X11R6/bin/blackbox
/usr/X11R6/bin/bsetbg
/usr/X11R6/bin/bsetroot
/usr/share/blackbox
/usr/share/blackbox/menu
/usr/share/blackbox/nls
/usr/share/blackbox/nls/C
/usr/share/blackbox/nls/C/blackbox.cat
```

As you can see, the package list is the same, which is what you would assume.

Finding What RPM Package Owns a File

When a package has been installed, you may need to find out if a file on the system belongs to a package for maintenance purposes. To do this, you need to query (-q) the database again and also find where the file came from (-f), as we do in the following code lines:

```
bible:/media/dvd/suse/i586 # rpm -qf /usr/X11R6/bin/blackbox
blackbox-0.65.0-313
```

As you can see by the second line in the preceding example, the RPM database is fully aware that the file /usr/X11R6/bin/blackbox belongs to the Blackbox package.

Tip   If you do not know the full location of a binary file, you can use the which command and backticks to pass the full path of the binary to rpm -qvf. If you wanted to find the location of Blackbox, you could use which blackbox. Passing this to rpm -qvf is achieved by using the command rpm -qvf `which blackbox`. A backtick is not a single quote; it looks like a single quote slanted to the left on your keyboard.

Querying the database for file ownership is really useful when you want to upgrade a certain application, but you are unsure if it is controlled by the RPM system.

Listing the RPM Packages Installed on a System

When we have installed SUSE servers for customers, one of the first things we do is install a minimal system and then use YaST to install only the packages we need to run the specific server the customer wants — for example, Apache.

When all packages we need have been installed, we then remove any non-essential packages used for the running of the server. This lowers the security risk, mainly for local security exploits that could take place.

To see what packages you have on the system, you need to query the RPM database (-q) and list all (-a) RPM packages (see Listing 12-5).

Listing 12-5: Listing Installed RPM Packages

```
bible:/media/dvd/suse/i586 # rpm -qa
aaa_skel-2005.2.1
providers-2004.10.25
suse-release-10
dos2unix-3.1-303
netcat-1.10-869
mktemp-1.5-732
gle-3.0.6-648
gpart-0.1h-478
eject-2.0.13-190
usbutils-0.70-8
popt-1.7-207
ziptool-1.4.0-111
```

Again, we have cut the list down as we have a lot of packages installed, but you get the point.

Tip   The program sort is useful in this situation to sort the output of the rpm -qa command into an alphanumeric list. Using the pipe (|) command, you can redirect the output of the rpm -qa command through the sort command (rpm -qa |sort).

Once listed, you can go through the RPM list and remove any packages not needed.

Removing Installed Packages

After an RPM has been installed, you may need to remove it from the system for one reason or another. As it does when installing packages, RPM will check the dependencies of the package you want to remove. This check of dependencies is as important as checking package dependency during installation, because you could end up deleting files that another RPM package depends on.

To remove packages, you need to erase (-e) the package from the system. As with installation of packages, RPM checks to see if any other RPM packages on the system depend on the package you want to remove. If a package does depend on it, the removal will fail. See Listing 12-6 for an example.

Listing 12-6: **Removing a Dependent Package**

```
bible:/media/dvd/suse/i586 # rpm -e blackbox
error: Failed dependencies:
blackbox is needed by (installed) bbtools-2005.1.24-3
```

In this example, you have been told that the package bb-tools depends on the Blackbox package we are trying to remove. To resolve this, you have two options, one good and one bad:

✦ The bad option, which can prove marginally useful during both installation and removal of packages, is to tell RPM to ignore package dependencies. This should never really be used when removing a package, because as in the case of bbtools, other packages will stop working.

However, during package installation, you may know for certain that a dependency that RPM is aware of is in fact resolved by a source-compiled library you have installed, or are testing. To tell RPM to not check for dependencies, use the -nodeps parameter as well as the usual rpm -Uvh.

✦ The good option (you do want to be a good administrator, don't you?) is to remove the dependent package as well as the package you originally wanted to remove, as shown in the following:

```
bible:/media/dvd/suse/i586 # rpm -e blackbox bbtools
```

Caution

You may have noticed a very important characteristic of package removal, one common with most things in Unix — that is, when you are root, you are not warned that you are removing files. This holds true when removing packages. You were not asked to confirm the removal of bbtools and blackbox; rpm assumed you knew what you were doing.

Verifying an RPM

If you want to verify whether an RPM is correctly installed, you can use the rpm -V command. Using the verify command will check the files, their permissions, and also if the package's dependencies are installed so that it can function correctly.

```
bible:~ # rpm -V logcheck
bible:~ #
```

If rpm -V returns nothing, then the RPM itself has been successfully verified and all is well.

On the other hand, if something is wrong with the package, you are told what file in the package is different from the original installed file from the RPM.

```
bible:~ # rpm -V i4l-isdnlog
S.5....T c /etc/isdn/isdn.conf
bible:~ #
```

For each file in an RPM that differs from the norm, you receive a letter that dictates what the difference was and why. Table 12-1 details what the differences can be and their respective status letters (or number).

<table>
<tr><td colspan="2" align="center">Table 12-1
RPM Verification Output</td></tr>
<tr><td>*Status*</td><td>*Description*</td></tr>
<tr><td>S</td><td>Different file size.</td></tr>
<tr><td>M</td><td>The file mode is different.</td></tr>
<tr><td>5</td><td>The MD5 sum differs.</td></tr>
<tr><td>D</td><td>If this is a device file, the major or minor number is different.</td></tr>
<tr><td>L</td><td>If this is a file link, then its status is different from what is expected.</td></tr>
<tr><td>U</td><td>The owner of the file differs.</td></tr>
<tr><td>G</td><td>The group owner differs.</td></tr>
<tr><td>T</td><td>The modification time differs (the file contents have changed since being installed).</td></tr>
</table>

So in the case of the /etc/isdn/isdn.conf example given previously, the current file differs in size (S), its MD5 sum is different (5), and the modification time is different (T). This might lead you to assume that the configuration file has changed since installation.

Note   As with the RPM list command (rpm -qa), you can verify all the packages installed on the system with rpm -Va.

Using RPM is not as difficult as most new users think. As we hope you can see, RPM provides a very useful tool for your arsenal, and any competent administrator or user should know how to use it.

For more information, see the rpm man page, which lists the full range of what RPM can do.

Creating an RPM

Every application begins its life in source code form, and to make an executable you need to compile it for your architecture. When you compile software, you have to define certain parameters that the source code is compiled under. This could be software optimization, file installation locations, or options to enable or disable certain software functionality.

Once compiled, the software is installed into the system to be able to run on its own. This process is repeated for each iteration of the software release that you want to install. However, this process does not control the software versioning, and there is a great danger that older library versions of software could conflict with the software when you upgrade.

The RPM system enables you to semi-automate this process with the definition of a specification or spec file. The *spec file* defines the location of the source code, preparing the code for compilation and installation of the source code in one manageable package. Inside the spec file is also a definition of the version of the code and the location of all files the RPM contains. This allows for updates to overwrite (effectively removing the old software and installing the new), negating the impact of the traditional configure, compile, and install with source code.

Distribution RPMS

Each Linux distribution that bases its software on RPM files will compile the software distribution for you as well as release source RPM packages. A source RPM package is an RPM containing the source code for the software as well as instructions on how to prepare and compile the software. The RPM will also contain the spec file.

SUSE uses the auto-build system to automate the process of compiling the same source RPM files to create binary RPMs for all the supported architectures (Intel 32/64, AMD64, PPC, and zSeries). This provides SUSE with an advantage over the other distributions in that all architectures are based on exactly the same source base. This means that you can use Linux on a desktop for development work and there is a 99 percent chance that you can recompile and run on a mainframe because all the libraries are the same, from the same code base.

Source Code

A large proportion of source code actually includes a spec file in the source distribution, which means you can compile into an RPM and use software versioning to control the installation.

Compiling Source Code

To transform source code (C, C++, Fortran, and so on) to a machine architecture binary, you use a compiler. A compiler takes the source code and analyzes it for syntactical and semantic errors (much like checking the spelling and grammar of text), tokenizing (splitting the source code into smaller, quantifiable chunks), and then producing a binary runtime. This runtime is linked to any libraries it relies upon to run.

The internals of these operations are handled for the C programming language by gcc (GNU C Compiler). It is unlikely you will have to use gcc directly unless you want to produce applications in Linux (or any other Unix), but it is useful to know it exists and is the main contributor to the creation of Linux applications.

If you wrote the standard "Hello World!" application in C:

```
#include <stdio.h>
int main () {
printf ("Hello World!\n");
}
```

and saved this file as hello.c, you could then compile this into a binary runtime using gcc:

```
gcc hello.c –ohello
```

Notice that there is no space between -o (output file) and the name of the output file.

When the compilation has finished, you will have a binary runtime called hello in the current directory. Running the file produces the desired results.

```
bible:~ # ./hello
Hello World!
```

The hello binary has been compiled and linked to system libraries it relies on correctly, and works as it should, by producing Hello World!.

It is beyond the scope of this book to go into programming in Linux, but if you are interested in more information, pick up the excellent *Beginning Linux Programming, Third Edition*, by Neil Matthew, Richard Stones, and Alan Cox (Wrox, 2003).

An RPM package is only as good as the person who created it. All of the intelligence that you saw in RPM earlier in the chapter is controlled by how the RPM is created. Earlier, we talked briefly about spec files and how they are used to control package creation. We will now create an RPM from a small program and show how it all fits together.

The RPM Environment

You will create a spec file later in the chapter, but first you need to see how the process works.

SUSE uses the directory `/usr/src/packages` to build and create an RPM package. This directory contains subdirectories, and Table 12-2 shows the reasoning behind this.

Table 12-2
The RPM Source Directories

Directory	Description
BUILD	This is where your original source code is unpacked and compiled.
SOURCES	This is a placeholder for source files before they are unpacked.
SPECS	This contains the spec files for the package you are creating.
SRPMS	If you are creating source RPMS, they are stored here in source RPM once built.
RPMS	The final resting place for your packaged RPM. This directory is further subdivided into architecture type (i386, i586, i686, and so on).

The architecture of an RPM package can be a subset of a general architecture; for example, Intel can be i386 (386-based, works on all Intel-based machines). The i586/i686/Athlon architectures will usually contain specific optimizations for the higher Intel/AMD processors.

Other architectures could be ppc (Power PC based), s390 (zSeries/System 390 based), AXP (Alpha processor), and so on. We will deal specifically with the Intel-based architectures, but we wanted you to be aware that other architectures do exist, and RPM does consider these.

The Spec File

The spec file is composed of four main components: the header, preparation, build options, and file list.

The RPM Header

The header is the description of the software name, release, and the location of the source file; see Listing 12-7 for an example.

Listing 12-7: **The RPM Header**

```
Summary:        Logcheck system log analyzer
Name:           logcheck
Version:        1.1.2
Release:        2
Vendor:          Craig Rowland <crowland@psionic.com>
Packager:        Justin Davies <justin@palmcoder.net>
License:        GPL
Group:           Applications/System
Source0:        http://www.palmcoder.net/files/suse-rpms/10/%{name}-%{version}.
                tar.gz
URL:             http://www.palmcoder.net/files/suse-rpms/10
Requires:       cron
Requires:       /usr/sbin/sendmail
BuildRoot:       /tmp/%{name}-buildroot

%description
Logcheck is a software package that is designed to automatically run and
check system log files for security violations and unusual activity.
Logcheck utilizes a program called logtail that remembers the last
position it read from in a log file and uses this position on
subsequent runs to process new information.
```

Some of the header options are self-explanatory, such as the Summary and package Name. However, a few need further explanation.

✦ One of the most important parts of this header file is the version and release.

- **Version** — The major version number of the package, which usually refers to the main source version.

- **Release** — The sub-version of the release. This could be used for updates to the main package for bugs and so on.

✦ **Vendor** — The name of the company or person who wrote the software, whereas the *Packager* is the name of the person that maintains the RPM package release.

✦ **License** — What the package/source code is released under. In this case, logcheck is released under the GPL license.

✦ **Group** — A defined package group list is maintained to control the general section the software falls under. The Group definition is used to tell the user what type of application it is that they are installing and does not affect the RPM itself. When using graphical user interface (GUI) tools to view RPM packages, the Group definition is used to group applications under the headings found in the GROUPS file located at

`/usr/share/doc/packages/rpm/GROUPS`. The file contains each group followed by a subsection of the group:

- Amusements/Games
- Amusements/Graphics
- Applications/Archiving
- Applications/Communications
- Applications/Databases
- Applications/Editors
- Applications/Emulators
- Applications/Engineering
- Applications/File
- Applications/Internet
- Applications/Multimedia
- Applications/Productivity
- Applications/Publishing
- Applications/System
- Applications/Text
- Development/Debuggers
- Development/Languages
- Development/Libraries
- Development/System
- Development/Tools
- Documentation
- System Environment/Base
- System Environment/Daemons
- System Environment/Kernel
- System Environment/Libraries
- System Environment/Shells
- User Interface/Desktops
- User Interface/X
- User Interface/X Hardware Support

✦ **Source** — Refers to the location of the source for the RPM. This is extremely important because the RPM build process uses this location when it prepares the source distribution. Even though this entry refers to a web address, the last portion is used as the filename of the source tarball, located in /usr/src/packages/SOURCES.

✦ **Requires** — Tells RPM that this package depends on the cron RPM package and the existence of /usr/sbin/sendmail.

✦ **BuildRoot** — The location where RPM will prepare the entities that are part of the final binary RPM.

✦ **Description** — A long form extension of the summary. It provides an overview of what the package does and is a good place to let the end user know what capabilities the package provides.

The RPM %prep Section

When you have defined the RPM header, you need to prepare the source code for compilation. The first thing that needs to happen is that you untar the source distribution. RPM uses the macro %setup to do this, as follows:

```
%prep
%setup -q
```

The %setup macro untars the source file into the BUILD directory. The -q option suppresses the output when unpacking the source.

The %build Macro

After you have prepped the source, you need to compile the code for your system.

The %build macro enables you to tell RPM how to compile the source code. You can use any shell command here, which could be a configure script or a simple make for the Makefile. In this case, you are just running make in the source directory to compile logcheck.

```
%build
make
```

The macro enters the directory of the source code and runs any programs you define in the %build section. Anything you run on the command line to compile the application can be entered here.

Next, you have to create the %install macro (see Listing 12-8).

Listing 12-8: **The %install Section for logcheck**

```
%install
rm -rf $RPM_BUILD_ROOT
mkdir -p $RPM_BUILD_ROOT/usr/sbin
mkdir -p $RPM_BUILD_ROOT/etc/logcheck
mkdir -p $RPM_BUILD_ROOT/etc/cron.hourly

install ./systems/linux/logcheck.hacking $RPM_BUILD_ROOT/etc/logcheck
install ./systems/linux/logcheck.violations $RPM_BUILD_ROOT/etc/logcheck
install ./systems/linux/logcheck.violations.ignore $RPM_BUILD_ROOT/etc/logcheck
install ./systems/linux/logcheck.ignore $RPM_BUILD_ROOT/etc/logcheck
install ./systems/linux/logcheck.sh  $RPM_BUILD_ROOT/usr/sbin
install ./src/logtail  $RPM_BUILD_ROOT/usr/sbin

cat <<EOF > $RPM_BUILD_ROOT/etc/cron.hourly/logcheck
#!/bin/sh
exec /usr/sbin/logcheck.sh
EOF
```

The `%install` macro is the most involved section because you have to use it to prepare the `RPM_BUILD_ROOT` for RPM packaging.

1. First, you need to make sure you start a fresh RPM build in case a previous
   build took place and did not complete successfully. This is done with the
   `r m -rf $RPM_BUILD_ROOT` directive.

2. Next, you have to create the target directories for the installed files. In this
   example, the `logcheck` binaries are located in `/usr/sbin` and the configuration
   files are located in `/etc/logcheck`.

> **Note**
>
> The `RPM_BUILD_ROOT` is an *effective root*. This means that it is a representation
> of where files would be located after the RPM has been installed in the root (/)
> directory.

3. The `install` program is effectively the same as `cp`. It copies a file from one location to another. Here you are copying files to the location they would be in an
   installed system, under `RPM_BUILD_ROOT`.

4. The `cat` entry is a nice way of creating a file out of text using redirection. The
   redirection will enter the text following the `cat` program until an EOF (end of
   file) is found. This will create an entry in `/etc/cron.hourly` for `logcheck` to
   run once an hour.

The %clean Macro

After your RPM has been created, the `%clean` macro is executed. The `%clean macro` is used to clean up your system after an RPM build. As with the other macros in the spec file, the `%clean` macro you define is automatically executed during the RPM build process, in this case, after the RPM has successfully been built.

```
%clean
rm -rf $RPM_BUILD_ROOT
```

The %files Macro

RPM needs to know what files to archive into a binary RPM. The `%files` macro contains a list of files relative to `RPM_BUILD_ROOT`. Listing 12-9 shows an example.

Listing 12-9: **The %files Macro for logcheck**

```
%files
%defattr(644,root,root,755)
%doc CHANGES CREDITS README* systems/linux/README*
%attr(700,root,root) %dir /etc/logcheck
%attr(600,root,root) %config /etc/logcheck/*
%attr(700,root,root) %config /etc/cron.hourly/logcheck
%attr(755,root,root) /usr/sbin/logcheck.sh
%attr(755,root,root) /usr/sbin/logtail
```

The entries you want to note in this file are as follows:

✦ The `%defattr` macro sets the default file permissions for all files installed, unless explicitly stated for each file entry.

✦ One important `%files` macro entry is the `%doc` macro. It is used to specify that the files listed are documentation. In SUSE, all RPM documentation is stored in `/usr/share/doc/packages/rpmname`. Any files set as `%doc` type will be installed into `/usr/share/doc/packages/logcheck`.

✦ The `%attr` macro, like `%defattr`, sets the file permissions of the file specified. In the case of the `logcheck` configuration files, you have said that only root is allowed to access the files.

✦ The `%config` entry specifies that the file specified is a configuration file. When an RPM file is upgraded, any configuration files belonging to the RPM are "kept back" so that any changes you may have made are not lost.

Compiling an RPM from the Spec File

To set up your environment for compiling the RPM, the source file has to be located in /usr/src/packages/SOURCES. You need to use the rpmbuild program to take the spec file and compile the source based on the configuration you have specified. The -bb argument is used to specify that you want to build (b) and binary (b) package.

You can see in Listing 12-10 how the build process follows the spec file you have created, going through %prep, %setup, and %files to compile a binary RPM.

Listing 12-10: **Using rpmbuild to Compile the logcheck Source**

```
bible:/tmp # rpmbuild -bb /tmp/logcheck.spec
Executing(%prep): /bin/sh -e /var/tmp/rpm-tmp.48125
+ umask 022
+ cd /usr/src/packages/BUILD
+ cd /usr/src/packages/BUILD
+ rm -rf logcheck-1.1.2
+ /usr/bin/gzip -dc /usr/src/packages/SOURCES/logcheck-1.1.2.tar.gz
+ tar -xf -
+ STATUS=0
+ '[' 0 -ne 0 ']'
+ cd logcheck-1.1.2
++ /usr/bin/id -u
+ '[' 0 = 0 ']'
+ /bin/chown -Rhf root .
++ /usr/bin/id -u
+ '[' 0 = 0 ']'
+ /bin/chgrp -Rhf root .
+ /bin/chmod -Rf a+rX,g-w,o-w .
+ exit 0
Executing(%build): /bin/sh -e /var/tmp/rpm-tmp.48125
+ umask 022
+ cd /usr/src/packages/BUILD
+ /bin/rm -rf /tmp/logcheck-buildroot
++ dirname /tmp/logcheck-buildroot
+ /bin/mkdir -p /tmp
+ /bin/mkdir /tmp/logcheck-buildroot
+ cd logcheck-1.1.2
+ make
Making logcheck
cc -O -o ./src/logtail ./src/logtail.c
src/logtail.c: In function `main':
src/logtail.c:56: warning: return type of `main' is not `int'
+ exit 0
Executing(%install): /bin/sh -e /var/tmp/rpm-tmp.85959
```

Continued

Listing 12-10 *(continued)*

```
+ umask 022
+ cd /usr/src/packages/BUILD
+ cd logcheck-1.1.2
+ rm -rf /tmp/logcheck-buildroot
+ mkdir -p /tmp/logcheck-buildroot/usr/sbin
+ mkdir -p /tmp/logcheck-buildroot/etc/logcheck
+ mkdir -p /tmp/logcheck-buildroot/etc/cron.hourly
+ install ./systems/linux/logcheck.hacking /tmp/logcheck-buildroot/etc/logcheck
+ install ./systems/linux/logcheck.violations /tmp/logcheck-buildroot/etc/logcheck
+ install ./systems/linux/logcheck.violations.ignore /tmp/logcheck-buildroot/etc/logcheck
+ install ./systems/linux/logcheck.ignore /tmp/logcheck-buildroot/etc/logcheck
+ install ./systems/linux/logcheck.sh /tmp/logcheck-buildroot/usr/sbin
+ install ./src/logtail /tmp/logcheck-buildroot/usr/sbin
+ cat
+ RPM_BUILD_ROOT=/tmp/logcheck-buildroot
+ export RPM_BUILD_ROOT
+ test -x /usr/sbin/Check -a 0 = 0 -o -x /usr/sbin/Check -a '!' -z /tmp/logcheck-buildroot
+ echo 'I call /usr/sbin/Check...'
I call /usr/sbin/Check...
+ /usr/sbin/Check
+ /usr/lib/rpm/brp-compress
Processing files: logcheck-1.1.2-2
Executing(%doc): /bin/sh -e /var/tmp/rpm-tmp.11584
+ umask 022
+ cd /usr/src/packages/BUILD
+ cd logcheck-1.1.2
+ DOCDIR=/tmp/logcheck-buildroot/usr/share/doc/packages/logcheck
+ export DOCDIR
+ rm -rf /tmp/logcheck-buildroot/usr/share/doc/packages/logcheck
+ /bin/mkdir -p /tmp/logcheck-buildroot/usr/share/doc/packages/logcheck
+ cp -pr CHANGES CREDITS README README.how.to.interpret README.keywords
systems/linux/README.linux systems/linux/README.linux.IMPORTANT /tmp/logcheck-
buildroot/usr/share/doc/packages/logcheck
+ exit 0
Finding  Provides: /usr/lib/rpm/find-provides
Finding  Requires: /usr/lib/rpm/find-requires
Requires(rpmlib): rpmlib(PayloadFilesHavePrefix) <= 4.0-1 rpmlib(CompressedFileNames) <=
3.0.4-1
Requires: cron /usr/sbin/sendmail /bin/sh libc.so.6 libc.so.6(GLIBC_2.0) libc.so.6(GLIBC_2.1)
Checking for unpackaged file(s): /usr/lib/rpm/check-files /tmp/logcheck-buildroot
Wrote: /usr/src/packages/RPMS/i586/logcheck-1.1.2-2.i586.rpm
Executing(%clean): /bin/sh -e /var/tmp/rpm-tmp.14217
+ umask 022
+ cd /usr/src/packages/BUILD
+ cd logcheck-1.1.2
+ rm -rf /tmp/logcheck-buildroot
+ exit 0
```

The RPM has been successfully created. In the next section, you check the RPM and install it.

Checking the Finished RPM

When an RPM has been created, it is stored in /usr/src/packages/RPMS/i586. For other architectures (s390, ppc, and so on), RPMs are saved in the relevant architecture subdirectory.

You can check the existence of the file and also list the files in the package just as you did earlier in the chapter with the rpm -qlp command, as shown in Listing 12-11.

Listing 12-11: **Listing the Files in the logcheck RPM**

```
bible:/usr/src/packages/RPMS/i586 # rpm -qlp logcheck-
1.1.2-2.i586.rpm
/etc/cron.hourly/logcheck
/etc/logcheck
/etc/logcheck/logcheck.hacking
/etc/logcheck/logcheck.ignore
/etc/logcheck/logcheck.violations
/etc/logcheck/logcheck.violations.ignore
/usr/sbin/logcheck.sh
/usr/sbin/logtail
/usr/share/doc/packages/logcheck
/usr/share/doc/packages/logcheck/CHANGES
/usr/share/doc/packages/logcheck/CREDITS
/usr/share/doc/packages/logcheck/README
/usr/share/doc/packages/logcheck/README.how.to.interpret
/usr/share/doc/packages/logcheck/README.keywords
/usr/share/doc/packages/logcheck/README.linux
/usr/share/doc/packages/logcheck/README.linux.IMPORTANT
```

So you can see the RPM is there and looks correct based on your configuration in the spec file. Now you are ready to install the RPM, as shown in Listing 12-12, with rpm -Uvh (upgrade, verbose, and show hash marks).

Listing 12-12: **Installing the logcheck RPM**

```
bible:/usr/src/packages/RPMS/i586 # rpm -Uvh logcheck-1.1.2-2.i586.rpm
Preparing...                ######################################### [100%]
```

```
1:logcheck                       ######################################### [100%]
```

The RPM you have taken from source, created the spec file for, and compiled into a binary RPM is finally integrated into our system.

RPM creation is something that the distributors have to do for every release, bug-fix, and update of a package. SUSE includes over 3,000 packages already, so the possibility of not having software that fulfills your need is quite slim. However, in the event that you can't find a package, like logcheck, RPM creation is a useful skill to have.

Ultimately, knowing how an RPM is built and what RPM authors can do with an RPM package proves useful when you are working with packages themselves. It enables you to see how dependencies, post-installation scripts, and file specifications impact how your packages work when installed.

✦   ✦   ✦

Working with Files

In a way, "Working with Files" could have been the title
of the whole book. After all, just about everything you do
with your system is working with files. In fact, the Unix philosophy states that *everything is a file*, and it's almost true.

In this chapter we look at some of the common tools for examining and manipulating files. We also look at working with the
most common file formats and compressing and archiving
files. Finally, we touch on issues surrounding file attributes
and access control lists (ACLs).

Listing, Copying, and Moving Files

We covered the fundamental concepts of listing, copying, and
moving files in Chapter 2. In this section, we review those concepts and expand on them slightly.

The Command-Line Tools

You can list files at the command line with the `ls` command, or
you can use commands such as `mv` or `rm` to work with those
files.

Using ls

We doubt that many people know all of the options to the
`ls` command, and we shall certainly not list them all here. If
you're curious, read the man page (`man ls`) or, better, the info
pages (`info coreutils ls`). But there are a few important things
to note about the behavior of `ls`. If you don't use the

-a or -A option, you will not see the hidden files (that is, those with names starting with a dot). It can be easy to forget about this possibility — for example, consider the following:

```
user@bible:~> rmdir directory/
rmdir: `directory/': Directory not empty
user@bible:~> cd directory/
user@bible:~> ls
user@bible:~>
user@bible:~> ls -a
.  ..  .afile
```

Here we tried to remove the directory that appeared to be empty because the ls command on its own produced no output. But ls -a shows that there is a hidden file in it, which is why the rmdir command failed (rmdir removes only empty directories).

As mentioned in Chapter 2, symbolic links are objects that point to other files and directories. In a standard directory listing, symbolic links show up as regular files, but ls provides the -l option to provide more information about files and directories as well as to help you to identify any symbolic links in the directory. For example, create a symbolic link in this directory and then look at it with the standard ls command:

```
user@bible:~/directory> ln -s ../otherdir/bfile alink
user@bible:~/directory> touch afile
user@bible:~/directory> ls
afile  alink
```

Using the ls -l command clearly shows that this file is a symbolic link:

```
user@bible:~/directory> ls -l
total 0
-rw-r--r--  1 user users  0 2004-06-20 10:10 afile
lrwxrwxrwx  1 user users 26 2004-06-20 10:32 alink -> ../otherdir/bfile
```

Unless you are looking at a directory with a very large number of files in it, ls -la is quite a good way to use the ls command. If there is anything unexpected about the sizes or ownerships of the files, you will be able to notice it, and dot files will be displayed.

The -t option to ls can be very useful. Suppose, for example, you have recently done something that has caused a file to be created in a large directory, but you have forgotten or don't know the name of the file. The ls -lat command lists the files in order of modification date and time, so the new or newly modified files will be at the top of the listing.

If you want to get a full recursive listing of all files beneath a particular directory, the command ls -laR is what you want. This can be particularly useful if you are doing some detective work to find out, for example, what is being changed when you make some change to a system using a graphical or other configuration tool, but you don't know which file or files are being changed. If you use ls -laR before and after making the change, writing the output to a file, you can then compare the two files and work out what has happened.

```
root@bible: / # ls -laR>/tmp/listing1
```

(Some change to the system.)

```
root@bible: / # ls -laR>/tmp/listing2
root@bible: / # diff /tmp/listing1 /tmp/listing2
```

Here we have made some change to the system at the step marked "(Some change to system.)," before and after which we created separate files containing a listing of the files existing at that time. Using diff, you can see what has changed.

Occasionally it can be useful to know that ls -i shows you the inodes to which the files are attached in the underlying filesystem. In particular, this can help you to understand hard links:

```
user@bible:~/directory> touch afile
user@bible:~/directory> touch bfile
user@bible:~/directory> ln afile cfile
user@bible:~/directory> ls -la
total 8
drwxr-xr-x   2 user users 4096 2004-06-20 10:44 .
drwxr-xr-x  32 user users 4096 2004-06-20 10:31 ..
-rw-r--r--   2 user users    0 2004-06-20 10:44 afile
-rw-r--r--   1 user users    0 2004-06-20 10:44 bfile
-rw-r--r--   2 user users    0 2004-06-20 10:44 cfile
```

The total 8 message is initially somewhat confusing. The number that follows the total is the total number of files and links to files in the specified directory, not just the total number of files. If you add the values in the second column, counting '..' (which is a link to the parent directory of the current directory) as 1, you'll get the number 8.

```
user@bible:~/directory> ls -il|sort -n
total 0
1259203 -rw-r--r--   2 user users 0 2004-06-20 10:44 afile
1259203 -rw-r--r--   2 user users 0 2004-06-20 10:44 cfile
1259206 -rw-r--r--   1 user users 0 2004-06-20 10:44 bfile
```

The inode numbers confirm that afile and cfile refer to the same file.

Note   r m cfile leaves the file untouched: the r m command really removes links to files rather than the files themselves — when there are no links left, you can't access the file.

The way in which the ls command displays its output depends on a set of default options, which are stored in the $LS_OPTIONS environment variable. This setting is in turn set up in the file /etc/bash.bashrc. If you examine the contents of this variable, you will find something like the following:

```
user@bible:~ > echo $LS_OPTIONS
-N --color=tty -T 0
```

This means that these options are passed to ls whenever it is run. You can override these options by setting and exporting a different LS_OPTIONS variable:

```
user@bible:~ > export LS_OPTIONS='— color=never -T 0'
```

Then you will see the same layout, but without any colorized entries. Any options that can be passed to ls can be included in this variable.

If you want to set a permanently different option for yourself, you can set and export the LS_OPTIONS variable by adding a line similar to that just given to your .bashrc file.

Tip   The color scheme that ls uses to colorize its output is determined by the LS_COLORS variable. By default this is taken from the file /etc/DIR_COLORS, but you can override the defaults by copying that file to ~/.dir_colors and editing it as required.

Using mv

It sometimes strikes people as odd that m v is a command both for moving and for renaming files. Actually it's quite logical: If you move a file from the current directory to somewhere else, what happens is that the file appears over there and disappears here. If you rename the file, the copy with the new name appears, and the copy with the old name disappears. And of course you can copy the file to a new location and a new name with just one invocation of the m v command. For example:

```
user@bible:~> mv afile /tmp/
```

moves afile to the /tmp directory and

```
user@bible:~> mv afile bfile
```

renames afile to bfile in the current directory, while

```
user@bible:~> mv afile /tmp/bfile
```

moves afile to the /tmp directory and renames the file to bfile at the same time.

Using rm

Take care. The rm command removes files and doesn't (by default) give you any second chances, so it is dangerous. There are various ways to use rm to make it less final, but none of them are totally satisfactory.

You may choose to use rm -i in place of rm; this makes it interactive, and you will be prompted before the file is actually removed:

```
user@bible:~/directory> ls
afile
user@bible:~/directory> rm -i afile
rm: remove regular empty file `afile'? y
user@bible:~/directory>
```

If you like this, you can create an alias in the file .alias in your home directory (or in your .bashrc file) to make rm always behave like rm -i. You can add a line like this:

```
alias rm='rm -i'
```

to ~/.alias. When you log in the next time, you will see this behavior:

```
user@bible:~/directory> ls
afile
user@bible:~/directory> rm afile
rm: remove regular empty file `afile'? y
user@bible:~/directory>
```

So rm is behaving like rm -i. If you don't want to be prompted, you will now need to use rm -f.

Note   The only problem with doing this is that it gives you a false sense of security: If you are logged in on a system where you have not set up the alias, you may remember too late that this safety blanket was not available. In some ways the best advice is to always think hard about what you're doing before you press the Return key (and always keep regular backups).

Some people use other more elaborate solutions to take the sting out of rm, such as

There is also the possible problem that when you delete more than one file with the same name you are not sure which one still exists in the trash directory.

You can use r m recursively with the -r option. The r m -rf command recursively removes a directory and everything in it. The r m -rf / (as root) command removes everything on your system.

File Managers

A file manager is a tool that enables you to look at the layout of the files and directories on your system and to perform various actions on the files (copy, move, delete, open, and so on). There are three particularly useful choices for a file manager: Konqueror, Nautilus, and m c. If you are using KDE, then by default you are likely to use Konqueror as your graphical file manager. If you are using GNOME, the same applies to Nautilus. m c (the Midnight Commander) is a text-based file manager that has some very useful features.

Konqueror as a File Manager

If you want to do file listing and file management graphically, Konqueror's file manager mode is powerful. It has the advantage that it can show you previews of at least some of the files as it lists them. (You can configure this behavior to some extent in Konqueror's Settings menu.) When selecting files, remember KDE's one-click interface: People who are used to Windows will tend to left-click a file and then act surprised when it opens in an application.

To use Konqueror as a file manager, the best plan is to use it with a split view (Window ⇨ Split View Left/Right). Then you can drag files from one pane to the other to move or copy them. When you drag a file, you are offered three options: Move here, Copy here, and Link here. If you hold down the Shift key while you drag, a move is forced. If you hold down the Control key while you drag the file, a copy action will be forced. In general, it is best to choose the keystroke in advance; this way you remove the risk that your click will open the file.

A right-click inside a directory brings up a menu that includes the ability to create new directories or files and operations on the selected file such as Copy to and Move to.

Konqueror has recently added some nice additional functionality, including the ability to open a KdirStat window (displaying directory statistics: the sizes of files and subdirectories displayed graphically). You can also bring up a graphical tool that will do string replacement on all files in a directory (KFileReplace).

As we have noted elsewhere, Konqueror displays files across the network and includes the ability to display files on a machine accessed by ssh as if they were local.

In Konqueror, clicking an RPM file offers you the choice of installing it. Clicking a zip or tar archive seamlessly takes you inside it so that you can extract individual files.

For more discussion of Konqueror, see the KDE section of Chapter 8.

Nautilus as a File Manager

There is not a great deal of difference in choosing in terms of functionality between using Konqueror as a file manager and Nautilus. Again, it is capable of offering previews of many types of files. To move a file from one directory to another, you will need one window open on each directory; a simple drag will move, while dragging with the Control key held down will do a copy.

A nice feature of Nautilus is its CD creator functionality; you can get to this through the Go menu or by entering burn:/// in the location bar. When you have dropped a collection of files into this window, you can burn them to a CD simply by pressing the Burn to CD button.

Nautilus will also transparently open zip and tar archives and can access network shares including FTP, NFS, and Windows shares. Another nice feature is that fonts:/// shows all the fonts on the system.

Nautilus is introduced in the GNOME section of Chapter 8.

mc as a File Manager

m c offers you file manager capabilities in a non-graphical environment. By default, it opens with two panes, each open on the current directory. Navigation is accomplished through the use of arrow and function keys:

✦ F9 opens the menus and you can then navigate them with the arrow keys.

✦ F5 copies the selected file.

✦ Tab switches between the two panes.

Among the menu items are chmod and chown capabilities (allowing you to change file permissions and ownerships, respectively), and m c enables you to enter RPM files and extract files from them transparently. Of course, the fact that m c is a text-based application means that you can run it in a text console when the graphics are not running. The KDE konsole terminal emulator has a menu item (under Session) that starts an m c session or a root m c session at the current directory in a new tab.

Finding Files

Often you may want to find a file with a given name. There are two common ways to do this at the command line: the `find` command and the `locate` command.

Using find

The `find` command has a bewildering number of options, and you will sometimes see complex examples of the use of `find`. But in most cases where you will want to use it, the situation will be something like this: You believe that a file with a certain name exists somewhere below a certain directory (say `~/temp/`). Change to that directory and type:

```
user@bible:~/temp> find .
```

You will see everything below the current directory being listed. So if you are looking for `afile` and you type:

```
user@bible:~/temp> find . | grep afile
```

you will get some output showing the path to `afile` (or any file whose name includes the string `afile`) if it exists anywhere under the directory `~/temp`. In most cases this is all you need, although you will read elsewhere that the "correct" way to use the `find` command is to do this:

```
user@bible:~/temp> find . -name afile -print
```

This finds any file below the current directory with the exact name `afile`.

You may sometimes want to pipe the output of the `find` command to another program such as `cpio` (see more about `cpio` later in the chapter) or use `find`'s built-in `-exec` option to perform another command on the list of files `find` produces. For example:

```
find . -name afile -exec lpr {} \;
```

This executes the `lpr` command and prints any file that is found by the `find` command. Here the {} (curly brackets) represent each file that was in the output of `find`. The `\;` is needed to terminate the command.

Using locate

The `locate` command is part of the `findutils-locate` package. It gets its information about where files are on the system from a database that is normally updated once a day, so it cannot be used to find files that have been created or moved very recently unless you manually update the database.

To find a file using `locate` is as simple as this example:

```
user@bible:~ > locate traceroute
/usr/sbin/traceroute
/usr/sbin/traceroute6
/usr/share/man/man1/traceroute.1.gz
/usr/share/man/man1/traceroute6.1.gz
```

Note
The `locate` utility is located in `/usr/bin/locate`, but is installed only if you've installed the Experienced User set of packages on your system or subsequently installed this package on your system using YaST's software installation module.

Note that any file whose name contains the string given (in this case `traceroute`) will be found.

The updating of the `locate` database is done daily from the file `/etc/cron.daily/ updatedb`, which reads certain parameters from `/etc/sysconfig/locate`. In `/etc/sysconfig/locate` you can set whether or not you want the automatic updating to take place at all and which paths you want to be excluded from the database (by default, temporary and spool files are excluded, as are removable media).

If you want to update the database manually, run the command (as root) `/etc/ cron.daily/updatedb`. This is the command that is normally run automatically each day. It runs `find` across the whole system, and writes the results to the database file `/var/lib/localtedb`. It takes account of the settings in `/etc/ sysconfig/locate` and so calls `/usr/sbin/updatedb` with the correct options. As this command searches the entire system, it is, not surprisingly, fairly resource intensive.

Using Konqueror to Find Files

Konqueror has a menu option (Tools ➪ Find File) that searches for files under the directory being displayed when it is running in file manager mode (see Figure 13-1).

Finding Files in GNOME

The find files functionality in GNOME is separated from the Nautilus file manager itself. There is a small application called `gnome-search-tool` that can be accessed through the Actions menu on the desktop (Actions ➪ Search for Files), as shown in Figure 13-2.

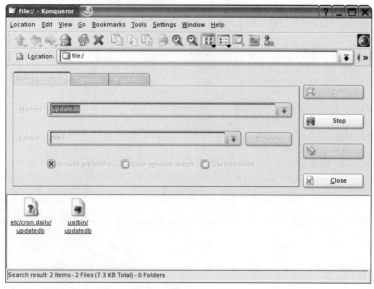

Figure 13-1: Konqueror finding files

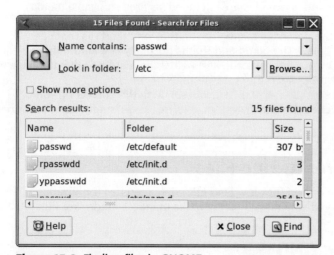

Figure 13-2: Finding files in GNOME

Finding Files in mc

m c also has find files functionality, with the capability to search for content within files. To use the find files functionality in m c, choose Find File from the Command menu (or press Alt+?). You can then enter a filename pattern and text content to search for in the dialog box that appears (see Figure 13-3).

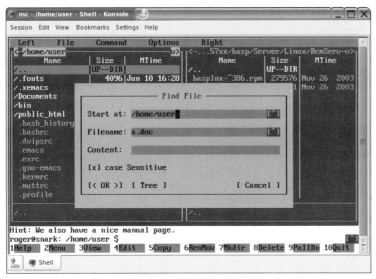

Figure 13-3: Finding files with mc

Looking at Files and File Types

We generally want to examine the contents of files because they contain some useful information, and storing, viewing, processing, and manipulating that information is our reason for using a computer at all. The problem is that there are many different types of files, and different ways of opening them.

In the world of Windows, the filename extension (.doc, .txt, and so on) is traditionally how the system knows what type of file it is dealing with. How the file is displayed in the Windows Explorer file manager and what application will open it is decided by the file extension.

The file Command

Linux does better than this: The command file is used to determine what a file really is by looking at it internally. For a very large number of file types, a "magic number" is included within the file that the file command looks up in the "magic number file" that is at /usr/share/misc/magic (this is the human readable form) and /usr/share/misc/magic.mgc (the compiled binary file created from /usr/share/misc/magic for speed of access). It can also distinguish files that do not have magic numbers by looking at characteristic contents (as seen, for example, in a variety of text files with markup).

To use the `file` command, simply type **file** followed by the file or files you want to analyze. For example:

```
user@bible:~/temp> file index.html
index.html: HTML document text

user@bible:~/temp> file realworddoc.doc
realworddoc.doc: Microsoft Office Document
```

We know that `index.html` is a real HTML file and `realworddoc.doc` is a real Microsoft Word document. However:

```
user@bible:~/temp> cp index.html strange.doc
user@bible:~/temp> file strange.doc
strange.doc: HTML document text
```

Here, `file` was not fooled by the fact that we changed the file extension of the file. Actually it isn't too hard to fool `file`, but you actually need to copy the first 8 bytes of the real Microsoft Word document into a new file to do so.

```
user@bible:~/temp> dd if=realworddoc.doc of=8bytes bs=1 count=8
user@bible:~/temp> cat 8bytes index.html > newfile.doc
user@bible:~/temp> file newfile.doc
newfile.doc: Microsoft Office Document
```

You can actually check how `file` did it:

```
user@bible:~/temp> grep Office /usr/share/misc/magic
0    string  \376\067\0\043              Microsoft Office Document
0    string  \320\317\021\340\241\261\032\341 Microsoft Office Document
0    string  \333\245-\0\0\0             Microsoft Office Document

user@bible:~/temp> od -b newfile.doc |more
0000000 320 317 021 340 241 261 032 341 074 041 104 117 103 124 131 120
[...]
```

The command `od` gives you an octal dump of the file, and you can see that it has the second of the possible signatures of an Office document at its start. Since you are piping the output of `od` to `more`, you can terminate the command at any time by pressing q to exit the `more` command.

strings, ghex2, khexedit, and antiword

If you are confronted with a file that the `file` command doesn't give very useful information about (perhaps it just reports "data"), it may be worth trying to view it with `cat -v`, with `less`, or with a text editor. If all you see is binary junk, you may still be able to find out something useful using the `strings` command, which searches inside a binary file for text strings and outputs them.

```
user@bible:~> strings filename
```

The output may give some useful clues. The applications ghex2 or khexedit may also be useful. These are graphical hex editors — that is, they enable you to view and edit binary files at the level of the bytes in them (which you will see represented in hexadecimal notation). A hex editor such as khexedit shows you a string representation of those bytes that represent text characters amongst the rest of the file in a separate pane.

Caution Changing binary files with a hex editor can easily render them totally useless, whether they are executables or data files.

The strings command can sometimes also be a quick way of looking inside Microsoft Office files. antiword is also useful; it tries to extract all the text from a Microsoft Word document. antiword works with almost all versions of the Microsoft Word .doc file format and is very quick. You can combine it with grep to check whether a particular file contains particular words. For example:

```
user@bible:~> antiword wordfile.doc | grep -i linux
```

checks whether the word linux appears in wordfile.doc. (The -i option tells grep not to care about upper- or lowercase.)

Cross-Reference The commands strings and antiword are both discussed in more detail in Chapter 10.

Viewing and Opening Different File Types and Formats

It would be both impossible and useless to try to make an exhaustive list of all the file formats the reader is likely to come across on Linux. However, in the next sections we note some of the most important file types and formats and comment on how to view or open them.

PostScript

PostScript is a page description language. Actually it is more than that — in fact it is a special-purpose programming language, but designed (by Adobe) for the job of describing how graphic elements and characters are laid out on a page. PostScript is a fully open and documented standard. A PostScript printer will accept a PostScript file and print it directly. If you have a different type of printer, the printing system will filter the PostScript appropriately before passing it to the printer, but PostScript is considered the *lingua franca* of printing in Linux. Applications that produce output for printing produce that output in the form of PostScript.

A PostScript file is a plain text file with a certain specific format. It always starts something like this:

```
%!PS-Adobe-3.0
%%Title: filename
```

Although raw PostScript looks odd at first glance, it is not difficult to learn how to write simple PostScript files to create pages with geometrical shapes and text on them, for example.

A PostScript file is typically called something like file.ps. An encapsulated PostScript file may have the file extension .eps. To view it you can use any of the programs gv, ggv, or kghostview. These all use ghostscript (gs) in the background to render the file in graphical form.

You can print a PostScript file directly from the command line with:

```
user@bible:~/tmp> lpr file.ps
```

Because of its importance as a format, there are a number of utilities for processing PostScript files in various ways:

✦ ps2ascii tries to extract text from a PostScript file.

✦ ps2pdf converts a PostScript file to PDF.

✦ The psutils package includes various utilities for splitting and joining PostScript files and for rearranging and resizing pages.

Any application that enables you to print to file will produce PostScript. Some applications also offer a print to PDF option.

Note   An encapsulated PostScript file (.eps) is a special type of PostScript file that includes information about its physical size (bounding box) and that is designed to be included inside another document.

PDF

PDF is related to PostScript and is also a fully documented format from Adobe. The application of choice for opening PDF has to be Adobe Acrobat Reader, acroread, but there are also xpdf and gpdf. The kghostview application also happily opens PDF files. However, acroread best takes advantage of all the advanced features of PDF (hyperlinks, text search, forms, and so on).

Again, a large number of utilities are available for dealing with PDF files, in particular pdftotext and pdf2ps, which try to do what their names imply.

Note   OpenOffice.org now has instant "export to PDF" functionality with a corresponding toolbar button.

DVI

A DVI file is a device-independent file and usually has the file extension .dvi. The DVI format is almost exclusively seen as the output of the TeX and LaTeX typesetting programs. Usually this is now seen as an intermediate stage in the production of PostScript; the program dvips converts a DVI file to PostScript. However, you can view DVI files directly, using xdvi or kdvi. (You may have to wait a surprisingly long time while the necessary fonts are generated.)

TeX and LaTeX Files

Among open source documentation, you will sometimes come across .tex files, which are usually LaTeX files. TeX is a markup-based typesetting system developed by Donald Knuth, and LaTeX is a widely used set of macros for TeX. If you need to create printable output from a LaTeX file that is not present, the command latex file.tex creates a .dvi file (see the previous section). This can be converted to PostScript with dvips file.dvi.

LaTeX is a wonderful way of making very attractive printed output and particularly for typesetting mathematics, but there is a learning curve.

HTML

HTML is a file format that needs no introduction. For editing HTML on Linux, the tool of choice is (in our view) emacs with one of its HTML modes. Another editor with very nice HTML editing capabilities is fte (the *folding text editor*), which makes it easy for you to "fold up" the content of tags so that you can see the large scale structure of the code.

There are also the quanta and bluefish HTML editors and the Mozilla composer, as well as HTML export in OpenOffice.org.

The tool tidy checks HTML for validity based on its DOCTYPE declaration.

If you need to extract just the text from web pages or local HTML files, one way to consider is using the lynx browser with the -dump option:

```
user@bible:~> lynx -dump http://lwn.net/ > lwn.txt
```

Graphics Formats

The graphics viewers and editors in SUSE can cope with a very large number of different graphics file formats. Pretty much any graphics file that you come across can be handled by GIMP (which should be your first choice if you need to edit a graphics file).

An occasionally useful feature of GIMP is that it can convert a PostScript file to a graphics format, and more generally it can convert between the whole range of formats that it understands.

Sound and Multimedia Formats

As far as sound is concerned, you can play `.mp3`, `.ogg`, and `.wav` files with a number of different applications, notably `xmms`, and MIDI files are catered to by more than one application.

The situation with movie files is not so simple.

The applications `kaffeine`, `noatun`, and `xine` are all capable of playing movies. The `kaffeine` application is a KDE front end for `xine`. The problem is that most movie formats require codecs (compressor-decompressors) that are encumbered by patents that prevent SUSE from distributing them. It is possible to obtain these codecs and add them to `xine`.

The RealPlayer application is included in SUSE Professional. This plays `.rm` and `.ram` files, which are common formats for sound and video clips on Internet news sites.

There are also third-party packages built for SUSE of the very capable `mplayer` multimedia application, which is capable of playing `.avi`, `.wmv`, `.mov` (QuickTime), MPEG, and other formats. With the addition of plug-ins for the various codecs, the `mplayer` package can cope with most formats. It can also use Windows dynamic link libraries (DLLs) for additional codecs. You can find SUSE packages for `mplayer` and the associated codecs at `http://packman.links2linux.org/` (a useful source of many additional packages for SUSE). In practice, using the `mplayer` package from here together with the add-on codecs is probably the best way to get support for the widest variety of video formats on SUSE Linux.

The home of the `mplayer` project is at `www.mplayerhq.hu/`. SUSE provides two mailing lists that are dedicated to information about multimedia on SUSE Linux (one in German and one in English). To subscribe to these (and other) SUSE mailing lists, see `www.suse.com/us/private/support/online_help/mailinglists/`.

CSV Files

CSV (comma-separated values) is a common format for interchanging data, particularly as an export format from various commercial applications running on Windows.

A CSV file consists of a set of lines of text. Each line is broken into fields by a field separator, which is usually the comma, and each field is usually surrounded by quotes.

```
"First Name","Second Name","Street Address","City"
"Peter","Rabbit","1, The Burrows","Peterborough"
```

OpenOffice.org imports a CSV file into its spreadsheet; how perfectly it will do this depends on the exact format of the file. CSV is actually an ugly format because the fields of the file may contain commas themselves, while the comma is the field separator. This means that the fields then have to be surrounded by quotes. But of course the fields may also contain quotes. So there are cases when importing a CSV file will fail on some records for reasons of this kind.

Tip   If you need to create a CSV file for some reason (for example, by exporting a spreadsheet file as CSV), it may be better to use a different symbol as the separator (for example), particularly if you are writing your own code to parse the file. Perl and Python both have modules for parsing CSV files.

XML Files

XML is self-describing data in the form of tagged text. XML stands for Extensible Markup Language. An XML file looks rather like an HTML file if you open it in a text editor. The difference is that XML allows arbitrary tags, but any given XML file will follow a DTD (Document Type Definition) or an XML Schema, which describes the tags it may include and whose elements may contain other elements. XML is growing in importance because of its use as a format for the exchange of information in e-commerce applications, and because of its usefulness as a base format from which to generate multiple versions of the same document (print, web, plain text, and so on).

As with HTML, if you need to make major edits to XML files, the best way is probably to use emacs together with the appropriate mode (see Figure 13-4). You will need to have the psgml package installed for this. The emacs editor will then be able to validate the XML document, load a DTD, offer you only the tags that are available at the current point in the document, close the open tag with a single keystroke, and much more.

Cross-Reference   For more information about emacs, see Chapter 11.

Office Formats

OpenOffice.org opens almost all Microsoft Word .doc, Excel .xls, and PowerPoint .ppt files, as well as its own and StarOffice native formats.

As noted earlier in the chapter, to quickly extract the text from a Word file, antiword can be useful. The "other" office applications on Linux (AbiWord, Gnumeric, Koffice) are generally not quite as good as OpenOffice.org at opening alien files.

You can *try* to educate your contacts to understand that if they want to send you a shopping list, it's not actually necessary to write it as a Word document and attach it to an email, but you won't always win. And if your contact requires a printable formatted file from you, send him PDF (exported from OpenOffice.org). If he wants to edit the file, you may have to save the file as some version of .doc.

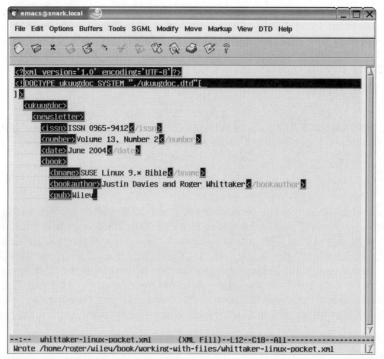

Figure 13-4: Editing XML in emacs

The .rtf (Rich Text Format) format is often mentioned as an "open" text-based format for interchanging documents. This file format was developed by Microsoft. It is a plain text format with markup, and there is an openly published specification for it, unlike the binary .doc files.

An RTF file is actually not so nice when you look inside it:

```
user@bible:~> less afile.rtf
{\rtf1\ansi\deff0\adeflang1025
{\fonttbl{\f0\froman\fprq2\fcharset0 Nimbus Roman No9 L{\*\falt Times New
Roman};}{\f1\froman\fprq2\fcharset0 Nimbus Roman N
o9 L{\*\falt Times New Roman};}{\f2\fswiss\fprq2\fcharset0 Nimbus Sans L{\*\falt
Arial};}{\f3\froman\fprq2\
[...]
\par {\loch\f4\fs22\lang2057\i0\b0 The key delivery of this project was
[...]
```

Since you are using the less program to paginate the output of the file afile.rtf, you can press q at any time to exit from less and return to the command prompt.

One problem is that it is difficult to extract the pure text from all the markup and formatting instructions. Another is that there have been several revisions of the RTF specification. But RTF files open well in any of the Linux word processing applications, including those that are have a smaller footprint than OpenOffice.org.

Working with Excel Files

Microsoft Excel files usually open just fine in OpenOffice.org or Gnumeric provided that they don't include complex macros, in which case you may have difficulties.

Note
OpenOffice.org has its own macro language, but this is not compatible with VBA (Visual Basic for Applications), which is used by Microsoft Office. In general, this means that you will have to convert or rewrite the macros in an Excel workbook to make it work in OpenOffice.org.

Working with Access Files

Microsoft Access databases are a problem in more ways than one: Until recently, there was no freely available open source Linux desktop application with similar functionality. That has changed with the release of Rekall under an open source license. Rekall is included in SUSE Linux Professional.

To deal with the files that Access creates (`.mdb` files), the Mdbtools project may be useful: `http://mdbtools.sourceforge.net/`.

Otherwise, the best approach is to use an intermediate format (such as `.csv` or an SQL dump) for export and import.

The OpenOffice.org Native File Formats

The OpenOffice.org native file formats are zipped archives that contain a variety of XML documents, as in the following example:

```
user@bible:~> file afile.sxw
afile.sxw: Zip archive data, at least v2.0 to extract

user@bible:~> zipinfo afile.sxw
Archive:  afile.sxw   9043 bytes   7 files
-rw----     2.0 fat       30 b- stor 23-Jun-04 11:39 mimetype
-rw----     2.0 fat       18 b- stor 23-Jun-04 11:39 layout-cache
-rw----     2.0 fat    10336 bl defN 23-Jun-04 11:39 content.xml
-rw----     2.0 fat    17791 bl defN 23-Jun-04 11:39 styles.xml
-rw----     2.0 fat     1158 b- stor 23-Jun-04 11:39 meta.xml
-rw----     2.0 fat     7064 bl defN 23-Jun-04 11:39 settings.xml
-rw----     2.0 fat      850 bl defN 23-Jun-04 11:39 META-INF/manifest.xml
7 files, 37247 bytes uncompressed, 8261 bytes compressed:   77.8%
```

XML is a structured markup language, which means that all OpenOffice documents are ultimately text documents, unlike the traditional Microsoft formats, which are binary. XML was designed as a portable document description format that separates information about the content of a document from the information about how the document is to be formatted, known as its presentation format. XML documents surround portions of the text with tags (more properly known as elements) that identify the way in which the associated text fits into the entire document. Tags identify portions of your document's content such as paragraphs, headings, text to be emphasized, quotations, lists and portions of lists, and so on. Writing and storing documents in XML makes them usable by any software package that understands XML, and therefore makes them more portable than documents stored in a format that is specific to a certain software package. This in turn means that, in principle at least, a set of OpenOffice.org documents can be processed with external scripts to extract or change information in them in some uniform way.

OpenOffice documents use a set of XML document descriptions that have been adopted as a draft standard by OASIS (Organization for the Advancement of Structured Information Standards). See `www.oasis-open.org` for more information about OASIS and the various standards that they are working on or sponsoring. This standard is known as the OpenDocument standard. Documents created in OpenOffice 2.0 will be fully compliant with this standard. Documents produced by versions of OpenOffice prior to version 2.0 are XML documents, but use a simpler XML document type definition.

For the complete OASIS OpenDocument standard, go to `www.oasis-open.org/committees/download.php/12573/OpenDocument-v1.0-os.sxw`. This is a version of the standard in OpenOffice format. A PDF version is also available at `www.oasis-open.org/committees/download.php/12572/OpenDocument-v1.0-os.pdf`.

Compressing Files

Two compression programs are in common use on Linux, `gzip` and `bzip2`; `gzip` is more common, but in general, `bzip2` leads to somewhat smaller file sizes. To compress a file using `gzip`, do this:

```
user@bible:~/temp> gzip afile
user@bible:~/temp> ls
afile.gz
```

The file `afile` has been compressed to the file `afile.gz`. To restore the original file you can use the `gunzip` command (or the equivalent `gzip -d`).

```
user@bible:~/temp> gunzip afile.gz
user@bible:~/temp> ls
afile
```

Notice how each time the original is no longer there. If you want to keep the original file while writing the compressed file, you can use the -c option (which writes the output to standard output) and redirect that output to a file.

By default, gzip keeps the original permissions and timestamp and restores them on decompression. With the -N option, the name is also preserved, even if you change the name of the compressed file.

The bzip2 program behaves in a very similar way to gzip:

```
user@bible:~/temp> bzip2 afile
user@bible:~/temp> ls
afile.bz2
```

To uncompress, you can use bunzip2 or the equivalent bzip2 -d:

```
user@bible:~/temp> bunzip2 afile.bz2
user@bible:~/temp> ls
afile
```

It is very common to see gzip and bzip2 being used together with tar, which is discussed later in the chapter.

One or two applications are capable of reading in files in the gzip format and uncompressing them and reading them on the fly. In particular, if you come across .ps.gz files (gzipped PostScript files), the programs gv and kghostview can read these as is without first decompressing them.

Also, a number of standard utilities have versions that first uncompress the file (assuming it to be gzipped). By convention, a letter *z* at the start of the name indicates this. For example:

- ✦ zgrep first uncompresses the file and then runs the grep command.

- ✦ zless and zmore are versions of less and more that first uncompress the file they are acting on.

Chapter 2 contains more information on the commands grep, less, and more.

Working with Archives

An *archive* is a directory tree that has been put together into a single file in such a way that it can be restored at a later date. Archives may also be compressed. The most common type of archive on Linux is the tar archive, but we also consider cpio and pax archives as well as zip archives. rpm package files (used as installation packages on SUSE, Red Hat, and other Linux distributions) are a special kind of archive, as are Debian packages (.deb).

Tip   A general point about unpacking archives: Sometimes badly behaved archives will unpack *into* the current directory rather than into a directory *under* the current directory. This can be annoying, so it is always a good idea to put the archive into a new directory of its own before you unpack it.

Working with tar Archives

To create an archive of a directory tree with tar, you can do something like this:

```
user@bible:~/temp> tar -cf directory.tar directory/
user@bible:~/temp> ls
directory  directory.tar
```

The preceding command creates (c), verbosely (v), the file (f) directory.tar, which is a tar archive, by running tar on directory.

If you do this with a directory containing a couple of small text files, and then you look at the resulting tar file (with cat), you will see that it is just a concatenation of the original files themselves together with additional information.

If you want to list the files in the archive:

```
user@bible:~/temp> tar -tf directory.tar
directory/
directory/afile
directory/bfile
```

Here the t option lists the contents of the file (f) directory.tar.

Using gzip Compression with tar

If you want to create a gzipped tar archive (the -z option implies compression, while the c means create):

```
user@bible:~/temp> tar -zcf directory.tgz directory/
user@bible:~/temp> ls
directory  directory.tgz
```

The original is still there, unlike when we compressed a single file with gzip. (Note that .tgz and .tar.gz are used interchangeably for filenames of gzipped tar archives.)

To list the files in this case, use the following:

```
user@bible:~/temp> tar -tzf directory.tgz
directory/
directory/afile
directory/bfile
```

Using bzip2 Compression with tar

If you want to use compression with bzip2 instead of gzip, the required option is -j rather than -z:

```
user@bible:~/temp> tar -jcf directory.tar.bz2 directory/
user@bible:~/temp> ls
directory  directory.tar.bz2

user@bible:~/temp> tar -jtf directory.tar.bz2
directory/
directory/afile
directory/bfile
```

Unpacking tar Archives

To unpack a tar archive, you need to use the -x option (for extract):

```
user@bible:~/temp> tar -xvf directory.tar
```

or

```
user@bible:~/temp> tar -zxvf directory.tgz
```

or

```
user@bible:~/temp> tar -jxvf directory.tar.bz2
```

Here the options have the following meanings:

- ✦ The -x option to tar means *extract*.
- ✦ The z option implies that you are uncompressing a tar archive where gzip compression has been used.
- ✦ The j option is needed if you are extracting an archive where bzip2 compression has been used.

Working with a Source Code tar Archive

Very commonly, programs that are distributed as source code are offered as compressed tar archives. When you have downloaded one of these, your first step is to copy it into a new directory somewhere and do either tar -zxvf or tar -jxvf to it. Then read the compilation and installation instructions (if you are lucky, the three commands ./configure followed by make followed by make install will do what you need).

If you have a tar archive from which you need just a single file, you can do this:

```
user@bible:~/temp> tar -xf directory.tar directory/afile
```

If `directory` does not exist, it will be created with just the named file or files inside it. If you need to do this kind of task, Konqueror's ability to read inside archives is useful to remember; this is one area where the graphical tools can be a great help.

Copying a Directory Tree with tar

You can use `tar` to back up an entire directory tree to another location while preserving permissions and ownerships. Here's a sample command:

```
root@bible:/somedir # tar cf - . |(cd /another/dir/; tar xvf -)
```

This creates a new directory structure under `/another/dir/` containing a mirror of the current directory. It does this by creating a `tar` file on standard output (the - symbol), and then changing `directory` to the destination and unpacking the `tar` file that it sees on standard input. This is not quite as neat as the `pax` command discussed later in the chapter, which does the same thing.

Working with cpio Archives

It is much less likely that you will need to work very often with `cpio` archives, so we show here just a simple example of creating an archive and extracting the files from it.

When creating an archive, `cpio` takes a list of filenames and uses them to decide which files to include in the archive:

```
user@bible:~/temp> ls | cpio -vo > ../temp.cpio
```

This lists the files in the current directory and passes the filenames to `cpio`, which creates an archive on standard output (the `-o` option), verbosely (the `-v` option).

If you want to create an archive containing everything under the current directory, you can use `find` to list all the relevant paths and pipe its output to `cpio`:

```
user@bible:~/temp> find . | cpio -vo > ../temp.cpio
```

To unpack an archive, use the following:

```
user@bible:~/another_directory > cpio -ivd < ../temp.cpio
```

This unpacks (the `i` option) the archive under the current directory, creating new directories as necessary (the `-d` option).

Working with zip Archives

The common zip archive format (associated with the DOS and Windows programs PKZIP and WinZip among others) is supported on Linux. To unzip a zip archive, simply do the following:

```
user@bible:~/temp> unzip zipfile.zip
```

To create a zip archive of the current directory:

```
user@bible:~/temp> zip -r ~/newzip.zip .
```

This will recursively zip up the current directory and create the zip file newzip.zip in you're your home directory (~).

The program zipinfo will give a listing and information about compression ratios:

```
user@bible:~/temp> zipinfo zipfile.zip
Archive:  zipfile.zip   7762 bytes   4 files
-rw-r--r--  2.3 unx      2048 bx stor 21-Jun-04 20:06 afile
-rw-r--r--  2.3 unx      4096 bx stor 21-Jun-04 20:07 bfile
drwxr-xr-x  2.3 unx         0 bx stor 21-Jun-04 20:10 directory/
-rw-r--r--  2.3 unx      2048 bx defN 21-Jun-04 20:10 directory/cfile
4 files, 8192 bytes uncompressed, 7230 bytes compressed:  11.7%
```

Unpacking RPM Packages

Typically, you can do everything you need to manipulate RPM packages using the rpm command, but it is sometimes useful to know that you can convert an RPM package to a cpio archive as follows:

```
user@bible:~/temp> rpm2cpio partimage-0.6.2-152.i586.rpm >partimage.cpio
```

You can then unpack the archive under the current directory with:

```
user@bible:~/temp> cpio -ivd < partimage.cpio
```

Here again, the i option unpacks the archive, while the d option creates the necessary directories as cpio verbosely (v) operates on the archive. You will find directories under the current directory corresponding to the system locations where rpm will install the particular files. This corresponds to what you see if you look inside the rpm package with m c, for example.

Using pax

A nice alternative to tar and cpio is pax, which is capable of unpacking archives in both these formats. Its command syntax is also simpler to learn than either tar or cpio, both of which can give a new user headaches. It also offers a neater solution than tar to the problem of exactly copying an entire directory tree complete with permissions, timestamps, and symbolic links from one place to another.

To create a pax archive file of the current directory, do the following:

```
user@bible:~/tmp> pax -wvf /tmp/archive.pax .
```

This writes (- w) verbosely (-v) the file (-f) /tmp/archive.pax, archiving the current directory (.).

To unpack the archive somewhere else, do the following:

```
root@bible:/another_directory # pax -rvf archive.pax
```

Here we are verbosely (v) reading (r) from the archive file, and pax by default writes out the archived directories and files to disk under the current directory. To be sure that all the permissions and ownerships will be restored, you will need to do this as root.

To list the files in the archive, simply do the following:

```
user@bible:/another_directory > pax -f archive.pax
```

If you have a gzipped tar file, you can unpack it with pax like this:

```
user@bible:~/tmp> pax -rzvf archive.tgz
```

Here the r option shows that you are reading from the archive, while the z indicates that you need gzip uncompression.

To unpack a cpio archive, do the following:

```
user@bible:~/tmp> pax -rvf archive.cpio
```

To copy a directory tree preserving all ownerships and permissions, do the following:

```
root@bible: / # pax -rvw -pe /source/ /path/to/destination/
```

Here you read (r) from the source directory and write (w) to the destination directory, while preserving (-p) everything (e) (in other words all ownerships and permissions).

Using ark

The ark graphical tool comes with KDE and can view and open various types of archives including tar, tar.gz, and zip archives. Its functionality is reasonably obvious and not unlike WinZip on Windows. See Figure 13-5 for an example.

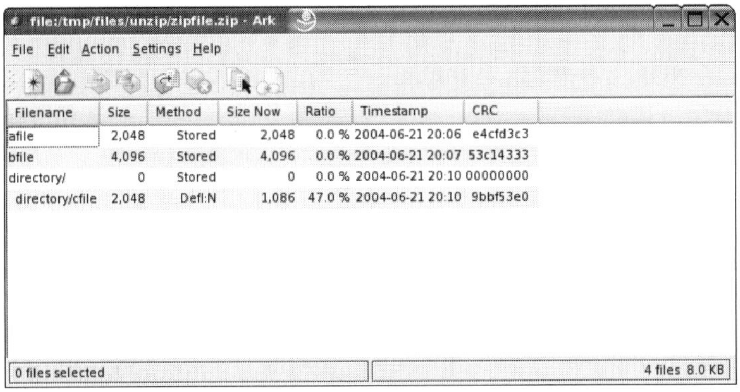

Figure 13-5: Opening a zip file with ark

Files Attributes and ACLs

In Chapter 2 we cover the basic concepts of file ownership and permissions. Less well known is the fact that there are two other mechanisms for controlling the access to and properties of files. In this section we give a brief introduction to the concepts of file attributes and file ACLs.

File Attributes

This is an additional layer of control over files above and beyond the standard Unix permissions system. File attributes are controlled by the chattr command. In general and in most situations, the attributes that this system allows are not widely used and not all of them are implemented on every filesystem, but most of the functionality of chattr is available on the common filesystems (ext2, ext3, and reiserfs).

The one attribute that is particularly interesting and that can be set with this command is the *immutable* attribute. It means that a file is made to behave in this interesting way. See the following example.

```
user@bible:~> ls -l afile
-rw-r--r--  1 user users 26 2004-06-23 15:21 afile

user@bible:~> rm afile
rm: remove write-protected regular file `afile'? y
rm: cannot remove `afile': Operation not permitted
```

According to the permissions that you see in the listing, you should certainly be able to delete the file, but attempting to do so results in an Operation not permitted alert.

Also, if you try to edit the file, you'll find that you can't write to it.

But the situation is even stranger than that:

```
user@bible:~> su
Password:

root@bible: /home/user/ # rm afile
rm: remove write-protected regular file `afile'? y
rm: cannot remove `afile': Operation not permitted
```

This looks very odd indeed: The owner can't delete the file, although he appears to have the right to do so, but even root can't delete the file. The reason is that the file has the immutable bit set:

```
root@bible: /home/user/ # lsattr afile
----i-------- afile
```

The file has the special file attribute *immutable* set, which effectively means that no one has the right to change the file.

To set a file to be immutable, do the following:

```
root@bible: /home/user/ # chattr +i afile
```

This adds (+) the immutable attribute (i).

To remove the attribute, do the following:

```
root@bible: /home/user/ # chattr -i afile
root@bible: /home/user/ # lsattr afile
------------- afile
```

There are easily imagined practical situations in which you might want to use this functionality to prevent accidental deletion. For example, you might want to set this attribute on certain configuration files so as to force yourself to think very hard before modifying them. Use of the immutable attribute on particular system files is also often recommended as a way of adding an additional level of security to the system.

For further details, see the chattr and lsattr man pages.

File ACLs

Relatively recently, Linux has gained the concept of file and directory ACLs (access control lists). In contrast to the file attributes discussed previously, which control the behavior of the file itself (making it undeletable or immutable, for example), file ACLs are all about who can access the file and in what way. These ACLs mean that the sharing of files and directories with specifically named users can now be achieved, where previously a complex design of users and multiple groups was the only way to bring this about.

The particular application where this is of importance is Samba, and it means that the owner of a file who is accessing that file by Samba from a Windows client can set sharing on that file in the same way as if the file were on a Windows machine.

Cross-Reference Chapter 18 contains more on Samba.

To use this ACL functionality, it is necessary that the partition on which the filesystem resides be mounted with the acl option. ACL functionality is now available regardless of which of the common filesystems you use (ext2, ext3, or reiserfs). To set ACLs on the command line, you use the command setfacl. getfacl reads the ACLs of a file.

If ACLs have been set, when you do an ls -l command, you will see this:

```
tom@bible:~> ls -l afile
-rw-r--r--+ 1 tom users 81 2004-06-23 15:59 afile
```

Note the extra plus (+) symbol after the permissions string. This shows that ACLs have been set on this file, but to actually find out what they are, you will need the getfacl command described later in this section.

If tom wants to modify the ACL to allow tanya to write to the file, he does this:

```
tom@bible:~> setfacl -m u:tanya:w bfile
```

Here tom is modifying (- m) the ACL to allow the user (u) tanya to write (w) to the file.

You can then get the ACL for the file like this:

```
tom@bible:~> getfacl bfile
# file: bfile
# owner: tom
# group: users
user::rw-
user:tanya:-w-
group::r--
mask::rw-
other::r—
```

So the change was made. For each user, you see the permissions shown in the usual r w x (read, write, execute) format. The user tanya now has write permission.

To remove the ACL that was just set:

```
tom@bible:~> setfacl -x u:tanya bfile
```

Here the -x means remove, so tom is removing the ACL that the user (u) tanya had on the file.

```
tom@bible:~> getfacl bfile
# file: bfile
# owner: tom
# group: users
user::rw-
group::r--
mask::r--
other::r-
```

Here tanya's special write permission has gone away.

Finally, familiarity with the techniques and concepts introduced in this chapter, as well as the content of Chapter 2, is necessary for anyone who wants to be able to work comfortably with a Linux system and its files. Some of the commands have a bewildering variety of options, but practicing with the examples given here and building on them is the best way to increase your skill and gain understanding.

✦   ✦   ✦

Working with the System

In this chapter we look at some of the more useful tools for working with your SUSE Linux system. First, we examine some of the tools that are available to you to deal with emergencies; if your system won't boot or is otherwise seriously damaged, SUSE's Rescue System and YaST System Repair running from the installation media can be very useful. We also look at different ways to deal with partitions and disk images and how to create CDs. We touch on the use of Webmin as an alternative to YaST for administrative tasks, and we give a (necessarily brief) introduction to shell scripting and scripting languages.

What all these sections have in common is that they all concern tools that give you more power over your system, and working with these tools will add to your understanding.

Tip   You should not be afraid to experiment, even with — indeed particularly with — the more scary and destructive examples given in this chapter. If you can, by all means set up a "sacrificial" system and play with the rescue and repair systems, with the partitioning tools, and so on. The knowledge that you gain may well be useful when (not *if*) things eventually go wrong.

System Rescue and Repair

You may find occasionally that you have problems you cannot solve from within the system itself. Most commonly, there may be something that is preventing the system from booting at all. This could be a misconfigured boot manager or a root partition that needs to have a filesystem check run on it manually. There is also the possibility that you have forgotten the root password and you need to remove it.

In This Chapter

Using the rescue and repair systems to recover from problems

Working with partitions and disk images

Burning CDs and DVDs

Using Webmin

Using shell aliases

Automating with shell scripts and scripting languages

◆   ◆   ◆   ◆

Booting from the Hard Disk with Special Boot Parameters

Sometimes it is enough to boot the system from hard disk, but into runlevel 1 (by simply typing the digit 1 as a boot parameter in the initial boot screen). Runlevel 1 is single-user mode, with no networking and without starting most services. So if there is a problem that is causing the boot process to fail at a later stage, you may be able to solve the problem by booting into runlevel 1 and making the necessary changes. You can run YaST or edit configuration files in this state, and then reboot or bring the system up to runlevel 3 or 5 with one of the commands init 3 or init 5.

Cross-Reference   Chapter 4 has more information on booting into specific runlevels.

If you have lost the root password, you can boot with the following parameter:

```
init=/bin/bash rw
```

This starts the system but bypasses the normal init system, instead taking you straight to a shell, without the need to log in, and mounting the root partition read-write. You can then, if necessary, remove the root password by editing the file /etc/shadow using vi and removing the encrypted password. You need to change it from looking something like the first line below to something like the second.

```
root:cJLgWo7eN1gqk:12629:0:10000::::
```

```
root::12629:0:10000::::
```

You can then reboot to runlevel 1 as described previously and you will be able to log in as root without a password, and then reset the password using the passwd command.

Booting into the Rescue System

The SUSE installation media offer a special option when you boot from them: One of the menu items is Rescue System. If you boot from the first CD or DVD and choose this option, a Linux system that runs in memory loads and does not mount any hard disk partitions. You can log into it as the root user without a password.

You can then mount any of the partitions on the hard disk to /mnt and make changes before rebooting. For example, if your root partition is /dev/hda1, you could do the following:

```
Rescue:~ # mount /dev/hda1 /mnt
```

followed by, for example:

```
Rescue:~ # vi /mnt/etc/fstab
```

if you needed to correct a problem with the file /etc/fstab.

Booting into YaST System Repair Mode

SUSE also provides a System Repair mode with YaST. If you boot from the installation media and choose the option Installation, but add the boot parameter repair=1, you enter a system similar to the Rescue System (running in memory and with no hard disk partitions mounted). The only difference is that YaST now runs in graphical mode. In this system you can use parts of YaST's standard functionality to repair a broken system. The main screen offers three options: Automatic Repair, Customized Repair, and Expert Tools.

If you choose Automatic Repair, the YaST system check repair runs through a series of tests and shows a commentary on the screen. Among the tests it runs are filesystem checks, verification of the package database, a check on the boot loader configuration, and a check of the initrd (the initial ramdisk used at boot time). If problems are found, it offers to attempt a repair.

The Customized Repair Screen

If you choose Customized Repair (see Figure 14-1), you can select or deselect the particular tests that you want to be run. If you have a good idea of what might be at fault, this reduces the time the tests and repairs need to run. The options are:

- ✦ Check Partition Tables
- ✦ Check Swap Areas
- ✦ Check File Systems
- ✦ Check fstab Entries
- ✦ Check Package Database
- ✦ Check Minimal Package Selection
- ✦ Verify Base Packages
- ✦ Check Boot Loader Configuration

The most useful of these are those concerned with filesystems and boot loaders.

- ✦ Although journaling filesystems means that filesystem corruption is unlikely, if it occurs and prevents the system from booting normally, this filesystem option is useful because it will run a filesystem check for you with the correct options.

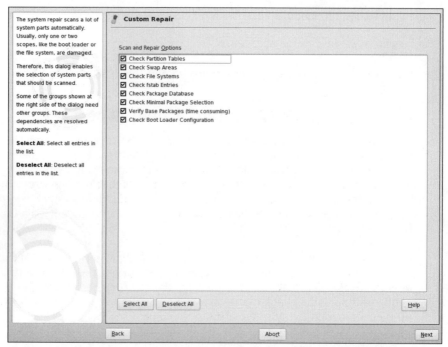

Figure 14-1: The YaST System Repair mode Customized Repair screen

✦ If you have a dual-boot system, and you have reinstalled Windows, the Windows installer may overwrite the Master Boot Record and prevent Linux from booting at all. The boot loader check can rewrite the boot loader (usually grub) so that both systems can be booted correctly.

If the package database does not correspond to the packages that are actually on the system, or if packages have become corrupt, the package checking tools can correct the problem.

The Expert Tools Screen

The Expert Tools screen, shown in Figure 14-2, offers some additional tools:

✦ Boot Loader Install

✦ Partitioning Tool

✦ Repair File System

✦ Recover Lost Partitions

✦ Save System Settings to Floppy Disk

✦ Verify Installed Software

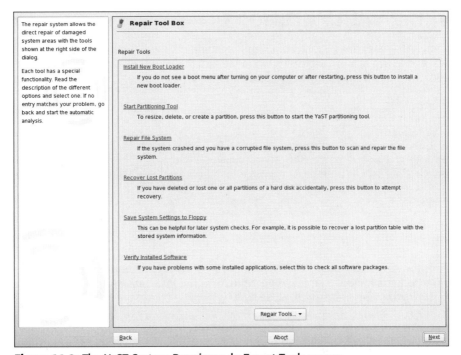

The repair system allows the direct repair of damaged system areas with the tools shown at the right side of the dialog.

Each tool has a special functionality. Read the description of the different options and select one. If no entry matches your problem, go back and start the automatic analysis.

Repair Tool Box

Repair Tools

Install New Boot Loader

If you do not see a boot menu after turning on your computer or after restarting, press this button to install a new boot loader.

Start Partitioning Tool

To resize, delete, or create a partition, press this button to start the YaST partitioning tool.

Repair File System

If the system crashed and you have a corrupted file system, press this button to scan and repair the file system.

Recover Lost Partitions

If you have deleted or lost one or all partitions of a hard disk accidentally, press this button to attempt recovery.

Save System Settings to Floppy

This can be helpful for later system checks. For example, it is possible to recover a lost partition table with the stored system information.

Verify Installed Software

If you have problems with some installed applications, select this to check all software packages.

Repair Tools... ▾

Back   Abort   Next

Figure 14-2: The YaST System Repair mode Expert Tools screen

Tip

In order to see all of these options, you will have to use the scroll bar at the right of the screen to scroll down. SUSE's Repair mode assumes a fixed screen height/width ratio and thus can't show all of these options at once.

The boot loader tool enables you to create a new boot loader configuration from scratch and install it to the Master Boot Record. The partitioning tool is YaST's standard partitioning module (clearly a dangerous tool; see the next section of this chapter).

The Repair File System and Verify Installed Software options have the same function as the equivalent items discussed in the previous section.

Recover Lost Partitions scans the disk and attempts to restore any partitions that might have been deleted from the partition table (possibly by reckless use of the partitioning tool or fdisk).

Finally, Save System Settings to Floppy Disk backs up important system files and the Master Boot Record to a floppy disk.

Working with Partitions

Each hard disk that you use in a Linux system will have a number of partitions on it (except in the rather rare cases when we write to raw disk devices). To list (-l) the disks and partitions that the system can see, type:

```
root@bible:/tmp # fdisk -l

Disk /dev/hda: 40.0 GB, 40007761920 bytes
16 heads, 63 sectors/track, 77520 cylinders
Units = cylinders of 1008 * 512 = 516096 bytes

   Device Boot     Start       End    Blocks   Id  System
/dev/hda1    *        1       12484  6291904+  83  Linux
/dev/hda2           12485     16646  2097648   82  Linux swap
/dev/hda3           16647     47854  15728832  83  Linux
/dev/hda4           47855     77520  14951664  83  Linux
```

This shows you the partitions that the system can see, whether or not they are mounted. It provides in more digestible form the information that can also be seen in the virtual file /proc/partitions:

```
root@bible:/tmp # cat /proc/partitions
major minor  #blocks  name

   3     0   39070080 hda
   3     1    6291904 hda1
   3     2    2097648 hda2
   3     3   15728832 hda3
   3     4   14951664 hda4
```

The fdisk -l command together with the outputs of mount and df -h are useful for understanding what you've got, how much of it, and where:

```
user@bible:~> mount
/dev/hda1 on / type reiserfs (rw,acl,user_xattr)
proc on /proc type proc (rw)
tmpfs on /dev/shm type tmpfs (rw)
devpts on /dev/pts type devpts (rw,mode=0620,gid=5)
/dev/hda3 on /home type ext3 (rw)
/dev/hda4 on /space type ext3 (rw)
usbfs on /proc/bus/usb type usbfs (rw)

user@bible:~> df -h
Filesystem         Size  Used Avail Use% Mounted on
/dev/hda1          6.1G  5.5G  599M  91% /
```

```
tmpfs              253M  8.0K  253M   1% /dev/shm
/dev/hda3           15G   12G  2.8G  81% /home
/dev/hda4           15G   12G  1.5G  89% /space
```

Before doing anything with your partitions, you should at least run the three commands we just mentioned. Together they should reassure you that you know what
partitions exist and what they contain and make it less likely that you will accidentally do something destructive.

When you work with partitions, most of your time is spent when you install the
system, and at that time you will be using YaST's partitioning capabilities. At other
times, if you simply want to create partitions on a new disk, you are likely to do this
using fdisk, but you can use YaST's partitioning module at any time from the YaST
menu or by typing (as root):

```
yast2 disk
```

You will first see a warning (see Figure 14-3).

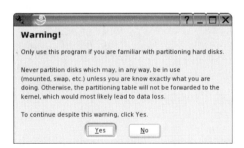

Figure 14-3: YaST's partitioning warning

Take that warning seriously, regardless of the tool that you are using to do
partitioning—one false move and you can destroy your system.

The main YaST partitioning scheme looks like what is shown in Figure 14-4.

Note   You may notice that YaST reports the starting and ending cylinders differently from
fdisk. That is because fdisk starts counting from 0, whereas YaST counts from 1.

YaST uses the functionality of parted rather than fdisk to do its job: This means
that in addition to creating and destroying partitions, it is also capable of resizing
them. It can also call ntfsresize to resize NTFS partitions.

**Cross-
Reference**   Partitions and the principles of partitioning are discussed in further detail in Chapters 1 and 3.

Figure 14-4: YaST's partitioning module

Partitioning Examples

On the x86 architecture, there are limitations on the number of partitions a disk can contain: There can be at most four primary partitions, one of which can be an extended partition. The extended partition can contain multiple logical partitions (up to a maximum of 60 on an IDE disk or 12 on a SCSI disk).

When working with partitioning tools, you should always ensure that any partitions you are going to change are not mounted before you start. You should also be absolutely sure that you know what partitions exist on the system and what they contain (as we stressed before): Keep a printed copy of the output of at least the commands fdisk -l, mount, and df -h on hand during the process. You can print any of these listings by redirecting the output of that command to the lpr command by using a pipe symbol, as in fdisk –l | lpr.

fdisk

To use fdisk to partition a disk, type the command **fdisk** followed by the device name of the disk concerned. Suppose that you had just added a new disk as the first disk on the second IDE controller:

```
root@bible : ~ # fdisk /dev/hdc
Command (m for help):
Command action
   a   toggle a bootable flag
   b   edit bsd disklabel
   c   toggle the dos compatibility flag
   d   delete a partition
   l   list known partition types
   m   print this menu
   n   add a new partition
   o   create a new empty DOS partition table
   p   print the partition table
   q   quit without saving changes
   s   create a new empty Sun disklabel
   t   change a partition's system id
   u   change display/entry units
   v   verify the partition table
   w   write table to disk and exit
   x   extra functionality (experts only)
```

Type **m** to see the menu as shown, and then **n** to add a new partition. At this point, p creates a primary partition; e creates an extended partition:

```
Command (m for help): n
Command action
   e   extended
   p   primary partition (1-4)
```

If you choose p, you see something like the following:

```
p
Partition number (1-4): 1
First cylinder (2-77520, default 2):
Using default value 2
Last cylinder or +size or +sizeM or +sizeK (2-1000, default 1000): +2000M
```

You can specify the size of the partition in terms of disk cylinders, or (more usefully) by typing a size in megabytes (here the +2000M). By default fdisk creates partitions of type Linux (with the hex code 83). If you want to change the partition type, you need to do t and then the relevant code (which is typically 83 for a data partition and 82 for swap, but you can create any number of foreign partition types).

When you think the correct partitions have been created, you can type **p** to print the partition table and then **w** to write it to disk.

Using YaST

YaST's partitioning module has the ability to create and delete partitions. It can also resize (non-destructively) certain types of partitions, including Windows partitions, which is a feature in great demand for dual-boot installations on previously Windows-only machines. YaST uses `parted` to do this but provides a user-friendly interface. Although the procedure is very reliable, we recommend that you back up all the data on the partition you want to resize before doing this. If, for example, the power suddenly failed during the resizing process, it's possible that the result would be a completely corrupt partition.

YaST's partitioning tool can be accessed from the main menu, or by typing (as root) the command `yast2 disk` (for a graphical interface) or `yast disk` for a text interface.

Note You cannot make changes to any partition that is mounted.

In YaST's partitioning module, you can select a partition by clicking it. You can then choose to delete, edit, or resize the partition. These options have the same functionality as the corresponding options available through the expert partitioning option during installation:

✦ **Delete**—Naturally asks for confirmation. In fact, none of the changes that you make in this module are carried out until you click the Apply button in the main screen, so you can still abort if you have made a mistake.

✦ **Edit**—Enables you to choose whether to format the partition, and if so, which type of filesystem to create in it. It also gives you the option of setting the mount point for the partition and setting the mount options that will be written to the `/etc/fstab` file.

✦ **Resize**—Offers you a graphical resizing tool with a slider and a display showing how much space the partition will take up after the operation and how much free space there will be.

In Figure 14-5, you see YaST graphically resizing an `ext2` partition.

Note One of the Expert Tools in the YaST System Repair mode discussed earlier in this chapter is YaST's graphical partitioning tool. This means that you can use the YaST partitioning tool "from the outside" with no partitions mounted.

Using parted

It is useful to be able to use `parted` from the command line when you need to change partitioning from the SUSE Rescue System. You might need to do this because you want to reclaim disk space from a partition that has empty space on it, but that has to be mounted in the running system (as `/` or `/usr`, for example).

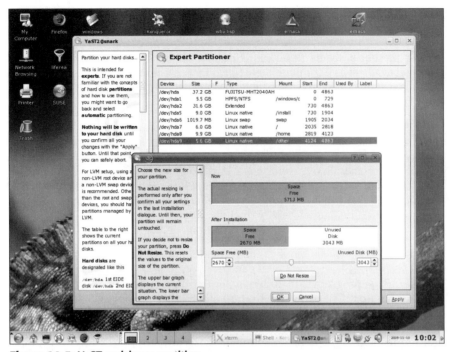

Figure 14-5: YaST resizing a partition

In that case, you boot from the installation medium and choose Rescue System from the boot menu. You can then log in as root (without a password) to a Linux system running in memory: None of the partitions will be mounted. parted offers you a prompt like this: (parted). To get help, type **help** or **?**. In the example that follows, we list (print) the partitions on /dev/hdc and then resize the second partition. The parted command resize 2 6677 8000 moves the end of the second partition from its current position at 8307 to 8000, while leaving the start of the partition unchanged.

```
# parted /dev/hdc

(parted) print
Disk geometry for /dev/hdc: 0.000-14324.625 megabytes
Disk label type: msdos
Minor   Start      End      Type     Filesystem  Flags
1        0.016   4042.000  primary   fat32      lba, type=0c
2     6677.000   8307.000  primary   ext2            type=83
3     8307.000  14324.000  primary   reiserfs        type=83

(parted) resize 2 6677 8000
```

parted enables you to copy a filesystem from a partition onto another partition and can create a filesystem on the partition as soon as it creates the partition.

> **Note**   At present it seems that parted does not handle EXT3 partitions very well: It regards them as EXT2 partitions of a type that it does not understand. On the other hand, unlike fdisk, parted is able to create large FAT partitions.

Commercial Partitioning Utilities

The commercial tools Acronis Disk Director (www.acronis.com) and PartitionMagic (www.powerquest.com/partitionmagic/) are also very popular and have friendly graphical interfaces. In our experience, PartitionMagic is easier to use than Acronis Disk Director. If you simply need to create or resize partitions (including NTFS), Linux now has tools that will do the job just as well as these commercial tools. They do have some additional functionality (including built-in boot managers, which make it rather easy to boot multiple Windows partitions on the same machine).

Using partimage

The partimage program is included in SUSE Professional and enables you to create an image file from a partition for backup and restore purposes. Because empty space is not included in the image, and because the image is compressed, it uses less space than simply writing out the partition to a file using dd (dd is discussed later in the chapter). The program includes a restore option. It possibly should not be regarded as totally mature but is certainly worth investigating. Figure 14-6 shows partimage up and running. If partimage is installed, simply (as root) type the command **partimage** to start it. The version of partimag that is provided with your system differs depending on the version of SUSE Linux Professional that you are using.

Making a Filesystem

When you have created a partition, you still need to create the filesystem of your choice on it (typically EXT2, EXT3, or ReiserFS). While YaST and parted include the ability to create a filesystem on the new partition, fdisk simply makes the partition. Do not confuse the fact that fdisk sets the partition identity hex code with actually creating the filesystem on the partition. To do that you will need to do one of the following (here we assume that you have just created the partition /dev/hdc3 and you now want to create a filesystem on it):

```
root@bible : ~ # mkfs -t ext2 /dev/hdc3

root@bible : ~ # mkfs -t reiserfs /dev/hdc3

root@bible : ~ # mkfs -t ext3 /dev/hdc3
```

Note that you must be root to create a filesystem.

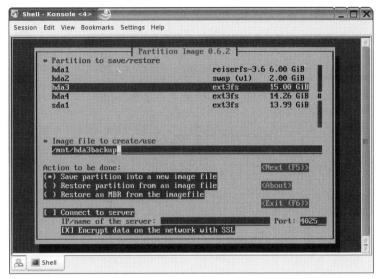

Figure 14-6: partimage

These commands use the mkfs command to make a filesystem of type (-t) ext2, reiserfs, or ext3, respectively, on the hard disk partition /dev/hdc3 (the third partition on the first disk on the second IDE controller).

Caution

> Again, note that these are seriously destructive commands: Be absolutely sure you know which partition you are dealing with before you issue an mkfs command.

Working with DVDs, CDs, and Floppies

It is very useful to be able to take a floppy disk, CD, or DVD and create an image file from it on your hard disk from which you can create new copies of the disk, possibly after modifying them first. You can even create a disk image of a hard disk partition or an entire hard disk if you have sufficient disk space.

Creating and Using Images of Existing Disks

Linux makes it easy to work with disk images because copying a disk (a floppy disk or a CD or a hard disk partition) to a file is a simple matter.

```
user@bible:~> dd if=/dev/fd0 of=floppy.img
```

The dd command reads the raw data from the device /dev/fd0 (the floppy disk) and writes it to the image file floppy.img.

You can now mount this image (you may need to become root):

```
root@bible : ~ # mount floppy.img /mnt -o loop
```

If you look in /mnt you see exactly the same files that you would have seen if you had mounted the floppy disk. You need the option -o loop to the mount command to mount a filesystem from a file rather than a disk device. (The -o loop option is discussed in more detail later in the chapter.)

If you want to write the image back to another floppy, use the following:

```
user@bible:~> dd if=floppy.img of=/dev/fd0
```

This is exactly the same process in reverse: Now the input to the dd command is the image file, and you are writing to the floppy disk.

Caution   Be very careful with the dd command. If you mix up the if= with the of= you could end up doing very serious damage, particularly if one of them is a hard disk partition.

You can do exactly the same thing with disk partitions:

```
root@bible : ~ # dd if=/dev/hda1 of=imagefile
```

In this case it is certainly best if /dev/hda1 is not mounted at the time.

This is something you might find yourself doing in the rescue system. For example, it's possible to imagine circumstances in which you might run the rescue system, get on the network, mount an NFS share from somewhere on the network, and then copy the disk partitions across to that share to back them up before doing something drastic to the system.

When you have copied the partition to a file, you can simply mount the file (with the -o loop option):

```
root@bible : ~ # mount imagefile /mnt -o loop
```

A CD image (ISO image) will work in exactly the same way; to copy a CD to an ISO image, do the following:

```
user@bible:~> dd if=/dev/cdrom of=cdimage.iso
```

Again, you can mount it:

```
root@bible : ~ # mount cdimage.iso /mnt -o loop
```

Creating and Using New Disk Images

Just as you can copy a partition to a file and mount it using the loopback device (using the -o loop option), you can create a file and then create a filesystem on it as if it were a disk partition. You can then write it out to a partition or to a removable device. For example:

```
root@bible: /tmp # dd if=/dev/zero of=image.dsk count=1440k bs=1
1474560+0 records in
1474560+0 records out
```

What you are doing here is creating a file of exactly the same size as a standard floppy disk image (1440k) by reading from the /dev/zero device (which simply outputs a stream of null bytes).

Now you can create a filesystem on the file image.dsk (you need to be root to do this):

```
root@bible: /tmp # mkfs -t ext2 image.dsk
mke2fs 1.34 (25-Jul-2003)
image.dsk is not a block special device.
Proceed anyway? (y,n) y
Filesystem label=
OS type: Linux
Block size=1024 (log=0)
Fragment size=1024 (log=0)
184 inodes, 1440 blocks
72 blocks (5.00%) reserved for the super user
First data block=1
1 block group
8192 blocks per group, 8192 fragments per group
184 inodes per group

Writing inode tables: done
Writing superblocks and filesystem accounting information: done

This filesystem will be automatically checked every 37 mounts or
180 days, whichever comes first.  Use tune2fs -c or -i to override.
```

You can then mount the filesystem and copy files onto it:

```
root@bible: /tmp # mount image.dsk /mnt -oloop
cp file1 file2 /mnt
```

Now you can write out the image to a floppy disk, but first you should unmount it:

```
root@bible: /tmp # umount mnt
root@bible: /tmp # dd if=image.dsk of=/dev/fd0
```

You now have a file containing an image of the filesystem and a floppy disk that actually contains that filesystem.

Creating ISO CD and DVD Images

Data CDs and DVDs almost always use the ISO 9660 filesystem (so called after the international standard that defines it). These images are therefore usually referred to as ISO images. You could also create CD or DVD images, CDs, and DVDs using standard Linux filesystems (ext2, for example), but these will not be useful for exchanging data with users of other operating systems.

Tip   It is not essential to use the ISO 9660 filesystem when you create images to burn to CD; you can create a suitably sized EXT2 loopback filesystem and simply copy the files you want to it and then burn a CD from it. (If you use k3b, it will detect that the image is not an ISO image, but you can force it to burn the image by pretending that it is.) But you won't be able to read (easily) the resulting CD on a non-Linux system. You may also have to mount it manually on Linux (with a command such as mount /dev/hdc /mnt) because subfs on current versions of SUSE will expect an ISO 9660 filesystem.

A quick way to save or back up a moderate amount of data is to create an ISO image containing that data and burn it to a CD or DVD.

The tool for creating ISO images is mkisofs. The man page for mkisofs is fairly bewildering to say the least because there is a very large number of options. But for most purposes, the recipe we discuss will probably do exactly what you want.

Suppose you have a directory work under your home directory. You want to create a CD containing this directory's contents, and you know that the total amount of data is not too big to fit on a CD.

```
user@bible:~> mkisofs -J -r -o work.iso work/
```

This makes a filesystem of type ISO 9660 and copies the contents of the directory work into it. This is very similar to the way that you created a filesystem image earlier in the chapter and then mounted it and wrote to it. The difference is that the mkisofs tool both creates the special ISO 9660 filesystem and writes the data to it in one action.

The options -J and -r here indicate that the ISO will have Joliet and Rock Ridge extensions (this should mean that the resulting CD works fine on Windows, Mac OS, and Linux systems). The -o indicates the name of the output file.

You should now be able to mount `work.iso` and check that it has been correctly created:

```
root@bible : ~ # mount work.iso /mnt -o loop
```

Burning CDs from the Command Line

There have been changes recently in the way Linux handles CD writers. Under the 2.4 kernel series, CD writers required the `ide-scsi` driver, which meant that they worked using SCSI emulation. In 2.6, this is no longer the case. As a result, the user-space tools have had to change somewhat.

If you want to burn disks from the command line, the tool to use is `cdrecord`. If you are running a 2.6 kernel and your CD writer is an ATAPI device (almost all are), then you will need to do something like this:

```
root@bible : ~ # cdrecord -v dev=/dev/hdc speed=8 -dao -data filename.iso
```

Here we are burning the image `filename.iso` to CD. The CD burner device is `/dev/hdc` (the first device on the second IDE channel), and we are burning the image in disk at once mode (`-dao`) to produce a data CD (`-data`). The speed has been specified as 8. This example assumes that we are running a 2.6 kernel.

If you are using a 2.4 kernel, ATAPI CD writers are treated as emulated SCSI devices using the `ide-scsi` module. In this case, the `dev=` parameter will refer to the SCSI device (for example, typically `dev=0,0,0` on a system with no real SCSI devices: `cdrecord --scanbus` helps to find the correct device numbers).

Burning CDs and DVDs Using k3b

The easiest way to create CDs and DVDs is by using `k3b`, which is a graphical tool included with all current versions of SUSE. Figure 14-7 shows a CD being burned in `k3b`.

The `k3b` application makes it easy for you to burn audio CDs, data CDs, mixed-mode CDs, video CDs (VCDs), eMovix CDs, audio DVDs, data DVDs, video DVDs, and eMovix DVDs from a convenient graphical interface. To specify the type of project that you want to create, select the appropriate type of project from the File ➪ New Project menu. If you simply want to burn an existing ISO image to a CD or DVD or extract the contents of a CD or DVD, the appropriate commands are available on the Tools ➪ CD or Tools ➪ DVD menus, respectively.

Selecting any of the CD or DVD formats from the File ➪ New Project menu displays a dialog box that enables you to drag and drop files from a browsable window at the top of the k3b display to the bottom half of the k3b display, which shows the working contents of the CD or DVD. As you drag and drop files, a graphical progress bar at the bottom of this window shows the amount of space that is currently used and the amount of space remaining on the type of output media that you selected.

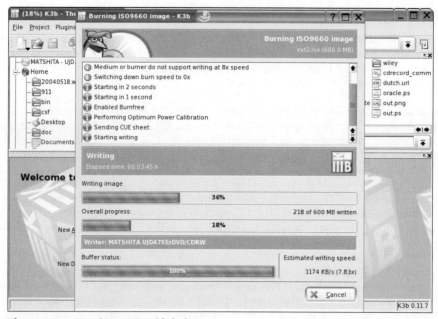

Figure 14-7: Burning a CD with k3b

Note   The k3b application enables you to create DVDs from existing DVDs or DVD directory structures. It does not include a *transcoder,* which is the software that creates the audio and video hierarchy used on audio and video DVDs. Maybe one of these days . . .

Once you've dragged and dropped all of the files that you want to include in your CD or DVD project, clicking the Burn button in the lower right corner of the k3b dialog box displays a pop-up dialog box that enables you to select the device that you want to write to and the speed at which you want to write your CD or DVD project. After you've specified these parameters, the dialog box shown in Figure 14-7 shows the progress dialog for creating your project.

The k3b application is extremely powerful, easy-to-use, and eliminates much of the traditional complexity associated with command-line CD and DVD creation. For detailed information about using and customizing k3b, see the K3b handbook, which is available from k3b's help menu.

Webmin

Webmin is a modular web-based administration tool that works on a wide variety of Linux versions and other Unix and Unix-like operating systems. It enables you to log in via a web page and perform administration tasks. Webmin then "does the right thing" and makes the necessary appropriate changes to configuration files.

Webmin is included in the SUSE Professional distribution and works well with SUSE, even on SLES. In some ways Webmin competes with YaST as a user-friendly system administration tool. In fact, it does some things well that YaST does not yet do, or does not yet do well.

Webmin's philosophy differs from that of YaST. YaST tends (for many purposes) to make changes in a two-stage process, first changing files under /etc/sysconfig and then carrying those forward to changes in the actual configuration files later when SuSEconfig runs. Webmin writes directly to the configuration files. Although SUSE ships versions of Webmin, it should not be regarded as supported by SUSE, and official SUSE versions are not included in SLES 8 or SLES 9, although Webmin itself includes support for SLES. That said, Webmin can be a very convenient alternative way to look after your system. It can also help you to get started with configuration files for particular purposes (Samba and BIND spring to mind) where writing them from scratch might be difficult the first time around.

Caution Do not use Webmin on a production machine without thinking carefully about the possible security implications. In particular, you will probably want to ensure that it is configured to work only over SSL and limit the hosts that can connect to it.

Tip Webmin is very sensitive to different versions of system libraries that may change across SUSE versions and updates to installed systems. If you encounter problems installing Webmin, check the official Webmin web site for the latest version (w w w .webmin.com) or a new development version (www.webmin.com/devel.html). If you still have problems installing or using Webmin, you may want to simply download the source archive and build a version that is completely compatible with your system.

Contacting a Running Webmin Process

When Webmin has been started, you should be able to access it through a browser by going to http://bible:10000 (or if name services are not available, the equivalent IP number followed by :10000). Of course, you can also use http://localhost:10000 from the machine itself. You will then see the login screen shown in Figure 14-8.

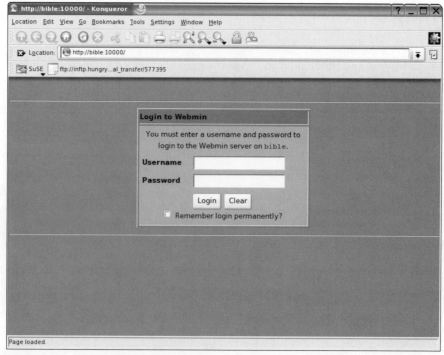

Figure 14-8: The Webmin login screen

You should change the security settings in Webmin as soon as you can to ensure either that it works only over SSL or to ensure that it allows logins only from trusted IP numbers. These actions can be done from icons in the Webmin Configuration screen after you choose the Webmin tab in the main screen (see Figure 14-9).

Webmin and YaST

The variety of modules that Webmin includes can be seen from the Networking tab and Servers tab (see Figure 14-10). These include items that have only recently become part of YaST (such as IPsec configuration and HTTP configuration) and others that are still not included in YaST (such as Point-to-Point Tunneling Protocol [PPTP] server and client, CVS server, MySQL server, and others).

Webmin provides a convenient alternative to YaST that you can use from anywhere. In the longer term it would be nice to see a web-enabled YaST. There have been vague indications (but no announcement) that such a thing might be forthcoming.

Figure 14-9: The Webmin main screen

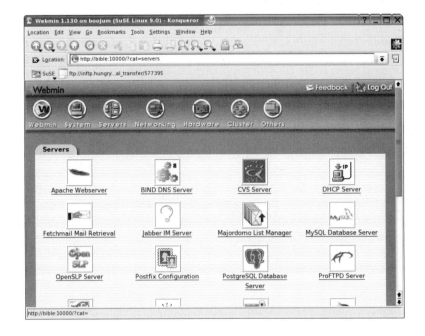

Figure 14-10: Webmin's Servers screen

It is interesting to compare the way Webmin and YaST do a job (which, frankly neither of them is ideally suited to) — adding a host to the DHCP configuration. Here we compare Webmin to YaST's DHCP server module in SUSE 9.3. While Webmin provides a web form to add all the details at once (see Figure 14-11), YaST required you to add each possible option separately by opening a drop-down list multiple times (see Figure 14-12). In either case, you would almost certainly have some difficulty if you did not already know something about the layout of the actual configuration file that is going to be written (/etc/dhcpd.conf). On the other hand, both tools save you from the kind of misery that you can suffer if you mislay a semicolon somewhere and the DHCP server will not start. Interestingly, YaST has since (in 10.0) retreated from attempting to configure hosts with fixed IP addresses in the DHCP configuration, illustrating the fact that creating GUI tools capable of writing all possible types of entries to system configuration files is a tricky problem.

The Webmin home page is at www.webmin.com. Among the resources linked from there is the 300-page *Book of Webmin* by Joe Cooper, which is available as a PDF file on the web site's Documentation page.

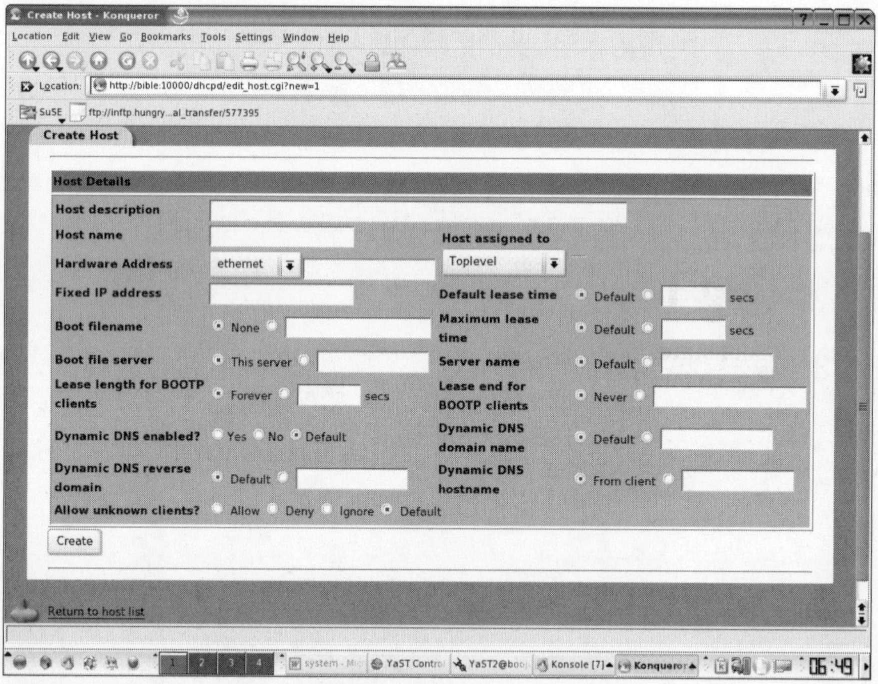

Figure 14-11: The Webmin DHCP server screen

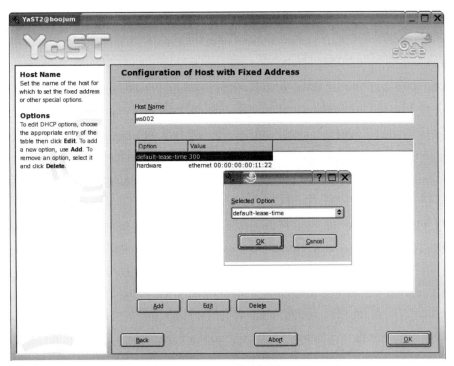

Figure 14-12: The YaST DHCP server screen in SUSE 9.3

Automating Tasks

A useful maxim states that if you have to do something manually more than three times, it's time to find a way to do it automatically. If the thing that you need to do manually is a complicated shell command, then maybe what you need is either an alias or a shell script to automate its effect.

Shell Aliases

If you have long compound commands that you regularly type, a bash *alias* is a nice way of reducing the amount of typing and thinking you have to do. You can create aliases at the command line (for the current session only) or permanently in the file ~/.alias.

For example, if you want to be able to use the single letter command b as an alias for the command ssh user@somemachine.mydomain.net, you can type:

```
user@bible:~> alias b='ssh user@somemachine.mydomain.net'
```

From now on in the current session if you type **b**, it will do the ssh command. To make that permanent, simply add the following:

```
alias b='ssh user@somemachine.mydomain.net'
```

to your .alias file. Then from the *next* time that you log in, the alias will be available. If you want to test it now, you will need to type **bash** to start a new bash shell.

To find out what aliases are defined, simply type the command **alias**.

There is no limit to the ingenuity you can apply to creating useful aliases: A long command combined from smaller commands connected together with pipes might be a good candidate for an alias. When you have constructed the command to do what you want, you can call it with a single small command. For example, to search the web server logs for a particular keyword, you might do this:

```
root@bible: /tmp # grep keyword /var/log/apache2/access_log
```

To create an alias for it, do the following:

```
root@bible: /tmp # alias k ='grep keyword /var/log/apache2/access_log'
```

Now you can simply type **k** to search the logs for keyword. Of course, before defining an alias, you should ensure that the alias you are about to define does not already exist as a command in the system.

Writing Shell Scripts

Although in principle a shell command that you define an alias for could be quite long and complex, in practice there can be problems, particularly if the command itself contains quotation marks. However, essentially you can create an alias only for a single command. So if you want to execute a more complex command and particularly if you want to be able to execute multiple commands, you are moving into the area of shell scripts. A *shell script* is a program written to be interpreted by the shell. Essentially it is just a list of shell commands to be executed one after the other, but it can contain conditionals and other programming constructs, giving it the power of a real program. Here we consider scripts to be run by the bash shell (bash scripts).

Shell scripts offer a simple means of automating tasks, provided those tasks are not too complex. If the length and complexity of a shell script goes beyond certain limits, then it might be that a shell script is not the best way to perform the task at hand.

Note   In the next sections, we offer some examples of simple shell scripts, the aim being to show their basic logic and act as a getting started guide. Like so much else in this book, shell scripting is a subject on which entire books have been written. Here we give a few examples of the basic concepts to get you started and experimenting.

Shell Variables

As a shell script is essentially just a string of shell commands, it understands the current environment variables. For example:

```
#! /bin/bash
echo "Hello" $USER
echo "Your current directory is" $PWD
```

Here $USER and $ PWD are the environment variables that are already accessible to the shell representing the current user and the working directory, respectively.

If you save this in a file scr1.sh, you have a simple shell script. The first line tells the system that it is to interpret the script using /bin/bash. This line applies if you make the script executable and run it directly, and it is important because it is possible that the user might be running a different shell. In fact, you can run the script in two different ways:

✦ Under the current shell by *sourcing* it:

```
fred@bible:~> source scr1.sh
Hello fred
Your current directory is /home/fred
```

✦ Use a dot as the source command:

```
fred@bible:~> . scr1.sh
Hello fred
Your current directory is /home/fred
```

You can also run the script by explicitly calling bash:

```
fred@bible:~> bash scr1.sh
```

Or, because /bin/sh is a symbolic link to /bin/bash, you can do the following:

```
fred@bible:~> sh scr1.sh
```

Alternatively, you can make the script executable and run it as a program. This is done by the chmod command, which adds executable permissions for all. Note that if you want to run the script in this way, it must have the first line:

```
#! /bin/bash
```

This tells the system that the interpreter needed to run the script is bash. If you source the script, this is not necessary.

```
fred@bible:~> chmod a+x scr1.sh
fred@bible:~> ./scr1.sh
Hello fred
Your current directory is /home/fred
```

A shell script can include the types of logical structures that one would expect to find in any programming language. For example, a for loop:

```
#! /bin/bash
for i in 1 2 3 4 5
do
  echo $i
done
```

Here $i represents the variable i, which takes the successive values in the loop.

Save this as scr2.sh, make it executable, and run it as you have previously, and you'll see the following:

```
fred@bible:~> chmod a+x scr2.sh
fred@bible:~> ./scr2.sh
1
2
3
4
5
```

Although you are unlikely to use numerical variables often except as basic counters in keeping track of a repeating process, you can do arithmetic in shell scripts:

```
#! /bin/bash
a=12
echo "a is "$a
echo "a+1 is " $((a+1))
```

This script produces output like this:

```
a is 12
a+1 is 13
```

Note   Notice that there should be no white space around the = sign; if there is, the variable a will not be assigned. Notice also the way that extra brackets were needed in $((a+1)).

Variables can equally represent strings:

```
#! /bin/bash
a=ABCDE
echo $a
echo ${a}FGHIJ

ABCDE
ABCDEFGHIJ
```

Here, to get the desired result, you had to write ${a}FGHIJ rather than $aFGHIJ, which would have represented a new and as yet undefined variable (named aFGHIJ). This ensures that bash interprets the last line as a request to echo the variable, which we defined as a, followed immediately by the string FGHIJ.

Suppose you want to produce word count data for all the files with the file extension .txt in the current directory.

```
#! /bin/bash
for i in *.txt
do
  wc -l $i
done
```

This produces output as shown in the following lines, indicating that you can loop over a set of files produced by *globbing*—the use of a notation such as *.txt.

```
3 1.txt
8 2.txt
17 3.txt
```

Clearly you could take this idea further to select, for example, certain lines from each of a set of files and append them to a file:

```
#! /bin/bash
for i in *.html
do
  grep -i \<title\> $i >>titles.list
done
```

This creates a file containing all lines of the form:

```
<title>Page Title</title>
```

from any of the HTML files in the current directory. Or you could do anything else that can be done with one or more commands acting on each file and direct the output to another.

Certain variables have built-in meanings. In particular, some variables represent the arguments that are given to the script when you run it (sometimes known as *positional parameters*). So, for example, consider a script showargs.sh with these contents:

```
#! /bin/bash
echo "the first argument is" $1
echo "the second argument is" $2
```

If you just run ./showargs.sh, you will see no output because the command line contains no arguments. But if you do the following:

```
user@bible:~ > ./showargs.sh this that
the first argument is this
the second argument is that
```

you get the output because you have provided a first argument, this, and a second argument, that.

Suppose you want to take the first two lines of one file and append them to the end of another file:

```
#! /bin/bash
head -2 $1 >> $2
```

Save this as append2.sh. Now, suppose you have files a and b with these contents:

```
a line 1
a line 2
a line 3
a line 4
a line 5
```

and

```
b line 1
b line 2
b line 3
b line 4
b line 5
```

To use the shell script append2.sh on files a and b, you run the following:

```
user@bible:~ > ./append2.sh a b
```

When the shell script is done, you can examine the results:

```
user@bible:~ > cat a
a line 1
a line 2
a line 3
a line 4
a line 5

user@bible:~ > cat b
b line 1
b line 2
b line 3
b line 4
b line 5
a line 1
a line 2
```

You can see that the shell script `append2.sh` has taken `a line 1` and `a line 2` and appended them to the end of file `b`.

This kind of operation has great simplicity and power at the same time if used with a little ingenuity. For example, many people do something like this:

```
#! /bin/bash
ssh $1 -l root
```

Save this output as a file with the name `root` in `~/bin` (the directory `bin` under your home directory, which should be in your path). Then you can simply type:

```
user@bible:~ > root remote
```

and you will be logging in as root to the machine `remote`. This example, although very simple, illustrates the value of being able to use arguments with a script, something you cannot do with an alias. Of course for this very simple use, you could define an alias like the following:

```
alias root='ssh -l root'
```

In general, however, a script can take as many arguments as you want. For example, you could modify the previous script to take both the user and the machine as arguments simply by making the second line `ssh $1 -l $2`. This functionality could not be achieved with an alias.

File Tests

In system shell scripts you will often see a test for the existence of a file; if the file exists, then the script may, for example, source it, delete it, rename it, or rewrite it in some way.

To test for the existence of a file with a given name, do the following:

```
#! /bin/bash
if [ -f masterpiece.doc ]
   then echo "found lost masterpiece"
else
   echo "a cultural tragedy for the whole of humanity"
fi
```

Note how the if has to be closed with fi. Note also that you need a space after the square bracket and before the -f file test.

There are many different file tests including -e (simple existence of a file), -f (existence of a regular file rather than a directory or device file), and -d (a directory), as well as tests based on permissions and modification dates, among others.

You can see examples of these in the standard .profile on SUSE, which contains these lines (commented out as it happens):

```
if [ -x /usr/bin/fortune ] ; then
   echo
   /usr/bin/fortune
   echo
fi
```

These lines cause the fortune program to run when you log in if it is installed. The test -x checks whether the current user has execute permission on /usr/bin/ fortune. (If you don't have it installed, you might enjoy trying it out.)

As another example, in /etc/init.d/xntpd, you see these lines:

```
NTP_CONF="/etc/ntp.conf"
if [ ! -f ${NTP_CONF} ]; then
    echo -n "Time server configuration file, ${NTP_CONF} does not exist."
```

In other words, if you find that the required file is not there, you output a statement to that effect.

Cases

While you are already looking at /etc/init.d for the previous example, it is a good time to note that the init scripts in /etc/init.d are a good place to see examples of the use of the case statement. The case statement provides a way of choosing what to do based on a particular decision. This simple example case.sh is enough to illustrate the principle:

```
#! /bin/bash
case $1 in
happy)
echo "What a nice day it is today"
;;
sad)
echo "What a gloomy day it is today"
;;
esac
```

So the script is deciding what it will output on the basis of the value of a variable (in this case the argument that was given). Such conditional branching is a key feature of any kind of programming:

```
user@bible:~ > ./case.sh happy
What a nice day it is today

user@bible:~ > ./case.sh sad
What a gloomy day it is today

user@bible:~ > ./case.sh mad
user@bible:~ >
```

Notice that the alternative tests are each followed by a right-hand parenthesis, and the conditional block as a whole is terminated by a double semicolon. The whole set of conditions is closed by esac.

Mailing from a Script

You may want to be informed of the progress or success of a script. One way to achieve this is to use the mail command in the script. It will look something like the following:

```
echo "many happy returns" | mail -s "Happy Birthday" user@otherdomain.net
```

This sends an email with the subject Happy Birthday and the content "many happy returns" to the address given. Note that the message body could have been obtained from a file on the system. Of course it's more likely that the kind of message being sent is something like "Backup complete," but there are almost certainly system administrators out there who use a cron job and a mail script to avoid the risk of forgetting their spouse's birthdays!

A more sophisticated way of using a block of text within a script is the so-called here-document. Within a script, the symbol << together with a string that defines the end of the block is used to define the block of text that is to be redirected to a command. Very often the string EOF is used as the *limit string*.

For example:

```
#! /bin/bash
cat <<EOF
Happy birthday to you
Happy birthday to you
EOF
```

If you run this, you will see the following:

```
Happy birthday to you
Happy birthday to you
```

To mail the greeting, do the following:

```
#! /bin/bash
mail -s "Birthday Greetings" user@otherdomain.net<<EOF
Happy birthday to you
Happy birthday to you
EOF
```

The Limits of Shell Scripting

A large amount of the basic infrastructure of the SUSE system rests on shell scripts. In particular, the whole init and runlevel system depends on a large number of interdependent shell scripts. These also read from files under /etc/sysconfig/ and elsewhere. They make heavy use of such basic standard commands as awk, sed, and grep and work very efficiently.

However, as a user or system administrator, you may not necessarily consider that shell scripts are the easiest or most elegant way to execute some logic to get something done. In general, shell scripts are best for the kinds of things they commonly do: relatively small scripts working at a fairly low level. For more complex tasks, people often turn to one of the dedicated scripting languages. In practice, that means either Perl or Python (or just possibly Ruby). If you are interested in creating dynamic web content, look also at the PHP inline scripting languages as well as CGI scripts written in either Perl or Python, and take your choice.

Shell Script Resources

You can find many good books available on shell scripting, including the following:

✦ *Mastering UNIX Shell Scripting* by Randal K. Michael (Wiley, 2003)

✦ *Linux Shell Scripting with Bash* by Ken Burtch (Sams, 2004)

✦ *Learning the bash Shell* by Cameron Newham and Bill Rosenblatt (O'Reilly, 1998)

✦ *Wicked Cool Shell Scripts* by Dave Taylor (No Starch Press, 2004)

Resources available on the web include:

✦ Advanced Bash-Scripting Guide (`www.tldp.org/LDP/abs/html/`)

✦ Bash Guide for Beginners (`http://tille.soti.org/training/bash/`)

✦ Heiner's SHELLdorado (`www.shelldorado.com/`)

Scripting Languages

Just as there are "religious wars" between the followers of `vi` and the devotees of `emacs` (as we discuss in Chapter 11) or the lovers of KDE and the true GNOME believers, so in the case of scripting languages something of a division exists between Perl and Python users.

✦ Perl is far more common, and arguably more versatile, if only because of the very large number of modules that have been written for it. It is possible to write much more compact code in Perl, which is full of shorthand and special notations.

✦ Python is newer, cleaner, and arguably more elegant. It is certainly the easier language to learn, and it is much easier to read another person's Python code than another person's Perl code.

The difference between them is perhaps best summed up in the Perl slogan, *"There's more than one way to do it,"* and the Python response to that, *"There should be one — and preferably only one — obvious way to do it."*

This is not the place to do more than briefly introduce either language; again there are many resources available on both of them (see the "Comments and Resources" section later in the chapter for some resource options).

If you know neither of them and you want to do useful scripting quickly, we advise you to learn Python. However, if you are likely to be working in an environment where you are required to maintain scripts that others have written, then Perl will very probably be the right first choice.

Here we simply offer a tiny example of a very simple task done in the two languages, and some pointers to further information.

Squid Log Reader Scripting Example

The Squid web proxy produces a log file that is not very readable. There are plenty of tools out there that turn the output of the Squid log into other formats including nice web output, but we wanted something simpler — just to be able to quickly look at the sites visited (and the dates and times) by a particular client on the network (192.168.2.4). The Squid log contains entries like these:

```
1058269843.343  54782 192.168.2.4 TCP_MISS/000 0 POST http://journeyplanner.
tfl.gov.uk/user/XSLT_TRIP_REQUEST2 - DIRECT/journeyplanner.tfl.gov.uk -

1058269847.816  40315 192.168.2.4 TCP_MISS/200 43728 POST http://journeyplanner.
tfl.gov.uk/user/XSLT_TRIP_REQUEST2 - DIRECT/journeyplanner.tfl.gov.uk text/html

1058269848.652    485 192.168.2.4 TCP_MISS/200 1728 GET http://journeyplanner.
tfl.gov.uk/user/templates/tfl/modal.css - DIRECT/journeyplanner.tfl.gov.uk text/css

1058269848.653    472 192.168.2.4 TCP_MISS/200 2035 GET http://journeyplanner.
tfl.gov.uk/user/templates/common/advanced.css - DIRECT/journeyplanner.tfl.gov.uk text/css
```

Each line is very long; they are shown wrapped here. Basically, we just want to get the correct date and time and the URL visited, and only if the client is 192.168.2.4.

Python Version

To achieve what we want in Python, we script the following:

```python
#! /usr/bin/env python
from time import localtime, strftime
infile = open('access.log', 'r')
for line in infile.readlines():
    bits = line.split()
    if bits[2] == '192.168.2.4':
        print strftime('%c', localtime(float(bits[0]))), bits[6]
```

Taking the script line by line, first we specify that the interpreter is Python (so that the script can be made executable as in the shell script examples earlier). We then import some functions from the Python standard library module time, to enable the formatting of the date and time. We then create a file handle (infile) to read from the file access.log. We loop over the lines of the file and split each line (according to white space) into a list (bits) of text strings. For each line whose third element (Python counts from 0) is the required IP address, we print the correctly formatted time and the URL.

Running this script on the fragment of the Squid log shown in the previous section gives this output:

```
Tue Jul 15 12:50:43 2003 http://journeyplanner.tfl.gov.uk/user/XSLT_TRIP_REQUEST2

Tue Jul 15 12:50:47 2003 http://journeyplanner.tfl.gov.uk/user/XSLT_TRIP_REQUEST2

Tue Jul 15 12:50:48 2003 http://journeyplanner.tfl.gov.uk/user/templates/tfl/
modal.css

Tue Jul 15 12:50:48 2003 http://journeyplanner.tfl.gov.uk/user/templates/common/
advanced.css
```

Again, the lines are wrapped, but you can see how the script has made the Squid log more readable for us, giving us only the information we absolutely need and want.

Perl Version

To achieve what we want in Perl, we script the following:

```perl
#! /usr/bin/perl
use Date::Calc::Object qw(:all);
Date::Calc->date_format(2);
open (LOG, "access.log");
while (<LOG>) {
   @bits = split(/\s+/);
   if (@bits[2]=="192.168.2.4") {
      $date = Date::Calc->gmtime(@bits[0]);
      print $date, ' ', @bits[6];
      print "\n";
   }
}
```

Here we define the interpreter to be Perl. The line starting with use again imports the necessary functionality to format the date from the appropriate Perl module, and the next line specifies a particular format for the date and time string that will be printed later. We then create a file handle (LOG), and the while statement loops over the lines of the file. The next line splits the line on white space, and again we print the required information if the third element matches the required IP address.

The output looks like this:

```
Tue 15-Jul-2003 11:50:43 http://journeyplanner.tfl.gov.uk/user/XSLT_TRIP_REQUEST2

Tue 15-Jul-2003 11:50:47 http://journeyplanner.tfl.gov.uk/user/XSLT_TRIP_REQUEST2

Tue 15-Jul-2003 11:50:48 http://journeyplanner.tfl.gov.uk/user/templates/tfl/
modal.css

Tue 15-Jul-2003 11:50:48 http://journeyplanner.tfl.gov.uk/user/templates/common/
advanced.css
```

Again, the script has made the Squid log more readable for us, giving us only the information we absolutely want.

Note the following about these two examples:

✦ In each case, we are importing modules concerned with calculating and displaying dates and times to provide functions that would not otherwise be available (Python: from time import localtime, strftime, Perl: use Date::Calc::Object qw(:all);).

✦ In each case we are defining a file handle to read the log file from (Python: infile = open('access.log', 'r'), Perl: open (LOG, "access.log");).

✦ In the case of Python, the list bits that we get by splitting the line does not require any special notation to denote its type. In Perl, we have to use @bits (for an array or list) and $date for a simple variable.

✦ In each case we begin the file with a line starting with `#!` that tells the system what interpreter to use. And the output differs in terms of the time zone shown.

Comments and Resources

For our money, Python is far cleaner, more readable, and easier to write. Others may not agree. Perl shares a lot of conventions with `shell` and `awk`, and handles regular expressions in a very neat way. Perl, being older and having a larger user base, has a wider variety of modules available and a wonderful automated system for getting and installing them — the Comprehensive Perl Archive Network (CPAN), which enables you to get and install modules with a single command.

Python Resources

If you are interested in pursuing scripting in Python, take a look at the following web sites:

✦ `www.python.org`

✦ `www.python.org/psf/`

✦ `http://starship.python.net`

You can also check out the information available in the `/usr/share/doc/packages/python` directory.

Additionally, you could consult the following books on the subject:

✦ *Python 2.1 Bible* by Dave Brueck and Stephen Tanner (Wiley, 2001)

✦ *Making Use of Python* by Rashi Gupta (Wiley, 2002)

✦ *Python Essential Reference* by David Beazley (New Riders, 2001)

✦ *Learning Python* by Mark Lutz and David Ascher (O'Reilly, 2003)

✦ *Programming Python* by Mark Lutz (O'Reilly, 2001)

Perl Resources

If you prefer to look into Perl, take a look at the following web sites:

✦ `www.cpan.org`

✦ `www.perl.com`

✦ `www.perl.org`

✦ `www.perlfoundation.org`

CPAN is a searchable site full of modules that add functionality to your Perl installation. But better still, you can download and install modules from CPAN with a single command, provided you know the names of the modules.

Information is also available in the directory `/usr/share/doc/packages/perl*`.

You can also use `perldoc` to get more information on Perl. For example, you can type **perldoc Date::Calc** to see documentation for the module we used in the example.

Finally, you can find a number of books on Perl including the following:

✦ *Perl For Dummies* by Paul Hoffman (Wiley, 2003)

✦ *Perl Weekend Crash Course* by Joe Merlino (Wiley, 2001)

✦ *Beginning Perl* by Simon Cozens with Peter Wainwright (Wrox Press, 2000)

✦ *Learning Perl* by Randal L. Schwartz and Tom Phoenix (O'Reilly, 2001)

✦ *Programming Perl* by Larry Wall, Tom Christiansen, and Jon Orwant (O'Reilly, 2000)

If some of the tools in this chapter were new to you, don't regard this simply as a reference to them that you will come back to in due course when you need them. Regard it more as an invitation to play. Set up a system that doesn't matter and experiment with some of the more potentially destructive tools. Try doing some willful damage to that system and try repairing it. This experience will be invaluable when the time comes that you need it.

If you have not worked with shell scripting or with scripting languages, take the introductions here as a starting point, and, making use of some of the resources listed, try out a few ideas with those, too.

✦   ✦   ✦

Linux Networking

Utilizing Linux in a networked environment, whether it is serving data or providing a service, is the main driving force for the operating system into the enterprise market. When you install SUSE, you are given the option to configure your network during system configuration. In this chapter, we delve into configuring the network using the command-line tools. Knowing how to use the tools directly as opposed to using the SUSE management tools is always the best way to learn how your system works.

Cross-Reference   We talked about configuring your network in Chapter 1. The network configuration after SUSE has been installed is exactly the same as the network configuration during installation. See Chapter 9 for more information on how to access your network configuration using the YaST tool.

Also, in this chapter we talk about `ping` and `traceroute`, which you can use to make life just that little bit easier when troubleshooting your network.

Finally, configuring your network when you use a wire-based network card is quite different from a wireless network card, and we discuss this issue in this chapter. And with Linux having support for Bluetooth, we discuss its uses and the applications that are available to set up and pair with your Bluetooth devices.

Configuring an IP Network

As we have talked about in previous chapters, there are many ways to do the same thing in Linux. You can configure your network through YaST, using `ifconfig`, using the SUSE network configuration files, and using the `ip` command. The next sections discuss configuring your IP network from the command line. Throughout the rest of this chapter, you will need to be logged in as root to complete network configuration.

ifconfig

If you need to view the configuration of your network, the `ifconfig` command is an easy and quick way to do this. As root, you can just type **ifconfig** to show the configuration of all active network ports (see Listing 15-1), both physical and virtual (we talk about virtual interfaces later in the chapter).

Listing 15-1: **Output of the ifconfig Command**

```
bible:~ # ifconfig
eth0      Link encap:Ethernet  HWaddr 00:03:FF:69:68:12
          inet addr:192.168.131.70  Bcast:192.168.131.255  Mask:255.255.255.0
          inet6 addr: fe80::203:ffff:fe69:6812/64 Scope:Link
          UP BROADCAST NOTRAILERS RUNNING MULTICAST  MTU:1500  Metric:1
          RX packets:30256 errors:0 dropped:0 overruns:0 frame:0
          TX packets:35690 errors:0 dropped:0 overruns:0 carrier:0
          collisions:0 txqueuelen:1000
          RX bytes:4048565 (3.8 Mb)  TX bytes:34473633 (32.8 Mb)
          Interrupt:11 Base address:0x1080

lo        Link encap:Local Loopback
          inet addr:127.0.0.1  Mask:255.0.0.0
          inet6 addr: ::1/128 Scope:Host
          UP LOOPBACK RUNNING  MTU:16436  Metric:1
          RX packets:3162 errors:0 dropped:0 overruns:0 frame:0
          TX packets:3162 errors:0 dropped:0 overruns:0 carrier:0
          collisions:0 txqueuelen:0
          RX bytes:1150733 (1.0 Mb)  TX bytes:1150733 (1.0 Mb)
```

Cross-Reference   The output of `ifconfig` can sometimes prove confusing for new users. See Chapter 6 for information on understanding most of the output.

Table 15-1 shows a breakdown of the `ifconfig` output.

Note   You may come across other flags that are attached to your network interface, a common one being the `PROMISC` flag. This flag means that your Ethernet adapter will actually listen to all packets traversing its link as opposed to listening only for packets destined for its own station.

Table 15-1
Output of ifconfig

Entry	Description
Link encap	Linux supports not only Ethernet, but other networking devices. This signifies what data link format is used. In this case we are using an Ethernet device.
Hwaddr	The hardware address (commonly referred to as the MAC address) of the Ethernet card.
inet addr	The IP address of the interface.
Bcast	The broadcast address.
Mask	The network mask.
Inet6 addr	The IPv6 address of the interface.
Scope	The scope of the IPv6 address.
UP	Flag to signify this interface is up or active.
BROADCAST	This interface will accept broadcast traffic (Ethernet, not IP).
NOTRAILERS	This interface does not support trailer encapsulation.
RUNNING	The interface is working.
MULTICAST	Interface supports multicasting.
MTU	The maximum transmission unit of the device—this is the largest amount of data this device can send in a single operation.
Metric	The metric is used in the routing algorithm. The higher the metric, the less likely the route would be used.
RX	Details about the number of received packets, including errors, dropped packets, buffer overruns, and frame count.
TX	Same as RX, but for transmitted packets.
Collisions	The amount of Ethernet collisions this station has detected.
txqueuelength	The size of the transmit buffer.
RX bytes	The amount of data in human-readable form that this station has received.
TX bytes	Same as RX bytes, but for transmitted bytes.
Interrupt	The IRQ (interrupt request) line this interface is attached to.
Base address	The hardware address of this network interface card (NIC).

Persistent Naming of Network Interfaces

In SUSE 9.3, SUSE changed the way network cards and interfaces were detected. In the past, network configuration and hardware initialization went hand in hand. In 9.3 the hardware configuration is separate from network configuration. If, for example, a network card has failed, the next network card to be detected will be allocated the interface name (eth0, for example). In multinetworked environments, this can prove fatal. If you need to be able to work with a specific network card, you should add the PERSISTENT_NAME=nic0 setting to the configuration file for the network card (/etc/sysconfig/network/ifcfg-*) where nic0 is the persistent name you want to give to the card. This name cannot be a normal interface name (eth0, wlan0, or so on) and must be unique so it does not interfere with the way SUSE 9.3 works with the network.

The problems caused by network interfaces' changing their names if persistent names were not set have been solved in SUSE 10.0, which has a means of remembering the name for each interface in the file /etc/udev/rules.d/30-net_persistent_names.rules. PERSISTENT_NAME should no longer be set in the /etc/sysconfig/network/ifcfg-* files.

To view only a specific network interface, you can pass the interface name to the ifconfig command. If you want to view details about eth0 (Ethernet 0) only, use ifconfig eth0.

Configuring an Interface with ifconfig

To configure an address for an interface with ifconfig, you need to specify the interface in question, the IP address, and traditionally the state of the interface (up or down). Consider the following example, which assigns an IP address to an interface with ifconfig:

```
bible:~ # ifconfig eth0 192.168.0.1 up
```

This configures the device eth0 with an IP address of 192.168.0.1 and sets the interface into an active configuration. When you are setting an IP address, the network and broadcast addresses are automatically set based on the IP address given (in a class-based configuration). If you want to specify a network mask for this interface, add the netmask option to the ifconfig command.

Note
If you want to set up a classless IP address to split the IP address into subnets, you could set up the interface with ifconfig eth0 192.168.0.1 netmask 255.255.255.240 up. This sets the network mask for the interface, which is used by the kernel to make routing decisions. Subnetting is discussed in more detail in Chapter 6.

Virtual Interfaces

If you have only one Ethernet adapter on your machine with the IP address of 192.168.0.5/24, but you have a machine on that network segment with the IP address of 10.0.2.3/24, you are going to have a tough time communicating with the 10.0.2.3 machine because your only network connection is on a different subnet than 10.0.2.3. The only way to communicate with this machine is to set your IP address to a machine in the 10.0.2.0/24 network. However, this is usually not an option as your connectivity to the outside world would probably be lost.

The quickest and easiest way to resolve this is to use a virtual interface. A *virtual interface* (also called a virtual adapter) is something you create and for all intents and purposes is seen as a new physical network interface. A virtual interface uses the physical connectivity of an existing network interface (in this case eth0) to be able to send and receive data. This does not affect the working of the main interface address (192.168.0.5), and it enables you to send and receive network traffic to both subnets.

One of the most common reasons for using virtual interfaces is when you need your computer to receive network traffic on multiple addresses on the same subnet. For example, if you were testing a new mail infrastructure with a separate SMTP and IMAP server, you could set up a test infrastructure on one machine running both the SMTP and IMAP server, but having them listening on 192.168.0.8 and 192.168.0.9, respectively. Using a virtual interface, you can test the connectivity from a desktop machine, and it seems, as far as the client machine is concerned, that the SMTP and IMAP services are running on separate machines.

To configure a virtual interface using ifconfig, you use exactly the same syntax as you do when setting up the IP address of eth0, with a slight twist. When specifying the network adapter to attach the virtual IP address to, you need to specify in the form of *realnetworkadapter:virtualinterface*. So, for your first virtual adapter connected to eth0, you use eth0:1.

```
bible:~ # ifconfig eth0:1 192.168.0.9 up
```

When the interface has been configured, you can then use it as you would any other real network interface you have on your system.

Setting Up Your Routes

When your interface has been configured, you usually need to configure at least a default route to talk to machines external to your network.

By default, when you configure a network address for an interface, the kernel routing table contains an entry for that interface. The reason for this entry is that even though you may not be communicating to machines on another network, the kernel still needs to know where to send traffic for machines on your local network.

Taking the address of 192.168.0.1/24 as an example, if you want to communicate with another machine on your network with an IP address of 192.168.0.233, the kernel needs to know that traffic for the 192.168.0.0/24 network needs to be sent through the eth0 device. This ensures that the machine 192.168.0.233 can physically (through Ethernet and IP) listen for traffic that has been sent to it over the same media as the sending host's Ethernet adaptor.

The route command is used to manipulate the routing table of the Linux kernel. The most common entry is the default *interface/network route* we just talked about. The other very important route for external communication is the default route. The *default route* is used as a catchall for all IP traffic that your machine cannot reach based on its routing table.

Taking 192.168.0.0/24 as the network, if you look at your default routing table, you can see you are able to access the 192.168.0.0/24 network (see Listing 15-2).

Listing 15-2: **Output of route -n with No Default Route**

```
bible:~ # route -n
Kernel IP routing table
Destination     Gateway        Genmask         Flags Metric Ref    Use Iface
192.168.0.0     0.0.0.0        255.255.255.0   U     0      0        0 eth0
127.0.0.0       0.0.0.0        255.0.0.0       U     0      0        0 lo
```

As you can see, this example uses the -n option to suppress the use of name resolution. When you suppress name resolution, it speeds up the execution of the command because it will not try to resolve an IP address to a name using your name resolver, which could at best be your local host's file or at worst be your network's DNS server.

You have two routes that have automatically been assigned by the kernel when the two devices, eth0 and lo, were created. If you need to talk to a machine in the 192.168.0.0/24 network, that traffic is routed to the eth0 device. The same is true for the 127.0.0.0/8 network, which is routed over the lo (loopback) adaptor.

However, if you want to communicate with a machine on any other network, say 10.0.0.0/24, you get an error that the machine cannot be found because you are currently unable to route packets outside of your network.

To combat this, you need to set up a *default route* for all traffic you do not know about. To do this, you create a default route with the following command:

```
bible:~ # route add default gw 192.168.0.254
```

Here you have used the route command to add a new route to the routing table. Table 15-2 explains the options used in the preceding command example.

Tip   The route command can also be used to add static routes for other networks (for example, if you know that a specific router attached to eth1 is servicing a destination network you want to reach without using your default route). For example, if you want to add a specific route for the 192.168.1.0 network, you can use route add -net 192.168.1.0/24 192.168.0.253. This routes traffic for 192.168.1.0/24 through the 192.168.0.253 router.

Table 15-2
The route Command-Line Options

Options	Description
Add	Adds a route to the routing table
Default	Specifies this is the default route
G w	Specifies that packets should be sent to this gateway
192.168.0.254	The IP address of the gateway/default router

When the default route has been added, you can take another look at the routing table (see Listing 15-3).

Listing 15-3: **The Updated Routing Table**

```
bible:~ # route -n
Kernel IP routing table
Destination    Gateway        Genmask        Flags Metric Ref    Use Iface
192.168.0.0    0.0.0.0        255.255.255.0  U     0      0        0 eth0
127.0.0.0      0.0.0.0        255.0.0.0      U     0      0        0 lo
0.0.0.0        192.168.0.254  0.0.0.0        UG    0      0        0 eth0
```

You can now see that the default (0.0.0.0) route has been added. Any traffic you do not know how to route locally will be sent to the machine/router 192.168.0.254. It is then up to the router to take care of helping the packet along its way to the destination.

Other Routes

In the previous section, we talked about network routes and the possible uses for them. We also briefly mentioned specifying a route to a specific network. You can actually specify a route to a specific IP address. The uses for this are a little bit more obscure than a network route, but are nonetheless useful.

We once had a customer that actually used a public IP address for one of their internal intranet machines. This machine was not actually accessible from the Internet, but the customer still chose to give it a real, routable address. We were designing a firewall/router for them, and once it was configured and working in production, they realized they could not access the intranet server that was located on another site. After much scratching of the head, we realized that they had a public routable address that to all intents and purposes should have been (according to the router) on the Internet. They absolutely refused to change the address, and after much protesting, we had to add a *host route* to this machine that was located on another site. This stopped the router from sending the requests to a random machine on the Internet with the same IP address as their intranet server.

Cross-Reference   Configuring a firewall/router is covered in Chapter 24.

This is why the use of private IP addresses is very useful. It means you control your local infrastructure without burdening a random server with requests that were not meant for it.

A host route specifies a static route to a single IP address and is useful for these one-off situations. If, on the other hand, you have a network that is not attached to your default gateway, or that is serviced by a specific router on your network — for example a wide area network (WAN) router — you can use a network route to specify that a dedicated router should be contacted for that specific network.

Adding a host route is quite simple, and in certain situations is very useful. Consider the following example:

```
bible:~ # route add -host 10.0.0.4 gw 192.168.0.250
```

You may note that adding a host route is very similar to adding the default route, apart from the fact you need to specify the host you are creating an entry for (-host 10.0.0.4).

To specify a network route, use the -net parameter.

Note   Note the hyphen in the -net and -host parameters. This is very important and should not be confused with the absence of the hyphen in the gw (gateway) route you have also worked with.

Setting up your routing is a very important part of your work with the network. Just as without the proper routing, the Internet would never work, your network needs to have the correct routing in place to function properly. The tool to help you do this is `route`.

routed

We have talked throughout this chapter about routing tables and how to add to them. Another type of routing is called *dynamic routing*. Manually adding routes to your servers if you have many routers across your organization can be quite cumbersome and a laborious task. With this in mind, dynamic routing presents its routing table across the network to any routers that understand the Routing Information Protocol (RIP). Routing tables are routinely interchanged using RIP, keeping routing tables on all RIP-aware routers updated about routes around your network.

SUSE includes the simple `routed` service that reads your routing table, routinely presents it to the network, and accepts routing information over RIP from other routers. This will drastically reduce your routing maintenance times as all network and host routes are updated automatically for you.

To use RIP, you must install the `routed` package using YaST and start the service with `rcrouted start`.

Once started, `routed` sends out routing table updates and also makes changes to your routing table when it receives updates from the network.

Using iproute

In the future, it is very likely that `ifconfig` and `route` will be phased out and replaced by the powerful iproute suite of programs. The iproute suite enables you to have much more granular control over your network configuration, but with a more involved process of configuring your network configuration that may be a hindrance to users new to the world of Linux.

We will show you how to configure your network card and routing with the `iproute` suite as well as how to view detailed information about your network.

The iproute suite's main command is `ip`. This command is used to set options for your network card, network configuration, and routing information. For each part of the network you want to configure, `ip` takes an object to work on. The objects you are concerned with are `link` (the network interface), `addr` (network configuration), and `route` (routing information).

Configuring Your Network Card

First, to configure your network card (not the network configuration), you use the
ip link command:

```
bible:~ # ip link set mtu 9000 dev eth0
```

Here, you have told ip to edit the link (network device) and set the maximum transmission unit (MTU) to 9000 on device eth0.

Note   Setting an MTU to 9000 is common on gigabit Ethernet devices, and this is commonly called a *jumbo frame*. As gigabit Ethernet works a lot faster, it gets to a
point where it is not efficient to send data in blocks of 1500 octets as is common
with 10- or 100-megabit devices. Setting the MTU to 9000 provides a much more
efficient way of transporting data very fast over gigabit Ethernet.

To view data about your Ethernet device, you can use the show option for the link
(network interface) object (see Listing 15-4).

Listing 15-4: **Viewing Information about Your Network Device**

```
bible:~ # ip link show
1: lo: <LOOPBACK,UP> mtu 16436 qdisc noqueue
link/loopback 00:00:00:00:00:00 brd 00:00:00:00:00:00
2: sit0: <NOARP> mtu 1480 qdisc noop                           link/sit 0.0.0.0 brd 0.0.0.0
3: eth0: <BROADCAST,MULTICAST,ALLMULTI,UP> mtu 1500 qdisc pfifo_fast qlen 100
link/ether fe:fd:d4:0d:d0:73 brd ff:ff:ff:ff:ff:ff
```

As is the case with the output of ifconfig, you are shown the hardware address,
MTU, and interface flags. The qdisc entry refers to the queue (or buffer) that is
associated with any traffic that is sent over the interface.

Configuring Your Network Address

As with the configuration of the network interface, you need to work on a certain
network object. To configure the addressing of a network interface, you need to
work with the addr (address) object. The ip addr command is similar to ifconfig in
what information it needs to configure the address.

```
bible:~ # ip addr add 192.168.0.5 dev eth0
```

As would be the case with ifconfig, you tell ip to edit the address of the device
eth0, adding the IP address of 192.168.0.5.

We talked about virtual adapters earlier in the chapter, and the configuration with ip is as simple (if not simpler) to configure. If you want your network interface to listen to more than one address, simply use the same format as shown for the initial network address with a different IP. This will add the address to the adapter, which can be viewed using the ip addr show command (see Listing 15-5).

Listing 15-5: **Viewing Network Configuration**

```
bible:~ # ip addr show
1: lo: <LOOPBACK,UP> mtu 16436 qdisc noqueue
   link/loopback 00:00:00:00:00:00 brd 00:00:00:00:00:00
   inet 127.0.0.1/8 brd 127.255.255.255 scope host lo
   inet6 ::1/128 scope host
      valid_lft forever preferred_lft forever
2: sit0: <NOARP> mtu 1480 qdisc noop
   link/sit 0.0.0.0 brd 0.0.0.0
3: eth0: <BROADCAST,MULTICAST,NOTRAILERS,UP> mtu 1500 qdisc pfifo_fast qlen 1000
   link/ether 00:03:ff:69:68:12 brd ff:ff:ff:ff:ff:ff
   inet 192.168.0.5/24 brd 192.168.0.255 scope global eth0
   inet6 fe80::203:ffff:fe69:6812/64 scope link
      valid_lft forever preferred_lft forever
```

Again, as with ifconfig, you are shown the IP address (inet) and broadcast address (brd) of the interfaces.

Configuring Your Routing

Whereas with ifconfig and route, you use separate commands to configure the network and routing, you use the ip command to configure the routing as well.

To configure routing, you need to edit the route object. You first add the default route to the Linux system:

```
bible:~ # ip route add default via 192.168.0.8
```

As you can see, this command is very similar to the way you set the default route using the route command with the exception of specifying the g w portion (which is now via).

The iproute suite of applications is just now coming into mainstream use and its operation set is very large and well defined. Take a look at the ip man page for more information about what you can do with the ip command.

The Wonderful World of ARP

On the level of Ethernet, each station (or node) listens for traffic destined to its physical (MAC) address. In Chapter 6, we talked about the layered model of the ISO OSI. This model can help your understanding here because when TCP/IP traffic has been encapsulated into an Ethernet frame, the destination Ethernet address is also added. However, at this level, the IP address does not come into play because this is purely Ethernet-based addressing. So how does the sending machine know what Ethernet address local traffic should have?

TCP/IP uses *Address Resolution Protocol* (ARP) to match an IP address to a local (to the network) address. When a machine needs to send data to a machine on its local network, it sends an ARP broadcast asking, "Who has the IP address 192.168.0.233?" The 192.168.0.233 machine (if alive) will respond saying, "I have that IP address, and my MAC address is XYZ." The sender then uses this MAC address as the destination in the Ethernet frame when it needs to send data to the 192.168.0.233 machine.

Now, if every time data needs to be sent to 192.168.0.233 the sending host were to do an ARP lookup, this would slow down the transfer of data. To combat this, Linux keeps an *ARP cache*. This cache contains a lookup table, correlating the IP address to the destination MAC address.

To view the ARP table, use the command `arp` (see Listing 15-6). In the following output, you can see how an IP address is correlated to a MAC address (for example, IP address `192.168.0.1` is associated with MAC (hardware) address `00:00:0F:00:00:01`).

Listing 15-6: **Viewing the ARP Cache**

```
bible:~ # arp -n
Address                HWtype  HWaddress         Flags Mask     Iface
192.168.0.1            ether   00:00:0F:00:00:01  C               eth0
192.168.0.233          ether   00:00:0F:00:00:02  C               eth0
```

Here, you have told `arp` to not resolve machine addresses as this will slow down the operation. Most network-based operations can use the `-n` parameter to stop host name lookups.

 Tip   If you want to remove an entry from the ARP cache (if the machine is taken down and another machine has the IP address associated with a stale hardware address), you can use the `arp -d` command. To remove the 192.168.0.1 ARP entry, use `arp -d 192.168.0.1`.

You can see the IP address of the nodes in question, the hardware type (`ether` is Ethernet), hardware address, and the flags associated with these entries.

> **Note**
>
> The ARP flags explain the status of a specific ARP entry. `C` means this is a complete associated entry. `M` specifies a permanent entry (it will not get flushed from the cache), and a published entry is signified by a `P`. A published entry is a way to allow your machine to answer ARP requests on behalf of other hosts. By default, your ARP cache is concerned only with your own machine's communications.

Taking Part in an IPX Network

Many universities use Novell for their core infrastructure. Novell NetWare has been extremely good at managing large pools of users (in the thousands), and this is why it is so popular with large organizations. A large proportion of universities have tens of thousands of user accounts that they must manage in an efficient manner. Linux is able to communicate with NetWare servers, mount NetWare file servers, send pop-up messages to other users, and so on.

The protocol now known as IPX was originally designed by Xerox as a protocol for local area networks. Novell took these protocols and enhanced them for their network products.

One of the first tasks that needs to be completed in taking part in an IPX network is to configure your network card and Linux to become IPX-aware. This can be completed by running the `ipx_configure` command. Think of `ipx_configure` as `ifconfig` for IPX.

The IPX utilities and helper applications for mounting NetWare file servers are contained in the `ncpfs` package. To configure your network interface to take part in an IPX network, you need to tell Linux that you want for it to create your IPX interface automatically and also select your primary interface. Consider the following example.

```
bible:~ # ipx_configure --auto_primary=on --auto_interface=on
bible:~ #
```

Here, you have told `ipx_configure` to automatically create the IPX interface (`auto_interface`) and also to select this interface as the primary IPX interface on the machine (`auto_primary`).

When configured, you can search for NetWare servers on your IPX network with the `slist` command (see Listing 15-7).

Listing 15-7: Listing NetWare Servers on Your Network

```
bible:~ # slist

Known NetWare File Servers                  Network    Node Address
----------------------------------------------------------------------
BIBLE                                       C0A80001   000000000001
```

As you can see, in this example, we just so happen to have a NetWare server on our network called BIBLE.

For this example, we have created a directory under /media called Netware on which to mount our server. To actually mount the server, you use the command ncpmount. It is very similar to the mount command you have already come across in the book, but because you need to tell the server the username you are authenticating as, you have a few extra things to bear in mind.

The ncpmount command takes the server name, the username, and the mount point under which you want to mount the server. In this case, you will log in to the server BIBLE as the user (-U) justin, mounting under /media/Netware.

```
bible:/ # ncpmount BIBLE -U justin /media/Netware/
Logging into BIBLE as JUSTIN
Password:
```

When mounted, you can use the NetWare file server as any other mounted filesystem.

Network Tools

When you have the network up and running, you need to take advantage and start using it. Any administrator will realize that sitting in front of a machine to administer it is laborious and time-consuming. Network tools such as Telnet and SSH provide a means to log in to a Linux machine, creating a virtual terminal for you to work at.

Telnet is a protocol that has been around for a very long time and is now considered quite antiquated and insecure as all transmissions through Telnet are in plain text. Because of this, most modern distributions disable the Telnet server out of the box. By default, you will be able to use SSH to connect to a server (discussed later in the chapter).

Caution It does not take a genius to be able to sniff traffic on a network, and anything that is sent over the network in plain text can be found using freely available network monitoring tools. Telnet itself has no concept of encryption, and your username and more important password are sent over the network in plain text. Imagine if you were using Telnet to connect to a machine over the Internet. All of the routers and networks your packets have to traverse could have a malicious user sniffing traffic for data. As soon as they find you connecting to a machine through Telnet and have your password, they can then log in to that machine and assume your identity.

Telnet is still in use today as its implementations are still widespread. SUSE does include a Telnet server and client, but the server is not enabled by default.

The SSH server and client are installed by default and are enabled out of the box. This forces you to use SSH for your terminal emulation, if you do not install the Telnet services.

The SSH protocol is an encrypted virtual terminal and so much more. SSH will connect to the server and initiate an encrypted connection. It will then negotiate a connection using a username and password, all encrypted. This stops any man-in-the-middle" attack from taking place as an encrypted link has been set up before user data has been sent.

Note A man-in-the-middle attack takes place when a malicious user intercepts network packets on your network and views the contents of them. In the example of Telnet, your passwords can easily be found by some malicious user's intercepting your network packets and analyzing these packets during the initialization of a Telnet session.

Not only can you set up a connection with a username and password, but also you can create a public and private key pair that will authenticate instead of a password. The great thing about using public/private keys is that unless you have physical access to the key, you will be unable to log in to the server, regardless of whether you know the password of a user.

Using Telnet

Telnet has more uses than just providing a virtual login to another server. We regularly use Telnet to check to see if services are working correctly and to check for configuration issues that may arise.

Using Telnet for Virtual Terminal Services

In its barest form, the telnet client takes one argument, the host name of the server you want to connect to (see Listing 15-8). In the following example, you will log in to the server bible using telnet.

Listing 15-8: Using telnet to Connect to a Remote Server

```
bible:~ # telnet bible
Trying 192.168.0.1...
Connected to bible.
Escape character is '^]'.
Welcome to SUSE LINUX Enterprise Server 9 (i586) - Kernel 2.6.5-97-default

bible login:
```

Once connected to the server, you are prompted to log in to the system as you would on your local system.

To force a disconnect from the remote machine, you can use the Ctrl+] (Control and right square bracket) key combination. This drops you to the telnet prompt. From this prompt, you can open another connection to a server using open servername or quit telnet by issuing the quit command. For more information about what you can do in the telnet prompt, type **help** and press Return.

Using Telnet for Testing

You can use Telnet for more than just a virtual terminal, however. We mentioned using telnet to test services that you have configured. Telnet provides a virtual terminal that opens a TCP connection to a specific port. This connection prints whatever text it is sent from the server (in this case, the Telnet server) and sends any data you type into the remote server.

Quite a few services work on this notion of sending their data in plain text form for their protocol. The two main candidates are Hypertext Transfer Protocol (HTTP) and Simple Mail Transport Protocol (SMTP).

To see a rundown of the SMTP protocol, we log in to the mail server on our local machine and send a test mail (see Listing 15-9).

Listing 15-9: Using telnet as a Protocol Tester

```
bible:~ # telnet localhost smtp
Trying 127.0.0.1...
Connected to localhost.
Escape character is '^]'.
220 bible.suse.com ESMTP Postfix
ehlo localhost
250-bible.suse.com
250-PIPELINING
```

```
250-SIZE 10240000
250-VRFY
250-ETRN
250 8BITMIME
mail from: justin@bible
250 Ok
rcpt to: justin@palmcoder.net
250 Ok
data
354 End data with <CR><LF>.<CR><LF>
This is a test mail that I am sending you.
Justin
.
250 Ok: queued as 6D5CF18490
```

We have used the SMTP protocol to specify that we are sending a mail to the user justin@palmcoder.net from the user justin@bible from the machine localhost (ehlo localhost). This is a standard SMTP protocol transaction that can be used to quickly test an SMTP server's ability to send mail to a specific user.

Cross-Reference   We discuss mail servers and a further example of using Telnet to test a service in Chapter 17.

The command line used, telnet localhost smtp, is the same command line used previously with the addition of the port specification (smtp). The port you connect to can either be in text form (as we used) or in numerical form. The port number for the SMTP protocol is port 25.

Note   From now on in the book, we will refer to TCP/IP ports more and more. A TCP/IP port can be thought of as a virtual plug that serves a specific purpose. Each port has a unique number and a number of well-known port numbers have been reserved for specific purposes. For example, port 80 is HTTP, port 25 is SMTP, and port 21 is FTP. View the file /etc/services for more information on what the well-known port numbers are.

If security is a concern for your organization, then Telnet should not be used to transmit sensitive information. As all information is plain text, it just is not safe.

Using SSH

SSH can be initially thought of as a secure extension to Telnet. It provides virtual terminal services that are encrypted to the user; this includes encrypting the password that the user sends to the server. However, SSH, is actually a suite of technologies that provide not only virtual terminal services, but also file transfer and tunneling services that prove extremely useful. In this section, we will talk first about the virtual terminal side of SSH and then move onto public/private key use and tunneling data through an SSH secure tunnel.

Using SSH for Virtual Terminal Services

Like its poorer cousin, the prime use of SSH is to log in securely to servers. SSH does not provide you with a login and password prompt as Telnet does. SSH partakes in the user authentication process when the connection is being negotiated (you will see why later). Because of this, SSH needs to know the username you want to use to connect to the server before it attempts a connection. If you just use SSH to connect to a remote server, the SSH client will assume you want to connect to the server as your current userid (see Listing 15-10).

Listing 15-10: Using SSH to Log in to a Remote Server as the Current Userid

```
justin@bible:~> ssh bible
The authenticity of host 'bible (192.168.0.1)' can't be established.
RSA key fingerprint is e3:0a:4b:1e:d5:55:80:24:e4:7d:5f:86:23:f2:1d:8a.
Are you sure you want to continue connecting (yes/no)? yes
Warning: Permanently added 'bible,192.168.0.1' (RSA) to the list of known hosts.
Password:
Last login: Wed May 12 13:30:36 2005 from console
Have a lot of fun...
justin@bible:~>
```

If you look at the output in the preceding listing, you notice quite an important thing happening when we attempted to log in to the machine bible. We were told that the machine has not been recognized and thus is not trusted. This is part of the security of the SSH protocol. You will see this warning for every machine you log in to for the first time. If you want to proceed and log in to the server, your client will make a note of the fingerprint of the remote server.

If you try to log in to the server again, but someone has maliciously tricked you into thinking you were connecting to your original server (when in fact it was a bogus server with the same name), SSH knows that the fingerprint of the machine is bogus and warns you of this when you log in.

As you can see, we were not asked for a username because the SSH client already knew we wanted to connect as the user justin.

If you want to connect to the SSH server as another user, you have two options; either use the -1 switch to specify the user or the more compact username@server notation. For example:

```
justin@bible:~> ssh root@bible
Password:
Last login: Tue Jul  6 04:23:05 2005
Have a lot of fun...
bible:~ #
```

Because we specified the username on the command line, we were asked for that user's password and not ours. In this case, we logged in as the user root.

Public and Private Keys

If you are bored of typing in passwords, or you want to make the process of remote authentication more secure, you can use public and private keys to identify yourself.

A PPK (Public Private Key) pair consists of two keys:

✦ One key that you keep to yourself and share with no one else (the *private key*).

✦ The other is a *public key* that you install on all servers you want to log in to that can be read by anybody.

PPKs are useless if you do not have the pair of keys. Even if someone finds your public key, they cannot use it detrimentally, because it is used only as the partner of the private key that you have kept secret.

To create a PPK, you need to run the ssh-keygen command. The ssh-keygen command takes quite a few arguments, but we will create a standard SSH2 key pair for our purposes. Consider the example shown in Listing 15-11.

Passphrases

You have two options for how you want to create your key pair—with or without a passphrase. A *passphrase* is a long string of characters that can be thought of as your password. A passphrase could be a sentence, or a piece of text you can remember, and can contain spaces. This does make the PPK much more secure because even if your private key has been compromised, the user still needs to know your passphrase. If you do not set a passphrase, you can then log in to a machine without entering a password or a passphrase, and you rely on the security of the PPK partnership and nothing else. If security is a big thing for you (and it should be), you should set a passphrase when asked.

Listing 15-11: **Creating a PPK Pair**

```
justin@bible:~> ssh-keygen -t dsa
Generating public/private dsa key pair.
Enter file in which to save the key (/home/justin/.ssh/id_dsa):
Enter passphrase (empty for no passphrase):
Enter same passphrase again:
Your identification has been saved in /home/justin/.ssh/id_dsa.
Your public key has been saved in /home/justin/.ssh/id_dsa.pub.
The key fingerprint is:
07:3d:01:94:6b:23:4d:d4:a3:8d:49:b5:b6:ac:ad:83 justin@bible
justin@bible:~>
```

In this example, we created a key pair using the DSA encryption algorithm. The SSH protocol has two levels, protocol 1 and protocol 2. Protocol 2 is inherently more secure. To make sure you create an SSH v2 key pair, pass either dsa or rsa as the key type with -t on the command line.

Our keys are saved in ~/.ssh/, providing us with a means to copy our public key over to another server so that we can log in. In the case of DSA, our public key is called id_dsa.pub and our private key is called id_dsa.

Note Your private key must always be kept private from any other user at all costs, particularly if you choose not to enter a passphrase.

On the machine on which we want to log in securely, we need to copy our public key over to the file ~/.ssh/authorized_keys (see Listing 15-12). The authorized keys file contains public keys for a specific user that will enable them to log in. Only this user will use the PPK pair; it is not system-wide.

Listing 15-12: **Copying Our Public SSH Key to Another Server**

```
justin@bible:~> scp .ssh/id_dsa.pub 192.168.131.70:.ssh/authorized_keys
The authenticity of host '192.168.131.70 (192.168.131.70)' can't be established.
RSA key fingerprint is e3:0a:4b:1e:d5:55:80:24:e4:7d:5f:86:23:f2:1d:8a.
Are you sure you want to continue connecting (yes/no)? yes
Warning: Permanently added '192.168.131.70' (RSA) to the list of known hosts.
Password:
id_dsa.pub                        100%  602    0.6KB/s   00:00
```

We will talk about the scp (secure copy) command later in the chapter. For now, note that it uses an encrypted channel to send files to and from remote servers.

When we have copied over our SSH public key to the file `authorized_keys`, we can then log in to the remote server with our passphrase as opposed to our password, as follows:

```
justin@bible:~> ssh 192.168.131.70
Enter passphrase for key '/home/justin/.ssh/id_dsa':
Last login: Tue Jul  6 04:31:19 2005 from bible.suse.com
Have a lot of fun...
```

Notice this time we were asked for our passphrase and not a password. The SSH server does not query the user database for our password but accepts the fact that we are trusted because we have a valid public and private key partnership.

If we had not entered a passphrase when we created the key pair, we would have been granted access to the system without any user intervention. Even though it is not as secure as the passphrase or the traditional password system, it proves invaluable when you need to write a script that automatically logs in to a remote server without any user intervention.

Using Secure Copy

Secure copy is an extension of the SSH shell system that uses your PPK pair (if available) to copy files to and from remote systems. We already came across the `scp` command earlier when we copied our public key to a remote server.

The `scp` command is very similar to SSH in the way it defines what server you are connecting to (as well as supporting the username@server notation). The addition of a file, remote server, and location specification is what makes this command special.

```
scp myfile justin@zen.palmcoder.net:/etc/myfile
```

This command copies the file `myfile` to the server `zen.palmcoder.net` as the user `Justin` in the `/etc/` directory. If you have a PPK defined, you will be prompted for that passphrase, as you would if you were logging in via SSH.

SCP is able to copy entire directories, as is the `cp` command. If the source file you specify to copy is in fact a directory, you need to add `-r` to the command line (before the specification on the source directory) for a recursive copy:

```
scp -r mydirectory justin@zen.palmcoder.net:/tmp/
```

This copies the entire contents of the directory `mydirectory` to the `/tmp` directory on `zen.palmcoder.net` as the user `justin`.

Note Notice the colon used in the `scp` command. It is very important and tells SCP that you are in fact copying data to another machine. If you omit the colon, it will do a straight copy to `justin@zen.palmcoder.net` in our example.

rsync

It is quite common that two servers may need to keep some data synchronized on a regular basis. You have a few options of doing this, including File Transfer Protocol (FTP), Network File System (NFS), or scp. The problem with these protocols is that it is difficult to know whether files have changed since last synchronizing them, and even if they have, the full file still needs to be copied.

rsync is an effective transfer protocol that has been designed to deal with these issues. We have used it many times to take backups of data from one server to upgrade to another physical machine, and it proves very useful when dealing with many gigabytes of data that may change many times throughout the day.

Another very good feature of rsync is the way you can compress the data stream that is sent from the server. This can help to reduce the amount of time it takes to synchronize data.

For example, rsync is great at keeping a web site synchronized to a local copy on one of our laptops just in case the worst happens. See Listing 15-13.

Listing 15-13: **Synchronizing a Web Site Directory**

```
bible:~/www # rsync -avrz -e ssh
www.palmcoder.net:/var/www/palmcoder/blogimages .
receiving file list ... done
blogimages/
blogimages/DSCN0156.thumb.jpg
blogimages/DSCN0191.thumb.jpg
blogimages/DSCN0718.jpg
blogimages/dscn0456.jpg
blogimages/palmcoder.gif

wrote 96 bytes  read 92643 bytes  10910.47 bytes/sec
total size is 96350  speedup is 1.04
```

You can see that we have chosen to copy a single small directory with multiple files. In this example, the rsync command uses the parameters -azrv that correspond to the following:

  ✦ -a—Enables an archive mode that keeps all of the file attributes of the files you are copying.

  ✦ -v—Verbose mode prints out so you can see the files you are copying.

  ✦ -r—Recursive copying traverses the directory structure of the directory you are copying.

  ✦ -z—Compresses the data stream.

In this example, we have also told `rsync` to use `ssh` to connect to the server. You do have an `rsync` server that can be used, but most people just use `ssh` to transport data because many servers are running `ssh` and not the `rsync` server.

> **Note** In the example, when specifying the server (`www.palmcoder.net`), we also specified the directory to copy over, separated by a colon (`:`). As we have not put a forward slash (`/`) at the end of the `blogimages` directory, `rsync` copies the directory and its contents to our local machine. If a forward slash were added to the directory specified, we would copy only the contents of the directory and not the directory itself. Be very wary about this because it is easy to copy something you were not expecting if you miss a forward slash.

If you want to make sure any files that were deleted from the originating server were actually deleted on the local machine when synchronized, you need to add the `-delete` parameter to the command-line options.

wget

If you need to download web pages or files from FTP quickly, you can use `wget`. It's a great tool to use if you need to get a file onto a server when you do not have a web browser, which is very common.

The `wget` command is used only to transfer files over HTTP and FTP. It is not to be confused with something like `rsync`, which is a general network copy system.

In its simplest form, all you have to do is pass the URL you want to download to the `wget` command (see Listing 15-14). This downloads the URL specified to the local directory.

Listing 15-14: Downloading a File over HTTP to Your Local Server

```
bible:~ # wget www.palmcoder.net/index.php
--03:26:23--  http://www.palmcoder.net/index.php
       => `index.php'
Resolving www.palmcoder.net... 212.13.208.115
Connecting to www.palmcoder.net[212.13.208.115]:80... connected.
HTTP request sent, awaiting response... 200 OK
Length: unspecified [text/html]

   0K ........                                    59.59 KB/s

03:26:23 (59.59 KB/s) - `index.php' saved [8608]
```

Here, you have an overview of how long it took to download the file and a real-time status indicator notifying you of how long you have left until the file has completely downloaded.

You can also use wget to mirror a web site by passing the recursive (-r) parameter to it. As we are all kind and gentle Internet users, we do not want to recursively follow links in every HTML document we come across, and the default depth to traverse to is five. If you want to recursively get only the first two levels of a site, you use -l 2.

```
bible:~ # wget -r -l 2 www.palmcoder.net
```

Network Troubleshooting

At some point or another you will have to fix network problems. It happens to the best of us and is an important part of the administration of a networked infrastructure. There are two very important tools at your disposal for diagnosing your network — the ping and traceroute programs.

ping

The ping program sends an ICMP (Internet Control Message Protocol) packet to an IP address, asking the remote machine to send back an echo packet. The ICMP packet is very small in the grand scheme of things and puts very little burden on your network. It tests the full route of the network from your client machine to the server, whether it is from the United Kingdom or Australia or a machine sitting next to you.

To ping a machine, you need to issue the ping command with the host name or IP of the machine you want to test. The ping process will either show you echo packets and how long it took for them to return to you or notify you that the machine could not be contacted. Take a look at Listing 15-15.

Listing 15-15: **Using ping to Test Network Connectivity**

```
thinkpad:~ # ping www.palmcoder.net
PING zen.palmcoder.net (212.13.208.115) 56(84) bytes of data.
64 bytes from sospan.palmcoder.net (212.13.208.115): icmp_seq=1 ttl=55 time=
27.0 ms
64 bytes from sospan.palmcoder.net (212.13.208.115): icmp_seq=2 ttl=55 time=
28.4 ms
64 bytes from sospan.palmcoder.net (212.13.208.115): icmp_seq=3 ttl=55 time=
30.0 ms
```

```
--- zen.palmcoder.net ping statistics ---
3 packets transmitted, 3 received, 0% packet loss, time 2001ms
rtt min/avg/max/mdev = 27.015/28.482/30.028/1.231 ms
```

Here, you can see the machine `thinkpad` sending an Internet Control Message Protocol (ICMP) echo request to the machine `zen`. When `zen` receives this ICMP echo request, it sends back an ICMP echo reply to the machine `thinkpad`. This back and forth happens until you press Ctrl+C to stop the sequence. After `ping` has been interrupted, you will be told the amount of packets that were lost (not replied) and an average of the time it took for the response to come back from the machine. On a slow or noisy network, you could well see dropped packets, which is never a good thing.

The `ping` program and its ICMP packet tell you only if the TCP/IP stack on the remote machine is up. It is not capable of telling you how well the machine is. You should not assume that just because the remote machine is "alive" that all services are running as they should on the machine. The `ping` program is really used only to test network connectivity.

traceroute

The `traceroute` program goes a bit further than the `ping` program, because it tells you what routers it used on the way to the destination machine.

The TCP/IP protocol uses the notion of Time to Live (TTL). This TTL is decreased by one as it moves through a router. As soon as the TTL reaches zero, the packet is destroyed. This stops TCP/IP packets from flooding a network when there is a routing loop. A *routing loop* is where your packet traverses the same router over and over again because of router misconfiguration. This is not common, but we have seen it on quite a few occasions in the Internet.

The `traceroute` program takes advantage of the TTL by initially specifying a TTL of 1. As your packet hits the first router, its TTL is decreased to zero and your client receives an ICMP packet informing you that your packet has been destroyed. To find the next router to your destination, `traceroute` sends a packet out to your server, with a TTL of 2. This time the packet goes one router further until the TTL is zero and you are notified that your packet has been destroyed. This happens until your packet eventually reaches your target machine.

The `traceroute` program helps you diagnose where a connectivity problem exists on the way to a server. This is useful as it can rule out whether the problem is local to your administrative domain or is someone else's problem. See Listing 15-16 for an example.

Listing 15-16: **Using the traceroute Program to Diagnose Network Problems**

```
thinkpad:~ # traceroute www.palmcoder.net
traceroute to www.palmcoder.net (212.13.208.115), 30 hops max, 40 byte packets
 1  192.168.1.1  2.734 ms   3.840 ms   3.231 ms
 2  217.41.132.74  17.986 ms   18.992 ms   19.735 ms
 3  217.41.132.1  21.366 ms   22.553 ms   24.021 ms
 4  217.41.132.106  30.135 ms   32.597 ms   33.552 ms
 5  194.106.33.67  34.500 ms   22.508 ms   24.022 ms
 6  194.106.32.12  28.242 ms   30.509 ms   31.278 ms
 7  195.66.226.103  30.782 ms   31.283 ms   32.833 ms
 8  194.153.169.25  34.975 ms   35.234 ms   37.647 ms
 9  212.13.195.93  39.701 ms   40.441 ms   41.401 ms
10  212.13.210.20  41.606 ms   44.235 ms   45.992 ms
11  sospan.palmcoder.net (212.13.208.115)  47.959 ms   33.374 ms   30.918 ms
```

For each router that traceroute passes, you see the router's IP address and three timings. When the router is queried, the query actually happens three times to allow you to glean an average response time from the router.

Wireless Networking

One of the best of the networking technologies that have come along in the past few years is wireless networking. Wireless networking is having its quickest adoption in the laptop market, and many machines now come with the Centrino chipset from Intel.

If your laptop does not include an onboard wireless chipset, you will probably find a good PCMCIA (an expansion slot for laptops) card that provides wireless support for you. A lot of Linux users have had great results with the Cisco wireless cards.

If you are not sure whether your wireless networking card is supported in Linux, or you are looking to purchase one, Google is always your friend. Use Google to search for the term "Linux" and the model number of the wireless networking card you are interested in.

Starting with SUSE 9.3 and in subsequent releases, SUSE has added a lot more support for the popular Centrino chipset. The firmware files for these chipsets are now included in the distribution and are configurable in the same way as a normal network card under YaST.

ndiswrapper

If you do not use one of the popular wireless cards supported out of the box in SUSE, you can potentially use ndiswrapper. ndiswrapper is a great system that will enable you to wrap a Linux kernel driver around a Windows network card driver to be able to provide you with support for pretty much any network card out there.

> **Note**
>
> Before you start with the configuration of your networking with ndiswrapper, you must make sure you download the correct Windows drivers. If you are using a 64-bit laptop (for example, an AMD 64), you must download the 64-bit version of the driver. Similarly for a 32-bit laptop, you must use the 32-bit Windows drivers.

To get ndiswrapper working:

1. You need to install the ndiswrapper package using YaST. For more information about how to install new applications under SUSE, refer to Chapter 1.

2. In the YaST package search screen, search for ndiswrapper and select it for installation.

3. After ndiswrapper has been installed, you will need to download or copy the Windows driver package to your SUSE installation. We use the A-Link WL54H chipset as an example.

4. When downloaded, unarchive the package (Windows drivers usually come as a zip file, so in this case use the unzip command — see Listing 15-17).

Listing 15-17: Using unzip to Unarchive a Windows Network Driver

```
linux:~ # unzip WL54driver2.2.6.0.zip
Archive:  WL54driver2.2.6.0.zip
 inflating: RaLink2_RT2560.exe
  creating: Win2K/
 inflating: Win2K/rt2500.cat
 inflating: Win2K/Rt2500.INF
 inflating: Win2K/rt2500.sys
  creating: Win9xMe/
 inflating: Win9xMe/Rt2500.INF
 inflating: Win9xMe/rt25009x.sys
  creating: WinXP/
 inflating: WinXP/rt2500.cat
 inflating: WinXP/Rt2500.INF
 inflating: WinXP/rt2500.sys
```

5. After the driver archive has been unarchived, you need to install the driver under ndiswrapper. If you want to support WPA (Wi-FI protected access), you will need to use Windows XP version of the drivers. To install the driver, you need to use ndiswrapper -i (install). See Listing 15-18.

Listing 15-18: Using ndiswrapper to Install a Windows Network Driver

```
linux:~/Win2K # ndiswrapper -i Rt2500.INF
Installing rt2500
linux:~/Win2K #
```

6. After the driver has been installed, you can then check whether ndiswrapper has successfully recognized it by listing the driver it has installed using the -l option (list). See Listing 15-19.

Listing 15-19: Listing ndiswrapper Drivers

```
linux:~/Win2K # ndiswrapper -l
Installed ndis drivers:
rt2500   driver present
linux:~/Win2K #
```

7. If you are happy with the installed driver, you can load the ndiswrapper module into the kernel and continue configuring your wireless network. See Listing 15-20.

Listing 15-20: Installing the ndiswrapper Driver into the Kernel

```
linux:~/Win2K # ndiswrapper -m
linux:~/Win2K # modprobe ndiswrapper
linux:~/Win2K #
```

The `ndiswrapper - m` command creates the module configuration and an alias for your wireless network adapter so that the `ndiswrapper` module is always loaded when you need to access your wireless network card.

Now that the `ndiswrapper` driver has been installed, you can access your Windows wireless card like any other Linux-enabled driver.

Configuring Your Wireless Network

One of the first things you need to do to configure and join a wireless network is to search for any wireless base stations that are within range. To do this you need to use the `iwlist` command (see Listing 15-21).

Listing 15-21: **Searching for a Wireless Network**

```
thinkpad:~ # iwlist eth1 scan
eth1      Scan completed :
      Cell 01 - Address: 00:30:BD:62:80:7A
              ESSID:"WLAN"
              Mode:Master
              Frequency:2.462GHz
              Bit Rate:1Mb/s
              Bit Rate:2Mb/s
              Bit Rate:5.5Mb/s
              Bit Rate:11Mb/s
              Quality:20/100  Signal level:-78 dBm  Noise level:-98 dBm
              Encryption key:off
```

The `iwlist` command returns all wireless networks in range as well as the frequency and signal strength. In this case, you have found the network WLAN that you need to join and configure.

To join a wireless network, you use the `iwconfig` command, which is effectively `ifconfig` for wireless networks.

```
thinkpad:~ # iwconfig eth1 essid WLAN
```

The `iwconfig` command takes two very important parameters, the interface your wireless network card has been attached to (`eth1`) and the ESSID (the network name of your wireless network) of the wireless LAN you want to connect to.

When the command has completed, you can then enable DHCP (Dynamic Host Configuration Protocol) for that interface. SUSE includes `ifup-dhcp` and `ifdown-dhcp` to attach a DHCP client to the network card. In this example, you attach the DHCP process to `eth1`, which has now been configured and attached to the WLAN wireless network.

```
thinkpad:~ # ifup-dhcp eth1
Starting DHCP Client Daemon on eth1... . IP/Netmask: 192.168.1.80 / 255.255.255.0
```

You can see that the wireless network has picked up 192.168.1.80/24 as our network configuration.

 Cross-Reference   For more information on using DHCP, take a look at Chapter 20.

Bluetooth

Bluetooth is another great technology that is helping drive mobile technology further and further. Bluetooth under Linux is quite mature, and KDE also includes programs to take advantage of your Bluetooth system.

For Bluetooth to work under Linux, do the following:

1. Install the `bluez-*` Bluetooth stack packages using YaST's package manager.

2. When installed, make sure Bluetooth has been turned on in your laptop (on the Thinkpad, press Fn+F5).

3. When running, start the Bluetooth service with `rcbluetooth start`.

4. When running, you need to bring up your Bluetooth network device with the `hciconfig hci0 up` command.

As usual with the Bluetooth stack on other operating systems, you can scan for discoverable devices in range of the personal area network. To scan for Bluetooth devices, use the `hcitool` command:

```
thinkpad:~ # hcitool scan
Scanning ...
    00:0E:07:24:7E:D5        Justin's Phone
    00:0A:95:2F:D6:78        tibook
```

This scan has found two Bluetooth-aware devices in discoverable mode, my Powerbook and my T610 mobile phone.

When you have found a Bluetooth device, use the `l2ping` command to check connectivity (see Listing 15-22).

Listing 15-22: **Checking Connectivity with l2ping**

```
thinkpad:~ # l2ping 00:0E:07:24:7E:D5
Ping: 00:0E:07:24:7E:D5 from 00:20:E0:73:EF:7F (data size 20) ...
0 bytes from 00:0E:07:24:7E:D5 id 200 time 46.77ms
0 bytes from 00:0E:07:24:7E:D5 id 201 time 50.29ms
0 bytes from 00:0E:07:24:7E:D5 id 202 time 30.28ms
0 bytes from 00:0E:07:24:7E:D5 id 203 time 43.26ms
4 sent, 4 received, 0% loss
```

As with the TCP/IP-based ping command, the Bluetooth stack sends an echo request to the Bluetooth ID specified and displays the time it takes to receive a ping response back from the device.

Note   It is beyond the scope of this quick introduction to Bluetooth on Linux to discuss configuring General Packet Radio Service (GPRS), but if you have a GPRS-capable phone, you can now configure your dial-up settings to take advantage of this on the road.

For a quick use of Bluetooth, you can use the obexftp command to put and get files from a device. For a T610, you can view the hardware configuration by getting the file telecom/devinfo.txt. To do this you can issue the obexftp command. Listing 15-23 shows an example of getting a file over Bluetooth.

Listing 15-23: **Getting a File from a T610 Over Bluetooth**

```
thinkpad:~ # obexftp -b 00:0E:07:24:7E:D5 --get telecom/devinfo.txt
No custom transport
Connecting...bt: 1
done
Receiving telecom/devinfo.txt... done
Disconnecting...done
```

In this use of obexftp, we made sure it used Bluetooth (-b), the Bluetooth address, the process (get), and the file we wanted to transfer. In this case, the file devinfo .txt will be downloaded to the current directory.

You can do a huge amount of things with Bluetooth in Linux, and it all depends on what device you are communicating with.

As we have talked about throughout this chapter, networking is core to the use of Linux. Unless you are using your system as a standalone machine (for a desktop, for example), you need to be able to configure networking to be able to connect yourself to the outside world or other machines on your network. With the recent addition of wireless technology to new laptops (wireless Ethernet and Bluetooth), you'll find yourself relying more and more on these new technologies to be able to carry out your day-to-day tasks.

Every modern Linux distribution offers a way to configure at the least the network card in your machine. YaST also enables you to configure your wireless connection and modem through the same interface that we have talked about. This is just another arrow to the rather large bow that YaST provides you.

Do not think that you must know all of the options for ifconfig or route or feel compelled to use these tools for your network configuration work. It is certainly a lot faster to configure networking with YaST. However, this chapter has shown it is important that you understand what happens under the hood and how to use these very important tools to configure and diagnose your network.

✦   ✦   ✦

Implementing Network Services in SUSE Linux

Part IV describes the setup of the major network services on a SUSE system, including setting up web servers, mail servers, and file and print servers.

Setting Up a Web Site with the Apache Web Server

✦ ✦ ✦ ✦

In This Chapter

Hosting a web site

Configuring the
Apache web server

Securing your server

✦ ✦ ✦ ✦

The beginning of the World Wide Web as we know it can be traced back to two different continents. In Europe in 1990, Tim Berners-Lee put together the pieces of software that today, make the Web what it is, while a few years later, North American programmers at the University of Illinois' National Center for Supercomputing Applications (NCSA) developed and released what became the world's first widely used web client and server software.

The roots of the Apache web server can be traced to the NCSA HTTPd Web Server, because in 1995 Brian Behlendorf started collecting software patches that various web server administrators had applied to the last version of HTTPd. These initial series of patches, traded on a mailing list between eight individuals, formed the basis of "a patchy" web server that in April of 1995 saw the first public release in a beta version labeled 0.6.2. By the end of December, this ad hoc group had the first stable version of Apache, and within a year it had surpassed NCSA HTTPd web server software as the most-used web server on the Internet.

Since then the Apache web server has been adopted by companies such as Yahoo! and Amazon.com as the software to run their web sites, providing the core business operations to customers around the world. Companies such as IBM, Sun, and SUSE have developed products and services that use and cater to users of the Apache web server, a multimillion-dollar segment of the open source industry. Today 70 percent of the web servers serving content to the public on the Web report themselves as some variation of the Apache web server.

The informal group of developers that originally made up the Apache Group has grown and changed over the years as well. In 1999 the Apache Software Foundation (ASF) was created. Incorporated as a 501(c)(3) non-profit corporation in the United States, the foundation was formed primarily to provide a legal structure for the continued open, collaborative software development of the Apache web server and other related projects. The ASF does this by supplying hardware and communication and business infrastructure from which companies and individuals can donate resources for individual volunteers to work from in developing the web server and other related software. The legal structure of the ASF also shelters developers from legal suits directed at projects funded by the ASF and provides legal protection for the Apache brand.

The web server itself has undergone a number of revisions over the years. Since 1995 there have been six different branches of code under development and put into use all over the world, the most popular branch being Apache 1.3. As of this writing over 7 million web sites run some version of Apache 1.3. However, the 1.3 branch of Apache is on its way out the door. While this branch it still maintained by the Apache developers, with bug fixes and security patches, the future of the Apache web server has already arrived.

At the annual gathering of Apache developers and administrators, known as ApacheCon, in 2000 the developers released the next generation of the web server, Apache 2.0 with the first public alpha release. Unlike the previous versions of Apache, which can still find the structure of their code dating back to the NCSA days, if not the actual code itself, Apache 2.0 is a complete rewriting of the web server from the bottom up.

With the new version the Apache developers focused on improving key aspects of the web server's overall performance: portability, scalability, configuration, and I/O processing. By April of 2002 the Apache developers had released the first stable version of the new server, known as version 2.0.35. Since then the developers have moved on to refining the web server with a new development branch known as 2.1. As with the Linux kernel development, the Apache developers have started, with Apache 2.0, to number their releases such that all even number releases, such as 2.0, 2.2, and 2.4, will be considered stable releases that retain forward compatibility to later stable version of Apache. Consequently, any odd number version, 2.1, 2.3, 2.5, and so on, will be development versions, under consideration for the next stable branch of Apache.

Today the Apache web server itself, along with the projects developed in conjunction with the Apache Software Foundation, is a veritable Swiss army knife for network professionals and system administrators. Besides acting as a web server for corporations, organizations, and individuals, the Apache web server can be used as a proxy, mail, MP3, and application server, to name just a few additional options available through numerous add-on modules.

This chapter covers using Apache as a web server in a SUSE environment. Specifically, it explores how to configure and run the Apache web server for hosting one or many web sites on one SUSE powered server. This chapter also covers some of the basic issues concerning security and access control that you might need to consider.

Of course, most web sites these days provide dynamic access to information that is not contained within a plain HTML web page. In many cases the information that may seem to the end users to come from one resource has in fact been put together by some web-based application from information that can reside in a database, the web server's memory, and a text file. In some cases these pages, such as a form for processing a customer's shipping information, is processed using Perl or shell scripts through the Common Gateway Interface (CGI). In others, a computer language embedded within the web server application, such as PHP, takes advantage of system resources already dedicated to the running of the web sever. As such, after taking a look at how to get a basic Apache web server up and running, this chapter reviews how to take advantage of CGIs and embedded languages such as PHP with the Apache web server and SUSE.

Configuring Apache

After you install the Apache web server from the SUSE distribution disks, it's time to set up a working environment for Apache. As with other key tools within the SUSE distribution, Apache is configurable at the command line by editing files or in the YaST GUI configuration tool. However, the YaST tool requires a bit of knowledge about a web server in general and common Apache configuration options in particular. The easiest way to pick up this knowledge is to look at the Apache configuration file through your favorite text editor.

The main Apache web server configuration, located at /etc/apache2/httpd .conf, is a plain text file containing directives for controlling the behavior of the overall web server, web sites, or files as needed. The main configuration file can also incorporate Apache-related directives in other text files using the Include directive and changes to the main configuration files are recognized only when the server is started or restarted.

Note   Apache 2 has been included in versions of SUSE since 9.1, including SLES 9. This chapter contains configuration that will help you get Apache 2 up and running.

To configure Apache, to start the service, and so on you must be logged in as root.

To manage the multilayered options the web server provides, the configuration file is broken down into three main sections:

✦ **Global Environment Section** — This section contains directives that affect the overall operation of the Apache web server.

✦ **Main Server Section** — This section provides configuration options dedicated to the operation of the primary web site.

✦ **Virtual Host Section** — Here you can apply the same configuration options available in the main server configuration section to any virtual host.

Note

Virtual hosts are discussed later in the chapter.

The syntax itself for the configuration file is pretty straightforward; each line within the file contains one directive and if needed the backslash (\) may be used as the last character on a line to indicate that the directive continues onto the next line.

Directives themselves are case insensitive, but arguments to directives are often case sensitive. As with many programming languages, the hash character (#) is considered the token to denote the beginning of comments; however, comments may not be included on a line after a configuration directive. Blank lines and white space occurring before a directive are ignored allowing directives to be spaced as needed for additional clarity. The syntax of a configuration can be checked before invoking the web server process by using the apache2ctl configtest tool provided by the ASF.

For example the following command-line argument tests the configuration file at /etc/apache2/httpd.conf. Note that if the configuration syntax is valid, apache2ctl returns Syntax O K.

```
apache2ctl configtest
Syntax OK
```

However, if an error has been made — for example, the DocumentRoot directive, which points to where all of the main documents the web server serves for client requests are kept, is not defined — then the configuration test returns the proper error message.

```
apache2ctl configtest
Syntax error on line 449 of /etc/apache2/httpd.conf:
DocumentRoot takes one argument, Root directory of the document tree
```

Should apache2ctl not be available on the system, the httpd binary itself can also be used to verify the syntax of a configuration file:

```
/usr/sbin/httpd2 -t
Syntax OK
```

Global Directives

As mentioned, the directives within this section affect the overall operation of the Apache web server; the most important of these options include controls for the number of concurrent requests the server will handle and how to treat those requests after they have been accepted, all of which directly relate to the performance of the web server at large, including a number of options for controlling the management of Apache processes during runtime.

The traditional processing model for Apache on Linux is known as Prefork. Within this method, upon startup the Apache parent process, running as root, creates a number of child processes, the number of which and user type is predefined in the configuration file using the `user` directive. The child processes handle requests on a one-to-one basis for resources managed by the web server. If a spike of requests is beyond the allotment of the currently running child process, the parent process will fork off more processes to catch up. The root parent process, however, is limited to a predefined maximum number of child processes, since creating additional child processes is a resource-expensive exercise. Since forking a process is a time- and resource-consuming exercise, the goal behind the Prefork model is to have the child processes forked and ready before they are needed.

There are a number of directives for controlling the Prefork processing module, including:

✦ **StartServers** — The number of server processes the parent process is to start with

✦ **MinSpareServers** — The minimum number of server processes to keep available

✦ **MaxSpareServers** — The maximum number of server processes to be kept available

✦ **MaxClients** — The maximum number of server processes allowed running at any given time

✦ **MaxRequestsPerChild** — The maximum number of requests a server process handles

The following shows a typical Apache server performance configuration:

```
StartServers         5
MinSpareServers       5
MaxSpareServers        10
MaxClients          150
MaxRequestsPerChild     0
```

In this example configuration the Apache root process forks off five child processes to handle any initial traffic the server may encounter. The parent process then monitors the pool of processes and, as a process handles a network request for a given resource, adds or subtracts processes to the waiting pool, keeping handy a minimum of five child processes and no more than ten processes. The parent process will create no more than 150 processes, should the web site see a peak in traffic. This limit is used to keep the incoming requests from overwhelming the resources on which the server is running.

Since `MaxRequestsPerChild` is set to zero, the parent process enables a child process to handle an unlimited number of network requests during the child's lifetime. If this directive were set to a positive number, the parent server would limit the total number of requests the child process could handle over its lifetime — that is, if the child process is limited to handling only ten requests, after the child has finished processing its tenth network request, the parent process would terminate the process and create a new child process to handle ten more. This results in two specific benefits:

✦ It limits the amount of memory that any one process can consume, limiting the chance of any accidental memory leakage.

✦ By giving processes a finite lifetime, it helps reduce the number of processes when the server load reduces.

With version 2.0 of the Apache web server the ASF programmers have introduced the concept of Multi-Processing Modules (MPMs). MPMs provide a better solution for handling multiple process models that can vary from platform to platform. In addition it also helps Apache 2.0 in reaching a greater operating system (OS) independence within the core web server code, a stated goal of the developers in undertaking the 2.0 development.

While there are a number of new developments in relation to MPMs for Linux and other platforms, the default configuration for Apache 2.0 remains the Prefork processing method, which, for Apache 2.0, is configured and runs in the same manner as Prefork for Apache 1.3.

Main Server

The Main Server section covers directives used to manage the operation of the primary web site to which the Apache web server is host. In addition the values used for the directives set in the main server section are used as the default values for any configuration done within the Virtual Host section.

The most commonly used configuration options within the Main Server and Virtual Host section are containers that operate on the configuration of particular resources in the filesystem or webspace.

✦ **Filesystem** — The view of the resources as seen by the operating system. For example, on SUSE Linux, the web pages for Apache to serve reside at `/srv/www` on the filesystem.

✦ **Webspace** — The view of the resources as seen by the web server and by the client. For example the path `/dir/` in the webspace might correspond to the path `/srv/www/htdocs/dir/` in the filesystem. Of course, the webspace need not map directly to the filesystem, since web pages may be generated dynamically from databases or other locations.

The `<Directory>` and `<Files>` containers, however, are batches of directives
that apply to resources as seen from the filesystem. Directives enclosed in a
`<Directory>` container apply to the named filesystem directory and all subdirectories therein. For example, in the following configuration, directory indexes will be
enabled for the `/srv/www/htdocsl/dir` directory and all subdirectories.

```
<Directory /srv/www/htdocs/dir>
Options +Indexes
</Directory>
```

Directives enclosed in the `<Files>` container apply to any file with the specified
name, regardless of what directory it resides in. For example, the following configuration directives deny access to any file named `private.html` regardless of where it
is found.

```
<Files private.html>
Order allow,deny
Deny from all
</Files>
```

If, however, a directive needs to focus on a file found in a particular part of the
filesystem, the `<Files>` and `<Directory>` containers can be nested, allowing for granular control of resources within the configuration file.

```
<Directory /srv/www/htdocs/dir>
<Files private.html>
Order allow,deny
Deny from all
</Files>
</Directory>
```

In the preceding example, the configuration will deny access to
`/srv/www/htdocs/`
`dir/private.html` and any files named `private.html` within any subdirectories found
within `/srv/www/htdocs/dir/`.

In the area of webspace, the `<Location>` directive operates on the configuration of
resources found from within this point of view. The following configuration example
prevents access to any URL-path that begins with the string `/private`, such as
`<http://www.suse.com/private>`

```
<Location /private>
Order Allow,Deny
Deny from all
</Location>
```

Unlike the `<Directory>` or `<Files>` containers, the `<Location>` directive need not
have anything to do with a resource located on the filesystem. This is useful for
dynamically generated content that has no physical location on the filesystem. An

example can be seen with the Apache module `mod_status`, which provides dynamic information about the running Apache processes. The dynamic information is mapped to a particular URL, usually `/server-status`. Since no file exists at a corresponding filesystem location, any directives, just as the `Order` and `Deny` directive previously mentioned, must be contained within the `<Location>` container.

```
<Location /server-status>
Order Allow,Deny
Deny from all
</Location>
```

Note   Why all the fuss about containers representing resources from the point of view of the filesystem or webspace? Generally directives placed in the main configuration file apply to the entire site. Thus, to manage the configuration for only a section or specific resource contained within a site the directive containers such as `<Directory>`, `<Files>`, and `<Location>` are necessary.

Virtual Hosts

Apache has the capability to serve more than one web site simultaneously. This is known as *virtual hosting*. To provide for this ability the web server configuration provides the `<VirtualHost>` container for a web administrator to maintain multiple domains/host names on one server.

At the basic level, the Virtual Host section is simply a reimplementation of the directives found in the Main Server section, only directed in relation to a specific Virtual Host. Moreover, since the Virtual Hosts section inherits, as its default settings, any configurations defined within the Main Server Configuration, the directives within the Virtual Host section simply need to focus on what is different. Take a look at Listing 16-1.

Listing 16-1: **Defining a virtual host**

```
# VirtualHost for the subdomain apache.suse.com
<VirtualHost 192.168.2.34>
ServerName apache.suse.com
DocumentRoot /srv/www/apache.suse.com/html
ErrorLog logs/apache.suse.com-error_log
CustomLog logs/apache.suse.com access_log combined

<Directory "/srv/www/apache.suse.com/html">
Options Indexes FollowSymLinks
Order allow,deny
Allow from all
</Directory>
</VirtualHost>
```

This virtual host, which is a web site running under the subdomain apache for suse.com, is binding itself to the IP address 192.168.2.34. Since no port is specified for this virtual host, the default port, 80, which would be specified in the Main Server section, is inherited as the default port to run this site on. The name of the site is apache.suse.com and the document root, where the main resources in the filesystem space can be found for this site, is /srv/www/apache.suse.com/html. Moreover the logs for this site will go in the file separate from those used for the Main Server. Finally, the options for access content with the document root have been laid out within the Directory container.

To facilitate the migration of existing websites from Apache 1.3 to 2.0, the ASF programmers looked to minimize the changes that have taken place to the Main Server and Virtual Host configuration sections. This is not to be read as meaning the developers did not change the underlying functionality or code, but simply to mean the group tried to keep from complicating any migration with a round of completely new directives and syntax. However, web administrators should be aware that some directives have been eliminated and the behavior of others may have changed. Further reading of the Apache documentation is therefore recommended for anyone who may be making the switch.

Security

Security is a big issue when it comes to computers these days and can mean different things to different people. To an administrator it can mean the following questions: Is the server locked down and the software up-to-date and free of any known vulnerabilities? To an application developer it might mean that the user has been verified and that the customer data has been stored in a safe, reusable manner. To the user of the web site it could mean that the personal data remains in limited hands and that, while in transit, is encrypted to limit eavesdropping.

All of these concerns are valid fundamental concerns. However, from the Apache web server's perspective all of these issues come down to three basic concepts: authentication, authorization, and access control.

✦ **Authentication** is any process by which the web site verifies the identity of a user in question, that in essence they are who they claim they are.

✦ **Authorization** is any process by which someone is allowed to gain access to information that they want to have.

✦ **Access control** is the process of limiting users access to information that they may not have access to.

With the basic web server setup these processes are managed by the Apache modules mod_auth and mod_access. You can use these modules' configuration directives in the main server configuration file, httpd.conf, or in per-directory configuration files, .htaccess.

Setting Up User Access

The most common security issue for a web site is the need to password protect a directory or file. To do this, the first step is the creation of a password file. The password file needs to reside somewhere outside of the webspace. For example, if the web site's documents reside at /srv/www/htdocs/dir on the filesystem, then the password file needs to reside somewhere outside of that space, such as /etc/http-passwd.

Creating the file is simple; just use the htpasswd2 utility that comes with the Apache RPM. The utility will ask for a password for the username given as a command line option and will ask that the password be re-entered for verification. If all goes well, the file will be created with the new entry.

```
htpasswd2 -c /etc/http-passwd paul
New password:
Re-type new password:
Adding password for user paul
```

In the preceding example, a password file is created (-c) in the /etc/http-passwd directory and a user, paul, and associated password for that user was entered into the newly created password file.

To add names to an existing password file, simply omit the -c flag.

```
htpasswd2 /etc/http-passwd justin
New password:
Re-type new password:
Adding password for user justin
```

After the password file has been properly populated with usernames and passwords, the next step is to configure the server to request a password and tell the server which users are allowed access. If, for example, there is a need to password protect a private directory, this can be done within the httpd.conf file using the <Directory> container.

```
<Directory /srv/www/htdocs/private>
AuthType Basic
AuthName "Restricted Directory"
AuthUserFile /etc/http-passwd
Require user paul
</Directory>
```

In the <Directory> container:

✦ The AuthType directive selects what HTTP method is used to authenticate the user; the most common method is Basic and is implemented by mod_auth.

Note | The `Basic` authentication method implemented by the Apache web server module `mod_auth` passes the username and password over the network between the client and the server in an unencrypted clear text manner. The Apache web server does support other authentication methods such as `AuthType Digest`, which is implemented by the Apache web server module `mod_auth_digest`. The `Digest` authentication type provides a more secure password system by sending only an MD5 hash of the password over the network. However, this authentication type works only with latest version of the major web browsers currently available.

✦ The `AuthName` directive sets the Realm that is requiring authorization before access. The realm name provides two major functions:

- First, the client application often presents this information to the user as part of the password dialog box.

- Second, it is used by the client to determine what password to send for a given authenticated area should there be more than one protected area on the same web site.

✦ The `AuthUserFile` directive sets the path to the password file that was created with `htpasswd`.

✦ The `Require` directive provides the authorization part of the process by defining for the web server, after a valid authentication, the users that are allowed to access the defined realm.

Setting Up Group Access

The previous example will let only one user in, `paul`. In most cases this is not very practical, as most sites will need to allow more than one person in. This can be accomplished in two different manners.

✦ Instead of the `Require user paul` directive that will allow only the user `paul` access to the directory, `Require valid-user` will allow anyone in the password file access to the directory after correctly entering their password.

✦ Another option is to create a group file that associates a group name with a list of users listed in a file. The format of this file is straightforward and can be accomplished with one's favorite editor.

```
GroupName: paul justin roger
```

The directory container will need to know where the password file and the group file are located. Since there can be more than one group listed within the group file, which group may gain access will also need to be specified.

```
<Directory /srv/www/htdocs/private>
AuthType Basic
AuthName "By Invite Only"
AuthUserFile /etc/http-passwd
```

```
AuthGroupFile /etc/http-groups
Require group GroupName
</Directory>
```

Anyone that has been properly authenticated and is listed in the group `GroupName` will be let in to the "By Invite Only" realm.

An issue with the `Basic` authentication is that the username and password must be verified every time a request is made for a resource from the server, be it an HTML page, an image, or any other resource from the protected directory. This can slow things down a little in regards to the responsiveness of the web server. In fact, the amount that the web server slows down is proportional to the size of the password file. Remember the Apache web server has to open up that file and go down the list in order of users until it gets to the user in question, every time a page is loaded.

A consequence of this is that there is a practical limit to how many users can be listed in one password file. While the limit will vary depending on the configuration of a particular server, chances are after a few hundred entries the performance of the web server will suffer and a different authentication method option may be needed.

Such a method can be found in the `mod_auth_dbm` module. `mod_auth_dbm` provides the `AuthDBMUserFile` directive allowing the use of files used with the `dbm-manage` program. Another possible option is `mod_auth_mysql`. The `mod_auth_mysql` module allows the Apache web server to connect to a backend MySQL database where username and passwords can be stored and accessed with greater efficiency.

Note Going any further about authentication on your Apache web server is beyond the scope of this book. However, if you are interested in delving deep into the topic of security and Apache, you can check out a book like *Maximum Apache Security* (Sams, 2002) for more information.

The Common Gateway Interface

The Common Gateway Interface (CGI) defines a way in which a web server can interact with external programs, often referred to as CGI programs or CGI scripts, for generation of dynamic content based on a client request. To configure the Apache web server to interact with a CGI program the first task to complete is to let the web server know where the CGI programs reside.

One method is with the `ScriptAlias` directive, which tells Apache that a particular directory has been set aside for CGI programs. Apache will assume that every file in a given directory is a CGI program. Thus the web server will attempt to execute a program when a client requests a particular resource. The `ScriptAlias` directive is much like the `Alias` directive, which defines a URL webspace that is mapped to a particular directory on the filesystem. Consider the following example:

```
ScriptAlias /cgi-bin/ /srv/www/cgi-bin/
```

For the given example, the directive marks the target directory, /srv/www/cgi-bin, as containing CGI scripts that will be processed by the Apache mod_cgi module 's cgi-script handler. Moreover, the mapping defined by this directive would result in any request for resources at http://oursuseserver/cgi-bin/ causing the server to run a script located in /srv/www/cgi-bin/.

However, CGI programs can also be invoked from arbitrary directories. For CGI programs to reside anywhere in the directory of a site, two configuration steps need to be completed. First, the cgi-script handler must be activated using the AddHandler directive. Second, ExecCGI must be specified in the Options directive for any directory or subdirectories that may contain a CGI program.

```
AddHandler cgi-script .cgi
...
<Directory /srv/www/htdocs/dir>
Options +ExecCGI
</Directory>
```

The AddHandler directive tells the server to treat all files with the .cgi file extension as CGI programs. In addition the <Directory> container with the Options +ExecCGI directive tells Apache to permit the execution of CGI programs that reside in the directory /srv/www/htdocs/dir or any subdirectories therein.

Listing 16-2 is a Perl script and an example CGI program that prints a welcome message to a client along with the date.

Listing 16-2: **A Perl CGI script**

```
#!/usr/bin/perl
# example.cgi
# An example script written to print a welcome message and the current
date
$thismonth =
('jan','feb','mar','apr','may','jun','jul','aug','sep','oct','nov','dec')[(lo
caltime)[4]];
$thisyear = (localtime)[5];
$thisday = (localtime)[3];


print "Content-type: text/html\n\n";
print "<html><title>This is a test, this is only a test</title><body>.\n\n";
print "Hello, World.<br/><br/>";
print "Today is: ";
if ($thisday < 10) {
print $thismonth," 0",$thisday;
```

Continued

Listing 16-2 *(continued)*

```
} else {
print $thismonth," ",$thisday;
}
$thisyear-100;
if ($thisyear < 10) {
print " 0", $thisyear;
} else {
print " ",$thisyear;
}
print "</body></html>";
```

Note that the first line of the output from a CGI program is a MIME-type header. This is an HTTP header that tells the client what sort of content it is receiving; in the case of this script, the client will be receiving content of the text/html variety. Secondly, the remaining output is in HTML, a format that the client web browser is expecting and will be able to display.

However, this script is not quite ready for prime time. When the Apache web server starts up, it is running with the permissions of a user separate of that from the user who create the script. Thus the filesystem permissions of the file need to be changed so that it can be read and executed by whatever user the webserver is running as.

```
chmod a+x example.cgi
```

See Chapter 2 for more detail on using chmod.

All should be set. But most of the time when starting out, a CGI program or script will fail, maybe because of a problem with the program itself, a syntax or logic error. Remember the web server error logs are your friends. More often than not, if anything goes wrong, it will generate a message in the error log. Look there first (/var/log/apache2/error_log). The error_log file contains errors about why something did not work. This could be an error from a PHP script or a Perl script, for example, and you will have to use your skills in these languages to understand what the log files are telling you.

Learn to read and manage the error (and access) logs that the web server creates, and you will find that almost all the problems are quickly identified and solved.

We discuss Apache logs in Chapter 7.

Creating Dynamic Content with PHP

The Apache web server is a highly modular server. The most popular module for use with it is `mod_php`. PHP is short for what is officially called PHP: Hypertext Preprocessor and was created by Rasmus Lerdorf, a developer, who in 1994 was looking for a tool to keep track of who was looking at his resume. PHP is a robust open-source development language that provides the tools and flexibility to accomplish virtually any task.

PHP is a customized, server-embedded scripting language. That is, PHP has many of the features of a complete programming language, but allows for the embedding of code in otherwise normal HTML files for the creation of dynamic content.

A server-side technology simply means that the client viewing the web page needs no special application, because it is the web server, with PHP installed, that takes the extra step of processing any PHP code within the requested document before sending it to the user. From this extra step PHP can then perform any operation such as accessing a database. Thus, it enables a web developer to dynamically construct a web page based on data gathered from a third source and then communicate that data through almost any means provided by the Internet.

How is this different from a CGI script written in Perl? First off, unlike a Perl CGI script — which will run as a separate process, invoking a Perl interpreter to run the script and piping the output to standard out for the web server — PHP runs an interpreter within the Apache web server processes, ready to run at a moment's notice. However, the real benefit can be seen in what web authors can do with little or no knowledge of the inner workings between the CGI and, for example, a back-end database with which the script may be communicating.

Note The Perl scripting language can also be embedded within the Apache web server using the `mod_perl` module. With `mod_perl` and some modification to existing CGI scripts written in Perl you can see the same runtime advantages as scripts written with PHP.

To include the basic functionality of PHP in the core server, extending the features of the web server, you use the `LoadModule` directive. Apache will also need to know what files to parse using the PHP module. This is done using the `AddType` directive. After you restart the Apache daemon, all will be set.

```
LoadModule php4_module libexec/libphp4.so
AddType application/x-httpd-php .php
```

Note To use the PHP language, you will need to install the RPM. To do this, load YaST and select Install and Remove Software. You can then search for *php*, which will return the PHP packages that you can install on your system. Select the `php4` package. For more information on installing new software, refer to Chapter 1.

The LoadModule directive points the Apache web server to the actual PHP module that will be loaded by the web server for processing PHP scripts. The AddType directive maps the given filename extension, .php, onto the specified content type.

To test the module, create the following file, example.php, and try to access it through the web server. If all works well, a text message that includes the welcome message "Hi, I'm a PHP script!" and the current date is displayed within the web browser window. If the script fails, you'll see an error message, either from the web server or the PHP module, depending on what the issue is.

```
<html>
<title>Example</title>
<body>

<?php
echo "Hi, I'm a PHP script!";
echo "Today is:";
echo date ("l dS of F Y h:i:s A" );
?php>


</body>
</html>
```

Note   For more information on using PHP, you can turn to *PHP5 and MySQL Bible* by Tim Converse, Joyce Park, and Clark Morgan (Wiley, 2004).

For SUSE users there are a number of resources for finding and installing the web server, including the Apache Software Foundation and SUSE.

While configuration of the web server is a snap, a number of tools such as graphical user interface (GUI) tools like Webmin (www.webmin.com) are designed to ease the configuration of the web server by providing all configuration options in a basic point-and-click interface. And, of course, don't forget about YaST!

In fact, all of this shows that the Apache web server is a powerful tool. However, this chapter hasn't even begun to cover the tip of the iceberg. A number of resources exist to provide details of all that can be done with the Apache web server and its corresponding open source license. These web sites include:

✦ The ASF main site (www.apache.org)

✦ Apache Week (www.apacheweek.com), a newsletter dedicated to covering news of the web server and related projects

✦ Planet Apache (www.planetapache.org), a web site dedicated to collecting the latest blog postings from Apache developers worldwide

As with Linux, the Apache web server is a powerful, rapidly evolving platform developed in accordance with the open source model. It has become a key tool of the Internet infrastructure that allows for the World Wide Web to exist as we know it today. In fact it has been pointed out by a number of industry observers that the rapid growth and adoption of the Internet, of web applications and services, and resources such as Google and Slashdot, could not have happened as it did during the 1990s without flexible, open source tools such as Linux, Apache, and PHP. Starting with your SUSE Linux install, it is a simple jump to start building a web site that can be of use both to you alone or to millions.

✦   ✦   ✦

Mail Servers — Postfix, Sendmail, Qpopper, and Cyrus

◆　◆　◆　◆

In This Chapter

Sending mail via SMTP

Configuring Postfix

Configuring sendmail

Configuring Qpopper

Configuring Cyrus

Choosing a mail client

◆　◆　◆　◆

One of the primary uses for Linux on the Internet (aside from Apache) is for mail servers — both from the position of an MTA (Postfix, sendmail, Exim, and so on) and an MDA (Cyrus, Qpopper, and so on).

The terms MTA, MDA, and MUA are generic ways of referring to the components in a mail system.

- ◆ **Mail Transfer Agent (MTA)** — The component of the mail system that handles the receiving and sending of mail over the SMTP protocol.

- ◆ **Mail Delivery Agent (MDA)** — Controls the delivery of mail into a user's mailbox. An MDA also deals with the presentation of mail to a user over POP3 or IMAP.

- ◆ **Mail User Agent (MUA)** — The component that the end user employs to read mail. This could be Evolution, Outlook, `mail`, `mutt`, or any other choice of MUA on the market.

A few very popular MTAs have arrived on the scene, with the grandfather of them all being sendmail.

Linux is extremely well suited to the hosting of mail, and the authors have worked on very large mail infrastructures where Linux has been prevalent. This chapter discusses using Linux as a mail server, and focuses in particular on sendmail or Postfix as an MTA and Qpopper and Cyrus as MDAs.

How Mail Is Sent and Received

When mail is sent to a user, many things have to happen behind the scenes. Here we take an example of Roger sending an email to Justin at different domains.

1. Roger, a KDE user, uses kmail to compose a message to justin@ palmcoder.net. Roger's mail configuration states that his SMTP (outbound) mail server is mail.disruptive.org.uk, so kmail connects over port 25 (SMTP) to the host and attempts to send the mail to justin@palm coder.net.

2. When connected, Roger's mail server checks the sanity of the connection and the mail itself (which is discussed later in this section). All being well, the mail is accepted, and Roger's mail server then attempts to send the mail to its final recipient, Justin.

3. Roger's mail server knows that mail for palmcoder.net is not handled by its local MTA and proceeds to do an MX lookup for palmcoder.net.

   An MX is a Mail Exchange domain name system (DNS) record that points to the mail server for palmcoder.net. The MX record is the backbone of Internet mail and provides a means for any domain to be resolved to a specific host that handles mail for it.

   In the case of address@palmcoder.net, the DNS MX record is

   MX   10 mail.palmcoder.net.

   Cross-Reference In Chapter 21, we talk more about how a DNS record works, but for now, realize that the MX record for palmcoder.net points to mail.palmcoder.net.

4. Going back to Roger's mail server, once an MX record has successfully been retrieved, the mail server attempts to connect to mail.palmcoder.net over port 25 and deliver Roger's original mail to Justin. The same sanity checks take place by Justin's mail server as to whether it should accept the mail connection and the mail recipient given in the SMTP negotiation.

5. As the mail is destined for justin@palmcoder.net, Justin's mail server accepts the connection and delivers the mail to Justin's mailbox locally (or to another process, depending on how your mail server is configured).

After mail has been delivered to your mailbox, it is stored until you retrieve it. It is the MDA that actually presents the mail to the user for retrieval. Do not confuse your mail client with an MDA; it is used only to retrieve your mail and to read it!

Popular MDAs are POP3 and IMAP; these two protocols enable users to log in to a mail server and retrieve their messages, as an MDA should do. These are discussed later in the chapter.

Postfix

SUSE's MTA of choice is Postfix. Postfix was designed by Witse Venema, who at the time had an internship at IBM, with the idea to build from the ground up a secure and scalable MTA. The most popular MTA, sendmail, is often considered difficult to come to grips with because the configuration format is obscure.

Postfix's reliability and security features, as well as having a much simpler *parameter=value* configuration format, have helped it balloon to an extremely popular MTA.

Postfix is constantly being maintained by Venema and other developers. Bugs are fixed in a timely manner, and new versions with additional features are released regularly.

> **Note**
>
> In general, the speed at which bugs and security updates are released is astonishing — not just for Postfix, but also for the kernel and other high-traffic software releases. The last thing you need when relying on a piece of software is to not have the backup from the developers to fix security issues (although this is a rare occurrence in the Linux world compared with other operating systems) or implement new features.

When installed, by default, Postfix is configured to accept mail locally for users existing in your machine's domain. Postfix's default security settings also stop your machine from acting as an open relay.

> **Note**
>
> An *open relay* is a mail server that allows any user to send mail through your mail server, regardless of his or her location (in your local network or the Internet). This has proven to be a large contributor to the existence of spam as malicious users can use your mail server to send large quantities of mail on the back of your network bandwidth.

The built-in security features of Postfix have contributed to its success, and these security features can be extended even further by adding granularity for UCE (unsolicited commercial email) and user authentication for relay controls.

Postfix is commonly configured in three main ways to provide MTA services to your organization, and we discuss these throughout the chapter:

✦ Always-on, Internet facing mail server.

✦ Dial-up/laptop mail server mainly used for sending mail from your machine only.

✦ Local mail delivery only. This is used to mainly route mail messages that originate from your local machine and is the default for a SUSE installation.

Local mail delivery is also capable of connecting to other Simple Mail Transport Protocol (SMTP) servers if mail is sent using the Postfix mail system, and we discuss this later in the chapter.

Postfix Configuration

Postfix configuration is held in the file /etc/postfix/main.cf. This file contains all configuration entries for general Postfix configuration as well as the locations of secondary configuration files for specific Postfix subsystems.

To familiarize you with the Postfix configuration, we will run through the default Postfix main.cf file, highlighting the important configuration options. The default main.cf file is heavily commented to give you a means to understand what the option means. In Listing 17-1, we have taken out the comments to conserve space, but take a look at your main.cf file while looking through this to see how it fits in with your configuration.

When editing the Postfix configuration files and restarting the Postfix system, you must be logged in as root.

Listing 17-1: **Postfix main.cf file Example**

```
queue_directory = /var/spool/postfix
command_directory = /usr/sbin
daemon_directory = /usr/lib/postfix
mail_owner = postfix
unknown_local_recipient_reject_code = 450
debug_peer_level = 2
debugger_command =
      PATH=/bin:/usr/bin:/usr/local/bin:/usr/X11R6/bin
      xxgdb $daemon_directory/$process_name $process_id & sleep 5
sendmail_path = /usr/sbin/sendmail
newaliases_path = /usr/bin/newaliases
mailq_path = /usr/bin/mailq
setgid_group = maildrop
manpage_directory = /usr/share/man
sample_directory = /usr/share/doc/packages/postfix/samples
readme_directory = /usr/share/doc/packages/postfix/README_FILES
mail_spool_directory = /var/mail
canonical_maps = hash:/etc/postfix/canonical
virtual_maps = hash:/etc/postfix/virtual
relocated_maps = hash:/etc/postfix/relocated
transport_maps = hash:/etc/postfix/transport
sender_canonical_maps = hash:/etc/postfix/sender_canonical
masquerade_exceptions = root
masquerade_classes = envelope_sender, header_sender, header_recipient
myhostname = linux.site
program_directory = /usr/lib/postfix
inet_interfaces = 127.0.0.1
masquerade_domains =
mydestination = $myhostname, localhost.$mydomain
```

```
defer_transports =
disable_dns_lookups = no
relayhost =
content_filter =
mailbox_command =
mailbox_transport =
smtpd_sender_restrictions = hash:/etc/postfix/access
smtpd_client_restrictions =
smtpd_helo_required = no
smtpd_helo_restrictions =
strict_rfc821_envelopes = no
smtpd_recipient_restrictions =
permit_mynetworks,reject_unauth_destination
smtp_sasl_auth_enable = no
smtpd_sasl_auth_enable = no
smtpd_use_tls = no
smtp_use_tls = no
alias_maps = hash:/etc/aliases
mailbox_size_limit = 0
message_size_limit = 10240000
```

Configuration Parameters

The Postfix configuration format is quite easy to follow if you have some background in Linux and the SMTP protocol, which is one of its strengths. The next sections provide a breakdown of the configuration file's options with a description of the parameter uses.

queue_directory

When mail is received by Postfix, it is held in the mail queue for further processing until it is delivered to the user's mailbox. Each mail is stored in a separate file in the queue directory for Postfix to pick up when needed. This is the location of the mail queue.

command_directory

This is the location of all Postfix-based commands.

daemon_directory

This is the location of Postfix server processes.

mail_owner

This shows the user who Postfix runs as.

unknown_local_recipient_reject_code

When a user does not exist on the system (for mail delivery), this is the SMTP code that is returned to the client. In this case, 450 means service temporarily unavailable. This tells the sending mail server that it should try again at a later date rather than produce a permanent error and lose the mail.

debug_peer_level

If you need to debug any problems with mail being received, the debug peer level sets how verbose Postfix will be when the host name connected is listed in debug_peer_list. If you want to have a certain SMTP connection debugged, you have to add a debug_peer_list entry in the main.cf file.

debugger_command

If you need to debug the run time of Postfix, this parameter specifies the debugger to use.

sendmail_path

As sendmail is seen as the de facto MTA for Unix in general, Postfix provides a send-mail-compatible interface to its services to allow applications specifically designed to send a query mail with the sendmail command. This provides the location of this command to Postfix.

newaliases_path

When you add an aliased account to the aliases map, you need to run newaliases to tell Postfix about them. This is the location of the newaliases command. Later in the chapter we discuss aliases in detail.

mailq_path

The mailq command is used to query the Postfix mail queue. It is very useful to use when you need to know what mails are stuck in your system and also the reason why they have not been sent.

setgid_group

As a security measure, Postfix does not allow all users to write to the mail queue (for mail drops) and instead uses a totally separate group ID for the directory as well as for queue commands. This parameter specifies the group to use.

manpage_directory

This is the location of the Postfix man pages.

sample_directory

This is the location of the sample Postfix configuration files.

readme_directory

This is the location of the Postfix documentation.

mail_spool_directory
This shows the location of the user's spool directory. In a traditional mail system, this directory contains a file named after the mail recipient, containing all of his or her mail.

canonical_maps
This shows the location of the canonical map. Whereas an alias changes only the recipient of an incoming mail, the canonical map can change the sender address of an outgoing mail. If the user `justin@susebible.com` has an incoming alias of `justin.davies@susebible.com`, you can use a canonical map to specify that an outgoing mail from `justin@susebible.com` will be rewritten to `justin.davies@susebible.com`.

```
justin justin.davies
```

virtual_maps
This shows the location of the virtual map. If you need to set up a Postfix virtual domain (we discuss virtual domains later in the chapter), the virtual map is used to set up the association of a virtual domain and the users that receive mail for the domain.

For example, if you want to receive mail for the `wiley.com` domain and associate the users `justin`, `roger`, `aimee`, and `jane` to this domain, you need to specify the `wiley.com` domain as virtual and also associate the users to receive the mail for the domain.

```
wiley.com virtual
justin@wiley.com justin
roger@wiley.com justin
aimee@wiley.com aimee
jane@wiley.com jane
```

With this configuration, any mail for the listed virtual users is delivered to the local users specified on the right-hand side. These users must exist on the local system as if the mail were delivered directly to them in a standard domain setup.

relocated_maps
When a user has left a company (more specifically, the mail system), the relocated map is used to inform the sender that this user has moved to another address.

transport_maps
This shows the location of the transport map. If you want to route any traffic for a certain domain to a specific mail host, you can specify a transport entry in the transport map.

For example, if you wanted to route all mail for the domain `editors.wiley.com` to the machine `editorsmail.wiley.com`, you need to specify the `smtp` host for the domain.

```
editors.wiley.com smtp:editorsmail.wiley.com
```

So, if a mail for `debra@editors.wiley.com` arrives at the mail server, it will be sent automatically over SMTP to the machine `editorsmail.wiley.com`.

sender_canonical_maps

This shows the location of rewrite mail rules for senders. If you want to specify a canonical map to rewrite only outgoing mail addresses, then a `sender_canonical_maps` entry needs to exist in the file `main.cf`. If you want to rewrite only incoming addresses (as an aliases map does), then you need to specify a `recipient_canonical_maps` entry.

masquerade_exceptions

This shows address masquerading exceptions. We discuss this later in the "Presentation to the Outside World" section of the chapter.

masquerade_classes

This lists what to masquerade.

myhostname

This is the host name of the server Postfix is running on. Postfix checks the host name of the system at startup, but this command enables you to force Postfix to think it is running on another machine. We discuss where the host name parameter fits into Postfix in the "Configuring an Always-On Server" section of the chapter.

program_directory

This is the location of Postfix server process helpers.

inet_interfaces

This shows the network interfaces that Postfix listens on for incoming SMTP connections. This helps to limit where mail can be received from in a multi-interface server.

masquerade_domains

These are the domains to masquerade. We discuss this in the "Presentation to the Outside World" section later in the chapter.

mydestination

These are the domains for which this mail server accepts mail. This is discussed in the "Creating Virtual Domains" section later in the chapter.

defer_transports

This lists what transfer protocols to defer. This is discussed later in the "Dial-Up Server Configuration" section of the chapter.

disable_dns_lookups

This sets whether or not to try to translate IP addresses to host names for accounting purposes. It is usually a good idea to have this turned on unless your mail server receives very large quantities of mail.

relayhost

Sometimes called a *smarthost*, this is the machine to which you forward all mail that is not local to your Postfix server's domain of control.

content_filter

The content filter clause is usually used to pass mail to a virus checker for your mail. The content filter defines a server and port that all of your mail is sent through for further processing before being re-inserted in the Postfix workflow. It is the responsibility of the content filter you define to re-inject your mail into the system.

mailbox_command

The `mailbox` command is the program used to deliver mail to a user's mailbox. A common configuration for this is the Cyrus deliver program that injects the mail message into the user's IMAP mailbox. This is discussed later in the chapter when we talk about Cyrus.

mailbox_transport

The mailbox transport is very similar to the `mailbox` command. Instead of using a specific program directly to deliver the user's mail, it uses a protocol that can be user-defined in the `master.cf` file. It is commonly used to deliver mail over LMTP (Local Mail Transport Protocol) to a Cyrus IMAP mailstore. We briefly talk about the `master.cf` file when we talk about Cyrus later in the chapter.

smtpd_sender_restrictions

This sets restrictions on the information a client sends to describe itself when connecting to the Postfix server when attempting to send mail.

smtpd_client_restrictions

This sets what restrictions bind clients connecting over SMTP to the Postfix server. We discuss these settings when we discuss stopping spam later in the chapter.

smtpd_helo_required

This specifies whether an SMTP connection should be initiated with the HELO or EHLO command. This should be used when trying to restrict non-standard servers trying to send mail to or through your server. If you want to enforce strict rules for HELO/EHLO, also use the `smtpd_helo_restrictions`.

HELO and EHLO

A HELO is the first part in a handshake (so called because that is how we civilly start a conversation). When an SMTP server receives a HELO from the client, it then responds with the capabilities of the SMTP server itself. As the SMTP grew, more features were added. For backward compatibility, the HELO command responded with the very standard response of what the SMTP server can do. If an SMTP client can understand extended SMTP commands, it can start the conversation with an EHLO (Extended HELO). In response to this, the SMTP server tells the client what extra functionality it has. One of the main uses for EHLO is to initiate a Secure Sockets Layer (SSL) SMTP connection.

smtpd_helo_restrictions

If the HELO/EHLO requirement has been set, you can use HELO restrictions to enforce strict checks on what a connecting machine tells you is its host name.

strict_rfc821_envelopes

If you want clients connecting to Postfix to have to strictly use RFC 821 envelope addresses (fully qualified and enclosed in angle brackets), then this option will deny any MAIL FROM: RCPT TO: non-RFC addresses.

Tip   It may be a bad idea to set this, because there are many broken mail servers that assume they can get away without the angle brackets, and so on.

smtpd_recipient_restrictions

This deals specifically with the recipient specified in the SMTP transfer (RCPT TO). You can tell Postfix to check that the recipient's address is fully qualified or that the recipient domain is hosted on the Postfix installation.

smtp_sasl_auth_enable

This designates whether or not to enable SMTP authentication for connecting clients. By itself it will allow users to authenticate to the Postfix server, but you need to add `permit_sasl_authenticated` to `smtpd_recipient_restrictions` to allow relaying when the user has successfully authenticated. You also have to set up your Simple Authentication and Security Layer (SASL) password system correctly for the user/password database to be queried.

smtpd_use_tls

This enables Transport Layer Security (TLS)–encrypted connections to the Postfix server. For more information on providing an encrypted link to your mail server, take a look at `www.aet.tu-cottbus.de/personen/jaenicke/postfix_tls/`.

smtp_use_tls

This enables SMTP client requests. This will tell Postfix to make a secure TLS connection if it sees that the server it is sending mail to accept TLS connections. To check if a server accepts TLS connections, connect to port 25 via Telnet and send ehlo <your_host_name>. If the server supports TLS, it will report a STARTTLS back to you in the extended HELO (EHLO) response.

alias_maps

The location of the compiled alias databases. These could be stored in Lightweight Directory Access Protocol (LDAP), Network Information System (NIS), or in a local aliases file that has been compiled with postalias.

mailbox_size_limit

This specifies the maximum size of the user's mailbox. This is relevant only to a standard mbox format. If you use maildir mailbox format, it refers to the individual message files, not all messages collectively.

message_size_limit

This specifies the maximum size of a mail message coming into or leaving the Postfix server.

Postfix Terminology and Use

The configuration options we just discussed represent only a small amount of what can be done with Postfix. We now talk about how this all works together and what it provides to you as a mail server administrator.

Note   Any parameter that starts with an SMTPD controls some part of an *incoming* SMTP-based connection. Similarly, any parameters starting with SMTP refer to *outgoing* (to other SMTP servers) connections.

Configuring and Securing Your Relay Policy

Postfix's relaying policy (allowing users to send mail through the mail sever) is dictated by default via the mynetworks parameter. The mynetworks parameter tells Postfix what networks or specific hosts are trusted by Postfix to allow mail to be sent through the mail server to any destination based on this trust. When the mynetworks parameter has been set, you can then use the variable to explicitly tell Postfix the networks that your installation trusts.

Figure 17-1 shows an example setup for your always-connected corporate mail server. You can see where the mynetworks parameter comes into use. By default, the mynetworks parameter contains your localhost network (127.0.0.0/8) and your network connections that have been configured in your system.

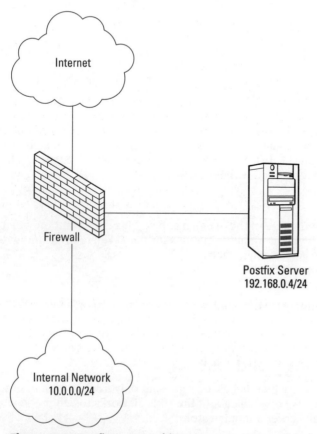

Figure 17-1: Postfix server architecture

In this example, you can see the Postfix server in the DMZ (demilitarized zone) on an IP address of 192.168.0.4/24. Your internal network is in the subnet of 10.0.0.0/24. Given Postfix's default mynetworks parameter, the 10.0.0.0/24 network will not be allowed to relay mail through Postfix because it is not part of the Postfix server's network. To remedy this, you need to add the 10.0.0.0/24 network to the mynetworks clause:

```
mynetworks = 127.0.0.0/8, 192.168.0.0/24, 10.0.0.0/24
```

This entry now allows relaying from localhost, the DMZ network, and also your internal network.

When mynetworks has been configured, the parameter smtpd_recipient_ restrictions actually allows the relaying to take place. As you can see from the default main.cf configuration we talked about before, this parameter has two objectives:

✦ To allow all relays from machines that are in `mynetworks`

✦ To deny all other relays using the `reject_unauth_destination` (reject all unauthorized connections) clause

Caution

Be careful with what you put into the `mynetworks` clause because this is the easiest way to configure Postfix to be an open relay. We pointed out the DMZ issue so you can understand that even if you think that locally the configuration is secure, as soon as you add the Internet to that equation, it can get a lot more difficult to see the bigger picture.

Postfix also allows relaying to any domains listed in `relay_domains`. This parameter by default contains whatever is in the `$mydomain` parameter, which by default is your machine's configured domain. If you use the default setting, any untrusted sender (not in `mynetworks`) can relay mail through Postfix to any user at `$mydomain`. It should be obvious why this is the default, as this would mean that Postfix would accept mail for the domain it is hosting.

Creating Virtual Domains

Another parameter that is very useful is `mydestination`. In a real world example, we host our domain, `palmcoder.net`, and also the domain `planetsuse.org`. Even though by default our Postfix installation configures itself to accept mail for the `palmcoder.net` domain, we need to tell it that it should accept mail for the `planetsuse.org` domain (if we don't, the mail will be rejected). To do this, we add an updated `mydestination` clause.

```
mydestination = palmcoder.net, planetsuse.org
```

In this example, we are creating a *virtual domain* — that is, a domain that physically (in terms of our server's configuration) does not exist, but we are hosting in the same realm as palmcoder.net (our physical server domain).

Our login on this server is `justin`, and it exists as a real user. Any mail for `justin@palmcoder.net` is delivered to Justin's mailbox, and with the `mydestination` clause, any mail for `justin@planetsuse.org` is delivered to the same mailbox.

This works because Postfix believes it is the final destination for `palmcoder.net` and `planetsuse.org`. When the mail has gone through the mail system, Postfix will decide that the user `justin` does indeed exist and will deliver any mail on any domain that is listed in `mydestination` to `justin`.

This type of virtual domain is called a *sendmail virtual domain* because it makes no distinction between one user and another regardless of the destination domain listed in the `mydestination` clause.

If you want to make that distinction, you use a Postfix-style virtual domain that correlates the fact that a user and domain make up a unique user on the system.

Presentation to the Outside World

It is always advisable to make mail sent from your network as Internet friendly as possible. Why? If you are running Postfix on a laptop, and you send mail using the system's `mail` command, and if you have not configured address rewriting, the mail will be sent in the form of `username@fullmachinename`. This is not pretty to see and can prove problematic for people trying to reply to you. To get around these problems, you need to masquerade your mail headers so that they are clean before they leave the system.

The `masquerade_domains` parameter controls this behavior by rewriting the domain portion of a mail message before it leaves Postfix. For example, if your machine is called `foo.bar.com`, and your domain is `bar.com`, you need to remove the "foo" component. The `masquerade_domains` parameter can take your domain as a parameter to combat this.

```
masquerade_domains = bar.com
```

This tells Postfix that for anything that is below `bar.com` (which includes `foo.bar.com`), rewrite the address to `bar.com`.

If you do not want to masquerade all users' addresses, as is common for the root user so that you know what machine the email was from internally, then you use the `masquerade_exceptions` parameter:

```
masquerade_exceptions = root
```

Configuring an Always-On Server

In this section, we take our example of Figure 17-1 and modify the default configuration to set up an always-on, Internet-facing mail server.

In Listing 17-2, you can see the updated configuration for the domain `palmcoder.net` with some omissions for clarity.

Listing 17-2: **Updated Postfix main.cf Configuration**

```
mail_spool_directory = /var/mail
canonical_maps = hash:/etc/postfix/canonical
virtual_maps = hash:/etc/postfix/virtual
relocated_maps = hash:/etc/postfix/relocated
transport_maps = hash:/etc/postfix/transport
sender_canonical_maps = hash:/etc/postfix/sender_canonical
masquerade_exceptions = root
masquerade_classes = envelope_sender, header_sender, header_recipient
myhostname = laptop.palmcoder.net
program_directory = /usr/lib/postfix
inet_interfaces = 127.0.0.1, 192.168.0.4
masquerade_domains = palmcoder.net
mydestination = $myhostname, localhost.$mydomain, $mydomain
```

```
disable_dns_lookups = no
smtpd_sender_restrictions = hash:/etc/postfix/access
smtpd_helo_required = no
smtpd_recipient_restrictions =
permit_mynetworks,reject_unauth_destination
alias_maps = hash:/etc/aliases
mailbox_size_limit = 0
message_size_limit = 10240000
```

In this example, we have configured Postfix to accept mail for `$mydomain`, which is found when Postfix strips off the domain portion of `$myhostname`. We could have explicitly set the domain, but the less retyping of any configuration changes, the better. This is the default behavior of Postfix, but it is better to explicitly set this in the configuration for verbosity.

The `inet_interfaces` clause has been manually changed to listen on the real network address of the Ethernet card. (We have substituted the real address and replaced it with a non-routable one.) By default, the SUSE Postfix configuration listens only on the loopback address, which means your installation will not receive mail from the outside world.

Dial-Up Server Configuration

This scenario is unlikely to be used these days as most mail clients hold off from sending mail when you are offline, but the configuration is still relevant to other situations.

When you do not have a constant connection to the Internet, it is a good idea to stop Postfix from attempting to send mail when it is not connected to the Internet. To do this, you need to defer the sending for a later date by telling Postfix that it should defer sending mail via SMTP using the `defer_transports` parameter.

```
defer_transports = smtp
```

When the machine is connected to the Internet, you then need to tell Postfix to send the mail it has queued. The `sendmail` command can be used to queue up mails, as follows:

```
sendmail -q
```

When the command has completed, use the `mailq` command to query whether your mails have been sent. The `mailq` command also tells you if there are any mails stuck in the queue for any reason. Common problems will be that Postfix cannot communicate with another mail server because of connectivity problems or the local mail cannot be delivered because a user is over quota.

To stop your machine from unnecessarily trying to look up host names when processing mail in the queue, you need to turn off address lookups via DNS, so you
need to change the default `disable_dns_lookups` parameter as follows:

```
disable_dns_lookups = yes
```

Usually if you are on a dial-up, you will pass on all of your mail to another, dedicated mail server for further handling, in which case you need to configure a relay
host using the `relayhost` parameter:

```
relayhost = mail.palmcoder.net
```

Now, any mail that is not local to your mail server will be sent through SMTP to the
machine `mail.palmcoder.net`.

Note   The `relayhost` parameter is used in larger sites where the use of department mail
servers propagates mail through an organization with a central mail hub.

Stopping Spam

Spam, or UCE (unsolicited commercial email), is the bane of any Internet user's life,
and an administrator is more than aware of how much mail is worthless junk. To
combat this, you can use Postfix's UCE controls to limit the amount of spam that
travels through your systems.

We have already touched upon the restriction of relaying through your mail server,
which is part of the problem of spam. Another way to stop spam is by making sure
connections to the mail server are true to the RFC SMTP standard. With this comes
the increased risk of false positives. False positives happen when Postfix sees that a
non-standard connection is taking place and rejects the mail. This could happen
when the sending mail server does not properly conform to the RFC, not because it
is malicious, but because it is based on the legacy that mail servers are understanding when it comes to slight errors in the way an SMTP transaction takes place.

To be more stringent with what data a connecting machine sends to Postfix, you
can restrict their access and the format that data is in with the
`smtpd_sender_restrictions` parameter. Consider the following example:

```
smtpd_sender_restrictions = reject_unknown_sender_domain,
reject_non_fqdn_sender, permit
```

This rejects any mail from a user whose domain does not exist in the Internet
domain system. This will stop spammers from trying to use a fictitious domain
component in their MAIL FROM: clause. The `reject_non_fqdn_sender` rejects any
mail where the format of the MAIL FROM: does not include a fully qualified domain
name (of the form `domain.tld`).

Note   A *TLD*, or *top-level domain*, encapsulates the `.com`, `.org`, `.net`, `.co.uk`, and so on domains and is the defined and controlled domain format for the Internet. An Internet *fully qualified domain name* (FQDN) is always composed of a domain and a TLD. For example, `palmcoder.net` is an FQDN.

Restricting client connections to a mail server is always tricky because you do not want to produce false positives as it will drastically impact what mail you receive. To help with this, RBL (Real-time Black Hole) servers are in place that list known spammers' addresses in real time to enable you to rely on rejecting mail connections. This is an extremely useful idea that takes away a large proportion of your spam catching and gives it to a trusted, free service.

To enable RBL server lookups, you need to use the `reject_rbl_client` parameter in the `smtpd_client_restrictions`.

```
smtpd_client_restrictions = permit_mynetworks, reject_rbl_client
relays.ordb.org, reject_unknown_client
```

This allows connections from `mynetworks`, rejects mail from spam artists listed in the `ordb` database, and also rejects mail from unknown clients (clients that do not have an entry in the Internet DNS).

This just scratches the surface of what can be done with Postfix but gives you enough to get started configuring your own mail server. The Postfix documentation is some of the best out there and can be found at the Postfix site at `www.postfix.org`.

sendmail

As mentioned earlier in this chapter, sendmail is the most popular mail transfer agent in use on Linux and Unix systems today, but is not used by default on SUSE systems because its configuration syntax is somewhat cryptic. However, if you are installing a SUSE system in an environment where sendmail is the default MTA, you'd be hard pressed to argue for using a different MTA on your SUSE box.

sendmail was written by Eric Allman, whose `delivermail` program was the original ARPANET mail delivery system provided with 4.0 BSD Unix and early versions of 4.1 BSD. However, as the ARPANET transitioned to newer protocols (such as TCP), `delivermail` proved to be too inflexible, largely due to the fact that it used compiled-in configuration information. `sendmail` was developed to be dynamically reconfigurable by modifying an external configuration file and was first delivered with later versions of BSD 4.1. Although many alternate MTA software packages have been developed since then, sendmail is still the default MTA provided with most Unix and Unix-like systems. The source code for sendmail has always been freely available. Development of sendmail continues in both the Open Source community (www.sendmail.org) and at a company named Sendmail www.sendmail.com), where Eric Allman is CTO, and a next-generation version of sendmail is actively under development.

This section explains how to install, configure, and initiate sendmail on a SUSE system.

Installing sendmail

As mentioned previously, sendmail is never installed by default on a SUSE system. To install sendmail, you will need to remove Postfix, the default MTA on SUSE Linux systems, or any other MTA that you may previously have installed. SUSE's use of RPM as a core database for tracking installed packages and associated files simplifies adding and removing entire packages, but YaST makes the process even easier.

To install sendmail on your SUSE Linux system:

1. Start YaST, then select Software, and finally, select Install and Remove Software. Click the Administrator Mode button and enter the system's root password to proceed to the actual software installation screen.

2. To locate the sendmail package, enter **sendmail** in the Search text box and click the Search button. The sendmail package displays in the package list at the top right of this dialog. Click the check box to indicate that you want to install the package and the Accept button in the lower right portion of the Install and Remove Software pane.

3. If you configured your SUSE system as a server system, YaST automatically installed Postfix for you as part of the basic server installation. If this is the case, YaST displays the Dependency Conflict dialog box shown in Figure 17-2. As you can see from this figure, YaST automatically detects that sendmail conflicts with the Postfix MTA that is currently installed.

   To resolve this conflict, click the Remove the Conflicting Package button, which is shown selected in Figure 17-2. Click OK - Try Again to proceed.

4. If the media containing the sendmail package is not already in your CD or DVD drive, YaST prompts you to insert the appropriate CD or DVD and proceeds with the installation.

5. After installation is complete, YaST displays a dialog asking if you want to install other packages. Click No and then click OK to close YaST's Install and Remove Software pane.

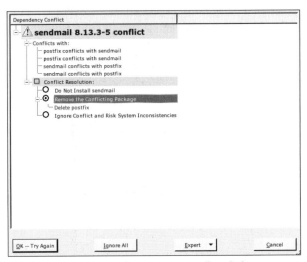

Figure 17-2: YaST2's dependency conflict dialog

Configuring sendmail

sendmail's primary configuration information is stored in the file /etc/sendmail .cf. Additional configuration information is stored in the directory /etc/mail. The file /etc/sendmail.cf is a text file that contains configuration information consisting of name/value pairs on separate lines of the file.

Most systems that run sendmail create the file /etc/sendmail.cf from another file, sendmail.mc, which is often stored in the /etc/mail (Linux systems such as Red Hat) or /usr/lib/mail/cf (Solaris) directory. The file sendmail.cf is generated from sendmail.mc using the m 4 command, which is a macro processor that expands the condensed configuration information in sendmail.mc into the more verbose but more complete sendmail.cf file.

Luckily, SUSE simplifies sendmail configuration by providing a graphical configuration mechanism in YaST. The YaST configuration module for sendmail and the shell scripts and configuration files that it uses were all installed automatically as part of SUSE's sendmail package. Configuring any MTA in YaST is done in the same location, which is Network Services ⇨ Mail Transfer Agent. The underlying scripts implement any changes or additional options provided by different support MTAs on SUSE Linux, such as Postfix, sendmail, and Exim. This section describes the most common configuration options that you may want to set or change in YaST's sendmail configuration module.

After starting YaST's MTA configuration module (Network Services ⇨ Mail Transfer Agent), the screen shown in Figure 17-3 will appear.

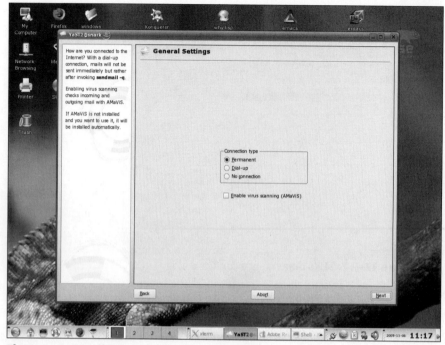

Figure 17-3: Specifying your network connection

On this screen, you identify the type of network connection that is used by the host on which you are running sendmail. If you want to automatically include virus scanning as part of receiving incoming mail, click the Enable virus scanning (AMaViS) check box. (If this package is not already installed, YaST will prompt you for the appropriate CD or DVD media at the end of the sendmail configuration process.) After selecting the appropriate options on this screen, click Next. The screen shown in Figure 17-4 displays.

If you are configuring sendmail on a host where you want to be able to receive and deliver mail, but your site uses a central mail server for relaying email to the Internet or other local networks, enter the name of this central server on this screen. If sendmail will need to authenticate to this server in order to send mail through it, click Authentication and enter the name and password of the user that sendmail should use to authenticate. (This is often a user named "sendmail," for whom a specific account has been created.) Click OK to record any changes that you have made and return to the Outgoing mail pane, or click Back to return to the Outgoing mail pane without making any changes.

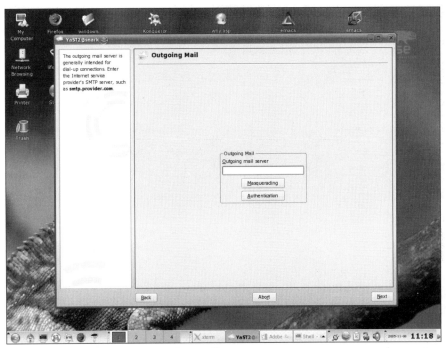

Figure 17-4: Specifying an outgoing mail server

If you want mail sent from the host that you are configuring to appear to be from a different domain, click Masquerade and enter the information about that domain that you want to appear in the headers of mail sent by sendmail. This pane also enables you to configure sendmail to make mail from specific local users to appear to come from selected locations, which can be useful for mail from system accounts that you do not want to reflect the name of the specific host from which they were sent. Click OK to record any changes that you have made and return to the Outgoing mail pane, or click Back to return to the Outgoing mail pane without making any changes.

Click Next to continue the configuration process and display the screen shown in Figure 17-5.

The most important setting on this panel is the Accept remote SMTP connections setting. By default, sendmail listens on a system's loopback interface and uses that to locally deliver mail that has also been sent locally. You will therefore need to enable the Accept remote SMTP connections setting if you want your system to be able to accept and deliver mail sent from other systems (such as if you are setting up a system that will deliver or relay mail sent by other systems).

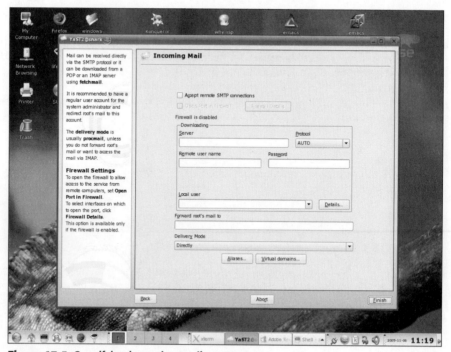

Figure 17-5: Specifying incoming mail parameters

The other settings on this panel enable you to specify a port that sendmail can use to retrieve and send mail, and to identify a remote mail server from which sendmail should retrieve mail for local delivery.

This panel also enables you to specify a central address to which you would like mail to the root user on your current system to be delivered. This is the most common example of email aliasing, which is the ability to specify the destination to which mail addressed to a specific local user should be forwarded or delivered. Clicking the Aliases button displays a screen that enables you to add other email aliases, which will be stored in the file /etc/mail/aliases. Similarly, clicking the Virtual domains button enables you to specify the addresses to which mail addressed to non-local users should be forwarded or delivered.

Click Finish to complete your configuration of sendmail. If you enabled antivirus scanning and the AMaViS package is not already installed, YaST will prompt you for the appropriate CD or DVD media at this point. If this is the case, insert the appropriate media and wait for the installation to complete.

YaST completes the sendmail configuration process by running SUSEConfig for you, which generates and updates /etc/sendmail.cf for you, as well as any of the files in /etc/mail that have been affected by your configuration changes.

Starting sendmail

Installing sendmail as described in the previous section also installs the sendmail startup script /etc/init.d/sendmail and creates symbolic links that automatically start and stop sendmail at run levels 3 (/etc/init.d/rc3.d/S14sendmail and /etc/init.d/rc3.d/K08sendmail, respectively) and 5 (/etc/init.d/rc5.d/S14sendmail and /etc/init.d/rc5.d/K08sendmail, respectively). To start sendmail, execute the startup script manually, as in the following example:

```
#/etc/init.d/sendmail start
```

To verify that sendmail is running and its current status, you can use a command such as the following:

```
$ ps -p `pidof sendmail`
UPID    TTY  STAT START TIME COMMAND
root    ?    Ss   05:31 0:00 sendmail: accepting connections
```

Note

If the ps -p command returns the error message ERROR: List of process IDs must follow –p, the pidof command returned NULL because sendmail is not running on your system. Try restarting sendmail using the startup script, as described previously. If you still receive an error message, try executing the ps – A command and using grep to search for sendmail in its output (ps – A |grep –I sendmail).

This shows that the sendmail daemon is running as root. Alternately, you could connect to the mail port (port 25) using your host's loopback address to verify that the sendmail daemon will respond to incoming requests, as in the following example:

```
$ telnet 127.0.0.1 25
Trying 127.0.0.1...
Connected to 127.0.0.1.
Escape character is '^]'.
220 laptop.vonhagen.org ESMTP Sendmail 8.13.3/8.13.3/SuSE Linux 0.7; \
   Thu, 9 Jun 2005 05:38:28 -0400
QUIT
221 2.0.0 laptop.vonhagen.org closing connection
Connection closed by foreign host.
```

If you configured sendmail to accept remote SMTP connections, you should also verify this by connection to the mail port on your host's externally visible IP address.

Getting More Information about sendmail

SUSE's YaST tool vastly simplifies the configuration and administration of sendmail compared with the tasks required on other Linux and Unix systems. As mentioned in the beginning of this section, the primary reason that people choose a mail transfer agent other than sendmail is the complexity of its configuration files, which are totally hidden by YaST's graphical interface. If you decide to use sendmail, you may eventually want to delve more deeply into manual aspects of its configuration. A number of excellent books dedicated to sendmail are currently available, as are a number of online resources. The best online resource for information about sendmail is the home page for the Sendmail Consortium, which maintains and develops the freeware version of sendmail. Go to www.sendmail.org for a good deal of information local to their site, as well as pointers to many of the best sites on the Internet for sendmail information.

Qpopper

When your MTA is configured, you need to be able to access your mail using a mail client by connecting to an MDA. You have three ways of remotely accessing your mail:

✦ By logging in to the server and accessing the mail spool directly

✦ Through Internet Message Access Protocol (IMAP)

✦ Through Post Office Protocol (POP3)

We will talk about POP3 and IMAP in this section of the chapter, starting with POP3.

POP3 enables you to receive your mail from a server and store it on your local disk. When the mail has been received from the server, it is deleted from the server. POP3 is a good mail storage option for laptop users as your mail is always local to your machine.

IMAP takes a different approach by always storing your mail messages on the server. This gives you the added benefit of being able to access all of your mail (including subfolders) wherever you are. If you use POP3, you are able to see all of your mail that you have downloaded only if you have your laptop or desktop machine that you use to download your POP3 mail with you.

One of the best POP3 servers is Qpopper. In addition to being the standard for POP3 retrieval, it is actively maintained and also supports extended authentication methods from the standard cleartext username and passwords.

You will need to install Qpopper using YaST, and then enable POP3 access in /etc/inetd.conf. Open /etc/inetd.conf and uncomment the popper line relating to POP3 (see Listing 17-3).

Listing 17-3: **Enabling Qpopper in inetd**

```
# Pop et al
```

```
#
# pop2    stream  tcp     nowait  root    /usr/sbin/tcpd  ipop2d
# pop3    stream  tcp     nowait  root    /usr/sbin/tcpd  ipop3d
# pop3s   stream  tcp     nowait  root    /usr/sbin/tcpd  ipop3d
pop3      stream  tcp     nowait  root    /usr/sbin/tcpd  /usr/sbin/popper -s
#
```

> **Note**   The network process `inetd` accepts connections from standard ports and passes control over to a specific application. Whereas Postfix listens on port 25 in daemon mode, Qpopper relies on `inetd` to provide its listening services.

When enabled, start `inetd` to enable POP3 access to your mail.

```
bible:~ # rcinetd start
Starting inetd                                        done
```

Once started, you can test connectivity with Telnet as we discuss in more detail in Chapter 15. Listing 17-4 shows an example.

Listing 17-4: **Testing the POP3 Server with Telnet**

```
bible:~ # telnet localhost 110
Trying 127.0.0.1...
Connected to localhost.
Escape character is '^]'.
+OK ready   <2282.1088970620@bible>
user justin
+OK Password required for justin.
pass password
+OK justin has 1 visible message (0 hidden) in 544 octets.
```

As you can see, the user `justin` has one unread mail that is 544 octets in length.

You can pass other parameters to Qpopper to extend its functionality. For example, if you want to allow your users to enter their usernames in uppercase or mixed case format, you can add `-c` to the Qpopper command line in `inetd.conf` to enable this. Another common parameter is `-R` to disable reverse name lookups (so that the host name and not the IP address is stored in the system log).

If you want to store your Qpopper options in a configuration file instead of specifying them on the command line through `inetd.conf`, you need to call Qpopper with the `-f` parameter (to set the configuration file):

```
# Pop et al
#
```

```
# pop2   stream  tcp     nowait  root    /usr/sbin/tcpd  ipop2d
# pop3   stream  tcp     nowait  root    /usr/sbin/tcpd  ipop3d
# pop3s  stream  tcp     nowait  root    /usr/sbin/tcpd  ipop3d
pop3     stream  tcp     nowait  root    /usr/sbin/tcpd  /usr/sbin/popper -f
/etc/qpopper.conf
#
```

If you want to set the parameters discussed previously in the qpopper.conf configuration, you have to use a full text representation of the parameters:

```
set statistics
set downcase-user
set reverse-lookup=false
```

Qpopper has many options that you can enable on the command line in /etc/inetd.conf or by specifying a configuration file on the command line containing parameters.

For more information on what you can do with Qpopper, take a look at the popper(8) man page.

Fetchmail

In certain situations, you may need to pull your email from a POP or IMAP server to your local mail server. The fetchmail program was designed to contact an MDA and fetch the mail and then pass it through your local SMTP server for delivery.

For fetchmail to successfully run, you need to know the address of your MDA server, the username, password, and the protocol to use (POP3/IMAP).

The fetchmail program then connects to the MUA and transports the messages to your SMTP server for further processing. When you run fetchmail with the required options, it delivers mail to the user you are running the command as.

```
justin@bible:~> fetchmail mail.bible.suse.com -p pop3
Enter password for justin@mail.bible.suse.com:
1 message for justin at mail.bible.suse.com (720 octets).
reading message justin@mail.bible.suse.com:1 of 1 (720 octets)  flushed
```

In the example, the user is currently logged in as justin, so the mail will be delivered through SMTP to the user justin@localhost.

In the fetchmail run in the previous example, we told fetchmail the server (mail.bible.suse.com) and the protocol (-p pop3). The fetchmail program is clever enough to know that we also need a password, so it asks us for it. When a message has been "flushed," it is delivered through SMTP.

If you are using a dial-up Postfix configuration, you can use `fetchmail` to automatically download your POP mail through SMTP to your mail server. Some Internet service providers (ISPs) routinely poll a static IP address that you have been assigned and automatically have your mail delivered through SMTP, but these services usually cost more money and are few and far between.

Cyrus IMAPD

POP3 is a good mail delivery agent for most situations, but if you like your mail controlled from a central server, with access to all your mail and folders from a remote site regardless of whether your mail is stored locally, then IMAP is the answer.

IMAP is a *connection-based* protocol. What that means is that you need a connection to the server to read your mail. Some MUAs enable you to read your mail locally and offline while not connected, but the server holds the up-to-date representation of your mail.

There are two main contenders in the Unix IMAP server space, University of Washington and Cyrus IMAPD. Both IMAP servers are extremely good at what they do, and we have chosen Cyrus as our focus because it is the IMAP server of choice by SUSE (it is the IMAP server used in OpenExchange).

The Cyrus IMAP server is extremely scalable and is capable of handling thousands of mail accounts. If more scalability is needed, you can use a Murder of Cyrus (a cluster of Cyrus servers) to provide a distributed IMAP server farm.

To use Cyrus, you need to add a system user (in our case, we will use `justin`) to the Cyrus database. All authentication is still handled through the user's system password, but the Cyrus database needs to provide a namespace for the user, including folders and access control lists.

Configuring the Cyrus User

When Cyrus has been installed through YaST, a few administrative tasks need to take place before you can log in as a user. First, we need to talk about how Cyrus works and interacts with the system. The Cyrus IMAP process is controlled by the user `cyrus`. With most daemon processes, the user who owns the process is usually a placeholder to run the daemon and nothing else. In the case of Cyrus, the `cyrus` system user plays an important part by not only running the IMAPD process but also by being the user that IMAP administration is conducted under.

With this in mind, you need to set a password for the `cyrus` user. To do this, as root, run the `passwd` command for the `cyrus` user:

```
bible:~ # passwd cyrus
Changing password for cyrus.
```

```
New password:
Re-enter new password:
Password changed
```

When set, you need to start the cyrus and saslauthd services.

Note

The saslauthd service is the Cyrus SASL authentication daemon. SASL is a general-purpose authentication mechanism that can be used in client and server environments. Cyrus IMAP relies on the SASL library to provide authentication services.

Adding Users to Cyrus

When those services are started, you need to add users to the Cyrus database to provide mail services for them. We will take the user justin (who must exist in the system) as an example. To add a user to the Cyrus system, become the cyrus user and connect to the Cyrus IMAP server with the cyradm command (Cyrus administration tool):

```
bible:~ # su - cyrus
cyrus@bible:~> cyradm localhost
IMAP Password:
localhost>
```

When connected, you can use the c m (create mailbox) command to create the user justin's inbox:

```
localhost> cm user.justin
localhost> lm
user.justin (\HasNoChildren)
localhost>
```

Here you have told Cyrus to create the mailbox user.justin. This may seem odd, but it is a standard way to configure Cyrus for user mailboxes. Cyrus works on a hierarchical mailbox structure, not only for the users, but also for system mailboxes. These system mailboxes could be mailboxes that are shared between many users for bulletins, for example.

Creating a Shared Mailbox

If you want to create a mailbox that is shared between certain users, use the c m command to create the mailbox and also set the access control list (ACL) for users on the mailbox.

For example, if you have three users, justin, roger, and aimee, on the system, and you want them to be able to store and view messages in this folder, but not to be able to delete any, you can look up the access control codes in Table 17-1 and set the ACL on that folder using the s am command (set ACL on folder).

Note

If you ever need to find out what Cyrus commands you can use, type **help** in the Cyrus command shell.

Table 17-1
Cyrus ACL Settings

ACL Code	Description
L	List the folder—that is, be able to view the folder in a folder list.
r	Read the contents of the folder.
s	Set the seen flag on a message in the folder.
w	Write to the folder—that is, store a message in the folder.
i	Insert or append a message to the folder.
p	Send a mail to the folder.
c	Create (subfolder) or delete the folder.
d	Delete a message in the folder.
a	Administrative rights on the folder, set ACLs.

To set an ACL on the folder, you need three pieces of information: the user you want to set the ACL for, the mailbox, and the ACL settings themselves. Consider the example in Listing 17-5.

Listing 17-5: Setting ACLs on a Shared Mailbox

```
localhost> sam share aimee lrwsip
localhost> sam share roger lrwsip
localhost> sam share justin lrwsip
localhost> lam share
roger lrswip
justin lrswip
anyone lrs
aimee lrswip
```

Here, we have allowed the users justin, roger, and aimee to list the folder, read the contents of the folder, set the seen flag on a message, store a message in the folder, and also send a message directly to the folder. We have not allowed them to delete any messages in the folder, so all is as we originally wanted.

When set, the ACLs come into effect immediately. Copying mails to the shared folder will work, but deleting them will not. This enables you as the administrator to set up a non-volatile, non-destructive mail store for a group of users with fine-grained access controls.

Integrating Cyrus and Postfix

So now that you know how Cyrus works, you need to set up Postfix to use Cyrus to store the user's mail.

In /etc/postfix/main.cf, you need to set the mailbox_transport to use the service cyrus. The service cyrus is preconfigured in /etc/postfix/master.cf. This file contains definitions for SMTP services as well as any user-defined services that can be used in parameters such as mailbox_transport. So you edit /etc/postfix/main.cf and change the mailbox_transport as follows:

```
mailbox_transport = cyrus
```

When /etc/postfix/main.cf is edited, restart Postfix with rcpostfix.

Tip   To make sure Postfix or any other service (such as inetd, or cyrus in this chapter) starts when you boot the system, use chkconfig -a servicename.

Any mail sent to users will now be delivered to their mailboxes using the cyrus service. The cyrus service calls the Cyrus deliver command to take the mail message and deliver it to the defined user's IMAP mailbox for his or her retrieval instead of the local mail spool.

Setting an Alias for Root's Mail in Cyrus

One thing that you need to consider when using Cyrus in this type of environment is that any mail to a user that is not in the Cyrus database will be rejected by Cyrus. This is especially true for the root user. It is not a good idea to store the root user mail in Cyrus, so most people configure an alias for root's mail to be delivered to a non-administrative user. Here we configure root's mail to be delivered to the user justin:

1. Open the file /etc/aliases and add an entry for the root user:

   ```
   root:    justin
   ```

   This tells Postfix that any mail for root should actually be delivered to the user justin.

2. When /etc/aliases is edited, run the postalias command:

   ```
   bible:~ # postalias /etc/aliases
   ```

3. You then need to reload Postfix's databases to commit the new alias.

Choosing a Mail Client

When your mail server is configured, you need to be able to read your email. You will find many mail clients available, the most popular being `mutt`, `pine`, `kmail`, and evolution. We briefly describe the benefits of all of the systems and where they are most commonly used.

The Command-Line Clients

If you have only command-line access to your mail, you will probably want to use `mail` or `mutt`.

mail

The `mail` command is the most basic mail client of all and is used to send mail and receive it using the command line. If you want to send mail with the `mail` command, just enter `mail` and the person you want to send mail to.

```
bible:~ # mail justin@wileybible.com
Subject: Hello there
This is a test
.
EOT
```

Here, we have been asked for the subject of the mail, and we are then ready to type our mail message. Notice that at no point during this transaction are we given guidance on what to do. This is stereotypical Unix commands at their best!

When the message has been entered, you then need to enter a period on a line by itself and then press Enter/Return. This will send the mail to the recipient specified.

To read mail with the `mail` command, enter `mail` at the command line and press Enter/Return.

You are then presented with a list of mails in your mailbox that you can read. To read a message, just enter the number of the mail you want to read:

```
bible:~ # mail
mailx version nail 10.6 11/15/03. Type ? for help.
"/var/mail/justin": 1 message 1 new
>N  1 justin@wileybible.com   Thu Sep 30 11:30  14/452   "Hello there"
&
```

Pressing 1 and Return will show you the mail message you just sent.

`mail` is installed by default on most Unix systems and can be used as a last resort to read your mail. It is also good because you can use the `mail` command to send mail through a shell script if you have a list of email addresses you need to send something to (but not for spam).

mutt

mutt is a more feature-filled command-line mail client that can display your mail in a formatted list and also employs mail message threading. It is a lot more interactive than mail, but can be used on the command line as your daily mail client. If you want to use mutt, install it through the YaST package manager.

The Graphical Mail Clients

For Linux users, the choice of mail client usually boils down to the desktop product they use. KDE comes with the kmail client, whereas Gnome comes with the Evolution mail client. Both are quite different beasts.

kmail

kmail is a very nice, well-rounded mail client that can connect to POP, IMAP, and also local mail spools to read your mail. You can set up mail rules to send mail to specific folders based on certain parameters and can also connect to mail servers over SSL.

Evolution

Evolution is more of an "Outlook for Linux" application in that it incorporates not only mail, but calendaring, address book, and tasks under the same roof. Whereas with kmail you use separate applications for this functionality, Evolution has them built in.

Note   Recently, Ximian open sourced their Connector product, which also enables you to connect your Ximian Evolution client to a Microsoft Exchange 2000/2003 server and access your calendars and so on.

Mail Systems on Linux

Mail on Linux is a funny thing; there are many ways to provide mail services on any Unix system in general, from using sendmail or Postfix as an MTA to Qpopper or Cyrus as an MDA, all the way to choosing from among numerous MUAs for reading your mail. At the end of the day, it is up to you how you want to configure mail on your system. We've given you enough information to proceed, and you will quickly find the variety of choices available will enable you to implement a solution that meets your needs.

✦   ✦   ✦

Setting Up Windows Interoperability with Samba

Regardless of how you feel about Microsoft Windows, it's impossible to ignore that most businesses use it for their day-to-day activities. The prevalence of Windows makes it important for Linux systems to be able to access Windows resources such as Windows file servers and printers. Similarly, the power of Linux as a corporate computing resource makes it important for Windows systems to be able to access file servers and printers that may run on Linux systems. Interoperability with other types of computer systems and network communication mechanisms is an important aspect of the power and flexibility of Linux and is one of the keys to its being adopted in both the home- and enterprise-computing environments.

Interoperability between Windows and Linux network resources is provided by a set of client/server applications that are part of a set of applications known as the Samba software suite. Linux systems that need to be able to access Windows resources (and therefore need to be able to act as a client of those Windows resources) do so by running a Samba client application. Linux systems that need to export resources to Windows users do so by running a Samba server that makes those resources available over the network in a form that Windows systems can access.

This chapter explains how to configure both Samba clients and servers, explains various authentication models for Samba servers, and discusses some graphical and command-line utilities that make it easier to explore and interact with Windows resources from your SUSE Linux system. The last section highlights the Samba-related packages that are available in your SUSE distribution and explains how to locate and install any that you might not have initially installed on your system.

A Bit of Background

The SUSE Linux kernel features built-in connectivity with networked Windows resources by supporting the Windows Server Message Block (SMB) protocol that underlies most native Windows networking mechanisms. The SMB protocol is now considered a part of Microsoft's more general Common Internet File Services (CIFS), but its name lives on in the Samba software suite.

Acronyms reign supreme in the network world, most of which are related to the history of various standards and protocols. This is especially true for the long list of network protocols used by DOS and Windows systems. When Microsoft decided that network support was a good thing, it began entering the market by introducing the NetBIOS (Network Basic Input/Output System) standard in 1984 to define and control the characteristics of network communication from a DOS or Windows system. To implement this transport standard, Microsoft provided the NetBEUI (NetBIOS Extended User Interface) protocol. NetBEUI worked fine on the small corporate networks of the day but was missing basic features, such as routing, that were required as networks became larger and connection between distinct but connected networks became increasingly necessary. From 1985 through 1988, Microsoft worked with IBM and Intel to introduce and popularize SMB, which is a NetBIOS implementation that today runs over TCP/IP networks. If you're still collecting acronyms, SMB is the most common example of what is generically known as NBT (NetBIOS over TCP/IP, also known as NetBT).

As discussed in Chapter 6, TCP/IP has always been the networking protocol associated with Unix and Linux systems. Samba was originally developed by Andrew Tridgell ("tridge"), who initially began development of what would later become Samba on DEC and Sun workstations in 1991. He began work on porting Samba (then just known as NetBIOS for Unix or smbserver) in 1992. In 1994, J.R. Conlin and Dave Fenwick started an SMB-related newsgroup, comp.protocols.smb, as a forum for discussing Samba development; smbserver was renamed Samba in 1994 because of conflicts with the name of an existing product, and the rest is history.

Today, Samba is used on Linux, FreeBSD, NetBSD, Solaris, AIX, HP-UX, and any Unix and Unix-like system that you can think of. Similarly, most of the NAS (Network Attached Storage) systems that you can purchase today support NFS (the Network File System, discussed in Chapter 22) thanks to Sun's early release of the NFS specification and Windows networking courtesy of Samba.

SUSE Linux provides an up-to-date version of Samba Version 3. Version 3 introduces several significant enhancements over previous versions of Samba, including the following:

✦ Support for Microsoft Active Directory. This also provides support for Samba servers as member servers in Active Directory domains.

✦ Improved Unicode and internationalization support.

✦ Improved support for the updated printing system used by Windows 200X and Windows XP.

For detailed information on Samba 3.0 and migration issues for older Samba servers, see the Samba HOWTO collection. This set of documents is installed on your SUSE system as part of the `samba-doc` package, as described in "Samba-Related Packages in SUSE Linux" later in this chapter. When you have installed the `samba-doc` package, the Samba HOWTO collection is available in the file `/usr/share/doc/packages/samba/Samba-HOWTO-Collection.pdf`. You can also find the Samba HOWTO collection online at sites such as `www.comp.hkbu.edu.hk/docs/s/samba30/htmldocs/howto/`.

Setting Up and Using a Samba Client

Most desktop SUSE users who work in an environment where Windows systems are also used will want to configure and start a Samba client on their machines. Starting a Samba client on your system enables you to access Windows resources such as printers and file servers on your local network. A Samba client does not enable your system to export filesystems and printers to your local network—to do that, you will need to configure and start a Samba server on your system, as explained in "Setting Up a Samba Server," later in this chapter.

Note   If you have problems locating any of the YaST configuration options or applications described in this section, see the section entitled "Samba Client and Server Packages" later in this chapter for information about locating and installing any packages that may not have been installed during the installation process.

Configuring a Samba Client

Like most administrative tasks on a SUSE Linux system, configuring and starting a Samba client is most easily done through YaST. If you are running the X Window system KDE desktop (SUSE's default graphical environment), you can execute by selecting YaST from the Control Center menu, which is available by clicking the SUSE icon at the bottom-left corner of your KDE desktop. If you start YaST as the root user, the YaST dialog box is displayed, as shown in Figure 18-1.

Note   If you start YaST as any other user, the KDE su dialog box is displayed as shown in Figure 18-2. Enter your system's root password, and the system will start YaST for you as the root user.

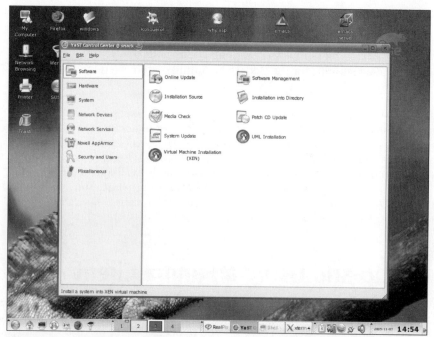

Figure 18-1: YaST initial screen

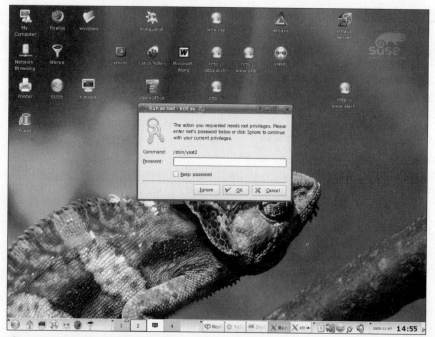

Figure 18-2: KDE su dialog box

To configure and start a Samba client, follow these steps:

1. Click the Network Services icon in the left pane of the YaST Control Center and scroll down the right pane until you see the Samba Client icon, as shown in Figure 18-3.

2. Click the Samba Client icon to display the Samba Client configuration pane, as shown in Figure 18-4.

   This screen enables you to set the name of an existing Windows domain or workgroup. Under Windows, the core difference between a domain and workgroup is where the administrative and authentication information is stored. Workgroups typically store authentication and connection information on each PC, while domains are administered from a central authentication and user database known as a domain controller. Domain controllers will be discussed in more detail later in this chapter in the sidebar "To PDC or Not to PDC."

Figure 18-3: Samba Client icon in YaST

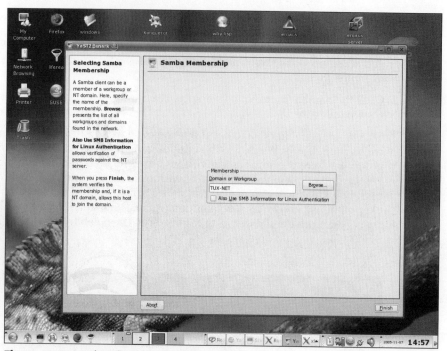

Figure 18-4: Samba Client configuration pane in YaST

3. When this screen is displayed, the default name TUX-NET appears in the Windows Domain or Workgroup text box.

   - If you know the name of the domain or workgroup that you want to join, position the cursor in this text box, type the domain or workgroup name, and click the Finish button.

   - If you do not know the exact name of the domain or workgroup that you want to join, click the Browse button to display a dialog box that shows the list of Windows domains and workgroups that can be detected on the network to which your system is attached.

Tip   If you are configuring your system to be a member of a Windows domain, the Samba Client configuration panel also provides the option of using the existing Windows authentication information provided by that domain when you log in to your Linux system. Selecting this option simplifies local system administration by using a single, central authentication mechanism, but may make it difficult for you to log in when your system is not connected to the network. Using a Windows domain as your primary authentication mechanism is done by adding an SMB Pluggable Authentication Module (PAM) to the authentication process on your system, as defined by the file /etc/pam.conf.

That's all there is to it — your system is now configured as a client of the selected domain or workgroup! Your credentials and rights to access the resources available in the selected domain or workgroup will be checked when you attempt to access those resources, as described in the following sections.

Browsing Available Windows Resources

SUSE Linux provides a number of different ways to browse Windows networks to identify and access available resources. The most common of these is to use the Konqueror browser, shown in Figure 18-5. SMB support in Konqueror is constantly being improved, so make sure that you have installed the latest version of the kdebase3 package using YaST's Online Update control (discussed in Chapter 9) if you encounter problems.

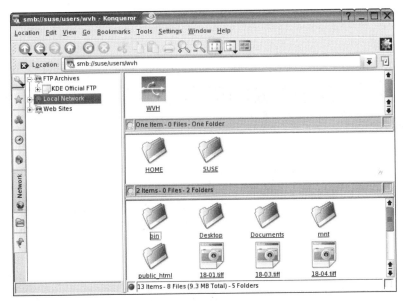

Figure 18-5: Browsing SMB resources in Konqueror

To browse resources on your local network using Konqueror, click the My Computer icon on your desktop, and select the Network icon from the column of icons at the left. Click the Local Network entry in the left pane, and select the Windows Network icon from the right pane to display icons for any available domains and workgroups in the right pane. You can then drill down into any available domain or workgroup by clicking the icons that are subsequently displayed. Figure 18-5 shows local network resources after drilling down to the WVH workgroup and its HOME share in Konqueror.

Tip

If you are using the KDE desktop, you can create a permanent shortcut to the Local Network icon on your SUSE desktop by dragging the Local Network icon from Konqueror to your desktop and selecting Copy Here from the menu that is displayed. You can do the same thing by right-clicking Konqueror's Local Network icon, selecting the Copy To menu item, navigating your Home Folder's Desktop folder, and selecting the Copy Here menu command.

A fast alternative to using Konqueror to browse available Windows resources is to use a command-line utility called smbtree. This utility is installed as part of the samba-client package, and provides a fast listing of available SMB resources when executed from within konsole, xterm, or any other Linux terminal emulation utility. Figure 18-6 shows the output from running smbtree on a sample home network featuring two Samba servers that are both members of the WVH workgroup.

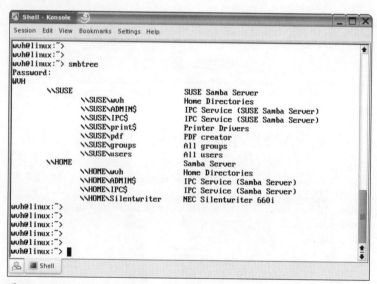

Figure 18-6: Browsing SMB resources using smbtree

Another useful package for browsing SMB resources is the open source project LinNeighborhood (www.bnro.de/~schmidjo/index.html). A package containing LinNeighborhood is included as a separately installable package in your SUSE Linux Professional distribution set. Figure 18-7 shows LinNeighborhood displaying the same set of resources shown in Figures 18-5 and 18-6.

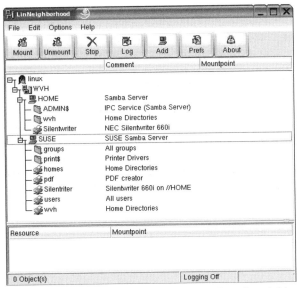

Figure 18-7: Browsing SMB resources using LinNeighborhood

Mounting a Shared Windows Drive

There are many different ways to mount a shared Windows drive on your SUSE system, the easiest of which is to use the standard Linux mount command. For example, to mount an SMB share named wvh that is available on an SMB server named home, mount that share on the directory /mnt/smb, and access those files as the Windows user wvh, you would execute a command such as the following as the root user:

```
# mount -t smbfs -o username=wvh //home/wvh /mnt/smb
```

The previous command line can be broken down as follows:

✦ -t smbfs—Identifies the type of filesystem that you are mounting as an smbfs filesystem (SMB filesystem).

✦ -o username=wvh—Passes the username=wvh option to the mount command, which identifies your Windows user login as wvh.

✦ //home/wvh—The name of the Windows directory that you want to mount on your SUSE system. In this example, this is a directory named wvh on a Windows file server named home.

✦ /mnt/smb—The directory on your SUSE system where you want to mount the specified Windows directory.

The directory on which you want to mount the SMB share must already exist. The `mount` command actually executes a command called `smbmount`, which is usually a symbolic link to the command `/sbin/mount.smbfs`. After executing this command, you will be prompted for the Windows password associated with the specified user.

Tip

You can also execute a command as a user other than the root user by using the `sudo` command, which lets users execute commands as privileged users (sudo means "do with a substitute user ID"). The privileged commands and the users who can perform them are listed in the file `/etc/sudoers`. If you have a valid entry in the `/etc/sudoers` file, you will be prompted for your password and then again for the Windows password associated with the specified user. If you do not have a valid entry in the `/etc/sudoers` file, there isn't much point in using the `sudo` command, but if you do you will be prompted for the root password and then again for the Windows password associated with the specified user. You can enable users to execute privileged commands by executing the `visudo` command as the root user, which enables you to edit the `/etc/sudoers` file using the `vi` text editor. For more information about the `sudo` command, execute the `man sudo` command in a console window or xterm. For more information about the `/etc/sudoers` file, execute the command `man sudoers`.

Tip

Just like any other partitions or network drives, you can automatically mount SMB shares when your system boots by adding them to your system's `/etc/fstab` file. To do this, create a standard `/etc/fstab` entry such as the following:

```
//SUSE/wvh /mnt/smb/wvh smbfs
username=wvh,password=foo,uid=578,gid=500 0 0
```

The first field defines the name of the SMB share that you want to mount, the second field is the directory on your system where you want to mount the drive, and the third field is the type of filesystem that you are mounting. The fourth field provides options that you want to use when mounting the SMB share, and the fifth and sixth fields define when you want to back up the filesystem and when you want to check the consistency of the filesystem at boot time. These values are almost always 0 (zero) for networked filesystems, which means never.

For SMB shares, the mount parameters that you have to pass in the mount options field include the username that you want to use for authentication with the Samba server, your password, and the user and group IDs that you want to associate with the mounted filesystem so that only you can read and write files in the Samba share. Because you have to enter your password, you should also make sure that the `/etc/fstab` file is not publicly readable by executing a command such as `chmod 600 /etc/fstab`, or else anyone in the know can view the file and find out your Windows password — probably not a good idea.

Using a Windows Printer from Linux

To access a networked Windows printer from your Linux system using Samba, you must have created a printer definition entry for that printer using YaST. You can then print to it as you would to any other local or networked printer.

To create a printer definition for a Windows printer after installing and configuring the Samba client software, follow these steps:

1. Start YaST as explained earlier in this chapter in the section "Configuring a Samba Client." Click the Hardware icon in the left pane, and select the printer icon from the right pane. The screen shown in Figure 18-8 is displayed.

2. Click the Add button to begin creating a new printer definition. The dialog shown in Figure 18-9 is displayed.

3. Select the Print via SMB Network Server option and click the Next button to display the dialog box shown in Figure 18-10.

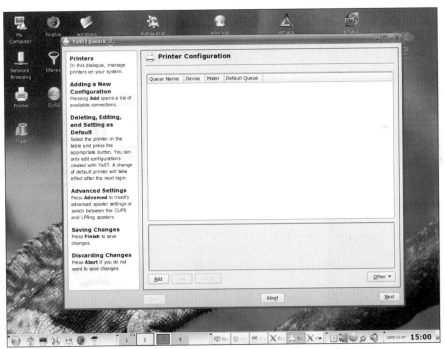

Figure 18-8: The initial printer configuration dialog box in YaST

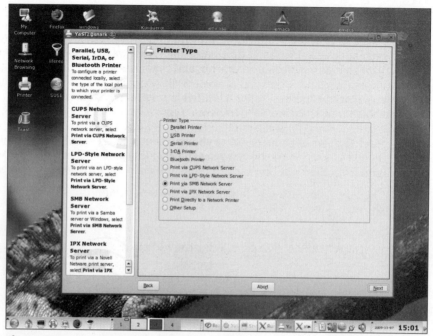

Figure 18-9: Specifying the printer type in YaST

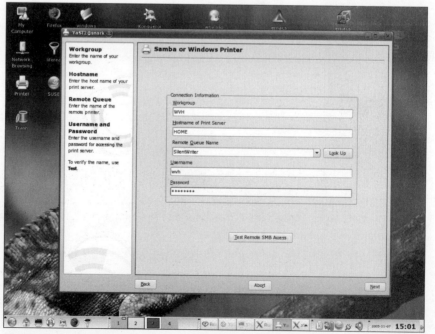

Figure 18-10: Defining a Samba or Windows printer in YaST

4. Enter the name of the workgroup or domain in which the printer is located, the name of the host that controls printing to that printer, and the name of the print queue associated with that printer on the specified host. These must not contain spaces. You must also enter the Windows login name of a user that is authorized to print to that printer, and that user's password. After entering these values, click the Test Remote SMB Access button to make sure that all of the values that you have specified are correct. If they are, a pop-up message is displayed that tells you that your system can connect to the specified printer. If the values are not correct, an error dialog box is displayed, and you should recheck the values that you have entered. If you need assistance identifying the correct values, contact the system administrator of your Windows network.

When you have entered valid values and verified them, click the Next button to proceed. The dialog shown in Figure 18-11 is displayed.

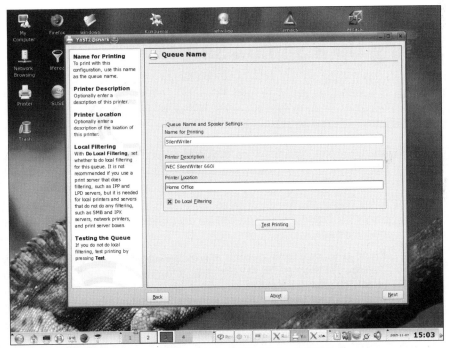

Figure 18-11: Setting queue values for an SMB printer in YaST

5. Enter the name that you want to associate with the specified SMB printer. This will be the queue or printer name that you specify to commands such as lpr in order to print to this printer over the network, and can be any name that you like. You can also enter description and location information for the printer, although these values are optional.

6. Next, deselect the Do Local Filtering check box. Because the printer is already configured on the remote SMB server, you do not need to do any local preprocessing in order to print to it.

At this point, you can click the Test printing button to send a test printout to the remote printer. A dialog box that gives you a choice of sending a text or graphical printout to the remote printer is displayed. If the remote printer can print graphics, you should send a graphical test sheet to it in order to make sure that it is correctly configured. The graphical test sheet also contains text, so it will test both capabilities.

Tip

If you print a test sheet at this point, make sure that you pick it up. It will contain the username and password that you used to access the remote printer—not something you want to leave lying around!

7. When the test sheet prints successfully, click the Next button to display the next screen and click Finish to complete and save your new printer definition.

Setting Up a Samba Server

Like most administrative tasks on a SUSE Linux system, configuring and starting a Samba server is most easily done through YaST. You can start YaST in the same way as discussed earlier in the chapter in the section "Configuring a Samba Client." To configure and start a Samba server, follow these steps:

1. Click the Network Services icon in the left pane of the YaST Control Center and scroll down the right pane until you see the Samba Server icon, as shown in Figure 18-12.

2. Click the Samba Server icon to start the Samba Server configuration, as shown in Figure 18-13. You will be prompted for the Windows workgroup or domain name.

Note

If you have problems locating any of the configuration options or applications described in this section, see the section "Samba Client and Server Packages" later in this chapter for information about locating and installing any packages that might not have been installed during the installation process.

Figure 18-12: Samba Server icon in YaST

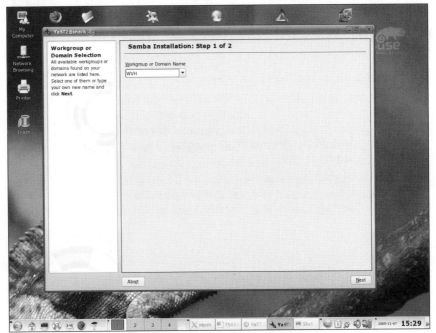

Figure 18-13: Initial Samba Server configuration screen in YaST

3. You can now choose whether the server should be a PDC (Primary Domain Controller) or not as in Figure 18-14.

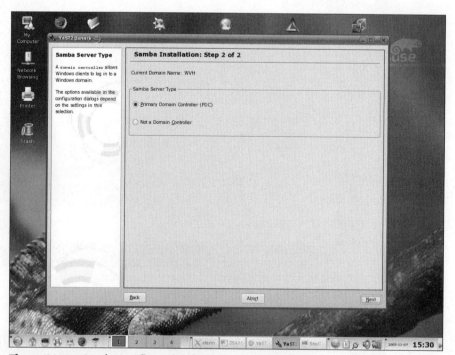

Figure 18-14: Samba configuration in YaST: second screen

4. The next screen has three tabs:

- Start-up. Here you decide whether the Samba service should be started at boot time (in production you will normally want to do this) or manually (Figure 18-15). Here you also have the option to open the necessary port on the firewall (if you are running one) to allow connections to the Samba server.

- Shares. Here the Samba shares which will be offered by the server are listed. You can add any directory as a share in this tab and provide it with the name which will be seen by Windows clients (Figure 18-16).

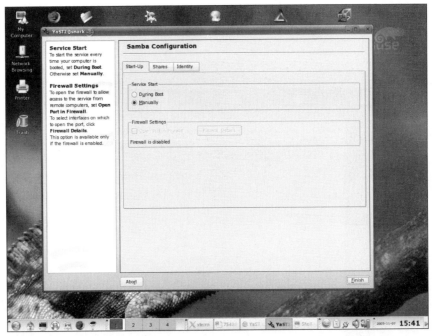

Figure 18-15: Samba configuration: Start-up tab

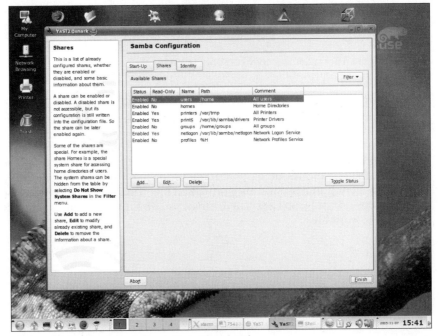

Figure 18-16: Samba configuration: Shares tab

- Identity. Here you have another chance to set the Windows domain or workgroup name, to decide whether the server is a PDC or not, and to set the Windows NetBIOS hostname (the name by which the server will be seen according to the native Windows naming scheme) (Figure 18-17).

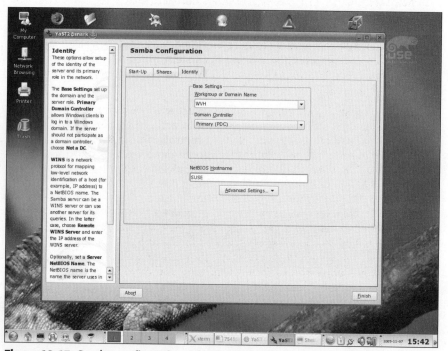

Figure 18-17: Samba configuration: Identity tab

5. By default, your Samba server will authenticate users by looking them up in a Samba password file, which is a text file that is explained in the following section of this chapter, "Creating and Managing the Samba Password File." To set alternative sources of authentication information, click the Advanced Settings button in the Identity tab (seen in Figure 18-17), and then choose User Authentucation Sources. The screen shown in Figure 18-18 is displayed. Specifying an alternate authentication mechanism is a completely optional step — most Samba servers in small and home environments use a Samba password file.

To PDC or Not to PDC

A domain controller supplies authentication information for a Windows domain. You will rarely want your Samba server to act as a primary domain controller if you want your Samba server to join an existing Windows domain (such as at the office) because your existing Windows domain probably already has a primary domain controller (which probably runs on a Windows system). Starting a second primary domain controller on an existing Windows domain will certainly confuse any Windows systems that are already members of that domain and will definitely irritate your system administrator. However, if you are configuring your Samba server to host a new Windows domain, you will want it to act as the primary domain controller for that domain.

If you are configuring your Samba server to act as a backup for another Samba server in your domain, you may want to configure it to act as a backup domain controller. If you define a Samba server as a backup domain controller, your primary domain controller must also be a Samba server, because Samba cannot directly access authentication information that is stored in proprietary formats on a Windows primary domain controller. You will therefore have to configure your Samba backup domain controller to use the same authentication information as the primary domain controller. If your primary domain controller stores information in Lightweight Directory Access Protocol (LDAP), you can easily configure your backup domain controller to access the same LDAP server. If your primary domain controller stores authentication information in a Samba password file, you will have to replicate that file manually on your backup domain controller and make sure that the contents of the two files are always synchronized. Configuring and using an LDAP server is explained in Chapter 25. SUSE provides a number of tools for file synchronization, such as Unison, InterMezzo, and rsync, which are explained in the SUSE Administration Guide that you received with your SUSE distribution.

6. The dialog box shown in Figure 18-18 enables you to specify alternate and auxiliary authentication methods. You may want to specify multiple methods if you want to be able to try various authentication services in order before falling through to the default Samba password file (`/etc/samba/smbpasswd`).

To specify an alternate authentication mechanism, click the Add button on the dialog box shown in Figure 18-18 to display the pop-up dialog shown in Figure 18-19.

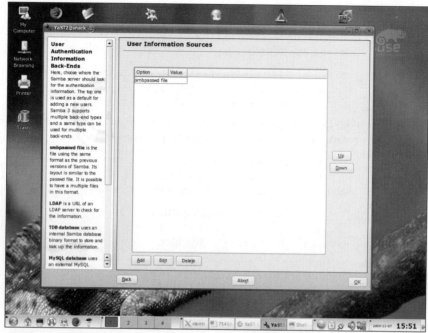

Figure 18-18: Customizing Samba server authentication

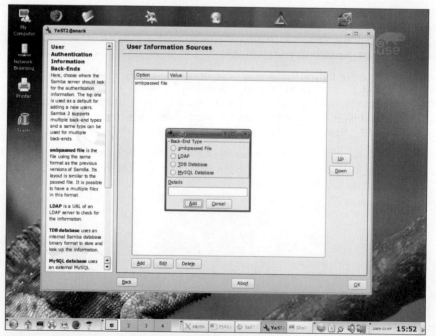

Figure 18-19: Samba server authentication alternatives

The pop-up dialog shown in Figure 18-19 lists alternate Samba authentication mechanisms that you can add to the default `smbpasswd` file selection that is displayed when you first configure a Samba server. Available authentication mechanisms are the following:

- **smbpasswd file (default)** — Useful in small networks, but provides a limited amount of information and requires manual replication when multiple Samba servers share a single `smbpasswd` file.

- **LDAP** — Suggested for large sites with multiple Samba servers that share authentication information or that already use LDAP for other purposes.

- **TDB database** — A trivial database that stores single name/value pairs. Not recommended for sites with more than 250 users or that require sharing authentication information across multiple Samba servers.

- **MySQL database** — A useful authentication mechanism for sites already running MySQL and using it to store authentication information. Requires that you specify the identifier of the MySQL database that holds the authentication table as an argument in the pop-up menu that is displayed after you select this option. You can then add appropriate entries to the Samba configuration file (discussed later in this chapter) to identify the columns in your MySQL table that contain different portions of your user and authentication information.

If you select multiple authentication mechanisms, you can reorder them by selecting one and clicking the Up button to move it to the top of the authentication series or clicking the Down button to move it to the bottom of the authentication series.

7. Click the Finish button to proceed. You will now be prompted for a Samba root password (Figure 18-20).

8. The configuration is now complete, and the YaST Samba server module will exit.

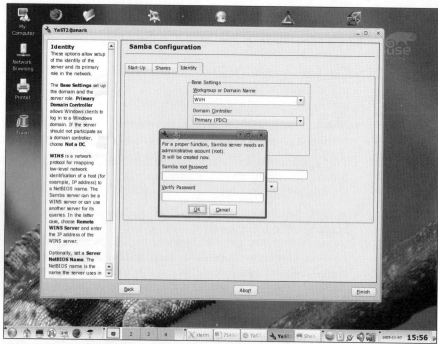

Figure 18-20: Setting the Samba administrative password

Creating and Managing the Samba Password File

Many Samba servers that serve as a PDC or that use workgroup authentication use a Samba-specific password file to store Windows username and password information. On SUSE systems, this file is /etc/samba/smbpasswd. Entries in this file are created and updated using a utility that is also named smpasswd. This file is used only by Samba servers — Samba clients use the authentication mechanisms that are provided by the Samba or Windows servers that you are connecting to.

If the smbpasswd file is the only authentication mechanism that you specified when you configured your Samba server, you must create a username and password entry in this file for each user that you want to be able to access any resources that require authentication on that Samba server.

To create a Samba authentication entry for a specified user, use the smbpasswd command's -a (add) option and provide the name of that user as an argument to the -a option, as in the following example:

```
# smbpasswd -a wvh
New SMB password:
Retype SMB password:
```

Enter the password that you want to assign to the specified user when prompted for it — the password is not echoed to the screen as you type. When you have entered the specified user's Samba password, you must type it again to verify that you didn't mistype the password.

The user that you are adding to the Samba password file must be a valid Linux user on your system, for whom an entry exists in the standard Linux /etc/passwd file.

If you execute the smbpasswd command without an argument, the command attempts to change the password for the current user. If you specify a username without specifying the -a option, the smbpasswd command attempts to change the Samba password for the specified user.

For complete information about the smbpasswd command, see the online manual page for the command, available by typing man smbpasswd in any konsole, xterm, or other terminal emulation window.

Working with the Winbind Daemon

The Winbind daemon, winbindd, enables the Linux name switch service (NSS) to retrieve user and group information from a Windows primary domain controller (PDC). This provides a networked authentication mechanism similar to the Network Information System (NIS and NIS+) often used in computing environments that make heavy use of Sun's Network File System (NFS). The Winbind daemon enables Windows users to log in on a Linux machine using the Windows credentials provided by the PDC without requiring any local user and group entries in the Linux password file.

To use winbindd, you must do the following:

1. Add Winbind entries to the /etc/nsswitch.conf file that tells your Linux system the services that it can use for authentication and the order in which those services should be queried for valid authentication information. These entries should look like the following:

```
passwd:      files winbind
group:       files winbind
```

2. Modify the auth (authentication) entries in all of the Pluggable Authentication Module (PAM) configuration files in the directory /etc/pam.d to contain authentication entries such as the following:

```
auth    required      /lib/security/pam_securetty.so
auth    required      /lib/security/pam_nologin.so
auth    sufficient    /lib/security/pam_winbind.so
auth    required      /lib/security/pam_pwdb.so use_first_pass shadow
nullok
```

3. Modify the account entries in all of the PAM configuration files in /etc/pam.d to contain an account entry such as the following:

```
account required /lib/security/pam_winbind.so
```

4. Join the existing Windows domain by executing Samba's net command, as in the following example, where PDC is the name or IP address of your Windows primary domain controller and USER is any user with administrative privileges in that domain:

```
net join -S PDC -U USER
```

5. Add appropriate winbind entries to the [global] section of your Samba server's configuration file, /etc/samba/smb.conf. The entries that you should add are the following, where MYDOMAIN is the name of the Windows domain for which the PDC you specified in the previous step provides authentication information:

```
winbind separator = +
winbind cache time = 10
template shell = /bin/bash
template homedir = /home/%D/%U
idmap uid = 10000-20000
idmap gid = 10000-20000
workgroup = MYDOMAIN
security = domain
password server = *
```

6. Start the Winbind daemon (/usr/sbin/winbindd) on your SUSE system, and restart the Samba daemon and NetBIOS name daemon by executing the following commands:

```
/etc/rc.d/nmbd restart
/etc/rc.d/smbd restart
```

Any user with an entry in your Windows PDC should now be able to log in on your SUSE system using a username of the form "DOMAIN+username" and his or her Windows password.

If you are using Winbind, you will also want to add a startup entry for the Winbind daemon to the startup scripts for your system's default runlevel, as in the following example for a system whose default runlevel is 5:

```
ln -s /etc/rc.d/winbind /etc/rc.d/rc5.d/S14winbind
```

Tip If you have problems configuring or using the Winbind daemon, you can use the `wbinfo` command to query the PDC through the `winbindd` daemon. The information that it returns can help you diagnose Winbind problems by seeing how the `winbindd` daemon translates various Windows authentication information. For complete information about the `wbinfo` command, type **man wbinfo** from the command line within any konsole, xterm, or other terminal emulation window on your SUSE system.

Command-Line Utilities for Samba

The Samba software suite includes a number of utilities that you may find useful when interacting with Windows networks from the Linux command line. The next few sections provide a brief introduction to some of the more useful ones. You can obtain a complete listing of all of the utilities on your SUSE system that are related to Samba by using the `apropos` command to identify any commands related to Samba or the SMB protocol, as in the following examples:

```
wvh@linux:~> apropos samba
net (8)          - Tool for administration of Samba and remote CIFS servers.
smb.conf (5)     - The configuration file for the Samba suite
cupsaddsmb (8)   - export printers to samba for windows clients
lmhosts (5)      - The Samba NetBIOS hosts file

wvh@linux:~> apropos SMB
smbspool (8)     - send a print file to an SMB printer
fs (5)           - Linux filesystem types: minix, ext, ext2, ext3, xia,
                   msdos, umsdos, vfat, proc, nfs, iso9660, hpfs, sysv,
                   smb, ncpfs
smbget (1)       - wget-like utility for download files over SMB
smbmnt (8)       - helper utility for mounting SMB filesystems
smb.conf (5)     - The configuration file for the Samba suite
cupsaddsmb (8)   - export printers to samba for windows clients
testparm (1)     - check an smb.conf configuration file for internal
                   correctness
findsmb (1)      - list info about machines that respond to SMB name
                   queries on a subnet
smbcquotas (1)   - Set or get QUOTAs of NTFS 5 shares
smbumount (8)    - smbfs umount for normal users
smbsh (1)        - Allows access to remote SMB shares using UNIX commands
smbmount (8)     - mount an smbfs filesystem
smbtar (1)       - shell script for backing up SMB/CIFS shares directly
                   to UNIX tape drives
smbcacls (1)     - Set or get ACLs on an NT file or directory names
smbclient (1)    - ftp-like client to access SMB/CIFS resources on servers
smbtree (1)      - A text based smb network browser
```

The Samba- and SMB-related commands that are available on your system will depend on the Samba packages that you installed on your system, as explained in the section "Samba Client and Server Packages," later in this chapter.

To obtain complete information about any of these commands, execute the command `man command` from any konsole, xterm, or other terminal emulation window on your SUSE system, where `command` is the name of the command about which you want information.

The Samba Configuration File

Samba is configured through settings that are stored in a text-format configuration file, which is located in the file `/etc/samba/smb.conf` on your SUSE system. The huge number of settings available in this file provides an interesting demonstration of the flexibility and power of the Samba software suite.

The Samba software suite provides excellent documentation about configuring and using every aspect of Samba. In addition, a number of excellent books are available on Samba and Samba 3 at your favorite brick and mortar or online bookstore. One of the best online general resources for Samba is its HOWTO collection, which is actually a single integrated document culled from many different sources by the Samba team. This document is installed as part of the `samba-doc` package on your SUSE system, and is also available online at many locations, including `www.samba.org/samba/docs/man/Samba-HOWTO-Collection/` from the master Samba web site.

The Samba HOWTO Collection for Samba 3 provides over 45 examples of Samba configuration files, showing how to configure Samba for scenarios ranging from an anonymous print server to a full-blown SMB server that functions as a primary domain controller. Rather than rehashing existing documentation, this section provides an overview of the format and main sections available in a Samba configuration file.

A standard Samba configuration file is divided into a number of primary sections, each delimited by the name of that section enclosed within square brackets. The only mandatory section of a Samba configuration file is the [global] section, which sets values for the Samba server itself, such as the name of the workgroup or domain that the Samba server exports (if it is a PDC) or belongs to (if it is not a PDC). Other than this section, the `smb.conf` file can contain any number of other sections, each of which describes the attributes of a shared resource that is exported by your Samba server. The sections and associated resources in the default `smb.conf` file provided with SUSE Linux are the following:

✦ **[global]** — General configuration settings, such as authentication and domain/workgroup information, that apply to all subsequent portions of the `smb.conf` file. As mentioned in the preceding paragraph, your `smb.conf` file must contain a [global] section, which is customized to reflect how your Samba server interacts with your local Windows domain or workgroup.

✦ **[groups]** — Configuration settings for a summary share that exports directories that are owned and writable by Linux groups.

✦ **[homes]** — Configuration settings for user home directories as exported by the Samba server.

✦ **[pdf]** — Configuration settings for a PDF file generator that is provided as a default printer in Samba.

✦ **[print$]** — Configuration settings for a general share that is intended to hold print drivers that Windows users can use to print to Windows printers via Samba.

✦ **[printers]** — Configuration settings for printers that are available via Samba.

✦ **[users]** — Configuration settings for a summary share that exports all Linux user home directories.

If you define additional shared resources using the Advanced dialog box available by clicking the Advanced button shown previously in Figure 18-17, an smb.conf section will be created for each additional resource. The Shares tab in the YaST Samba server configuration already seen in Figure 18-16 allows you to create additional Samba shared resource sections.

The SUSE Administration Guide provides examples of additional resources that you may want to define and discusses the configuration settings that you should use to manage access to those resources.

Tip If you manually modify your Samba configuration file, Samba includes a useful utility called testparm that reads and parses a Samba configuration file and identifies any syntax errors that are present. You should always use this utility after making changes to your smb.conf file but before restarting your Samba server to ensure that the file itself is correct before trying to diagnose problems with the values that you specified.

Samba Client and Server Packages

SUSE Linux comes with a large number of Samba-related packages. You can use YaST to add packages manually after completing your initial SUSE Linux installation or to query your system to determine the Samba-related packages that were installed as part of the type of installation that you selected during the installation process.

In this section, we list the Samba- and SMB-related packages provided with SUSE Linux Professional; we also discuss which of these packages are installed by the different installation types and package sets you can select when installing SUSE Linux.

Samba-Related Packages in SUSE Linux

SUSE Linux Professional provides the following Samba-related packages:

- ✦ gnome-vfs — Provides Samba/SMB support for the Nautilus file manager used by the GNOME desktop environment.

- ✦ kdebase3-samba — Libraries and applications required for accessing and displaying Samba and SMB resources from the KDE desktop and in applications such as the Konqueror web browser.

- ✦ samba — Libraries, applications, configuration files, and documentation for the Samba server.

- ✦ samba-client — Libraries, applications, configuration files, and documentation for the Samba client.

- ✦ samba-doc — Extensive Samba documentation.

- ✦ samba-pdb — Libraries and configuration information for using a database to hold Samba user and authentication information.

- ✦ samba-python — Libraries, Python code, and documentation for interacting with Samba and SMB resources using the Python programming language.

- ✦ samba-vscan — Libraries and associated documentation for performing virus-checking on resources exported by a Samba server.

- ✦ samba-winbind — Libraries, applications, and documentation associated with the Winbind daemon discussed earlier in this chapter.

- ✦ yast2-samba-client — Modules, documentation, and configuration information for YaST's Samba Client configuration option.

- ✦ yast2-samba-server — Modules, documentation, and configuration information for YaST's Samba Client Server configuration option.

When Samba-Related Packages Are Installed

SUSE Linux installs the Samba Client software as part of its default installation option. If you installed the default version of SUSE Linux and want to run only a Samba client, you do not need to add any additional packages.

If you selected another type of installation (such as the Minimal or Minimal+X11 install options) or customized the list of packages that you were installing, you may not have installed the Samba Client software and the administrative package that is used to configure a Samba client or server in YaST and YaST2.

Similarly, the Samba server software is installed only if you selected the Detailed Package Selection option during installation and did any of the following:

✦ Added the complete set of Network packages

✦ Selected the complete set of Samba packages from within the Network package set

✦ Selected the `samba` package during installation

The next two sections provide an overview of installing other Samba-related packages in SUSE's text and graphical versions of YaST.

Installing Samba Packages without a Graphical Interface

If you did not install any graphical interface on your SUSE system by installing any or all of the X11, KDE, or GNOME package sets, SUSE provides a non-graphical version of YaST that you can use to install packages without requiring the X Window system. Figure 18-21 shows the non-graphical version of YaST, which is the program `/sbin/yast` on your SUSE system.

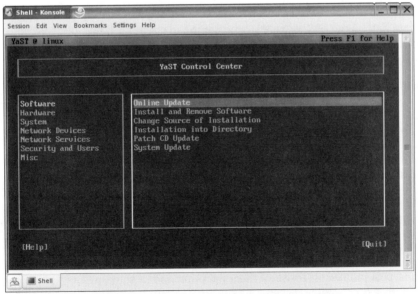

Figure 18-21: Main screen of the non-graphical version of YaST

The non-graphical version of YaST is organized in the same way as the graphical version discussed in the next section, and you can search for packages in the same way, selecting them by pressing the Spacebar when a package is selected in YaST.

The figures throughout this chapter use the graphical version of YaST, more properly known as YaST2, because this is the version of YaST that most people will use (and should, if possible).

Tip   You can run both a Samba client and server without a graphical interface on your system, but you will either have to use YaST in text mode to configure your Samba client or server, or manually edit the configuration files discussed earlier in this chapter and then manually add the Samba client and server to your system's startup procedures.

Installing Samba Packages

If you have problems configuring a Samba client or server or cannot find the YaST Samba Client or Server configuration icons described earlier in this chapter, you can use YaST to verify which Samba packages are installed on your system and install others if necessary. To do this, log in to your system as the root user and start YaST by selecting YaST from the Control Center menu, which is available by clicking the SUSE icon at the bottom-left corner of your KDE desktop, and clicking the Software icon in the left pane. Next, click the Install and Remove Software icon in the right pane to display the Package Selection dialog's Search panel.

To locate Samba-related packages, type **samba** in the Search text box and click the Search button. A listing of available Samba-related packages displays in the Package list of the Search dialog box (see Figure 18-22). The version numbers of the packages that are available will differ depending on the version of SUSE Linux that you are using.

Any packages that are currently installed are preceded by a checkmark. You can select other packages for installation by selecting the check box that precedes their entry in the package list window and clicking the Accept button.

Tip   Some of the Samba documentation is provided in PDF (Portable Document Format) files. You will also need to install Adobe Acrobat Reader (provided in the standard X11 package set), ghostview (provided in the Hacker package set), xpdf (provided in the hacker package set), or another PDF viewer in order to display and read this file on your SUSE system.

Note   Most RPM packages automatically restart any services that they require as part of the post-installation phase of the rpm command. If some part of Samba is not working for you after installing a new package, you can always restart Samba and associated processes by executing the commands /etc/init.d/nmb restart and /etc/init.d/smb restart as the root user.

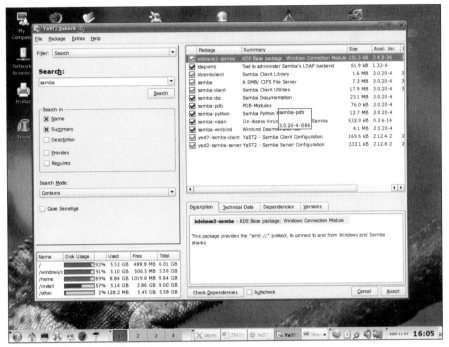

Figure 18-22: Samba packages available in SUSE Linux

The capability to interoperate with other types of computer systems, especially Windows systems, is one of the greatest strengths of Linux. The Samba client and server applications discussed in this chapter make it easy to integrate Linux systems into any networked Windows file and print server environment. A Samba client makes it easy to access existing Windows server resources from your Linux system. A Samba server makes it easy for you to export resources from your SUSE system to the networked Windows environment. Regardless of which way you need to go, or if you need to do both, SUSE provides great graphical tools for Samba client and server configuration through its YaST system administration utility.

✦   ✦   ✦

Setting Up Printing with CUPS

In the early days of Linux, printing was difficult to set up and equally difficult to manage. The print system was known as LPD (line printer daemon). Just as with X configuration, in the early days, at least, grown men wept. I still have bitter memories from 1997 of trying to make sense of the Linux Printing HOWTO and then, when I thought I had cracked it, ending up with a huge stack of paper covered in apparent garbage (raw PostScript code).

Fortunately, those days are gone. The standard now is CUPS (the Common Unix Print System) which implements (among other protocols) IPP (the Internet Printing Protocol). CUPS is also used by Mac OS X and is available for other forms of Unix.

A CUPS server can act as a print server for clients running all operating systems, including Windows. This means that it is not necessary for a Linux server to run Samba (see Chapter 18) to offer printing services to Windows clients.

On SUSE Linux, as one would expect, the configuration of printing has been integrated into YaST. For simple purposes YaST's printer configuration tool is all you need to set up printing both for a single machine and for a print server for a small local network. If you need a print server with more complex requirements, then a knowledge of the CUPS configuration files and possibly also its web interface is useful.

SUSE's default CUPS setup differs only slightly from the standard CUPS defaults. This means that a simple setup for a locally attached printer or a simple network print server works using YaST—you don't need to use the CUPS administration tools.

Printing in Linux: The Role of PostScript

As we hinted previously, the essentials of printing in Linux have their origins in the way printing was handled in traditional Unix systems, which originally printed to line printers that were only capable of printing lines of text characters.

The first printers with graphical capabilities used the PostScript language. As a result PostScript became a standard page description language. PostScript was introduced by Adobe Systems and dates back to 1982. It is both a page description language and a printer control language (that is, it describes the layout of the text and graphical elements on the page and can directly control the printer if the printer uses PostScript as its "native language"). PostScript is actually a full programming language: it is possible to include loops and other programming constructs in PostScript files, which can make the output arbitrarily complicated.

When other printer languages became common, PostScript was still used for the internal representation of the page on Unix systems: the PostScript file was then sent to the printer through a filter that converted it into the printer's native printer language.

Printers from different manufacturers use different control languages to describe the pages they are going to print. In the case of HP printers, this will be one of the versions of PCL (printer control language, which is currently at version 6). Epson printers use a language called ESC/P. Whatever the "native language" of the printer is, when an application wants to print, the PostScript code which the application outputs will need to be converted from PostScript to that native language.

This basic method still applies: normally the Ghostscript program together with the PPD files (PostScript Printer Description files, which describe the capabilities of the printer and how the conversion is to be made) provide the method whereby the PostScript is transformed into the printer's own language.

PostScript as a file format (normally PostScript files have names with the extension .ps) is widely used in Linux documentation and as a way of exchanging formatted printable materials. The programs gv, kghostview, ggv, and others will display PostScript on the screen. A PostScript file is in fact simply a text file with drawing instructions and text characters in it; if you are curious, view a PostScript file with a pager (such as less) or a text editor.

A full description of PostScript is available in documents known as the BLUE BOOK and the RED BOOK, which are available at www-cdf.fnal.gov/offline/PostScript/BLUEBOOK.PDF and http://partners.adobe.com/public/developer/en/ps/PLRM.pdf.

Setting Up a Locally Connected Printer

To begin setting up a printer using YaST, start YaST and from the Hardware menu, select Printer, or from the command line type:

```
yast2 printer
```

You will see the window shown in Figure 19-1.

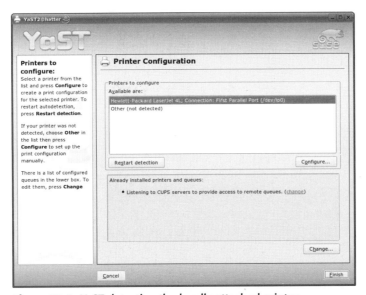

Figure 19-1: YaST detecting the locally attached printer

YaST usually detects any directly attached local printers (such as parallel or USB printers) immediately. For example, in Figure 19-1 a Laserjet 4L was detected on the parallel port.

If the printer has been correctly detected, continue by selecting Configure. Figure 19-2 shows YaST's suggested configuration.

You will find some options here that you can change. In particular, you can change the name that YaST has chosen for the printer (based on its model — in our example `laserjet4l`) to something more descriptive (like `reception` or `marketing`), and you can change the suggested PPD file that will be used. In general, you should accept the recommendation offered by YaST, but you may be able to change the quality of printing, particularly for graphics, by experimenting with the alternative PPD files (see Figure 19-3).

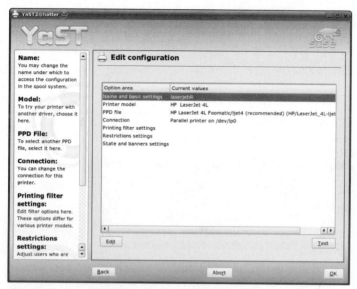

Figure 19-2: YaST's printer module: suggested configuration

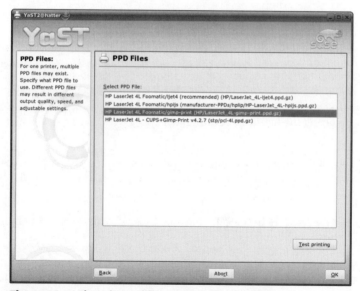

Figure 19-3: Choosing a different PPD file in YaST

About CUPS

CUPS (the Common Unix Printing System) is a network printing system. Whether or not you are printing to a local or a remote printer using CUPS, you will be using a network printing protocol (typically IPP, around which CUPS is based) to connect to `cupsd`, the CUPS daemon. By default CUPS offers a network service on port 631. IPP is essentially an extension of HTTP. Hence the CUPS configuration files look rather like Apache's configuration files.

CUPS offers an administrative interface over HTTP that can be accessed through a URL, such as `http://localhost:631/`. (The SUSE documentation and default settings do not particularly encourage the use of the web administration interface in CUPS, and for simple setups you will not need it.)

A CUPS server that is attached to a printer can advertise its presence on the network by putting out broadcasts; the clients that will print through it learn about the existence of the server from these broadcasts, and if the server allows them to do so, they can print through it without further configuration.

A CUPS server can also print to remote printers using a variety of protocols, including Windows printer shares and direct printing to a network printer.

The CUPS project web pages are at `www.cups.org`.

You can now print a test page. If all is well, the printer will now produce a nice page with a SUSE logo at the top, a photograph of a real chameleon and various colored test images. If nothing comes out of the printer, check that the cable is properly connected. Particularly in the case of a parallel printer, be sure that the cable is not damaged at either end (if a pin is missing or broken on the connector, you can spend a long time wondering why the printer is detected, but no test page is emerging).

In almost all cases, setting up a local printer is as simple as this. There are two problems that might occur. Your printer might not be listed by YaST, and worse, it might not be supported at all.

Printers Not Listed by YaST

If the printer is not listed, this does not necessarily mean that it is not going to work. If the printer is a new one from one of the major vendors such as HP or Epson, there's actually a very good chance that it is a variant of one of the printers that is listed by YaST, but is a slightly changed model that has come on the market recently. So the best strategy is to select the closest model that you can find manually. Then try printing a test page and see what happens. In many cases this will work fine. The information about your printer at `www.linuxprinting.org` may help with this process.

Unsupported Printers

Unfortunately, some printers just won't work on Linux. There is a class of printers known as GDI printers. These tend to be cheap and frankly rather nasty printers; they are designed to interact directly with the Windows graphics device interface, and they do not have an independent open printer control language. These printers are either unsupported or poorly supported in Linux. (This is in a way the printing equivalent of the Winmodem problem.) The best place to get good information about whether particular printers will work is at www.linuxprinting.org, where there is a database of printers currently supported by CUPS as well as good general information and a buyer's guide that has good advice about which printers to avoid.

Printing from Applications

After you have set up a printer, printing from any application should work without problems. In the case of KDE applications, printing is handled through Kprinter (see Figure 19-4), which is a common printing interface with nice features like the ability to print multiple pages on one page. Kprinter both acts as a common print dialog box in all KDE applications and can be used as a standalone printing application. In KDE, you can print files simply by dragging them from Konqueror and dropping them into the Kprinter window. In addition to printing to available printers that have been set up, Kprinter supports printing to files in PostScript and PDF.

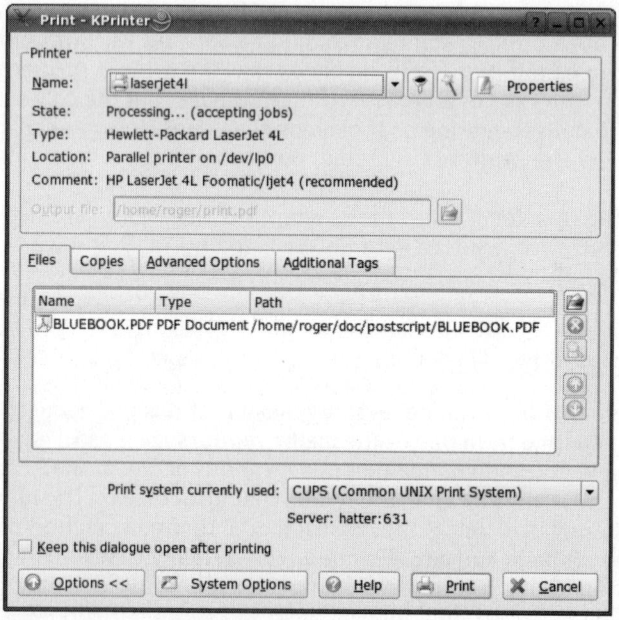

Figure 19-4: Using Kprinter

KDE also has a print monitor. When Kprinter has sent a job for printing, the print status monitor Kjobviewer appears (initially as an icon in the notification area system tray) to show the progress of the print jobs.

Other applications may print directly to the print system rather than going through `kprinter`.

GNOME has its own print tools: the print dialog boxes in the native GNOME applications, and `gnome-cups-manager`, which includes both a print queue viewer and a tool for adding printers. We would tend to advise sticking to YaST for that job, however.

Printing from the Command Line

After printing is set up, you can print various types of files from the command line. The basic command to print a file is `lpr` (or `lp` — they are essentially equivalent, but there are two commands for historical reasons):

```
lpr bible.ps
```

The previous command prints the postscript file `bible.ps` to the default printer.

The file is interpreted as a PostScript file and rendered correctly on the page. In the same way, you can print other standard file types directly from the command line, because appropriate filters to convert them are included in the print system. For example, the following commands will all work (assuming the files really are in the formats suggested by their filenames):

```
lpr bible.pdf
lpr bible.png
lpr bible.jpg
lpr bible.html
```

In the case of PostScript and PDF files, this method is entirely safe and will always produce the desired result. Other file types might sometimes be detected incorrectly. In that case there is a risk that it might try to render the result as plain text on the paper, which is not what you want. In general for HTML and graphics file types, it makes more sense to open them in a screen viewer first (Konqueror or GIMP, for example) and then print using that application's print dialog box. This usually gives you some additional control over the appearance of the final printed copy in any case.

Canceling a Print Job from the Command Line

Sometimes you want to cancel a job that has already been submitted. You need to look at the print queue, select a job, and then remove it.

lpq

The command `lpq` shows the print queue—for example:

```
roger@hatter:~> lpq
laserjet41 is ready
no entries
```

That means that there's nothing left in the print queue. However, if there are jobs in the queue, you will see something like this:

```
Rank   Owner   Job    File(s)           Total Size
laserjet41 is ready and printing
active  roger   118    (stdin)           2725888 bytes
active  roger   119    bible.pdf         1354558 bytes
```

Note   The command `lpq` shows the default print queue. If there is more than one queue and you want to display another queue, then you need to use the option `-P` to specify it, like this:

```
lpq -P laserjet41
```

The Commands cancel and lprm

You could now type `cancel 119` or `lprm 119` to remove the second of these jobs from the queue. Of course, you must be the owner of the job to do this. You may often find that you're too late—the job has gone to the printer and is in the printer's memory. Whether you can easily cancel the job at that stage depends on the printer.

Setting Up a Simple Print Server on the Local Network

If you have successfully set up a printer on the local machine, you have also successfully set up a print server for the local network. The SUSE default settings in the CUPS configuration file `/etc/cups/cupsd.conf` ensure this. If you look at `/etc/cups/cupsd.conf`, in the section Browsing Options, this is controlled by the lines:

```
BrowseAllow @LOCAL
BrowseDeny All
```

The CUPS server advertises itself on the local network and is ready to accept jobs from other machines after they have been set up correctly to print to it. Of course, you can change this behavior if you want to, but for the time being we assume that you have the default configuration on the machine that has the printer attached.

In this example, the printer is attached to the machine hatter, and we are setting up printing on another SUSE Linux machine.

1. Start the YaST printer module. If no printers have been set up before, choose Configure, and you will see a dialog box similar to the one in Figure 19-5.

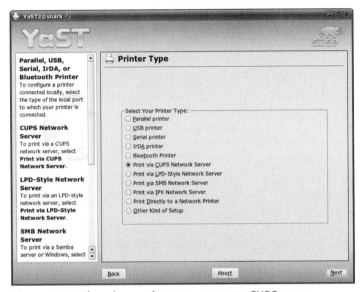

Figure 19-5: Choosing a printer type: remote CUPS server

2. Select Print via CUPS network server and then, in the next screen, choose CUPS Client-Only configuration. You will be asked to give the server name, as shown in Figure 19-6 (or you can allow YaST to detect it, or choose it from a list of all hosts on the network).

3. After you have clicked OK and Finish, you should be able to print to the machine hatter.

Starting and Stopping the CUPS Server

On SUSE, CUPS is started and stopped by the commands rccups start and rccups stop. It is just another service controlled in the usual way. If you make changes to the CUPS configuration files, you will need to restart CUPS for the changes to take effect.

You can check that CUPS is running with the command rccups status. By default, CUPS will be started in runlevels 2, 3, and 5.

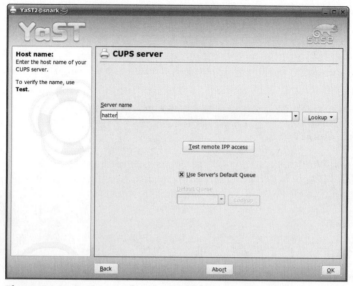

Figure 19-6: Setting up the remote CUPS server in YaST

Checking that the Remote CUPS Server Is Available

From the client machine, you may want to be sure that CUPS is running on the server and available across the network. You can check this by using a command like:

```
telnet hatter 631
```

If you see output like this, CUPS is available across the network:

```
Trying 192.168.2.6...
Connected to hatter.
Escape character is '^]'.
```

Now use Ctrl+] and enter **quit** to disconnect.

If there is a problem you may see this:

```
Trying 192.168.2.6...
telnet: connect to address 192.168.2.6: Connection refused
```

In this case there could be a problem with the network, CUPS might not be running, or there could be a firewall rule on hatter blocking the connection.

Setting Up a Windows Client to Print to the CUPS Server

Recent versions of Windows support the IPP protocol, so you can set them up to print to a CUPS server.

Note To use IPP printing on Windows 95 and 98 you need to download the file `wpnpins.exe` from `www.microsoft.com/windows98/downloads/contents/WUPreviews/IPP/`.

Printing from a Windows client using IPP is an alternative to using Samba as the print server on Linux. The printer does not appear as a Windows shared printer from the point of view of the Windows client, and unfortunately this means that you can't just browse for it as you would for a Windows shared printer or Samba printer. You have to enter the specific URI in the Windows Add Printer Wizard dialog box. Figure 19-7 shows what to expect. The URI that is required is made up of the name or IP number of the CUPS server followed by :631 (the IPP port number), followed by /printers/, and finally the name of the print queue on the server. Hence, you see in our example `http://hatter:631/printers/laserjet4l`.

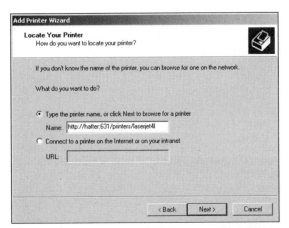

Figure 19-7: Setting up printing to a remote CUPS server in Windows

Printing from Linux to Other Types of Remote Printers

When you add a printer using YaST, a bewildering variety of alternatives are presented. In most cases, if you need the particular protocol or connection type, you will know about it in advance. The most common cases that you are likely to need to set up are printing to a Windows or Samba shared printer and printing directly to a network printer. In YaST these correspond to the Print via SMB Network Server and Print Directly to a Network Printer options.

Printing to an SMB Network Server

This could be a Windows machine that is sharing its printer or a Samba server. From the client's point of view they look just the same.

One thing to note here is that YaST wants to be able to find the server on the network by DNS; it won't automatically use Windows network names. So it is possible in some circumstances that you might need to add an entry to /etc/hosts for the SMB print server before YaST will be able to find it. Otherwise, this will just work.

Printing Directly to a Network Printer

Printers that are directly attached to the network will usually be doing direct TCP port printing and will be listening on port 9100 (the first of the options that YaST's dialog box offers). Setting this up is simple provided you know which printer you want to print to. YaST will scan the network and display a list of available printers for you to choose from in any case.

Using the CUPS Web Interface

The CUPS web interface can be viewed from a browser using port 631 (see Figure 19-8). By default, SUSE's settings allow only administrative changes through the browser interface when connecting from the local machine. This can be changed in the cupsd.conf file, but for now we will look at administering the server from a browser running on itself. So from the local machine, you need to browse to http://localhost:631.

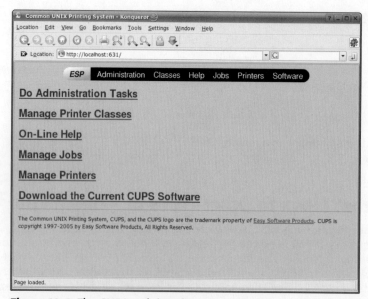

Figure 19-8: The CUPS web interface

If you click the link Do Administrative Tasks or other links that require administrative privileges, an authentication dialog box is displayed (see Figure 19-9).

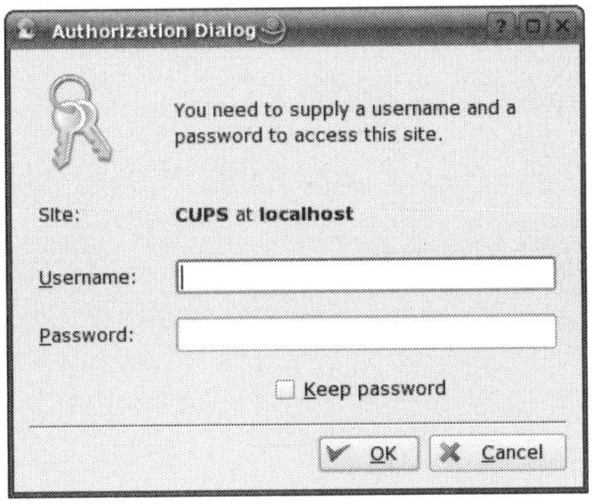

Figure 19-9: The CUPS web interface with authentication dialog box

The SUSE default settings will not allow you to get past this point unless you have first created a CUPS user from the command line using a command like the following:

```
lppasswd -a printman
```

This adds (-a) a CUPS user and prompts you for a password (it's rather fussy about what kind of password it will accept). After doing this, printman is a CUPS user. printman did not need to be a user in /etc/passwd. This is rather like setting up HTTP user authentication. Now you can log into the administrative interface as this user and administer the CUPS server. When you are logged in, you can perform all administration tasks from the web interface, including adding printers. The changes you make will then be written back to the CUPS configuration files.

The user information is specific to CUPS and is stored in the file /etc/cups/passwd.md5.

Working with Classes in CUPS

One of the nice features of CUPS is the fact that you can create a class of printers (for example, a group of printers in a certain physical location). The class will consist of a set of printers to which the CUPS server can print, whether locally connected or across the network. After a class is set up, users' print jobs will be printed on any one of the printers in the class to which they have access.

In the web interface, you can add a class (you will be prompted for its name, location and description, which can all be arbitrary). You then add printers to the class from the list of printers that CUPS already knows about. Figure 19-10 shows adding a class in the CUPS web interface.

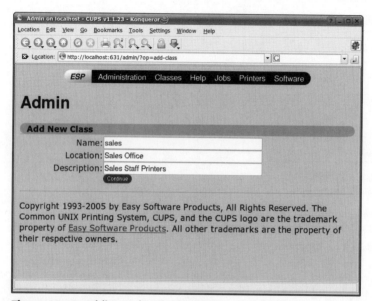

Figure 19-10: Adding a class in the CUPS web interface

After the class is set up, the CUPS server offers the class as a print queue. From a client you can then select that queue to print to in the YaST printer module (see Figure 19-11).

For example, if you are configuring a Windows system to print to the class queue called sales, you would choose http://hatter:631/printers/sales.

Allowing Remote Access to the CUPS Web Interface

As we mentioned earlier in the chapter, by default, CUPS does not allow you to log in to its web interface from a remote location. If you want to change this, you have to edit the file /etc/cups/cupsd.conf. In the section starting

```
<Location /admin>
```

add a line

```
Allow from @LOCAL
```

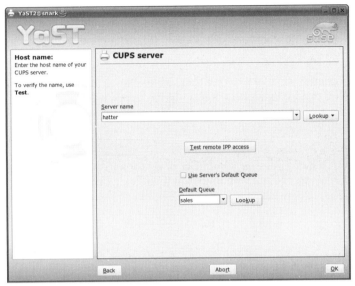

Figure 19-11: Selecting a class as default queue in YaST

Then save the file and restart CUPS:

```
rccups restart
```

Now you can use the web interface from other machines on the local network. Of course you could restrict this to a single IP address if you wanted by replacing @LOCAL by that IP address.

The CUPS Command-Line Tools and Configuration Files

CUPS also provides a set of command-line tools that can do all the administration that the web interface allows. These are the commands provided by the cups-client package; in particular the lpinfo, lpadmin, and lpoptions commands provide the functionality that the web interface provides, but from the command line.

In general, to avoid problems, you should use the available tools in the following order of preference:

✦ The YaST printer module for basic setup

✦ The CUPS web interface

✦ The CUPS command-line tools

In other words, do what you can with YaST. If you can't do a task with YaST, use the CUPS web interface and use the command-line tools only if you have to.

lpinfo

lpinfo shows the potential ways of printing that are available. lpinfo –v shows the potential devices that can be used for printing. lpinfo – m shows the available printer drivers.

lpadmin

The command lpadmin has a very large number of options to administer printing. You will probably prefer to use the web interface if you can, but here are one or two examples:

```
lpadmin –h hatter –p laserjet41 –u allow:roger,justin
```

allows the users roger and justin to print to the queue laserjet41 on the CUPS server hatter.

```
lpdamin –h hatter –p laserjet41 –u deny:badman
```

prevents the user badman from printing to the queue laserjet41 on the CUPS server hatter.

```
lpadmin –p newprinter –c sales
```

Typing this command on hatter will add the printer newprinter to the class sales of printers that we set up earlier.

lpoptions

The command lpoptions can be used to view the current options for a queue or to set new options.

```
root@hatter:~ # lpoptions -p laserjet41 -l
REt/REt Setting: Dark Light *Medium Off
TonerDensity/Toner Density: 1 2 *3 4 5
Dithering/Floyd-Steinberg Dithering: *Normal FSDithered
Manualfeed/Manual Feed of Paper: Off On
InputSlot/Media Source: *Default Tray1 Tray2 Tray3 Tray4 Envelope Manual Auto
Copies/Number of Copies: *1 2 3 4 5 6 7 8 9 10 11 12 13 [. . .] 100
PageSize/Page Size: *A4 Letter 11x17 A3 A5 B5 Env10 EnvC5 EnvDL EnvISOB5 EnvMonarch
Executive Legal
PageRegion/PageRegion: A4 Letter 11x17 A3 A5 B5 Env10 EnvC5 EnvDL EnvISOB5 EnvMonarch
Executive Legal
Resolution/Resolution: 75x75dpi 150x150dpi *300x300dpi
Economode/Toner Saving: *Off On
```

To change an option, do something like this:

```
lpoptions -p laserjet4l -o TonerDensity=5 -o Resolution=150x150dpi
```

This changes the Toner Density and Resolution to new settings.

lpstat

lpstat has many options to provide status information. For example:

```
roger@hatter:~ > lpstat -s
system default destination: laserjet4l
members of class sales:
     laserjet4l
device for laserjet4l: parallel:/dev/lp0
```

This is a summary (-s) of information about the printing system.

lpstat -r tells you whether the CUPS scheduler is available. lpstat -p gives you a
listing of printers and their current status. lpstat -t gives fuller status information.
lpstat -R shows the current print jobs with their owners and ranking in the queue.

The CUPS Configuration Files

The configuration files are in the directory /etc/cups/. The most important files
are cupsd.conf, printers.conf, classes.conf, and lpoptions. Apart from making
changes to cupsd.conf to change authentication settings (which hosts can connect
and so on), in general it is best to make changes from YaST or using the web interface or the command tools, and let CUPS write the configuration files itself. There is
a danger that otherwise you may find that the changes you have made will be overwritten when you use the graphical tools later.

The CUPS Logs

CUPS logs its activity in three log files: /var/log/cups/access_log,
/var/log/cups/page_log, and /var/log/cups/error_log. The names are self-
explanatory.

access_log

The file access_log shows access to the CUPS server in a rather similar way to the
Apache web server logs. It shows the requesting host name and the date for each
access to the CUPS server.

page_log

The file page_log shows the user and the job name, as well as the number of pages printed. Each page printed shows in the file as a serial number against the same job number. By analyzing the page log you can do user accounting. There are a number of tools available for this, including PyKota (www.librelogiciel.com/software/PyKota/).

error_log

This file is not really so much an error log as a place where CUPS logs everything else about its activity. It is useful for debugging problems because it shows what CUPS is doing in the background, for example, which filters are being used to print files and so on.

Other Tools

There are some additional tools (not part of the CUPS package) that are useful for printing.

kprinter

The KDE interface includes the kprinter tool, which handles printing from all KDE applications. You can set other programs to print via kprinter, too. It has the ability to manage (among other things) paper sizes and printing multiple pages to a single physical page.

xpp

xpp is the X Printing Panel, a graphical application similar in conception to kprinter, but independent of KDE. You can use it to browse for files to print, choose print queues to send them to, and choose various options regarding the appearance of the output, the number of copies, and so on.

gtklp

The gtklp package provides the gtklp graphical printing tool. This tool is similar in functionality to xpp but has a cleaner interface. It allows, among other things, scaling and color adjustment when printing image files.

Documentation

As is always the case with SUSE Linux, you can find a great deal of documentation to support you as you set up your printing, both locally and on your networks.

CUPS Online Documentation

The CUPS documentation is installed on the system and can be viewed either through the CUPS web interface locally at `http://localhost:631/documentation.html` or on the CUPS web site at `www.cups.org/documentation.php`. The commands `lp`, `lpr`, `lpadmin`, `lpoptions`, `lpstat`, `lpq` and `lprm` and other CUPS commands all have `man` pages.

The CUPS Book

There is an official CUPS book: *CUPS: Common UNIX Printing System* by Michael Sweet (Sams). The table of contents is at `www.cups.org/book/index.php`.

SUSE Printing Documentation

You can find a good many articles on printing on the SUSE support database, usefully grouped together into a category: `http://portal.suse.com/sdb/en/categories/Printing.html`.

The SUSE Professional Administration guide has a chapter on Printer Administration.

IPP Documentation

You can find more information about IPP on the Printer Working Group's site at `www.pwg.org/ipp/`. This includes links to the relevant RFC documents.

CUPS and the SUSE YaST printer module make setting up printing relatively easy. CUPS has far more capabilities than can be covered here. If you intend to use CUPS in a large networked environment, you should read the full documentation to find out more, in particular about such features as page and job accounting.

✦   ✦   ✦

Configuring and Using DHCP Services

◆ ◆ ◆ ◆

In This Chapter

DHCP overview

Configuring DHCP servers in YaST

Configuring DHCP servers manually

Using DHCP clients

◆ ◆ ◆ ◆

Today's networks are more complex than ever before. In addition to traditional requirements that each user's desktop system be connected to the network, many other devices such as printers, fax machines, laptop and notebook computers, and personal digital assistants (PDAs) now typically require network connections. Because today's networks typically use numerous IP addresses, system administrators must manage the set of IP addresses available to them more effectively within an enterprise and on specific network segments.

Devices like PDAs and notebooks, laptops, and other portable computers bring special requirements to network administration, because they are not always connected to the network and almost always move from place to place. Permanently allocating specific IP addresses to each PDA and portable computer basically wastes those IP addresses when the systems are not connected to the network and may not even be possible in a network environment with many different subnets and associated ranges of IP addresses. For example, if your office and main conference room are on different subnets, you cannot simply move your laptop from one location to another, plug it in, and transparently reconnect to the network.

To allocate and manage IP addresses more efficiently, and enable more flexible network configuration in general, today's networks use a variety of protocols for dynamically obtaining and managing IP addresses and associated network information. This chapter discusses the *Dynamic Host Configuration Protocol (DHCP)*, which is the most common and popular dynamic networking configuration mechanism used today.

What Is DHCP?

DHCP is the latest in a long line of protocols used to provide an IP address and related information to devices that cannot or are designed not to store such information as part of their configuration. Some devices do not have non-transient memory in which an IP address can be stored, which means that the device must request an IP address each time it boots. Even in devices that do have writable storage such as Flash or NVRAM that can preserve configuration information across reboots, not storing an IP address is a common design decision because it provides flexibility in network device configurations. Devices that are designed to dynamically request configuration information each time they boot retain no permanent knowledge of their network environment, which can therefore be flexibly reconfigured without any need to reconfigure the network device itself except by rebooting it.

The oldest of the network boot protocols is the Reverse Address Resolution Protocol (RARP). The processes that service RARP requests, known as RARP daemons, return an IP address based on a configuration file that provides an explicit mapping between a network device's Media Access Control (MAC) address and a specific IP address. A MAC address is a 12-digit hexadecimal number that is stored in the network device and is usually expressed in colon-separated pairs such as MM:MM:MM:SS:SS:SS, where the digits represented by M identify the manufacturer and the digits represented by S specify the serial number assigned to that device by the manufacturer.

RARP daemons can provide only an IP address to a network device. After an IP address has been assigned, network devices that use RARP typically also contain hard-coded instructions in their boot sequence that retrieve other mandatory configuration information, such as a boot image, through a simple download protocol such as the Trivial File Transfer Protocol (TFTP). Because the mapping between MAC and IP addresses is flexible, the name of the file containing additional configuration or boot information must be based on the MAC address, because that is the only non-transient information that is available about the device.

To provide additional flexibility during the boot process for network devices, the Bootstrap Protocol (BOOTP) was introduced as a next-generation network boot protocol. BOOTP is more advanced than RARP because it enables a network device to retrieve both its IP address and the name of a file to download and boot (usually referred to as a boot image). While this provides additional flexibility, standard BOOTP daemons still typically use a configuration file to map MAC addresses to specific IP addresses and associated boot images.

The need to maintain a static mapping between MAC and IP addresses has three main shortcomings:

✦ It limits the number of devices that can use a BOOTP daemon because a limited number of IP addresses are available and the BOOTP configuration file must have a unique, pre-defined IP address for each device that can used BOOTP.

✦ Predefined IP addresses limit BOOTP devices to specific network segments, because the subnet address must also be pre-defined.

✦ Even if different network segments run their own BOOTP daemons, BOOTP requests are typically invoked only at boot time, which requires rebooting devices whenever they are moved across network segment boundaries.

DHCP was developed to provide the flexibility required in modern networked environments, which typically contain multiple subnets and large numbers of networked devices. DHCP is a client/server protocol that is both more powerful and more flexible than its predecessors. DHCP does not require a predefined mapping between MAC and IP addresses; it delivers an IP address to any authorized network device that requests one. DHCP daemons maintain a pool of available IP addresses that are leased to DHCP-aware devices (which are typically referred to as clients of a DHCP server) for a period of time specified in your DHCP server configuration. When the lease expires, the DHCP client can renew the lease to continue using that IP address. If the device is no longer present, the associated IP address is returned to the pool of IP addresses that are available for assignment.

In addition to this increased flexibility in IP address assignment, DHCP delivers a much wider range of network configuration information than previous network boot protocols. DHCP servers can provide DHCP clients with an IP address, host and domain name information, network gateway and other routing information, the address(es) of DNS name servers, and so on. DHCP servers provide backward compatibility with BOOTP daemons and can service BOOTP requests, although they can deliver only the range of information supported by BOOTP.

DHCP is both a boot time and runtime protocol, meaning that network devices can change their IP addresses after they have booted and while they are running. To be able to do this, they must run a DHCP client process that supports dynamic network reconfiguration. The interaction between a DHCP client and a DHCP server is as follows:

1. An unconfigured client sends out a *DHCP discover* packet to the network to see if a DHCP server exists that can answer a request for configuration information.

2. If a server does exist, it sends a response (using the client's MAC address) saying that it can help the client out of a sticky situation with a *DHCP offer*. If a server does not reply with a DHCP offer, the client will retransmit a DHCP discover to try to contact a DHCP server.

3. When a response has been received by the client, the client sends a unicast response to the server asking it for configuration information *(DHCP request)*.

4. The server finally responds back to the client with a *DHCP ACK response* containing the information the client requested.

It is up to the client to ask the server for certain information that it will use. Simply configuring a DHCP server to provide a large amount of information (time servers, WINS servers, and so on) does not mean the client will use that information.

Much of the DHCP software and the standard to which Linux DHCP software adheres is maintained by the Internet Systems Consortium (ISC), whose home page is at www.isc.org. By default, SUSE systems use the DHCP server software from the ISC but use a customized and enhanced DHCP client, dhcpcd, as described in the next section.

The current DHCP protocol and associated BOOTP information are defined in several Internet Request For Comment (RFC) documents: RFC 2131, "Dynamic Host Configuration Protocol" (www.faqs.org/rfcs/rfc2131.html) and RFC 2132, "DHCP Options and BOOTP Vendor Extensions" (http://www.faqs.org/rfcs/rfc2132.html). The original DHCP RFC was RFC 1541, "Dynamic Host Configuration Protocol" (http://www.faqs.org/rfcs/rfc1541.html), which was made obsolete by RFC 2131.

SUSE DHCP Server Packages

The SUSE Linux Professional distribution provides the following DHCP-related packages. Whether or not a specific package is installed on your system depends on the type of installation that you selected.

✦ dhcp — Common files used by both the ISC DHCP server (dhcp-server) and client (dhcp-client) packages.

✦ dhcp-client — An alternative DHCP client from the ISC. This DHCP client uses the same configuration file as the standard dhcpcd client (/etc/dhclient.conf) and also supports additional configuration through a configuration script (/sbin/dhclient-script) that is called by the dhcp-client daemon.

✦ dhcp-devel — Libraries and headers for developing with the Internet Systems Consortium (ISC) dhcpctl API.

✦ dhcp-relay — The ISC DHCP relay agent that routes DHCP messages across physical network segments.

✦ dhcp-server — Provides the ISC DHCP server and associated configuration and documentation files.

✦ dhcp-tools — Provides the dhcpdump and dhcping diagnostic utilities for DHCP. The dhcpdump utility parses tcpdump output and displays DHCP packets for easier analysis. The dhcping utility enables a system administrator to check if a remote DHCP server is up and running.

✦ dhcp6 — A DHCP client and server for IPv6.

✦ dhcpcd — The default DHCP client software used on SUSE systems. The dhcpcd daemon retrieves an IP address and other information from a DHCP server, automatically configures the network interface, and manages lease renewal and release.

✦ yast2-dhcp-server — Support for DHCP server configuration using the SUSE YaST administrative tool.

Setting Up a DHCP Server Using YaST

The SUSE YaST administrative tool makes it easy to configure a DHCP server and integrate it into your system's boot process. This section discusses how to use YaST to configure and autostart a DHCP server for the first time and how to reconfigure an existing DHCP server in YaST.

Like most graphical interfaces to server configuration files, YaST automatically creates and maintains a fully functional DHCP server configuration file for you. However, in more advanced networking and DHCP environments, you may want to edit the configuration file manually to add support for obscure DHCP features or simply to create a more structured and easily deployed DHCP server configuration. For complete information about the format and all possible options in a DHCP server configuration file, see the section "Manually Configuring a DHCP Server" later in this chapter. You can also obtain reference information for the file dhcpd.conf using the man dhcpd.conf command, or consult an online reference site such as www.isc.org/index.pl?/sw/dhcp/ or www.unix.org.ua/orelly/networking/tcpip/appd_03.htm.

Tip
Before you install and configure a DHCP server, you must have already configured at least one network interface on your system. It is generally a good idea to run your DHCP server or servers on systems with fixed IP addresses, which simplifies identifying them and performing subsequent administrative tasks.

Using the YaST DHCP Server Wizard

The first time that you configure a DHCP server in YaST, YaST provides an easy-to-use DHCP Server Wizard that walks you through the basic stages of DHCP server configuration. After you have set up a DHCP server, YaST provides a slightly different interface to the same configuration information, which is discussed in the following section.

To set up and configure a DHCP server for the first time using YaST, do the following:

1. Start YaST and select the Network Services item from the left pane, and select DHCP Server. You will see a screen that lists all available Ethernet interfaces on your system (see Figure 20-1).

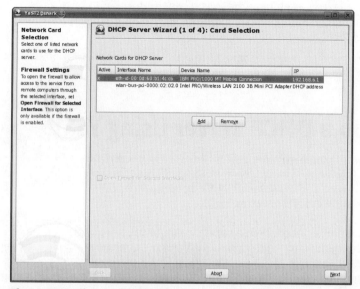

Figure 20-1: The Card Selection screen of the YaST DHCP Server Wizard

> **Note**
>
> If you are trying to configure a DHCP server but have not installed the necessary software, YaST prompts you to install the dhcp-server package and requests the installation DVD or correct installation CDs.

2. Select the network interface on which you want your DHCP server to listen for client DHCP requests. If you are running a firewall, click the Open Firewall for Selected Interface check box. If you do not open the firewall to enable DHCP connections, no other host will see your DHCP server. Click next to display the Global Settings screen (see Figure 20-2).

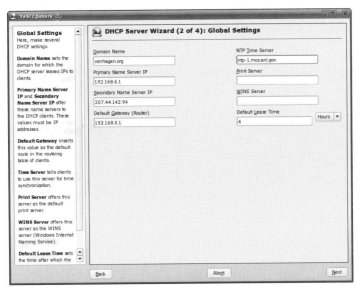

Figure 20-2: The Global Settings screen in YaST's DHCP Server Wizard

3. Enter the name of the domain for which the DHCP server will be answering DHCP client requests, the IP addresses of up to two DNS servers, and the default gateway for your network. If you want systems that obtain network configuration information from your DHCP server to contact an NTP (Network Time Protocol) server to synchronize their clocks, you can optionally specify the name or IP address of the NTP server that you want them to use. You can also optionally specify the name or IP address of a print server and WINS (Windows Internet Name Service) server, on your network. (A WINS server maps NetBIOS names to IP addresses) Finally, you have the option to modify the default duration of IP address leases by entering a new numeric value and specifying the correct units. Figure 20-2 shows some sample values entered for one of the authors' home networks. Click Next to proceed to the screen shown in Figure 20-3.

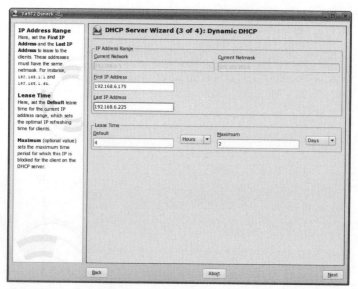

Figure 20-3: The Dynamic DHCP Screen in the YaST DHCP Server Wizard

Tip

If you can't set any of the values on the screen shown in Figure 20-3, chances are that some aspect of the network interface you've selected isn't correctly configured, or that network interface is already being configured by DHCP. For example, if the system on which you are configuring a DHCP server already receives domain or DNS information from another DHCP server, you cannot override those values in your DHCP server. As suggested previously, it is generally a good idea to run a DHCP server on a system and network interface that is statically configured. This not only makes it easier to locate and contact this system in the event of network or DHCP problems, but also provides you with complete control over the DHCP configuration information that is provided by that DHCP server.

4. The Dynamic DHCP screen enables you to specify the range of the IP addresses that your DHCP server can deliver to DHCP clients. Enter the lowest and highest IP addresses that you want your DHCP server to be able to allocate to a client. You must enter a range of IP addresses that are not already in use anywhere on your network and which are valid IP addresses for your network. After entering these values, click Next to proceed to the screen shown in Figure 20-4.

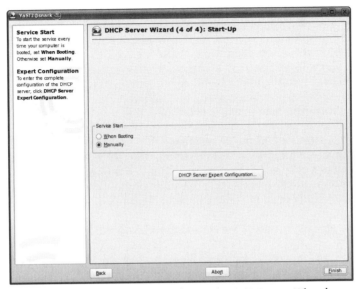

Figure 20-4: The final screen in the YaST DHCP Server Wizard

5. To configure your DHCP server to start automatically whenever you boot your system, click Start DHCP Server When Booting. At this point, you can click Finish to close the DHCP Server Wizard, or click the DHCP Server Expert Configuration button to further modify your configuration information and enter the existing YaST DHCP Server configuration interface that is discussed in the next section.

6. If you selected Finish in the previous step, the DHCP Server Configuration Wizard exits, but your DHCP Server is not actually running yet. To start your DHCP server manually, start or go to a Konsole or other X terminal window, use the su command to become the root user, and execute the following command to start your DHCP server:

```
/etc/init.d/dhcpd start
```

Tip   As previously mentioned, the DHCP Server Wizard displays only the first time you configure a DHCP Server on your system. Subsequent administration is done using the very similar YaST screens discussed in the next section. If you want to re-run the DHCP Server Configuration wizard at any time, you can do so by removing the DHCP server configuration file, /etc/dhcpd.conf.

Reconfiguring an Existing DHCP Server in YaST

As explained in the previous section, YaST provides an easy-to-use and intuitive interface for DHCP server configuration. If you use YaST to configure an existing DHCP server, you will see the YaST screens and dialog discussed in this section. If you have not already configured a DHCP server on your system, YaST walks you through the configuration process using the YaST DHCP Server Configuration Wizard, which was explained in the previous section.

The YaST screens for configuring an existing DHCP server are very similar to those in its DHCP Server Configuration Wizard, except that they do not walk you through a specific sequence of screens. You can select any of the YaST DHCP Server configuration screens at any time by selecting the same of that screen from the tree view in the DHCP Server configuration screen show in Figure 20-5.

To reconfigure an existing DHCP server using YaST, do the following:

1. Start YaST and select the Network Services item from the left pane, and choose DHCP Server. You will see the screen shown in Figure 20-5.

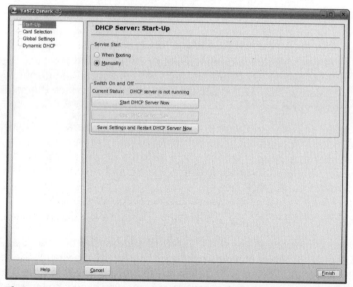

Figure 20-5: The DHCP Server configuration editor's Start-Up screen

2. To modify whether the DHCP server starts automatically, click either the Start DHCP Server When Booting or Start DHCP Server Manually radio buttons. This screen also enables you to start the DHCP server if it is not already running or to save any configuration changes that you have made on other DHCP Server configuration screens and to restart the DHCP server with those settings.

3. To change the Ethernet interface on which your DHCP server is listening for DHCP client requests, click the Card Selection item from the tree view at left in the YaST DHCP Server configuration editor. A screen like the one shown in Figure 20-6 is displayed, in which all available Ethernet interfaces on your system are listed. To specify that the DHCP server listens on another Ethernet interface, simply select the name of that interface from the choices listed on this screen.

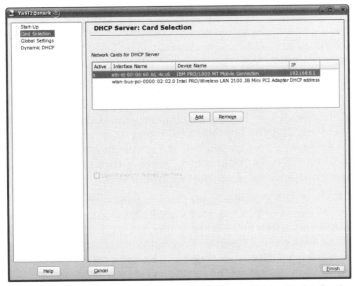

Figure 20-6: The DHCP Server configuration editor's Card Selection screen

4. To change any of the basic network information provided to DHCP clients by your DHCP server, click the Global Settings item from the tree view on the left in the YaST DHCP Server configuration editor. This displays a screen like the one shown in Figure 20-7. To update any of these entries or add a new value, select the appropriate field and enter the new information.

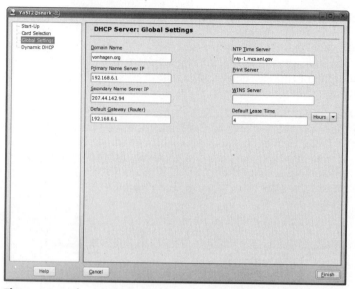

Figure 20-7: The DHCP Server configuration editor's Global Settings screen

5. To modify the range of addresses that your DHCP server can provide in response to DHCP client requests or the duration of the IP address leases given to clients, click the Dynamic DHCP item from the tree view at left in the YaST DHCP Server configuration editor. This displays a screen like the one shown in Figure 20-8. To update any of these entries or add a new value, select the appropriate field and enter the new information.

6. To exit the YaST DHCP Server configuration editor, click Finish. If you have made changes to your DHCP server's configuration, you may first want to go to the DHCP Server Start-Up screen shown in Figure 20-5 and click the Save Settings and Restart DHCP Server Now button to make those changes take effect immediately. Otherwise, those changes will take effect the next time you restart your DHCP server or the next time you reboot your system if you have configured the DHCP server to start automatically at boot time.

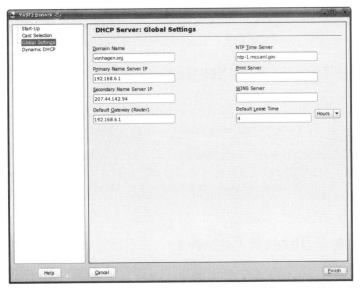

Figure 20-8: The DHCP Server configuration editor's Dynamic DHCP screen

Manually Configuring a DHCP Server

While YaST provides a convenient interface for configuring standard DHCP servers, you can achieve much finer-grained configuration if you configure a DHCP server manually by editing its configuration file. Configuration options for the DHCP server are stored in /etc/dhcpd.conf. The default file is heavily commented, so standard configuration is quite easy. In this section, we will configure a standard server, giving out IP addresses on a range of 192.168.0.10–192.168.0.250 inclusive. We add the relevant configuration options to the /etc/dhcpd.conf configuration file throughout the rest of this section.

Note When configuring your DHCP server, one of the first things you need to think about is whether this server is to be an authoritative DHCP server. When you say that a DHCP server is *authoritative*, you are telling it that it controls DHCP service for the local network. This helps to stop "rogue" servers from confusing your clients.

IP Address Ranges

It is common that you will use DHCP in a small network segment that contains permanent IP assignments for your servers. In this case, you need to exclude some IP addresses from being assigned to your DHCP clients so that duplicate addresses are not created.

Assuming that your servers are between 192.168.0.1 and 192.168.0.9, you can create a range of available IP addresses using the range parameter:

```
range 192.168.0.10 192.168.0.250;
```

This distributes the defined range across your network when a request comes in for DHCP.

Assigning a Default Gateway

Another common network configuration option is to set the default router for your network clients. To do this, you need to specify the option routers parameter.

```
option routers 192.168.0.8;
```

In this example, you have a gateway on your network with the IP address of 192.168.0.8.

Configuring Name Services

To resolve hosts, you need to configure your nameserver addresses and also a domain for the host. This is accomplished by using the domain-name-servers and domain-name options.

```
option domain-name-servers 192.168.0.2, 192.168.0.3;
option domain-name "wileybible.com";
```

ddns-update-style

When using dynamic DNS (updating a DNS server with the name and IP address of an assigned host), you need to specify an update style. There are two on the table at the moment, awaiting standardization. Previous versions of DHCP used an ad hoc mode, and the interim solution until standardization is the interim keyword. Regardless of whether you are using dynamic DNS, you must specify a ddns-update-style in the configuration file. The ad hoc version of dynamic DNS has been deprecated, so the standard is to use interim. As we are not using dynamic DNS in this implementation, we specify none, as we did in Listing 20-1. For more information on using Dynamic DNS with DHCP, take a look at www.mattfoster.clara.co.uk/ddns.htm.

To put this all together, you need to specify a subnet class that defines the address scheme and the options discussed previously (see Listing 20-1).

Listing 20-1: /etc/dhcpd.conf Configuration for a Test Network

```
authoritative;
ddns-update-style none;

subnet 192.168.0.0 netmask 255.255.255.0 {

range 192.168.0.10 192.168.0.250;
option routers 192.168.0.8;
option domain-name-server 192.168.0.2, 192.168.0.3;
option domain-name "wileybible.com";
option time-servers 192.168.0.2;
}
```

Putting all of this together, we have specified that this DHCP server is authoritative for the local network and that we are not using dynamic DNS.

Next, we specify a subnet on the network (192.168.0.0/24).

In this subnet we are allocating IP addresses from a pool between 192.168.0.10 and 192.168.0.250, with a default gateway of 192.168.0.8, and the DNS servers are located at 192.168.0.2 and 192.168.0.3 with a search domain of wileybible.com.

We have also told the client machine that it should synchronize its time with the server 192.168.0.2 (option time-servers).

When configured, you need to specify which network interface DHCP will listen on to provide its service. To do this, edit the /etc/sysconfig/dhcpd file and edit the DHCPD_INTERFACE parameter. If you have multiple Ethernet adapters in your system, it is important to set this explicitly; otherwise, you will probably find your DHCP server running on the wrong network portion. For example, to tell DHCPD to work with the eth0 network interface, use the following:

```
DHCPD_INTERFACE="eth0"
```

When set, start (or restart if currently running) the DHCP server with rcdhcpd start.

Tip   To make sure dhcpd starts when your system boots up, use chkconfig -a dhcpd.

Host Specification

If you have a specific host that needs explicit settings, you can set this with the host section in dhcpd.conf.

For the host specification to work, you need to specify the hardware address of the machine you want to configure. This can be found by issuing the ifconfig command for the interface in question on the client machine. See Listing 20-2 for an example.

Listing 20-2: **Output of ifconfig**

```
bible:~ # ifconfig
eth0      Link encap:Ethernet  HWaddr 00:03:FF:69:68:12
          inet addr:192.168.131.70  Bcast:192.168.131.255  Mask:255.255.255.0
          inet6 addr: fe80::203:ffff:fe69:6812/64 Scope:Link
          UP BROADCAST NOTRAILERS RUNNING MULTICAST  MTU:1500  Metric:1
          RX packets:30256 errors:0 dropped:0 overruns:0 frame:0
          TX packets:35690 errors:0 dropped:0 overruns:0 carrier:0
          collisions:0 txqueuelen:1000
          RX bytes:4048565 (3.8 Mb)  TX bytes:34473633 (32.8 Mb)
          Interrupt:11 Base address:0x1080
```

You can see that in the preceding output for ifconfig, you have found the hardware address (HWaddr) 00:03:FF:69:68:12 for the eth0 interface.

Once you find the hardware address of the machine in question, you can define a host entry in /etc/dhcpd.conf.

```
host bible {
option host-name "bible.wiley.com";
hardware ethernet 00:03:FF:69:68:12;
fixed-address 192.168.0.8;
}
```

The important parts of the host configuration are the hardware ethernet and the fixed-address parameters:

✦ The hardware ethernet parameter needs to be the Hwaddr that is specified through the ifconfig command.

✦ The fixed-address parameter is the IP address that will be used for this host specifically.

Defining Host Groups

If you need to specify explicit configurations for a group of machines, you can use a group definition. A group definition enables you to define a group of machines with a specific configuration that also inherits the global configuration. Consider Listing 20-3.

Listing 20-3: Defining a Host Group

```
group {
   option subnet-mask 255.255.255.0;
   option domain-name-server 192.168.0.2, 192.168.0.3;
   option domain-name "wileybible.com";

   host bible {
   option host-name "bible.wiley.com";
   hardware ethernet 00:03:FF:69:68:12;
   fixed-address 192.168.0.8;
   }

   host sospan {
   option host-name "sospan.wiley.com";
   hardware ethernet 00:03:FF:69:68:13;
   fixed-address 192.168.0.9;
   }
}
```

We now have two machines, bible and sospan, defined as static hosts in dhcpd.conf. Specifically for those machines we have defined only their host name (host-name) and their IP address (fixed-address). As we have defined a group that encompasses the host definitions, these hosts also inherit the subnet mask, DNS servers, and domain name settings.

Note   Make sure you do not forget the opening and closing curly brackets when you define a group.

Specifying Leases

A DHCP client keeps its information for a finite amount of time. You can specify the amount of time (in seconds) a client keeps the DHCP information using the default-lease-time. If the client does not specify a lease expiry time, the server's preference will be used. If a client does specify a lease time, the server can enforce a maximum time, max-lease-time, overriding the client's preference.

Specifying both options puts a limit on the upper and lower lease time allowed for clients to hold the DHCP configuration. (Again, you add both options to /etc/dhcpd.conf.)

```
default-lease-time 43200 # 12 hours
max-lease-time 86400 # 24 hours
```

This example specifies a lower limit of 12 hours, and an upper limit of 24 hours until a lease is renewed on the client.

Other DHCP Options

DHCP is an extremely powerful configuration tool when you have many client machines that must be configured. It is not just limited to IP address allocation and can be extended to encompass a large proportion of network configuration, from WINS servers to network time servers.

View the dhcp-options man page for more information on what options your DHCP server can present to your network clients.

Starting and Stopping DHCP Clients

To be able to use DHCP, your client machines must know how to actually send DHCP requests to the network for configuration. In SUSE, you can use the Network Configuration of YaST (Network Devices ➪ Network Card) to configure a network interface to use DHCP.

Another useful way to send a DHCP request is with ifup-dhcp and ifdown-dhcp. If you are using a wireless network, or you want to bring up a network interface temporarily using DHCP, then you can use the ifup-dhcp command:

```
bible:~ # ifup-dhcp eth0
Starting DHCP Client Daemon on eth0... . . .
```

This command starts the DHCP client and attaches it to the eth0 interface.

In the event that you want to remove the DHCP client from a network interface, thus removing its dynamic network configuration, you need to use the ifdown-dhcp command:

```
bible:~ # ifdown-dhcp eth0
```

This removes the DHCP client from the network card specified, in this case eth0.

Troubleshooting DHCP Clients and Servers

You will rarely encounter problems with starting or using a DHCP server, which makes these problems even more frustrating when they occur. On the other hand, DHCP client problems are quite common, usually resulting from the presence of multiple, unsynchronized DHCP servers on your network. This section provides some tips for identifying and resolving DHCP client and server problems.

Troubleshooting DHCP Clients

Most of the problems that you may see in DHCP environments are related to DHCP clients that somehow retrieve erroneous information from a DHCP server. This is almost always the result of people starting DHCP servers on other systems that either serve the same range of IP addresses as your DHCP server or serve an entirely different set of IP addresses.

If a DHCP client on your system retrieves an IP address that is in the same range as those delivered by your DHCP server but any other aspect of its network configuration differs, you will have to look for another DHCP server on your network that delivers the same range of IP addresses but provides slightly different network configuration information. If a DHCP client on your system retrieves an IP address that is in a completely different range of IP addresses, some user on your network has probably either started a DHCP server that is misconfigured or has accidentally started a DHCP meant for one Ethernet interface on another Ethernet interface. The latter is a common problem in network environments that include multihomed systems, which are systems with multiple Ethernet interfaces, each connected to a separate network.

Regardless of the type of erroneous information that DHCP clients are retrieving, you can use the dhcpcd-test utility (part of the dhcpcd package) to examine the information that they are retrieving from a DHCP server. To use this utility, execute the dhcpcd-test command followed by the name of an Ethernet interface on your system. Listing 20-4 is an example of the information retrieved from a DHCP server for the Ethernet interface, which is a wireless card on my laptop.

Listing 20-4: **Retrieving Information from a DHCP Server**

```
# dhcpcd-test eth1
dhcpcd: MAC address = 00:02:2d:31:b8:c8
IPADDR=192.168.6.242
NETMASK=255.255.255.0
NETWORK=192.168.6.0
BROADCAST=192.168.6.255
GATEWAY=192.168.6.1
```

Continued

Listing 20-4: *(continued)*

```
DOMAIN='vonhagen.org'
DNS=204.127.202.4,216.148.227.68
DHCPSID=192.168.6.200
DHCPGIADDR=0.0.0.0
DHCPSIADDR=192.168.6.200
DHCPCHADDR=00:02:2D:31:B8:C8
DHCPSHADDR=00:30:65:3C:7E:22
DHCPSNAME=''
LEASETIME=4080
RENEWALTIME=2040
REBINDTIME=3570
INTERFACE='eth1'
CLASSID='Linux 2.6.11.4-20a-default i686'
CLIENTID=00:02:2D:31:B8:C8
```

Pay particular information to the DHCPSIADDR value, which is the IP address of the
DHCP server from which this information was retrieved. If this is not the IP address
of the system on which your official DHCP server is running, track down that system and either terminate or reconfigure its DHCP server or restart it on the correct
Ethernet interface.

Troubleshooting DHCP Servers

If DHCP clients are not able to contact your DHCP server, use YaST to install the
dhcp-tools package discussed earlier in this chapter in the "SUSE DHCP Server
Packages" section. This package provides the dhcping utility, which you can use to
attempt to contact your DHCP server and retrieve an IP address. The basic syntax
of this command is the following:

```
dhcping -c valid-IP-address -s DHCP-server-IP-address
```

You must substitute the IP address of your client for valid-IP-address and the IP
address of the DHCP server that you are trying to contact for DHCP-server-IP-
address. This command will either respond with the message "no answer" if it was
unable to contact the DHCP server or the message "Got answer from: DHCP-server-
IP-address" if the command was successful.

You can use the dhcpdump command to obtain more detailed information about
DHCP traffic on your network. The dhcpdump command, also provided in the dhcp-
tools package, filters DHCP-related information from packet capture information
retrieved by the tcpdump command, as in Listing 20-5.

Listing 20-5: **Using tcpdump**

```
# tcpdump -lenx -s 1500 | dhcpdump
 Error in packet: .
  TIME: 01:27:46.168382
    IP: 192.168.6.200.1024 (00:30:65:3c:7e:22) > \
      255.255.255.255.514 (ff:ff:ff:ff:ff:ff)
n    OP: 60 (Boot file size)  HTYPE: 49 ((null))
  HLEN: 52
  HOPS: 50
   XID: 3e303537
  SECS: 14112
 FLAGS: 33fc
CIADDR: 48.32.68.72
YIADDR: 67.80.32.83
SIADDR: 69.82.86.69
GIADDR: 82.32.79.102
CHADDR: 66:65:72:65:64:20:20:20:20:20:20:20:20:20:7c:20
 SNAME: Offering: 192.168.6.243  To: 00112F8D94B8  By: 192.168.6.200.
 FNAME: .
---------------------------------------------------------------------
 Error in packet: :
  TIME: 01:28:15.044104
    IP: 192.168.6.246.2190 (00:06:25:07:f7:0e) > 192.168.6.255.2190 (ff:ff:ff:ff:ff:ff)
    OP: 116 (SMTP server)
 HTYPE: 105 (Static route)
  HLEN: 118
  HOPS: 111
   XID: 636f6e6e
  SECS: 25955
 FLAGS: 73c9
CIADDR: 49.10.115.119
YIADDR: 118.101.114.115
SIADDR: 105.111.110.61
GIADDR: 55.46.49.97
CHADDR: 2d:30:32:2d:32:2d:32:34:30:0a:6d:65:74:68:6f:64
 SNAME: =broadcast
identity=2400000804DC8FA
machine=Living Room
platform=tcd/Series2
services=TiVo-ServeTcdVideo-1:2191/tvbus_v3,TiVoMediaServer:80/http

 .
 FNAME: =tcd/Series2
services=TiVo-ServeTcdVideo-1:2191/tvbus_v3,TiVoMediaServer:80/http

 .
---------------------------------------------------------------------
 2 packets captured
 2 packets received by filter
 0 packets dropped by kernel
```

This output shows two packets that are identified as DHCP traffic. The first shows an attempt to contact the DHCP server at the IP address 192.168.6.200, which was successful and which is offering the IP address 192.168.6.245 to the client. The second, unrelated packet shows broadcast DHCP traffic from a TiVo on the author's home network, which is requesting SMTP server contact information.

Wrapping Up

DHCP is something that any administrator needs to know when it is no longer practical to assign static IP addresses to the hosts on your network. Thanks to the power and flexibility of YaST and the other administrative tools provided with SUSE Linux, DHCP can be quickly and easily configured to provide TCP/IP information to all of the hosts on your network, eliminating the need to do SABWA—system administration by walking around.

✦   ✦   ✦

Configuring a DNS Server

We have talked about a few backbone services of the
Internet in this book, but one of the most important
ones is the role of the nameserver. Imagine life without names;
going to your favorite search engine (e.g., www.google.com)
would involve your having to type http://66.102.11.104.
Not so bad, but if you had ten favorite sites, you would have
to remember all of those addresses. As TCP/IP needs to use
IP addresses to make a connection to another machine, the
Domain Name System (DNS) is important to bridge the gap
between the human and the computer. The role of DNS is not
just to translate names to IP addresses, but also to form the
basis for mail server lookups and reverse name lookups
(IP addresses to names).

The most popular DNS server on the Internet is BIND
(Berkeley Internet Name Daemon). BIND truly is an open
source success, on the par with Apache. Both are terribly
important to the function of the Internet, and both are very
well-written pieces of software.

Some DNS Theory

As is customary in the Unix world, DNS is distributed and
hierarchical in design. The DNS management is controlled
locally in a domain, and this is something that may need to be
explained. The dictionary tells us that domain is a " territory
over which rule or control is exercised." The term *domain* has
been used to describe a domain name, but its meaning is still
the same, a territory over which control is exercised.

Take our domain of `palmcoder.net` — we control all the information about the `palm-coder.net` territory on the Internet, and any mistakes or misconfiguration in DNS are under our control. This takes away a huge management burden from a central authority. With millions of web sites in the world, it would take more than an army of monkeys to smoothly run the Internet.

Even though domain control is up to the masses, a central control still needs to exist to allow everyone to query data in the distributed system. These centrally managed servers are called the *root DNS servers*. They control the top-level domains (TLDs) of the Internet, and this helps to facilitate the idea of a massively distributed network.

Top-Level Domains

Top-level domains (TLDs) encompass the `.com`, `.net`, `.org`, `.co.uk`, and other similar domains on the Internet. These top-level domains contain information about lower-level domains in the DNS address space. For example, `palmcoder.net` is under the control of the `.net` namespace (not the Microsoft programming architecture!).

In Figure 21-1, you can see that `palmcoder.net` falls under the administrative domain of the `.net` TLD.

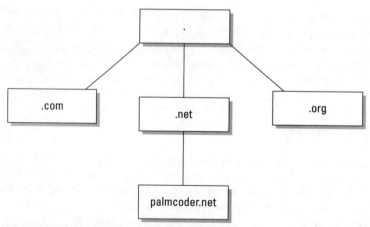

Figure 21-1: Top-level domain organization

There are many top-level domains that serve to segregate the domain name space. Table 21-1 lists some of the most common ones.

Table 21-1 Top-Level Domains	
TLD	**Use**
.com	Commercial organizations
.net	Network of machines
.org	Non-profit organizations
.mil	U.S. military
.gov	U.S. government
.co.uk	U.K. company

How Does a DNS Search Work?

We can take a look at how a DNS search takes place to put the idea of a distributed, hierarchical system into context.

1. Take our laptop as an example—the name lookup system is configured to get all name translations from our DNS server at 192.168.1.1. When we go to `www.google.com`, the laptop contacts 192.168.1.1 and asks it for the address of `www.google.com`. As our DNS server is a caching server (we talk about this later in the chapter), it contacts a public DNS server to see if it knows it.

2. The public DNS server at 194.106.56.6 accepts our DNS request and attempts to find the IP address of Google for us. As this public DNS server does not know the address directly (it does not control the Google domain), it asks a root DNS server if it knows the IP address of Google. Because the root name-servers do not control the Google domain, they tell our Internet service provider's domain server that it should ask the DNS server that controls the `.com` domain.

3. The public DNS server then queries the `.com` DNS server for the IP address of `www.google.com`. As the `.com` DNS server does not know the address directly, it refers the ISP DNS to the DNS server that controls the `google.com` domain (which the `.com` server knows about).

4. The ISP then asks the `google.com` DNS server if it knows the address of `www.google.com`. This time we strike it lucky, as the Google nameserver knows the address and returns this IP address to our ISP's DNS server.

5. When the ISP's DNS server knows the IP address, it passes this address back to our local DNS server, which finally returns it to our laptop.

As you can see, the DNS system works by servers cooperating with each other to find the answer to a DNS query. This helps to alleviate the burden of name resolution on a single root DNS server or a small group of root DNS servers.

Caching

You can imagine that with all the machines in the world wanting the IP address of Google that it would severely impact the performance of the root, .com, and Google DNS servers. To combat this, most local DNS servers cache the result of a query for a period of time that is called a *TTL (Time to Live)*. Until this countdown is reached, subsequent DNS lookups for www.google.com will be answered by the local DNS server.

In this chapter, we talk about configuring a forwarding/caching server, and we also create a small domain to control.

Configuring BIND for Caching and Forwarding

After installing the BIND DNS server using YaST, you need to edit its main configuration file /etc/named.conf. When you are configuring BIND to act as a central DNS server for your home or an organization, it is always a good idea to tap into your Internet service provider's DNS server as a resource to provide you with public DNS lookups. When you rely on another DNS server to go and find your DNS lookups, it is called a forwarder because it literally forwards your DNS lookups to another DNS server with the added benefit of caching the response so that future lookups of the data are returned locally by your DNS server.

Note   BIND is available with both the Professional and Enterprise versions of SUSE.

To edit DNS server settings from now on, you will have to be logged in as the root user.

Tip   You can also configure your DNS client and server through YaST. This chapter concentrates on direct configuration of the services so that you know how the system works. If you want to configure a DNS server, start YaST and navigate to Network Services ➪ DNS Server. If you want to configure your DNS client, navigate to Network Services ➪ DNS and Host Name.

The important entry in /etc/named.conf is the forwarders declaration. A *forwarder* is a DNS server that your DNS server passes requests to when your DNS installation does not know the answer.

```
forwarders { 194.106.56.6; 192.106.33.42; };
```

We have used two DNS servers for resilience purposes in this example, so that if the first DNS server cannot be contacted, the second one will be used. Note that a semicolon separates the forwarders, and the line is delimited with a semicolon.

Note When a BIND server has been configured as a forwarder, it automatically caches any answers it receives from the Internet DNS servers. No extra configuration is needed to enable this caching functionality.

When the `forwarders` declaration is configured, start the nameserver with `rcnamed`:

```
bible:~ # rcnamed start
Starting name server BIND 9                         done
```

To automatically set `named` to start when your system boots, use `chkconfig -a named`.

Before you start testing the DNS server, you need to configure the system resolver. To do this, you need to edit the `/etc/resolv.conf` file. Change the nameserver entry to point to your newly created DNS server. In this case, this is 127.0.0.1.

```
search palmcoder.net
nameserver 127.0.0.1
```

When the DNS server is started, you can look up a host name on the Internet to check that the forwarder and DNS are working correctly. The `dig` program is used to query a DNS server for information (see Listing 21-1), and we use it throughout this chapter for this purpose.

Using dig

The `dig` program is being phased in as a replacement for the `nslookup` application. With `dig`, you can query specific record types in a DNS zone. To query a specific record type, use the -t option. For example:

✦ To query the MX record of `palmcoder.net`, use `dig -t m x palmcoder.net`.

✦ For a nameserver (NS), use `dig -t ns palmcoder.net`.

✦ For an address record (A), use `dig -a www.palmcoder.net`.

Listing 21-1: Using dig to Test a DNS Server

```
bible:~ # dig www.palmcoder.net
;; Warning: ID mismatch: expected ID 23997, got 50172
;; Warning: ID mismatch: expected ID 23997, got 50172

; <<>> DiG 9.2.3 <<>> www.palmcoder.net
;; global options: printcmd
;; Got answer:
;; ->>HEADER<<- opcode: QUERY, status: NOERROR, id: 23997
;; flags: qr rd ra; QUERY: 1, ANSWER: 2, AUTHORITY: 1, ADDITIONAL: 0
```

Continued

Listing 21-1 *(continued)*

```
;; QUESTION SECTION:
;www.palmcoder.net.            IN     A

;; ANSWER SECTION:
www.palmcoder.net.     38396   IN      CNAME   zen.palmcoder.net.
zen.palmcoder.net.     38400   IN      A       212.13.208.115

;; AUTHORITY SECTION:
palmcoder.net.         38400   IN      NS      zen.palmcoder.net.

;; Query time: 443 msec
;; SERVER: 127.0.0.1#53(127.0.0.1)
;; WHEN: Tue Jul  6 10:02:21 2004
;; MSG SIZE  rcvd: 83
```

Tip   In the past, the name resolver tool `nslookup` was used in place of `dig`; `nslookup` is now deprecated, but is included in most Linux distributions. If you want to do a quick name resolution, using `nslookup hostname` returns the IP address.

The output of `dig` may be confusing if you have never used it before, but its response to a name query is logical when you understand what DNS does. The output contains three basic parts:

✦ The first part of the response is the QUESTION section. The QUESTION is what was sent originally to the DNS server. In this case, you asked for the A record of `www.palmcoder.net`. (Note that we talk about record types later in the chapter.)

✦ The second part is the ANSWER section. The answer is the response to your question. In this case, you have been told the `www.palmcoder.net` is a CNAME of `zen.palmcoder.net`, and `zen`'s address is 212.13.208.115.

✦ Finally, you have the AUTHORITY section. The authority is the controlling server's IP address in the NS record.

Using host

A user-friendly replacement for the `nslookup` program that enables you to query the DNS for information about a domain is `host`. Using `host`, you can query a specific domain record and by default look up the address mapping of a host name.

```
bible:~ # host www.palmcoder.net
www.palmcoder.net is an alias for zen.palmcoder.net.
zen.palmcoder.net has address 212.13.208.115
```

In this example, host has queried the nameserver that is authoritative for the palm-coder.net domain and has found that the host name www.palmcoder.net is actually a CNAME for zen.palmcoder.net with an address of 212.13.208.115.

If you want to find a specific domain record for a domain, you use the -t option, specifying the record type:

```
bible:~ # host -t mx palmcoder.net
palmcoder.net mail is handled by 10 mail.palmcoder.net.
palmcoder.net mail is handled by 20 pirhana.bytemark.co.uk.
```

Here, host has queried the nameserver that is authoritative for palmcoder.net, asking for the MX record for the domain. It has found that there are two mail exchangers, mail.palmcoder.net and pirhana.bytemark.co.uk, with mail.palmcoder.net taking precedence over pirhana.bytemark.co.uk.

Examining Record Types

Before we delve into creating a zone (an administrative domain) in DNS, we need to talk about *record types*. We briefly touched upon the fact that DNS provides not only host name–to–IP address translation, but also mail server information.

A record type tells DNS what kind of information it is storing. This record type is also something you can explicitly query. For example, you can query the MX record for a domain to find out what mail server to use when sending a recipient in the domain mail. Services that rely on DNS (such as mail or name resolution) query a specific record in the DNS database for specific hosts. This drastically reduces the amount of traffic that is produced because you see only the data you explicitly asked for, and not the whole record. What makes this happen is the use of record types. With DNS, you have six main record types to keep in mind:

- ✦ **The Address record** — The most common record in DNS is the Address record. An Address record is used to translate a host name to an IP address.

- ✦ **The Pointer record** — A Pointer record is the reverse of an Address record. It translates an IP address to a host name.

- ✦ **The CNAME record** — If you want to create an alias of one host to another, a CNAME entry is used.

- ✦ **The MX record** — An MX record is used to define a Mail Exchanger for the domain (or zone) you have created.

- ✦ **The NS record** — The NS record is used to define the nameserver for this domain.

- ✦ **The SOA record** — The Start of Authority (SOA) is effectively the header for the zone in question. It contains information about the zone itself and is mandatory.

Working with Zones

A *zone* is a description, or a definition, of a domain (or subdomain). The zone is what makes up the database full of records for a domain. *Zone files* are separate files located in `/var/lib/named` and are text files containing the data for the zone. BIND defines its zones in `/etc/named.conf` by specifying the location of these zone files.

In this section you will see how a DNS zone is constructed and what information you can store for a specific zone.

We use `palmcoder.net` as an example of a zone (see Listing 21-2) and will go through the DNS records and explain their uses.

Listing 21-2: **The palmcoder.net Zone**

```
palmcoder.net.   IN      SOA      zen.palmcoder.net. justin.palmcoder.net. (
                 200407111
                 10800
                 3600
                 604800
                 38400 )
                 NS      zen
                 MX      10 mail
                 MX      20 pirhana.bytemark.co.uk.

zen                      A       212.13.208.115
www                      CNAME   zen
mail                     A       212.13.208.115
sospan                   CNAME   zen
shuttle                  A       195.137.34.245
```

The Start of Authority

At the start of the zone, you have the SOA record. The Start of Authority dictates that this zone is authoritative for the domain in question, `palmcoder.net`.

> **Note** Notice that `palmcoder.net` ends in a full stop (a period for our American cousins). This is extremely important in the zone file for any domain. As you saw in Figure 21-1, the top of the DNS tree is the root of the DNS tree. A full stop is the delimiter for the end of the DNS tree, following the `palmcoder.net` domain all the way up the tree, the full domain name is `palmcoder.net` (with the full stop). If a full stop is not found, as in the `zen` record listed at the end in the example, the SOA's domain will be appended to the host name in the record.

The SOA can be further analyzed to break down the record's uses.

The SOA Server

After the definition of the domain you are managing, you need to define the server that is authoritative for the domain. It may seem bizarre, but you are referring to a name, not an IP address in this case, because BIND is aware that it needs to find the IP address for the server from its zone file (it may sound like a vicious circle, but it does work). In Listing 21-2, for example, the SOA for `palmcoder.net` is `zen.palmcoder.net`.

The Hostmaster

As with most things on the Internet, it is common practice to provide a technical contact for the service. In this case, it is the email address `justin.palmcoder.net`. You will notice that there is no @ sign in the email address, but a full stop (period). The hostmaster for the `palmcoder.net` zone is `justin.palmcoder.net` (justin@palmcoder.net).

 Tip

If the email address of the hostmaster contains a full stop, you need to "escape" it. For example, if your email address is `justin.davies@palmcoder.net`, the hostmaster entry is `justin\.davies.palmcoder.net`.

The SOA Record

The brackets around the rest of the data dictate that everything else up to the closing bracket is part of the SOA record. All time settings are in seconds.

The Serial Number

The first entry is the serial number for the zone. This is one of the most important parts of the SOA because it must be changed any time you edit the zone file. It is the serial number that tells other DNS servers that are querying your DNS server that data has changed. If you do not change the serial number, your changes will not get propagated through the system.

The general form of the serial number is the date, followed by an arbitrary number. For the 24th of July, you use 2005072401 (July 24, 2005). Notice that the date is in reverse, with the year (2005), month (07), and day (24), with an additional two digits able to represent multiple changes in one day.

The Refresh Rate

If you have a slave DNS server in your system (as a backup to your master), the refresh rate tells the slave server how often to check for updates to the zone. If you look back at Listing 21-2, you will see the refresh rate set to 10,800 seconds (3 hours).

The Retry Rate

If your slave server cannot contact the master, the retry rate is how often it will attempt to contact the master. In Listing 21-2, we have set the retry rate to 3,600 seconds (1 hour).

The Expiry Time

If the slave server cannot update the zone data in this time, it stops functioning. In Listing 21-2, we have set the expiry time to 604,800 seconds (1 week).

The Time to Live

When a server caches your DNS data (for example, if a home DNS server looks up www.palmcoder.net), this is how long that data will stay in the cache until a fresh query is sent to the authoritative server. This is a very important entry because any changes you make to your zone will not propagate potentially until this TTL has expired. In Listing 21-2, we have set the TTL to 38,400 seconds (10 hours).

The NS Entry

Every zone should have an NS (nameserver) entry, and in this case, the nameserver for palmcoder.net is the machine zen (remember that with no full stop, it gets expanded to zen.palmcoder.net).

The Mail Exchanger

If you want to receive mail for your domain, you must specify an MX record for it. The MX record is used to define the host that receives mail for this domain. When an SMTP server needs to find the host that handles mail for a domain, it will query the MX record for the machine to connect to.

You can see a number in the second field of this record, and this is very important. The number is a preference order for the MX host specified. The lower the number, the higher the preference. So in this case, all SMTP transactions for this domain will attempt to connect to mail.palmcoder.net, and if that fails they will try the machine pirhana.bytemark.co.uk (the backup MX server).

Note   The host machine for the domain is called mail.palmcoder.net according to its IP entry in DNS, but we have an alias configured, calling the machine zen. When defining an MX record, you must not use a CNAME record; it must be an Address record.

The Address Record

We have defined a machine called `zen` (no full stop), with the IP address of 212.13.208.115. This is the bread and butter of the Internet here, folks; savor it! This is the record that points a host name to an IP address, and it is no different from the record used for `www.google.com`.

The CNAME Record

To create an alias of a host so that a lookup returns the same IP address, you use a CNAME record. It is an alias for a host name, and we have found it most commonly used to define the address `www.hostname.tld` when the web server is on the same host as the DNS server.

When you have it composed, the zone file can be saved as a standard text file. You then need to add the zone to the `named.conf` file so that BIND can load and serve the zone to the network.

Adding the Zone to named.conf

To add the zone to the BIND server, you need to create a zone reference in `named.conf`:

```
zone "palmcoder.net" {
    type master;
    file "/var/named/palmcoder.net";
};
```

This defines the zone `palmcoder.net`, which is the master for this zone and is located in the file `/var/lib/named/palmcoder.net`. When the zone is defined, you need to reload the DNS server's data with `rcnamed reload`:

```
bible:~ # rcnamed reload
Reloading name server BIND 9                           done
```

Note   When you define a node, you must specify the type of the zone itself. In this case, we have defined the zone as a *master*. This means that this zone definition is the authority for this domain. Other options you can use are *slave* — this zone definition is in fact a secondary DNS server that obtains its zone information from a primary (master) DNS server; and *forward* — this zone definition refers any queries for this domain to another DNS server with the use of a `forwarders` definition.

You can now use `dig` to test your new DNS zone (see Listing 21-3).

> ## Listing 21-3: **Testing the DNS Zone with dig**
>
> ```
> bible:~ # dig -t MX palmcoder.net
>
> ; <<>> DiG 9.2.3 <<>> -t MX palmcoder.net
> ;; global options:  printcmd
> ;; Got answer:
> ;; ->>HEADER<<- opcode: QUERY, status: NOERROR, id: 5484
> ;; flags: qr aa rd ra; QUERY: 1, ANSWER: 2, AUTHORITY: 1, ADDITIONAL: 2
>
> ;; QUESTION SECTION:
> ;palmcoder.net.                 IN      MX
>
> ;; ANSWER SECTION:
> palmcoder.net.          38400   IN      MX      10 mail.palmcoder.net.
> palmcoder.net.          38400   IN      MX      20 pirhana.bytemark.co.uk.
>
> ;; AUTHORITY SECTION:
> palmcoder.net.          38400   IN      NS      zen.palmcoder.net.
>
> ;; ADDITIONAL SECTION:
> mail.palmcoder.net.     38400   IN      A       212.13.208.115
> zen.palmcoder.net.      38400   IN      A       212.13.208.115
>
> ;; Query time: 57 msec
> ;; SERVER: 127.0.0.1#53(127.0.0.1)
> ;; WHEN: Tue Jul  6 10:44:00 2004
> ;; MSG SIZE  rcvd: 147
> ```

We have specifically asked the DNS server for the MX record (using the -t option) for palmcoder.net that we just created. Comparing this with the zone, you can see this information is correct.

The Reverse Zone

If you want to be able to resolve IP addresses to host names, you need to set up a *reverse zone* for the domain. A reverse zone is very similar to a forward zone with the IP address–to–host name records being called *pointers*.

When you are setting up a public DNS server that controls a domain (as in the case of palmcoder.net), it is unlikely that you will be able to use a reverse zone, and the authority for the range of IP addresses your ISP has allocated to you will be controlled by their DNS servers. You will be very lucky to find an ISP that will hand over delegation of an IP address in the DNS system to you.

When you are running a DNS server in a network where you control the IP address allocation (for example, using non-routable addresses), a reverse zone is possible.

We will take the following zone as the internal forward representation (see Listing 21-4) and work back from that.

Listing 21-4: **Internal DNS Representation**

```
intpalmcoder.net.  IN    SOA    ns.intpalmcoder.net. admin.intpalmcoder.net. (
                   200407111
                   10800
                   3600
                   604800
                   38400 )
               NS    zen
               MX    10 mail

mail           A    192.168.0.2
files          A    192.168.0.5
intranet       A    192.168.0.10
```

In this zone definition, we have used the default zone values as before, with the addition of a nameserver entry of `zen.palmcoder.net` and a mail exchanger entry of `mail.palmcoder.net`. We have also defined address entries for `mail.palmcoder.net` of 192.168.0.2, `files.palmcoder.net` with an address of 192.168.0.5, and `intranet.palmcoder.net` with an address of 192.168.0.10.

Now that we have the internal network configuration, we can create the reverse zone to allow our internal IP addresses to be resolved into their respective host names (see Listing 21-5).

Listing 21-5: **Reverse Zone for 192.168.0.0/24**

```
@ IN   SOA    ns.intpalmcoder.net. admin.intpalmcoder.net. (
              200407111
              10800
              3600
              604800
              38400 )

       NS     ns.intpalmcoder.net.
2      PTR    mail.intpalmcoder.net.
5      PTR    files.intpalmcoder.net.
10     PTR    intranet.intpalmcoder.net.
```

In the reverse zone definition, you can see the first entry in the file has been replaced with the @ symbol. The @ symbol is very important and is interpreted as the zone this file relates to. In the case of a reverse map, the zone is `0.168.192.in-addr.arpa`. The `in-addr.arpa` is a special address that signifies this is an IP address lookup. The zone itself is a reverse of the IP address we are looking for.

In much the same way that the `intpalmcoder.net` zone contains an entry for each host, which is appended with the zone name, the reverse map is the same. This is why the zone is the subnet component of the addresses you are interested in.

For each reverse address, you have to specify the host name in its full form because the zone that contains the reverse map has no idea what forward domain it refers to. Whereas in the case of forward domains, you can let BIND take care of the host name completion, you must specify the fully qualified domain name (FQDN) with the full stop.

Regardless of whether you have a large corporate network or a small home network with an asymmetric digital subscriber line (ADSL), you will probably want to use a DNS server. In the case of a home network with multiple machines, you can make your life a lot easier by configuring a forwarding/caching server to speed up your general Internet use, as well as referring to your home networked machines by name (you do have a large network at home like ours, don't you?).

As for the corporate network, you have to implement an internal DNS infrastructure to maintain the accessibility of your servers, and perhaps your dynamically addressed client machines. If you have a large number of Internet-connected client machines, using a caching server can alleviate the amount of time and root server queries that your organization generates. If you have 1,000 client machines surfing the Internet all day, you can significantly decrease the amount of time your users have to wait for repeated name lookups.

DNS is a very important part of the Internet, and you will find it is important in your network, no matter how large.

✦   ✦   ✦

Working with NFS and NIS

NFS is the Network File System, which was pioneered by Sun and has become a standard in the world of Unix. With NFS, clients can mount filesystems across the network that are being offered by NFS servers and can work with them as if they were filesystems mounted from local disks. NFS is a simple and widely used method of sharing files across the network.

NIS is a distributed authentication mechanism that was developed as a companion to NFS. NIS provides an easy, centralized way of using the same user and group accounts and system configuration information within a network of systems running NFS. This eliminates the need for a system administrator to manually synchronize and update user and group accounts across all of the systems on a network.

In this chapter, we look at how to mount NFS file systems on client systems and how to set up an NFS server to make networked file systems available (known as exporting them). We then explore how to set up an NIS server and share the authentication and system information that it provides on all of the NFS client systems on your network.

Mounting NFS Filesystems

A machine that is offering directories to share across the network by NFS is an NFS server. A machine that mounts one of these shares for its own use is an NFS client.

First, we look at the client side of things; we will assume that an NFS server is available and look at how to mount a share that an NFS server is offering. At this stage all you need to know is that an NFS server on the network is capable of offering one or more of its directories in such a way that other machines on the network can mount them. For example, if you know that the server bible has made the directory /share available by NFS, you can mount the share on the client machine by a command as simple as this:

```
root@client: ~ # mount bible:/share /mnt
```

You should now be able to change the directory to /mnt and see the files that exist in the directory /share on bible.

Tip   If this command hangs, it is possible that portmap might not be running on client: check this with rcportmap status. If necessary, issue the command rcportmap start or rcportmap restart. Of course, the reason for the problem might be on the server, in which case it is more likely that you will see an error like the following:

```
mount: RPC: Remote system error - Connection refused
```

Mounting NFS Filesystems at Boot Time

It is possible that you may want to mount particular NFS filesystems at boot time. You may also want to allow non-root users on the client to mount NFS shares themselves. In either of these cases, you will need to include a suitable entry in the file /etc/fstab. Just as this file controls the local filesystems that are to be mounted, it can also control the mounting of NFS shares.

For example, with this entry in /etc/fstab on the client:

```
bible:/test   /testmount   nfs   user,noauto,ro        0 0
```

any user on the client can mount (read-only) the specified directory from bible on the specified mount point simply by issuing the command mount /testmount.

To force the directory to be mounted automatically, you might use the following:

```
bible:/test   /testmount   nfs   rw          0 0
```

This line in /etc/fstab ensures that the NFS share is mounted read-write whenever the system boots, provided that the service nfs is set to start in runlevel 3 on the client. See Chapter 3 for more information about the use of /etc/fstab for setting mount options for filesystems.

Tip To see what filesystems are mounted (including NFS mounts), simply type **mount**.

Using mount Options

Most of the control over how NFS behaves is based on the server; however, there are some options to the `mount` command that make a difference.

You may want to force a read-only mount (even if the server is offering the share read-write). At the command line, you type:

```
root@client: ~ # mount bible:/share /mnt -o ro
```

In other words, mount the directory `/share` from the server `bible` (which is being made available by NFS) on the mount point `/mnt`, with the option (`-o`) to the mount command `ro`, which means read-only.

You can also specify a hard or soft mount:

✦ **Hard mount**—Ensures that in the event that the NFS server becomes unavailable, a program that is accessing the mount hangs but will be able to recover once the server comes back on line.

✦ **Soft mount**—The NFS client will report an error to the requesting program; not all programs handle this correctly and there is a possibility of data corruption.

To specify a hard mount, you add the keyword `hard` to the options (after the `-o`) for the `mount` command. For example:

```
root@client: ~ # mount bible:/share /mnt -o ro,hard
```

In fact, `hard` is the default so you do not need to specify it explicitly. The NFS HOWTO recommends the options `hard,intr` unless there is a good reason to do otherwise. The option `intr` ensures that if the server is no longer responding, the program that is accessing the mount can be interrupted by a kill signal.

You can also try to force the connection to be carried over the TCP transport rather than UDP by adding `tcp` to the list of options to the `mount` command. UDP is the default, and NFS over UDP is stateless; this means that the server can be restarted without breaking the connection. However, it is also less efficient if any packets are being dropped on the network, because if you use TCP, every packet is acknowledged and is resent if it does not arrive. With UDP, only the completion of the entire request is acknowledged.

Other options to the mount command are `rsize` and `wsize`, which set block sizes in bytes for reads and writes, respectively. Performance can be expected to improve if these are set to 8,192 rather than the default of 1,024. The `mount` command looks like this:

```
root@client: ~ # mount bible:/share /mnt -o rsize=8192 wsize=8192
```

Under some circumstances, better performance may be achieved with different values, but if these parameters are too far removed from their defaults, problems occur.

> **Note**
>
> Increasing these values is recommended because newer Linux kernels perform read-ahead for values of `rsize` greater than the machine page size, which on the x86 architecture is 4,096. So a value of `rsize` greater than 8,192 will improve NFS read performance. The value needs to be a multiple of 1,024, and should not be greater than 16,384.

rcnfs start and rcnfs stop

On a SUSE system, the operation of the NFS client is treated as a service and has its own startup scripts in `/etc/init.d` and the related command `rcnfs`. The commands `rcnfs start` and `rcnfs stop` (run as root) start and stop the NFS client service and mount and unmount (if possible) any NFS shares that are included in `/etc/fstab`. The unmounting fails if the mount point is in use. If the service `nfs` is not set to start in runlevels 3 and 5, the Network File Systems specified in `/etc/fstab` will not be imported until one of the commands `rcnfs start` or `mount -a` is issued (as root).

If the NFS client service is set to start in its default runlevels, it will take a long time to time out if for some reason the server is unavailable when the client machine boots; this can be avoided by adding the option `bg` (for background) to the options in `/etc/fstab`. In this case, if the first mount attempt fails, it continues to try to do the mount in the background rather than making everything else wait until timeout occurs. The line you need in `/etc/fstab` might look like this:

```
bible:/test    /testmount    nfs    rw,bg              0 0
```

YaST's NFS Client Module

YaST's NFS client module simply writes information to the `/etc/fstab` file about NFS mounts that you want to be available there (and that you want to be mounted with `rcnfs start`). You can see an example of the module in Figure 22-1.

The YaST NFS client module can be started with the command (as root) `yast2 nfs` or `yast nfs` for the text version. It is available through the YaST Network Services menu.

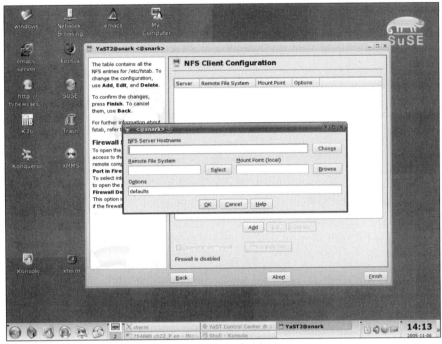

Figure 22-1: Configuring the NFS client with YaST

The NFS Server

Two NFS server implementations are available on SUSE. One is the kernel-based NFS server; the other is an implementation that runs in user space and is included in the package nfs-server. If you use the kernel-based NFS server, you need the package nfs-utils. If you install the user space nfs-server package, you need to uninstall nfs-utils because the packages conflict. The description that follows does not depend on which implementation is being used.

Note

The default kernel-based NFS server can be expected to give better performance. It has certain limitations including the inability to export directories that are mounted below the directory being exported. The user space implementation, although possibly slower, enables you to offer an NFS share that itself contains a subdirectory on which another filesystem is mounted. The client will be able to mount the share and navigate to that subdirectory, something that is not possible with the kernel-based implementation.

The NFS server is started with the command `rcnfsserver start`. To run an NFS server at all times, you need to check that the following services `nfsserver`, `nfsboot`, `nfslock`, and `portmap` are all set to run in their default runlevels.

You can use the YaST runlevel module (YaST ⇨ System ⇨ Runlevel Editor) for this, or alternatively:

```
root@bible: ~ # chkconfig nfsserver on
root@bible: ~ # chkconfig nfslock on
root@bible: ~ # chkconfig nfsboot on
root@bible: ~ # chkconfig portmap on
```

The exports File

The sharing of directories by NFS is controlled by the file `/etc/exports`, which contains a list of directories with details of the hosts they may be exported to and other options. A simple example such as `/etc/exports` might contain just the following line:

```
/test   client(rw)
```

This will export the directory `/test` to the host `client`. The option `r w` (read-write) is set. If you restart the NFS server, you see this:

```
Shutting down kernel based NFS server                          done
Starting kernel based NFS server exportfs: /etc/exports [8]: No 'sync' or 'async' option specified
for export "*:/home".
 Assuming default behaviour ('sync').
 NOTE: this default has changed from previous versions        done
```

To avoid this message, add `sync` or `async` to the options:

```
/test   client(rw,sync)
```

The default option `sync` means that the NFS server waits for local disk writes to complete, thus minimizing the risk of data corruption if the server suddenly fails.

If `async` is specified, the opposite is the case, meaning that if communication between client and server fails, corrupt data might be written to the client.

Note that there should be no space between the client name(s) and the options. If there is, the NFS server interprets the line differently; in the preceding example, it would offer `/test` to machine `client` with the default options and to any other machine with the options `rw,sync`. This is unfortunate because it is an easy mistake to make in creating the file. However, to indicate that you want to export to any machine, you should preferably use the * notation.

If you want to export `/test` to any machine, use the following:

```
/test   *(rw,sync)
```

Having made a change in /etc/exports, use the command nfsserver reload to make the NFS server re-read the configuration without restarting it.

You can specify an IP number or range, or a Domain Name System (DNS) name (provided it can be resolved) as the client or clients to export to. So any of the following work:

```
/test client(rw,sync)
/test 192.168.1.26(rw,sync)
/test 192.168.1.0/255.255.255.0(rw,sync)
/test 192.168.1.0/24(rw,sync)
```

The option r w (read-write) is set in all the preceding lines. However, the option ro allows read-only access only if you want.

As we noted previously, the /etc/exports file is simply a collection of lines like those we've shown. The comment character is #. So the following might be a simple complete /etc/exports:

```
# See the exports(5) manpage for a description of the syntax of this file.
# This file contains a list of all directories that are to be exported to
# other computers via NFS (Network File System).
# This file used by rpc.nfsd and rpc.mountd. See their manpages for details
# on how to make changes in this file effective.

/data2/ *(sync)
/home/peter/ rabbit(rw,root_squash,sync)
/home/david/ *(rw,root_squash,sync)
/media/cdrom/ *(sync)
```

In this example, the comments at the top are all that you will see in /etc/exports on a new installation. The directory /data2 is exported read-only (that's the default if neither ro or r w is specified) to any host. Peter's home directory is exported read-write with the root_squash option, but only to his machine named rabbit. If he becomes root on rabbit, he still won't have root privileges over the files in the share. The CD drive is exported to all hosts.

Setting Root, User, and Group Client Privileges

By default, the root user on the client is mapped to the anonymous user nobody on the server, which means that the root user on the client does not have full root privileges over the files on the mounted share. This default option can be made explicit by specifying root_squash. The opposite of this is no_root_squash, which allows the root user on the client full root privileges on the NFS share.

Note Unless there is a special reason to do otherwise, filesystems should be exported with the root_squash option.

The option `all_squash` is similar but maps all users to the user `nobody`. When the share is mounted, a normal user on the client will not be able to write to the share unless the permissions on the directory allow others to write to it. And any file that is created in this way will be owned by user `nobody` and group `nogroup`.

When using the `all_squash` option, you can also specify explicitly the user ID (UID) and group ID (GID) that you want users to be mapped to rather than the defaults for the user `nobody`. For example:

```
/test client(rw,sync,all_squash,anonuid=1999,anongid=1999)
```

This enables you to create a user on the server with the stated UID and GID and suitably arrange that user's permissions on the share.

Creating the exports File with YaST

The YaST NFS server module (`yast2 nfs_server`) can write the `/etc/exports` file for you. As with the NFS client module, there is probably no great advantage for most people in being able to configure this with a graphical tool, as it simply asks for the information that will be written in the configuration file. Some people may prefer this method simply because it makes it slightly less likely that a single typo will mess up your configuration. Figure 22-2 shows an example of the NFS server module in action.

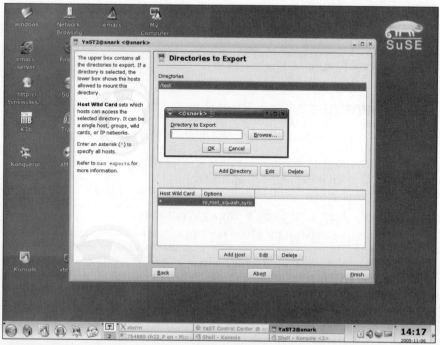

Figure 22-2: Configuring the NFS server with YaST

When you start the module, it first asks whether or not the NFS server should be started and then provides an interface that enables you to add a directory (to be exported) and specify the hosts and the options for that share. These are precisely the options discussed previously, and you have to type them in by hand.

The exportfs Command

The `exportfs` command can be used to handle the exporting of directories directly from the command line. To export all directories listed in /etc/exports, use `exportfs -a`.

If /etc/exports has changed, `exportfs -r` rereads /etc/exports and changes the state of the directories being exported accordingly. This is like doing `rcnfsserver reload`.

You can export a directory that is not mentioned in /etc/exports by doing something like this:

```
root@bible: ~ # exportfs -iv -o rw,sync client:/tmp
```

The `-iv` option tells `exportfs` to ignore /etc/exports and be verbose. The `-o` introduces the options, and the command as a whole exports the directory /tmp to the machine client.

With the option `-u`, the command unexports a currently exported directory:

```
root@bible: ~ # exportfs -u client:/tmp
```

To unexport all directories mentioned in /etc/exports, do `exportfs -au`.

The showmount Command

The command `showmount` provides information about mounts on an NFS server.

```
user@client: ~ > showmount -e bible
```

This command lists the exports list for the server bible. Typically this will be the contents of /etc/exports, but if changes have been made without using `exportfs` as described in the previous section, these will be reflected in the output.

```
root@bible: ~ # exportfs -i -o rw,sync client:/home

user@client: ~ > showmount -e bible
/test    *
/home    client
```

In the preceding example, you can see /home, which you just configured, and /test, which was included in /etc/exports.

If you want information about what is actually being mounted from bible, use the -a option:

```
user@client: ~ > showmount -a bible
All mount points on bible:
client:/test
```

This shows that the directory /test on bible is currently mounted by client.

showmount -d bible shows just the directories being mounted:

```
user@client: ~ > showmount -d bible
Directories on bible:
/test
```

Caution   The information given by showmount can sometimes include stale information about old mounts that are no longer present. This can happen, for example, if a client reboots without unmounting the NFS mount. To correct this situation, you can, if necessary, remove the file /var/lib/nfs/rmtab on the server and restart the NFS server.

Problems with Mounting NFS Shares

If you find that you cannot mount a share that you think should work, the first thing to check is whether the NFS server is actually running. Check the /etc/exports file on the server carefully, and be sure that you have done exportfs -r or rcnfs server reload since making any changes to it. The command rpcinfo can be useful; if all is well, its output should look something like this:

```
user@client: ~ > rpcinfo -p bible
   program vers proto    port
    100000    2   tcp     111   portmapper
    100000    2   udp     111   portmapper
    100003    2   udp    2049   nfs
    100003    3   udp    2049   nfs
    100003    4   udp    2049   nfs
    100227    3   udp    2049   nfs_acl
    100003    2   tcp    2049   nfs
    100003    3   tcp    2049   nfs
    100003    4   tcp    2049   nfs
    100227    3   tcp    2049   nfs_acl
    100021    1   udp   32771   nlockmgr
    100021    3   udp   32771   nlockmgr
    100021    4   udp   32771   nlockmgr
    100024    1   udp   32771   status
    100021    1   tcp   32830   nlockmgr
    100021    3   tcp   32830   nlockmgr
    100021    4   tcp   32830   nlockmgr
```

```
100024   1   tcp   32830   status
100005   1   udp     629   mountd
100005   1   tcp     633   mountd
100005   2   udp     629   mountd
100005   2   tcp     633   mountd
100005   3   udp     629   mountd
100005   3   tcp     633   mountd
```

If you don't see entries for nfs and mountd in this listing, then something is seriously wrong; perhaps the NFS server has not registered itself with the portmapper. Try stopping the NFS server, the portmap service, and the network and then starting them in the reverse order.

NFS Security Considerations

NFS has inherent security problems. Just as with SMB shares, you certainly should not make it available beyond the private network.

The lists of allowed client IPs or host names in the exports file are no defense against someone who is able to alter a machine's IP address (which with physical access in practice means anyone). The point made in the previous section about UIDs means that a user may have the wrong permissions on another user's files on the server, but if a user has root access on a client (again, with physical access that means anyone), they can become any user they want.

NFS security will improve when the client side becomes fully compliant with the NFS version 4 standard. In the future, it will be possible to use secure authentication to secure NFS on Linux. In the meantime, no measures to tighten NFS security should be regarded as totally effective. The subject is discussed further in the NFS HOWTO document at http://nfs.sourceforge.net/nfs-howto/.

Finally, NFS provides a very simple and transparent way of sharing filesystems across a network. It is likely to be an essential part of any network infrastructure, which includes Linux or Unix systems both as server and client. The information in this chapter should enable you to work with NFS on both the client and the server.

Using NIS for Authentication

As touched upon when discussing the root_squash and all_squash options, the question of ensuring consistent user and group IDs across a network of NFS clients and servers is not a trivial one. The previous section focused on ensuring that the root user on an NFS client system didn't get undue privileges to files owned by root on a file system that is exported by an NFS server. However, the same basic problem is also present for normal users. If a user's ID differs on the NFS server and client, then that user will not be able to do everything he or she should be able to do with his or her files. This means that you need to take steps to ensure that the group IDs (GIDs) and user IDs (UIDs) on the server and the clients are identical. These are the numerical IDs that you will find in the files /etc/passwd and /etc/group.

In a small environment with just a few NFS clients, it may be feasible to simply ensure that the UID that each user has on each client machine is identical to the user's UID on the server. However, this becomes unmanageable for any significant number of users and clients. Therefore, larger environments require an automated system of ensuring that the UIDs and GIDs on the server and client match up. This is usually achieved using either the Network Information System (NIS) or Lightweight Directory Access Protocol (LDAP) (see Chapter 25). NIS is a networked authentication system that was designed to work with NFS. This section explains how to set up an NIS server and how to ensure that client systems use that server for authentication information.

Tip   For additional information about NIS, see the NIS HOWTO at www.linux-nis.org/nis-howto/HOWTO/NIS-HOWTO.html.

Setting Up an NIS Server Using YaST

As mentioned earlier, NIS is the most commonly used distributed authentication mechanism today, largely because it is shipped free with almost all Unix and Unix-like systems. Another reason for the prevalence of NIS is that it's incredibly easy to set up, as shown in this section, which walks you through the process of setting up an NIS server. The SUSE YaST administration tool further simplifies NIS set up and configuration. Configuring other systems so that they get their authentication information from NIS (and are then known as NIS clients) is explained later in this chapter.

To use YaST to configure a system to function as an NIS server, do the following:

1. Start YaST's NIS Server configuration module from the Control Center or by typing the yast2 nis_server command from a root shell or using sudo. This displays the dialog box shown in Figure 22-3.

2. Select the Create NIS Master Server option button and click Next to display the dialog box shown in Figure 22-4 displays.

3. Enter the name of the NIS domain for which you are setting up a server. You can also optionally enable users to change their NIS passwords by selecting the Allow changes to passwords option button. You may also want to allow users to change their login shells by clicking the Allow changes to login shell option button—there may still be a /bin/csh user on one of your systems. Click Next to display the dialog box shown in Figure 22-5.

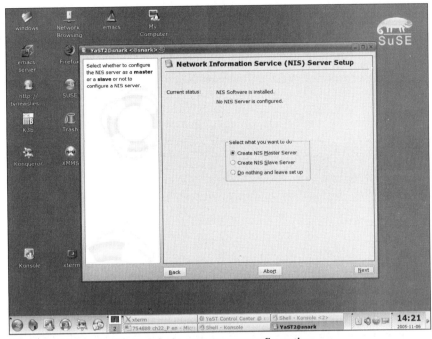

Figure 22-3: The YaST module for NIS Server configuration

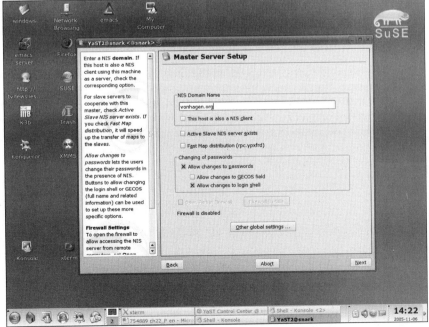

Figure 22-4: Specifying the NIS domain and capabilities in YaST

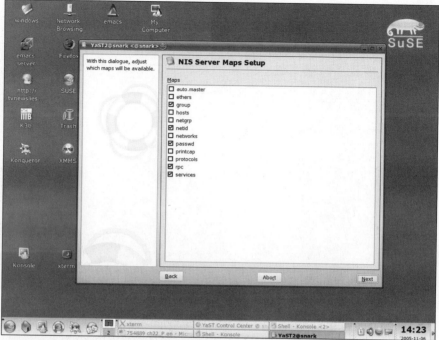

Figure 22-5: Selecting NIS maps to export

4. Select the user, group, and system configuration files, known as maps in NIS terminology, that you want the NIS server to distribute to client systems. Then click Next to display the dialog box shown in Figure 22-6.

5. Specify network masks that define which hosts can use the authentication information provided by the NIS server that you are configuring. Hosts can contact the NIS server for authentication information if the bit-wise AND of a specified netmask and the host's IP address is equal to one of the values specified for network in this dialog box. The netmask/network pair 0.0.0.0/0.0.0.0, therefore, enables any host to contact this NIS server. This is safe only if your network is not connected to the Internet or if you have a firewall between your network and the Internet that disables NIS and NFS RPC traffic. Click Finish to continue.

6. The YaST nis_server module updates your system and starts the NIS server. You are now ready to configure (and test) the NIS client as described later in this chapter, in the section "Configuring Clients for NIS."

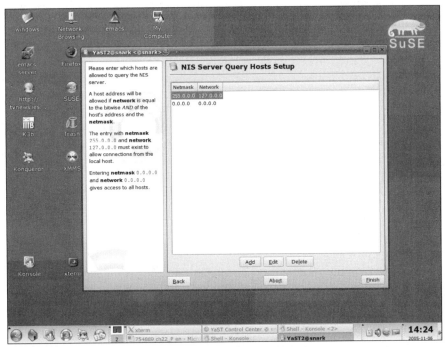

Figure 22-6: Specifying IP addresses that can use this NIS server

Setting Up an NIS Server Manually

This section explains how to set up an NIS server from the command line. YaST removes the need to do this manually, and you don't need to follow the instructions in this section if you've set up an NIS server using YaST. However, it's still convenient to know exactly what changes need be made under the hood in order to set up an NIS server. An NIS server that is configured using the instructions in this section exports the default password, group, host, and so on maps (files) found on the NIS server system. In a production environment, you would want to do substantially more customization before initiating NIS throughout your computing environment. You would also want to customize the NIS configuration files /var/yp/securenets, /etc/yp.conf, and /etc/ypserv.conf.

To set up an NIS server, log in as or use the su command to become root on the system you will be configuring as an NIS server, and do the following:

1. Make sure that the NIS software is installed on your Linux system. At a minimum, you will need the /bin/domainname, /usr/sbin/ypserv, and /usr/lib/yp/ ypinit programs.

2. Next, make sure that the `/etc/passwd` file has an entry for your personal account, which should also be found in the password file on the system you will be configuring as an NIS client. In the following section ("Configuring Clients for NIS"), we will use this entry to verify that NIS is working correctly.

3. Set the domain name of your new NIS domain. This should not be the same as the name of your TCP/IP domain, to avoid confusing DNS and potentially compromising security in your domain. To set the NIS domain name (in this case to the domain `foo.com`), issue a command like the following:

```
/bin/domainname foo.com
```

This NIS domain name is saved for reuse in the file `/etc/defaultdomain`.

4. Start the NIS server process using a command like the following:

```
/usr/sbin/ypserv
```

5. Initialize the NIS databases using a command like the following:

```
/usr/lib/yp/ypinit -m
```

You will see output like the following:

```
At this point, we have to construct a list of the hosts which will run NIS
servers.
  distfs.vonhagen.org is in the list of NIS server hosts.
Please continue to add the names for the other hosts, one per line.
When you are done with the list, type a <control D>.
next host to add:  distfs.vonhagen.org
next host to add:
```

6. When prompted for the name of any other NIS servers in your domain, press Ctrl+D. You will see output like the following:

```
The current list of NIS servers looks like this:
distfs.vonhagen.org
Is this correct?  [y/n: y]
```

7. Press return to respond yes. You will then see output listing the files that have been generated and added to the NIS database. This output looks like the following, where the domain name you specified will appear instead of the word *yourdomain*:

```
We need some  minutes to build the databases...
Building /var/yp/ws.com/ypservers...
Running /var/yp/Makefile...
gmake[1]: Entering directory `/var/yp/yourdomain'
Updating passwd.byname...
Updating passwd.byuid...
Updating group.byname...
```

```
Updating group.bygid...
Updating hosts.byname...
Updating hosts.byaddr...
Updating rpc.byname...
Updating rpc.bynumber...
Updating services.byname...
Updating services.byservicename...
Updating netid.byname...
Updating protocols.bynumber...
Updating protocols.byname...
Updating mail.aliases...
gmake[1]: Leaving directory `/var/yp/yourdomain'
```

That's all there is to it! Your new NIS server is up and running. You can now test that it is working correctly by following the instructions in the following section.

Configuring Clients for NIS

This section explains how to set up an NIS client of the server started in the previous section. As with setting up an NIS server, NIS clients can be configured using command-line utilities or by taking advantage of YaST's graphical administrative interface. The following two sections explain how to configure an NIS client using each of these methods.

Configuring an NIS Client using YaST

YaST makes NIS client configuration almost trivial, using a single dialog box to collect information about the NIS domain that you want your client to use. To configure a system as an NIS client using YaST, do the following:

1. Start YaST's NIS client configuration module by executing the command `yast2 nis` as root or using `sudo`. This displays the dialog shown in Figure 22-7.

2. Click the Use NIS option button, and enter the name of the NIS domain that you want the client system to contact for authentication information. If your client system uses DHCP to deliver NIS server information, click Automatic Setup (through DHCP). If you want the NIS Client to search the local network by broadcasting if a connection to the specified NFS server fails, click the Broadcast option button.

3. Click Finish. YaST modifies your system's configuration files to use NIS and exits after those modifications have been made.

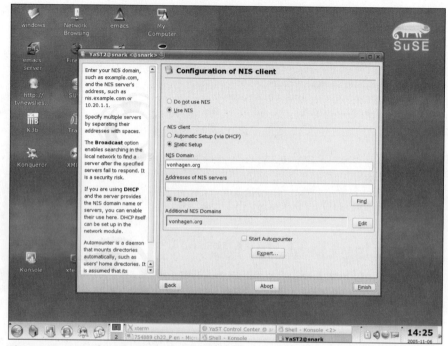

Figure 22-7: Configuring an NIS client in YaST

Configuring an NIS Client Manually

As mentioned previously, it is interesting to understand exactly what's going on under the hood when configuring an NIS client. This section explains how to configure a system to be an NIS client without using graphical utilities.

To do some pre-configuration, log in as or su to root on the client system and edit the /etc/nsswitch.conf file on the system you are using as an NIS client. Find the line that tells your system how to locate password entries and modify that line to look like the following:

```
passwd:     nis [NOTFOUND=return] files
```

This tells your system to look for password information in NIS and fail if the appropriate information isn't found.

Next, save a copy of your system's password file and then remove all entries in the existing password file after the entry for "piranha." As the last line of the new, shorter password file, add the following:

```
+::::::
```

This tells NIS to append the contents of the password map (file) retrieved from the NIS server whenever password information is requested.

Note that the entries for any individual accounts (including your own) have been removed from the abbreviated password file. This enables you to do a fairly simple test to determine whether NIS is working. If you can log in using an account that is not present in the password file on your client system but which is present in the password file on your NIS server system, then you can determine that NIS is working correctly.

To set up an NIS client, log in as root or use the su command to become root on the system you are using as an NIS client and do the following:

1. Make sure that the NIS client software is installed on your Linux system. At a minimum, you will need the /bin/domainname and /sbin/ypbind programs.

2. Make sure that the directory /var/yp exists and create it if it does not.

3. Set the domain name of the NIS domain to which this new client will belong. This should be the same name as the domain name set earlier in this chapter. To set the NIS domain name (in this case to the domain foo.com), issue a command like the following:

   /bin/domainname foo.com

4. Start the NIS client process using a command like the following:

   /sbin/ypbind

To verify that NIS is working correctly, use the telnet or ssh commands from the NIS client system to contact the client and attempt to log in as yourself. Remember that your password file entry is present in the password file on the NIS server, but not in the password file on the NIS client.

You should be able to log in successfully. Congratulations—you're running NIS! You should now modify your system's startup sequence to add the /etc/init.d/ypserv startup script.

Wrapping Up

NFS and NIS provide a powerful but easy-to-configure combination of a distributed filesystem and a distributed authentication service. SUSE's administrative tools simplify both NFS and NIS configuration, making it easy to create both NFS/NIS clients and servers.

✦   ✦   ✦

Running an FTP Server on SUSE

✦ ✦ ✦ ✦

In This Chapter

Security issues
with FTP

Setting up an
anonymous FTP
server with vsftpd

Allowing user access

Allowing upload
access

Allowing anonymous
uploads

Using pure-ftpd

✦ ✦ ✦ ✦

FTP is the File Transfer Protocol, which is best known as a way of allowing anonymous downloads from public Internet servers.

Traditionally, Unix systems ran an FTP daemon by default, and users expected to be able to move files to and from their home directories using an FTP client from elsewhere. This was a convenient way of accessing the system without logging on, and was available from any kind of client. This type of use of FTP has come to be seen as both insecure and unnecessary:

✦ It is regarded as insecure because typically username/password pairs were sent across the network in plain text, and so it was vulnerable to password theft by network sniffing. Just as telnet and rsh are regarded as insecure, use of FTP on a public network should generally be regarded with caution.

✦ However, this type of use of FTP is also usually unnecessary for just the same reason that telnet and rsh are unnecessary: because of the availability of the ssh family of programs (ssh, scp, sftp). These provide totally secure ways of achieving the same ends. (The availability of nice client implementations such as KDE's "fish" ioslave also means that you can view the directories on the server graphically from the client while transferring the files.)

FTP's poor security reputation has been made ever worse by the fact that some FTP implementations have suffered at times from serious vulnerabilities, including exploits allowing full root access to the client through the use of buffer overflows and the like.

Another important point is that if your FTP server is intended to allow uploads, you will need to think carefully about security. Any mail server that allows open relaying will be ruthlessly exploited for that purpose within hours. In much the same way, if you run an FTP server on the Internet that allows anonymous uploads, if you are not very careful, it will be filled up in no time with "warez" (illegal pirated material) and worse (pornography). This is certainly something to avoid. In most countries you could be held legally responsible for the fact that illegal content is residing on your server, despite the fact that someone else put it there. And the bandwidth costs resulting from this unauthorized usage can be considerable.

So a default SUSE installation does not have a running FTP daemon. SUSE actually offers a choice of two FTP servers: `pure-ftpd` and `vsftpd`. This chapter looks in detail at the use of `vsftpd` (Very Secure FTP Daemon). We also discuss `pure-ftpd`, but in less detail — the principles are similar, but the detailed setup differs. Both `vsftpd` and `pure-ftpd` are popular and well-regarded FTP servers among the open source community. Like many of the alternatives mentioned elsewhere in this book, the choice between them is largely a matter of taste.

The example FTP sessions are standard command-line FTP from a Linux client: These are intended to show the behavior clearly, but exactly the same results (in terms of functionality) can be seen with a graphical FTP client on any operating system.

vsftpd as an Anonymous FTP Server

An FTP server is most commonly used as a server for anonymous downloads. We look at this setup first.

An anonymous FTP server is a server that allows anyone to log in with the username `ftp` or `anonymous` and download files. If you use a browser to access an anonymous FTP site, the browser passes the login information to the site without the user having to think about it. User FTP, which we consider later, refers to an FTP server on which specified users have accounts that they can access with their username and password. Traditionally, Unix and Linux systems ran an FTP server by default, and users could access their home directories remotely by FTP. For the security reasons discussed previously, this is no longer standard practice except on a trusted internal network.

`vsftpd` is typically run from `xinetd`. If `vsftpd` is installed, you now need to enable it as a service to be started from `xinetd`. This can easily be done using YaST: Network Services ⇨ Network Services (inetd). The `xinetd` daemon itself should be enabled, and the FTP service should be toggled to on (see Figure 23-1). Now whenever the system boots into runlevel 3 or 5, the `xinetd` daemon will run and will start the `vsftpd` FTP daemon.

> **Note** The `xinetd` daemon is the extended Internet services daemon, sometimes described as a super-server. The purpose of `xinetd` is to control the starting of various network services, which are not started at boot time, but remain dormant until a request for the particular service arrives, at which point `xinetd` passes the request on the relevant program (in our case `vsftpd`). Each service that can be handled by `xinetd` has a corresponding file in the directory `/etc/xinetd.d/`. These files con-

trol how `xinetd` starts the service; the actual configuration file is elsewhere. So the file to edit to control the behavior of `vsftpd` is `/etc/vsftpd.conf`, not `/etc/xinetd.d/vsftpd`. The easiest way to control which services `xinetd` manages is through YaST's Network Services module as described in the main text.

The behavior of `vsftpd` is controlled by the file `/etc/vsftpd.conf`. The comment at the top of the file reads:

```
# Example config file /etc/vsftpd.conf
#
# The default compiled in settings are fairly paranoid. This sample file
# loosens things up a bit, to make the ftp daemon more usable.
# Please see vsftpd.conf.5 for all compiled in defaults.
#
# If you do not change anything here you will have a minimum setup for an
# anonymous FTP server.
```

And so once you have enabled `vsftpd`, you should be able to connect by FTP as follows:

```
user@client: /home/user $ ftp bible
Connected to bible.
220 (vsFTPd 2.0.2)
Name (bible:user):
```

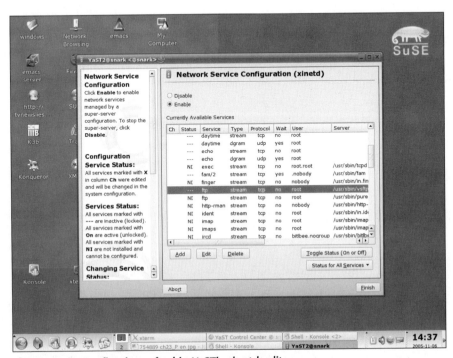

Figure 23-1: Configuring vsftpd in YaST's xinetd editor

Notice that the FTP server assumes a default username the same as that on the client. At this point, if you accept the default and press Return, or enter another username known to the system bible, you will see this:

```
530 This FTP server is anonymous only.
ftp: Login failed.
ftp>
```

But if you log in with either of the usernames ftp or anonymous, you can offer any password (traditionally this should be a valid email address, but the server will accept anything, including an empty password), and you are logged in.

```
user@client: /home/user > ftp bible
Connected to bible.
220 (vsFTPd 2.0.2)
Name (bible:user):ftp
331 Please specify the password.
Password:
230 Login successful.
Remote system type is UNIX.
Using binary mode to transfer files.
ftp>
```

If you now type **ls** to list files on the FTP server, you will (not surprisingly) find that there is nothing there:

```
ftp> ls
229 Entering Extended Passive Mode (|||37477|)
150 Here comes the directory listing.
226 Directory send OK.
ftp>
```

The location on the server that acts as the FTP server's root for anonymous FTP is /srv/ftp/ (just as the Apache web server's root is normally /srv/www/). So whatever files and directories you place there will be visible to FTP clients. If you now copy a file to /srv/ftp/, you will be able to download it by FTP by using the FTP get command:

```
ftp> get afile
local: afile remote: afile
229 Entering Extended Passive Mode (|||19160|)
150 Opening BINARY mode data connection for afile (4096 bytes).
226 File send OK.
ftp>
```

If you look at /var/log/messages on the server, you will see that vsftpd has logged the login:

```
Jul 25 16:41:06 bible vsftpd: Sun Jul 25 16:41:06 2004 [pid 23139] CONNECT: Client
"192.168.2.3"
```

```
Jul 25 16:41:13 bible vsftpd: Sun Jul 25 16:41:13 2004 [pid 23138] [ftp] OK LOGIN: Client
"192.168.2.3", anon password "password"
```

Each download is also logged.

Note that you can force vsftpd to write its logs to its own log file by making a small change to /etc/vsftpd.conf. Simply make sure that the following lines are present:

```
log_ftp_protocol=YES
xferlog_enable=YES
vsftpd_log_file=/var/log/vsftpd.log
```

Then comment out or remove the line:

```
syslog_enable=YES
```

You can create a customized FTP banner by including a line like this in the configuration file:

```
ftpd_banner="Welcome to our very fine FTP service."
```

When users log in using text mode FTP or a dedicated FTP client, they will see the following message before the login prompt:

```
220 "Welcome to our very fine FTP service."
Name (localhost:user):
```

This can be used to offer service messages, but is not useful for users connecting with a browser. It may be useful to include the files README or README.html, which these users can click.

You can also place a file named .message in /srv/ftp/ or any of its subdirectories. When the user changes to a directory with such a file in it, the file's contents will be displayed.

```
ftp> cd pub
250-This directory contains useful files
250 Directory successfully changed.
ftp>
```

The file /srv/ftp/pub/.message contained just the line:

```
This directory contains useful files
```

vsftpd allows passive FTP connections unless you set

```
pasv_enable=NO
```

in the configuration file. You almost certainly want to allow passive connections, as otherwise many clients connecting from behind a firewall will be unable to connect.

Note Active FTP operates on both server port 20 (for data transfers) and port 21 (for control commands) and involves a reply connection from the server to the client, which may be blocked by a firewall behind which the client is sitting. Passive FTP involves only server port 21 and is unlikely to cause problems with a standard firewall configuration that allows established connections. For more on firewall configuration, see Chapter 24.

Note that all options in the configuration file are specified in the form:

```
option=value
```

and that there should be no white space before or after the = sign.

For a standard anonymous Internet FTP download server, you have done all you need to do.

Setting Up User FTP with vsftpd

In this section we assume that you want users with accounts on the system to be able to access their home directories by FTP.

Caution Again, please be aware that this could constitute a security risk if the system is available to the Internet, and you should think carefully about whether you want to do it.

One common reason why you might want to do this is to set up a system to receive incoming files; you can set up "artificial" users to own each home directory for each type of incoming file. You can then give the relevant usernames and passwords to each person needing the ability to upload to these directories.

You need to make further changes in the configuration file /etc/vsftpd.conf. You need to enable these lines:

```
local_enable=YES
chroot_local_user=YES
```

The second of these lines means that users will not be able to change directories out of their own home directories. Users will be locked in a "chroot jail."

If you now log in as a user, you will see something similar to Listing 23-1.

Listing 23-1: **Logging in to FTP Server as a User**

```
user@client: /home/user > ftp bible
Connected to bible.
220 (vsFTPd 2.0.2)
```

```
Name (bible:user): user
331 Please specify the password.
Password:
230 Login successful.
Remote system type is UNIX.
Using binary mode to transfer files.
ftp> pwd
257 "/"
ftp>
```

If you don't specify chroot_local_user=YES, the pwd command returns the following:

```
257 "/home/user"
```

You are then able to do the following:

```
ftp> cd ..
250 Directory successfully changed.
```

This enables you to access, at least in principle, the entire filesystem on the server.

Allowing Uploads

With the setup described so far, users cannot upload files to the FTP server. See Listing 23-2.

Listing 23-2: **Attempting to Upload Files to an FTP Server**

```
user@client: /home/user > ftp bible
Connected to bible.
220 (vsFTPd 2.0.2)
Name (bible:user): user
331 Please specify the password.
Password:
230 Login successful.
Remote system type is UNIX.
Using binary mode to transfer files.
ftp> put afilelocal: afile remote: afile
229 Entering Extended Passive Mode (|||16553|)
550 Permission denied.
ftp>
```

If you want to enable existing local users to upload files, you need to set the following in /etc/vsftpd.conf:

```
write_enable=YES
```

If you have done this, a new user FTP session like the one shown in Listing 23-2 will succeed in uploading to the user's home directory.

If you also want to allow uploads from anonymous logins (ftp or anonymous), you need to enable the following:

```
anon_upload_enable=YES
```

There will have to be directories on the server with permissions allowing these writes: By default, this will not be the case. We cannot stress enough the dangers of allowing anonymous FTP writes unless you have thought carefully about what you are doing. In particular, the writable directory certainly should not be the root of the FTP directory structure /srv/ftp/. You should also consider creating a write-only setup, by creating a directory such as /srv/ftp/incoming/ owned by user ftp and group ftp, and with restrictive permissions. The permissions on this directory should not allow others to write to it or list it. In fact, the setup works fine if you set permissions 300 on /srv/ftp/incoming/.

Listing the root FTP directory now shows:

```
root@bible: /srv/ftp # ls -lA
d-wx------  2 ftp  ftp  144 Aug 10 17:31 incoming
```

These permissions mean that the anonymous FTP user cannot list the directory, but the FTP daemon can still write to the directory, so uploading will work. If the setting for the anonymous umask in the configuration file is left at its default value of 077, files that are uploaded will not be downloadable because they will have permissions 600 on the server and will not be readable by others.

If you set

```
anon_umask=022
```

in /etc/vsftpd.conf, then files that have been uploaded are anonymously downloadable again, although the incoming directory is still not listable. This is almost certainly very undesirable, except in a trusted environment, because then confederates of anyone who has parked files on your server will be able to download them.

The root FTP directory /srv/ftp/ itself should be owned by user root and group root, and there should be no subdirectory that is readable, writable, and listable.

Cross-Reference   See Chapter 2 for more information about permissions.

An anonymous FTP session looks something like Listing 23-3.

Listing 23-3: **Successfully Uploading Files**

```
user@client: /home/user > ftp bible
Connected to bible.
220 (vsFTPd 2.0.2)
Name (bible:user): ftp
331 Please specify the password.
Password:
230 Login successful.
Remote system type is UNIX.
Using binary mode to transfer files.
ftp> cd incoming
250 Directory successfully changed.
ftp> put afile
local: afile remote: afile
229 Entering Extended Passive Mode (|||62494|)
150 Ok to send data.
226 File receive OK.
ftp> ls
229 Entering Extended Passive Mode (|||50259|)
150 Here comes the directory listing.
226 Transfer done (but failed to open directory).
ftp>
```

Notice how the put command succeeds, but the ls command fails. As we planned, the anonymous login now permits uploads, but restricts directory listing. Further, the uploaded files cannot be downloaded again by other users, so this is a fairly secure setup.

Using pure-ftpd

The principles discussed in this chapter with reference to vsftpd apply equally to pure-ftpd, but there are some differences in detail.

You can set up pure-ftpd to start in one of two ways: either as a service that starts at boot time or from xinetd as described for vsftpd.

If you choose the first method, you need to edit the configuration file /etc/pure-ftpd/pure-ftpd.conf and then run the command rcpure-ftpd start. To ensure that it starts at boot time, you need to run the command chkconfig pure-ftpd on or use YaST's runlevel editor. Despite the slightly confusing wording at the beginning of the configuration file, if you use this method the configuration file *will* be read when it starts, thanks to SUSE's init script.

If you choose to run `pure-ftpd` from `xinetd`, it does not read its configuration file when it starts up. You need to edit the file `/etc/xinetd.d/pure-ftpd` to include a line

```
server_args = ...
```

To find out what needs to go after the = sign, you will need to run this command:

```
# /usr/sbin/pure-config-args /etc/pure-ftpd/pure-ftpd.conf
```

This parses the configuration file and converts the information in it to a long list of command-line switches that you can paste in. If you change the configuration file, you will need to repeat this process. For this reason alone, the first method of running `pure-ftpd` seems to be preferable, at least until you have created the configuration you want.

Further Information

You can find much useful information in the comments in the configuration file `/etc/vsftpd.conf`, in the man page for the configuration file:

```
man 5 vstfpd.conf
```

and under `/usr/share/doc/packages/vsftpd/`, including example configuration files for particular setups.

The home page for the `vsftpd` project is `http://vsftpd.beasts.org/`.

For `pure-ftpd`, there is also a man page (`man pure-ftpd`) and some documentation in `/usr/share/doc/packages/pure-ftpd/`. The home page for the project is at `www.pureftpd.org/`.

Enough has probably been said in this chapter to convince you that you should think hard about whether or not you actually need to run an FTP server. FTP for users who have accounts on the machine is inherently insecure, and also unnecessary given the availability of `ssh`, `scp`, and `sftp`. If you need to run a server to offer files for anonymous download, and if the expected volume is not enormous, you may choose to offer those files by HTTP. If you want to run an anonymous upload server, check carefully that it is not open to any kind of abuse, and monitor its usage.

✦   ✦   ✦

Implementing Firewalls in SUSE Linux

You have likely heard of a firewall before — your organization doubtlessly has one, and your asymmetric digital subscriber line (ADSL) router probably has one, too. Linux has had support for packet filtering (discussed later in the chapter) for quite a while now in some incarnation or another.

A *firewall* is a line of defense between two networks. It is used to explicitly allow network traffic to and from your networks, allowing you as an administrator to control what traffic can go where in your network. Many organizations not only use firewalls to protect their corporate network from the Internet, but also to protect one department from another. For example, is there any reason to allow the Sales department access to your Research and Development department? This also helps to slow down the spread of a malicious user or virus code through your network if it is compromised because only explicit traffic or protocols can communicate with other networks.

Many companies provide firewall appliances that offer the user a graphical user interface to the firewall internals. With most asymmetric digital subscriber line (ADSL) routers, you also have the added bonus of a firewall. One of the most popular firewall appliances used is the Cisco Pix. As with most things Cisco, it is aimed at the business end of the market and knowledge of firewalls and how they work is needed.

If you do not have a firewall solution at home or in the office, you can use an old PC to provide firewall services. A firewall does not need large amounts of memory or disk space because all the machine does is move packets from one network interface to another while analyzing network information. Linux firewalls are bound by the speed of the processor. We have implemented a firewall server on an old Pentium 75 with 16MB of memory before, and it worked perfectly fine for a home network.

The first Linux firewalling support came with the `ipfwadm` in the 2.0.*x* kernel series. With each major release of the kernel, the firewalling code has been rewritten, with 2.2.*x* came `ipchains`, and the 2.4.*x* kernel brought us to `iptables`.

The Linux firewalling, as we said, is packet filter–based. A packet filter will act upon a network packet, dealing with the parameters that can be queried in the TCP/IP headers. For example, you can produce a rule that takes into consideration the source of the packet (the source IP address), the destination (destination IP address), the protocol (for example, TCP), the port (SSH), and the TCP options (SYN).

Taking all of these into consideration, you can define a rule that describes a very specific scenario for a network connection. Putting numerous rules together, you can produce a very powerful firewall.

With the introduction of `iptables`, we were given the godsend that was stateful firewalls. `iptables` is something that most Linux administrators should know, especially when you need to secure your network or individual machines from a network attack. They are relatively simple to use and extremely powerful when done correctly. All kudos to Rusty Russell (the lead `iptables` developer) for implementing this feature as it allowed us to produce tight firewalls with fewer rules. We will talk about stateful firewalls and what they do in this chapter, as well as a few scenario-based `iptables` rules.

Why Use a Firewall?

A firewall, whether Linux-based or not, should always be used to protect machines connected to the Internet. A firewall, by its very nature, is designed to control what can be accomplished over the network, and it is very unlikely you want your 200 Windows machines to be connected to the Internet in full view of any malicious person that comes along (and bare Windows machines on the Internet are like drops of blood in a 10-mile radius of a pack of sharks!).

Most people think that a firewall is there to stop crackers from the Internet, but the fact of the matter is that your users are untrusted, too. It is all well and good to trust your users when you have security checked them and have run psychoanalytical tests to see if they have a predisposition for breaking the rules you have imposed on them. However, internal situations aren't always so simple. Take the following example.

We had a customer whose firewall was very tight at deterring Internet-based attacks and didn't let in anything that did not need to be there. For their internal users, there were no restrictions on connections to the Internet. All users were trusted and all good guys. Their email and operating systems on the other hand were not, and they started receiving emails with viruses that arbitrarily scanned thousands of hosts on the Internet to carry on propagating throughout the ether. The customer found this out only because the company's Internet service provider (ISP) called him to say his connection would be closed if the scanning did not stop.

This virus came through email to the user, and because Simple Mail Transport Protocol (SMTP) traffic was allowed through the mail server, there was nothing to stop it. This is an important point. A packet filtering firewall does not stop viruses that are transported using HTTP, SMTP, and so on. It stops TCP/IP traffic only on certain ports.

We used the logging facilities of `iptables` to track the source of these problems, and we proceeded to remove the virus (the customer subsequently installed virus scanners on all machines).

To combat these internal problems in the future, we tightened the security of the organization from a network standpoint. We restricted what could be accessed on the Internet from the internal network apart from the essentials. This stopped port scans from exiting the network and stopped most incarnations of virus transmission over Internet protocols.

Note   *Port scanning* is when a machine automatically tries to connect to a range of TCP/IP ports on a machine to see if there are any services listening. It is used not only by crackers, but also by legitimate users who want to see what services are available on a server. You should port scan only hosts that you have been allowed to interrogate. Port scanning a machine usually triggers alarms on a system, and you may get into trouble depending on what the administrator is feeling like that day.

This example fully illustrates that network security must be considered as a whole, not just as a threat from the Internet.

Configuring a Firewall with iptables

To configure a firewall on Linux, you need to get used to the `iptables` command, which is used to manipulate the kernel packet filtering settings from user space. (Refer to Chapter 6 for more information on TCP/IP, because an understanding of TCP/IP is needed.)

Note   The terms *user space* and *kernel space* are used a lot in the Unix community. When something runs in kernel space, it is under the control and the constraints of the kernel. Something running in kernel space could be a kernel module or the packet filtering code. When something is in user space, it uses the system libraries and is not under the strict control of the kernel. We use `iptables` (user space) to tell the kernel space filtering code (`netfilter`) what it needs to do with the TCP/IP packets it receives. When a TCP/IP packet is received by the kernel, it is passed and acted upon in kernel space by the `netfilter` code.

The kernel filtering code uses chains to signify where a packet is in the kernel. Figure 24-1 shows an overview of how the kernel sees a TCP/IP packet. This also helps us to see how `iptables` interacts with these packets later in the chapter.

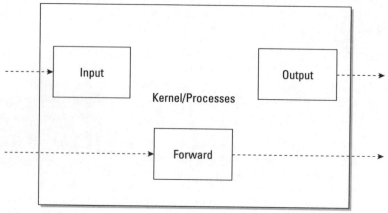

Figure 24-1: Overview of the kernel chains

The filtering chains are extremely important to the operation of the filtering code because they determine whether or not a packet should be interpreted by the kernel.

The chains themselves represent the final destination of the packet:

✦ **INPUT** — The packet is destined for the firewall itself.

✦ **OUTPUT** — The packet originated from the firewall.

✦ **FORWARD** — The packet is passing through the firewall (neither originates from nor is destined for the firewall).

Consider these examples to show how the chains work in a normal firewall:

✦ My firewall at home is Linux based, and it does a few things that most small firewalls do: It provides my non-routable addresses with a public Internet address through Network Address Translation (NAT), and runs an SSH server for me to log in remotely to my network.

Note   When setting up a firewall appliance, you need to enable IP forwarding. *IP forwarding* allows packets to be routed from one network interface to another in the Linux machine. This is integral to the whole process of routing packets and the Linux machine's acting as a router. Most `iptables` firewalls that protect a network run on low-cost, low CPU–powered hardware.

When a TCP/IP packet leaves my laptop, it is sent to the default route, which is my `iptables` firewall on my router. When the firewall receives the packet, it analyzes it to find its destination. As it sees that the packet is not destined for the machine itself, it is sent to the FORWARD chain.

When in the FORWARD chain, the packet will traverse all firewall rules until it is either dropped or is sent to the outbound network interface (my ADSL router) for further processing.

The important part of the scenario is that any non-local packets (destined or originating from the machine) are passed to the forward chain (for forwarding!).

✦ When I use SSH to connect to my firewall from the Internet, a TCP/IP packet attempts to open an SSH connection for me. In the same way that the packet will reach the firewall as in the forwarding example, the kernel analyzes the packet to see where it is destined. As my machine is the final destination for the packet, it is inserted into the INPUT chain for further processing. If the packet is allowed through, it is passed over to the kernel to be handed over to the user space (which is normal when no firewalling is used).

✦ The OUTPUT chain is slightly different because it does not deal with traffic from the network. An OUTPUT chain is triggered only when a packet originates from the machine itself. For example, if you are logged in to the machine and initiate an FTP connection to the outside world, this is considered a packet that traverses the OUTPUT chain.

Implementing an iptables Firewall

As a general rule of thumb when talking about network security, you should deny all and allow some. This means that by default you should not allow any network traffic at all to a machine, and then enable only what is needed for the operation of your firewall/network/server.

> **Note** In the rest of the examples in this chapter, you must be logged in as root because you are changing memory belonging to the kernel through the `iptables` command, and that requires a privileged user.

To make this easier, `netfilter` provides a default policy for each chain (INPUT, OUTPUT, FORWARD). You can set this policy to drop all packets that do not trigger a rule (that is, are not explicitly allowed).

The Linux filtering code is always running, but by default, the policy for the chains is ACCEPT (see Listing 24-1).

Listing 24-1: **The Default Filtering Rules**

```
bible:~ # iptables -L
Chain INPUT (policy ACCEPT)
target    prot opt source          destination

Chain FORWARD (policy ACCEPT)
target    prot opt source          destination

Chain OUTPUT (policy ACCEPT)
target    prot opt source          destination
```

For each chain, the output of `iptables -L` (list rules) contains information on the target (ACCEPT, DROP, and REJECT are the most common targets), the TCP/IP protocol, and the packet source and destination.

iptables Targets

When a TCP/IP packet is analyzed, a decision is made about what to do if that packet matches a rule. If the packet matches a rule, it is sent to a `netfilter` target, most likely ACCEPT, DROP, or REJECT.

We'll use an incoming SSH connection to a firewall as an example. It will be a TCP connection on port 22 on the INPUT rule at a bare minimum. If you have a rule that describes this packet, you need to tell the `netfilter` system to ACCEPT this packet into the TCP/IP stack for further processing by the kernel.

However, you could tell `netfilter` to DROP or REJECT the packet:

✦ When a packet is sent to the DROP target, it simply disappears and the sending machine does not know this has happened until it times out.

✦ When a packet is subject to the REJECT target, the sending machine is notified through an Internet Control Message Protocol (ICMP) message that the port was not reachable (that is, it was stopped).

Tip

If you configure the default policy of all chains to DROP/REJECT all non-triggered packets, it is unlikely you need to use these as targets because any packets that have not been explicitly ACCEPTed will be subject to the DROP/REJECT target.

Stateful Firewall

The `netfilter` firewalling code provides a stateful firewall, and this is a great new feature of the `netfilter` code. In the past, it was up to the administrator to track all connections through the firewall, which produced a lot of rules that were difficult to manage. With a stateful firewall, `netfilter` keeps a record of connection states. With this information, `netfilter` can track a connection initiation and match up related network traffic.

For example, previously, if you wanted to allow an incoming connection to SSH on the firewall, you had to first allow the incoming connection and also the return traffic from the SSH server to the client. With stateful firewalls, you can tell the firewall to manage the subsequent outgoing connection automatically because it is aware that an incoming connection to the machine will produce traffic in the opposite direction. It does this by storing the state of a connection and acting upon it with connection tracking.

To enable the stateful connection tracking, you need to enable states in the firewall. We discuss this in a small firewall script later in the chapter.

Setting Your First Rules

Before you touch upon setting more specific rules, you need to set the default policy for the firewall and enable some state rules (see Listing 24-2).

Listing 24-2: **Setting Initial Firewall Rules**

```
bible:~ # iptables -P INPUT DROP
bible:~ # iptables -P OUTPUT DROP
bible:~ # iptables -P FORWARD DROP
bible:~ # iptables -A INPUT -m state --state ESTABLISHED,RELATED -j ACCEPT
bible:~ # iptables -A FORWARD -m state --state ESTABLISHED,RELATED -j ACCEPT
bible:~ # iptables -A OUTPUT -m state --state NEW,ESTABLISHED,RELATED -j ACCEPT
```

Here, you have set the default policy for all chains to drop the packets. At this moment in time, all network connections, regardless of their originating address, will be dropped.

To set or change the policy of a chain, you need to specify that this is a policy edit (-P), the chain (INPUT, OUTPUT, or FORWARD), and also what to do with the packet.

It's a secure feeling knowing that any connection from the Internet that you do not need is dropped and the sender has to wait for a timeout before being notified. Imagine someone running a port scan of all 64,000 available ports on a TCP/IP machine. If they have to wait for a timeout on each port, it will take them quite a few hours to complete the full scan. It provides a kind of tar pit for any malicious users.

This is also true for internal connection, too. If your users are interested in what they can and cannot connect to, without reading the network rules, then making them wait will, one hopes, deter them from pushing the network too hard.

You have also configured the stateful firewall with the -m state declaration. This tells the firewall that you will allow any established or related connections on the INPUT chain.

This may seem like quite a big security hole, but bear in mind that it will allow *only* a connection that has been established, not a *new* connection. For the stateful rules to kick in, you would have already had to allow a *new* connection through the chain.

Depending on how paranoid you are about security, you may not want to allow all *new* connections from the firewall itself. However, if you want to use the firewall machine as a server, or want to be able to "bounce" from the machine to other hosts without the burden of setting up new rules for every protocol or TCP port you want to connect to, it is quite useful.

At this point, your firewall is locked down with the exception of allowing outgoing connections.

Now, suppose you want to allow an incoming SSH connection to the firewall.

Adding a Rule

When you add a rule proper, you need to specify as much information as possible to have full control over the TCP/IP packets you are allowing into the trusted network.

At a minimum, you need the chain, protocol, and destination port. With just this information, you do not have a very good rule, because it does not specify the interface you are allowing the SSH connection to. Another option that can be set is the connection type:

✦ **NEW** — This is a new connection; no other traffic is associated with this packet.

✦ **ESTABLISHED** — This packet is from a machine you already have a connection to (remember, you both send and receive data when a connection exists).

✦ **RELATED** — This packet is related to an existing connection. The FTP protocol, for example, makes a connection to the FTP server, and the FTP server actually makes a separate connection to the client. This separate connection from the server to the client is a RELATED connection.

```
iptables -A INPUT -p tcp -dport ssh -i eth0 -j ACCEPT
```

In this example, you have told `netfilter` that you want to append (-A) a rule to the INPUT chain, specifying the TCP protocol (-p tcp), with a destination port (-dport) of `ssh` (port 22), incoming (-i) on the `eth0` interface, and finally that you want to ACCEPT the packet (-j ACCEPT). The -j parameter means "jump to a target." Remember that `netfilter` rules are in a chain, so you are saying, "Stop processing this chain because you have a match and jump to the target." In this case, ACCEPT.

Note   The `-dport` parameter can take either a numerical port number or a service name that is specified in `/etc/services`.

When setting up a rule for connections, you really need to know how the protocol works. In the case of SSH, it is well known that it is a TCP protocol, running on port 22. With this in mind, it is relatively easy to write a rule for it.

It is up to you as to how you want to write the rule regarding the state of the connection, but because the initial INPUT state rule has allowed all ESTABLISHED and RELATED connections, you do not need to explicitly set the state to NEW because you have effectively allowed all connection types for SSH by not explicitly setting them.

Caution   When you do not specify something explicitly with an `iptables` rule, it is assumed that you want the default setting. For example, if you did not set the interface for the incoming connection, `netfilter` would have allowed an SSH connection on all network interfaces. This is indeed the same for the protocol type and the destination port. Be very careful how you write your rules, and make sure you explicitly set everything you want to control; otherwise you will probably let in more than you think.

For any incoming connections you want to have on a firewall, you can append a rule in the same way you did with the SSH connection.

The Order of Rules

You must be very conscious of the order you set rules in a chain because `netfilter` passes the TCP/IP packet through the rules in the order they are inserted into the kernel. If you want to insert a rule at the top of the list (that is, making it the first rule that is executed), you can use the -I (insert) parameter to `iptables`.

For example, if you are allowing SSH into your firewall from the Internet, but you know that you do not want a certain IP address to have access to SSH, you have to insert the REJECT/DROP rule before the general SSH rule:

```
iptables -A INPUT -p tcp -dport ssh -i eth0 -j ACCEPT
iptables -I INPUT -p tcp -dport ssh -i eth0 -s 10.32.1.4 -j DROP
```

In this example, using the -s option to specify a source IP address, we have inserted the DROP rule before the general SSH acceptance rule.

When a TCP/IP packet has been inserted into a chain, it is checked in order with each rule. If one of the rules matches the TCP/IP packet, it is then sent to the target specified (ACCEPT, DROP, REJECT) immediately. In the case of our inserted SSH DROP rule, it fires off packets destined for the SSH port to the DROP target before it gets to the ACCEPT SSH rule.

In essence, all the TCP/IP packets sequentially go through every rule in the chain until they are directed to a target. If none of the rules fires off a packet to a target, that packet is dealt with by the default policy, which is to kill the packet in this case.

Network Address Translation

While one of the main uses of netfilter is its packet filtering functions, another very important aspect of netfilter is its NAT functions.

Network Address Translation (NAT) is the process whereby the source or destination IP address of a packet is seamlessly changed when it passes through the firewall.

Cross-Reference Chapter 6 contains more information about NAT.

Source NAT

Source NAT (SNAT) works on packets forwarded through the firewall before a packet leaves for the outbound network. For this to work, you must deal with the packets before any routing decisions have been made, and the POSTROUTING chain must be used to implement Source NAT.

The main purpose of SNAT is to hide private networks behind a firewall with a public IP address. This drastically reduces the cost of acquiring public IP addresses and allows you to use non-routable addresses in your internal network.

Note The POSTROUTING chain deals with any packets that are about to be sent out to the network card. This includes any packets that are routed onto other destinations. In the case of SNAT, this is the only chain that you want to use because, for example, it makes no sense to source NAT traffic coming into the firewall INPUT chain.

Figure 24-2 details a home network that uses netfilter to SNAT our internal network.

In this scenario, all of the machines are behind a netfilter firewall that not only protects the machines, but also provides SNAT for outgoing connections. For SNAT to work, IP forwarding must be enabled. To do this, enter a 1 into /proc/sys/net/ipv4/ip_forward.

```
bible:~ # echo 1 > /proc/sys/net/ipv4/ip_forward
```

This will immediately enable IP forwarding on your Linux machine. This is a volatile operation, and once your machine has been rebooted, IP forwarding will be turned off by default.

To set IP forwarding on by default, edit the file /etc/sysconfig/sysctl and change IP_FORWARD from no to yes and re-run SuSEconfig. While editing the sysctl file, make sure that DISABLE_ECN is set to yes.

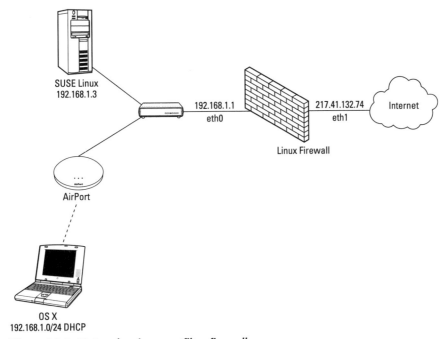

Figure 24-2: Network using a netfilter firewall

Tip

ECN is short for Enhanced Congestion Notification. This is a new feature of TCP/IP that allows machines to notify you that a network route is congested. It is a great feature, but unfortunately is not in widespread circulation and can stop your network traffic from traversing the Internet correctly if it goes through a router that does not support ECN. We have been on customer sites where their networks just stopped working for certain sites for no reason. Turning off ECN fixed this.

When IP forwarding has been enabled, you can insert the SNAT rule into the POSTROUTING chain.

In the home network, you need to source NAT all the internal traffic (192.168.1.0/24) to the firewall public address of 217.41.132.74. To do this, you need to insert a SNAT rule into the NAT table.

Note

The NAT table is used specifically for address translation rules. This includes source and destination address translation.

```
bible:~ # iptables -t nat -A POSTROUTING -s 192.168.1.0/24 -o eth1 -j SNAT -to 217.41.132.74
```

Here, we have told `iptables` to edit the `nat` table (-t nat) by appending a rule to the POSTROUTING chain. We have stated that any traffic from the 192.168.1.0/24 net-

work (-s) and destined to leave the firewall through eth1 (-o) should be source
address NAT'd to 217.41.132.74.

In the example, note that we have tried to be as descriptive as possible concerning
what traffic should be subject to the SNAT, detailing the source IP address (specifying the network address with netmask) and the network adaptor that the traffic will
leave on.

You know that the traffic you need to be SNAT'd will leave the eth1 interface
because you want to SNAT only traffic that is heading out to the Internet.
This can be through the eth1 interface only.

Any traffic that is sent back to the machines behind the firewall (for example, during the three-way handshake) will be translated back by the firewall (it remembers
connection states) and the destination address will automatically be set to the
address of the machine on the private network that initiated the connection.

Allowing the Packets to be Forwarded

It is all well and good setting up SNAT, but the astute of you will probably realize
that you have already told netfilter not to allow any forwarded traffic through the
firewall (the default FORWARD policy is DROP). To correct this, you need to allow
the firewall to forward these packets before they can be manipulated by the SNAT
rule.

To do this, you need to enable forwarding for traffic from the private network to the
Internet:

```
bible:~ # iptables -A FORWARD -s 192.168.1.0/24 -i eth0 -o eth1 -j  ACCEPT
```

Here, iptables is being used to append (- A) to the FORWARD chain (any traffic that
enters and then leaves the firewall on separate interfaces). Any traffic from the
192.168.1.0/24 network entering the firewall on interface eth0 and leaving on interface eth1 will be allowed through.

So, in this example, we have told netfilter that any traffic from the 192.168.1.0/24
network coming in on eth0 and leaving the firewall on eth1 should be allowed
through. Again, we are relying on the fact that any traffic coming in on eth0 and
leaving on eth1 that is from 192.168.1.0/24 will be traffic we want to go out to the
Internet.

Tip

In this example, we have been quite liberal in what we are allowing our users to
access on the Internet. It is usually the policy of most companies that IM clients,
P2P, and IRC should not be allowed from the corporate network. As it stands,
users can access anything on the Internet as if they were directly connected. For
the home network example, this is fine because the users are trusted. However, if
you are implementing a corporate firewall, you will probably need to have quite a

few DROP rules in the FORWARD chain, or do the right thing and deny everything and allow only essential traffic (maybe only HTTP).

Destination NAT

Destination NAT (DNAT) is a nice feature when building `netfilter` firewalls. It does the exact opposite of the SNAT function by translating the destination address of a network packet into another address.

Imagine in the example in Figure 24-2 that you had a mail server on your desktop machine. If you want to give access to that machine to Internet users, you can't just tell the firewall that you want everyone to access the IP 192.168.1.3 over port 25; because this is a non-routable address, Internet users would never be able to reach it. To combat this, you can tell `netfilter` that any traffic destined for port 25 on the public firewall address should be redirected to the machine 192.168.1.3. Any return traffic to the initiating machine will have the source address of the firewall, making the connection routable. And as far as the initiating machine is concerned, it has no idea that the machine it is actually talking to is hidden behind a firewall and is on a non-routable address.

To create the illusion, you need to add a DNAT rule to the NAT table for the Simple Mail Transport Protocol (SMTP) service.

```
bible:~ # iptables -t nat -A PREROUTING -p tcp --dport smtp -i eth1 -j DNAT -to-
destination=192.168.1.3
```

Here, `iptables` has been told to work on the NAT table (`-t nat`) by appending to the PREROUTING chain. You have stated that any traffic that is TCP (`-p tcp`)–based, with a destination port of SMTP (25), and entering the firewall on `eth1` should be destination NAT'd to 192.168.1.3.

In this case, all traffic for port 25 (SMTP) on the public network interface of the firewall will have its destination address changed to 192.168.1.3. The port destination of 25 will be untouched (we will come to this later).

Note　　When enabling DNAT, you have to insert the rules into the PREROUTING chain because a routing decision has to be made on the final destination of the packet. At this point in the `netfilter` processing in the PREROUTING chain, the final destination address has not been inserted into the packet, so the routing decision is still yet to be made after this for successful delivery.

In the same regard as SNAT, you still need to allow traffic destined on port 25 to 192.168.1.3 to be forwarded through the firewall.

```
bible:~ # iptables -A FORWARD -p tcp -dport 25 -d 192.168.1.3 -i eth1 -o eth0 -j ACCEPT
```

Here, `iptables` will append to the FORWARD chain, allowing through any TCP traffic that is destined for the SMTP port on 192.168.1.3 entering the firewall on `eth1` and leaving on `eth0`.

When set, all traffic destined for port 25 on the firewall public interface is successfully forwarded to 192.168.1.3.

Redirecting Traffic

What if you want to redirect traffic to a different port on the firewall? This is very common when you are setting up a transparent HTTP proxy with something like Squid or another content proxy.

A redirection rule does not redirect to an IP, only a port. This makes it a local rule to the firewall only. With this in mind, any redirect rules must have a matching INPUT rule allowing the traffic to be accepted on the redirected port.

```
bible:~ # iptables -t nat -A PREROUTING -p tcp --dport 80 -i eth0 -s 192.168.1.0/24 -j REDIRECT
--to-port=3128
bible:~ # iptables -A INPUT -p tcp --dport 3128 -s 192.168.1.0/24 -j ACCEPT
```

In the first instance, we have told `iptables` to append to the PREROUTING chain in the NAT table. Any traffic that is TCP-based, destined for port 80 (HTTP), entering the firewall in `eth0` from 192.168.1.0/24 should be redirected to port 3128 on the firewall itself.

In the second instance, we have appended to the INPUT chain (traffic destined for the firewall itself), allowing TCP traffic destined for port 3128 (the standard Squid proxy port number) from the 192.168.1.0/24 network.

So, any outbound traffic (to the Internet) that is for port 80 (HTTP) will be redirected to port 3128. Assuming that you have Squid running and properly configured as a transparent proxy, all of your web traffic will be automatically cached.

 Cross-Reference For more information on Squid, see Chapter 26.

Allowing ICMP Traffic

It is all well and good having a secure firewall, but you still need to be able to receive ICMP traffic so that your users, you, and other Internet users are aware if there is a problem.

Internet Control Message Protocol (ICMP) is integral to the working of the Internet. ICMP is used to send status and error messages about the state of the network to interested parties. For example, when you `ping` a machine, the `ping` packet and its echo are sent over ICMP. If you cannot access a machine because its network connectivity is not working, you are told this over ICMP, which your application interprets and tells you "Destination Unreachable."

One traditional cracker attempt to subvert your network is by issuing an ICMP redirect message. This tells a server that a route is unavailable and traffic for that destination should be routed through another destination.

As a minimum, you should allow destination unreachable, source quench (when you need to send smaller packets), and Time to Live (TTL) errors, which is when the packet has traveled through too many routers without reaching its destination. It is up to you if you want to allow `ping` requests or not. Traditionally, you do not enable these as it gives malicious users another tool during initial investigation for an attack.

To allow these types of ICMP traffic, you need to allow inbound ICMP and some outbound ICMP packets:

```
bible:~ # iptables -I INPUT -p icmp --icmp-type destination-unreachable -j ACCEPT
bible:~ # iptables -I INPUT -p icmp --icmp-type source-quench -j ACCEPT
bible:~ # iptables -I INPUT -p icmp --icmp-type time-exceeded -j ACCEPT
```

For each ICMP protocol type you have allowed, you are accepting incoming (that is, destined for the firewall) ICMP traffic that reports destination unreachable, source quench, and TTL exceeded.

Allowing Loopback

It is advisable that you allow loopback traffic on your firewall because many services that you usually assume can communicate internally with each other will fail if you don't. To do this, you can specify that the loopback device should not be restricted:

```
bible:~ # iptables -A INPUT -i lo -j ACCEPT
bible:~ # iptables -A OUTPUT -o lo -j ACCEPT
```

In this example, by appending to the INPUT chain you accept any type of traffic that is destined for (`-i`) or sent out (`-o`) of the loopback (`lo`) device.

As the loopback device is not capable of forwarding packets, you do not need to enable traffic through the FORWARD chain.

Logging Dropped Packets

When your firewall has been configured to your liking, you will want to log any traffic that has not been explicitly sanctioned by you. To do this, you need a final rule before the packet hits the default policy for the chain that uses a target of LOG.

The LOG target interprets the TCP/IP packet and logs it via the syslog facility for you to monitor unauthorized traffic.

Just logging raw, unauthorized traffic is quite difficult to manage, and thankfully the LOG target enables you to specify a log prefix to distinguish the entry based on the chain it originated from:

```
bible:~ # iptables -A INPUT -j LOG --log-prefix=INPUT:
bible:~ # iptables -A OUTPUT -j LOG --log-prefix=OUTPUT:
bible:~ # iptables -A FORWARD -j LOG --log-prefix=FORWARD:
```

In this example, for each chain that a packet traverses, you have appended a rule that will send all packets to the LOG target (-j LOG). The -log-prefix parameter will make sure each packet that is logged is prefixed by INPUT:, OUTPUT:, or FORWARD: (depending on the chain the rule has been appended to).

Any traffic that does not get triggered by a rule will be logged using the LOG target before hitting the default policy. For each chain, you are logging the packet details, with a prefix relating to the chain it originated from.

Caution

The location of the LOG rules is of paramount importance. If the LOG target were inserted at the beginning of the chain, all traffic, whether it is allowed or not, would be logged. You will find your logs filling up very quickly if you make this mistake.

Using SuSEfirewall2

SUSE includes its own sysconfig-based firewall script called SuSEfirewall2. The SuSEfirewall script has come a long way since its conception many years ago and provides a robust feature set that can be configured through YaST.

For new users who need to set up a quick firewall, this is the perfect option. We would have suggested in years gone by that you should write your own firewall script, but if you do not feel the need to be able to control your rules explicitly, SuSEfirewall produces a robust secure firewall for most environments.

To configure a small firewall for use at home using the YaST management system, follow these steps:

1. In YaST, select Security and Users ➪ Firewall (see Figure 24-3). When the module is loaded, you can continue with the firewall configuration.

2. Once the firewall configuration has been loaded, you will be asked how you want the SuSEfirewall to start on your system (Figure 24-4). If this system needs to be constantly protected, you will need to make sure "When Booting" is selected. Using the initial configuration screen, you will also be able to manually stop or start the firewall (you could also do this on the command line using rcSuSEfirewall2 start/stop).

3. To select the network interfaces that will take part in the firewall configuration, click on "Interfaces." It is very important that you get this right; otherwise, your configuration will be the wrong way round and will not work as you expect. In the sample network configuration previously in the chapter, you had eth0 as the internal network interface and eth1 as the external public interface, so set that here as well (see Figure 24-5).

Figure 24-3: Loading the Firewall YaST module

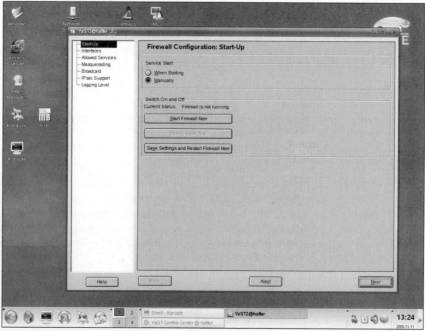

Figure 24-4: Configuring firewall startup

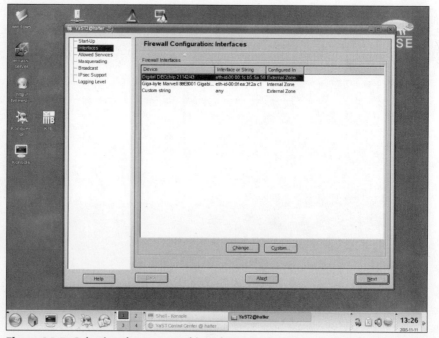

Figure 24-5: Selecting the protected interfaces

4. You need to select what services are allowed into the firewall (see Figure 24-6). To add a new service to the firewall, select the service from the drop-down list, and click "Add." This is the same as defining an INPUT chain rule. Be very careful what you want to allow into the firewall because if any of these services are compromised, a cracker will have access to your first line of defense. If you want to stop all access from your internal network to the firewall directly, select "Project Firewall from Internal Zone."

5. With many firewalls, you will want to masquerade all outgoing connections. To do this, click on "Masquerading." If you wish to masquerade all outgoing network connections from the internal network to your external network interface, select "Masquerade Networks."

   If you wish to Destination NAT an incoming connection to another internal machine, click "Add" to define a masquerade rule.

   You will be presented with the "Add Masquerade Redirect Rule" (Figure 24-7). To define a masquerade rule, you will need to edit the Source Network (0/0 for all Internet machines), the receiving port, the destination address, and the destination port.

   Once you are happy with your masquerade rule, click "Add."

6. It is always a good idea to log any malicious packets that hit the firewall, and you can choose how verbose you want to be. In Figure 24-8, you can see that we've chosen to log all denied packets, and log only critical allowed packets.

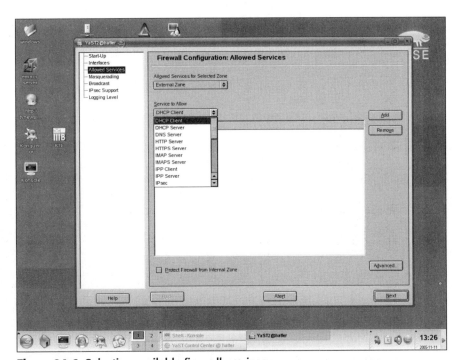

Figure 24-6: Selecting available firewall services

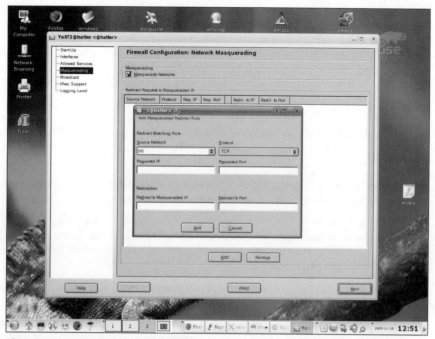

Figure 24-7: Enabling Masquerading

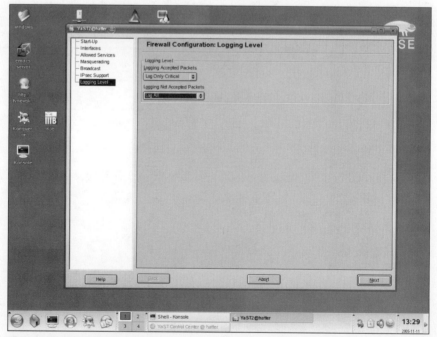

Figure 24-8: Configuring logging

7. When you are happy with the configuration, click Next to save and continue to commit your firewall. You will be presented with an overview of your firewall configuration. If you are happy with the configuration, click "Accept."

When saved, your firewall configuration will be implemented. If you notice any strange behavior on your network after this, check the logs on your firewall for dropped packets.

What Next?

Firewalls are the first step in protecting your network. They are sometimes all that stand between you and crackers. Many organizations incorporate a multitier, multivendor firewall solution to provide as much security as possible. Keep two things in mind:

✦ The first and most important rule of firewall building is to design it first! Sit down with the relevant departments in your organization to see what is needed and then come up with a conceptual diagram that describes what you need to do before typing a single rule.

✦ And remember, deny all, and then enable specific services that are needed. Better that than leave a massive backdoor in your firewall.

iptables is a huge topic, and we've given you the best bits to help you move forward. However, the best way to learn is to set up a small network and test out some rules to see how it works. For more information, the iptables man page is excellently written, and the iptables team has some great documentation on the iptables web site at www.netfilter.org.

✦   ✦   ✦

Working with LDAP in SUSE

Back in the day, the only way to centrally manage your users and services was to use Network Information System (NIS). NIS was an endeavor by Sun to help Unix administrators manage their users without having to create user accounts locally on all machines.

NIS is capable of maintaining user account information, user groups, services, hosts, and many more pieces of information that, historically, needed to be managed on a local level.

NIS was great for what it did at the time, but it had a few shortcomings; one problem, in particular, was that it wasn't great at dealing with very large amounts of data. We don't mean the physical size of the data, but the management of that data. NIS uses flat files as input to the NIS database, which does not bode well in large infrastructures. One other major drawback of NIS was that it could not store any other information apart from account and systems data.

One way around this management problem is to use a tree to organize data in a manageable fashion. This is where LDAP comes to the rescue.

Lightweight Directory Access Protocol (LDAP) organizes data in a hierarchical structure, allowing you to organize information based on departments, or any other distinguishing method.

When introducing people to LDAP, we have always found that it is not an easy concept to explain because it is not easily compared to any existing technology. In this chapter, we give you an overview of what LDAP is, its uses, how to populate an LDAP server with information, and also a scenario that is common to the use of LDAP, including configuration.

What Is LDAP?

LDAP is not a specific server. Much in the same way that Domain Name System (DNS) and Simple Mail Transport Protocol (SMTP) are conceptual protocols, LDAP describes the organization of data, access to the data, and the protocol used to talk to an LDAP server.

The Linux LDAP implementation is the extremely popular OpenLDAP server. It has been around for a very long time and uses the LDAP specification as a base to implement new features.

Note   LDAP is a part of many organizations although many people in those organizations aren't even aware of its use. The Active Directory service from Microsoft is heavily based on the LDAP protocol, as is Novell's eDirectory implementation.

The main distinguishing factor of LDAP is in the way it stores its information. All data in an LDAP database is stored in a tree. LDAP is an inverse tree in the same way that your filesystem is. At the top of the LDAP tree, you have the base object, usually the organization. Below this, you then have objects that are part of the LDAP tree, or you can also have a further split using subtrees.

Figure 25-1 puts this structure into a diagram.

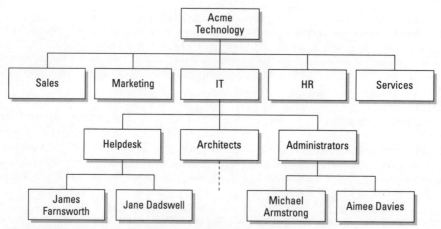

Figure 25-1: Conceptual overview of LDAP

When thinking about LDAP, try to think not on a technology level, but on an organizational level. LDAP design should follow the organization of what you are storing data about. For our example, we will take the organization of a fictional company called Acme Technology. Acme, like many organizations, has departments that deal with certain parts of the business (Sales, Marketing, HR, IT, the Board, and so on), and we will model this in our LDAP server.

We have taken the IT department and expanded it slightly to include job title and also some people in the organization. You may be thinking that this looks a lot like a standard organizational chart that you see when you start a company, and this is how you should view it.

All the people in the organization belong to a department, which belongs to the organization, and this methodology is how you should see LDAP. You can see that the tree structure lends itself very well to organizational data, whether it is just for an address book or user accounts.

LDAP Objects

LDAP uses *objects* to store data. Take the user object as an example. You can store a lot of information about a user: first and last name, location, telephone, fax, pager, mobile, and maybe a picture of that person. LDAP uses classes to define what information can be stored about that object, commonly known as object attributes.

Objects can be a business, a car, a person, a stock item, or a desk. Any data about these objects can be defined and stored in an LDAP server.

LDAP is very particular about what information you store in the LDAP server because it needs to maintain the integrity of all data. To do this, an object is specifically defined so that it *must* include certain data, *may* contain other data about an object, and will include *nothing* else. This may seem restrictive, but it stops any data that does not concern the object being stored.

For example, take the employee Jane Dadswell; the record *must* contain her first, middle, and last name; employee ID; Social Security number; telephone number; email address; date of birth; and her location (the list is not exhaustive, and we expect you can come up with more). One the other hand, her record *may* contain information about her car (if she has one), pager number (if she has one), picture, and home telephone number.

Any other data will not be allowed because the object is strictly defined to store only certain information. The object definitions are in the LDAP schema, which we talk about later in the chapter. At this point, you just need to be aware that there are very tight restrictions on what data is associated with an object, and that many object definitions exist for many situations.

The Hierarchy

You know that LDAP is a hierarchical database, but you may not be aware of all of the benefits of this.

Imagine on your filesystem, you have a home directory for a user called Justin: /home/justin. Inside this directory, you have a subdirectory called Documents, with a further subdirectory of Finances. Another user, Roger, has a home directory of /home/roger. Roger also stores information about his finances in his Documents directory.

It just so happens that Roger and Justin both have a file called finances_2004.xml in their Finance directories. Even with the same filename, these two files do not impact each other because their location is different throughout the filesystem tree.

LDAP works the same way. If a person called John Doe joins Acme as an HR assistant and another John Doe (it is a popular name!) joins IT as an architect, their locations in the tree mean that their information is uniquely identified by the path to that data. Figure 25-2 shows another diagram of Acme with some LDAP thrown in to explain how LDAP uses the tree design.

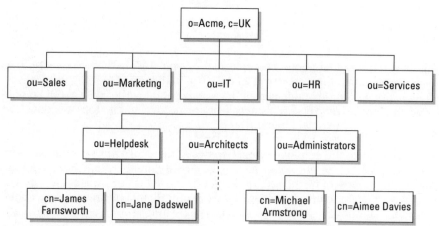

Figure 25-2: Acme organization in LDAP

We have replaced the organizational chart with an LDAP structure. Reading back from Jane Dadswell, much like you read back from the finances_2004.xml file, you can uniquely identify this person in the organization. In the case of Jane Dadswell, her unique entry is cn="Jane Dadswell", ou=Helpdesk, ou=IT, o=Acme, c=UK.

Note   Notice the quotes around Jane Dadswell in the previous entry. This is to make sure the space is included in the cn for Jane.

From this information, you see that Jane Dadswell is in the organization Acme (in the UK), the department of IT, and the subdepartment of Helpdesk.

The person Jane Dadswell is unique in the organization, working on the Helpdesk, and is unique in the LDAP directory. This unique identifier is called the Distinguished Name (dn), and we will refer to this throughout the rest of the chapter.

This is a quick introduction to how LDAP stores its data, and throughout the rest of the chapter, you will learn by example about using LDAP in the Acme organization, taking the organizational chart as a basis for its design.

Designing an LDAP directory is something that has to be done correctly. If you have an up-to-date organizational chart that effectively represents your organization, your life will be a lot easier.

Implementing the LDAP Server

When you have installed the OpenLDAP server using YaST, you need to do some initial configuration. The LDAP server is configured in the file `/etc/openldap/slapd.conf` and is heavily commented. The two very important parts you need to configure before even starting to populate the server are the `basedn` and the `administrator` account.

Configuring the Administrator

The `basedn` is the very top of the LDAP tree. In the base of Acme, the `basedn` will be `o=Acme, c=UK`. The o component means Organization, whereas the c component refers to the country. As with everything in LDAP, there are strict rules on naming the `basedn`. The most common elements are the `o=` and `c=` definitions, but also the general domain component (dc) is used to refer to the fully qualified domain name (FQDN) of the organization. In the case of Acme, you could use a `basedn` of `dc=Acme, dc=co, dc=uk`. However, as we are designing the LDAP structure from an organizational chart, we will use the organizational terms. To edit the LDAP configuration files, you must be root. When you have set the username and password for the administrator, you can be any user as long as you can authenticate as the administrator when connecting to OpenLDAP.

1. In the `slapd.conf` file, find the entry for the `suffix` and the `rootdn` (the administrator user) and change it to reflect your organization.

```
suffix          "o=Acme,c=UK"
rootdn          "cn=admin,o=Acme,c=UK"
```

The `rootdn` should reflect your `basedn` with a user component. In this case, we have used the `cn` definition for the user (Common Name).

2. When the `suffix` and the `rootdn` have been defined, you need to configure the administrator password. There are a few ways to do this — insecure and secure. Obviously, you want to set up the password securely.

Note The `rootdn` is not an entry in the LDAP directory but the account information for the LDAP administrator.

To produce an encrypted password, you need to use the `slappasswd` command:

```
bible:/etc/openldap # slappasswd
New password:
Re-enter new password:
{SSHA}F13k4cAbh0IAxbpKNhH7uVcTL4HGzsJ+
bible:/etc/openldap #
```

Caution You can define the password using cleartext (the password is just entered into the `slapd.conf`), if you want to do a quick and dirty implementation, but it is highly advisable to insert the encrypted form of the password.

3. After you enter the password you want to use twice, the `slappasswd` command returns an encrypted password that can be used in `slapd.conf`.

4. When you have the encrypted password, you need to find the `rootpw` entry in `slapd.conf` and enter it there.

```
rootpw          {SSHA}F13k4cAbh0IAxbpKNhH7uVcTL4HGzsJ+
```

Testing the LDAP Server

When the initial `slapd.conf` configuration has taken place, you need to start the LDAP server with `rcldap`:

```
bible:/etc/openldap # rcldap start
Starting ldap-server                                    done
```

When started, you can use the `ldapsearch` command to bind (connect to) the LDAP server with the administrator account (see Listing 25-1). Unlike an anonymous bind, we are authenticating to the LDAP server.

Tip To start OpenLDAP automatically when the system boots, use `chkconfig`: `chkconfig -a ldap`.

You can connect to the LDAP server with an anonymous bind, which means you have not presented authentication credentials to the LDAP server, and you are limited in what you can read and write to the server based on the default access control list (ACL) settings.

Listing 25-1: **Authenticating to the LDAP Server**

```
bible:/etc/openldap # ldapsearch -x -D "cn=admin,o=Acme,c=UK" -W
Enter LDAP Password:
# extended LDIF
#
# LDAPv3
# base <> with scope sub
# filter: (objectclass=*)
# requesting: ALL
#

# search result
search: 2
result: 32 No such object

# numResponses: 1
```

As you do not have anything in the LDAP server, you will not receive any responses.

The ldapsearch command is extremely powerful, not only for diagnostic purposes, but also for viewing data in the LDAP server. In Listing 25-1, we used the -D option to specify the bindDN with which to connect to the LDAP server, as well as the -W option to tell ldapsearch to ask us for the bind password.

Note We also used the -x option to tell ldapsearch to do a simple bind to the LDAP server. If you do not specify -x, you need to bind using a Simple Authentication and Security Layer (SASL) mechanism. We will not discuss SASL authentication in this chapter because this is just an introduction to LDAP. For more information on configuring OpenLDAP with SASL, refer to the OpenLDAP documentation in /usr/share/doc/packages/openldap2.

Adding Information

When the LDAP server is up and running, you can populate the server with your information. Some tools available for LDAP help with the initial population of LDAP data, as well as migrating existing users on the system to the LDAP directory. Here, we will populate the server with information using an LDIF (LDAP Data Interchange Format) file.

Note

PADL (the reverse of LDAP) provides some infrastructure tools that integrate with LDAP, providing a much easier environment for an administrator to work in. They also have designed the Pluggable Authentication Modules (PAM) LDAP and name switch service (NSS) LDAP modules that allow a Unix machine to query the LDAP server for user information. We discuss PAM/NSS LDAP integration later in the chapter. Download the PADL migration tools from `www.padl.com/download/MigrationTools.tgz`.

LDIF

An LDIF file is a text file containing LDAP data in a protocol defined fashion. You need to create an LDIF file that defines not only the data to be stored, but also the structure of the LDAP server. Use your favorite text editor to create the LDIF file. In Listing 25-2, we have created one you can work from that reflects the Acme organization.

Listing 25-2: **LDIF File for Acme**

```
dn: o=Acme,c=UK
o: Acme
objectClass: top
objectClass: organization

dn: ou=Sales,o=Acme,c=UK
ou: Sales
objectClass: top
objectClass: organizationalUnit

dn: ou=Marketing,o=Acme,c=UK
ou: Marketing
objectClass: top
objectClass: organizationalUnit

dn: ou=IT,o=Acme,c=UK
ou: IT
objectClass: top
objectClass: organizationalUnit

dn: ou=HR,o=Acme,c=UK
ou: HR
objectClass: top
objectClass: organizationalUnit

dn: ou=Services,o=Acme,c=UK
ou: Services
objectClass: top
objectClass: organizationalUnit
```

```
dn: ou=Helpdesk,ou=IT,o=Acme,c=UK
ou: Helpdesk
objectClass: top
objectClass: organizationalUnit

dn: ou=Architects,ou=IT,o=Acme,c=UK
ou: Architects
objectClass: top
objectClass: organizationalUnit

dn: ou=Administrators,ou=IT,o=Acme,c=UK
ou: Administrators
objectClass: top
objectClass: organizationalUnit
```

Caution   It is of paramount importance when constructing an LDIF file that there are no trailing spaces after any data in a record. It is a common mistake when people create an LDIF entry that there is a trailing space, and in the case of an LDIF entry, this will create havoc with data when it is inserted into the LDAP server. Data that looks correct in the LDIF file will not be the same once it is in the LDAP server. Also, the order of the LDIF entries is important.

Most of the entries are identical apart from the ou (organizational unit) they are defining. We will go through the file to help you understand what the entries mean.

Each entry has a specific DN that is unique across the tree. For example, the Architects' organizational unit tells us that the Architects are in the organizational unit of IT, in the Acme organization. Referring back to the organizational chart of Acme, you can see this is reflected correctly. (We hope you see how easy it is to compile the initial population of the LDAP server when you have access to the organizational chart!)

Each entry defines the structure of the LDAP server and does not actually enter information that you are interested in at this point. Apart from the first entry, you are creating an organizational unit that will hold data about people in that department.

Dissecting an Object

An entry is composed of the DN, the object being created (in this case, the organizational unit), and two object class definitions. We talked about objects and restrictions on what can be stored in each object, and the objectClass entry is what defines this.

The top objectClass is very special as it says that all objects should be defined by an objectClass. It may seem bizarre that there is an object class that defines that an object must have a class, but it means that the LDAP structure is totally modular and not hard-coded.

The `organizationalUnit objectClass` defines the object to be an organizational unit. There are many other `objectClasses` that define a massive set of objects that can be used to describe anything that would traditionally fit into an LDAP server. We will come across more throughout the chapter.

Note   An object may be defined by multiple object classes to be able to provide a large breadth of information. We will see this in practice when dealing with people, but for now, understand that it is not just one object class, one object.

Inserting the LDIF File

When the LDIF file that contains an organizational structure has been created, you need to enter that information into the LDAP server. First, make sure your LDAP server is running:

```
bible:~ # rcldap status
Checking for service ldap:                    running
```

When the LDAP server is running, you need to add the entries (see Listing 25-3).

Listing 25-3: **Inserting LDIF Entries into LDAP**

```
bible:~ # ldapadd  -D "cn=admin,o=Acme,c=UK"  -x -W -f /tmp/top.ldif
Enter LDAP Password:
adding new entry "o=Acme,c=UK"

adding new entry "ou=Sales,o=Acme,c=UK "

adding new entry "ou=Marketing,o=Acme,c=UK"

adding new entry "ou=IT,o=Acme,c=UK"

adding new entry "ou=HR,o=Acme,c=UK"

adding new entry "ou=Services,o=Acme,c=UK"

adding new entry "ou=Helpdesk,ou=IT,o=Acme,c=UK"

adding new entry "ou=Architects,ou=IT,o=Acme,c=UK"

adding new entry "ou=Administrators,ou=IT,o=Acme,c=UK"
```

The `ldapadd` command is similar in use to the `ldapsearch` command. You need to bind (`-D`) as the administrator, with a simple bind (`-x`) and get `ldapadd` to ask you for the password (- w). The only difference is the -f parameter to specify the location of the LDIF file we have created. All being well, the entries defined in the LDIF file will be added to the LDAP server.

Now that you have the organizational structure in the LDAP server, you need to populate it with some objects.

Adding User Data to the LDAP Server

You need to define what information you will hold about users before you create the LDIF files. As you are going to use this information to hold user accounts as well as information about users, you will use the inetOrgPerson, person, posixAccount, shadowAccount, and organizationalPerson object classes.

Note

> You can find more information about the data you can use in an LDIF file and also in an LDAP server in the OpenLDAP schemas. These are located in /etc/open ldap/schema.

Referring to the schema in /etc/openldap/schema, you can see that the person object class can contain the information shown in Table 25-1.

Table 25-1	
person Object Class	
Element	*Description*
sn	Second name[a]
cn	Common name[a]
UserPassword	Password
TelephoneNumber	Contact number
SeeAlso	Freeform referral entry
Description	Description of the user

[a]Must be in the object data

Each object class defines what each object can contain, and this information is defined in the LDAP schema files. For more information on what is included in an object class, view the schema files in /etc/openldap/schema.

You now need to construct an LDIF file for the users. In Listing 25-4, we detail one of the users so that you can see how her profile would look in this organization.

Listing 25-4: **LDIF Listing for Aimee Davies**

```
dn: uid=aimee,ou=Administrators,ou=IT,o=Acme,c=UK
uid: aimee
cn: Aimee Davies
givenName: Aimee
sn: Davies
objectClass: person
objectClass: organizationalPerson
objectClass: inetOrgPerson
objectClass: posixAccount
objectClass: top
objectClass: shadowAccount
userPassword: {crypt}ESLp8vFJWpVEE
shadowLastChange: 12572
shadowMax: 99999
shadowWarning: 7
loginShell: /bin/bash
uidNumber: 1000
gidNumber: 100
homeDirectory: /home/aimee
telephoneNumber: 555-1027
o: Acme UK
gecos: Aimee Davies
```

We have constructed an LDIF file for the administrator Aimee Davies, including account information allowing her to use the LDAP data as a Unix authentication source.

To construct the initial LDIF file, we used the PADL migration tools to transfer a standard user account from /etc/passwd to an LDIF format file, editing this file to add the extra information about the organization and also her telephone number.

You can add each user in the organization to the specific organizational unit that reflects the organizational chart. Using the ldapsearch command, you can now view the data in the LDAP server (see Listing 25-5). You use the -b option to tell ldapsearch that it should search from the o=Acme,c=UK base of the LDAP tree. This enables you to search a certain portion of the LDAP tree, not the whole tree.

Listing 25-5: **Output of ldapsearch for the Entire LDAP Database**

```
bible:/etc/openldap/schema # ldapsearch -x -b "o=Acme,c=UK"
# extended LDIF
#
# LDAPv3
# base <o=Acme,c=UK> with scope sub
```

```
# filter: (objectclass=*)
# requesting: ALL
#

# Acme, UK
dn: o=Acme,c=UK
o: Acme
objectClass: top
objectClass: organization

# Sales, Acme, UK
dn: ou=Sales,o=Acme,c=UK
ou: Sales
objectClass: top
objectClass: organizationalUnit

# Marketing, Acme, UK
dn: ou=Marketing,o=Acme,c=UK
ou: Marketing
objectClass: top
objectClass: organizationalUnit

# IT, Acme, UK
dn: ou=IT,o=Acme,c=UK
ou: IT
objectClass: top
objectClass: organizationalUnit

# HR, Acme, UK
dn: ou=HR,o=Acme,c=UK
ou: HR
objectClass: top
objectClass: organizationalUnit

# Services, Acme, UK
dn: ou=Services,o=Acme,c=UK
ou: Services
objectClass: top
objectClass: organizationalUnit

# Helpdesk, IT, Acme, UK
dn: ou=Helpdesk,ou=IT,o=Acme,c=UK
ou: Helpdesk
objectClass: top
objectClass: organizationalUnit

# Architects, IT, Acme, UK
dn: ou=Architects,ou=IT,o=Acme,c=UK
ou: Architects
objectClass: top
objectClass: organizationalUnit
```

Continued

Listing 25-5: *(continued)*

```
# Administrators, IT, Acme, UK
dn: ou=Administrators,ou=IT,o=Acme,c=UK
ou: Administrators
objectClass: top
objectClass: organizationalUnit

# aimee, Administrators, IT, Acme, UK
dn: uid=aimee,ou=Administrators,ou=IT,o=Acme,c=UK
uid: aimee
cn: Aimee Davies
givenName: Aimee
sn: Davies
objectClass: person
objectClass: organizationalPerson
objectClass: inetOrgPerson
objectClass: posixAccount
objectClass: top
objectClass: shadowAccount
userPassword:: e2NyeXB0fUVTTHHA4dkZKV3BWRUU=
shadowLastChange: 12572
shadowMax: 99999
shadowWarning: 7
loginShell: /bin/bash
uidNumber: 1000
gidNumber: 100
homeDirectory: /home/aimee
telephoneNumber: 555-1027
o: Acme UK
gecos: Aimee Davies

# search result
search: 2
result: 0 Success

# numResponses: 11
# numEntries: 10
```

The initial population of the LDAP server with the organization structure and the addition of the person Aimee Davies is reflected in Listing 25-5.

If you want to see only Aimee's telephone number, use the `ldapsearch` command to filter the output (see Listing 25-6).

Listing 25-6: **Searching for a Specific User and Filtering**

```
bible:/etc/openldap/schema # ldapsearch -x -b "o=Acme,c=UK" "uid=aimee" telephoneNumber
# extended LDIF
#
# LDAPv3
# base <o=Acme,c=UK> with scope sub
# filter: uid=aimee
# requesting: telephoneNumber
#

# aimee, Administrators, IT, Acme, UK
dn: uid=aimee,ou=Administrators,ou=IT,o=Acme,c=UK
telephoneNumber: 555-1027

# search result
search: 2
result: 0 Success

# numResponses: 2
# numEntries: 1
```

In the previous listing, we used the standard `ldapsearch` parameters, added a term
to search for (in quotes), and also the object data we want to view.

The term to search for should be unique to a user account; otherwise you will
receive multiple entries. In the case of the organization, we know that the UID of a
person is unique, as it must be when used as a username in Unix. If you want to
search specifically for an entry, you can explicitly search for the whole of the DN
for the user.

Pluggable Authentication Modules

Before Pluggable Authentication Modules (PAM) came along, any application that
needed to authenticate a user had to read the `/etc/passwd` and `/etc/shadow` files
directly. This restricted how data about users was stored because the data always
had to be in a text file.

PAM provides authentication modules that can obtain user accounts from numerous sources, an LDAP server, a SQL database, or a Windows Active directory, for
example.

PAM works by having a configuration file for each service that needs to authenticate users. For example, the login process has a separate PAM configuration file, as does the imap service.

These service configuration files are stored in /etc/pam.d and contain information about how the process gets information about the user, their account data, and passwords. Each file can contain four types of entries, discussed in Table 25-2.

Table 25-2	
PAM Configuration Entries	
Entry	*Description*
account	Used to check whether the user is allowed to log in, what the account expiry is, and so on.
password	Used to change the user's password.
auth	Used to check the user's password.
session	Used to enable or disable features of the user's session after he or she has authenticated. This can be used to mount the user's home directory automatically.

Note PAM is not just used for usernames and passwords; it is a general authentication library and can be used to check a smart card owned by the user to authenticate or maybe in the future to read biometric data from the user, such as facial recognition.

For each entry type, you can specify a PAM module to handle the account, password, authentication, or session data related to a user account.

For example, if you just want to allow the imap service to authenticate user data to the system /etc/passwd and /etc/shadow, you need at minimum an account and authentication entry. This enables a user to log in if his or her account is active and to also check whether the password provided by the user is correct.

```
auth      required /lib/security/pam-unix.so nullok
account   required /lib/security/pam-unix.so
```

This file has quite a bit of information in it, and you can see an entry for auth and account. The second, third, and fourth fields are also very important when configuring PAM for your service.

The second field determines how the data received back from the PAM module (specified in field three) is acted upon. When a PAM module is used, it returns either a success or a failure back to the process (in this case imap) that tried to authenticate the user. It is this failure that will stop you from logging in for one reason or another, if there is a problem with your account (expiry, for example) or your authentication credentials (incorrect username or password).

The second field can be one of the following:

✦ required — If a failure is encountered by the module, it results in an overall failure of the PAM system for the service (imap). Even if the authentication fails, execution of the remaining definitions in the service configuration continues.

✦ requisite — If a failure occurs, PAM returns a failure immediately and stops executing the rest of the modules in the configuration file.

✦ sufficient — If this PAM module returns a success from the system, it returns an overall success even if a previous PAM module returned a failure (useful to use with the required action).

✦ optional — If authentication succeeds or fails, it is enforced only if this is the only entry for this type of service (account, password, auth, or session).

The third and fourth fields are the location of the PAM module on the filesystem and also any parameters you need to pass to the module. For example, if you want to authenticate users against a MySQL database (using pam_mysql), you need to pass the database name, table name, the user and password column, and also the username and password of the MySQL user that can connect to the database.

In the example we have for the imap service, we have said that for the auth and account authentication methods, the authentication must succeed in both entries (which makes sense because if the user and password are incorrect or the account has been disabled, we do not want the user to log in). Both of these entries use the pam-unix.so module, which queries the standard Unix authentication database (/etc/passwd and /etc/shadow). And finally for the auth entry, we have told the pam-unix module that it is okay if the user provides us with an empty password (if the user has a blank password for example — bad idea!).

Integrating LDAP into Linux

When you have user accounts stored in LDAP, you can authenticate your users against them. Three things need to take place to make this happen:

1. When the system needs to find information about a user (UID, home directory, or so on), it queries the name switch service. The NSS is a core component

that allows glibc to find information from the system. This includes user, group, and host data.

The NSS is controlled through the /etc/nsswitch.conf file, and you need to change its default lookup of files (explicitly checking /etc/passwd and so on) to query the LDAP server defined in /etc/ldap.conf.

```
passwd: files ldap
group:  files ldap
```

When set, restart the Name Service Cache Daemon (NSCD) with rcnscd restart.

Tip   NSCD is the bane of an LDAP user's life. NSCD caches NSS lookups on the system so that subsequent lookups do not need to query the original NSS source. If bizarre things are happening when you use LDAP to authenticate users, try restarting the NSCD cache and see if that fixes the problem.

2. Tell your LDAP system to use a specific LDAP to source its data. To do this, you need to edit the file /etc/ldap.conf. This file defines certain LDAP client information, most importantly the LDAP server and the default search base (as we used previously with the -b command-line option). In this environment, the ldap.conf file contains a server specification of localhost, because this is where the LDAP data is, and also a base of o=Acme,c=UK.

```
host 127.0.0.1
base o=Acme,c=UK
```

3. Configure PAM to use the LDAP server. This has been greatly simplified in recent times with the use of the /etc/security/pam_unix2.conf file.

Edit the pam_unix2.conf file and edit the auth, password, and account entries.

```
auth:     use_ldap nullok
account:      use_ldap
password:     use_ldap nullok
```

This instructs any PAM entries using pam_unix2 to try the LDAP server for information.

When PAM and NSS have been configured, run SuSEconfig to commit your configuration changes. You should now be able to log in to the system as a user stored in LDAP. Because you have told NSS to use files and then LDAP for information, the root account that is stored in /etc/passwd is safe.

If you are having a problem authenticating as a normal user, check what /var/log/messages says about it. You will usually see a good description of the problem.

Setting the ACL on the LDAP Server

You finally need to configure the access controls for the LDAP server so that users can change their password using the `passwd` command.

The default access control list (ACL) in SUSE enables all people (authenticated and anonymous) to read all data in the LDAP server. When storing passwords, even encrypted ones, this is not a good security model. You need to tell OpenLDAP to allow only authenticated users to view their encrypted passwords (both read and write), as well as the administrator, but not any other users.

To do this, set a specific ACL on the `userPassword` entry in an object in the `/etc/openldap/slapd.conf` file:

```
access to attrs=userPassword
     by dn="cn=admin,o=Acme,c=UK" write
     by anonymous auth
     by self write
     by * none
```

As you are not using the default ACL (because you have triggered your own), you also need to give users access to all other data in the LDAP server.

Caution   As with the design of the LDAP server, you should also take great care when designing your ACL scheme. We have only a small ACL scheme here to keep the amount of information you have to manage to a minimum, but on a corporate system, there is a lot of data that should not be viewable by all users. For example, you do not want your coworker to see what your salary is, do you?

When setting an ACL for all users to read the rest of the information in an object, it is customary to set the ACL for the administrator user to clarify the desired outcome of the ACL. By default, the administrator has full control over all data in the LDAP server.

```
access to *
     by dn="cn=admin,o=Acme,c=UK" write
     by * read
```

How Can LDAP Help You?

In this chapter, we have just scratched the surface of what you can do with LDAP, but you can see it provides a good structure to mirror an organization. Let's face it — the better your systems mirror the organizational structure of the company, the better they will work with your workflow.

LDAP is extremely good at storing and retrieving data; it can search through extremely large data sets in a very short amount of time. LDAP should not be used as an online transaction processing (OLTP) database because it is not great at writing data to the directory. Given that 95 percent of transactions taking place on an LDAP server are retrievals of stored information (How often will your salary be updated? Likely not as often as you would like!), this is to be expected.

We are great fans of LDAP since working with it, and if designed correctly, it will save you a lot of time in the long run.

✦   ✦   ✦

Setting Up a Web Proxy with Squid

Squid is the most popular open source caching web proxy server. This means that it fetches and holds local copies of pages and images from the web. Client machines requesting these objects obtain them from the Squid proxy server rather than directly. There are several good reasons (and possibly also some bad ones) why people use Squid and other caching web proxies.

✦ A web cache on the local network means that objects (web pages, images, and so on) that have already been requested do not need to be fetched again from their original location, but can be served from the cache instead. This improves performance for users and reduces bandwidth usage.

✦ At the same time, using a proxy can give an organization a great deal of control over how and when users access the web and can log all web access. Squid can also be used to prevent access to undesirable sites, sometimes in conjunction with additional software that maintains blacklists of these sites.

✦ The use of a web proxy (and Squid also caches for FTP) means that you can set up a firewall in such a way that users do not have direct access from their PCs to the Internet; their HTTP and FTP traffic is handled by Squid, and their Simple Mail Transport Protocol (SMTP) traffic is handled by the mail server. Typically, users may have no direct TCP/IP access to the outside world. This simplifies security but may also rob users of the ability to connect to other services.

When a web proxy is up and running (and, most probably, direct HTTP through the firewall is blocked), traditionally all users' browsers need to be configured with the appropriate proxy setting. This leads to administrative problems. There are a number of solutions to these, including a very elegant one that we shall discuss later.

Getting Started with Squid on SUSE

The SUSE installation media contain the Squid installation package; first, you need to install this in the usual way using YaST. Squid is included in the YaST installation selection Network/Server.

For this discussion, we assume that you are setting up Squid on a machine on your network that has adequate access to the outside world.

Depending on which version of SUSE you are running, simply installing and starting Squid may not be enough. SLES 9 and older versions of SUSE Professional come with Squid configuration files that may need some work before Squid will start in a simple configuration.

If you do not encounter the difficulties mentioned in this section, you can proceed to the following section; exactly how easy it is to get Squid running depends on which SUSE version you are running.

Start Squid with the command `rcsquid start`. You may see something like this:

```
root@proxy: /tmp/ # rcsquid start
Starting WWW-proxy squid  (/var/cache/squid)/usr/sbin/rcsquid: line 135: 14165 Aborted
$SQUID_BIN -z -F >/dev/null 2>&1
 - Could not create cache_dir !
                                     failed
```

If you see this error message, there is a little bit of work to do.

Here Squid wants to create its cache directories under `/var/cache/squid/`, but it doesn't know how to do this because the necessary option is not set in the configuration file `/etc/squid/squid.conf`. At this stage, `/var/cache/squid` is empty.

The configuration file `/etc/squid/squid.conf` as shipped contains a fair amount of information about the default settings and descriptions of the meanings of the various valid parameters.

You need to enable the following line so that the cache directories can be created:

```
# cache_dir ufs /var/cache/squid 100 16 256
```

Edit the file to uncomment this line by removing # from it.

```
cache_dir ufs /var/cache/squid 100 16 256
```

If you try again, you may see a similar error message until you also add a line like this:

```
visible_hostname bibleserver.local.net
```

Search the file for `visible_hostname`. You will see where it is explained, but you will have to edit the file by hand and add it. Squid will not start until it knows what host name it is advertising.

Now if you try again, you see that Squid is starting correctly:

```
root@proxy: /tmp/ # rcsquid start
Starting WWW-proxy squid                                  done
```

If you look in `/var/cache/squid/`, you will see that the cache directories have been created: The SUSE start script checks for their existence and creates them if necessary (so in fact you do not need to manually run `squid -z` as stated in Squid's own documentation).

Tip   Squid installs a considerable amount of useful documentation (including a fully commented configuration file) in the directory `/usr/share/doc/packages/squid/`.

If you now list `/var/cache/squid/`, you see 16 directories 0 0, 0 1, 0 2, . . . , 0F, each of which has 256 subdirectories 0 0, 0 1, . . . , FF. So you have a total of 4,096 directories in the cache directory structure. It is in these that Squid saves copies of the objects that it proxies. Clearly you could have changed these numbers by changing the values set in the configuration file for `cache_dir`. You can stop Squid (`rcsquid stop`), remove these directories, and change the value of the `cache_dir` parameter to, for example:

```
cache_dir ufs /var/cache/squid 100 256 256
```

If you now start Squid, you find that there are 256 directories under `/var/cache/squid` with 256 subdirectories each.

If the `rcsquid start` command used earlier worked correctly, you will probably want to force Squid to start at every boot by enabling it in the YaST runlevel editor, or by using the command `insserv squid`.

Squid runs by default on port 3128. This can also be changed in the configuration file (the other popular port for a proxy server is 8080). Now go to a client machine (of course, you can do this on the server, too) and set the proxy settings in your browser to `proxy:3128`, where `proxy` is the host name or IP number of the server where Squid is running. Then try to go to a web site.

You should see a page similar to Figure 26-1. This shows that you're successfully talking to Squid; however, so far Squid doesn't want to proxy for you. That is because you now need to set up at least one access control list (ACL) to refer to either the specific client or the local network and allow access.

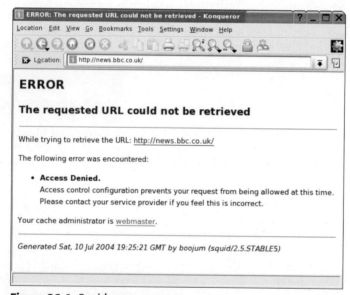

Figure 26-1: Squid error message

To do this, you need code similar to the following lines in the configuration file:

```
acl lan src 192.168.1.0/24
http_access allow lan
```

Here `lan` is an arbitrary name that is introduced in the first of these lines and referenced in the second. This allows access to any host in the 192.168.1.0 network.

Having made a change in the configuration file, you need to issue the command `rcsquid reload` so that the file will be reread. Now if you try to connect again from the client, you will find that you can access web sites. And in the Squid logs at `/var/log/squid`, you will start to see logging of that access.

Note   If necessary, you can also create separate ACLs for individual IP addresses.

If you are running SUSE 9.3 Professional or later, the Squid configuration file will work out of the box to proxy for clients on the local network, and you will be able to skip the preceding steps.

User Authentication

A common requirement is to add user authentication so that only known users within the network can get web access via Squid. The simplest way to do this is to make use of whatever authentication methods are available on the machine where Squid is running, using PAM (Pluggable Authentication Modules). To do this, you need something like the following in /etc/squid/squid.conf:

```
auth_param basic program /usr/sbin/pam_auth
```

This says that you should use PAM for authentication: Whatever authentication method is valid will now be employed, whether it be /etc/passwd, NIS, LDAP, or some other method. (See Chapter 25 for a discussion of PAM authorization.)

To force the authentication to take place, you need a line (following the one shown previously) like this:

```
acl lanauth proxy_auth REQUIRED
```

and a corresponding line later in the file like this:

```
http_access allow lanauth
```

Now when you try to access a web site for the first time from a client machine, you will see a dialog box similar to the one shown in Figure 26-2.

If you can now authenticate with a username and password known to the server, everything will work.

Combining user authentication with the acl that defines the local network is best done using the following code:

```
acl lan src 192.168.1.0/24
auth_param basic program /usr/sbin/pam_auth
acl lanauth proxy_auth REQUIRED
http_access deny !lan
http_access allow lanauth
http_access allow lan
...
http_access deny all
```

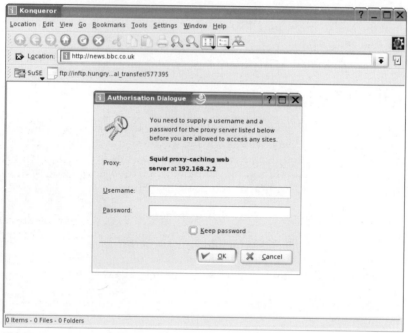

Figure 26-2: A user authentication dialog box

In other words, you deny anyone not on the desired network addresses before you force the authentication; then you allow the access from the network segment. As noted previously, if necessary, you can also set up separate ACLs for individual IP addresses.

This type of authentication uses the standard HTTP authentication method. This means that username/password pairs are being transmitted across the network in base64 encoded form (that is, not simple plain text, but not encrypted either). If a method of authentication is being used that is also available for other purposes on the server (as with the pam_auth example), there is an inherent security risk, which could potentially compromise users' accounts on the server.

This risk is avoided with the digest_pw_auth method. For this you need lines similar to the following in /etc/squid/squid.conf:

```
auth_param digest children 5
auth_param digest program /usr/sbin/digest_pw_auth /etc/squid/digestpw
auth_param digest realm Squid proxy-caching web server
```

Here you specify a password file /etc/squid/digestpw. You could have specified any suitable location for this file. With the current version of Squid, this file is a plain text file with entries of the form:

```
username:password
```

The passwords are stored in plain text (we understand this will change in future versions), so the file's ownership and permissions should be `squid:root` and `600`. In other words, it should be readable and writeable by the Squid user and not readable by anyone else.

Now when a client starts a session, Squid authenticates using the information in this file. However, this does not require a password to be sent across the network. Instead, the server and client each calculate an MD5 sum or one-way hash based on the password and the URL (and some additional per-session information offered by the server). The client sends the result of its calculation to the server, which compares them.

Most browsers will cooperate correctly with this form of authentication. However, we have seen some problems with Konqueror, but Internet Explorer, Mozilla, Netscape, Galeon, and Firefox all appear to work perfectly with it.

The other authentication methods that are shipped with SUSE's Squid package are all installed into `/usr/sbin/` and are `msnt_auth`, `ntlm_auth`, `smb_auth`, `yp_auth`, `getpwname_auth`, `ncsa_auth`, and `squid_ldap_auth`.

Thus, it is possible to use Windows, Samba, LDAP, or YP as the authentication method. However, for most of these, the remarks given previously about unencrypted passwords crossing from the client to the server hold true.

Restricting Access by Hardware Address

You have already seen how you can specify network or specific IP addresses in the ACLs in the configuration file. You can also restrict access to particular MAC addresses:

```
acl bible arp 00:11:22:33:44:55
http_access allow bible
```

This pair of lines allows the host bible to access the proxy. This works only if bible is directly connected to the same physical Ethernet network as the server. You can add multiple pairs of lines such as the previous lines for each permitted client machine on the network.

The Squid Log

The main Squid log is by default at `/var/log/squid/access.log`. Exactly what is logged here depends on the options chosen in the configuration file. The options are explained as comments in the standard configuration file shipped with the SUSE package. In particular, if you set

```
emulate_httpd_log on
```

in /etc/squid/squid.conf, the format of the log file will change to look more like Apache's access log. The difference can be seen in these two sample entries:

```
1089560809.055    159 192.168.2.111 TCP_MISS/200 768 GET
http://www.grokdoc.net/images/button_hr.png - DIRECT/152.2.210.81 image/png

192.168.2.111 - - [11/Jul/2004:16:57:54 +0100] "GET
http://news.bbc.co.uk/nol/shared/css/news.css HTTP/1.1" 200 15258 TCP_HIT:NONE
```

The first shows the standard layout, with the time first (in seconds since January 1, 1970), and the second shows the Apache-like layout.

Squid logs are very long and difficult to read, so a number of Squid log analysis tools are available. SUSE includes a tool called sarg (Squid Analysis Report Generator). If you want to use sarg, you must install it separately; it is not included in the Squid package. The sarg tool can be set to run daily from a cron job and produce HTML reports, which can be viewed through a browser, as in the example in Figure 26-3.

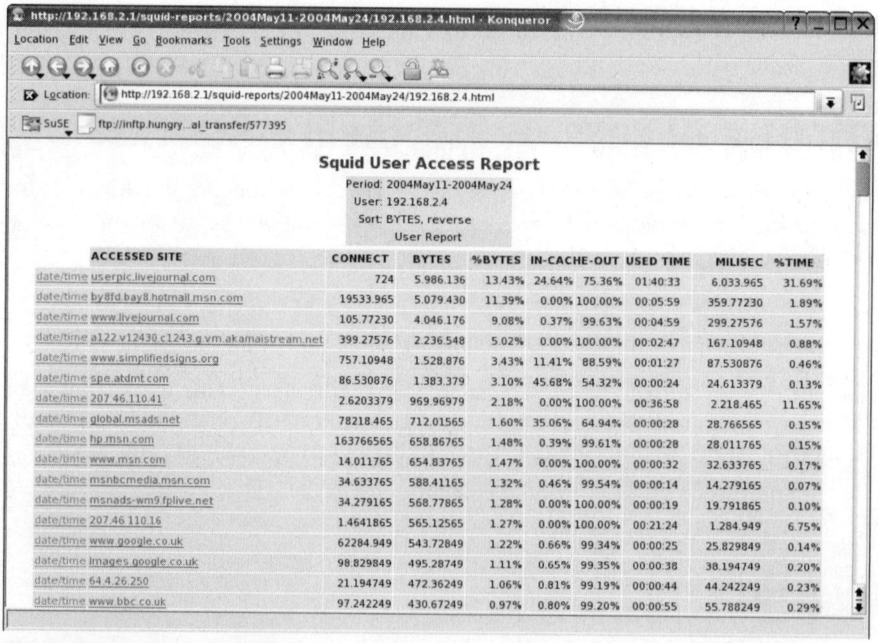

Figure 26-3: The sarg display

The reports combine a statistical analysis of usage with fine detail such as at what time a particular client or user accessed a particular site. The use of such a tool is clearly subject to certain ethical considerations; users will rightly consider that they have a right of privacy, but at the same time this must be weighed against a company's acceptable use policies.

Using Squid as a Transparent Proxy

One of the difficulties in running a web proxy is that each client browser has to be configured to use it. A much neater solution is to force all attempts to access a web site to go through the proxy. This can be achieved quite simply by using `iptables` firewall rules on the machine where Squid runs.

What you want to do is to intercept all outbound packets to external hosts on port 80 (and certain others perhaps) and redirect them to port 3128 on the server. Squid will then do the proxying. So you need `iptables` rules similar to this:

```
iptables -t nat -A PREROUTING -i eth0 -p tcp --dport 80 -j REDIRECT --to-port 3128
```

This assumes that `eth0` is the internal interface that is receiving the outgoing HTTP requests and that the machine where Squid is running is set as the gateway for the client machines.

Cross-Reference See also the discussion of firewall rules in Chapter 24. Note also that SuSEfirewall2 is capable of setting up the necessary rules for a transparent proxy. SuSEfirewall2 is also discussed in Chapter 24.

The Squid configuration file should include the following lines:

```
httpd_accel_host virtual
httpd_accel_port 80
httpd_accel_with_proxy on
httpd_accel_uses_host_header on
```

See also the LDP's "Transparent Proxy with Linux and Squid mini-HOWTO" by Daniel Kiracofe at `www.tldp.org/HOWTO/TransparentProxy.html`.

Note You cannot combine transparent proxying with authorization on the proxy. It has also been reported that in some circumstances there can be problems with remote sites that require authentication.

Using Cache Manager

Squid includes a tool, cachemgr.cgi, that is installed at /usr/share/doc/ packages/squid/scripts/cachemgr.cgi. If you copy this file to /srv/www/ cgi-bin/, you can then go to http://<squid-server>/cgi-bin/cachemgr.cgi and view comprehensive information about the state of the squid cache (see Figure 26-4). This assumes you have the Apache web server set up and running, so that it can run these CGI scripts (see Chapter 16).

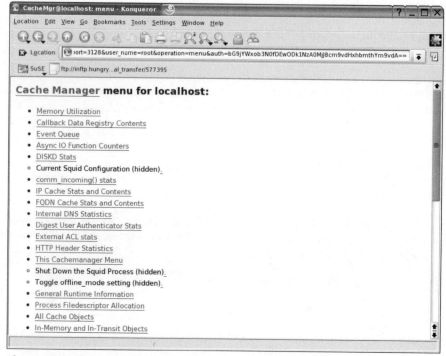

Figure 26-4: The Cache Manager menu

Using squidGuard

The squidGuard filter can be used with Squid to prevent access to undesirable sites. It is an additional package that you may need to install from the installation media. The maintainers of squidGuard also offer a set of blacklists of pornographic and other undesirable sites that squidGuard reads into a database in memory when it runs. Any requests for URLs in the database will be blocked by Squid.

In order to use squidGuard, you need an additional line in /etc/squid/squid.conf:

```
redirect_program /usr/sbin/squidGuard -c /etc/squidguard.conf
```

A convenient Webmin module for configuring squidGuard enables you to download and install the blacklists and configure the program in other ways. The module is available from www.niemueller.de/webmin/modules/squidguard/. (See Chap-ter 14 for a discussion of Webmin.)

When the blacklists are installed and squidGuard is configured, Squid calls squidGuard to check its database every time a request comes in.

A very basic but working configuration file /etc/squidguard.conf for squidGuard looks like this:

```
logdir /var/log/squidGuard
dbhome /var/lib/squidGuard/db
src grownups {
        ip              192.168.1.0/24
}
dest blacklist {
   domainlist blacklist/domains
   urllist    blacklist/urls
}
acl {
   grownups {
           pass !blacklist
   }
   default {
      pass none
      redirect http://www.bbc.co.uk
   }
}
```

Here, any client in the 192.168.1.0/24 network who requests any domain or URL included in the blacklist will be redirected to www.bbc.co.uk. In practice, you would want to replace this with a local page explaining why access was denied and explaining what to do if you think this was an error.

The information in this chapter is enough to get you started using Squid and the associated programs squidGuard and sarg on SUSE Linux. When correctly config-ured, Squid operates as an efficient proxy server and requires very little attention. If you are using squidGuard, you need to be aware that by its very nature it requires a good deal more attention if you are to keep its blacklists up to date.

✦   ✦   ✦

SUSE Linux in the Enterprise

Part V describes the place of SUSE Linux in the modern enterprise and covers the use of storage area networks (SANs). Configuration of the kernel is covered. A chapter is devoted to emulation and virtualization in SUSE Linux. Finally, the SUSE Linux OpenExchange Server, the Open Enterprise Server, and the Novell Linux Desktop are covered.

Enterprise Architecture

It is all well and good knowing how to configure Linux for your environment, but it is too often overlooked how to implement a solution to fit into your environment. This chapter comprises some best practices that we have come across with regards to Linux on the enterprise.

Enterprise often evokes images of men in suits, money, and starships. Here, the enterprise is a general concept of scalable, stable, and manageable systems that helps to turn business processes into automated and efficient systems. In fact, some people will never have to come into contact with certain elements of the enterprise: storage area networks (SANs), disaster recovery (DR) scenarios, and high-performance (HP) clustering to name a few.

> **Tip** The term *clustering* is widely used in the IT industry and many people associate this only with HP computing. *HP computing* is a term used to describe the use of many separate processors (whether in a multiprocessor or separate configuration). The other two common types of cluster are load balancing (using many servers to provide nonuniform computing power like a web farm) and high availability (HA), used to provide a failsafe solution to a service.

So the general architecture of a system, and specifically Linux, should always be considered with scalability and stability in mind. Total Cost of Ownership (TCO), availability statistics, and maintainable systems are very important when you have a large budget. But TCO, availability, and supportable systems are even more important as your IT budget decreases year after year. As Linux moves deeper into the enterprise, these concepts become ever more important not only to you, but also to the decision makers in the enterprise.

This chapter, which draws on experiences both from previous chapters and from the real world, is here to help you use SUSE in the enterprise, taking into account these issues, and helping you to move SUSE into your organization in a way that fits in with your policies, Quality Assurance (QA) requirements, and maintenance issues.

A Typical Organization

We take Acme as an example of an organization that is quite large (more than 1,000 users). Acme is heterogeneous, as are most organizations, with multiple sites and a DR policy. After all, if Acme loses its data, it loses its business; it does sell the best widgets in the world, and its customer lists, stock database, and distributors are all core to their business process. See Figure 27-1 for an example of Acme's worldwide architecture.

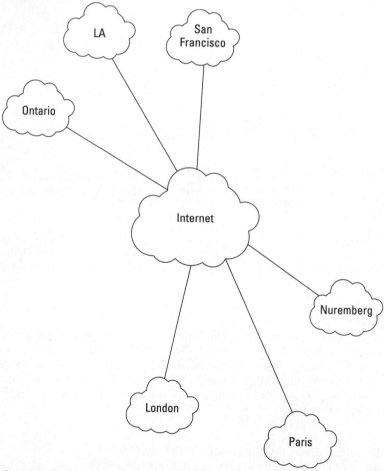

Figure 27-1: Acme's worldwide architecture

We will look at how Acme's technical organization is arranged and delve into specifics on where Linux can be used. We also take a further look into how Linux can be configured based on what we know from previous chapters.

We first delve into how Linux is used at one of Acme's offices — we'll use the London office as our prime example. We can assume that the other offices are very similar in their makeup. Acme is an open source embracer, as many enterprises over the past few years have been.

Where Can Linux Be Used?

Most IT directors ask this question first. The case for using Linux has already been made in the popular IT press, and organizations understand that Linux is now a viable option when anything Unix needs to be deployed.

The Datacenter

Independent Software Vendors (ISVs) now see Linux as a Tier 1 (primary) platform for their software, and we are not talking about a group of coders in a dark room. The big boys are at it, too — Oracle, IBM, SAP, and SAS to name a few. All see Linux as a platform that they can market and successfully sell upon, and the figures prove this, too.

Take Oracle as an example; it has been said that its primary platform for development is Linux. Other ports are secondary to this strategy. Linux will always see a new release of Oracle, just like the other major OS players (Microsoft, Sun, IBM, and so on). Oracle has made its database products available on many hardware platforms, including Intel (32/64-bit), PowerPC (PPC), and IBM zSeries (discussed later in this chapter).

This part of the market is called the datacenter and is where Linux is growing the fastest at the moment. We have seen many customers using Linux to run critical Oracle databases over the past few years; IBM software is also very strong in this space.

Infrastructure

Linux has traditionally been strong in this space, and it encompasses what organizations see as a core part of their IT infrastructure. Domain Name System (DNS), intranet, extranet, firewalls, email, file services, and print services all fall under this section of the enterprise. Market results have shown that Apache on Linux is extremely strong. And many organizations run their DNS on Linux without upper management even knowing.

Note   This is a very important point. It is fine asking MIS directors where they use Linux in their organization, but they might not even know that some of the people with their feet on the floor are implementing Linux in a stealth move to save money when budgets have been cut. Linux is very, very good in this space as this work-flow is something that has been a known quantity by developers and distributions alike. SUSE knows this, and the SUSE Standard Server caters to these core services.

Embedded Systems

This may be something you overlook in your organization, but Linux is already embedded in a lot of the systems within the enterprise.

While many people have questioned just how secure Linux is and its security continues to be a matter of great speculation, Linux is nevertheless known for its stability and its security. In reality, the security of any operating system is dictated by two things:

✦ The configuration and administrative actions that take place to secure the operating system out of the box

✦ The quality of the code that encompasses the operating system itself

Linux is not the be-all and end-all of operating system security. However, given that the code is open and under constant security, it comes pretty close to it. Some patches to the Linux kernel drastically overhaul the default Unix/POSIX security of the operating system, one of the most popular and secure being the Linux Intrusion Detection System (LIDS). The name is a misnomer, because it is not designed as a detection system, but to harden the kernel beyond recognition.

Because of this security, Linux has been used in many embedded systems and you may not even know about it. Many firewall appliances run Linux, and the fiber switches in IBM BladeCenter run on embedded Linux.

Running embedded Linux in an organization is not usually one of choice, but one of indirect choice when you buy a product for its feature set, not for the operating system that it runs. This is where embedded systems prove their worth in the marketplace, when the features of the appliance sell the product, and the operating system under the hood helps this with stability and provides the features that the user sees.

I Know Where, but How?

It used to be difficult selling Linux to the masses. In recent years, this hurdle has been overcome with Linux proving itself time and again. The problem that the industry now faces is how to deploy it.

With Novell's acquisition of SUSE, this has been less of a problem. Novell has traditionally done very well in large rollouts because of its management features. Novell Linux Desktop will help with bringing Linux to the arena of user presentation, and the bundling of the Novell network tools on the Linux kernel will help to provide the solid infrastructure needed to manage your infrastructure in a heterogeneous environment.

This is a SUSE book, but this is not to say that the other Linux vendors are not aware of the management and deployment issues facing the industry. With this in mind, nearly every distributor offers unattended installations, package management, and also configuration from a central location. This may seem trivial, but consider a 1,000-seat organization where all machines are running Linux (unlikely in the current Linux market). Unless you have deep pockets to fill your support infrastructure, you will want some way of controlling your Linux infrastructure. You would not do it yourself in a Microsoft environment, and you no longer have to do it yourself in a Linux environment.

No longer are organizations worried about support and maintenance from the Linux vendors. The major players are now offering supportable distributions, first-, second-, and third-line support, and professional services. IBM and Hewlett-Packard (HP) offer all of this, too, as well as the army of vendor business partners (BPs). With so much choice, there is no excuse for customers to worry about the supportability of their Linux infrastructure.

The business partner community is very important to SUSE, HP, and IBM as they provide an extension of the services the vendors can offer. Business partners usually employ technical resources that have had experience with the vendor in question (as has happened for us). You will find that a business partner is able to provide an unbiased outlook on the remedy for a problem, whereas the vendors will, of course, push for their products to fulfill that void.

Fulfilling Your Staff Requirements

With the support of an industry player behind you, the choice of whether to use your existing technology specialist or to call on a vendor/BP may be threatening to some. It is very common that organizations employ this community to implement new technology and then train their staff to maintain and grow their infrastructure.

Existing Unix specialists are the easiest to train on Linux as their background fits well with the Linux methodology. For other specialists (MCSE, CCNA, and so on), it proves more difficult. All vendors offer a well-defined training migration strategy for the enterprise customers, as well as individuals to follow to bring them up to speed and get certified on the technology. As Linux is essentially free, the accessibility of the software for new users is not an issue and helps to spread the use and knowledge of Linux in both the enterprise and home. In other words, getting internal staff proficient in Linux is the other issue new customers moving to Linux may have that can be crossed off the list.

Linux is now ready for the enterprise, it has been for the past 18 months, and it can only get stronger with vendors pushing the acceptance with knowledge transfer and tools that the enterprise is used to having.

Linux Enterprise Hardware: The Big Players

We have already alluded to the fact that many of the big technology players are involved with Linux and with bringing Linux into the enterprise. This section surveys some of the major companies and technologies that have placed Linux so firmly in the enterprise space.

We have always been big fans of ridiculously expensive hardware that runs Linux, and we think that is true for most *ubergeeks* (although we would never admit to being them!). The de facto hardware in the industry has to be Intel-based servers, and this covers the lower-end to mid-range workhorses.

Categorizing hardware in this way is very common when talking about the enterprise:

✦ The lower-end servers usually constitute file/print servers, mail servers, and infrastructure servers in the SMB (Small/Medium Business) market.

✦ Mid-range servers are usually the Unix-based servers — AIX, HPUX, and Solaris machines — and this is where Linux is gaining its ground at the moment. IBM and HP are well aware of this and have made sure Linux is a selling point of their mid-range servers. Sun Microsystems is still firmly gripping onto this market with Solaris and is unlikely to change this as it has invested so much in the pursuit of this market.

✦ The high-end market is the massively parallel single-footprint servers — for example, the SGI Altix, or IBM's powerhouse, the System/390 (zSeries) machines.

IBM

Two of IBM's platforms, the pSeries and zSeries, have proved to be amazingly good at running Linux. IBM has invested a lot into code development for Linux to take advantage of the mid- and high-end hardware architectures.

The zSeries

IBM's zSeries machines hold a special place in one of the authors' hearts as they started working on these machines when SUSE started its development lifecycle of Linux for the hardware.

The IBM zSeries has a long history within IBM and recently celebrated its 40-year history in the organization. The zSeries does not contain terabytes of memory, does not have the fastest processors in the world, and is not considered a supercomputer, but it is one of the most exciting things that has happened to Linux in recent years. The zSeries is extremely good at shifting data around in its system and moving data from disk, and it's very, very good at managing resources.

The zSeries has proved so popular with Linux users because you can potentially have 40,000 Linux systems running in one box, all running relatively well. What most people who have a few servers here and there fail to recognize is the utilization of their servers. The traditional utilization of a server is around 15 to 20 percent. This means that 80 percent of the cost of your server is not being returned to the company.

With the zSeries, you can run all of your Linux servers in one manageable machine and make sure your workloads are running at 99 percent hardware utilization. It manages this through partitioning of the system resources into a virtual machine for Linux to run on.

You can do this in a couple of ways:

✦ Using IBM's LPAR (Logical Partition) technology, you can split up the server into a number of partitions to run Linux under. This is good when dealing with a small number of virtual machines.

✦ These logical partitions can run z/OS (zSeries operating system), MVS (Multiple Virtual System), Linux, or VM (Virtual Machine). The VM operating system is extremely powerful and allows many more Linux images to run under the zSeries hardware. Using VM's resource management, you can dynamically allocate CPU power to a Linux image when the workflow needs it and decrease when you see a Linux image that is not utilizing the resources it has been given. With this model, you can guarantee that your hardware's cost is actually returning on your investment.

Note   The zSeries machines should not be considered when you have the need for huge processing power because they do not fit well with this profile. If you need powerful processing (HP computing), you should consider the pSeries or the 64-bit computing platforms from IBM or other vendors.

The pSeries

The pSeries machines are considered mid-range in IBM speak and are ideally suited for intense compute environments (HP computing). They do run Linux, both natively and in LPARs (the same idea as the zSeries), and they are extremely fast.

With the IBM release of the OpenPower architecture, they have produced a 64-bit processor that has a very efficient core, which, of course, Linux is able to take advantage of because IBM has added new features to the kernel and has designed the chip around its use in Linux. Apple licensed this technology for its 64-bit OS X platform, and whether you believe the hype or not, the benchmark results are very impressive.

IBM has taken this a step further and is incorporating the Power architecture with micropartitioning technology for the next generation of pSeries and 64-bit blade architectures.

Hewlett-Packard

HP is the second big player in the vendor arena and has been very strong in the Intel and traditional Unix space. The Superdome servers provide a very scalable hardware platform that can be partitioned to run multiple operating systems across the hardware resource.

The Superdome uses the Itanium processor to be able to run a mixture of Linux, Windows, and HP-UX. The partitioning (up to 16 partitions at the time of this writing) allows consolidation of both low and very high workloads into one manageable server.

64-bit Platforms

It is obvious that in the datacenter, the 32-bit architecture will die eventually. This can be backed up by the fact that most ISVs that work in the enterprise are already releasing their software for the 64-bit platforms.

SUSE has been a driving force in the 64-bit space as the hardware vendors have routinely called upon SUSE to implement the port to a new 64-bit architecture. SUSE has managed to control a large portion of the enterprise space because it is considered a de facto platform in the area.

The datacenter is not bound by the normal laws of the IT industry because it usually relies on a single application to provide a service. In an office environment, servers usually run a mixture of very specific applications on one server (or at least more than one application on a server).

The 64-bit architectures available at the time of this writing are the Itanium, Opteron, Athlon, and the IBM POWER architecture:

✦ The Intel Itanium has had a lot of bad press since its release, mainly because of its inability to run legacy 32-bit applications with any increase in performance from a comparable Xeon processor at the same clock speed. We would say this is an unfair point if it weren't for the price of servers with Itanium processors in them. Unless you are running a pure 64-bit environment, it is unlikely you will be considering an Itanium.

✦ The AMD Opteron is really a success of the 64-bit story as it is relatively cheap, with impressive performance statistics. You can now buy Opteron-based desktop machines for the home, and SUSE has realized this with the inclusion of a 64-bit SUSE distribution included with the boxed product.

✦ Intel now offers 64-bit processors with backward compatibility, in response to AMD's Opteron and AMD64 processors. Most Xeon processors are now designated EM64T (Extended Memory 64) and are compatible with AMD's 64-bit architecture — the 64-bit SUSE versions originally designed for Opteron run perfectly on these systems.

For any user installing the 64-bit version, you will see no difference during installation, or in the use of the system itself. The main difference is that the kernel, libraries, and applications have been compiled for the 64-bit environment. Faster application pipes, larger memory access, and legacy support for 32-bit applications are in the distribution and work very well. The distribution has been accepted as a great way to take advantage of your shiny new Opteron box.

✦ The IBM JS20 is specifically designed for the BladeCenter architecture and is definitely aimed at the consolidation of datacenter services. SUSE's pSeries distribution runs on the blade, and Linux was the first officially supported operating system on the architecture. We were lucky enough to borrow a BladeCenter with six JS20 blades for an expo in London recently, running DB2, WebSphere, and Tivoli, on SLES. The demo went very well, and the bundle was as stable as a 32-bit distribution on the HS20 (Xeon) blades.

If you need large memory support, a massive execution pipe, and a resilient system, the 64-bit systems are ripe for the picking. The problem you have now is very similar to picking a Linux distribution (SUSE); you need to choose a specific 64-bit technology.

Unless you have a BladeCenter, and you do not see a need for the technology, the JS20 blades are out. If you are worried about the price/performance of the Itanium, both the Opteron and the Xeon processors with EM64T are attractively priced. Both IBM and HP have Opteron and 64-bit Intel systems, and you can buy off-the-shelf boxes from retailers if you do not feel you need vendor support.

Blade Technology

The blade architecture has had a lot of press since its release, and for good reason. Both HP and IBM have blade technology that does practically the same thing, consolidation.

Linux is ideal for the blade architecture because it works wonderfully in its intended space — web, firewalls, and databases, that is, the real workhorses of an organization.

The blade architecture is a way to pack a lot of processing power into a small footprint, with IBM being able to pack 14 servers in a 7U space, and HP can do 20 blades in a 3U space.

Note   The term U is a standard way of describing the amount of rack space a server takes up: 1U is 1.8".

The blade architecture removes the need for large cabling requirements, and each physical blade is considered commodity hardware — if one blade goes down, you get your hot swap and replace it. It takes approximately 10 seconds to remove and replace a blade whereas with a standard 1U system it would take you at least 20 to 30 minutes. You can even automate a build on the blade and have your system up and running in a matter of minutes.

Note   In terms of computing, the term *commodity* is used to describe so-called throw-away hardware. If the server breaks, you do not need to worry too much because you can replace it either at low or no cost, with little impact to the service your servers provide. This is something unheard of a few years ago when talking about HP or IBM hardware, but the fact that you can have your blade replaced within 24 hours under warranty means you really don't have to worry about the availability of the hardware.

If you have many web, file, or database servers, you can consolidate a couple of racks into one with the blade architecture, hook your blades up to a SAN, and you have the same functionality, with a small footprint and less management hassles (always good for saving money).

As you can see in this survey of the big players in the enterprise, Linux has been a major part of their roadmaps to sell more software and hardware into this space. As these are the companies that define the enterprise, they know that Linux is something to be enhanced, marketed, and implemented.

SUSE made the decision to technically improve the distribution for the enterprise space without the marketing over three years ago, and both IBM and HP have realized this commitment by embracing SUSE in their strategies.

Plenty of vendors and Business Partners worldwide can provide you with more information on Linux. Both HP and IBM have great Linux sites (www.hp.com/linux and www.ibm.com/linux), whereas two of your authors' employers, SCC (www.scc.com) and CSF (www.csf.co.uk), can provide you with more information about the enterprise space on an unbiased level.

Putting It All Together

We have talked about many technical aspects of Linux in the book, and this chapter has been included for two reasons: to help you see where Linux fits in with the enterprise, and to help you see where the components we have talked about fit into a typical organization.

The final part of this chapter deals with the best practices we have come across for Linux in the enterprise.

Where Do I Put the Services?

A typical organization's IT infrastructure relies heavily on three things—file and print services, email, and user management. People need to store data, which is what computers were originally designed for; they need to send and keep hard copy documents to communicate with other people; and they need an account.

Figure 27-2 is an overview of the IT infrastructure of Acme's London office, detailing non-specific components of the infrastructure.

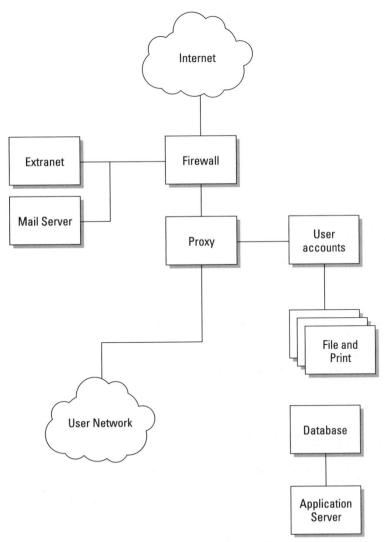

Figure 27-2: Generic overview of the London office IT infrastructure

Most organizations will have most of this network infrastructure installed some-where — with a firewall protecting the network connection to the Internet, an authentication server for user accounts, and some sort of file store.

The demilitarized zone (DMZ), hanging off to the left of the firewall, provides external services to the Internet from your organization. We have implemented an SMTP mail server as well as an HTTP server, hosting the company web site.

Note

> The DMZ is a portion of the firewall used to store services that must be accessed by the Internet. It is a more secure way of segregating your network than allowing Internet traffic to travel through your firewall into your internal network. With the DMZ you are able to control the traffic that enters the zone both from your internal users (for example, to a mail server) and from the Internet (again, to a mail server).

If your company needs to store some data about customers, you will invariably use a database to store this information, as well as use some kind of application server to access this data in a human-friendly format.

In Figure 27-3, we have replaced the generic infrastructure with Linux-specific services:

✦ Apache can serve as a web server, with Cyrus and Postfix doing mail server duty.

✦ `iptables` establishes a hardened firewall for the internal network.

✦ OpenLDAP provides the data store for all user accounts.

✦ Samba, as it is commonly used, provides the file storage for the network. This could be enhanced by providing a single Samba installation for each department if needed.

✦ Squid, the open source proxy server, is used to cache all HTTP and FTP traffic for the network, optimizing the bandwidth used to provide browsing facilities on your network.

✦ As for the database, Acme has chosen to use DB2 from IBM, as well as the WebSphere application server for access to the data.

Each Linux implementation in Figure 27-3 is considered extremely stable in this environment and cannot be considered new or unstable territory when it comes to making a decision about migration or implementation.

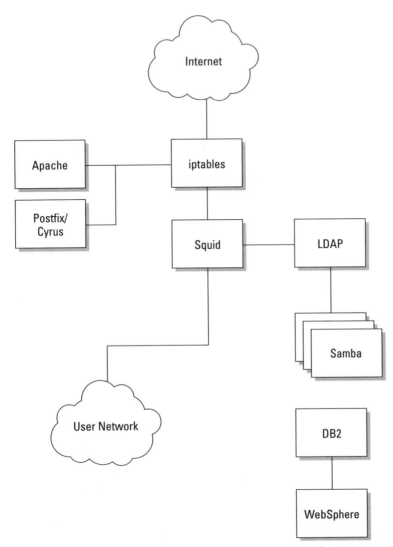

Figure 27-3: Linux implementations of the generic network components

Note

Of course, showing how integral Linux can be in your enterprise is only the tip of the iceberg when selling Linux to your organization. If upper management is sold on the Microsoft bandwagon, you will face an uphill struggle, and all of the TCO studies that you email around will make no difference. However, pushing the right buttons of the right people will work. Go to your CFO and tell her you can drastically reduce the cost of your IT infrastructure, or tell your CIO that you can do more computing with less hardware.

The following sections go into more detail about how SUSE Linux is working in the London office's IT infrastructure.

The Firewall

Depending on how secure you want to make your network from the Internet, you may have more than one firewall. Many security policies of banks dictate that you must have at least three firewalls made by different manufacturers even before you hit any internal network component (including switches). The thinking behind this is that a hacker may know one type of firewall, or an exploit may be available for one firewall, but will not work on the second-tier firewall.

We have included a DMZ in the overview, because this is very common in any organization. A DMZ is there to separate your Internet-facing servers from your internal network.

It is usually on a physically and logically separate network from the rest of your organization, and the communication between your network and the DMZ is usually very restricted, as is inter-DMZ communication. The less that can be accessed, the less chance there is of compromising a server.

Cross-Reference   For more on firewalls in SUSE Linux, see Chapter 24.

User Accounts

In this environment, you can see that an OpenLDAP server stores the user accounts for the entire network. This Lightweight Directory Access Protocol (LDAP) server is configured with referrals, which tell any clients looking for a specific account that is not on the local network to ask the originating LDAP server for the information. For example, if a user from Los Angeles has her laptop in the London office and tries to log in, her account will be sourced from the Los Angeles office directly by an LDAP referral.

The Samba file and print server communicates with the LDAP server to acquire user data for authentication purposes and with the Linux desktop machines using pluggable authentication modules (PAM) to source user account data. This design provides a single sign-on environment, which is something you could not do a few years ago.

With the single sign-on, the mail server also gets its user information from the site LDAP server, completing the authentication services for the London office. In the past few years, LDAP has been an integral component of nearly every operating system in one way or another. The Oracle database can also source user account data from an LDAP server, which also helps the Oracle Apps developers to deploy new applications.

Samba is covered in more detail in Chapter 18; LDAP and what it can do for you is discussed in Chapter 25.

File and Print Services

Samba is used to provide file and print services for the network, acting as a primary domain controller (PDC) for the network. Each Windows user's profile is stored on the Samba server, and the Samba server acts as a print router for the network. The back-end authentication service in Samba has also been configured to talk to the central LDAP server for all authentication and machine accounts.

The Web Proxy

Squid has been configured as a straight proxy, with no transparency through `iptables` because we are going to be authenticating our users before they can use the Internet. Each user has been configured to use a proxy for Internet use, and upon connection, the user will be asked to authenticate. This allows the administrator to monitor any unauthorized browsing and point this to a specific user.

Using Squid as a proxy server is covered in more detail in Chapter 26.

The whole solution works very well together in a proven and implemented environment and serves as a good example of what SUSE Linux can do in an enterprise environment, but it is unlikely that an organization would want to switch an existing environment over to this type of solution. Traditionally, organizations have a legacy infrastructure that cannot or they feel does not warrant migration. However, part of the solution could well be integrated into your environment in one way or another if the need is there.

That's the big part of moving Linux into your organization — finding where Linux fits. It is all well and good saying you want to implement Linux, but you will need to look for opportunities — you need to find a problem that can be solved, not a solution for a problem that does not exist.

Storage Area Networks

When it comes to the enterprise, storage is a major consideration. Attaching disks to each and every server will prove to be a massive administrative headache, not only from the point of view of physical space, but also because it will be extremely difficult to monitor and manage your storage infrastructure.

The solution to this is the *storage area network* (SAN). A SAN provides a central repository for all of your storage that is attached to a controller. This controller is then attached to a fiber switch that your servers then connect to.

Network Attached Storage

Another form of storage that has become increasingly popular in recent years is Network Attached Storage (NAS). Whereas a SAN is attached directly to the server, a NAS is accessed over the network using popular file access protocols such as Network File System (NFS) and Samba. With an NAS, the disks are directly attached to the NAS appliance and the storage is then shared out to the network. This helps to reduce drastically the cost of allocating storage to a pool of machines, but decreases the reliability and the speed of accessing the data, because you are sharing the networking resources to the NAS appliance.

NAS appliances usually offer features above and beyond your standard file server (which is essentially what an NAS is). One of the most popular servers, NetApp, provides remote mirroring to another NetApp for DR purposes and also takes snapshots, where you can make a copy of the data in a storage group instantly so that you can back up your data with minimal downtime to your applications. These are both technologies that until recently were available only in the SAN space.

Using the storage controller, you can create partitions (commonly called *logical unit numbers* or *LUNs*) that are presented to the server.

Figure 27-4 displays a SAN, with all of your SAN-attached servers connected to two fiber switches. These switches are in turn connected to the SAN controller, the real brains behind the storage system. It is up to the SAN controller to provide the storage from the disks connected to it, feeding this through to the servers through a fiber channel (through the switches).

Tip   Note in Figure 27-4 that we have detailed a number of servers attached to two switches for redundancy. This is a very important part of a SAN; if a link to the storage goes down, then your server will not work. Redundancy of a path to the storage is something that should not be considered lightly. If you have spent the money on a SAN, then spend a little more to make it redundant.

Accessing a SAN in Linux

The most common way to connect a server to a SAN is to use a host bus adapter (HBA), the most common being the Qlogic HBA. Qlogic support in Linux is very strong, and Qlogic fully supports its cards under Linux.

Even most hardware vendors rebadge QLA (Qlogic Adaptor) cards under their own name, which makes it a lot easier when using Linux, because a large proportion of the cards works out of the box.

Tip   For more information about Qlogic and the latest QLA drivers, visit `w w w .qlogic.com`.

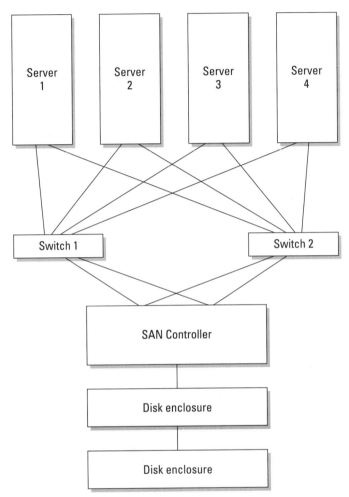

Figure 27-4: Overview of a SAN

If you are installing SUSE on a server, we always recommend that you disconnect the server from the SAN fabric. (This is a term that refers to the fiber network connecting all the devices.) It used to be that Linux installers could potentially pick up the LUNs accessible on the SAN before the onboard storage, and an unsuspecting administrator could install the operating system onto the SAN, or even worse, destroy data on a SAN.

A QLA card is seen by the Linux kernel as a SCSI card. Even though the SAN runs on fiber, it is still SCSI and is treated as such by the system. When the Qlogic card is initialized and scans the fiber for devices, if it finds any, it then assigns a SCSI device to that piece of storage, which is then accessible as a standard disk.

The LUN

A logical unit number (LUN) is a piece of storage created in the SAN. It is integral to the use and design of a SAN. An LUN is a number assigned to an area of storage, and from the point of view of the server does not have anything to do with a physical disk. When an LUN is created, it is likely that the defined LUN will span many disks, as shown in Figure 27-5.

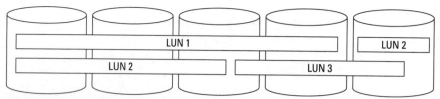

Figure 27-5: Composition of a LUN

Each LUN is presented as a single disk to the servers, and LUN masking can be used to direct an LUN to a specific server or servers. LUN masking is very important in a shared storage environment.

Imagine connecting five servers to a SAN and all servers having access to all created LUNs. If one server goes crazy and starts writing data to an LUN it is not supposed to, or accessing a file it should not, you will find your data corrupted very quickly.

LUN masking defines a mapping of LUNs to servers using the World Wide Name (WWN) of the server HBA. Defining an explicit mapping stops the previously mentioned situation from happening. A server that does not have a mapping has no idea an LUN exists, and the operating system does not have to know or be aware of how or why LUN masking works.

The important thing to remember about an LUN is that it is seen and accessed as a single-disk device in Linux. Partitions and filesystems are then created upon this LUN and used by Linux.

Shared Storage

In certain situations, it is useful to share a single LUN between servers. This is most common in a highly available cluster, such as a database. Take Oracle 9i RAC as an example; all the database table spaces are stored on a shared medium (in this case an SAN) and accessed by multiple instances of the database. As both database instances are accessing the same storage, the database needs to be aware of what files and portions of the files each is accessing. This is called *locking*. When an instance needs write access to a tablespace, it needs to lock a portion of the file so that the other instance does not try to write or destroy that data that is being worked upon.

Locking of files and of a Linux partition is something that must be considered when sharing storage between multiple servers. Most standard Linux filesystems are not cluster aware and will behave very badly when mounted on two separate servers. To combat this, cluster-aware filesystems have been created. A cluster filesystem understands that multiple servers may be accessing data at the same time, and understanding that, the filesystem may change out of the control of one of the servers. One of the most popular Linux clustered filesystems is Global Filesystem (GFS), now owned by Red Hat.

If you ever have to share data between more than one server in a disk environment, always be aware that you must use a cluster-aware filesystem.

Using the Qlogic Driver

The most common QLA card in circulation at the moment is the QLA2300 chipset, which is fully supported by SUSE. It is very likely that YaST would have found your Qlogic card during installation and would have configured the driver to load at boot time.

If you have installed the driver after installation, you may need to configure your SAN access manually from Linux:

1. Manually load the driver and see if you can access your storage.

   ```
   bible:~ # modprobe qla2300
   ```

   While the driver loads, you may see your system lock up. This is standard as the Qlogic driver initializes and is nothing to worry about.

2. Run dmesg to see what the Qlogic driver has found.

   You may see multiple SCSI devices found on the SAN fabric. The problem with this scenario is that you have created only one LUN on the storage and you can see two SCSI devices.

   This is because there are two links into the fabric, and each card has found the same LUN. To resolve this, you need to use the Qlogic failover driver. When a link to the SAN goes down, the driver switches the preferred path to a link that is up. During this time, all IO operations stall until the failover has happened.

3. Check the output of /proc/partitions to see what the kernel sees regarding disks on the system. You may see errors in /var/log/messages warning you that your new LUN does not have a valid partition table, and this is because it is a raw disk that needs to be initialized.

4. Load fdisk and create a partition on the disk (or many if needed). You can then access the disk as if it were any normal storage disk in the system.

For more information on using `fdisk` to create partitions, see Chapter 3.

When your storage has been configured, you should tell SUSE that it needs to load the Qlogic driver at boot time so that you can mount the filesystems using `fstab`. To do this, edit the file `/etc/sysconfig/kernel` and add the Qlogic driver to the M O D-ULES_LOADED_ON_BOOT list. Every module listed in MODULES_LOADED_ON_BOOT will be automatically loaded when the system boots. Each module listed is the module name without the .ko extension as found in `/lib/modules`.

```
MODULES_LOADED_ON_BOOT= "cdrom ide-cd ide-scsi qla2300"
```

Disaster Recovery

In recent years, *disaster recovery* (DR) has become a very important part of an organization. This is not only for the enterprise, but also for any company. DR can mean anything from storing backups of your network at a secure, off-site location to replicating data in real time to a DR site.

DR is not just about saving your data in the event of a disaster but also about a methodology on how to bring your business back up when the worst happens. Most organizations realize that the quicker they can bring a DR site up, the less they will lose. To do this, real-time data replication has become very popular recently.

Most SAN controllers support block-level replication over fiber to another location. This is a very costly DR solution. However, it is a solution that is very resilient and fast. The main problem is that you need to have a very fast connection to your DR site, which could involve laying dark fiber directly to the site, using a high-capacity link, and employing iSCSI or an IP to Fiber translator, which again is very costly.

Luckily, Linux has a block replication service called DRBD that mirrors a disk device over TCP/IP to another server. Philip Reisner wrote DRBD while writing his thesis and has employed very elegant ways to transfer data across the network.

DRBD works on the block level of a disk device so it has no understanding of files, directories, or filesystems. It transfers any changes to the device, whether they are metadata or file changes. DRBD works by storing a bitmap of the disk and transferring dirty data across the network based on changes to the bitmap to another device on the partner machine.

DRBD provides a shared storage system and is seen by Linux as a disk device in the same way that a SAN is seen. This also produces the same problem you have with sharing a disk between two machines with a standard Linux filesystem. With this in mind, you should never mount your DRBD device on both machines at the same time because you will probably corrupt your data at some point.

Setting Up a DRBD Pair

Before configuring DRBD, make sure it is installed using YaST. By default, the DRBD system is not installed. For more information on installing packages, refer to Chapter 1.

To configure the partners, you need to create a single DRBD configuration that is used on both machines, /etc/drbd.conf. A DRBD configuration file needs to contain a resource definition that describes the DRBD devices. This definition will contain the host names of the partners, IP addresses, and the devices you want to keep synchronized.

DRBD works on the block level, so you need to specify the partition, not the mount point, of the filesystem.

Note When defining your hosts, one must be the primary, and another the secondary node (synchronizing from one to the other). With this in mind, the secondary node's device you are synchronizing to must be the same as or bigger than the primary's node.

If you have multiple devices that you want to synchronize, you can specify multiple resource definitions in the same file. For example, if you want to synchronize /dev/sdb2 to 192.168.0.5 and synchronize /dev/sdb3 to 192.168.0.6, you can specify two separate resource definitions.

When you define a host in the DRBD definition section, you must specify the node name as returned by the uname -n command. This is paramount to the operation of DRBD, and if it is incorrect, DRBD will complain at startup.

Listing 27-1 is a sample DRBD configuration file for a partnership.

Listing 27-1: **Defining a Partnership in DRBD**

```
resource drbd0 {
net {

sync-max = 30M

}
  protocol = C
  fsckcmd  = /bin/true

# DB Server
  on node1 {
    device  = /dev/nb0
    disk    = /dev/sdb1
    address = 192.168.0.2
    port    = 7788
```

Continued

Listing 27-1 *(continued)*

```
    }

# DR DB Server
  on node2 {
    device  = /dev/nb0
    disk    = /dev/sda8
    address = 192.168.0.3
    port    = 7788
  }
}
```

We have defined two machines, node1 and node2; node1 is the primary node in the partnership (the first node defined).

As synchronization takes place over the network, it is a good idea to specify how much bandwidth can be used when sending data between machines. If you have to share your network bandwidth with other applications—which is usually true over a wide area network (WAN) link to a DR site—you do not want to saturate your connection for the sake of one DR configuration.

The net section enables you to configure any network-based operations that DRBD will use during synchronization. For example, here we have defined a maximum synchronization rate of 30 megabytes per second (Mbps) so as not to saturate our 100 Mbps link.

DRBD Protocols

A very important aspect of DRBD is the protocol used for synchronization. DRBD defines three protocols that can be used. They are listed in Table 27-1.

Table 27-1
DRBD Protocol Versions

Protocol Version	Description
A	Data is marked as written when it has been written to the local disk and the network buffer.
B	Data is marked as written when it has been written to the local disk and an acknowledgment has been received from the secondary node's network buffer.
C	Data is marked as written when it has been written to the local disk and an acknowledgment has been received when data has been written to the remote disk.

Each protocol version provides a different profile for writing data depending on your network and disk latency and also whether you need to guarantee your data has been saved to the remote disk or not.

✦ If you are using a high-latency connection, you may need to use protocol A. This effectively removes any issues you have with the network as the kernel returns a write operation as soon as it has been written to the local disk and sent to the network buffer. This is the fastest protocol you can use if your application needs near-local write efficiency.

✦ If you are using a low-latency network, protocol C guarantees data has been written to both machines' disks before a write is returned by the kernel. If you notice that your disk writes are taking too long when using this protocol, you may want a mid point between protocol A and C.

✦ Protocol B returns a write only when data has been written to the local disk and has been received by the remote network buffer. This decreases the amount of time it takes for local writes but also gives you some guarantee that your network is on the way to being written to the remote disk.

Choosing the best protocol is something that you must be comfortable with because it severely impacts the speed of local writes to the disk, thus slowing down the application that relies on the data being replicated. As we are more concerned with the integrity of the data and not the speed of the transfer, we have chosen protocol C.

Defining Your Hosts

When your network and protocol have been defined, you need to specify the hosts that will be taking part in the replication.

In Listing 27-1, we have defined `node1` first, telling DRBD that this is the primary node.

You need to define the IP address of the node, the raw device to replicate, and the name of the device as it will be used by the node itself.

Note After DRBD has been configured for a device, a DRBD device is created to be used as the device to be replicated. We have defined that `/dev/sdb1` should be replicated and that we will use the device `/dev/nb0` to access the replicated device. For example, we can use `mkreiserfs /dev/nb0` to create a Reiser filesystem that is replicated to the secondary node automatically.

For the sake of verbosity, we have also specified in the listing the TCP port that we will use for sending DRBD data over the network. And we have also made a similar configuration with the configuration that is specific to the secondary node.

When saved, you can copy the `drbd.conf` file to the secondary node as is and start DRBD with `rcdrbd start`.

When DRBD has started, check `/proc/drbd` for information on what DRBD is doing and whether the node is in primary or secondary mode.

Using DRBD

If the primary node in your DRBD cluster goes down, you will need to promote the secondary node to primary status so that you can mount the filesystem and start your applications. When the primary node comes back up, any data written to the secondary node is replicated to the primary node, and you can then reverse their roles and carry on normal operation.

To change the status of a node, you need to use the `drbdsetup` command. The `drbdsetup` command can be used to change the DRBD runtime environment, including the definition of host parameters.

To change from a secondary to a primary node in the event of a primary node failure, you need to tell DRBD to set the DRBD device to `primary`.

```
bible:~ # drbdsetup /dev/nb0 primary
```

This tells DRBD on the secondary node that it is safe to use the device and also that this device should be marked as the master when it comes to the owner of the data. This is important because if the old primary node comes back to life, you must maintain where the most recent copy of the data is.

If you have managed to fix the broken (old primary) node, the data from the new primary node is automatically transferred to the now secondary node. When this is complete, you need to set the new primary to secondary and the old primary to primary so that normal operation can resume.

To set the new primary to secondary, you need to use the `drbdsetup` command again:

```
bible:~ # drbdsetup /dev/nb0 secondary
```

When the roles have been reversed on both nodes, and the machine you originally designed as the primary is restored to its former glory, you can carry on to use its services as normal.

Finally, the enterprise is somewhere where your IT services *must* work, *must* be maintainable, and *must* be transparent to the end user. Saying that Linux is enterprise-ready means that at least those points must be satisfied, and only recently has this happened.

Now that customers are happy to use Linux in this enterprise space, things can only get better. More money into the Linux market will help to boost its scalability, stability, and usability in the long run!

✦ ✦ ✦

Emulation and Virtualization

Since the earliest days of Linux, there has been interest in running software designed for other systems on a Linux system. For obvious historical reasons, many people wanted ways to run applications written for MS-DOS (or other DOS variants) or Windows on Linux. There has also been an interest in finding ways of running Linux on top of Linux.

Initially the motivation for these attempts largely had to do with enabling desktop usage of DOS or Windows programs in a Linux environment. However, as time has gone by, and hardware has become more powerful, the emphasis has partly changed. There is now great interest in the idea of consolidating server loads by moving multiple existing systems into a virtual environment running on top of Linux.

Emulation versus Virtualization

We look at two main approaches in this chapter: emulation and virtualization. To some extent these two terms are interchangeable, and many forms of emulation involve a certain amount of virtualization.

Emulation refers to the idea of creating an environment (as a running program) that behaves in terms of input and output like the target system. For example, the dosemu program is an emulation of a DOS system. Although it is a program running under Linux, it responds to interactions from users just as a real DOS system would. Wine's Windows emulation behaves slightly differently. Strictly speaking, Wine's approach is not emulation (indeed the name Wine stands for "Wine is not an emulator") because there is not a process running that pretends to be a Windows system. What Wine does is to intercept calls by Windows programs to the operating system and libraries and replace them with calls to its own infrastructure, which results in the right behavior. User Mode Linux and

FAUmachine can be regarded as emulating Linux under Linux, because the guest Linux system runs as a process on top of Linux.

Virtualization implies (at least) that a virtual machine exists: in other words that there is a software environment which emulates (at least some aspects) of a real hardware machine. If you can emulate an entire hardware platform, then you are doing virtualization. The term is used most often in cases where there is also some mechanism for transferring some of the resources directly to the virtual environment, which is a requirement that the virtual machines must provide to ensure decent performance.

It is possible to emulate an entire hardware platform. For example, the bochs project emulates an entire PC environment. You can then install an operating system into this virtual PC. The operating system thinks that it is being installed into real hardware. When you start the emulator, the guest operating system boots within it and you have a virtual machine running on top of your real one.

This is the approach used by bochs, VMWare, QEMU, and Xen, but there are significant differences in how it is achieved. To get decent performance in a virtual machine, there needs to be a way of sharing some of the real hardware resources with the guest operating system. As noted previously, the term *virtualization* is usually used with the implication that as well as providing a virtual machine capability, some of the resources of the real hardware are "virtualized" and offered to the guest operating system. This is not the case with bochs, which is why it is so slow, although it provides an entire emulated PC environment. However, bochs can run on any Unix system on any hardware platform. VMWare, QEMU, and Xen do have the ability to virtualize real resources and hence provide better performance. To be able to virtualize real system resources in this way requires that the emulated system have the same architecture as (or in the case of Xen, very similar to) that of the real hardware.

The Xen virtualization system is creating a great deal of interest at the moment, as it is a way of running multiple virtual systems on a single server with minimal loss of performance. It also has the very powerful feature of allowing running systems to be migrated from one physical server to another with downtime measured of only fractions of a second. This makes it a serious competitor with VMWare's high-end server products. The only disadvantage is that at present Xen requires a slightly modified version of the operating system in order to be able to run it. This is not a problem for Linux (or indeed any open source system); current versions of SUSE already include the necessary modifications. However it does mean that at present it is not possible to run Windows operating systems within Xen. Future versions of Xen (3.0 onwards) running on new Intel and AMD processors (with Intel's VT and AMD's Pacifica extensions) will be able to run other operating systems unmodified, so soon Windows guest operating systems on Xen will also be possible.

DOS Emulation Using dosemu and dosbox

SUSE contains packages for two DOS emulators, dosemu and dosbox. They are similar, with the difference that dosbox is intended as a platform for running DOS games.

dosemu

The dosemu package that comes with SUSE includes a version of FreeDOS, and free software DOS clone. However, it is possible to replace this with MS-DOS or another DOS variant if you want to.

After the package is installed, all you need to do to run it is type either **dosemu** or **xdosemu**, and you will see a window with a DOS prompt (the first time you run it you are asked to confirm the path to the DOS version that it is going to run and to confirm that you accept the license). The virtual DOS C: drive that appears is in fact rooted at ~/dosemu/freedos/ and is copied from the master copy at /opt/dosemu/share/dosemu/freedos/. The virtual D: drive is simply your home directory (however, because DOS expects filenames to be in 8.3 format, long filenames are garbled). If you create a directory DOSPROG under your home directory and copy into it a DOS program that you want to run, you will then be able to run it simply by switching to the directory D:\DOSPROG within dosemu.

To exit from dosemu, type **exitemu** at the prompt, and the DOS session will close. Figure 28-1 shows dosemu displaying a typical DOS directory listing.

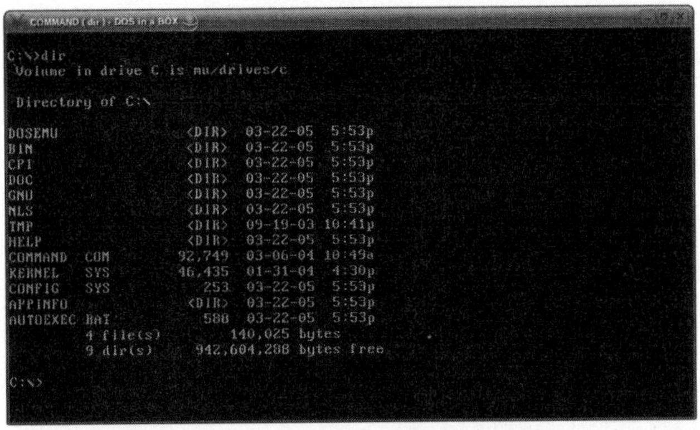

Figure 28-1: dosemu showing a directory listing

Many DOS programs will work fine in dosemu, but games and other programs that produce graphical output may fail.

dosbox

The `dosbox` package is similar to `dosemu`, although it is designed essentially for playing games. The web page at `http://dosbox.sourceforge.net` includes a long list of DOS games with comments on how well they work under `dosbox`. `dosbox` can run both real-mode and protected-mode DOS games, and its graphics support is remarkably good. When `dosbox` starts, you are presented with a DOS prompt showing the drive letter Z:. `dosbox` contains an internal mount command, so you can type, for example:

```
Z:\> mount C /home/roger/DOSPROG
```

Then when you switch to drive C: under `dosbox`, you will be able to run the DOS programs that you have saved in that directory. In Figure 28-2, `dosbox` is seen running a graphical DOS program, which fails under `dosemu`.

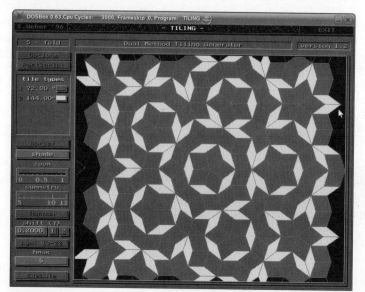

Figure 28-2: dosbox running Stefan Weber's Penrose tiling generator

Running Microsoft Windows Applications Using Wine

Even the most rabid Linux fanatic has to recognize that there are times when you must run Microsoft Windows applications for compatibility reasons with other applications or your co-workers. As discussed elsewhere in this chapter, one solution is to run software such as VMWare that emulates an entire Windows system. Within the context of this virtual machine, you can then install and execute the

Windows applications that you need to run because the virtual machine looks like an actual Windows system to the software. However, that seems like overkill when all you need to do is to edit a Word document that contains complex macros or tweak someone's *n*-dimensional Excel spreadsheet. Wouldn't it be nice to simply be able to run the one or two Windows applications that you need without the overhead and associated storage of a completely emulated Windows system?

Providing the ability to run Microsoft Windows applications natively on Linux and other Unix-like systems is the precise goal of the Wine (Wine Is Not an Emulator) Project (`www.winehq.com`). Wine is an open source implementation of the application programming interface (API) provided by Microsoft Windows and used by all Microsoft Windows applications. Wine runs in the X Window system environment on Linux and Unix. SUSE Linux includes a stable and tested version of Wine to enable many Microsoft Windows applications to install and execute normally on SUSE Linux systems.

Wine is one of the most popular and most misunderstood open source projects. Unlike emulators, which simulate the behavior of a given operating system or graphical environment and support its applications within that environment, Wine is a complete re-implementation of the API used by Windows applications. It therefore does not need to translate Windows API calls into equivalent Linux or X Window system calls on the fly. For example, Windows applications running under WINE call the same graphical APIs that they always called, but the implementation of those APIs immediately performs specific X Window system functions rather than the Windows functions that one would see if the application was running on a Microsoft Windows system. Very cool!

Wine is installed on SUSE Linux as part of the Office applications package. To install a Windows software package on Linux, execute the `wine` command, followed by the name of the installer for that package. For example, to install the Windows NX Client package on your Linux system, you would execute the following command:

```
$ wine nxclient-1.4.0-92.exe
```

Figure 28-3 shows a Windows installer running on a SUSE system under Wine. The first time that you run it on your Linux system, Wine creates a mock Windows directory hierarchy, as indicated by the message in the Konsole window in Figure 28-3. This mock Windows directory structure is located in the directory `~/.wine`, and contains a configuration directory, a `dosdevices` directory that provides DOS/Windows drive letter mappings, a `drive_c` directory that mirrors the directory structure that Windows expects to find on its boot drive, and three files that contain various system and user information and represent the Windows registry.

After you have installed a software package under Wine, you can execute any of the applications that it contains by specifying the `wine` command followed by the full pathname of the program that you want to run, as in the following example:

```
$ wine ~/.wine/drive_c/Program\ Files/NX\ Client\ for\ Windows\nxclient.exe
```

Figure 28-3: A Windows installer running under Wine

Due to the complexity and size of the Windows API, Wine is always a work in progress, and all Windows packages do not run correctly under Wine. For information about which Windows applications run correctly under Wine, see http://appdb.winehq.org.

> **Note**   A commercially supported version of Wine known as CrossOver Office is available from CodeWeavers (www.codeweavers.com). This version of Wine provides enhancements and bug fixes that enable it to run many more applications, such as the complete Microsoft Office suite, than the free version of Wine. The CodeWeavers folks are very good about working directly with the Wine community, are the leading commercial sponsor of the Wine project, and push all of their fixes into the open source version of Wine. CrossOver Office is an excellent investment if you need to run Office or other resource-intensive software packages on your Linux system. As a matter of fact, this section of this chapter was written in Word running under CodeWeavers' Wine implementation.

The bochs PC Emulator

The bochs project goes back a long way. It is a free (licensed under the GNU LGPL) PC hardware emulator that provides a complete emulation of PC hardware in software. As is the case with QEMU and VMWare (see later in the chapter), you can install an operating system into bochs. However, bochs does not offer virtualization of the underlying hardware to the guest. This means that it can be built and run on any Unix-like platform on any hardware architecture, but it also means that it is slow. For most practical purposes, if you want to run *x*86 operating systems as virtual machines on *x*86 hardware, then either QEMU (free) or VMWare (proprietary and commercial) will probably be a better first choice.

A bochs package is included in SUSE Linux. Install it in the usual way, and type the command **bochs**. A set of text menus appears in which you can set various options. You can write these to disk to create a configuration file for future use. After you have set the options, or bochs has read them from a configuration file, a graphical window will appear. Provided bochs knows how to find its virtual CD drive, you can begin installing an operating system, and you have created and configured a suitable file as a virtual hard disk, you can begin installing an operating system.

Because bochs is so slow, unless you have very powerful hardware to run it on, or you have an academic interest in the workings of emulation and the *x*86 processor family, you will probably conclude that for practical purposes either QEMU or VMWare is a more useful solution, particularly if you want to get real work done with your guest operating system.

Figure 28-4 shows the starting of a SUSE installation in bochs.

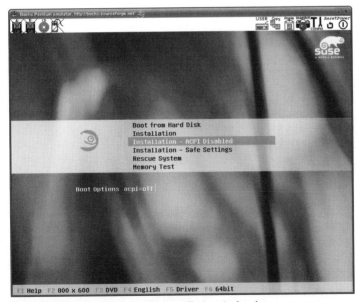

Figure 28-4: Starting a SUSE installation in bochs

Virtual Machines Using QEMU

QEMU is an open source hardware emulator. It can emulate an *x*86 system on *x*86, but can also both emulate and run on some other architectures. In particular, it can emulate and run on the PowerPC architecture.

QEMU packages are included in the SUSE distribution. QEMU is developed by Fabrice Bellard, and the latest version is always available from `http://fabrice.bellard.free.fr/qemu/`.

You can install most *x*86 operating systems in QEMU, including most versions of Windows and most Linux distributions.

QEMU manages to achieve reasonable speeds (between 5 to 10 times slower than native) by using dynamic translation of binary code. The author, Fabrice Bellard also offers a QEMU accelerator known as `kqemu` for the Linux host operating system. The accelerator is a special kernel module that improves the performance of QEMU very considerably (the QEMU web page claims that guest operating systems will run at better than half native speed if the accelerator is running; this is nothing like as good as Xen or VMWare, but is far better than `bochs`). It works by allowing QEMU to get access to the real underlying hardware, just as VMWare does. Certainly informal tests show that, for example, Microsoft Word on Windows 2000 under QEMU with the accelerator is considerably more responsive than the same version of Word under Wine running on the same machine.

The QEMU accelerator is distributed without cost but licensed as proprietary software (apparently the author is still undecided about its eventual license status, and is looking for some kind commercial sponsorship of the project). It seems that there are fairly widespread hopes that it will be released at some point under a genuinely free software license.

Installing and Running QEMU

To use QEMU without the accelerator module, all you need to do is to install the package on the SUSE media.

If you want to try a version that is newer than the one currently offered by SUSE, you can download a binary distribution from the QEMU web site, which can be installed simply by copying it to the root directory and unpacking it:

```
cp qemu-0.7.1-i386.tar.gz /
cd /
tar zxvf qemu-0.7.1.tar.gz
```

You can also build QEMU from source, although there is normally no real need to do so unless you want to apply some obscure options at compile time. If you want to use the accelerator module, you need to have a copy of the source distribution in order to build the module (see later in the chapter), but you do not actually need to build the core software from source: only the accelerator module.

QEMU needs a virtual hard disk onto which to install an operating system. It includes a tool that makes creating the virtual hard disk easy. This tool is the `qemu-img` command. To create a virtual hard disk of size 3GB, do the following:

```
qemu-img create test.dsk 3G
```

This creates a virtual disk called `test.dsk`

Then you can run an operating system installation either from a real CD or from a CD image. For example:

```
qemu -hda test.dsk -cdrom /dev/hdc -monitor stdio -boot d -m 192
```

This will start QEMU with `test.dsk` as the virtual hard disk (`-hda`), and using the real CD drive (`-cdrom /dev/hdc`). The option boot `-d` makes the virtual system boot from CD (think of drive D:), and `-m 192` gives it 192MB of memory. The extra option `-monitor stdio` provides a command-line monitor interface that you can use to interact with QEMU from the outside. You need this option if you are installing an operating system from more than one CD image, because you need it to force QEMU to change disks.

After the operating system has been installed into QEMU, you can run it using a command similar to the following:

```
qemu -hda test.dsk -monitor stdio -boot c -m 192
```

Here `-boot` c makes the system boot from hard disk (think of drive C:).

Figure 28-5 shows a Windows 2000 installation under way in QEMU.

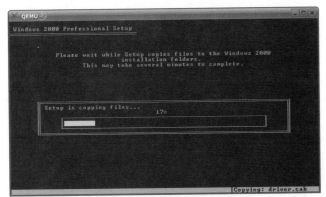

Figure 28-5: Installing Windows 2000 Professional under QEMU

Building and Using the QEMU Accelerator

If you want to use the QEMU accelerator, you will need to download the source distribution of QEMU and the source for the `kqemu` module. First unpack the source distribution somewhere:

```
tar zxvf qemu-0.7.1.tar.gz
```

This creates a directory `qemu-0.7.1` under the current directory. Copy and unpack the accelerator source tarball inside that directory:

```
cp kqemu-0.7.1-1.tar.gz qemu-0.7.1
cd qemu-0.7.1
tar zxvf kqemu-0.7.1.tar.gz
```

Then do the following:

```
cd kdqemu
make
make install
./install
```

In this case, `make install` does not actually install the module, but creates a script `install` which does the installation of the module when you run it.

The preceding process described requires the QEMU source code, but it doesn't require you to build QEMU from source, provided that you have exactly the same version of the binary distribution installed with which the accelerator module was distributed.

To run QEMU with the accelerator module loaded, you simply need to load the kernel module before starting QEMU by typing the command (as root):

```
modprobe kqemu
```

You should notice a significant improvement in the speed of the guest operating system.

Note that certain older versions of Windows (Windows 95/98) may fail to run under certain versions of QEMU if the `kqemu` module is loaded. Fortunately that is not such a hardship as these versions require fewer resources in any case. However, the author of QEMU is currently working on solving this problem.

With the accelerator, QEMU can compete well with VMWare for the straightforward task of running a single guest operating system on the desktop. We have found it a very user-friendly way of running both Windows and other PC operating systems under Linux, and on modern hardware performance is more than acceptable.

Using the Network in QEMU

Setting up networking between the guest operating system and the host operating system in QEMU is most easily done by using the *user-mode network stack* within QEMU. QEMU creates a network device on the host operating system that is visible to the guest systems and allows the guests to see the outside world.

To use this feature, you need to use the option `-user-net` when starting QEMU (on later versions this is the default, so you do not need to type the option). You will then find that by default a dedicated network interface is available on the host with address 10.0.2.2. QEMU then starts a DHCP server on this address (see Chapter 20 for more on DHCP), allowing the guest operating system to get a network address and to access the outside world.

If the guest operating system is a version of Windows, you can run QEMU with an additional command line option like `-smb /home/roger/shared`, which will share the named directory with the guest by running a built-in Samba server (see Chapter 18 for more on the Samba server).

It is also possible to do networking in QEMU using the `tun/tap` network interface. This requires some configuration and the loading of a kernel module in the host Linux system. Details of how to do this are included in the QEMU documentation.

QEMU Summary

For desktop purposes, if you simply want to run a single guest operating system graphically under Linux, QEMU probably offers everything that you need. VMWare (see the following section) has more options and is slightly easier to use, but is both proprietary and expensive. As they say, your mileage may vary, but the fact that QEMU is included in the SUSE distribution makes it particularly easy to install and use for straightforward tasks.

VMWare Virtual Machines

VMWare is a commercial and proprietary product similar in many ways to QEMU as described in the previous section. VMWare began as a desktop product for running Windows under Linux and vice versa, but now there are a variety of products on offer, including server versions (the VMWare GSX and ESX servers) that allow server consolidation by letting you migrate a variety of servers running different operating systems onto a single physical server.

VMWare Workstation

VMWare Workstation is a proprietary product and licenses are expensive, even for the workstation version. However, VMWare does offer 30-day evaluation licenses, and you can download the full product together with a 30-day key from the company's web site at `www.vmware.com`.

In this section, we discuss VMWare for Linux (the version that runs on Linux and enables you to install guest operating systems to run on top of Linux). You can also download a VMWare for Windows product.

VMWare Workstation Installation

The current version of VMWare at the time of writing is 5.0. It is offered both as a binary tar.gz archive and as an RPM package. For installation on SUSE Linux, choose the RPM package and install it from the command line:

```
rpm -Uvh VMware-workstation-5.0.0-13124.i386.rpm
```

If you now try to run the program you will almost certainly see something like this:

```
roger@bible: ~> vmware &
vmware is installed, but it has not been (correctly) configured
for this system. To (re-)configure it, invoke the following command:
/usr/bin/vmware-config.pl.
```

As root, you now have to run the command vmware-config.pl as stated in the error message. It is again likely that this will fail (but with different and obscure error messages) the first time that you try it. You need to have the kernel source installed for this to work, and you also need to have done at least a partial kernel build in the past. You also need the standard build tools (gcc, make, and so on) to be installed.

So if the kernel source package is not installed, install it using YaST and then run (as root) the following commands:

```
cd /usr/src/linux
make cloneconfig
make
```

(See Chapter 29 for more information on building the kernel.)

Now try the vmware-config.pl command once more, and it will take you through a series of questions (mainly about what kind of networking you want to set up for your virtual machines). Don't worry about giving wrong answers here; you can always run vmware-config.pl again at any future time to change the setup.

You can set up three types of networking\: host-only networking, NAT networking, and bridged networking.

- ✦ **Host-only networking** creates a private network between the host operating system and the virtual machines. You can give the virtual machines access to the outside world with host-only networking, but this requires manually setting up the necessary packet forwarding and routing on the host computer.
- ✦ **Bridged networking** makes the virtual machines appear on the real network with a publicly available IP address.

✦ The **NAT option** gives the virtual machines private addresses as if they were behind a gateway, but with NAT (Network Address Translation) access to the public network.

Starting VMWare

To start VMWare, simply type `vmware` at the prompt. If all is well, VMWare's graphical interface will start. At this point you will need to enter a license key, whether you have bought a full license or downloaded an evaluation license key. The key is entered using the following menu item: Help ⇨ Enter ⇨ *serial number.*

Now you can begin installing an operating system into VMWare. There are various settings that you should look at before beginning. In particular you can specify which operating system you want to install, and VMWare will optimize its settings accordingly. You can also choose whether to install from the real CD drive or from an ISO image on the filesystem (often a very convenient way of working). You can change the image if necessary during the installation when you are asked to swap disks. You can also alter the amount of memory that is to be assigned to the guest operating system. Clearly the memory you give the guest operating system is a significant factor in the way it performs. VMWare creates a virtual hard disk as one or more large files in the filesystem. For each virtual machine that you create, VMWare creates a directory containing these files and a few others; you can copy this directory to another physical machine and run the virtual machine there.

Figure 28-6 shows a SUSE system running within VMWare.

Advanced features of VMWare workstation include the ability to take snapshots of the state of a guest operating system and the ability to build teams of guests — very useful for testing the networking provided that you have enough memory available.

VMWare Workstation Compared with QEMU

VMWare's performance is better than that of QEMU, and it has some interesting special features (teams, snapshots, easy set-up of different types of networks, and so on). However, if you are simply looking for a way of testing alternative operating systems or running Windows under Linux, then QEMU (with the QEMU accelerator) will probably do everything you need.

VMWare Server Products

VMWare offers two highly sophisticated server versions, the VMWare GSX server and the VMWare ESX server. These are widely used for server consolidation purposes. The essential difference between them is that the GSX server is (like the workstation version) a program that runs on top of an operating system (Windows or Linux) and provides the capability to install virtual machines. The ESX server is a specialized cut-down operating system that runs on the bare metal and provides the same kind of facilities. It remains to be seen what the effect of enterprise utilization of Xen will be on VMWare's market share.

For more details of the server versions see www.vmware.com.

Figure 28-6: SUSE starting in VMWare 5

Creating and Using Virtual Machines with Xen

Xen is an open source virtual machine system designed for use on Linux systems. Xen was developed by the University of Cambridge's Computer Laboratory (www.cl.cam.ac.uk/Research/SRG/netos/xen). Xen enables you to run multiple operating system instances on a single hardware system, and currently supports running the Linux 2.4, Linux 2.6, and NetBSD operating systems. Ports of FreeBSD and Plan 9 are actively under development and should be available soon. SUSE Linux was the first commercial Linux vendor to ship a supported version of Xen, first including it in SUSE Linux 9.3.

Although largely similar in functionality to other virtual machine systems such as VMWare, Xen's approach is very different. The core of Xen is a small virtual machine manager application, known as a *monitor* or *hypervisor* (hyper-supervisor), which is what you initially boot on your system. This virtual machine monitor then boots a single instance of an operating system, which can be used to start any number of other operating system instances (known as virtual machines). The number of virtual machines that you can run on any given system depends on the amount of memory allocated to each and therefore the total amount of memory available on your system. The Xen virtual machine monitor reserves 64MB of memory for itself at boot time and then manages the hardware resources of the system on which the virtual machines are running, providing a central clearinghouse for all requests for hardware and network access by any of the virtual machines.

Xen requires a specially modified kernel. Each Xen virtual machine must have its own root filesystem, and any read-only filesystem can be shared between multiple Xen virtual machines. At the moment, networked filesystems such as NFS or Samba are the only filesystems that can be shared between Xen virtual machines, because these filesystems provide built-in locking and synchronization protocols for handling simultaneous writes by multiple operating systems.

Installing Xen

Xen is not installed by default on SUSE systems, but can be installed when you install your SUSE system if you specify Custom Package Selection and select the Xen Virtualization package. Xen can also be added to any installed SUSE system using the YaST Install Software module. Installing the Xen Virtualization package installs the Xen virtual machine monitor, a Linux kernel that has been modified for use with Xen, the Xen daemon (xend), and the Xen management utility (x m). It also installs the Linux bridge-utils package for bridged networking support and any necessary Python packages (because xend and x m are both written in Python).

If you install the Xen Virtualization package as part of your initial SUSE installation, the SUSE installer automatically adds the correct entries to your GRUB boot configuration file (/boot/grub/menu.lst). If you add the Xen Virtualization package to an existing SUSE Linux system, you may need to manually modify the GRUB boot configuration file to contain a stanza for Xen such as the following:

```
title XEN
  root (hd0,1)
  kernel /boot/xen.gz dom0_mem=524200
  module /boot/vmlinuz-xen root=/dev/hdb2 resume=/dev/hdb3 showopts
  module /boot/initrd-xen
```

The sample Xen boot stanza shown previously is modeled after your standard SUSE Linux boot entry, assuming that it looks something like the following:

```
title SUSE LINUX 10.0
  root (hd0,1)
```

```
kernel /boot/vmlinuz root=/dev/hdb2 resume=/dev/hdb3 showopts
initrd /boot/initrd
```

Your SUSE and Xen boot stanzas may contain other kernel options such as
vga=0x314 selinux=0 splash=silent.

The boot stanza for a Xen monitor and associated kernel identify the location of a
compressed version of the Xen virtual machine monitor in its kernel entry, which
also defines the amount of system memory to be reserved for the initial Linux system that you are booting under Xen. Xen uses the term *domain* to refer to a single
instance of an operating system environment. The initial Linux system that you
boot under Xen is known as *domain 0* in Xen terms. The Xen boot stanza in your
GRUB configuration file can either assign all available memory to your initial
domain, or can associate a specific amount of memory to that domain. If you
choose the former approach, you can subsequently reduce the amount of memory
associated to your primary domain using the x m balloon command. If you associate
only a specific subset of your system's available memory to domain 0, you can
associate specific amounts of memory to subsequent domains when you create
them, which is the option that we prefer. The Xen stanza shown previously allocated 512MB of the 1GB of memory available on the sample system to domain 0,
which enables you to directly specify the memory requirements of subsequent
domains in their configuration files. You may want to customize this value to assign
a specific amount of memory to domain 0 on your system. The maximum value that
you can use is the amount of memory available on your system, minus 64K for the
Xen monitor. The amount of memory allocated to domain 0 must currently be given
in kilobytes, although future versions of Xen plan to support more generic expressions of megabytes.

The remainder of a Xen boot stanza tells GRUB to load a Linux kernel that has been
prepared for use with Xen (/boot/vmlinuz-xen) as the system's primary Linux
instance, using a RAM disk with Xen functionality (/boot/initrd-xen) during the
boot process. It is a good idea to specify symbolic links for both the kernel and initial RAM disk so that you can subsequently install updated versions of both without
needing to modify your GRUB configuration file.

Creating Xen Virtual Machines Using YaST

SUSE's YaST provides a Virtual Machine Installation module that makes it easy to
create and configure Xen virtual machines. In order to use this module, you must
first be running a Xen-enabled kernel. You can then configure a Xen virtual machine
by doing the following:

   1. Start the Control Center and select YaST2 Modules, or start YaST2 directly.
   Select the Software topic from the left pane and click the Virtual Machine
   Installation (XEN) icon. If you are not already running as the root user, you will
   have to click the Administrator Mode button and enter the root password in
   the password dialog box. The screen shown in Figure 28-7 displays.

2. Click the Options heading to set the amount of memory and set other options for the virtual machine that you are creating. The screen shown in Figure 28-8 displays. The amount of memory allocated to the virtual machine must be less than the amount of available memory on your machine. Click Accept to continue.

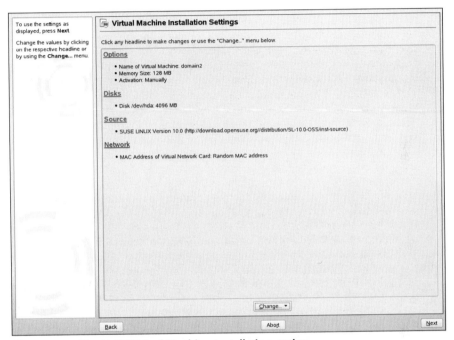

Figure 28-7: The YaST Virtual Machine Installation option

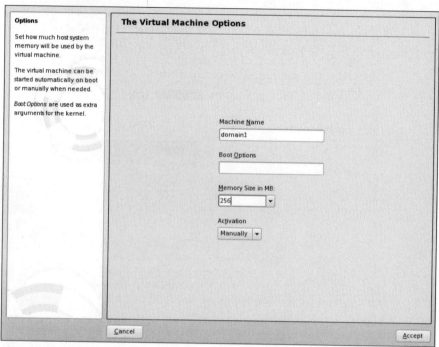

Figure 28-8: Setting Xen virtual machine options in YaST

Note You may need to adjust the amount of memory allocated to your main Xen domain in /boot/grub/menu.1st and reboot in order to make sure that sufficient free memory is available to enable you to create additional Xen domains.

3. Click the Disks heading to adjust the size or name of the virtual disk image that is being created. The screen shown in Figure 28-9 displays. Click Edit to modify the default entry or click add to specify a new one. I tend to use 4 GB (4096 MB) as the size of disk images for Xen domains, as this provides room to add applications, collect data from long-running applications, and so on. Click Accept to continue.

4. If you do not already have a network installation source defined, click Source to define one. YaST's Virtual machine Installation module requires the use of a networked install source such as FTP, HTTP, SMB, or NFS. This displays the standard YaST Installation Source dialog box. After defining a networked install source, that YaST module closes and the Virtual Machine Installation dialog box redisplays.

5. Click Network to customize the setting of the network interface used by the Xen domain that you are creating. It is rarely necessary to modify this.

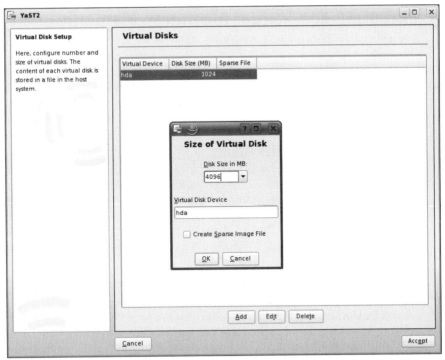

Figure 28-9: Setting Xen disk image options in YaST

   6. Click Next to proceed with the actual Xen Virtual Machine installation. YaST
   creates a root filesystem image and stores it in a subdirectory of /var/
   lib/xen/images with the same name as the virtual machine that you are
   creating. YaST also creates a template domain configuration file by the same
   name and stores it in /etc/xen.

That's all there is to it. You will still need to add information such as the name of
the Xen kernel to the template domain configuration file created in /etc/xen, but
YaST has done the hard part of creating a filesystem image for you. The next section explains how to manually customize a Xen domain configuration file.

Creating Xen Virtual Machines Manually

While the YaST Virtual Machine Installation (Xen) module simplifies the task of creating Xen virtual machines, it isn't completely customizable. You may want to migrate existing Xen virtual machines or install them in a way that no one could anticipate. For this reason, it's also useful to understand how to create and configure Xen virtual machines. The following sections discuss the various aspects of a Xen virtual machine and how to perform each step manually.

Creating Xen Root Filesystems

As mentioned previously, each operating system instance running under Xen must have its own root filesystem. The root filesystem used by Xen domain 0 is typically the root filesystem on your Linux system. Root filesystems for use by other Xen domains can easily be created using YaST. You can create these in one of two ways — by installing SUSE Linux into a filesystem or by using the YaST Virtual Machine Configuration module and doing filesystem creation/population as part of your virtual machine setup. This section explains the former approach.

The root filesystem used by an operating system running under Xen can be any root filesystem location supported by that operating system — a physical disk partition, an NFS-mounted root filesystem, a filesystem image contained in a file, and so on. These must be created in the standard fashion. When created, you can use the SUSE YaST administration suite to populate them from your SUSE installation media.

Tip   For convenience, many people create Xen root filesystems and associated swap partitions within logical volumes. This provides flexibility that enables you to subsequently increase the size of these filesystems or otherwise modify their configuration as needed, without requiring that you add disks or modify existing, physical partitions.

To use YaST to install a bootable SUSE distribution into a specified root filesystem location, mount the partition, NFS location, or file as `/var/tmp/dirinstall` on your SUSE system, and then start YaST. Select Software and then select Installation into Directory, which displays the screen shown in Figure 28-10.

This screen is analogous to the standard SUSE installation screen. You can change the packages installed into the new root filesystem by clicking Change or selecting the Software link. When you have made the modifications to the contents of the root filesystem for your new Xen domain, click Next to begin the installation process, which displays a standard installation screen (see Figure 28-11).

The standard SUSE installation process on a Linux system automatically creates user, group, and system configuration files in a target root filesystem during the installation process. Because the YaST Installation into Directory module populates only the root filesystem for Xen, you must perform a few manual steps before the filesystem is actually ready to be used with Xen.

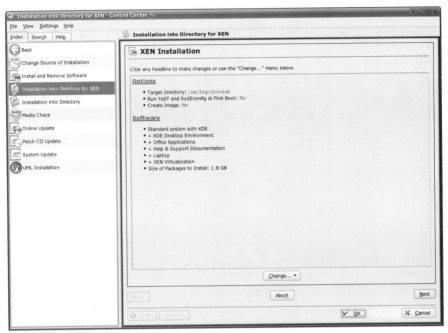

Figure 28-10: The YaST Installation into Directory option

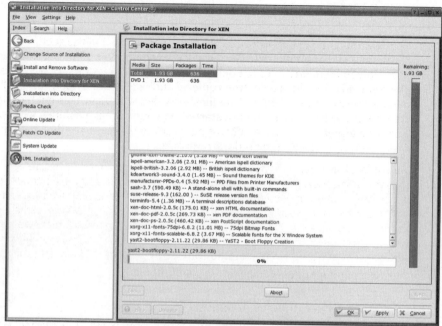

Figure 28-11: Installing into a directory using YaST

After the installation has completed, you should do the following:

1. Add any loadable kernel modules required for the Linux kernel to the new root filesystem. You can do this from the command line (as the root user) with a command like the following, where *xen-kernel-dir* is the name of the directory containing the loadable kernel modules associated with the Xen-enabled Linux kernel that you will be booting on a virtual machine:

```
(cd /lib/modules/; tar cf - xen-kernel-dir)| \
    (cd /var/tmp/install/lib/modules; tar -xf -)
```

2. Create appropriate /etc/passwd, /etc/shadow, and /etc/group files for the Xen domain in which you will use the root filesystem that you are creating. You can do this by simply copying those files from your primary root filesystem into the etc subdirectory of the directory in which you are creating a root filesystem for Xen.

3. Create an appropriate /etc/fstab file for the Xen system on which you will use the root filesystem that you are creating. The entries in this fstab file will reflect the names of partitions as seen by the Xen domain that you are creating, which will usually differ from their names on the Linux system where the files or partitions are actually stored. See the section later in this section entitled "Creating Xen Configuration Files" for information on how to specify the

name by which your Xen domain will see specific disk partitions or filesystem images.

4. Create appropriate startup/runlevel links. As discussed in the section "Creating Xen Configuration Files," the runlevel in which your Xen domains start up can be defined in the configuration file for each domain. We typically use runlevel 4, which is a custom runlevel and is also the default runlevel used in the example configuration files provided with Xen. This enables you to customize the processes that are started on your virtual machines without worrying about activating/deactivating a variety of processes that are normally started in the SUSE standard runlevels.

Tip

Thread-local storage, as implemented in current versions of glibc and its associated threading package, can cause problems with applications running under Xen. Its implementation under Xen can also be very slow. To disable thread-local storage under Xen and thus fall back to the simpler mechanisms used by earlier versions of glibc, move the file /lib/tls to /lib/tls.disabled in each root filesystem that you will be using with a Xen domain. If you do not do this, you will see a warning message to this effect in the console log for each Xen domain that you start other than domain 0.

Creating Swap Space for Xen Domains

After you have created a root filesystem for use with a new Xen domain, you should also prepare a swap file or partition for that same domain. Like any Linux system, any operating system instance running under Xen must also have an associated swap partition. This partition can be a file or disk partition, and should be formatted using the standard mkswap command.

Make sure that an entry for the swap partition exists in the etc/fstab file in the root filesystem for your Xen domain. As with the root filesystem, the entry for the swap partition in this fstab file will reflect the name of the swap partition as seen by the Xen domain that you are creating, which will usually differ from their names on the Linux system where the files or partitions are actually stored. See the following section, "Creating Xen Configuration Files," for information on how to specify the name by which your Xen domain will see your swap partition.

Creating Xen Configuration Files

Xen configuration files are typically stored in the directory /etc/xen and can have any name. The name of the Xen configuration used when starting a Xen domain other than domain 0 is specified on the x m command line, as explained in the following section.

The SUSE Xen implementation includes two sample configuration files that you can use as starting points for defining your own domains. The first, /etc/xen/xm example1, is a template for a simple domain configuration file and is the one that we'll focus on in this section. The second, /etc/xen/xmexample2, is a more complex domain configuration file that accepts command-line arguments and is suitable for use with Xen deployments in which you start a number of Xen domains that are similarly configured.

To create a configuration file for the domain that you are creating, copy the file `/etc/xen/xmexample1` to a file whose name represents the domain that you are creating. Next, edit this file using your favorite text editor and modify its values to reflect appropriate values for the domain that you are creating. The key items that you will want to customize are the following (listed in the order that you encounter them in the sample configuration file):

✦ `kernel = "/full/path/to/Xen/kernel"` — The full path of the Xen-enabled kernel that you want to boot on the Xen virtual machine which you are defining.

✦ `memory = amount-to-allocate-in-mb` — The amount of memory that you want to allocate to the virtual machine that you are defining, in megabytes.

✦ `name = "domain-name"` — The name that you want to associate with the virtual machine that you are creating. This can be any text string and need not be related to your network domain. It is just a unique identifier for the virtual machine.

✦ `nics=number-of-NICs` — The number of network interfaces that you want the virtual machine to create, excluding the loopback interface. The default value is 1, but we find it useful to set this value explicitly as a reminder of the number of network interfaces that the virtual machine will export.

✦ `vif = [ 'mac=aa:00:00:00:00:11, bridge=xen-br0' ]` — Specific information about each virtual network interface exported by the machine, consisting of a *MAC address/Ethernet-device* pair. Although technically optional, specifying an explicit MAC address for your virtual machine's Ethernet interface simplifies automatic network setup on systems such as SUSE, whose network startup scripts typically refer to a specific MAC address. The Ethernet-device value in this value pair is the name of the Ethernet bridge device on your host system that the bridge-tools package will automatically associated with the Xen virtual machine that you are defining.

✦ `disk = [ 'physical-partition-or-file-name,virtual-machine-partition-name,mode', 'phy:v0/vm1boot,hda1,w' ]` — Information about each disk that you want the virtual machine to be able to use or see. Each value consists of the physical name of a device or file that you are exporting to the virtual machine from the host system, the name of the device as seen by the virtual machine, and how the machine will use the disk. Possible values for *physical-partition-or-file-name* are values such as *phy:hdd2* (`/dev/hdd2` on the host system), *phy:v0/vm1boot* (the logical volume `vm1boot` in logical volume group 0 on the host system), *file:/home/wvh/xen/xenboot.img* (a file on the host system that contains an image of a root partition), and so on. The value of *virtual-machine-partition-name* is the name of the device as seen by the virtual machine. This enables you to map partitions/files on the host system to explicit partition names on the virtual machine, which you can then identify and refer to in the `etc/fstab` file on the virtual machine. The final value in each of these triplets is *mode*, which indicates how the virtual machine will use the specified partition or partition image. Possible values for mode are r (for read-only) and w (for a writable partition or partition image).

✦ root = "/dev/boot-partition mode" — The name of the root partition as seen by the virtual machine and its write-mode. This value will be passed to the virtual machine's kernel when booting the virtual machine. Possible values for */dev/boot-partition* are any of the partitions that you defined in the disk portion of your virtual machine configuration file. Possible values for *mode* are ro (read-only) and r w (read/write).

✦ extra = "run-level" — Any extra arguments that you want to pass to the kernel of the virtual machine when it boots. As mentioned previously, we typically use runlevel 4 for the default runlevel of Xen virtual machines, so we typically pass 4 to the kernel as an extra boot option. You could do the same by modifying the etc/inittab file in the virtual machine's root filesystem, setting the initdefault entry to 4, but we prefer to specify this on the host side so that it is easily overridden and is also clear to any user before they connect to a virtual machine.

After you've created your virtual machine's configuration file, you're ready to boot the machine.

Starting, Stopping, and Interacting with Xen Virtual Machines

Before you can start a Xen virtual machine, Xen's main daemon (xend) must be running on your host system. This daemon is usually started through the startup script /etc/init.d/xend, which was installed on your host system as part of the Xen package.

After you have started the Xen daemon, you can open a console to any of the virtual machines that you have defined by executing the x m console command. If you are starting a Xen virtual machine for the first time, you must specify its configuration file on the command line using the x m command's –c option. For example, to start the Xen virtual machine defined in the Xen configuration file /etc/xen/wvh_vm_1.conf, you would type the following command as the root user or via sudo:

```
xm console -c /etc/xen/wvh_vm_1.conf
```

This command starts the specified virtual machine and displays its console in the window in which you executed the command. For this reason, you may find it convenient to start each virtual machine console session in its own xterminal window, as in the following example:

```
xterm -e xm console -c /etc/xen/wvh_vm_1.conf &
```

This command opens a new `xterm` window and executes the specified `x m console` command within it. Figure 28-12 shows a SUSE system displaying an xterm containing a console session to a Xen virtual machine running on that same hardware.

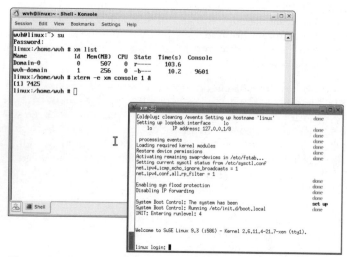

Figure 28-12: A console prompt for a Xen virtual machine

The `x m` command provides a number of other subcommands, our favorites of which are the `x m list` command, which lists the Xen domains that are active on the host system at the given moment, and the `x m shutdown` command, which you use to terminate a specified Xen virtual machine. Sample output from the `x m list` command on one of our host systems looks like the following:

```
# xm list
Name              Id  Mem(MB)  CPU  State  Time(s)  Console
Domain-0          0    507      0   r----   583.6
wvh-domain        1    256      0   -b---    10.5    9601
```

You can find out all of the available `x m` subcommands by executing the `x m help` command, which displays output like the following:

```
# xm help

call        Call xend api functions.
help        Print help.

Commands related to consoles:

console     Open a console to a domain.
```

consoles   Get information about domain consoles.

Commands on domains:

balloon   Set the domain's memory footprint using the balloon driver.
create   Create a domain.
destroy   Terminate a domain immediately.
domid   Convert a domain name to a domain id.
domname   Convert a domain id to a domain name.
list   List information about domains.
maxmem   Set domain memory limit.
migrate   Migrate a domain to another machine.
pause   Pause execution of a domain.
pincpu   Pin a domain to a cpu.
restore   Create a domain from a saved state.
save   Save domain state (and config) to file.
shutdown   Shutdown a domain.
sysrq   Send a sysrq to a domain.
unpause   Unpause a paused domain.

Commands related to the xen host (node):

dmesg   Read or clear Xen's message buffer.
info   Get information about the xen host.
log   Print the xend log.

Commands controlling scheduling:

atropos   Set atropos parameters.
bvt   Set BVT scheduler parameters.
bvt_ctxallow   Set the BVT scheduler context switch allowance.
rrobin   Set round robin slice.

Commands related to virtual block devices:

vbd-create   Create a new virtual block device for a domain
vbd-destroy   Destroy a domain's virtual block device
vbd-list   List virtual block devices for a domain.

Commands related to virtual network interfaces:

vif-list   List virtual network interfaces for a domain.

Try '/usr/sbin/xm help CMD' for help on CMD

Automating Xen Domain Startup

SUSE includes a convenient mechanism for automatically starting Xen domains on a host system through the /etc/init.d/xendomains startup script, which automatically starts any Xen virtual machines defined in configuration files found in the /etc/xen/auto directory on the host system. For example, to automatically start the Xen virtual machine defined in the configuration file /etc/xen/wvh_vm_1.conf, you would simply move this file to the directory /etc/xen/auto and then add the /etc/init.d/xendomains startup script to the boot sequence for the default run level on our host system.

More Information About Xen

Xen is still under development at the University of Cambridge's Computer Laboratory (www.cl.cam.ac.uk/Research/SRG/netos/xen). The developers of Xen have also started a company called XenSource (www.xensource.com) whose purpose is to commercialize Xen and support its use in enterprise environments. Both of these sites provide a good deal of information and other online resources to help you use Xen as a virtual solution to multimachine requirements.

Xen is an extremely interesting and exciting technology that is quite easy to set up and use on SUSE Linux systems thanks to its built-in support in YaST and modern SUSE Linux distributions.

User Mode Linux and FAUmachine

SUSE Linux has for some time included User Mode Linux (UML), which offers a way of running Linux on top of Linux as a user process. SUSE has more recently also begun to package FAUmachine, a similar project that comes from the University of Erlangen in Germany and that has evolved to allow the running of some non-Linux guest systems and some integration with QEMU.

UML has had some popularity in recent years as a way for hosting companies to offer full Linux servers with root access to their customers. It can be expected, however, with the extraordinary growth and maturity of Xen, that UML will soon be seen as largely superceded in this role. However, it remains an interesting way of running Linux under Linux on the desktop.

FAUmachine is an interesting alternative, indeed to some extent a variant of QEMU, in that there is some cooperation between the two projects. FAUmachine, like VMWare, offers a virtual BIOS, and after the system configuration has been written, a graphical installation goes ahead just as it would on real hardware. However, setup is complicated by the fact that special files are needed.

User Mode Linux Installation and Setup

There are a number of UML packages that need to be installed. In particular, you need to install the packages `yast2-uml`, `um-host-kernel`, `um-host-install-initrd` and `uml-utilities`. After this has been done, YaST will display an icon for the UML installation module in the Software section. Clicking this icon starts the UML installation. For this installation, you need to set up a networked installation source offered over NFS from `localhost` (copy the contents of the installation DVD to a directory and add that directory to `/etc/exports`, and restart the NFS server). A CD or DVD installation source will not work.

A new user is now created for UML (the first such user is called `uml0`, with a home directory `/home/uml0`). A virtual hard disk (a file called `umd0`) for UML is created in this directory, and the UML kernel executable that is used to run the UML session is also placed in this directory. The packages are installed into the virtual hard disk (you will see a text mode SUSE installation pop up in an `xterm` window). When the installation is complete, you can log in as the user `uml0` and run the executable (simply called `linux`) in that directory, and the UML instance will start. You will see the boot messages appearing in an `xterm` window.

FAUmachine Installation and Setup

After you have installed the FAUmachine packages, run the command `faum`. This starts a wizard that enables you to set up details of the virtual machine, and then you can start the machine itself. It boots in a nice graphical window. One of the major disadvantages of FAUmachine is that whatever version of Linux you want to run as a guest, you need a specially modified boot loader and kernel; otherwise performance will be slow, if not glacial. SUSE offers a variety of these as special additional packages, but not for the current SUSE version. At the current time of writing, FAUmachine must be regarded more as an academic project than a practical way of running guest operating systems under Linux, but there are reasons to think that it may improve very quickly as time goes on.

Other Emulators

SUSE provides a number of other open source emulators for legacy game systems and the like. These can be found in YaST's software selection: Package Groups ⇨ System ⇨ Emulators ⇨ Other.

The Kernel

The kernel is the heart of Linux; indeed, strictly speaking, the kernel *is* Linux—hence, the naming controversy. (Those who prefer the term GNU/Linux stress the fact that the system as a whole contains a Linux kernel and the GNU utilities.)

In this chapter we discuss the kernel in general and the SUSE kernel packages, and we explain how to configure and build a kernel. We also look at some of the problems involved with running third-party software that requires specific kernel versions.

Why You Probably Don't Need This Chapter

At one time, this would have been one of the most important chapters in the book. Knowing how to configure and recompile a kernel was a vital skill in the earlier years of Linux. This has changed for various reasons. The kernel is modular and vendors such as SUSE provide a kernel with virtually anything that you might need available as a module. This means that it is very unlikely that you will need to reconfigure and recompile to get support for some particular device; the support will already be there in the form of a loadable module. In most circumstances, SUSE will be unwilling to support you if you are not running the shipped kernel binaries.

Also, the relationship between the size of the kernel and the amount of memory on a system has changed beyond all recognition; the kernel has grown over the years, but average amounts of memory have rocketed. This means that the old motivation for creating a minimal, monolithic kernel supporting your hardware (which used to be a common practice) is no longer a factor.

Why You Might Need This Chapter

First of all, kernel configuration is interesting, and an understanding of the process is useful. You may have occasion to rebuild the kernel provided by SUSE in order to make an unusual configuration change to get support for experimental or unusual features that are not allowed for in the default configuration.

You might want to experiment with creating a monolithic kernel supporting the exact hardware on your system without loading anything as a module (although, as noted previously, this will not have a serious effect on performance).

You might also want to experiment with functionality that is available only in the form of kernel patches; to do this, you first need to patch the kernel source and then rebuild it.

But it is only in unusual cases that you will need to put most of this into practice; usually the work has been done for you by the nice people at SUSE. Note also that SUSE always provides experimental kernels as RPM packages (the "kernel of the day").

SUSE Kernels and Vanilla Kernels

Traditionally, the kernels shipped by SUSE and other commercial Linux vendors have always differed from the official kernels (often known as vanilla kernels) that are available from `www.kernel.org`. Exactly how much difference there has been has varied with time. During the long period when the 2.4 kernel series was the stable kernel and extensive development was being done on the 2.5 series, a large number of 2.5 features were backported into SUSE's 2.4 kernels. The 2.4 kernels with various backported features were standard for a long time until version 9.0 Professional and SUSE Linux Enterprise Server (SLES) 8.

The first release of the 2.6 kernel was in December 2003. SUSE moved to the 2.6 kernel with the SUSE Linux 9.1 release and SLES 9. Current SUSE kernels still contain a significant number of specific patches added by the SUSE team.

SUSE Linux versions 9.0 and SLES 8, SUSE Linux OpenExchange Server (SLOX), and Standard Server 8 use 2.4 series kernels.

Kernel Version Numbers

A Linux kernel has a version number like 2.6.12.4 (the latest stable version of the kernel at the time of this writing). The convention is that the stable kernel series has a middle number that is even. Thus 2.0, 2.2, 2.4, and 2.6 are successive stable kernel series. The odd numbers represent the development series: For a long period while the 2.4 kernels were the stable series, 2.5 kernels were being issued in the development toward the current stable 2.6 kernel. The third and fourth digits (in our example the 12.1) represent the number of the kernel within the 2.6 series. At the time of writing, a development 2.7 tree has not been opened. SUSE kernel packages have additional version information after the third digit of the version number. To find out what kernel you are currently running, use the command uname. The -r option limits the output to giving the release number.

```
user@bible: ~ > uname -r
2.6.11.4-21.7-default
```

This corresponds to the package name kernel-default-2.6.11.4-21.7. So this is a 2.6.11.4 kernel with the additional SUSE version information in the trailing digits.

The Binary Kernel Packages

SUSE provides a choice of binary kernel packages; typically during installation the correct kernel will be automatically selected and installed. The choices in SLES 9 on x86 are the packages kernel-bigsmp, kernel-default, kernel-smp, and kernel-debug (and the specific user mode Linux kernels). SUSE Professional 9.3 and above offer also the specific Xen kernels.

During the installation process, hardware detection ensures that a kernel package appropriate to your system is installed:

✦ For a machine with a single processor, that is the kernel_default package.

✦ For a multiprocessor machine, it is either kernel_smp or kernel_bigsmp.

✦ The kernel_debug package is not intended for production use but has all debugging options enabled.

Each binary kernel package contains not only the kernel itself, but also the additional files that are installed under /boot and the entire (very large) set of modules installed under /lib/modules/<version-number>/.

Note that the naming convention has changed from the previous less-descriptive k_deflt, k_smp, and so on. The different binary kernels are all generated from the same source, which as noted previously is a patched version of the vanilla sources. The kernel-syms package contains kernel symbol information for modules and is used to ensure that modules loaded match the running kernel.

Updated kernel packages are released relatively often, both for the purpose of adding functionality and to fix known problems including security issues. In the case of security issues, just as for other packages, details are available at www.suse.com/de/security/announcements/. Full details of updates for SLES can be found on the SUSE Linux Maintenance web site at http://portal.suse .com/psdb/index.html.

What Kernel Am I Running?

Use the command `uname -a` to see detailed information about which version of the kernel is running. If you look in `/boot` you should see a kernel and an `initrd` file with the same version number as the one revealed by the output of `uname -a` (there may of course be others). The symbolic link `vmlinuz` in `/boot` should point to the running kernel. If the `kernel-default` package is installed, there will also be a file `/boot/config-<version-number>-default`, which is the default kernel configuration file for the running kernel, and which will be identical to the current configuration unless you have already reconfigured and rebuilt your kernel. Note that if one of the other binary kernel packages is installed, the naming conventions will reflect the name of that package. So in the examples that follow, where we have `<version-number-default>` you might see, for example, `<version-number>-smp`.

The modules are installed under `/lib/modules/<version-number>-default/`.

Caution

In each case, `<version-number>` should agree. If you have installed the kernel package in the usual way, everything should be fine. However, if you boot a kernel (perhaps an older one) that does not correspond in terms of version number to the modules that are installed, the system may boot, but many things will not work. It is essential that the versions of the kernel and the modules match.

Upgrading a Kernel Package

Upgrading from one kernel package to another is simple; you just need to install the new package using the `rpm` command. If you want to retain the ability to run the old kernel, you should back up the files called `/boot/vmlinuz-<version number>` and `/boot/initrd-<version-number>` and also the directory `/lib/modules/<version-number>/` and restore them after you have installed the new kernel RPM. You also want to check that you have an entry in the GRUB configuration for the old kernel and possibly do a `mkinitrd` (see the section "Building the Kernel" later in the chapter). If you use LILO for booting, check the LILO configuration and rerun LILO before rebooting.

Kernel Configuration

To be able to build kernels, you obviously need the kernel source package (called `kernel-source`) installed. In addition, you need `gcc`, `make`, and a number of other packages. One of the SUSE installation package set options is Kernel development; if you have installed that selection, you should have everything you need.

If you want to base your kernel configuration on the currently running kernel, you have more than one way to begin.

The configuration of the kernel that is actually running is always available in
/proc/config.gz, a gzipped virtual file in the /proc filesystem, which is created in
memory on the fly by the running kernel (see Listing 29-1).

Listing 29-1: **Looking at the Configuration of the Running Kernel**

```
root@bible: /proc # zcat config.gz | more
#
# Automatically generated make config: don't edit
#
CONFIG_X86=y
CONFIG_MMU=y
CONFIG_UID16=y
CONFIG_GENERIC_ISA_DMA=y

#
# Code maturity level options
#
CONFIG_EXPERIMENTAL=y
CONFIG_CLEAN_COMPILE=y
# CONFIG_STANDALONE is not set
CONFIG_BROKEN_ON_SMP=y

#
# General setup
...
```

When you get bored with reading this, type q to quit more.

It is instructive to page through this file and look at the various options in it that
refer to the hardware, filesystems, and so on that are to be supported by the kernel.

✦ The =y at the end of lines means that the support for the relevant item is compiled into the kernel.

✦ Lines ending is not set clearly imply that the support is not included.

✦ Lines ending = m imply that the support is provided by a loadable kernel module rather than being compiled into the kernel itself. SUSE provides most functionality in the form of modules.

In a newly installed system, you should find that /usr/src/linux/.config is identical to /boot/config-<version-number>-default and to the content of /proc/con-
fig.gz when uncompressed.

The kernel build process takes place in /usr/src/linux/, which is a symbolic link to /usr/src/linux-<version number>/ (for example, /usr/src/ linux-2.6 .5-7.79/). The commands that you use to build the kernel must be issued in this directory because they refer to the top-level kernel makefile, which is /usr/src/linux/Makefile.

The configuration file for building the kernel is the file .config in this directory. If this file does not exist, you need to create it for the first time. If the kernel that is running is the exact same version that the source code is for, you can simply do this:

```
root@bible: /usr/src/linux-2.6.5-7.79/ # cp .config .config.bak
root@bible: /usr/src/linux-2.6.5-7.79/ # make cloneconfig
```

 Tip   Here we have backed up the existing .config file before creating a new one; whenever you use any of the tools in this section that create kernel configuration files, you may want to do this.

If the kernel source that you have installed is for a newer version of the kernel than the one that is running, you can do this:

```
root@bible:~ # zcat /proc/config.gz > /usr/src/linux/.config
root@bible:~ # cd /usr/src/linux/
root@bible: /usr/src/linux-2.6.5-7.79/ # make oldconfig
```

Alternatively, the command make cloneconfig has exactly the same effect. If the version of the kernel source is newer than the running kernel, then the command make oldconfig is what you need.

Creating a new kernel configuration can be done in essentially one of three ways.

✦ If you type the following:

```
root@bible: ~ # cd /usr/src/linux/
root@bible: /usr/src/linux-2.6.5-7.79/ # make config
```

(note that the version number you see on the directory depends on the kernel source version that is installed), you will see something like this:

```
root@bible: /usr/src/linux-2.6.5-7.79/ # make config
scripts/kconfig/conf arch/i386/Kconfig
drivers/char/lirc/Kconfig:102:warning: 'select' used by config symbol 'LIRC_SIR' refer to undefined
symbol 'LIRC_SIR_IRDA'
#
# using defaults found in .config
#
*
* Linux Kernel Configuration
*
```

```
*
* Code maturity level options
*
Prompt for development and/or incomplete code/drivers (EXPERIMENTAL) [Y/n/?] Y
  Select only drivers expected to compile cleanly (CLEAN_COMPILE) [Y/n/?] Y
  Select only drivers that don't need compile-time external firmware (STANDALONE) [N/y/?]
*
* General setup
*
Support for paging of anonymous memory (swap) (SWAP) [Y/n/?]
```

This is simply a series of questions and answers; there is no way to go back, and it certainly could not be described as user friendly.

✦ A more pleasant method is the following:

```
root@bible: /usr/src/linux-2.6.5-7.79 # make menuconfig
```

This requires the ncurses-devel package to be installed. You will see a screen something like the one in Figure 29-1.

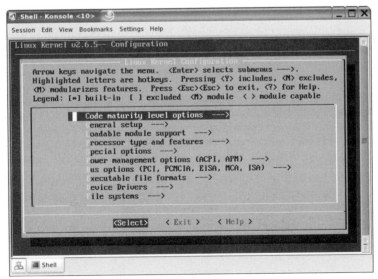

Figure 29-1: Using make menuconfig for kernel configuration

This is a much nicer text-based, menu-driven interface that splits the items into sections and submenus. When you have completed your selections, save the configuration file (see Figure 29-2).

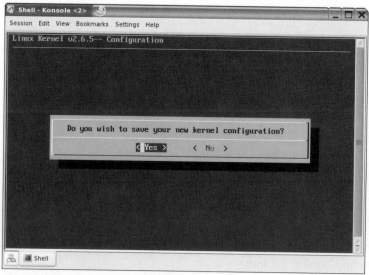

Figure 29-2: Saving the configuration

✦ However, the nicest interface is the graphical one that you can get by running the following command:

root@bible: /usr/src/linux-2.6.5-7.79 # make xconfig

This requires the qt3-devel package to be installed to create the graphical user interface. This contains exactly the same information as the other two systems but is easier to navigate and is a new interface (previously make xconfig used the less elegant Tk graphical toolkit to create its graphical user interface). See Figures 29-3 and 29-4 for examples of the interface.

A nice feature of this interface is that if you choose Options ➪ Show all Options, you can see the name of each kernel configuration variable, the possible values it can have, and its current setting.

Tip

There is also an option make gconfig that uses the GTK+ libraries for a GNOME-like interface.

Whichever interface you use for configuring the kernel, most items offer the choice of y, m , or n (in the xconfig interface these are represented by a tick in the check box, a dot in the check box, and an empty check box, respectively):

✦ y means "Compile this option into the kernel."

✦ m means "Compile this option as a module."

✦ n means "Don't include this option."

When you have saved your configuration, you will have a new .config file. This is the one you will use when you start building the kernel.

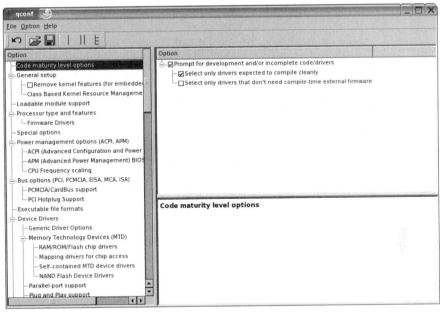

Figure 29-3: Using make xconfig for kernel configuration

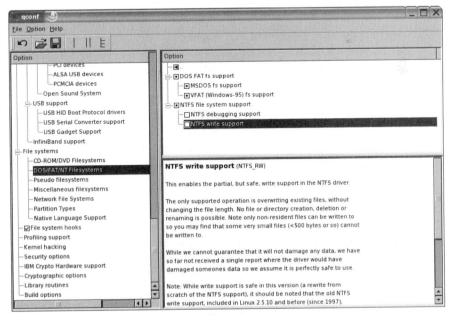

Figure 29-4: Selecting options in the xconfig interface

Building the Kernel

Now, assuming the architecture is *x*86, you need to do the following:

```
root@bible: /usr/src/linux-2.6.5-7.79/ # make bzImage
```

Historically, the b stands for big, and the z indicates that it is a compressed image. On other architectures, the command you need is different. Details specific to SUSE are available at www.suse.de/~agruen/kernel-doc/.

This is where the real work gets done. In the 2.6 kernels, by default you see slightly less output on the screen than before (see Listing 29-2).

Listing 29-2: **Output from the Kernel Build Process**

```
root@bible: /usr/src/linux-2.6.5-7.79/ # make bzImage
  SPLIT   include/linux/autoconf.h -> include/config/*
make[1]: `arch/i386/kernel/asm-offsets.s' is up to date.
  CHK     include/linux/compile.h
  UPD     include/linux/compile.h
  CC      init/version.o
  LD      init/built-in.o
  CC      init/kerntypes.o
  IKCFG   kernel/ikconfig.h
  GZIP    kernel/config_data.gz
  IKCFG   kernel/config_data.h
  CC      kernel/configs.o
  LD      kernel/built-in.o
  GEN     .version
  CHK     include/linux/compile.h
  UPD     include/linux/compile.h
  CC      init/version.o
[...]
```

When the build process has completed successfully, you will see a message similar to this:

```
Root device is (3, 1)
Boot sector 512 bytes.
Setup is 5039 bytes.
System is 1426 kB
Kernel: arch/i386/boot/bzImage is ready
```

You can now navigate to that directory and see the file that has been created.

```
root@bible: ~ # cd /usr/src/linux/arch/i386/boot/
root@bible: /usr/src/linux-2.6.5-7.79/arch/i386/boot/ # ls -l bzImage
```

You should see a brand-new file `bzImage` with a timestamp showing that it has just been created.

When you've made the `bzImage`, you have several more steps to perform:

1. Build the modules:

`root@bible: /usr/src/linux-2.6.5-7.79/ # make modules`

> Note that if you simply issue the command `make` or `make all`, the `bzImage` and the modules will be built in one step.

2. Install the kernel and the modules:

`root@bible: /usr/src/linux-2.6.5-7.79/ # make install`

> This copies the `bzImage` file to the `/boot` directory. (Before you do this you may want to back up the old kernel, particularly if it has the same version number.)

`root@bible: /usr/src/linux-2.6.5-7.79/ # make modules_install`

3. Create a new initial ramdisk to correspond to the new kernel:

`root@bible: /usr/src/linux-2.6.5-7.79/ # mkinitrd`

4. Check that both the new and old kernels are referenced in the GRUB menu so that you can go back to the old kernel if you need to. Edit the file `/boot/grub/menu.lst` to confirm this.

> If you use LILO for booting, you need to edit `/etc/lilo.conf` to ensure that both the new and old kernels are included *and* run the `lilo` command.

Now you can reboot and select the new kernel.

Caution　If you have compiled things into the kernel that were previously being loaded as modules, it is important that these modules themselves should not be loaded when the new kernel is booted; otherwise, unexpected problems could occur. You may need to adjust `/etc/modprobe.conf` in this case.

Tip　There is a useful document (by Andreas Gruenbacher) about working with the 2.6 kernel sources on SUSE systems in the directory `/usr/share/doc/packages/kernel-source/`. There is also a sample showing the principles of creating and building kernel modules.

Rebuilding the km_* Packages

A number of packages have names beginning with `km_`. These packages contain source code for additional external kernel modules that you may need to compile separately to add support for certain things. For example, the `km_ocfs` package adds support for the Oracle Cluster File System (OCFS), and the `km_smartlink-softmodem` package adds support for a certain class of winmodems.

You can find these packages by searching for "km_" in the YaST software module.

To make use of these packages, you must have the source for the running kernel installed.

When you install these packages, they install the relevant source code to a directory under `/usr/src/kernel-modules/`. To add support for OCFS, for example, change to the directory `/usr/src/kernel-modules/ocfs2/`, and then issue the following commands:

```
# make modules KERNEL_SOURCE=/usr/src/linux
# make install KERNEL_SOURCE=/usr/src/linux
```

Alternatively, you can issue this command:

```
# make -C /usr/src/linux SUBDIRS=$PWD modules
```

This runs the `make` command in `/usr/src/linux` while referring to the current directory to find the module code.

You will then find that the module has been built and installed as:

```
/lib/modules/<version-number>-default/extra/ocfs2.ko
```

If you install a new kernel, you will need to rebuild these modules, whether or not you build the new kernel from source.

Kernel of the Day

The SUSE FTP server always has a so-called kernel of the day, which is the latest test kernel, with versions available for each supported architecture. This is available at `ftp://ftp.suse.com/pub/projects/kernel/kotd/`. It goes without saying that these kernels should be used only with caution, because they have not been officially released and are provided for testing purposes.

The Kernel and Third-Party Software

Third-party commercial software that requires low-level kernel support is some-times run only on or with particular kernel versions. In the worst case this is because the vendor ships binary-only kernel modules, but even when a module source is shipped that needs to be built against the running kernel, it can be limited to very specific kernel versions. This can be a real problem, particularly when a ker-nel update is recommended by SUSE (for example, for security reasons) and ven-dors are slow to respond. The problem can be worse if you are trying to run two such pieces of software at the same time.

Consider the following example of this kind of problem in a production environ-ment: A customer needed to run a piece of proprietary software allowing multipath access to storage area network (SAN) storage and at the same time needed to run a third-party clustering solution with kernel modules for its filesystem. Although both of these products supported the version of SLES that the customer was running, when you looked at the small print, things were more difficult because only one ver-sion of the kernel package among the various updates provided by SUSE worked with both products. And that kernel version was not the latest and had been offi-cially superceded because of a security patch.

These problems will persist until all third-party vendors gain a better understand-ing of the dynamics of Linux and realize that releasing their code in a more flexible and open way does not necessarily prevent them from making money from their products.

When certain third-party modules load, you will see a message of the form:

```
Warning: loading <module file> will taint the kernel: non-GPL license - Proprietary. [...]
See <http://www.tux.org/lkml/#export-tainted> for information about tainted modules
Module <module file> loaded, with warnings
```

This indicates that a module with a non-GPL license is being loaded into the kernel. This warning is not simply about software ideology: When proprietary (and particu-larly binary-only) modules are loaded, little can be done to debug any problems they may cause.

Loading Kernel Modules

In the 2.6 kernel, kernel modules have filenames ending with .ko (rather than .o as in 2.4). To check what modules are loaded:

```
root@bible: ~ # lsmod
Module              Size  Used by
nls_cp437           6016  0
vfat               14208  0
```

```
fat                    43584   1 vfat
usb_storage            60096   0
nls_iso8859_1           4352   2
udf                    85380   0
nls_utf8                2304   0
[...]
```

Dependencies between modules are indicated in the last column of the output.

To load a module manually, you use the following:

```
root@bible: ~ # modprobe tulip
```

To unload a module, use the following:

```
root@bible: ~ # rmmod tulip
```

The automatic loading of modules is now (in 2.6 kernels) controlled by the file `/etc/modprobe.conf`, which has replaced the `/etc/modules.conf` file.

The file `/lib/modules/<version-number>-default/modules.dep` contains a listing of all the dependencies between available modules. This file can be regenerated if necessary by the command `depmod -a`.

Kernel Parameters at Boot Time

You can pass parameters to the kernel at boot time either permanently by editing the GRUB configuration file or temporarily by typing at the boot prompt. These control the behavior of the kernel when it boots in various ways. Current versions of SUSE use the `showopts` keyword in the GRUB configuration file, which has the unfortunate effect of hiding the parameters that are being passed. Actually what this keyword does is to hide the options that are listed before it and show those that appear after it.

If you remove `showopts` from the default entry line in `/boot/grub/menu.lst`, then at the next boot you will see exactly which boot parameters are being passed to the kernel when it loads. You will also be able to edit these parameters in the initial boot screen.

A list of supported parameters and their meanings are in the file:

```
/usr/src/linux/Documentation/kernel-parameters.txt
```

A few examples of parameters that you might want to pass at boot time are as follows:

✦ `root=/dev/hda3` — Sets the root device

✦ `vga=791` — Sets the framebuffer resolution to 1024×768

See Chapter 8 for more information on framebuffer graphics and resolution.

✦ `acpi=off` — Disables Advanced Configuration and Power Interface (ACPI), often required on troublesome hardware

✦ `ide=nodma` — Disables Direct Memory Access (DMA) access to IDE disks

✦ `noapic` — Does not use the APIC interrupt controller

These last three will be seen as part of the failsafe entry in `/boot/grub/menu.lst` because each of them can solve common problems with particular hardware.

The Initial Ramdisk

As the system boots, it needs drivers for the disk controllers and the filesystems on the hard disk; otherwise, it will not be able to mount the disks. The necessary drivers may not be included in the kernel itself but loaded as drivers. This is not a problem on the running system but can create a "chicken and egg" situation at boot time. This problem is solved by loading the initrd into memory at boot time. (Typically the initrd loaded is whatever is pointed to by the symbolic link `/boot/initrd`, but a different initrd can be specified if required in the GRUB menu `/boot/grub/menu.lst`. The initrd is in fact a compressed EXT2 filesystem that is decompressed and loaded into memory at initial boot time.) The initrd and the kernel are loaded in the same way: either directly from known physical locations on the boot device (in the case of LILO) or through the use of a boot loader that is capable of reading the filesystem from the outside (in the case of GRUB). The initrd is then mounted temporarily by the kernel prior to the mounting of the disk partitions. Exactly what the initrd includes is set in the file `/etc/sysconfig/kernel` in the INI-TRD_MODULES variable. On a desktop machine, this may simply look like this:

```
INITRD_MODULES="reiserfs"
```

If you have SCSI disks, it will almost certainly need to include a driver for the disk controller. This will normally be handled correctly during installation, but there are occasions when you may need to change this manually. Having done so, you will need to run the command `mkinitrd` to create a new initrd with the correct modules included. After the initrd has been created, if you reboot, the necessary support should be present.

See Chapter 4 for a description of the booting process.

Although the process described in this chapter for configuring and building a kernel from source is an interesting one, it is probably not something you will often need to do in practice. If you are running SLES in a production environment, SUSE will probably not give you support for a self-built kernel unless they themselves have recommended this course of action for a specific reason.

It is, however, certainly useful to have some familiarity with the process, and it is interesting and instructive to look around in /usr/src/linux/, particularly in the Documentation subdirectory.

✦   ✦   ✦

SUSE Linux OpenExchange Server

The SUSE Linux OpenExchange Server, developed by SUSE in conjunction with Netline, consists of Netline's proprietary application server integrated into SLES 8. After the takeover of SUSE by Novell, Netline released its software under the GPL under the name OPEN-XCHANGE, and a decision was made that SUSE would no longer bundle the software and that Netline would offer the next version independently. This means that it is possible to run OPEN-XCHANGE on other versions of Linux. Netline remains a partner of Novell, which continues to support SLOX 4.* (based on SLES 8), and Novell and Netline will provide joint support to customers upgrading from SLOX 4.* to the commercial version of OPEN-XCHANGE (which has recently become available at the time of writing) on newer versions of SLES.

This chapter describes SLOX 4.1.

The SUSE Linux OpenExchange Server (SLOX) provides mid-range mail and collaboration services, with a web interface to configure the system and for users to access the groupware functionality. *Groupware* and *collaboration* are terms used to describe shared calendaring capabilities, address books, and groups of people working together using computers.

One of SLOX's most important features is its integration with Outlook, allowing existing Exchange users to use SLOX with little impact on their daily work. SLOX cannot replace all of the Exchange functionality that some users rely on, but this is constantly being worked on by the Netline developers who write the groupware component of SLOX.

SLOX is based on four core components, three of which are open source. We investigate these services in detail throughout the chapter and show you how to get up and running with SLOX in as little time as possible.

Cross-Reference
We recommend that you also read up on Postfix/Cyrus and LDAP in Chapters 17 and 25 because the content in those chapters will help with your understanding of some of the subjects in this chapter.

Licensing SLOX

There are two main sides to the licensing of SLOX. If you are just using the mail and webmail features, you do not need a license for your users because the groupware functionality is a separate license, with ten licenses being included with the standard SLOX box.

The license is based solely on the amount of concurrent users who have been using the groupware functionality at the same time. So if you have 100 SLOX users, with 20 of them using the groupware functionality (calendaring, tasks, and so on), you have to buy at most 20 groupware licenses if all of those users are to use groupware at the same time.

A groupware session is triggered as active if a user is logged in to groupware functionality through the web interface, or if they are using the o/iSLOX connectors from Windows and Outlook. Any other connection through IMAP/POP3, SMTP, or by reading mail through the web interface is not classified as a groupware session, and you do not need to license those users. You can limit what users can access through the web interface to stop them from using the groupware functionality if needed.

Installing SLOX

The SLOX base operating system is SUSE Enterprise Server 8, and the installation process is very similar to later SUSE versions that we have discussed in the book already. We will go through an overview of the installation process in this chapter, concentrating on the SLOX-specific installation procedure. The latest version of SLOX at the time of this writing is 4.1.

Tip
If you have an existing SLOX installation at version 4, we highly recommend you upgrade to 4.1 as it includes not only bug fixes, but also new features and speed increases that you and your users will appreciate.

If you have received the SLOX 4.1 CD, use it for the boot media and not the original SLOX 4 boot CD.

Note   We work with SLOX 4.1 throughout the rest of the chapter. If you have not received a 4.1 update CD, contact your SUSE representative who will arrange for a copy to be sent to you or download the update from the SUSE maintenance web site (`http://portal.suse.de`).

Starting the SLOX Installation

When you are ready to start, insert the SLOX 4.1 CD into your server and boot it up, proceeding with the installation.

If you have standard hardware, select Installation. If you have hardware that does not play nicely with the SUSE kernel (obscure hardware or so forth), then select Installation – Safe Settings. As with the installation of SUSE we discussed in Chapter 1, you are given other boot options to choose from depending on your requirements (see Figure 30-1).

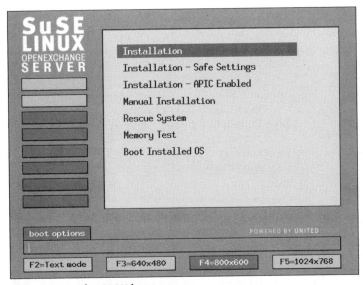

Figure 30-1: The SLOX boot menu

As with the SUSE installation, YaST proceeds to initialize itself and load up the installation routine to continue the installation.

Select your system language and proceed to the next stage by pressing the Accept button. You are then presented with the system overview screen. It is likely that you will want to change the default partitioning scheme to reflect your system configuration. For example, you may want to make sure /var is on a storage area network (SAN) because this is where your Postfix mail queue, LDAP data, PostgreSQL, and Cyrus mail store are located.

With SLOX, you cannot change the package selection during installation because it has already been predefined.

> **Tip** We are not happy with this because by default it installs a full KDE environment. Because this is a server environment, you really should have only the bare minimum of installed applications to provide the service the system has been designed for. To get around this issue, you can load YaST after installation and remove any packages that are not needed (such as X).

Figure 30-2 is the familiar system overview you saw in Chapter 1. From here you can change any installation setting you need in order to be happy with your newly installed system.

When you are happy with your system configuration, press the Accept button. You are then warned that you are about to initialize your disks based on the configuration you have chosen. When you have proceeded with the partitioning/formatting, YaST starts installing the SLOX system.

As YaST installs SLOX, you are asked to switch media between the UnitedLinux and SLOX disks a few times. When all packages have been installed, YaST initializes the system configuration and proceeds to boot to SLOX and continue with the configuration of SLOX itself.

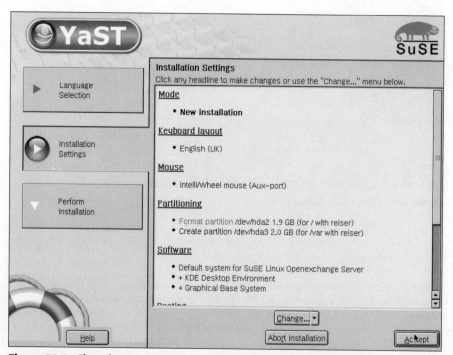

Figure 30-2: Changing your system configuration before installation

Configuring UnitedLinux

The SLOX system's base operating system is the now deprecated UnitedLinux. SUSE, Caldera, and TurboLinux, along with the major vendors, decided that a base, certified Linux distribution was needed so that vendors could certify against it. Since the SCO lawsuit, UnitedLinux has been disbanded, but SUSE has still used the UnitedLinux base as the certified platform for SUSE Linux Enterprise Server (SLES) 8 and SLOX. As SUSE was the distributor that UnitedLinux was written by, this has not impacted the supportability by SUSE of any business products they provide. The configuration of UnitedLinux is very similar to the installation of a normal SUSE system:

1. When the system configuration has been saved and YaST has booted into your installed system, you will be asked for the root password (see Figure 30-3).

2. Configure the X Windows environment (see Figure 30-4). If this is a small internal mail server, you may want to configure X so that you can use the web browser on the server for configuration. We prefer to disable X and use a management node to configure the server over a web browser and also remove the X system completely because it is not needed for SLOX to run.

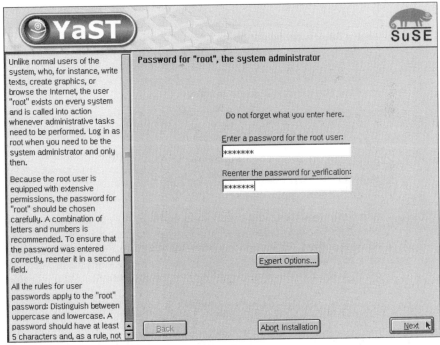

Figure 30-3: Setting the root user password

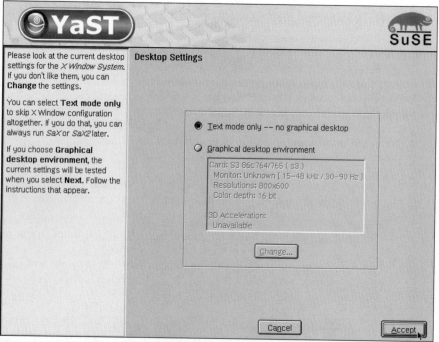

Figure 30-4: X configuration

3. When you are happy with the X configuration, YaST will run SuSEconfig to commit the changes to the system.

4. As with the standard SUSE installation, you will be asked to configure ancillary hardware (see Figure 30-5). If you want to use SLOX to provide printing for your network, you can configure it here.

5. When you are happy with the hardware configuration, configure your network (see Figure 30-6). Select the network card you want to configure for connectivity and press Configure to continue with the IP configuration.

Note

When the network configuration is saved in SLOX, it is not easy to change it at a later date because some configuration for the running services relies on the IP address of the SLOX installation being static for the life of the installation. It is possible to change it, but it may prove to be more hassle than it is worth. With this in mind, make sure the IP address you need to assign to SLOX is the final address for your network.

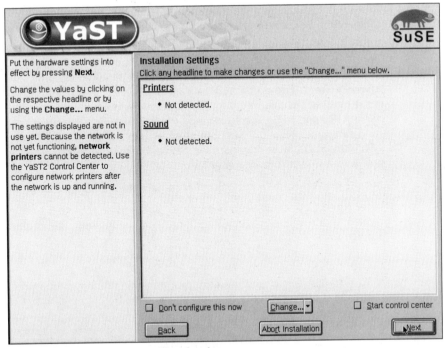

Figure 30-5: Configuring ancillary hardware

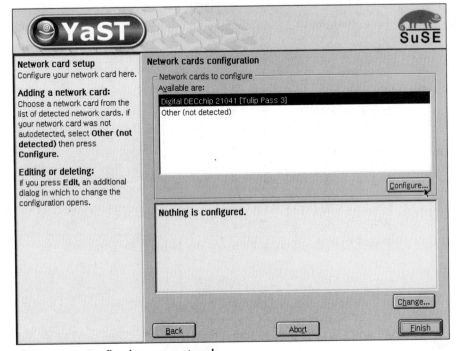

Figure 30-6: Configuring your network

6. As with normal SUSE installation, enter the IP and subnet mask of the node (see Figure 30-7) and click Next.

7. When configuring the name resolution (see Figure 30-8), you must be sure that your DNS server can do external lookups for Internet servers. This is needed because SLOX will have to do many MX lookups when sending mail to other Internet users. The domain name your SLOX server is given will also dictate what mail, out of the box, your SLOX server receives. For example, we have set the domain to be susebible.com. By default, SLOX is able to receive mail for user@susebible.com without any further configuration. You can further configure SLOX after it is installed to receive mail for other domains, and we talk about this later in the chapter.

8. Set the default route for the SLOX installation (see Figure 30-9).

9. After the network has been configured, you will be returned to the network overview screen (see Figure 30-10); check your settings and click Finish to save your network configuration.

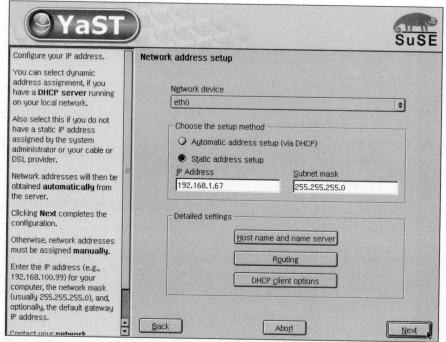

Figure 30-7: Configuring the IP address of the SLOX installation

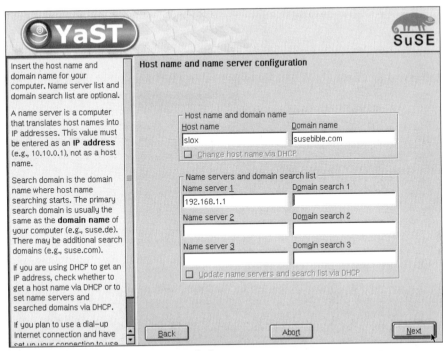

Figure 30-8: Configuring name resolution

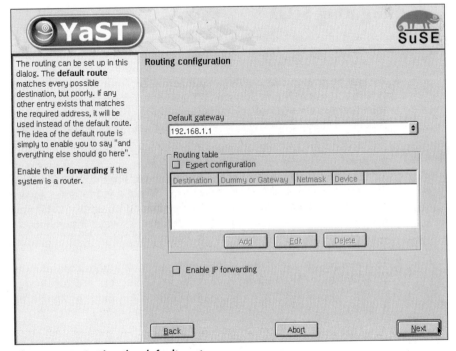

Figure 30-9: Setting the default route

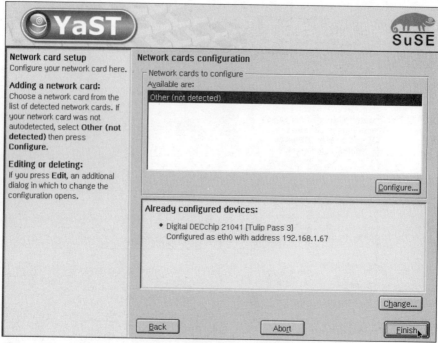

Figure 30-10: Checking network configuration

Configuring SLOX

When UnitedLinux has been configured, you move on to the SLOX-specific configuration:

1. We will be configuring SLOX as an Internet-facing mail server, talking to an external Domain Name System (DNS) server (Internet lookup capable). With this in mind, we will not configure an internal DNS or Samba server because this is not needed for the operation of the mail server and is very rarely used in an existing network.

Note

> If you want to configure a DNS and Samba server, you need to set the workgroup (or Windows domain name) of the Samba server. For the DNS and Dynamic Host Configuration Protocol (DHCP) server, you do not need to enter any more information for the servers to work. The configuration of Samba, DNS, and DHCP is then handled through the SLOX web interface. For more information on Samba, DNS, and DHCP, refer to Chapters 18, 20, and 21.

2. To move past the DNS and Samba configuration and to continue on to the LDAP server configuration, click Next. LDAP server configuration (see Figure 30-11) is integral to the operation of SLOX because all configuration, user, and address book functionality is stored here.

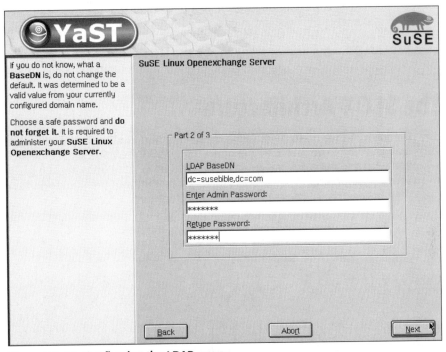

Figure 30-11: Configuring the LDAP server

As with the base used in Chapter 25, the LDAP basedn, it is very important to get this right the first time. Most people use the domain component (dc) to describe the Internet domain that refers to the organization. The basedn you choose will not impact how SLOX runs, but it is important that if you are using this LDAP server as your central authentication server and as a mail server that you choose a basedn that will fit in with your network.

Cross-
Reference

For more information on naming basedn and on LDAP in general, see Chapter 25.

Remember that the admin password is not the same as the root password. It is used for the administration of SLOX itself, not the UnitedLinux system. When you log in to the web administrative interface, you will use this password to authenticate as the SLOX administrator.

3. When you are happy with the LDAP server configuration, set the organization name and the country of origin. This is used for presentation purposes in SLOX only. For example, if you set the organization name to Wiley SUSE Bible, this will appear as the organization that a user belongs to when they are added to SLOX through the web interface. The same is true for the country that your SLOX installation resides in.

4. When the SLOX configuration has been finalized, click the Finish button to save your settings and start the SLOX services.

Your SLOX system is now ready to use and start adding users.

The SLOX Architecture

Before we move on to discuss administering and configuring SLOX in more detail, it makes sense to understand the underlying SLOX architecture. To be able to provide you with a feature-rich service, SLOX relies on certain open source and closed source components. Figure 30-12 gives an overview of the components and how they fit together in the overall SLOX architecture.

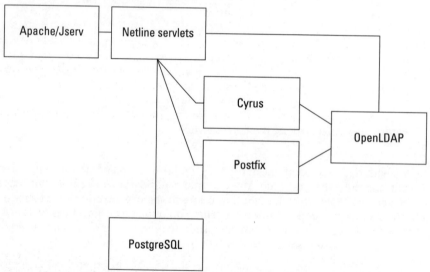

Figure 30-12: Conceptual overview of SLOX components

PostgreSQL

All groupware-related data, calendar items, tasks, notes, and so forth are stored in the PostgreSQL database itself. When the user synchronizes his or her data through Outlook, or accesses any calendar or tasks data, the PostgreSQL database is queried. This can lead to a high amount of traffic if your system is used a lot.

During the creation of a user, information is stored in the Cyrus mail store, PostgreSQL database, and LDAP server.

OpenLDAP

The LDAP server stores the virtual domain information, aliases, address books (both personal to the user and the global address book), and user accounts. It is *the* most important part of your SLOX environment and defines the profile of your SLOX server. You should routinely back up your LDAP server as well as the mail store when deciding on what to save.

Whenever a user logs in, the LDAP server is queried multiple times for both the user authentication data and user settings and also to load up the server configuration for the duration of the session.

Netline Servlets

The Netline servlets provide the groupware functionality of SLOX. This is also where the very important WebDAV (Web-based Distributed Authoring and Versioning) interface is presented to the clients. During the writing of the book, Netline has released an open source version of their application environment. For more information on the Netline program, go to www.open-xchange.org. This is great news because it means the functionality and scalability of the Netline servlets will, we hope, increase dramatically in a short space of time.

 Note As all the groupware services are Java servlets, you will see at least one Java process spawn when any groupware activity takes place.

WebDAV

Most of the groupware data is stored and queried over WebDAV. This is only for the i/oSLOX connectors (which we talk about later in the chapter). If you have any applications that you want to interface with SLOX, you can access calendars, tasks, and projects through a WebDAV interface.

WebDAV is a protocol that allows you to access and query files over HTTP, very much like a mixture of FTP and HTTP. As most vendors have embraced this technology, it provides an excellent opportunity for third-party application vendors, or you, to write bolt-on applications that can talk to SLOX directly. For example, we had a customer who wanted to tie in a student database into the user's calendars directly for their timetables. This is all possible through the WebDAV interface, which most operating systems support very well.

Cyrus and Postfix

All mail-based services are provided by Postfix and Cyrus, both very scalable and reliable mail services.

Cyrus and Postfix both rely on the user data stored in LDAP to function correctly. Any user who wants to make an Internet Message Access Protocol (IMAP) connection must exist in the LDAP server to be allowed access to any other SLOX service.

Any configuration changes you want to make to Postfix can be done either through the web interface or through the Postfix configuration files. The same is true of the Cyrus IMAP server. For more information on Postfix and Cyrus, refer to Chapter 17.

Administrating SLOX

To administrate SLOX, you need to log in to the SLOX interface using a web browser. The administrative user who has full control over SLOX is called cyrus. The cyrus user can control users, services, mail spools, and the monitoring of the SLOX system using the administrative interface.

To log in to your SLOX installation, open a web browser and enter the IP address of the SLOX server.

Note   If you were a clever administrator, you would have entered the IP address of your SLOX installation into your DNS servers. In this case, you can use the name of the SLOX server to browse to it.

Log in with the username cyrus and the password that you set during the SLOX installation (see Figure 30-13).

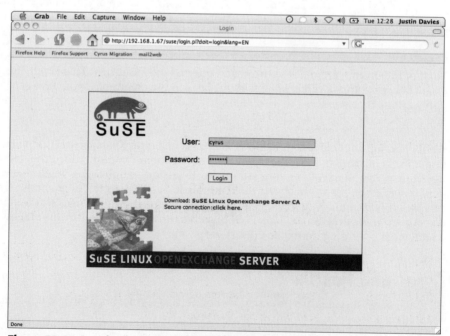

Figure 30-13: Logging in to the SLOX administrative interface

When logged in, you are presented with the initial configuration screen (see Figure 30-14). You can configure any aspect of SLOX through the web interface without having to know any Linux or SLOX-specific technology.

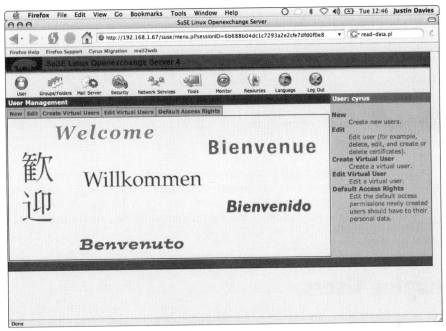

Figure 30-14: The initial configuration screen

There are numerous sections to the SLOX configuration interface. We will go through the most common ones throughout the rest of the chapter. Table 30-1 details what each section refers to.

Table 30-1
SLOX Configuration Sections

Section	Description
User	Create, edit, and delete user accounts. You can also create virtual users here.
Groups/Folders	Create, edit, and delete user groups and shared folders.
Mail Server	Postfix/Cyrus configuration.
Security	Apache, SSL, and services security information.

Continued

	Table 30-1 *(continued)*
Section	**Description**
Network Services	Configuration of miscellaneous network services and the creation of virtual domains.
Tools	LDAP browser, configuration file editing; send a mail to all users.
Monitor	Check the status of the mail queue, system load, services, and so on.
Resources	Manage groupware resources.
Language	System language.
Log Out	Self-explanatory.

 Tip

Wherever you are in SLOX, you can always click the question mark to get help about the specific part of SLOX you are configuring at that time. The context-sensitive help icon (the question mark) is usually located at the top-right of the section you are working on, or next to the field about which you may want to find out more information.

Managing Users

The most important components of a mail system are the users and their accounts. Without these, there is no point in running a mail system. In this example, we create a new user called justin who will also receive mail for the virtual domain wiley.com. There are a few procedures that you need to go through that may not be obvious if you have never used SLOX before to create the virtual domain. We detail this in the rest of the section.

Creating the User

To create a user, click the User section and then the New subsection. You are presented with a form to fill in to create a new user (see Figure 30-15).

We have added the user justin, with his full name, password, and alias information. Everything else in the entry is the default based on the questions asked during installation.

Aliases

An email alias enables justin to receive mail using a different email address from the default. Some organizations use the default First.Lastname@domain.tld; with this in mind, SUSE can create this alias by default for you (if you want). However, we have created another alias for the user justin, called jdavies, because this structure is also quite common.

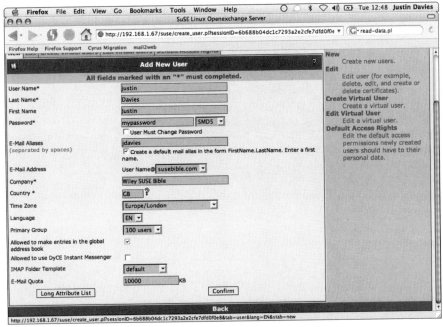

Figure 30-15: Creating a new user

So the user justin can be contacted on justin@susebible.com, jdavies@wileybible.com, and justin.davies@susebible.com. A lot of email addresses for one person, but it does help when people need to guess your email address when they have lost your business card.

Caution It is helpful to create these kinds of aliases for your users, but it does have a downside. If spammers can guess your email address, you could end up with unwanted mail. Check with your company policy on email aliases before you roll this out into production.

When you are happy with the user, you can save the account by pressing Confirm.

Checking the User Data

If you want to view any data about a user on the system, select the Edit subsection (see Figure 30-16). You will be presented with a filter that you can use to narrow down a search for a user, or just leave it as "*" to list all users. Click Apply Filter to search for the users.

When you have found the user account, select it and click User Data. You are presented with the details that you previously filled in for the user. If you want to be able to edit all information relating to a user, such as his or her birthday, title, and so on, click Long attribute list to get a screen like the one shown in Figure 30-17.

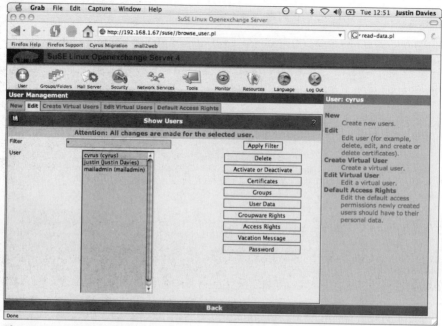

Figure 30-16: Searching for users

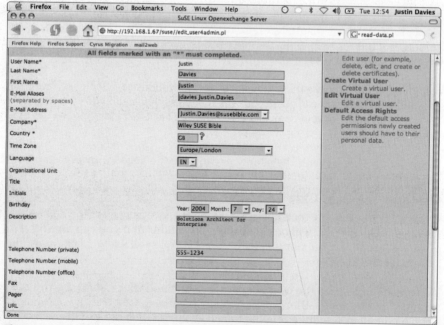

Figure 30-17: Listing all information about a user

Creating a Virtual Domain

When the user has been created, you need to create the virtual domain for which you also want to receive mail. This machine is specifically for the SUSE Bible authors and editors, but we also want to be able to receive mail for the wiley.com domain.

To create a virtual domain, select the Network Services section and then select the Virtual Domains subsection. You will arrive at the screen shown in Figure 30-18.

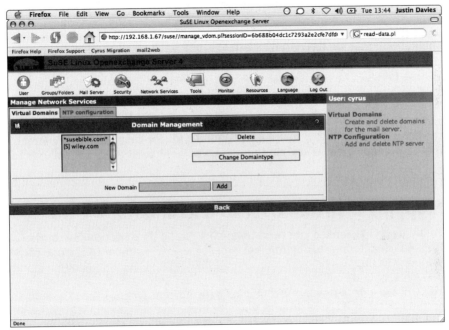

Figure 30-18: Creating a virtual domain

To create a new virtual domain, enter the new domain and press Add. This adds the domain to the SLOX configuration.

Notice that there is a letter next to the domain on the domain list. This letter signifies what type of domain you are creating:

✦ In a Sendmail [S] virtual domain, a single, flat namespace is used. If you have wiley.com and susebible.com as domains hosted on this mail server, you must use unique mail recipients.

For example, as we have already created the user justin, any mail for justin@wiley.com and justin@susebible.com will go to the same person, justin.

For most people, this is fine because their organization may have a few domains that they have acquired over the years that they want to work across the organization.

✦ A Postfix [P] virtual domain, on the other hand, segregates virtual domain users from each other. So justin@susebible.com and justin@wiley.com are seen as two separate email accounts. If you want mail from justin@wiley.com to be received by the user justin, you will have to tell Postfix to do this for you.

Each virtual domain type has pros and cons, and you need to make a decision on what virtual domain type you want to use. We are going to use a Sendmail-style virtual domain because we have only a small mail server and want to let our users choose between having a wiley.com and a susebible.com address.

When the domain has been created, suppose you want to make all mail for info@wiley.com go to the user justin. (Apparently the editors were so happy with the book that they asked Justin if he wanted a job looking after any general inquiries coming into Wiley!) In that case, you have to assign a virtual user to a real user.

Mapping a Virtual User to a Real User

To create a virtual user, you need to go back to the User section. Select the Create Virtual Users subsection. You will see a screen similar to the one shown in Figure 30-19.

You will see a drop-down box that shows the current virtual domains configured on the system and also a filter as you saw in the user list. Select the domain you for which you want to create a virtual user and also the real system user you want that mail to go to. When you are happy with your configuration, click Create to save your configuration. Now, all mail for info@wiley.com will be received by the user justin.

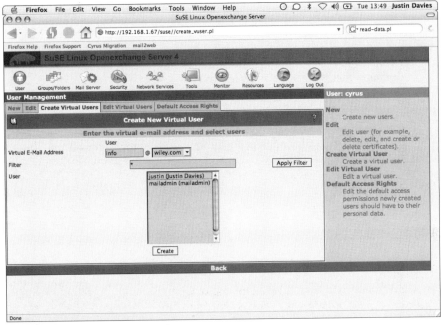

Figure 30-19: Creating a virtual user

Configuring the Postfix Subsystem

The default SLOX installation provides you with a working mail server infrastructure for your organization, but if you want to tweak your settings, this can all be done through the web interface.

Postfix enables your users to authenticate to the mail server when they are not on the trusted network. (See Chapter 17 for information on trusting users.) This means that if some of your users are on a dial-up connection, they can send mail through the mail server for people who are not in your domain.

To do this, select the Mail Server section and click the Postfix subsection. You will see a screen similar to the one shown in Figure 30-20.

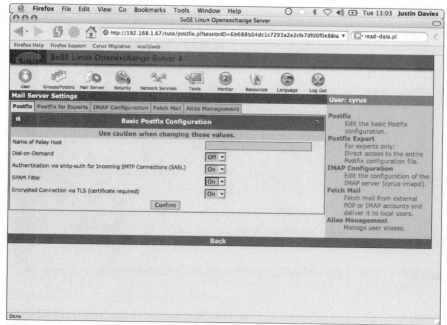

Figure 30-20: Editing the Postfix server configuration

Enabling SMTP-AUTH

To enable SMTP authentication, change the drop-down box for authentication through SMTP-AUTH to On and click the Confirm button.

Your users will now be able to configure their mail clients to send authentication information to the SMTP server before they attempt to send any mail.

Note   The mail server will not ask the client for authentication details for the user. It is up to the client to tell the mail server it wants to authenticate itself before sending mail. With this in mind, a mail client must support the SMTP-AUTH standard to be able to authenticate to an SMTP server.

Enabling Spam Prevention

As with most things in the world, there are people who want to spoil email for the rest of us. Spammers are out there, sending useless mail by the thousands, and most people's mailboxes are full of this spam.

SLOX includes the excellent SpamAssassin prevention mechanism to check each email that is received by the mail server based on things such as keywords, the format of the mail (HTML as opposed to plain text), inclusion of images, and so on. If the mail is deemed spam, it is sent to the user's spam folder so the user can see it and decide whether to keep it or not. (This helps to stop any false positives losing user's mail.)

To enable spam prevention, change the SPAM Filter drop-down box to On and click Confirm to save the changes.

Managing the Cyrus Subsystem

To set Cyrus-specific configuration options, select the Mail Server section and the IMAP Configuration subsection (see Figure 30-21).

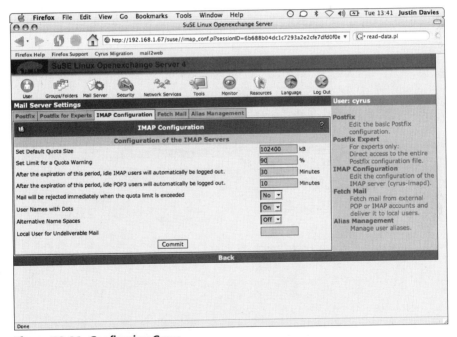

Figure 30-21: Configuring Cyrus

When we created the user justin, we had the quota set to a default. If you want to allow subsequent users to have a higher (or lower) disk quota, you can set it (in kilobytes) on this screen.

Click Commit to save your changes.

Tip   It is always a good idea to make sure users are aware they are over their quota limits, but still allow their mail to be delivered; otherwise, they may lose important correspondence. If you want to allow this functionality, set Mail will be rejected immediately when quota limit is exceeded to No.

Managing Groups and Folders

If you want to organize your users into groups or want to create shared mail folders for certain users, you can do this through the web interface.

Creating a Group of Users

Select the Groups/Folders section, and then the Create Groups subsection (see Figure 30-22).

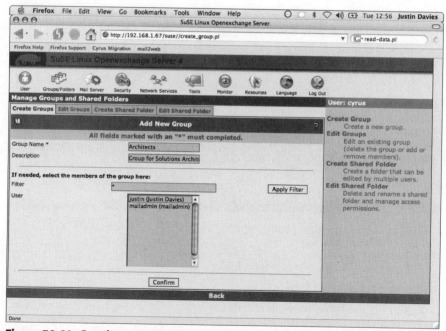

Figure 30-22: Creating a new group

Again, you will be presented with the now familiar filter for all of your users. To create a group, enter the group name and a description for the group. Using the filter, select the users you want to be contained in the group and click the Confirm button.

You can add users to the group during their creation, or select the Edit Groups subsection.

Creating a Shared Folder

A shared folder is a part of IMAP that proves very useful. Instead of setting a mail alias for multiple users, you can deliver mail directly to a folder that those users can access. This cuts down the amount of mail that is sent through the system and also saves space in the user's quota. To create a new shared folder, follow these steps:

1. Select the Create Shared Folder subsection (see Figure 30-23).

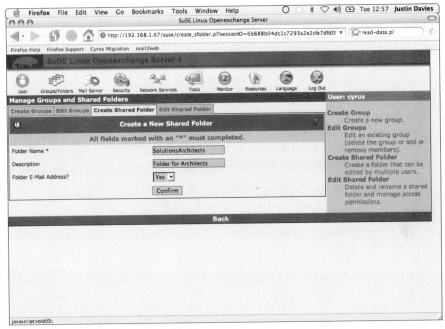

Figure 30-23: Creating a shared folder

2. You will be asked to enter the name of the folder as well as a description. If you want to allow mail to be sent directly to the folder (through `foldername@domain.tld`), make sure the Folder E-mail Address is set to Yes. When you are happy with the configuration, click Confirm.

3. You are then presented with the access control list (ACL) configuration, which enables you to select the users and the access that they have to the folder. See Figure 30-24.

As we have already created a group of users, we can tell SLOX that we want just those users to have access to this folder.

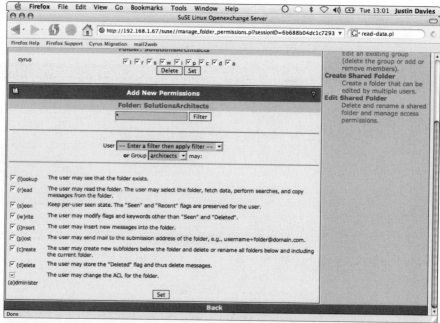

Figure 30-24: Setting the access controls on a shared folder

4. Either select a group that you want to give access to, or use the filter to select specific users.

As with the ACLs in the Cyrus IMAP server, you need to set the access control on the folder. We trust our architects, so we have given them full access to the folder. To save your ACL changes, click Set. The ACLs are implemented immediately.

Checking System Resources

If you want to monitor the health of your SLOX system, you can either log in directly to the box, or you can use the web interface to give you an overview of running services, system load, and the status of the mail queue.

Click in the Monitor section and select the component of the system you want to view. The System Statistics view, shown in Figure 30-25, will give you a history of the system load, free memory, and the CPU usage of the SLOX server. This can help when you monitor how well your hardware is coping with the load and see peaks in the mail system for your busiest times.

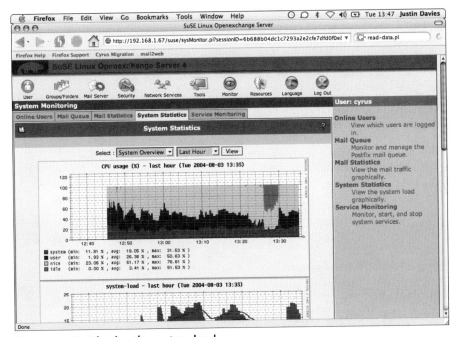

Figure 30-25: Viewing the system load

You can view the performance statistics of the SLOX server over a period of time if you want (for example, the last month) or narrow it down to one day. These are good statistics to have when asking management for more hardware!

The User Perspective

When you have configured SLOX to your network and added your users, they can start using the functionality of SLOX through the web interface or the i/oSLOX connectors. To log in as a normal user, go to the URL for your SLOX installation and enter the credentials of the user you want to log in as.

When you initially log in to SLOX as a normal user, you are presented with an overview of your groupware for the day (see Figure 30-26). This is very much the same as the Outlook Today screen.

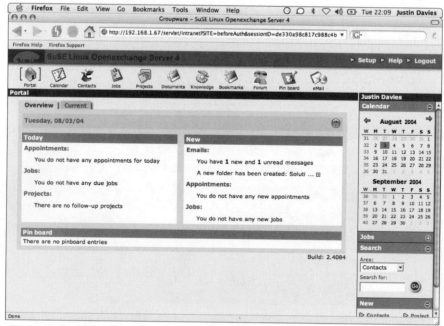

Figure 30-26: The Portal screen

Reading Your Mail

To view your mail through the web interface, select the eMail icon from the list of icons across the top of the Portal screen. You will be presented with an easy-to-use email client that you should be familiar with if you have ever used any of the popular webmail services (see Figure 30-27).

On the left side of the screen is a list of the folders that you have through IMAP. If you created an IMAP account on your desktop email client, these are visible as any normal email folder on the right.

Notice in the Inbox that we have a new email that was generated when we created the SolutionsArchitects folder earlier in the chapter. When you select an email from the top pane, it is displayed in the lower window, just as it is with the preview pane of most email clients.

If you need to send a message, you can simply select the New Message option in the top-left section of the screen. A New message screen displays, as shown in Figure 30-28, and you can compose an email to send just as you do in any email client.

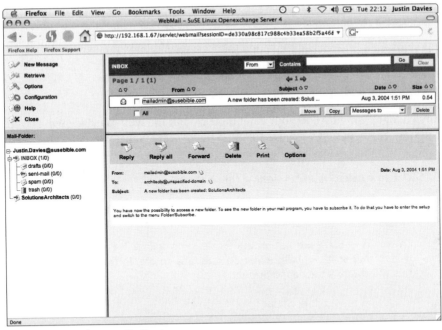

Figure 30-27: The email client

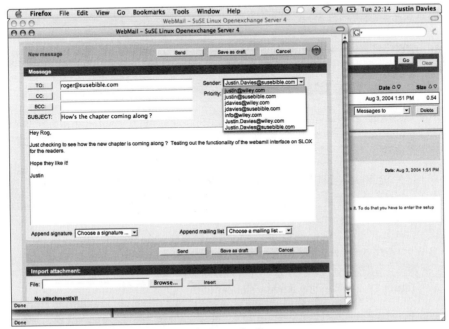

Figure 30-28: Sending an email with the web client

Notice that we have a few aliases and also a virtual user assigned to us, so we have a list of possible From email addresses we can choose to use. This is a very powerful feature when you have to reply to mail that has been sent to a specific alias or virtual user that is under your control.

The Calendar

Any changes you make to your calendar through the web interface will be replicated to your Outlook calendar the next time you synchronize. This is also true for other groupware sections that map onto the Outlook functionality.

To add a new calendar entry, follow these steps:

1. Select the Calendar section and click the icon that looks like a star. A screen similar to the one shown in Figure 30-29 is displayed.

The icons in SLOX are not always that easy to follow. It is usually a good rule of thumb that anything with a star on it means *create*. In the case of the calendar, this will create a new appointment.

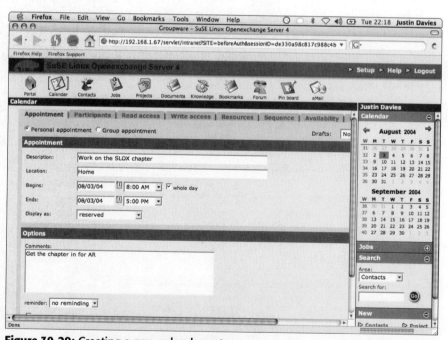

Figure 30-29: Creating a new calendar entry

2. As with most calendaring applications, you can select begin and end times for the entry, choose to make this entry an all-day event, select what date you want to create it on, and also set a reminder for the entry. When you are happy with the calendar entry, click Save.

3. When the entry has been created, you can select that day on the calendar along the right side of the screen and check to see what your calendar looks like for that day.

Jobs (tasks)

The task list is actually called Jobs in SLOX. Many of our customers have found it annoying that there is a difference in the name between Outlook and SLOX. To create a new job, follow these steps:

1. Select the Jobs section and click the new icon (the star!). A screen similar to the one shown in Figure 30-30 is displayed.

2. With the new task, you can set the amount complete, a due date, and a cost associated with the task itself. This is a kind of mini-project definition and not just a task that you may be used to. To commit the new task to the system, click the Save button.

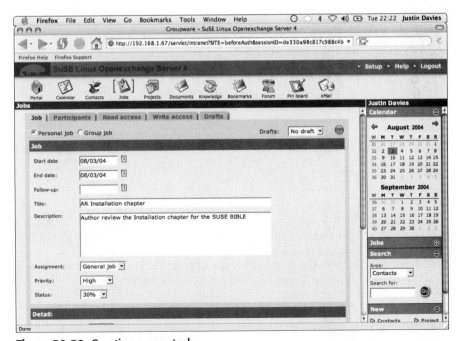

Figure 30-30: Creating a new task

3. When a task has been created, you can view it in the task list along with the millions of other things you probably have to do in one day (we all know that there aren't enough hours in the day, right?) by clicking the Jobs section in the main menu bar.

Creating Documents

SLOX has the capability to manage your documents and versioning for those documents through the Documents section of its interface (see Figure 30-31). It is not the most ideal document management system in the world, but it serves its purpose.

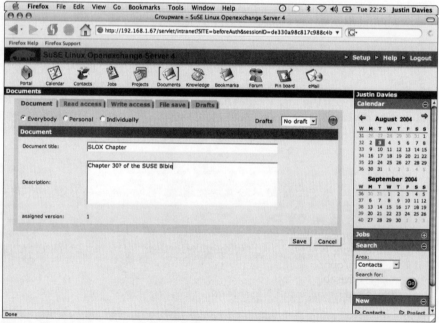

Figure 30-31: Creating a new document

When you create a document, you can set a description and also an ACL for the file (by clicking Read access or Write access) so that other users can access it.

When you have set the description on a file, click the File save tab to actually upload the file you want to version control (see Figure 30-32).

When the file has been uploaded, SLOX sets the size and MIME type automatically as well as the filename that users will see when they browse the document tree.

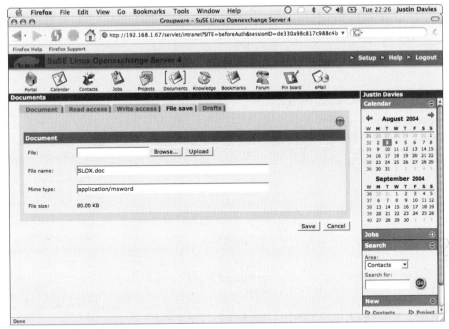

Figure 30-32: Uploading a new file

When you have saved the file, you can view its details in the document tree by hovering your mouse over the entry.

Tip   When you upload a file, its details are stored in the database, but the file itself is referenced on the filesystem of the SLOX installation. The file itself will be saved under `/var/opt/comfire/filespool`. If you are heavily using the document system, it is advisable to store the `/var/opt/comfire/filespool` directory on a separately sized partition or SAN partition.

Creating a Note

In SLOX, notes are called Pinboard entries. A note is just a small sticky note for you to remind yourself of something that can be displayed on your portal screen when you log in to SLOX as a normal user. Again, these Pinboard entries are not as elegant as some people would like, but they do serve the purpose they have been designed to fulfill.

To create a Pinboard entry, click the Pinboard section and then the new icon (yes, the star). You can create your note in the screen shown in Figure 30-33.

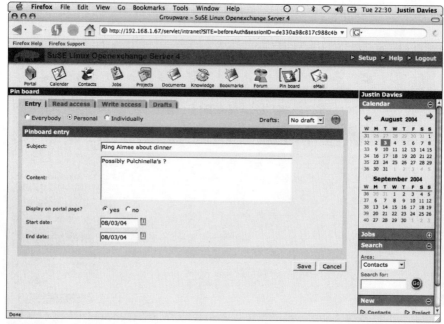

Figure 30-33: Creating a note

To save the note, click Save. The note will then be viewable from the Portal page.

Creating a New Contact

A SLOX user has two address books, private and public:

✦ The private address book should be used to store personal contacts, or those contacts that are not relevant to running the business.

✦ The public address book contains all SLOX users' details and also any contacts that you save as public. You can write to the public address book only if the administrator gave you public write access when your account was created or has since given you access after your account was created.

To access contacts, you select the Contacts section. Clicking the new (star) icon will present you with a new contact form. It is quite thorough in the information you can store about the person or organization you want to add an address for (see Figure 30-34).

When you are happy with the contact information, click the Save button to insert the entry into the LDAP server.

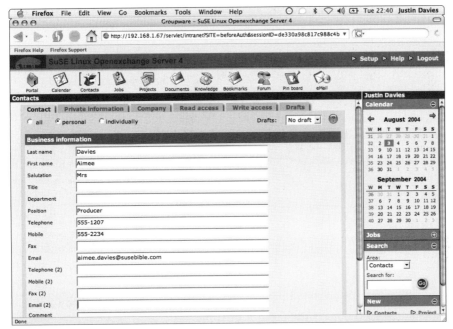

Figure 30-34: Creating a new contact

Setting a contact to *all* allows other users to see the contact information. If you want this contact to be private to you, set its visibility to *personal*. Finally, you can give certain users explicit access to the entry by selecting *individually* and use the Read/Write access links to set the access control list.

Taking another look at the address book, you can see the new entry is listed along with the other SLOX users. If you created a personal entry, the new entry is visible only to you.

If you click the entry in the address book, you can view the details entered for the entry and also view an industry standard vCard entry by clicking the vCard tab.

Viewing Your New Portal Page

After you have entered all of your new information for the day, you can take a look at your Portal page and see if it has changed. As you can see in Figure 30-35, a lot of the information we entered for our examples is pertinent to today, including a note, calendar entry, and an update about an undelivered mail.

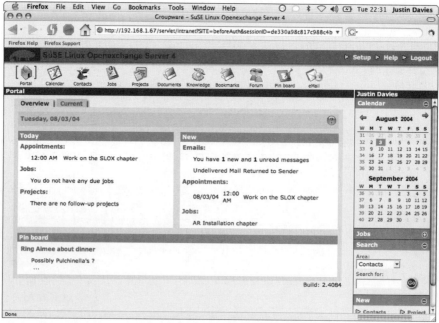

Figure 30-35: Viewing the updated Portal page

Any information that is relevant to today will be displayed for you in the Portal page, very much like the Outlook Today page. This is a great little feature that enables you to see what you have going on for the day and is something that is considered a given feature in any personal information manager (PIM) application.

Using the Outlook Connectors

SUSE and Netline have provided a connector for Windows Clients that will allow you to access the groupware functionality of SLOX through Outlook. Both products provide a way to access the services, but both do it in a different way.

iSLOX

The iSLOX connector provides a real-time connector for SLOX that does not save any data for you to read offline at a later point. In much the same way as an IMAP connection gives you access to mail for the duration of a connection to the server, iSLOX provides access to SLOX data for the duration of a server connection.

With iSLOX you can change permissions on a folder in the same way you do with a connection to a Microsoft Exchange server.

oSLOX

The oSLOX connector provides a connection to the SLOX server by synchronizing data at an interval to your Outlook PST file directly. With oSLOX, you cannot change permissions on your folders, and you have to create a separate IMAP profile to read your mail.

Using oSLOX has two main advantages:

✦ If you use oSLOX, all of your SLOX data is stored locally on your computer for offline use. If any of your users are accessing SLOX from a laptop, you should use the oSLOX connector.

✦ You can statistically distribute the load on the SLOX server by increasing the time your clients synchronize to the server. For example, if you have 100 users and you set the synchronization time to 5 minutes, you can distribute the load of WebDAV connections to 20 connections per minute (at best), which drastically reduces the impact of concurrent groupware users on your installation. This also helps to distribute the amount of groupware licenses that are needed for concurrent connections.

Throughout the rest of the chapter, we will use the Netline oSLOX connector to make a connection to the SLOX server.

Using oSLOX

To download the oSLOX connector, follow these steps:

1. Go to http://sdb.suse.de/download/i386/update/Openexchange-Server/4/images/ and log in with your SUSE support credentials (you received this when you registered your version of SLOX).

2. Download the latest oSLOX version.

When you have downloaded the oSLOX connector, run it by double-clicking the installation file.

Note   The oSLOX file you have downloaded is the application itself, not an installation binary. It is advisable to drop the executable into your Program Files directory and place a link in your Startup folder so that it runs whenever you log in.

To configure the oSLOX component:

1. Select the Outlook profile with which you want to use oSLOX (see Figure 30-36).

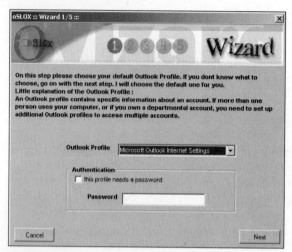

Figure 30-36: Selecting the Outlook profile to use with oSLOX

When you have selected the profile you want to use, click Next to continue with the server configuration.

2. For the next screen (see Figure 30-37), you need to know the IP address of your SLOX server; you also need to enter the username and password that you use to connect to the web interface.

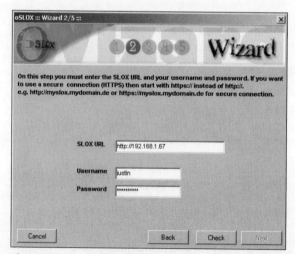

Figure 30-37: Configuring your server connection

When you are happy with your settings, click the Check button to test the server connection and your credentials. If all has gone well, click Next to continue to folder configuration (see Figure 30-38).

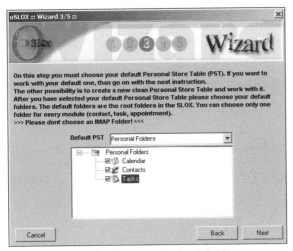

Figure 30-38: Selecting your Outlook folders

3. Select the Outlook folders you want to synchronize. This will probably be all of your standard folders (Contacts, Calendar, and Tasks). Click Next when you are finished.

4. Choose what SLOX public folders (not mail folders) you want to subscribe to (see Figure 30-39). If you or your administrator has created a SLOX public folder (for contacts, calendars, and so on), you will see them listed here. Select the folders you want to subscribe to, or you can select always all to have access to all publicly accessible folders. Click Next to continue.

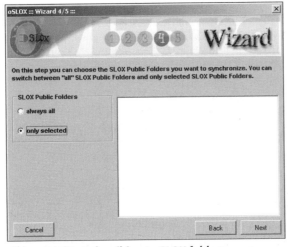

Figure 30-39: Subscribing to SLOX folders

5. In the screen shown in Figure 30-40, you can configure oSLOX to synchronize to the server automatically at a given interval, or you can manually synchronize your data (we see this in the next section of the chapter). If you have a lot of users on the SLOX installation, the longer the synchronization interval, the more you will spread the load (statistically) on the server itself. Click Start to make oSlox run in the background and synchronize at the interval you have selected.

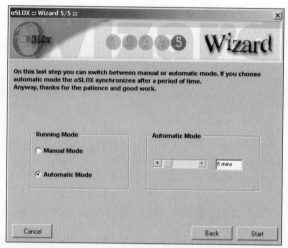

Figure 30-40: Configuring synchronization time

Your First Synchronization

If you have existing entries in your Outlook PST file, it is a good idea to do a synchronization to the SLOX server so that your data is replicated. If you do not have any existing data (meaning this is a brand-new Outlook user), then only entries on the SLOX server will be replicated.

To synchronize your data, follow these steps:

1. Right-click the oSLOX taskbar icon (visible in Figure 30-41) and select Open. This opens the oSLOX manager, which enables you to force a synchronization and to change your oSLOX settings.

2. Click the sync button to start synchronization. As we have created only a few SLOX entries, we will not produce a lot of traffic.

When that completes, we will have synchronized three contacts (Justin, Roger, and Aimee), one appointment (the all-day task created earlier in the chapter), and a task (the AR task we created).

Now take a look at what Outlook has in its Today screen (see Figure 30-42).

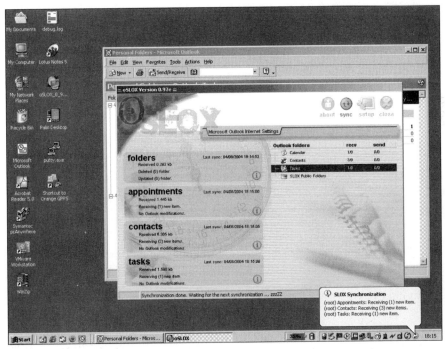

Figure 30-41: Forcing a synchronization

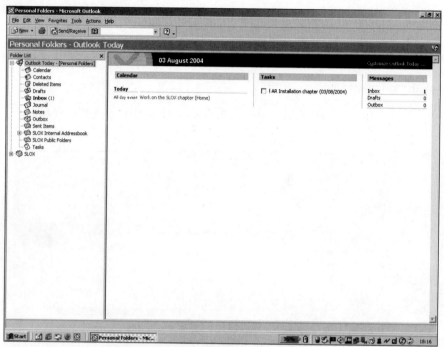

Figure 30-42: The synchronized Outlook data

Finally, you can see how creating an Outlook appointment impacts the SLOX web interface. Figure 30-43 shows a new appointment being created in Outlook.

After forcing a synchronization, you can see how that looks in the web interface (see Figure 30-44).

As expected, the appointment has been synchronized to the server correctly and is in our SLOX calendar.

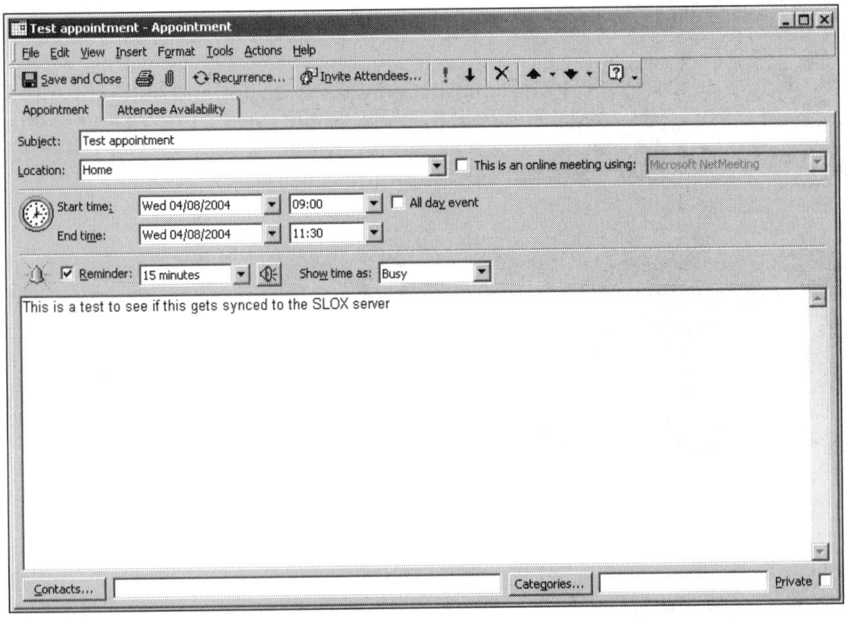

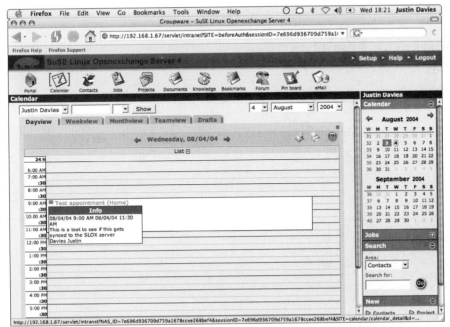

Figure 30-43: Creating an Outlook appointment

Figure 30-44: The SLOX web interface after an Outlook synchronization

To SLOX or Not to SLOX?

SLOX provides a perfect groupware infrastructure for small to medium organizations. You should ask SUSE for a Not for Resale version of the product or a test copy to see if it fits in with your current expectations of a groupware product. Alternatively, you can look at Netline's new OPEN-XCHANGE product. Details are available at www.openexchange.com.

It provides 80 to 90 percent of the functionality you get in an Exchange/Outlook environment, and the other functionality you may not even miss. The only way you will know is to try out the full functionality of the product.

With all of that out of the way, SLOX is an excellent groupware replacement for organizations that need a small to medium install base. In terms of cost, it is cheaper than Exchange; it is also more stable and it is cluster aware.

✦   ✦   ✦

The Novell Open Enterprise Server

Novell's Open Enterprise Server (released in March 2005) is the biggest single outcome resulting from Novell's acquisition of SUSE. Had the takeover not occurred, the SUSE Linux Enterprise Server and SUSE Linux Professional would have continued to develop much as they did. Also, another business desktop Linux release would have occurred, replacing SLD (see Chapter 33). But the Open Enterprise Server comes into a different category.

Novell's NetWare network operating system was the market leader in its field in the early 1990s when there was no competing Microsoft product with comparable functionality. After the release of Microsoft Windows NT 4, other commercial competitors in this field dropped out, and Novell's market share was damaged. But many large organizations continued to choose NetWare on account of its stability and reliability. Novell surrounded the NetWare operating system with a variety of services tailored to the needs of large organizations: in particular NDS (Novell Directory Services) and its successor eDirectory, which again were market leaders in their field prior to the release of Microsoft Active Directory.

Novell's motives for the takeover of SUSE Linux were various. NetWare as an operating system was becoming more of a burden to maintain and develop at a time when it was losing market share. The open source world was solving the same problems in developing Linux, which had reached a point where it was regarded as stable and suitable for enterprise use. Novell wanted to be able to offer the same set of services as before, but running on Linux and leveraging the power of the Linux development model, rather than being tied purely to its own development team. At the same time, Novell saw that many customers wanted Linux for its own sake and wanted to play in that market. It therefore made a lot of sense to buy a Linux company and at the same time put a massive effort into porting all the traditional services associated with the name of Novell to Linux.

Novell's strategy is thus:

✦ To offer pure Linux solutions to those who want them, with the assurance of the maintenance and support services that are available on the SLES.

✦ To offer an upgrade path to existing NetWare customers based on Linux, but including the same services and configuration tools that they have become used to.

✦ To offer this enhanced hybrid solution also to new customers.

Novell has recognized the power of the open source development method, and has in general pleased the open source community by many of its actions in releasing various code bases as open source. However, at the same time the top end of the software stack offered by Novell is quite unashamedly proprietary.

Open Enterprise Server (OES) consists of those proprietary elements, currently running on a choice of either Linux or NetWare. Novell has made no statements about how long the NetWare option will continue to exist, but one can only assume that in time (though the transition period may be long) Linux will eventually be the only choice for the underlying operating system.

In this chapter we can take only a brief look at OES and what it offers. It is a large subject, encompassing as it does most of Novell's large pieces of software. As the saying goes, it requires a whole book to itself. In fact, Novell has already produced two large books on the subject, and more books from third parties can be expected in the near future. In this chapter we also look only at the Linux-based version of OES.

OES components

OES provides a great deal of functionality. The most important services that it provides are listed in this section. Most of these functions (or the associated administrative tools) are accessed through a web interface (see Figure 31-1).

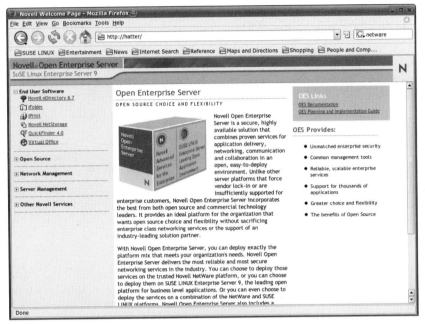

Figure 31-1: The OES web interface start page

eDirectory

Novell's eDirectory is a directory service similar in purpose to OpenLDAP (see Chapter 25) or Microsoft Active Directory. eDirectory holds the information about all groups, users, services, servers, and hardware throughout the organization. All the other services provided by OES depend on eDirectory for the information they need about users and services on the system.

iManager

iManager is the web-based interface for configuring the system. Within iManager there are tools to set up and modify all the services in OES. Figure 31-2 shows the iManager user creation interface.

Linux User Management

This component enables users who are already set up on OES to be treated as Linux users with a home directory and shell account on the server. Users connecting from Linux clients (running Novell Linux Desktop, for example) who are able to authenticate against the eDirectory server need to be set up in this way.

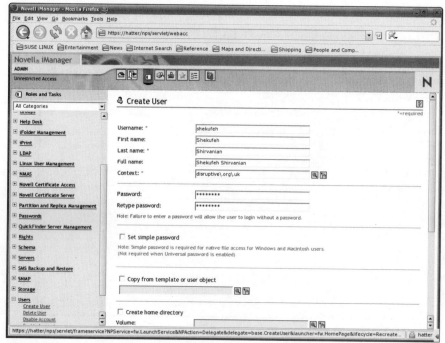

Figure 31-2: Creating a user in iManager

eGuide

eGuide, shown in Figure 31-3, is a tool that provides web access to the contents of the eDirectory server. In particular, it makes it easy for users to find information about others within the organization. Users can be permitted to edit the information about themselves through eGuide and to add photographs.

iFolder

iFolder provides server-based storage and file synchronization for user files and is accessible from anywhere. An iFolder server holds the user files in an encrypted form. The iFolder client can be installed on Windows or Linux and enables users to create a folder that automatically connects to the server and synchronizes the files within it. The iFolder files can also be viewed and accessed through a web browser using NetStorage (see the brief discussion of NetStorage later in this chapter), if it has been configured to allow this. See also the discussion of the iFolder client in Chapter 32.

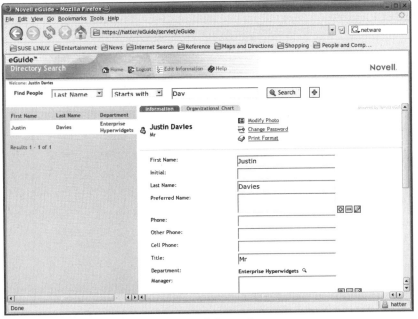

Figure 31-3: Using eGuide to edit user information

iPrint

iPrint is an enhanced version of Novell's NDPS (Novell Distributed Print Services), which supports IPP (see Chapter 19). It enables users to locate and set up printers anywhere on the network through a web interface that can be configured to show a map of the building (or indeed of a whole worldwide organization) with the locations and capabilities of printers indicated. The system also transparently handles the use by the client of the necessary printer driver.

NetStorage

NetStorage provides web-based access to user files on the server (using the WebDav protocol). Thus, user directories that are available to the user across the network by NetWare Core Protocol (NCP) or Samba may also be made accessible through a web interface across the local network or across the Internet.

QuickFinder

QuickFinder is a web-based search tool. It can create an index of the OES web server's document root or of the entire file system, or a restricted subset defined by the administrator (see Figure 31-4). Users can then search for particular terms: the results that they see will depend on whether they have the credentials to view them. QuickFinder can search within many file formats, including PDF and Microsoft Word files.

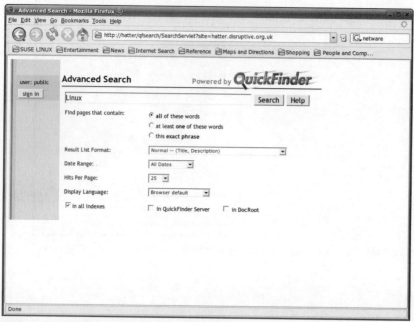

Figure 31-4: The QuickFinder search interface

Virtual Office

Virtual Office is a web-based collaboration tool that enables users to create and join virtual teams and publish and share files and other information through the web interface.

Novell Remote Manager

Novell Remote Manager (NRM) is an administrator's tool that provides a complete web-based view of the server's status. It shows hardware information, the process list, current connections, memory usage, installed packages and indeed most of the information that you could gather at the command line when logged in to the server, but it offers the information through a friendly web interface. NRM runs on port 8009. In Figure 31-5, Remote Manager is seen displaying the process list.

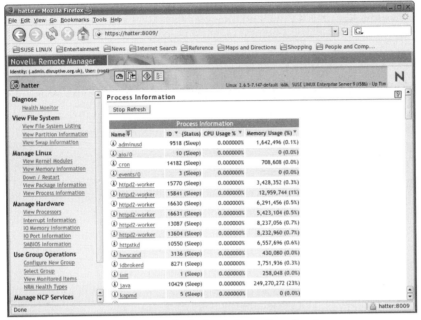

Figure 31-5: Remote Manager displaying information about server processes

Novell Storage Services

Novell Storage Services (NSS) is Novell's proprietary storage system. It includes its own file system (which is part of OES and is implemented through a set of kernel module with names beginning nss) and the ability to manage storage volumes arranged into pools. NSS manages the low-level storage of files on disk, while the files are offered to the clients by NCP and Samba described in the next two short sections.

Novell NCP server

NCP is the NetWare Core Protocol. OES offers user directories across the network both by NCP (the traditional NetWare protocol) and by Samba. Client machines with the NetWare client installed use the NCP protocol to access their files. Currently there is not a full implementation of the NetWare client for Linux.

Novell Samba server

The version of Samba (see Chapter 18) included in OES has been modified to integrate it into the eDirectory framework so that user authentication is against the eDirectory server. Windows and Linux clients can use Samba to manage and view files on the server.

Novell Cluster Services

Novell Cluster Services can manage multiple OES servers attached to the same storage area network (SAN). Its main purpose is to manage connections from a number of servers to SAN storage over fiber channel or iSCSI (SCSI over IPI), and allocate the volumes on the storage to the various servers attached to the SAN.

Obtaining OES

OES is available as a download for evaluation purposes from `www.novell.com/products/openenterpriseserver/eval.html`. The download consists of three CD images in addition to the SLES 9 disk set that is a required part of the installation. The evaluation CD images contain a full version of the software.

It is also possible to add OES to an already existing pre-installed SLES 9 installation, provided that Service Pack 1 has already been applied.

Installing OES

To start the installation, boot the machine from the first of the three OES CDs. This will start the familiar YaST installer, just like any other SUSE installation. Initially, apart from some additional license information, there is nothing unusual about the installation; it proceeds just as described in Chapter 1. There is an extra step where you are required at an early stage to decide what type of server you are installing. Figure 31-6 shows the general options at this stage.

For a full installation of OES, choose the default Full installation, but note that this does not include, for example, the iFolder server. To change the software selection that you have chosen in this screen, choose Detailed Selection to use the usual YaST interface to add individual packages or selections. Here we describe Full installation with iFolder2 server added as an option.

After you have set the partitioning, package selections, and all the other options in the main installation screen, YaST will proceed with the partitioning and create the file systems, and then will copy the entire contents of OES CDs 1 and 2 to a temporary location on the hard disk. Installation will then proceed, partly from the packages that have already been copied temporarily to the hard disk, and partly from the SLES 9 disk set which you will be prompted for as installation proceeds.

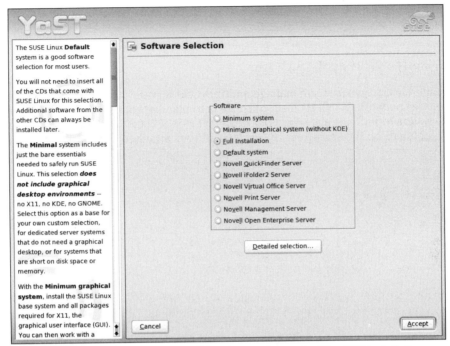

Figure 31-6: The Installation types dialog box at the start of the OES installation

Note that if you are installing from scratch, you will not be prompted for the SLES 9 Service Pack 1 disk set; certain necessary updates are included on the OES CDs, or will be completed through online updates afterwards.

At the end of the package installation there are various extra stages compared to a standard SUSE Linux or SLES installation.

After configuring a fixed IP number, host, domain names, and default route in the usual way, you are presented with a screen in which the SSL certificate authority is configured, and OpenLDAP. Unless you have very special reasons to do otherwise, you should accept the defaults here: in OES, eDirectory takes the place of OpenLDAP, so you should leave this unconfigured.

Next, you are asked whether you want to configure OES now or later: choose to do so now. In the next screen (see Figure 31-7), you are asked to configure eDirectory.

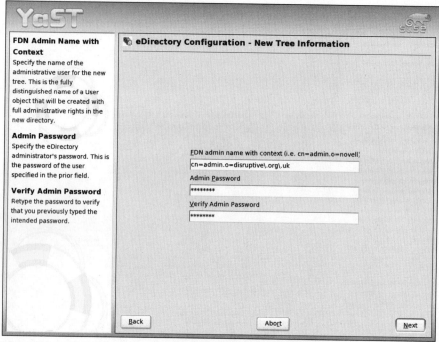

Figure 31-7: The eDirectory configuration during the installation of OES

Here, the administrator name and context should be in the form shown in Figure 31-7. In the dialect of LDAP used by eDirectory the cn= is separated from the o= by a dot rather than a comma, and so the dots within the domain name need to be escaped by backslashes. So you need to enter something like:

```
cn=admin.o=disruptive\.org\.uk
```

The next screen sets port numbers; there should normally be no reason to change anything here.

In the next screen you are given the opportunity to set an NTP (time) server and configure SLP (Server Location Protocol) if necessary; with a single OES server, this is optional.

If you have chosen to install iFolder, you now have to set an IP alias (an additional IP number) and an additional host name for the iFolder server, regardless of the fact that it will be running on the same machine as the rest of the OES installation (see Figure 31-8).

The setting up and starting of the eDirectory server now takes quite a while.

Following this, the installation will be complete.

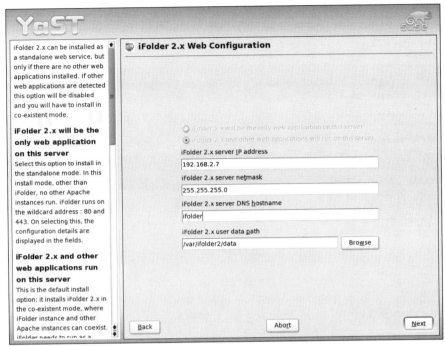

Figure 31-8: Setting additional network properties for the iFolder server

OES Licensing

The Novell Open Enterprise Server is quite unashamedly proprietary, and its licensing cost depends on the number of users and the additional services which you want to run. You can find price lists (in dollars and euros) at `www.novell.com/products/openenterpriseserver/pricing.html` and `www.novell.com/products/openenterpriseserver/pricing_euro.html`.

Post-Installation Configuration of OES

Although OES installs YaST modules for most of its specific services, this is not the way to configure them under normal circumstances. In fact, if you try to do this, you will in most cases see a warning telling you that you should not proceed unless your intention is to completely re-install that particular component.

OES runs a web interface, and all normal configuration can be done through it. Most of the configuration is through the iManager interface, as mentioned earlier, which is accessed through `https://<servername>/nps/`.

In practice Mozilla or Firefox seem to be better at working with the OES web interface than Konqueror.

Most of the configuration of OES depends heavily on the information that is held in eDirectory. In many cases, when you are asked to complete a web form entry box to select an object; an object selector window can be opened by clicking a small magnifying glass icon. This enables you to select the object in eDirectory that you need to configure.

For example, in Figure 31-9 we are about to launch the iFolder Management tool.

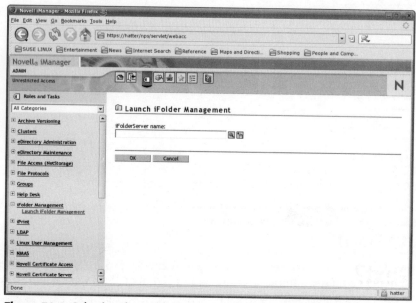

Figure 31-9: Selecting the iFolder server in the iManager web interface

The iFolder server name either can be typed into the web form or can be selected from the object selector window (see Figure 31-10). This makes working with the interface easier, because the object names are not always obvious (as in this case, where we need to choose iFolder_server01.disruptive\.org\.uk).

The same process is used throughout whenever objects are to be selected for configuration. Everything that we can work with in OES is an object in the eDirectory database, including printers, servers, users, groups, storage volumes, and anything else that can be configured.

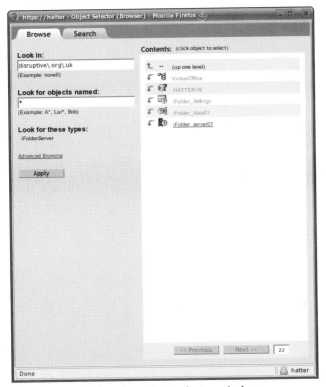

Figure 31-10: Using the object selector window

What Next?

The Open Enterprise Server is Novell's attempt to create a new generation of server products for enterprise customers. It is instructive that they have understood that in the long term the only way to achieve this is on a Linux base. It will be interesting to watch how OES develops and whether it can gain serious market share for Novell.

If you are involved in administering a large mixed network, OES must surely be one option that you should look at as a way forward. Most of the functionality that you would then have at your disposal can be achieved with Linux and open source tools alone (Samba, OpenLDAP and so on), but OES also gives you an integrated set of easy interfaces and robust underlying software that ease the problems of managing the entire infrastructure once it has been set up.

Further Information

For further information, you can go to Novell's main pages for the OES at `www`
`.novell.com/products/openenterpriseserver/index.html`.

Also, there are two books on OES published by Novell:

✦ *SUSE Linux and Novell Open Enterprise Server Administrator's Handbook* by
Mike Latimer and Jeffrey Harris (Novell Press, 2005)

✦ *Expanding Choice: Moving to Linux and Open Source with Novell Open Enterprise
Server* by Jason Williams, Peter Clegg, and Emmett Dulaney (Novell Press, 2005)

✦   ✦   ✦

Business Desktop Linux: The Novell Linux Desktop

The vexed question of whether this year is the year of Linux on the desktop has been with us for some time now. The potential of Linux as an enterprise desktop operating system is clear, but the difficulties for a large organization in making the move are also formidable.

There have been some high-profile decisions to move to Linux desktops: one of SUSE's early coups in this area was the decision by the town of Schwaebisch Hall in Germany in 2002 to move to Linux desktops. That migration has now taken place. SUSE and IBM achieved a great deal of publicity the following year when the City of Munich made a similar decision in principle, despite a dramatic last-minute counter-offer from Steve Ballmer of Microsoft. The history of the Munich Linux move since the initial decision has not been all good news for IBM or for Novell, however; the city has decided to use a specially modified Debian distribution and has chosen to contract out the implementation and support to relatively small local companies. The time scale for the migration has also been put back relative to the original plans. The outcome of the Munich migration will be of great interest to other large organizations. There certainly is a growing interest, particularly in public sector organizations in Europe, in making this move, which is combined with a growing suspicion of proprietary file formats (for example the Norwegian government recently announced a policy that proprietary file formats are not to be used in government work). The release of OpenOffice.org 2.0 using as default the OASIS OpenDocument Format can only fuel this general trend.

There is also a growing realization that getting locked in to the next versions of the Microsoft Office file formats might not be what everybody wants. In August 2005 the Commonwealth of Massachusetts announced that state agencies must adopt applications capable of supporting the OpenDocument file formats by January 1, 2007. It will be interesting to see whether Microsoft responds to this type of move by offering support for these formats in Microsoft Office, or whether this leads to file format wars in which the ultimate winner might be OpenOffice.org.

The fact that OpenOffice.org is cross-platform software and runs on Windows as well as Linux means that migration to a fully open source desktop can be done in stages: first moving to OpenOffice.org on Windows and then changing the underlying operating system. This was the method adopted internally at Novell, with great success.

The Technical Background

Most of the pieces of the puzzle required for Linux to take its place on the desktops in large organizations are in place; indeed they have been for some time now.

The majority of users in the majority of organizations use their computers for a relatively limited range of functions, almost entirely confined to email, web browsing, word processing, and spreadsheets. Native Linux applications for all these are available and equivalent in functionality to the Microsoft equivalents.

   ✦ There is a very capable email client in Evolution, which has a look and feel similar to Microsoft Outlook. Evolution is able to connect to Microsoft Exchange mail servers, an essential capability for a desktop mail client in many large enterprises during the period of transition.

   ✦ There is OpenOffice.org, which in its 1.1.x versions is able to read and write to Microsoft Office file formats with a high degree of fidelity in terms of formatting. (Version 2.0, which is in late beta at the time of this writing, is even further improved in terms of file format compatibility and supports the OASIS Open Document Format, which could become a standard for office-type file formats in the future.)

   ✦ As web browsers, Firefox and Konqueror provide a better user experience and better security than Microsoft Internet Explorer.

So for the core office functionality, Linux on the desktop has everything that it needs. The problems lie with the more unusual or stubborn applications.

The Stubborn Applications

In almost every large organization there are some specialist applications for which no Linux alternative exists. These may be commercial, off-the-shelf applications for particular purposes (such as, for example, computer-aided design), or they may be applications that have been created in-house. If an organization wants to migrate to Linux, there are a number of answers to such stubborn problems.

✦ The simplest is to accept that not all users need to migrate to Linux. If a particular group of workers really does require particular software that runs only on Windows, then maybe it makes sense to leave that group of workers out of the migration plan, at least initially. If the great bulk of workers who only need the core applications can be catered for, real progress has been made.

✦ The other answers to the problem of Windows applications that cannot be replaced are the use of Windows emulation using Wine, (or the CodeWeavers CrossOver Office version of Wine), or delivery of the applications over the network.

Wine and CrossOver Office are discussed in Chapter 28. The principle of Wine is that the Windows binary runs directly on Linux; all the system calls that it makes are intercepted and reinterpreted by Wine. Many Windows applications will run perfectly (if rather slowly) in this environment, but not all Windows applications will run correctly. CodeWeavers has worked very hard to ensure that the most popular Windows applications will run well, but there is no guarantee that your particular stubborn application will run if it is not on their list.

The alternative that will work in every case is to offer the stubborn application across the network from a Windows remote desktop, terminal server, or Citrix server. Users can access the application using an ICA (Intelligent Console Architecture) or RDP (Remote Desktop Protocol) client on the Linux desktop. The major disadvantage of this approach is the cost of licensing.

Commercial Desktop Distributions

Although there has been no doubt that there is a viable business model for commercial enterprise server Linux distributions (a fact that has been amply demonstrated by the commercial success of SUSE/Novell and Red Hat), whether there is a real market for a commercial form of Desktop Linux is at the time of writing still something of a moot question.

It is at least arguable that the business model that has worked well for the server versions is not quite suited to the desktop market, where the need for support and maintenance from the vendor is much less acute.

There are a number of niche commercial distributions in the desktop area, the most important being Xandros and Linspire (formerly known as Lindows, but forced to renounce that name by legal action). Both these companies are staying afloat, but have not made serious inroads into the commercial market for business desktop operating systems.

✦ Xandros is a business desktop version of Linux that has been tailored towards the ability to join a Windows network seamlessly, particularly from the point of view of authentication against the Windows domain, login scripts, and group policy profiles. Xandros offers a KDE desktop with its own look and feel and also a proprietary file manager with some interesting features.

✦ As their original name implies, Linspire's approach was to create a Linux desktop as similar as possible to Microsoft Windows as far as user experience was concerned. Earlier versions bundled CodeWeavers software for running Windows applications, and there was a business model based on an additional cost for the ability to run particular applications. Linspire has more recently made it clear that they are more interested in file compatibility. Among other things they have produced a modified version of OpenOffice.org with changes to make it save files by default in Microsoft formats. As of this writing, they have not released enterprise management tools. Their business model is now based on an annual subscription to a download and installation service that offers a large number of packages (both open source and proprietary) that are packaged specifically for Linspire.

One of the essential requirements for a business desktop OS (at least if it is installed locally on every client throughout the enterprise) is a management system that can look after a large number of installations and update and maintain them remotely. Xandros now offers such tools; at the time of writing, Linspire does not, but has announced that management tools will be available in the near future.

Other Approaches

All the desktop solutions we have discussed so far, and Novell's Novell Linux Desktop (NLD) offering assume a local installation on each machine. This is essentially the approach of replacing the existing local Windows installation on each desk with a Linux installation. As noted previously, such a solution, if it is to be adopted on a large scale, requires some kind of system dedicated to the central management of software installation and updates.

There is an interesting alternative to this approach, which is the idea of a diskless Linux thin client. There are a number of projects in this area, of which the best known is LTSP (the Linux Terminal Server Project). In such a setup, the client PC boots across the network (if the network card is capable of PXE booting, this just works) and gets an address by DHCP (see Chapter 20), loads a kernel from the LTSP server and mounts a minimal Linux filesystem by NFS (see Chapter 22) from the server, and starts a local X display. It then runs all applications on the server with only the display happening locally. No management of any kind is required for the client, which has nothing installed on it. If a client fails, it can simply be unplugged and replaced.

This type of technology is not new, but it has become more attractive recently because of two factors.

✦ First, the relative power of the server hardware that is available makes it possible to run many more clients from one server than was previously possible.

✦ Second, the other previously limiting factor for this type of solution, the heavy network traffic produced by large numbers of multiple X sessions, can be overcome by using a new technology called NX, which compresses the X protocol and drastically reduces the resulting network traffic. An NX server can also be used in connection with a Citrix server to deliver Windows applications to Linux desktops.

There is more information about LTSP at `www.ltsp.org`. The FreeNX project at `http://freenx.berlios.de` is based on work done and released as open source by NoMachine (`www.nomachine.com`).

Note that there is no reason why the Linux version running on the LTSP server should not be one of the business desktop–specific versions mentioned here, including NLD, so a combination of the two approaches is possible.

SLD and NLD

SUSE first offered a business desktop version in 2002; this was the SUSE Linux Desktop (SLD), which was based on the code of SLES 8. It was essentially similar to SUSE Personal/Professional 8.1, but had some extra features including a bundled licensed version of CrossOver Office (a commercial version of the Wine Windows emulation software discussed in Chapter 28) and a Citrix client. Take-up was not particularly strong, despite the good publicity that came out of the Munich announcement. There was also a very sensible caution on the part of the SUSE marketing team who did not want to over-hype the product, leading to unfulfilled expectations or disappointment. The explicit statement was made that SLD was not for everyone, and then, as now, the market sectors most suited to the product were identified and clearly stated.

Following the release of SLES 9, Novell Linux Desktop (NLD) 9 was released. It was based on the SLES 9 code base, but with recent versions of the KDE and GNOME desktops included, and a great deal of attention paid to usability issues. In particular, the version of OpenOffice.org included with NLD 9 (OpenOffice.org Novell edition) was set up to take on the native appearance of whichever desktop environment it is running in. NLD 9 includes support for Novell's ZENworks Linux Management (ZLM).

Novell still adopts a fairly cautious standpoint in marketing NLD, quite explicitly saying that NLD is not for everyone. They strongly recommend it in certain market sectors, particularly where users require only a limited set of applications, but they are still not trying to promote it to all and sundry as a direct replacement or competitor to Windows on the desktop. As the product matures, and particularly as the management options offered by ZLM (ZENworks Linux Management) improve, Novell's approach can be expected to gradually become more aggressive.

The pattern of releases will continue: NLD 10 is expected to be released early in 2006 following the release of SLES 10.

NLD Installation

Installing NLD is very similar to installing any other SUSE Linux–based product (see Chapter 1). The look and feel of the YaST installer has been altered to fit in with the general branding of NLD, but in almost all respects the installation proceeds just like an installation of SUSE Linux Professional. There is a moment early in the installation just before the installation proposal is made where a screen pops up asking whether you want a GNOME- or KDE-based installation (the default is GNOME). For a moment you may think that this screen is preventing you from making changes in the installation proposal; that is not so, but you have to decide between the two options before you can proceed.

Special Features of NLD

NLD has some special features that were not traditionally part of SUSE Linux.

iFolder Client

The Novell iFolder is a system that enables users to back up and store files on a server. The iFolder server stores the files in an encrypted form and makes them available both through the desktop iFolder client and through a web page.

There are clients available for both Linux and Windows. Anywhere that you have set up an iFolder client to access your files on the iFolder server, you will see exactly the same files in the shared directory.

To run the iFolder client on NLD, you need access to an iFolder server across the network, and you need to have been set up as a user on that server.

When you first run the iFolder client, you will be prompted for a username, password, and iFolder server (see Figure 32-1). You may also be prompted for a pass phrase that was provided when your iFolder server account was set up.

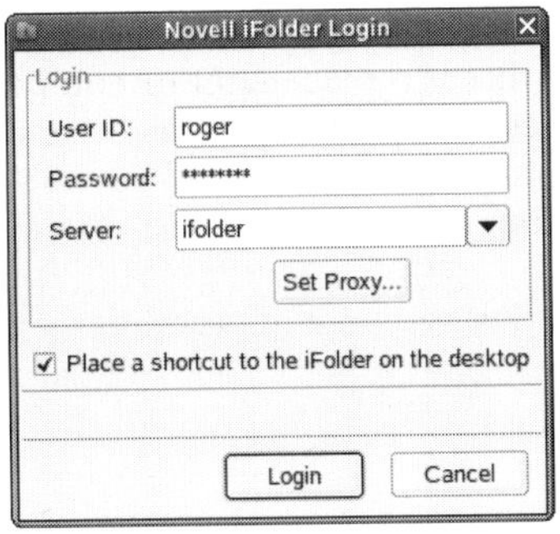

Figure 32-1: The iFolder Login dialog box

You are then prompted for the location of the iFolder that will be set up (see Figure 32-2). A desktop icon is created by default (a folder icon with a red letter i on it). From the user's point of view, this folder behaves like a normal directory; you can copy files to and from it freely.

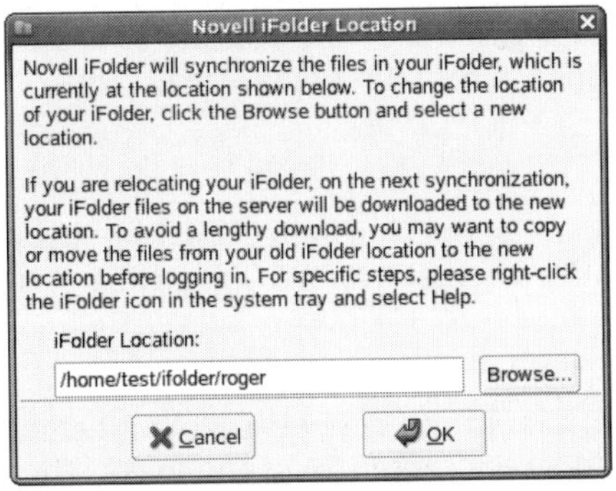

Figure 32-2: iFolder local folder setup

Whenever the iFolder client is running, this folder will be automatically synchronized with the data on the iFolder server (note, however, that on the server the data is stored in an encrypted form).

While the iFolder client is running, there is a small icon in the notification area (panel or system tray). Clicking on this icon provides status information, including the history and current status of synchronization with the server (see Figure 32-3).

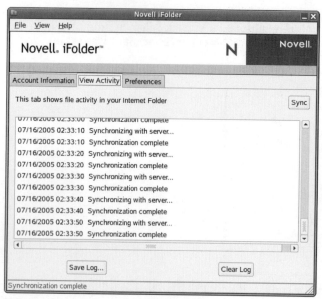

Figure 32-3: iFolder status information

Note An iFolder client has been added to SUSE Linux 10.0, supporting version 3 of the Novell iFolder protocol. The client is open source software; Novell's iFolder server is proprietary. However, as the protocol is published, it is possible to create an open source server, and this has been done in the form of the Simias server.

Terminal Server Client

There is a multipurpose terminal server client, shown in Figure 32-4, that has support for Remote Desktop Protocol (RDP), ICA, Virtual Network Computing (VNC), and other protocols. This enables you to connect to a Windows server that is offering remote desktop or Windows terminal server services (see Figure 32-5), a Citrix server, or any desktop that is offering connections by VNC.

Citrix Client

This is the official Linux client distributed by Citrix. It enables you to connect to a Citrix server and includes the ability to run specific single Windows applications from the server as well as connecting to an entire desktop, among other things.

Red Carpet Updates

NLD uses Red Carpet rather than YOU (YaST Online Update) as its software update system. To use this system, you choose the menu item (FIXME). The first time you run Red Carpet, you have to enter an activation code and subscribe to the NLD9 software channel. Then you can use the system to keep the software included in NLD up-to-date in roughly the same way that YOU does it on other SUSE/Novell Linux versions.

Figure 32-4: The Terminal Server client connection dialog box

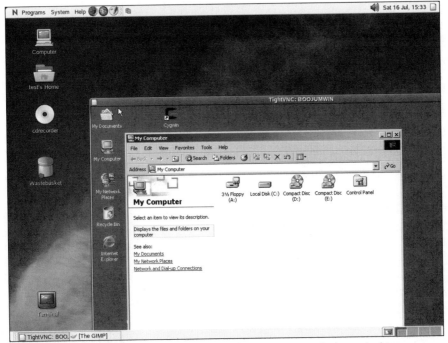

Figure 32-5: The Terminal Server client displaying remote Windows desktop

The Red Carpet client connects either directly to Novell's server or can connect to a local server running ZENworks Linux Management (which is a Novell management server for managing Linux machines, and includes the Red Carpet server software). ZENworks Linux Management is part of the wider ZENworks product that can also manage Windows and NetWare machines across the network.

The Future of NLD

Novell has been working very hard with the open source community on usability issues in the area of desktop software. The Novell OpenOffice.org team has contributed a great deal to the development of the office suite and its integration into the wider desktop environment. Novell is also very interested in upgrading existing customers with NetWare on the server and Windows on the desktop to OES (Open Enterprise Server — see Chapter 31) on the server and NLD on the desktop. As a result NLD can be said to be an important part of Novell's long-term strategy for the future of its Linux offerings.

For More Information

For more information, you can check out the following two books on the specific subject of the Novell Linux Desktop:

✦ *Novell Linux Desktop 9 Administrator's Handbook* by Emmett Dulaney (Novell Press, August 2005)

✦ *Novell Linux Desktop 9 User's Handbook* by Jim Pyles, Maries Perry, and Emmett Dulaney (Que, November 2005)

You may also find *Linux Desktop Hacks* by Nicholas Petreley and Jono Bacon (O'Reilly, April 2005) of interest.

✦   ✦   ✦

What's on the DVD

This appendix provides you with information on the contents of the DVD that accompanies this book.

System Requirements

Make sure that your computer meets the minimum system requirements listed in this section. If your computer doesn't match up to most of these requirements, you may have a problem using the contents of the DVD.

+ PC with a Pentium or AMD processor running at 90 MHz or faster.

+ At least 128MB of total RAM installed on your computer; for best performance, we recommend at least 256MB.

+ A DVD-ROM drive.

What's on the DVD

The DVD included with this book contains the SUSE Linux Professional Edition version 10.0 distribution for computers with x86, AMD64 or EM64T processors. This will install on most modern computers with an Intel or AMD processor. As you read the book, you will find more information about what is included in the Professional distribution, but it contains everything you need to get started with SUSE Linux. To order the SUSE Linux 10.0 source code, go to `www.wiley.com/go/ suselinux10bible` to download a coupon with further details.

For more information about installing the SUSE Linux Professional Edition version 10.0 included on the DVD, see Chapter 1.

Note that the retail version of SUSE Linux Professional (currently version 10.1) also contains a set of installation CDs, and a printed manual. The retail version also includes printed manuals and entitles the buyer to installation support (for details see www.novell.com/support/products/suselinux/conditions.html).

Caution

Note that the DVD contains a complete distribution of the Linux operating system. As this is a complete operating system, installing it will by default destroy all data on your computer, although a dual-boot installation is possible (allowing you to keep your existing operating system and choose between operating systems at boot-time). We recommend that you back up all important files before attempting a dual-boot installation.

This version of SUSE Linux is offered without any support from SUSE, Novell, or John Wiley & Sons, and any loss of data or other damage as a result of using this DVD is your own responsibility.

Troubleshooting

If you have difficulty installing or using any of the materials on the companion DVD, try the following solutions:

+ Ensure that you have a DVD-ROM drive and that this is set as the boot device in your computer's BIOS.

+ Ensure that your computer has sufficient memory (RAM). You will need at least 128MB of RAM and preferably 256MB to install this version of Linux.

+ Read the sections of this book referring to the installation procedure, particularly Chapter 1.

+ For other problems, see the SUSE support database at http://portal.suse.com/sdb/en/index.html

Customer Care

If you have trouble with the DVD, please call the Wiley Product Technical Support phone number at (800) 762-2974. Outside the United States, call (317) 572-3994. You can also contact Wiley Product Technical Support at www.wiley.com/techsupport. John Wiley & Sons will provide technical support only for installation and other general quality control items. For technical support on the applications themselves, consult the program's vendor or author.

To place additional orders or to request information about other Wiley products, please call (877) 762-2974.

✦　　✦　　✦

Index

Continued

Continued

G

Continued

U

Continued

GNU General Public License

Version 2, June 1991

Copyright © 1989, 1991 Free Software Foundation, Inc.

59 Temple Place - Suite 330, Boston, MA 02111-1307, USA

Everyone is permitted to copy and distribute verbatim copies of this license document, but changing it is not allowed.

Preamble

The licenses for most software are designed to take away your freedom to share and change it. By contrast, the GNU General Public License is intended to guarantee your freedom to share and change free software—to make sure the software is free for all its users. This General Public License applies to most of the Free Software Foundation's software and to any other program whose authors commit to using it. (Some other Free Software Foundation software is covered by the GNU Library General Public License instead.) You can apply it to your programs, too.

When we speak of free software, we are referring to freedom, not price. Our General Public Licenses are designed to make sure that you have the freedom to distribute copies of free software (and charge for this service if you wish), that you receive source code or can get it if you want it, that you can change the software or use pieces of it in new free programs; and that you know you can do these things.

To protect your rights, we need to make restrictions that forbid anyone to deny you these rights or to ask you to surrender the rights. These restrictions translate to certain responsibilities for you if you distribute copies of the software, or if you modify it.

For example, if you distribute copies of such a program, whether gratis or for a fee, you must give the recipients all the rights that you have. You must make sure that they, too, receive or can get the source code. And you must show them these terms so they know their rights.

We protect your rights with two steps: (1) copyright the software, and (2) offer you this license which gives you legal permission to copy, distribute and/or modify the software.

Also, for each author's protection and ours, we want to make certain that everyone understands that there is no warranty for this free software. If the software is modified by someone else and passed on, we want its recipients to know that what they have is not the original, so that any problems introduced by others will not reflect on the original authors' reputations.

Finally, any free program is threatened constantly by software patents. We wish to avoid the danger that redistributors of a free program will individually obtain patent licenses, in effect making the program proprietary. To prevent this, we have made it clear that any patent must be licensed for everyone's free use or not licensed at all.

The precise terms and conditions for copying, distribution and modification follow.

Terms and Conditions for Copying, Distribution and Modification

0. This License applies to any program or other work which contains a notice placed by the copyright holder saying it may be distributed under the terms of this General Public License. The "Program", below, refers to any such program or work, and a "work based on the Program" means either the Program or any derivative work under copyright law: that is to say, a work containing the Program or a portion of it, either verbatim or with modifications and/or translated into another language. (Hereinafter, translation is included without limitation in the term "modification".) Each licensee is addressed as "you".

Activities other than copying, distribution and modification are not covered by this License; they are outside its scope. The act of running the Program is not restricted, and the output from the Program is covered only if its contents constitute a work based on the Program (independent of having been made by running the Program). Whether that is true depends on what the Program does.

1. You may copy and distribute verbatim copies of the Program's source code as you receive it, in any medium, provided that you conspicuously and appropriately publish on each copy an appropriate copyright notice and disclaimer of warranty; keep intact all the notices that refer to this License and to the absence of any warranty; and give any other recipients of the Program a copy of this License along with the Program.

You may charge a fee for the physical act of transferring a copy, and you may at your option offer warranty protection in exchange for a fee.

2. You may modify your copy or copies of the Program or any portion of it, thus forming a work based on the Program, and copy and distribute such modifications or work under the terms of Section 1 above, provided that you also meet all of these conditions:

a) You must cause the modified files to carry prominent notices stating that you changed the files and the date of any change.

b) You must cause any work that you distribute or publish, that in whole or in part contains or is derived from the Program or any part thereof, to be licensed as a whole at no charge to all third parties under the terms of this License.

c) If the modified program normally reads commands interactively when run, you must cause it, when started running for such interactive use in the most ordinary way, to print or display an announcement including an appropriate copyright notice and a notice that there is no warranty (or else, saying that you provide a warranty) and that users may redistribute the program under these conditions, and telling the user how to view a copy of this License. (Exception: if the Program itself is interactive but does not normally print such an announcement, your work based on the Program is not required to print an announcement.)

These requirements apply to the modified work as a whole. If identifiable sections of that work are not derived from the Program, and can be reasonably considered independent and separate works in themselves, then this License, and its terms, do not apply to those sections when you distribute them as separate works. But when you distribute the same sections as part of a whole which is a work based on the Program, the distribution of the whole must be on the terms of this License, whose permissions for other licensees extend to the entire whole, and thus to each and every part regardless of who wrote it.

Thus, it is not the intent of this section to claim rights or contest your rights to work written entirely by you; rather, the intent is to exercise the right to control the distribution of derivative or collective works based on the Program.

In addition, mere aggregation of another work not based on the Program with the Program (or with a work based on the Program) on a volume of a storage or distribution medium does not bring the other work under the scope of this License.

3. You may copy and distribute the Program (or a work based on it, under Section 2) in object code or executable form under the terms of Sections 1 and 2 above provided that you also do one of the following:

   a) Accompany it with the complete corresponding machine-readable source code, which must be distributed under the terms of Sections 1 and 2 above on a medium customarily used for software interchange; or,

   b) Accompany it with a written offer, valid for at least three years, to give any third party, for a charge no more than your cost of physically performing source distribution, a complete machine-readable copy of the corresponding source code, to be distributed under the terms of Sections 1 and 2 above on a medium customarily used for software interchange; or,

   c) Accompany it with the information you received as to the offer to distribute corresponding source code. (This alternative is allowed only for noncommercial distribution and only if you received the program in object code or executable form with such an offer, in accord with Subsection b above.)

The source code for a work means the preferred form of the work for making modifications to it. For an executable work, complete source code means all the source code for all modules it contains, plus any associated interface definition files, plus the scripts used to control compilation and installation of the executable. However, as a special exception, the source code distributed need not include anything that is normally distributed (in either source or binary form) with the major components (compiler, kernel, and so on) of the operating system on which the executable runs, unless that component itself accompanies the executable.

If distribution of executable or object code is made by offering access to copy from a designated place, then offering equivalent access to copy the source code from the same place counts as distribution of the source code, even though third parties are not compelled to copy the source along with the object code.

4. You may not copy, modify, sublicense, or distribute the Program except as expressly provided under this License. Any attempt otherwise to copy, modify, sublicense or distribute the Program is void, and will automatically terminate your rights under this License. However, parties who have received copies, or rights, from you under this License will not have their licenses terminated so long as such parties remain in full compliance.

5. You are not required to accept this License, since you have not signed it. However, nothing else grants you permission to modify or distribute the Program or its derivative works. These actions are prohibited by law if you do not accept this License. Therefore, by modifying or distributing the Program (or any work based on the Program), you indicate your acceptance of this License to do so, and all its terms and conditions for copying, distributing or modifying the Program or works based on it.

6. Each time you redistribute the Program (or any work based on the Program), the recipient automatically receives a license from the original licensor to copy, distribute or modify the Program subject to these terms and conditions. You may not impose any further restrictions on the recipients' exercise of the rights granted herein. You are not responsible for enforcing compliance by third parties to this License.

7. If, as a consequence of a court judgment or allegation of patent infringement or for any other reason (not limited to patent issues), conditions are imposed on you (whether by court order, agreement or otherwise) that contradict the conditions of this License, they do not excuse you from the conditions of this License. If you cannot distribute so as to satisfy simultaneously your obligations under this License and any other pertinent obligations, then as a consequence you may not distribute the Program at all. For example, if a patent license would not permit royalty-free redistribution of the Program by all those who receive copies directly or indirectly through you, then the only way you could satisfy both it and this License would be to refrain entirely from distribution of the Program.

   If any portion of this section is held invalid or unenforceable under any particular circumstance, the balance of the section is intended to apply and the section as a whole is intended to apply in other circumstances.

   It is not the purpose of this section to induce you to infringe any patents or other property right claims or to contest validity of any such claims; this section has the sole purpose of protecting the integrity of the free software distribution system, which is implemented by public license practices. Many people have made generous contributions to the wide range of software distributed through that system in reliance on consistent application of that system; it is up to the author/donor to decide if he or she is willing to distribute software through any other system and a licensee cannot impose that choice.

   This section is intended to make thoroughly clear what is believed to be a consequence of the rest of this License.

8. If the distribution and/or use of the Program is restricted in certain countries either by patents or by copyrighted interfaces, the original copyright holder who places the Program under this License may add an explicit geographical distribution limitation excluding those countries, so that distribution is permitted only in or among countries not thus excluded. In such case, this License incorporates the limitation as if written in the body of this License.

9. The Free Software Foundation may publish revised and/or new versions of the General Public License from time to time. Such new versions will be similar in spirit to the present version, but may differ in detail to address new problems or concerns.

   Each version is given a distinguishing version number. If the Program specifies a version number of this License which applies to it and "any later version", you have the option of following the terms and conditions either of that version or of any later version published by the Free Software Foundation. If the Program does not specify a version number of this License, you may choose any version ever published by the Free Software Foundation.

10. If you wish to incorporate parts of the Program into other free programs whose distribution conditions are different, write to the author to ask for permission. For software which is copyrighted by the Free Software Foundation, write to the Free Software Foundation; we sometimes make exceptions for this. Our decision will be guided by the two goals of preserving the free status of all derivatives of our free software and of promoting the sharing and reuse of software generally.

NO WARRANTY

11. BECAUSE THE PROGRAM IS LICENSED FREE OF CHARGE, THERE IS NO WARRANTY FOR THE PROGRAM, TO THE EXTENT PERMITTED BY APPLICABLE LAW. EXCEPT WHEN OTHERWISE STATED IN WRITING THE COPYRIGHT HOLDERS AND/OR OTHER PARTIES PROVIDE THE PROGRAM "AS IS" WITHOUT WARRANTY OF ANY KIND, EITHER EXPRESSED OR IMPLIED, INCLUDING, BUT NOT LIMITED TO, THE IMPLIED WARRANTIES OF MERCHANTABILITY AND FITNESS FOR A PARTICULAR PURPOSE. THE ENTIRE RISK AS TO THE QUALITY AND PERFORMANCE OF THE PROGRAM IS WITH YOU. SHOULD THE PROGRAM PROVE DEFECTIVE, YOU ASSUME THE COST OF ALL NECESSARY SERVICING, REPAIR OR CORRECTION.

12. IN NO EVENT UNLESS REQUIRED BY APPLICABLE LAW OR AGREED TO IN WRITING WILL ANY COPYRIGHT HOLDER, OR ANY OTHER PARTY WHO MAY MODIFY AND/OR REDISTRIBUTE THE PROGRAM AS PERMITTED ABOVE, BE LIABLE TO YOU FOR DAMAGES, INCLUDING ANY GENERAL, SPECIAL, INCIDENTAL OR CONSEQUENTIAL DAMAGES ARISING OUT OF THE USE OR INABILITY TO USE THE PROGRAM (INCLUDING BUT NOT LIMITED TO LOSS OF DATA OR DATA BEING RENDERED INACCURATE OR LOSSES SUSTAINED BY YOU OR THIRD PARTIES OR A FAILURE OF THE PROGRAM TO OPERATE WITH ANY OTHER PROGRAMS), EVEN IF SUCH HOLDER OR OTHER PARTY HAS BEEN ADVISED OF THE POSSIBILITY OF SUCH DAMAGES.

END OF TERMS AND CONDITIONS